EUROPE INSET

PROJECTIONS FOR THE YEAR 2000 (in US dollars)

NA = data Not Available

Country	GNP 2000 (millions of $)	($ per capita)
Afghanistan	NA	NA
Albania	1,158	299
Algeria	50,824	1,580
American Samoa	NA	NA
Angola	NA	NA
Antigua & Barbuda	526	7,486
Argentina	297,779	8,190
Armenia	2,195	534
Australia	370,977	18,892
Austria	222,669	26,737
Azerbaijan	5,069	619
Bahamas, The	3,486	11,570
Bahrain	5,201	7,721
Bangladesh	34,059	251
Barbados	1,649	6,212
Belarus	30,000	2,827
Belgium	257,193	25,042
Belize	783	3,206
Benin	2,645	408
Bhutan	385	217
Bolivia	7,057	853
Bosnia & Herzegovina	NA	NA
Botswana	6,060	3,440
Brazil	561,470	3,150
Brunei	NA	NA
Bulgaria	9,545	1,193
Burkina Faso	3,552	298
Burundi	1,402	192
Cambodia	NA	NA
Cameroon	10,259	661
Canada	646,885	21,252
Cape Verde	479	1,007
Central African Republic	1,434	366
Chad	1,535	211
Channel Islands	NA	NA
Chile	62,849	4,082
China	971,276	753
Colombia	66,080	1,638
Comoros	325	476
Congo	2,763	877
Costa Rica	9,964	2,539
Côte d'Ivoire	9,837	567
Croatia	NA	NA
Cuba	NA	NA
Cyprus	11,400	14,582
Czech Republic	30,657	2,970
Denmark	150,632	28,618
Djibouti	522	646
Dominica	263	3,723
Dominican Republic	9,362	1,102
Ecuador	16,477	1,241
Egypt	45,111	691
El Salvador	8,896	1,434
Equatorial Guinea	209	399
Estonia	4,563	2,931
Ethiopia	NA	NA
Fiji	2,055	2,545
Finland	106,447	20,415
France	1,522,060	25,332
French Polynesia	NA	NA
Gabon	5,832	3,919
Gambia, The	513	391
Georgia	2,277	406
Germany	2,262,063	26,873
Ghana	9,575	473
Greece	86,900	8,090
Grenada	288	3,189
Guadeloupe	NA	NA
Guam	NA	NA
Guatemala	14,304	1,170
Guinea	4,228	553
Guinea-Bissau	300	249
Guyana	303	366
Haiti	NA	NA
Honduras	3,960	577
Hong Kong	159,568	25,610
Hungary	36,533	3,679
Iceland	6,826	23,786
India	372,272	358
Indonesia	214,285	1,015
Iran	NA	NA
Iraq	NA	NA
Ireland	60,006	16,813
Israel	103,614	16,113
Italy	1,312,709	22,384
Jamaica	4,311	1,690
Japan	5,044,204	39,314
Jordan	5,953	1,118
Kazakstan	26,520	1,441
Kenya	8,464	271
Kiribati	57	649
Korea, North	NA	NA
Korea, South	564,371	11,982
Kuwait	34,370	24,951
Kyrgyzstan	4,021	798
Laos	1,822	332
Latvia	5,029	1,957
Lebanon	NA	NA
Lesotho	1,585	698
Liberia	NA	NA
Libya	NA	NA
Lithuania	4,571	1,162
Luxembourg	18,355	43,179
Macao	NA	NA
Macedonia, FYR	NA	NA
Madagascar	3,640	231
Malawi	2,623	225
Malaysia	102,173	4,575
Maldives	309	1,048
Mali	3,012	269
Malta	NA	NA
Martinique	NA	NA
Mauritania	1,314	510
Mauritius	5,279	4,414
Mayotte	NA	NA
Mexico	397,324	4,048
Micronesia, Fed. States	NA	NA
Moldova	4,785	1,061
Mongolia	1,143	397
Morocco	34,699	1,101
Mozambique	1,871	93
Myanmar	NA	NA
Namibia	3,724	1,941
Nepal	4,291	176
Netherlands	381,272	23,784
Netherlands Antilles	NA	NA
New Caledonia	NA	NA
New Zealand	48,373	13,217
Nicaragua	1,509	317
Niger	2,767	263
Nigeria	47,395	371
Norway	121,716	27,275
Oman	13,642	6,085
Pakistan	72,953	481
Panama	7,501	2,548
Papua New Guinea	5,860	1,206
Paraguay	9,330	1,645
Peru	38,353	1,456
Philippines	71,379	927
Poland	93,722	2,371
Portugal	103,003	10,895
Puerto Rico	30,300	7,948
Qatar	10,783	15,389
Reunion	NA	NA
Romania	22,790	1,001
Russia	333,271	2,182
Rwanda	1,709	187
Sao Tome & Principe	47	317
Saudi Arabia	NA	NA
Senegal	7,174	724
Seychelles	621	8,341
Sierra Leone	765	143
Singapore	90,585	27,821
Slovak Republic	10,199	1,856
Slovenia	NA	NA
Solomon Islands	377	895
Somalia	NA	NA
South Africa	146,231	3,051
Spain	670,243	16,898
Sri Lanka	13,931	723
St. Kitts & Nevis	257	6,437
St. Lucia	727	4,073
St. Vincent & Gren.	339	2,900
Sudan	NA	NA
Suriname	568	1,403
Swaziland	1,558	1,360
Sweden	236,284	26,016
Switzerland	285,886	38,232
Syria	NA	NA
Taiwan	391,514	17,402
Tajikistan	2,797	406
Tanzania	3,408	104
Thailand	213,764	3,267
Togo	1,588	308
Tonga	163	1,790
Trinidad & Tobago	4,953	3,529
Tunisia	20,587	2,072
Turkey	169,777	2,473
Turkmenistan	NA	NA
Uganda	4,938	220
Ukraine	97,354	1,829
United Arab Emirates	49,933	23,264
United Kingdom	1,165,240	19,664
United States	7,387,947	26,902
Uruguay	15,773	4,811
Uzbekistan	24,256	935
Vanuatu	244	1,247
Venezuela	74,958	3,038
Viet Nam	19,518	234
Virgin Islands (U.S.)	NA	NA
Western Samoa	164	974
Yemen	NA	NA
Yugoslavia	NA	NA
Zaire	NA	NA
Zambia	4,406	418
Zimbabwe	6,976	530

P9-CKY-234

PRINCIPLES OF GLOBAL MARKETING

PRINCIPLES OF

GLOBAL MARKETING

Warren J. Keegan

Lubin Graduate School of Business
Pace University ~ New York City and Westchester, New York

Mark C. Green

Department of Management, Accounting, and Economics
Simpson College ~ Indianola, Iowa

Prentice Hall
Upper Saddle River, New Jersey 07458

Production Coordinator: David Cotugno
Manufacturing Supervisor: Arnold Vila
Manufacturing Manager: Vincent Scelta
Senior Designer: Ann France
Design Director: Patricia Wosczyk
Interior Designer: Lorraine Castellano
Copy Editor: WordCrafters Editorial Services, Inc.
Permissions Editor: The Permissions Group
Project Management and Proofreading: University Graphics Production Services
Cover Art: Shamen Liao, Inc.
Cover Designer: Wendy Helft, Design

Copyright © 1997 by Prentice-Hall, Inc.
A Simon & Schuster Company
Upper Saddle River, New Jersey 07458

Library of Congress Cataloging-in-Publication Data

Keegan, Warren J.
     Principles of global marketing / Warren J. Keegan, Mark C. Green.
          p.   cm.
     Includes bibliographical references and index.
     ISBN 0-13-722299-8
     1. Export marketing—Management.   2. Export marketing—Management—
     Case studies.   I. Green, Mark C.   II. Keegan, Warren J.
     Multinational marketing management.   III. Title.
     HF1416.K443   1997
     658.8'48—dc20   96–22966
                                                                  CIP

Prentice-Hall International (UK) Limited, *London*
Prentice-Hall of Australia Pty. Limited, *Sydney*
Prentice-Hall Canada inc., *Toronto*
Prentice-Hall Hispanoamericana, S.A., *Mexico*
Prentice-Hall of India Private Limited, *New Delhi*
Prentice-Hall of Japan, Inc., *Tokyo*
Simon & Schuster Asia Pte. Ltd., *Singapore*
Editora Prentice-Hall do Brasil, Ltda., *Rio de Janeiro*

Printed in the United States of America

10 9 8 7 6 5 4

To Polly

WJK

To Lisa, Lauren, Thomas, and Jonathan

MCG

Brief Contents

Contents

Preface

Principles of Global Marketing traces its ancestry to *Multinational Marketing Management,* a book that broke new ground in the field of international marketing when it was published in 1974. The first edition moved beyond the traditional export trade approach and adopted a strategic approach that reflected the growing importance of multinational corporations, the latest findings of research, and the most advanced experience of practitioners. This book combined text with classroom-tested, graduate-level cases and was an immediate worldwide success. Now titled *Global Marketing Management,* the book is currently in its fifth edition. The objectives of each revision have been not only to reflect current practice, but also to anticipate the direction of development in the field and maintain the book's authoritative position as the leading MBA graduate-level and reference text for practitioners of international marketing.

Principles of Global Marketing continues the groundbreaking tradition of this book. PGM takes a strategic and environmental approach by outlining the major dimensions of the economic, social and cultural, political, legal, and financial environments and providing a set of conceptual and analytical tools that will prepare students to successfully apply the 4P's (product, price, place, promotion) to global marketing.

This book has been written with today's student in mind. Business schools and faculty have increasingly recognized international marketing as an integral course in the modern curriculum. The authors realized that none of the available textbooks conveyed the dynamism and excitement that makes global marketing such a fascinating and timely topic of study, and have drawn on their direct experience in every world region: the Americas (North and South), Asia (East, Central, and South), Europe (West, Central, and East), Africa, and the Middle East. The result is a text that addresses the need of students in every part of the world for a textbook that is both readable and accessible.

Each chapter contains several color illustrations that bring global marketing to life. Chapter-opening vignettes introduce a company, a country, a product, or a global marketing issue that directly relate to chapter themes and content. In addition, every chapter contains one or more real-world boxed examples. These focus on: global marketing in action, risks and gambles, behind-the-scenes descriptions of things you don't necessarily discover by reading *The New York Times;* issues that are "open to discussion," and the fascinating cultural differences that challenge the global marketer.

We made a special effort to include outstanding cases in *Principles of Global Marketing.* The cases are short and can be covered in an efficient manner. At the same time, they introduce issues that will stimulate student interest and learning, provoke class discussion, and enhance the classroom experience for instructor and student alike. Every chapter and case has been classroom-tested.

Great care has been taken to produce the most comprehensive supplements available for any text on global marketing. Following is a list of the ancillary materials that are available to institutions that adopt this text.

INSTRUCTOR'S RESOURCE MANUAL WITH TEST ITEM FILE

This manual has been assembled based on the authors' combined experience teaching global marketing. Included are sample syllabi, chapter summaries, answers to end-of-chapter discussion questions, case tips, case teaching suggestions, answers to end-of-case questions, transparency masters with informative notes, video teaching tips, video resource list, list of supplementary materials that pertain to class material which can be obtained from outside sources. The Test Bank includes approximately 1000 true/false, multiple-choice, short-answer, and essay questions. The authors wrote the questions to ensure high-quality and correlation to the text.

PRENTICE HALL CUSTOM TEST (DOS AND WINDOWS VERSIONS)

Based on the #1 best-selling, state-of-the-art software program developed by Engineering Software Associates (ESA), *Prentice Hall Custom Test* merges the Test Item File with a powerful software package. Custom Test's user-friendliness allows the instructor to create tailor-made, error-free tests quickly and easily. Whether you work in a Windows or DOS format, with Custom Test, you can create the test, administer it traditionally or on-line, and evaluate and track the student's performance—all with the click of a mouse.

TRANSPARENCIES

Notes are provided in the Instructor's Resource Manual to aid with the presentation of 75 full-color overhead transparencies of major text concepts.

ELECTRONIC TRANSPARENCIES

A disk with Microsoft PowerPoint 4.0 for Windows color presentation is available to institutions that adopt this text.

VIDEOS

Several different videos are available to help illustrate the practice of global marketing.

- The New York Festivals International Advertising Awards winners reels, Volumes I–III give students examples of the most effective television and cinema advertising from over 25 countries, and let them compare and contrast international consumer persuasion tactics firsthand.
- Corporation case videos demonstrate the global marketing activities of well-known companies. Among others, MTV's approach to global standardization vs. adaptation issues, DHL's strategy for worldwide delivery, and Land's End's direct marketing techniques for Asian and European consumers, are explored.

We were meticulous about excluding extraneous information that would distract students from the core elements of the discipline thereby allowing instructors the time to include readings, cases, or projects of their choice in the class syllabus. One of the constant challenges to authors of books about the global market is the rate of change. Yesterday's impossible becomes today's reality. Books are quickly outdated by events. We recognize this fact and in the second year of the book's publication will offer on-line support, to include answers to frequently asked questions, updates on cases and statistics, and comments on trends and new developments. In addition, readers will have access to an interactive home page that will provide an opportunity for students and faculty around the world to share questions, answers, and insights about global marketing.

ACKNOWLEDGMENTS

This book reflects the contributions, labor, and insights of many people. I would like to thank my students, clients, and colleagues for their reflections and contributions. There are so many, it is difficult to single out individuals, but I would especially like to thank: Peter Allen, Jaime Alverez, James L. Bauer, Steve Blank, Jean Boddewyn, Lawrence G. Bridwell, Steve Burgess, Victoria Chaney, Arthur Centonze, Bertrand De Frondeville, John Dory, Bob Fulmer, Steve Kobrin, Jean-Marc de Leersnyder, Susan Douglas, Donald Gibson, Jim Gould, Handi Irawan Djuwadi, Salah Hassan, David Heenan, Peter Hoefer, Robert Isaak, Hermawan Kartajaya, Suren Kaushik, Mark Keegan, Hermann Kopp, Jem Li, Raymond Lopez, John Miranda, Dorothy Minkus-McKenna, Stan Paliwoda, Howard Perlmutter, Robert Radway, Alan Rugman, John Ryans, Rolf Seringhaus, Donald Sexton, Francoise Simon, Oleg Smirnoff, Ralph Z. Sorenson, Earl Spencer, Moshe Speter, John Stearns, William Stolze, John Stopford, Jim Stoner, Martin Topol, Robert Vambery, Terry Vavra, Len Vickers, Dianna Powell Ward, Colin Watson, Kathy Winsted, Dominique Xardel, George Yip, Margaret Young, and Alan Zimmerman.

I would especially like to acknowledge the many contributions of the students in my doctoral seminar on global strategic marketing. My faculty assistants, Jennifer Fish and Katariina Hytonen provided valuable research assistance, and my secretaries, Gail White and Mary O'Connor provided, as always, excellent secretarial support with a cheerful attitude.

The talented and creative support of our editor, David Borkowsky has been invaluable. David was quick to recognize the great potential of this manuscript and encourage our collaboration.

Warren J. Keegan

I am indebted to many colleagues and friends who carefully read and critiqued individual chapters of manuscript. Their comments helped us to improve the clarity and readability of the text. In particular, I would like to thank Jerry Anderson, Susan Anderson, Margaret Aten, Frank Colella, Cherie Francisco, Bob Gieber, Lisa Green, Kathy Hill, Derek Hulme, Kate Joeckel, Simon Lambert, Brian Larson, Eduardo Magalhaes, Keith Miller, Mark Miller, and Marilyn Mueller.

I would also like to acknowledge the many Simpson College students who supported the writing effort by suggesting improvements to the manuscript as it evolved over several semesters. Special thanks go to Anita Archibold, Donni Alley, Kim Bakker, Melinda Baumgarten, Alison Beaver, Stephanie Bowman, Colleen Crowley, Jennifer Feuling, Nan Freeman, Mary Gehrmann, Alexander Gilfanov, Alissa Harter, Wouter Herzberger, Clay Hess, Juli Holmes, Todd Jones, Danielle Kuehl, Todd Larson, Kari Langbehn, Melissa Morrison, Kathy Myers, Hope Nafziger, Nicole Noelck, Alexandre Plokhov, Jen Popovich, Leslie Reynolds, Julie Roberts, Jennifer Schulz, Kevin Schwery, Sascha Silvaratnam, Brad Sperbeck, and Menghen Zhou.

A special note of thanks goes to Kristie Ellingson at Dunn Library for her tireless efforts to expedite the interlibrary loan process.

To Bryan Ferry, Loreena McKennitt, Sam Phillips, and Pink Floyd, thanks for the ambiance and the atmospherics.

Mark C. Green

Reviewers

We are grateful to the many reviewers of this text who teach global marketing on three continents. The suggestions, insights, and examples they provided were extremely helpful in crafting our final product.

Douglas N. Behrman
Florida State University

Paul Chao
University of Northern Iowa

John S. Ewing
California State University—Chico

Tom Gillpatrick
Portland State University

Rolf Hackmann
Western Illinois University

Richard T. Hise
Texas A & M University

Alican Kavas
Michigan State University

Hiroshi Kosaka
Josai University (Japan)

Hugh Kramer
University of Hawaii—Manoa

Kenneth Lord
Niagara University

John Lox
Mississippi State University

Charles S. Madden
Baylor University

Lalita Manrai
University of Delaware

Carla Millar
City University Business School (England)

David J. Moore
University of Michigan

Alphonso Ogbuehi
Christopher Newport University

Agnes Olszewski
Seton Hall University

Anne C. Perry
The American University

Alfred Quinton
Trenton State College

David McHardy Reid
University of Hong Kong

Jan N. Sajkiewicz
Duquesne University

Dean C. Siewers
Rochester Institute of Technology

David Snyder
Canisius College

John Thanopoulos
The University of Akron

Brian Toyne
University of South Carolina

Bert Valencia
American Graduate School of International Management

Gerald L. Waddle
Clemson University

PRINCIPLES OF GLOBAL MARKETING

Introduction to Global Marketing

We live in a global marketplace. As you read this book, you may be sitting in a chair imported from Brazil or at a desk imported from Denmark. You may have purchased these items from IKEA, the Swedish global furniture retailer. The computer on your desk could be either a low-priced PC clone from Taiwan, or perhaps a Macintosh designed in the United States and manufactured in Ireland. Your shoes are likely to be from Italy, and the coffee you are sipping is from Latin America or Africa. You might be listening to the latest Paul Simon CD (featuring musicians from South Africa), thanks to your boombox's built-in CD player, the technology for which was developed jointly by two companies—one Japanese and the other Dutch. Your sweater could be the latest fashion from Italy's Benetton. What time is it now? When you check your watch, can you tell where it was made? It may be from Japan, Hong Kong, Singapore, the Philippines, or Switzerland. Welcome to the 1990s. Yesterday's marketing fantasy has become today's reality: A global marketplace has emerged.

In the past 150 years, a sweeping transformation has profoundly affected the people and industries of many nations. Prior to 1840, students sitting at their desks would not have had any item in their possession that was manufactured more than a few miles from where they lived—with the possible exception of the books they were reading. Some countries—most notably Great Britain—were actively involved in international trade in the mid-19th century. However, since World War II there has been an unparalleled expansion into global markets by companies that previously served only customers located in the home country. Two decades ago, the phrase "global marketing" did not even exist. Today, businesses look to global marketing for the realization of their full commercial potential. That is why you may own some of the products described in the preceding paragraph, no matter whether you live in Asia, Europe, or North or South America. But there is another, even more critical reason why companies need to take global marketing seriously: survival. A company that fails to become global in outlook risks losing its domestic business to competitors having lower costs, greater experience, and better products.

But what is global marketing? How does it differ from "regular" market-

---

[1]Noel M. Tichy and Stratford Sherman, *Control Your Destiny or Someone Else Will* (New York: Harper Business, 1994), p. 222.

ing? Marketing is the process of planning and executing the conception, pricing, promotion, and distribution of ideas, goods, and services to create exchanges that satisfy individual and organization goals.[2] Marketing activities center on an organization's efforts to satisfy customer wants and needs with products and services that offer competitive value. The marketing mix (product, price, place, and promotion) comprises a contemporary marketer's primary tools.[3] Marketing is a universal discipline as applicable in Argentina as it is in Zimbabwe.

This book is about *global marketing*. An organization that engages in **global marketing** focuses its resources on global market opportunities and threats. One difference between "regular" marketing and "global" marketing is in the scope of activities. A company that engages in global marketing conducts important business activities outside the home country market. Another difference is that global marketing involves an understanding of specific concepts, considerations, and strategies that must be skillfully applied in conjunction with universal marketing fundamentals to ensure success in global markets. This book concentrates on the major dimensions of global marketing. A brief overview of marketing is presented below, although the authors assume that the reader has completed an introductory marketing course or has equivalent experience.

OVERVIEW OF MARKETING

Marketing is often described as one of the functional areas of a business, distinct from finance and operations. Effective coordination of marketing with other functional areas is increasingly viewed as an important organizational task. The activities involved in product design, manufacture, marketing, and after-sales service can be described as comprising a **value chain**. Decisions at every stage, from idea conception to support after the sale, should be assessed in terms of their ability to create value for customers.

To ensure that marketers are involved in design and manufacturing decisions from the start, some organizations are applying a concept known as *boundaryless marketing*. The goal is to eliminate the communication barriers between marketing and the other functional areas. This orients all company personnel to issues of customer value. A company that subscribes to the concept of boundaryless marketing—GE, for example—makes everyone in the organization responsible for and participate in marketing. "Everyone" includes receptionists, designers, manufacturing employees, and customer service representatives. Figure 1–1 shows how the value chain and the concept of boundaryless marketing fit together.

All activities performed by a company—marketing included, of course—should be performed with two fundamental goals in mind: to create customer value and to achieve competitive advantage. Focus, or the concentration of attention, is required if a company is to achieve these goals. Many enterprises, large and small, have achieved success by understanding and applying this principle. However, a company may be forced to shift its focus in response to fundamental industry changes. For example, IBM's original success in the data processing industry was a result of focusing on customer needs and wants better than any other company. After decades of success, however, IBM remained focused on main-

[2]Peter D. Bennett, ed., *Dictionary of Marketing Terms, Second Edition* (Chicago: NTC Business Books, 1995), p. 166.
[3]For a recent review of the strengths and limitations of the 4P classification, see Walter van Waterschoot and Christophe Van den Bulte, "The 4P Classification of the Marketing Mix Revisited," *Journal of Marketing* (October 1992), pp. 83–93.

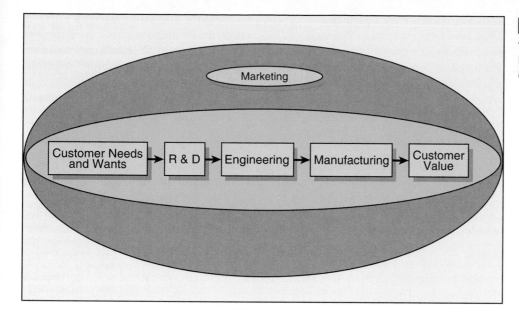

FIGURE 1–1

THE VALUE CHAIN AND
BOUNDARYLESS
MARKETING

Marketing

Customer Needs
and Wants → R & D → Engineering → Manufacturing → Customer
Value

frame computers despite the fact that customers were increasingly turning to PCs. IBM was a key player in the early days of the PC revolution, but its corporate culture was still oriented toward mainframes. "Big Blue" faltered in the early 1990s—it lost more than $8 billion in 1993—in part because competitors specializing in PCs had become even *more* clearly focused on what PC customers needed and wanted, namely low prices and increased speed. A few years ago, PC buyers might have been willing to pay more for an IBM machine; in today's market, the IBM name on a computer does not necessarily command a premium price when compared with Compaq, Dell, and other brands. The value of the Compaq brand in 1994 was calculated to exceed $4 billion—a 50 percent increase over 1993.[4]

Customer Value and the Value Equation

For any organization operating anywhere in the world, the essence of marketing is to surpass the competition at the task of creating perceived value for customers. The **value equation** is a guide to this task:

$$V = B/P$$
where V = Value, B = Benefits, and P = Price

The marketing mix is integral to the equation because benefits are a combination of the product, promotion, and distribution. As a general rule, value as perceived by the customer—the variable to the left of the equal sign—can be increased in two basic ways. The numerator can be increased by improving benefits associated with the product itself, distribution, or communications. Alternatively, value can be increased by reducing price.[5] Companies using price as a competitive weapon may enjoy an ample supply of low-wage labor or access to cheap raw materials. Companies can also reduce prices if costs are low due to efficiencies in manufacturing. If a company is able to offer both superior product, distribution, or promotion benefits *and* lower prices relative to the competition, it enjoys an extremely advantageous position. This is precisely how Toyota, Nissan, and other Japanese automakers made significant gains in the American market in the 1980s. They

---

[4]Alexandra Ourusoff, "Brands: What's Hot. What's Not," *Financial World* (Aug. 2, 1994), pp. 40+.
[5]With certain categories of differentiated goods, including designer clothing and other luxury products, higher price is associated with increased value.

offered cars that were higher in quality and lower in price than those made by Chrysler, Ford, and General Motors. Needless to say, to become a market success a product must come up to a threshold of acceptable quality. The Yugo automobile achieved a modest level of U.S. sales in the 1980s (despite a "don't buy" rating from a consumer magazine) because its sticker price of $3,999 made it the cheapest new car available. Built in Yugoslavia during the communist era, Yugo was a very low-quality product and ultimately failed in the market.

Competitive Advantage

When a company succeeds in creating more value for customers than do its competitors, that company is said to enjoy **competitive advantage** in an industry. Competitive advantage is measured relative to rivals in a given industry. For example, your local laundromat is in a local industry; its competitors are local. In a national industry, competitors will be national. In a global industry—automobiles, consumer electronics, watches, pharmaceuticals, steel, furniture, and a host of others—the competition is, likewise, global. Global marketing is essential if a company competes in a global industry.

Value, competitive advantage, and the focus required to achieve them are universal in their relevance. They should guide marketing efforts in any part of the world. Global marketing requires attention to these issues on a worldwide basis and the utilization of an information system capable of monitoring the globe for opportunities and threats. A fundamental premise of this book can be stated as follows: Companies that understand and engage in global marketing can offer more overall value to customers than can companies that do not have this understanding.

GLOBAL MARKETING: WHAT IT IS AND WHAT IT ISN'T

The discipline of marketing is universal. It is natural, however, that some marketing practices will vary from country to country. Why? Because the countries and the peoples of the world differ from one another. These differences mean that a successful marketing approach in one country will not *automatically* work in another country. Customer preferences, competitors, channels of distribution, and communication media may differ. An important task in global marketing is learning to recognize the extent to which marketing plans and programs can be extended worldwide, as well as the extent to which they must be adapted.

A second important task in global marketing is sorting through controversies among both academicians and business practitioners about the nature of the field itself. Much of the controversy dates back to Professor Theodore Levitt's 1983 article in the *Harvard Business Review* on "The Globalization of Markets." Professor Levitt argued that marketers were confronted with a "homogenous global village." Levitt advised organizations to develop standardized, high-quality world products and market them around the globe using standardized advertising, pricing, and distribution. Some well-publicized failures by Parker Pen and other companies seeking to follow Levitt's advice brought his proposals into question. The business press frequently quoted industry observers who disputed Levitt's views. For example, Carl Spielvogel, chairman and CEO of the Backer Spielvogel Bates Worldwide advertising agency, told *The Wall Street Journal*, "Theodore Levitt's comment about the world becoming homogenized is bunk. There are about two products that lend themselves to global marketing—and one of them is Coca-Cola."[6]

Indeed, it was global marketing that made Coke a worldwide success. However, that success was *not* based on a total standardization of marketing mix elements. For exam-

[6]Joanne Lipman, "Ad Fad: Marketers Turn Sour on Global Sales Pitch Harvard Guru Makes," *The Wall Street Journal* (May 12, 1988), p. 1.

ple, Coca-Cola achieved success in Japan by spending a great deal of time and money becoming an insider. That is, the company built a complete local infrastructure with its sales force and vending machine operations. Coke's success in Japan is a function of its ability to achieve "global localization," the ability to be as much of an insider as a local company but still reap the benefits that result from world-scale operations (Ohmae 1991).

What does the phrase *global localization* really mean? In a nutshell, it means that a successful global marketer must have the ability to "think globally and act locally." As we will see many times in this book, "global" marketing may include a combination of standard (e.g., the product itself) and nonstandard (e.g., distribution or packaging) approaches. A "global product" may be the "same" product everywhere and yet "different." Global marketing requires marketers to behave in a way that is global *and* local at the same time by responding to similarities and differences in world markets.

As the Coca-Cola Company demonstrated, the ability to think globally and act locally can be a source of competitive advantage. By adapting sales promotion, distribution, and customer service efforts to local needs, Coke established such strong brand preference that the company claims a 70 percent share of the soft drink market in Japan. At first, Coca-Cola managers did not understand the Japanese distribution system. However, with considerable investment of time and money, they succeeded in establishing a sales force that was as effective in Japan as it was in the United States. Today, Coca-Cola Japan generates higher profits than the U.S. operation. To complement cola sales, the Japanese unit has created new products such as Georgia-brand canned coffee expressly for the Japanese market (Reid 1995, 74).

Coke is a product embodying marketing mix elements that are both global and local in nature. In this book, we do *not* propose that global marketing is a "knee jerk" attempt

Some of Coke's many faces around the world. Although the basic design of the label is the same, the Coca-Cola name is frequently transliterated into local languages. In the left-hand column, the Arabic label (second from top) is read from right to left; the Chinese label (fourth from the top) translates "delicious/happiness." (Courtesy of the Coca Cola Corporation; Stock Boston, Inc.)

to impose a totally standardized approach to marketing around the world. A central issue in global marketing is how to tailor the global marketing concept to fit a particular product or business.[7]

Finally, it is necessary to understand that global marketing does *not* mean entering every country in the world. Global marketing *does* mean widening business horizons to encompass the world when scanning for opportunity and threat. The decision to enter markets outside the home country depends upon a company's resources, managerial mindset, and the nature of opportunity and threat. The Coca-Cola Company's soft drink products are distributed in more than 195 countries; in fact, the theme of a recent annual report was "A Global Business System Dedicated to Customer Service." Coke is the best-known, strongest brand in the world; its enviable global position has resulted in part from the Coca-Cola Company's willingness and ability to back its flagship product with a strong local marketing effort.

A number of other companies have successfully pursued global marketing by creating strong global brands. Philip Morris, for example, has made Marlboro the number one cigarette brand in the world. In automobiles, Daimler Benz has gained global recognition for its Mercedes nameplate. However, as shown in Table 1–1, global marketing strategies can also be based on product or system design, product positioning, packaging, distribution, customer service, and sourcing considerations. For example, McDonald's has designed a restaurant system that can be set up virtually anywhere in the world. Like Coca-Cola, McDonald's also customizes its menu offerings in accordance with local eating customs. Cisco Systems, which makes local area network routers that allow computers to communicate with each other, designs new products that can be programmed to operate under virtually any conditions in the world (Miles 1995, 50). Unilever uses a teddy bear in various world markets to communicate the benefits of the company's fabric softener. Harley-Davidson's motorcycles are perceived around the world as *the* all-American bike. Gillette uses the same packaging for its flagship Sensor razor everywhere in the world. Italy's Benetton utilizes a sophisticated distribution system to quickly deliver the latest fashions to its worldwide network of stores. The backbone of Caterpillar's global success is a network of dealers who support a promise of "24-hour parts and service" anywhere in the world. The success of Honda and Toyota in world markets was initially based on exporting cars from factories in Japan. Now, both companies have invested in manufacturing facilities in the United States and other countries from which they export. In 1994, Honda earned the distinction of being the number one exporter of cars from the United States by shipping more than 100,000 Accords and Civics to Japan and 35 other coun-

TABLE 1–1   EXAMPLES OF GLOBAL MARKETING

Global Marketing Strategy	Company/Home Country
Brand name	Coca-Cola (USA), Philip Morris (USA), Daimler-Benz (Germany)
Product design	McDonald's (USA), Toyota (Japan), Ford (USA), Cisco Systems (USA)
Product positioning	Unilever (UK/Netherlands), Harley-Davidson (USA)
Packaging	Gillette (USA)
Distribution	Benetton (Italy)
Customer service	Caterpillar (USA)
Sourcing	Toyota (Japan), Honda (Japan), Gap (USA)

[7]John A. Quelch and Edward J. Hoff, "Customizing Global Marketing," *Harvard Business Review* (May–June 1986), p. 59.

tries. The Gap focuses its marketing effort on the United States but relies on apparel factories in low-wage countries to supply most of its clothing.

The particular approach to global marketing that a company adopts will depend on industry conditions and its source or sources of competitive advantage. Should Harley-Davidson start manufacturing motorcycles in a low-wage country such as Mexico? Will American consumers continue to snap up American-built Toyotas? Should the Gap open stores in Japan? The answer to these questions is, "It all depends." Since Harley's competitive advantage is based in part on its "Made in the USA" positioning, shifting production outside the United States is not advisable. Toyota's success in the United States is partly attributable to its ability to transfer world-class manufacturing skills to America while using advertising to stress that its Camry is built by Americans with many components purchased in the United States. The Gap has about 40 stores outside the United States; most are in England. Japan may present an opportunity for the Gap to extend its basic competence in design and sourcing to another major market. On the other hand, the cost of entry into Japan, plus changing styles and customer preferences at home, may make it advisable for the Gap to continue to concentrate on trends in the U.S. fashion marketplace at this point in time.[8]

THE IMPORTANCE OF GLOBAL MARKETING

The largest national market in the world, the United States, today represents roughly 25 percent of the total world market for all products and services. Thus, U.S. companies wishing to achieve maximum growth potential must "go global," since 75 percent of world market potential is outside their home country. Coca-Cola is one U.S.-based company that understands this; 87 percent of its 1994 operating income and 67 percent of revenues were generated by its soft drink business outside the United States. Non-U.S. companies have an even greater motivation to seek market opportunities beyond their own borders; their opportunities include the 260 million people in the United States. For example, even though the dollar value of the home market for Japanese companies is the second largest in the free world (after the United States), the market *outside* Japan is 85 percent of the world potential for Japanese companies. For European countries, the picture is even more dramatic. Even though Germany is the largest single-country market in Europe, 94 percent of the world market potential for German companies is outside Germany.

Many companies have recognized the importance of conducting business activities outside the home country. Industries that were strictly national in scope only a few years ago are dominated today by a handful of global companies. The rise of the global corporation closely parallels the rise of the national corporation, which emerged from the local and regional corporation in the 1880s and 1890s in the United States. The auto industry provides a dramatic—and sobering—example. In the first quarter of the 20th century, there were thousands of auto companies in the world, and more than 500 in the United States alone. Today, fewer than 20 companies remain worldwide, and only three of them are American. In most industries, the companies that will survive and prosper in the next century will be global enterprises. Some companies that do not respond to the challenges and opportunities of globalization will be absorbed by more dynamic enterprises; others will simply disappear. Table 1–2 shows 25 of *The Wall Street Journal*'s Top 100 companies ranked in terms of market capitalization—that is, the market value of all shares of stock outstanding. Table 1–3 provides a different perspective: the top 25 of *Fortune* magazine's 1995 ranking of the 500 largest service and manufacturing companies by revenues. Comparing the two tables, it is striking to note that, while NTT (Nippon Telegraph &

---

[8]The challenges facing the Gap in the United States are aptly surveyed in Christina Duff, " 'Bobby Short Wore Khakis'—Who's He, and Who Cares?" *The Wall Street Journal* (Feb 16, 1995), pp. A1, A11.

TABLE 1–2	THE LARGEST CORPORATIONS BY MARKET VALUE ($ MILLIONS)

Company	Market Value
1. NTT (Japan)	$133,249
2. Royal Dutch/Shell Group (UK/Netherlands)	108,643
3. General Electric (USA)	99,939
4. Exxon (USA)	90,062
5. AT&T (USA)	83,464
6. Coca-Cola (USA)	83,180
7. Toyota Motor (Japan)	78,127
8. Fuji Bank (Japan)	70,754
9. Industrial Bank of Japan (Japan)	69,978
10. Mitsubishi Bank (Japan)	68,385
11. Roche Holding (Switzerland)	66,922
12. Sumimoto Bank (Japan)	65,647
13. Merck (USA)	63,844
14. IBM (USA)	63,220
15. Sanwa Bank (Japan)	62,277
16. Wal-Mart Stores (USA)	61,158
17. Philip Morris (USA)	60,510
18. Dai-Ichi Kangyo Bank (Japan)	58,841
19. Intel (USA)	53,833
20. Microsoft (USA)	53,000
21. Procter & Gamble (USA)	47,343
22. Johnson & Johnson (USA)	46,304
23. Motorola (USA)	44,982
24. Allianz Holding (Germany)	42,467
25. British Petroleum (UK)	41,858

Source: "The World's 100 Largest Public Companies," *The Wall Street Journal*, Oct. 2, 1995, p. R32. Data reflect market value on Dec. 31, 1994.

Telephone) has the highest market value, it ranked 16th in revenues and 129th in profits. One company that makes a strong showing in both rankings is GE: It is 3rd in market capitalization, 19th in revenues, but 5th in profits. Table 1–3 also highlights some of the problems Japanese companies have experienced in the mid-1990s. Japan's Nissan Motor, for example, ranks 12th in revenues but is near the bottom in terms of profitability. Nissan's problems stem in part from the yen's strength compared to currencies of major trading partners such as the United States.

MANAGEMENT ORIENTATIONS

The form and substance of a company's response to global market opportunities depend greatly on management's assumptions or beliefs—both conscious and unconscious—about the nature of the world. The world view of a company's personnel can be described as ethnocentric, polycentric, regiocentric, or geocentric.[9] Management at a company with a prevailing ethnocentric orientation may consciously make a decision to move in the direction of geocentrism. The orientations—collectively known as the EPRG framework—are summarized in Figure 1–2.

[9]Adapted from Howard Perlmutter, "The Tortuous Evolution of the Multinational Corporation," *Columbia Journal of World Business*, Jan.–Feb. 1969.

Ethnocentric Orientation

A person who assumes that his or her home country is superior to the rest of the world is said to have an **ethnocentric orientation**. Company personnel with an ethnocentric orientation see only similarities in markets and *assume* that the products and practices that succeed in the home country will, due to their demonstrated superiority, be successful anywhere. At some companies, the ethnocentric orientation means that opportunities outside the home country are ignored. Such companies are sometimes called *domestic companies*. Ethnocentric companies that do conduct business outside the home country can be described as *international companies*; they adhere to the notion that the products that succeed in the home country are superior and, therefore, can be sold everywhere without adaptation.

In the ethnocentric international company, foreign operations are viewed as being secondary or subordinate to domestic ones. An ethnocentric company operates under the assumption that "tried and true" headquarters knowledge and organizational capabilities can be applied in other parts of the world. While this can sometimes work to a company's advantage, valuable managerial knowledge and experience in local markets may go unnoticed. For a manufacturing firm, ethnocentrism means that foreign markets are viewed as a means of disposing of surplus domestic production. Plans for overseas markets are developed utilizing policies and procedures identical to those employed at home. No sys-

| TABLE 1–3 | THE *FORTUNE* GLOBAL 500: LARGEST CORPORATIONS BY REVENUES ($ MILLIONS) |

Company	Revenues	Profits	Profits Rank
1. Mitsubishi (Japan)	$175,835.6	$218.7	311
2. Mitsui (Japan)	171,490.5	263.8	283
3. Itochu (Japan)	167,824.7	81.6	400
4. Sumimoto (Japan)	162,475.9	73.2	408
5. General Motors (USA)	154,951.2	4,900.6	4
6. Marubeni (Japan)	150,187.4	104.4	373
7. Ford Motor (USA)	128,439.0	5,308.0	2
8. Exxon (USA)	101,459.0	5,100.0	3
9. Nissho Iwai (Japan)	100,875.5	52.7	419
10. Royal Dutch/Shell Group (UK/Netherlands)	94,881.3	6,235.6	1
11. Toyota Motor (Japan)	88,158.6	1,184.6	75
12. Wal-Mart Stores (USA)	83,412.4	2,681.0	17
13. Hitachi (Japan)	76,430.9	1,146.7	80
14. Nippon Life Insurance (Japan)	75,350.4	2,682.1	16
15. AT&T (USA)	75,094.0	4,676.0	7
16. Nippon Telegraph & Telephone (Japan)	70,843.6	767.9	129
17. Matsushita Electric Industrial (Japan)	69,946.7	911.0	106
18. Tomen (Japan)	69,901.5	10.2	451
19. General Electric (USA)	64,687.0	4,726.0	5
20. Daimler-Benz (Germany)	64,168.6	649.9	149
21. IBM (USA)	64,052.0	3,021.0	12
22. Mobil (USA)	59,621.0	1,079.0	84
23. Nissan Motor (Japan)	58,731.8	(1,671.7)	496
24. Nichimen (Japan)	56,202.6	39.7	430
25. Kanematsu (Japan)	55,856.1	(153.0)	469

Source: "The *Fortune* Global 500," *Fortune*, Aug. 7, 1995, p. F1. Figures cited from most recent fiscal year.

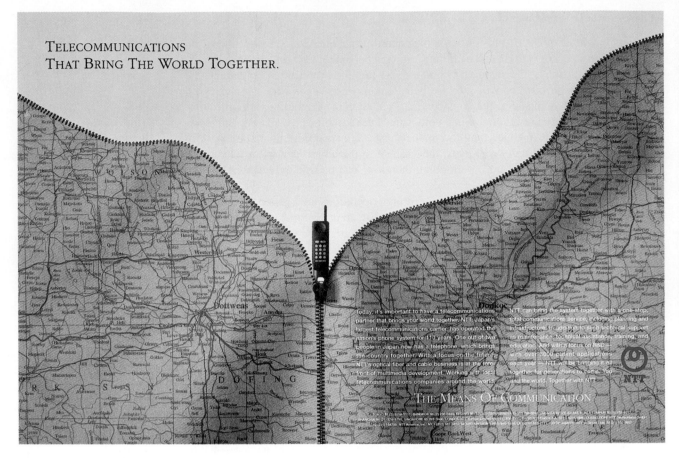

TELECOMMUNICATIONS
THAT BRING THE WORLD TOGETHER.

THE MEANS OF COMMUNICATION

NTT is promoting its international competitiveness as the telecommunications industry globalizes.

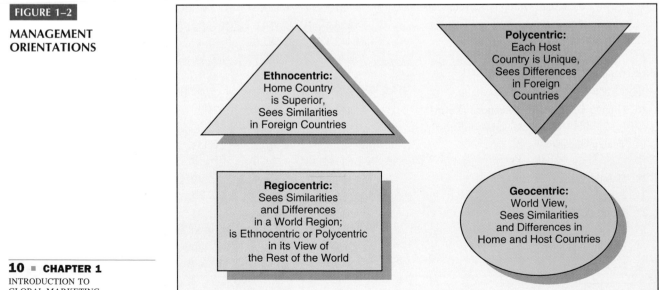

FIGURE 1–2

MANAGEMENT ORIENTATIONS

Ethnocentric:
Home Country
is Superior,
Sees Similarities
in Foreign Countries

Polycentric:
Each Host
Country is Unique,
Sees Differences
in Foreign
Countries

Regiocentric:
Sees Similarities
and Differences
in a World Region;
is Ethnocentric or Polycentric
in its View of
the Rest of the World

Geocentric:
World View,
Sees Similarities
and Differences in
Home and Host Countries

*A*s indicated in the opening paragraph of this chapter, global marketing is practiced by companies in many different countries. It was not so long ago, however, that some observers of the global scene predicted that American companies would dominate world trade. In his best-selling 1967 book *The American Challenge*, J. J. Servan-Schreiber warned that within 15 years, American-owned companies operating in Europe—IBM and GM, for example—would become the world's third greatest industrial power after the United States and the Soviet Union. He predicted dire consequences for Europe resulting from market domination by global corporations. He wrote:

> The Americans have been reorganizing their European operations. Everywhere they are setting up European-scale headquarters responsible for the firm's Continental business, with sweeping powers of decision and instructions not to pay any attention to national boundaries.[1]

He cautioned that European industry could eventually play a secondary role to U.S. industry, while Europe itself might become a mere satellite to the United States.

How accurate was Servan-Schreiber's vision? For one thing, the Soviet Union has ceased to exist. Also, many companies mentioned in his book—Union Carbide, CPC International, Celanese, and American Express, as well as IBM and GM—have indeed evolved considerably since the mid-1960s. At the time Servan-Schreiber's book was written, it was characteristic of many international companies for headquarters to keep tight control over every aspect of business strategy. Today, the way these same companies practice global marketing makes them distinctly different entities than the ones Servan-Schreiber was describing three decades ago. They have a different focus, vision, orientation, strategy, structure, operating style, and communications pattern; also, their policies relating to research and development, human resources, finance, sourcing, new product development, and investment have changed.

Moreover, today's global corporation, unlike the entities described by Servan-Schreiber, is not an exclusively American creation. Many industry sectors in Europe are alive and thriving. Numerous global corporations—including Nestlé, Philips, Volkswagen, and Unilever—are headquartered in Europe. They have not fallen into secondary roles, as Servan-Schreiber feared. Indeed, American companies have passed the baton to the Europeans as well as the Japanese in a number of key industries. For example, Thomson, a consumer electronics company headquartered in France, now owns the GE and RCA television businesses. Today, some of the biggest competitive challenges facing both Europe and the United States come from companies located in Japan, South Korea, and other Asian countries.

[1] J. J. Servan-Schreiber, *The American Challenge* (New York: Atheneum, 1968), p. 4.

tematic marketing research is conducted outside the home country, and no major modifications are made to products. Even if consumer needs or wants in international markets differ from those in the home country, those differences are ignored at headquarters.

Nissan's ethnocentric orientation was quite apparent during its first few years of exporting cars and trucks to America. Designed for mild Japanese winters, the vehicles were difficult to start in many parts of the United States during the cold winter months. In northern Japan, many car owners would put blankets over the hoods of their cars. Nissan's assumption was that Americans would do the same thing. Until the 1980s, Eli Lilly and Company operated as an ethnocentric company in which activity outside the United States was tightly controlled by headquarters and focused on selling products originally developed for the U.S. market (Malnight 1995, 125).

Fifty years ago, most business enterprises—and especially those located in a large country like the United States—could operate quite successfully with an ethnocentric orientation. Today, however, ethnocentrism is one of the biggest internal threats a company faces.

Polycentric Orientation

The **polycentric** orientation is the opposite of ethnocentrism. The term *polycentric* describes management's belief or assumption that each country in which a company does business is unique. This assumption lays the groundwork for each subsidiary to develop its own unique business and marketing strategies in order to succeed; the term *multinational company* is often used to describe such a structure. Until recently, Citicorp's fi-

nancial services around the world operated on a polycentric basis. James Bailey, a Citicorp executive, offered this description of the company: "We were like a medieval state. There was the king and his court and they were in charge, right? No. It was the land barons who were in charge. The king and his court might declare this or that, but the land barons went and did their thing."[10] Realizing that the financial services industry is globalizing, CEO John Reed is attempting to achieve a higher degree of integration between Citicorp's operating units. Like Jack Welch at GE, Reed is moving to instill a geocentric orientation throughout his company.

Regiocentric and Geocentric Orientations

In a company with a **regiocentric orientation,** management views regions as unique and seeks to develop an integrated regional strategy. For example, a U.S. company that focuses on the countries included in the North American Free Trade Agreement (NAFTA)—the United States, Canada, and Mexico—has a regiocentric orientation. Similarly, a European company that focuses its attention on Europe is regiocentric. A company with a **geocentric orientation** views the entire world as a potential market and strives to develop integrated world market strategies. A company whose management has a regiocentric or geocentric orientation is sometimes known as a *global* or *transnational company*.[11]

---

[10]Saul Hansell, "Uniting the Feudal Lords at Citicorp," *The New York Times* (Jan. 16, 1994), Sec. 3, p. 1.
[11]Although the definitions provided here are important, to avoid confusion we will use the term *global marketing* when describing the general activities of global companies. Another note of caution is in order: Usage of the terms *international*, *multinational*, and *global* varies widely. Alert readers of the business press are likely to recognize inconsistencies; usage does not always reflect the definitions provided here. In particular, companies that are (in the view of the authors as well as numerous other academics) global are often described as *multinational enterprises* (abbreviated MNE) or *multinational corporations* (abbreviated MNC). The United Nations prefers the term *transnational company* rather than *global company*. When we refer to an "international company" or a "multinational," we will do so in a way that maintains the distinctions described in the text.

The geocentric orientation represents a synthesis of ethnocentrism and polycentrism; it is a "world view" that sees similarities and differences in markets and countries, and seeks to create a global strategy that is fully responsive to local needs and wants. A regiocentric manager might be said to have a world view on a regional scale; the world outside the region of interest will be viewed with an ethnocentric or a polycentric orientation, or a combination of the two. Jack Welch's quote at the beginning of this chapter that "globalization must be taken for granted" in the 1990s implies that at least some company managers must have a geocentric orientation. However, recent research suggests that many companies are seeking to strengthen their regional competitiveness rather than moving directly to develop global responses to changes in the competitive environment (Morrison, Ricks & Roth 1991, 18).

The ethnocentric company is centralized in its marketing management, the polycentric company is decentralized, and the regiocentric and geocentric companies are integrated on a regional and global scale, respectively. A crucial difference between the orientations is the underlying assumption for each. The ethnocentric orientation is based on a belief in home-country superiority. The underlying assumption of the polycentric approach is that there are so many differences in cultural, economic, and marketing conditions in the world that it is impossible and futile to attempt to transfer experience across national boundaries.

FORCES AFFECTING GLOBAL INTEGRATION AND GLOBAL MARKETING

The remarkable growth of the global economy over the past 50 years has been shaped by the dynamic interplay of various driving and restraining forces. During most of those decades, companies from different parts of the world in different industries achieved great success by pursuing international, multinational, or global strategies. During the 1990s, changes in the business environment have presented a number of challenges to established ways of doing business. Today, the growing importance of global marketing stems from the fact that driving forces have more momentum than the restraining forces. The forces affecting global integration are shown in Figure 1–3.

Driving Forces

Regional economic agreements, converging market needs and wants, technology advances, improvements in communication and transportation technology, pressure to cut costs, pressure to improve quality, global economic growth, and opportunities for leverage all represent important driving forces; any industry subject to these forces is a candidate for globalization.

REGIONAL ECONOMIC AGREEMENTS • A number of multilateral trade agreements have accelerated the pace of global integration. NAFTA is already expanding trade

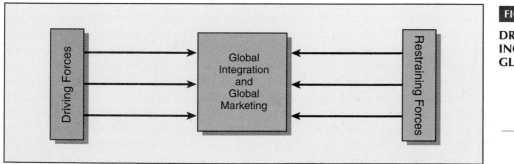

■ PHILIPS AND MATSUSHITA: HOW GLOBAL COMPANIES WIN

*U*ntil recently, Philips Electronics, headquartered in Eindhoven, Netherlands, was a classic example of a company with a polycentric orientation. Philips relied upon relatively autonomous national organizations (called "NOs" in company parlance) in each country. Each NO developed its own strategy. This approach worked quite well until Philips faced competition from Matsushita and other Japanese consumer electronics companies whose managements' orientations were geocentric. The difference in competitive advantage between Philips and its Japanese competition was dramatic. For example, Matsushita adopted a global strategy that focused its resources on serving a world market for home entertainment products. In television receivers, Matsushita offered European customers two basic models based on a single chassis. In contrast, Philips's European NOs offered customers seven different models based on four different chassis. If customers had demanded this variety, Philips would have been the stronger competitor. Unfortunately, the product designs created by the NOs were not based upon customer preferences. Customers wanted value in the form of quality, features, design—and price. Philips's decision to offer greater design variety was based not upon what customers were asking for but, rather, on Philips's structure and strategy. Each major country organization had its own engineering and manufacturing group. Each country unit had its own design and manufacturing operations. This polycentric, multinational approach was part of Philips's heritage and was attractive to NOs that had grown accustomed to functioning independently. However, the polycentric orientation was irrelevant to consumers, who were looking for value. They were getting more value from Matsushita's global strategy than from Philips's multinational strategy. Why? Matsushita's global strategy created value for consumers by lowering costs and, in turn, prices.

As a multinational company, Philips squandered resources in a duplication of effort that led to greater product variety. Variety entailed higher costs, which were passed on to consumers with no offsetting increase in consumer benefit. It is easy to understand how the right strategy resulted in Matsushita's success in the global consumer electronics industry. Since the Matsushita strategy offered greater customer value, Philips lost market share. Clearly, Philips needed a new company strategy. To meet the Japanese challenge, Philips executives consciously abandoned the polycentric, multinational approach and adopted a more geocentric orientation. A first step in this direction was to create industry groups in the Netherlands responsible for developing global strategies for R&D, marketing, and manufacturing.

among the United States, Canada, and Mexico. The General Agreement on Tariffs and Trade (GATT), which was ratified by more than 120 nations in 1994, has created the World Trade Organization to promote and protect free trade. In Europe, the expanding membership of the European Union is lowering boundaries to trade within the region.

MARKET NEEDS AND WANTS • A person studying markets around the world will discover cultural universals as well as differences. The common elements in human nature provide an underlying basis for the opportunity to create and serve global markets. The word *create* is deliberate. Most global markets do not exist in nature; they must be created by marketing effort. For example, no one *needs* soft drinks, and yet today in some countries per capita soft drink consumption *exceeds* the consumption of water. Marketing has driven this change in behavior, and today, the soft drink industry is a truly global one. Evidence is mounting that consumer needs and wants around the world are converging today as never before. This creates an opportunity for global marketing. Multinational companies pursuing strategies of product adaptation run the risk of falling victim to global competitors that have recognized opportunities to serve global customers.

Marlboro is an example of an enormously successful global brand. Targeted at urban smokers around the world, the brand appeals to the spirit of freedom, independence, and open space symbolized by the image of the cowboy in beautiful, open, American western settings. Notwithstanding recent competitive pressures in the United States that forced Philip Morris to cut prices to maintain market share, Marlboro remains popular throughout the world. The need addressed by Marlboro is universal, and therefore the basic appeal and execution of its advertising and positioning are global. Philip Morris, which markets Marlboro, is a global company that discovered years ago how the same basic market need can be met with a global approach.

TECHNOLOGY • Technology is a universal factor that crosses national and cultural boundaries. Technology is truly "stateless"; there are no cultural boundaries limiting its application. Once a technology is developed, it soon becomes available everywhere in the world. This phenomenon supports Professor Levitt's prediction concerning the emergence of global markets for standardized products. In his *Harvard Business Review* article, Levitt anticipated the communication revolution that has, in fact, become a driving force behind global marketing.[12] Satellite dishes, globe-spanning TV networks such as CNN and MTV, and the Internet are just a few of the technological factors underlying the emergence of a true global village. In regional markets such as Europe, the increasing overlap of advertising across national boundaries and the mobility of consumers have created opportunities for marketers to pursue pan-European product positionings.

COMMUNICATION AND TRANSPORTATION IMPROVEMENTS • The time and cost barriers associated with distance have fallen tremendously over the past 100 years. The jet airplane revolutionized communication by making it possible for people to travel around the world in less than 48 hours. Tourism enables people from many countries to see and experience the newest products being sold abroad. One essential characteristic of effective global business is face-to-face communication, among employees and between the company and its customers. Without modern jet travel, such communication would be difficult to sustain. In the 1990s, new communication technologies such as e-mail, fax, and video teleconferencing allow managers, executives, and customers to link up electronically from virtually any part of the world for a fraction of the cost of air travel.

A similar revolution has occurred in transportation technology. Physical distribution has declined in terms of cost; the time required for shipment has been greatly reduced as well. A letter from China to New York is now delivered in eight days—faster than domestic mail is delivered within many countries. The per-unit cost of shipping automobiles from Japan and Korea to the United States by specially designed auto-transport ships is less than the cost of overland shipping from Detroit to either U.S. coast.

PRODUCT DEVELOPMENT COSTS • The pressure for globalization is intense when new products require major investments and long periods of development time. The pharmaceutical industry provides a striking illustration of this driving force. According to the Pharmaceutical Manufacturers Association, the cost of developing a new drug in 1976 was $54 million; by 1982, the cost had increased to $87 million. By 1993, the cost of developing a new drug had reached $359 million (Malnight 1995, 123). Such costs must be recovered in the global marketplace, as no single national market is likely to be large enough to support investments of this size. As noted earlier, global marketing does not necessarily mean operating everywhere; in the $200 billion pharmaceutical industry, for example, seven countries account for 75 percent of sales.

QUALITY • Global marketing strategies can generate greater revenue and greater operating margins which, in turn, support design and manufacturing quality. A global and a domestic company may each spend 5 percent of sales on research and development, but the global company may have many times the total revenue of the domestic because it serves the world market. It is easy to understand how Nissan, Matsushita, Caterpillar, and other global companies can achieve world-class quality. Global companies "raise the bar" for all competitors in an industry. When a global company establishes a benchmark in

---

[12]Theodore Levitt, "The Globalization of Markets," *Harvard Business Review* (May–June 1983), p. 92.

quality, competitors must quickly make their own improvements and come up to par. Global competition has forced many U.S. manufacturers to improve quality; in a 1994 survey conducted by the International Mass Retail Association, 85 percent of respondents indicated they believed that U.S.-made goods had improved in recent years. That is a significant change from 1990, when only 67 percent of those surveyed thought the quality of U.S.-made goods had improved. For truly global products, uniformity can drive down research, engineering, design, and production costs across business functions. Quality, uniformity, and cost reduction were all driving forces behind Ford's development of its "World Car," which is sold in the United States as the Ford Contour and Mercury Mystique and in Europe as the Mondeo.

WORLD ECONOMIC TRENDS • There are three reasons why economic growth has been a driving force in the expansion of the international economy and the growth of global marketing. First, growth has created market opportunities that provide a major incentive for companies to expand globally. At the same time, slow growth in a company's domestic market can signal the need to look abroad for opportunities in nations or regions with high rates of growth.

Second, economic growth has reduced resistance that might otherwise have developed in response to the entry of foreign firms into domestic economies. When a country is growing rapidly, policy makers are likely to look favorably on outsiders. A growing country means growing markets; there is often plenty of opportunity for everyone. It is possible for a "foreign" company to enter a domestic economy and establish itself without taking business away from local firms. Without economic growth, global enterprises may take business away from domestic ones. Domestic businesses are more likely to seek governmental intervention to protect their local position if markets are not growing. Predictably, the worldwide recession of the early 1990s created pressure in most countries to limit access by foreigners to domestic markets.

The worldwide movement toward deregulation and privatization is another driving force. The trend toward privatization is opening up formerly closed markets significantly; tremendous opportunities are being created as a result. For example, when a nation's telephone company is a state monopoly, it is much easier to require it to buy only from national companies. An independent, private company will be more inclined to look for the best offer, regardless of the nationality of the supplier. Privatization of telephone systems around the world is creating huge opportunities for companies such as AT&T and Northern Telcom.

LEVERAGE • A global company possesses the unique opportunity to develop leverage. *Leverage* is simply some type of advantage that a company enjoys by virtue of the fact that it conducts business in more than one country. Four important types of leverage are experience transfers, scale economies, resource utilization, and global strategy.

Experience Transfers • A global company can leverage its experience in any market in the world. It can draw upon management practices, strategies, products, advertising appeals, or sales or promotional ideas that have been tested in actual markets and apply them in other comparable markets.

For example, Asea Brown Boveri (ABB), a giant industrial organization with 1,300 companies in 140 countries, has considerable experience with a well-tested management "model" that it transfers across national boundaries. The Zurich-based company knows that a company's headquarters can be run with a lean staff. When ABB acquired a Finnish company, it reduced the headquarters staff from 880 to 25 between 1986 and 1989. Headquarters staff at a German unit was reduced from 1,600 to 100 between 1988 and 1989. After acquiring Combustion Engineering (CE; an American company producing powerplant boilers), ABB *knew* from experience that the headquarters staff of 800 could be drastically reduced, in spite of the fact that CE had a justification for every one of the headquarters staff positions.

Scale Economies • The global company can take advantage of its greater manufacturing volume to obtain traditional scale advantages within a single factory. Also, finished products can be manufactured by combining components manufactured in scale-efficient plants in different countries. Japan's giant Matsushita Electric Company is a classic example of global marketing; it achieved scale economies by exporting VCRs, televisions, and other consumer electronics products throughout the world from world-scale factories in Japan. The importance of manufacturing scale has diminished somewhat as companies implement flexible manufacturing techniques and invest in factories outside the home country. However, scale economies were a cornerstone of Japanese success in the 1970s and 1980s.

Leverage from scale economies is not limited to manufacturing. Just as a domestic company can achieve economies in staffing by eliminating duplicate positions after an acquisition, a global company can achieve the same economies on a global scale by centralizing functional activities. The larger scale of the global company also creates opportunities to improve corporate staff competence and quality.

Resource Utilization • A major strength of the global company is its ability to scan the entire world to identify people, money, and raw materials that will enable it to compete most effectively in world markets. This is equally true for established companies and start-ups. For example, British Biotechnology Group, founded in 1986, raised $60 million from investors in the United States, Japan, and Great Britain. For a global company, it is not problematic if the value of the "home" currency rises or falls dramatically, because in this case there really is no such thing as a home currency. The world is full of currencies, and a global company seeks financial resources on the best available terms. In turn, it uses them where there is the greatest opportunity to serve a need at a profit.

Global Strategy • The global company's greatest single advantage can be its global strategy. A global strategy is built on an information system that scans the world business environment to identify opportunities, trends, threats, and resources. When opportunities are identified, the global company adheres to the three principles identified earlier: It leverages its skills and focuses its resources to create superior perceived value for customers and achieve competitive advantage. *The global strategy is a design to create a winning offering on a global scale.* This takes great discipline, much creativity, and constant effort. The reward is not just success—it's survival.

Restraining Forces

Despite the impact of the driving forces identified previously, several restraining forces may slow a company's efforts to engage in global marketing. Three important restraining forces are management myopia, organizational culture, and national controls. As we have noted, however, in today's world the driving forces dominate the restraining forces. That is why the importance of global marketing is steadily growing.

MANAGEMENT MYOPIA AND ORGANIZATIONAL CULTURE • In many cases, management simply ignores opportunities to pursue global marketing. A company that is "nearsighted" and ethnocentric will not expand geographically. Myopia is also a recipe for market disaster if headquarters attempts to dictate when it should listen. Global marketing does not work without a strong local team that can provide information about local market conditions. Executives at Parker Pen once attempted to implement a top-down marketing strategy that ignored experience gained by local market representatives. Costly market failures resulted in Parker's buyout by managers of the former U.K. subsidiary. Eventually, the Gillette Company acquired Parker.

In companies where subsidiary management "knows it all," there is no room for vision from the top. In companies where headquarters management is all-knowing, there is no room for local initiative or an in-depth knowledge of local needs and conditions. Executives and managers at successful global companies have learned how to integrate global vision and perspective with local market initiative and input. A striking theme emerged during interviews conducted by one of the authors with executives of successful global companies. That theme was the respect for local initiative and input by headquarters executives, and the corresponding respect for headquarters' vision by local executives.

NATIONAL CONTROLS • Every country protects local enterprise and interests by maintaining control over market access and entry in both low- and high-tech industries. Such control ranges from a monopoly controlling access to tobacco markets to national government control of broadcast, equipment, and data transmission markets. Today, tariff barriers have been largely removed in the high-income countries, thanks to GATT, NAFTA, and other economic agreements. However, nontariff barriers (NTBs) still make it difficult for companies to gain access to a domestic market. For example, utility companies in France are notorious for accepting bids from foreign equipment suppliers but, in the end, favoring national suppliers when awarding contracts.

OUTLINE OF THIS BOOK

This book was written for students and businesspersons interested in global marketing. Throughout the book, we present and discuss important concepts and tools specifically applicable to global marketing.

The book is divided into five parts. Part I begins with an overview of global marketing and the basic theory of global marketing. Chapters 2 through 7 comprise Part II, in which we cover the environments of global marketing: economic and regional market characteristics, including the location of income and population, patterns of trade and investment, and stages of market development; social and cultural elements; and legal and regulatory dimensions. The global financial framework and foreign exchange considerations are covered in Chapter 6. We discuss marketing information systems and research in Chapter 7.

Part III begins with Chapter 8 on market segmentation, targeting, and sourcing. Chapter 9 covers the basics of importing and exporting. Chapters 10 through 12 are devoted to various aspects of global strategy, including strategy alternatives for market entry and expansion, global strategic partnerships, and competitive advantage.

Part IV is devoted to global considerations pertaining to the marketing mix. The application of product, price, channel, and marketing communications decisions in response to global market opportunity and threat is covered in detail in Chapters 13 through 16.

Two final chapters make up Part V. Chapter 17 describes the organization and control of global marketing programs and examines the integrating and managerial dimensions of global marketing: planning, organization, control and the marketing audit, strategy implementation, and the future of global marketing. In the final chapter we offer some thoughts on the future of global marketing.

SUMMARY

Global marketing is the process of focusing the resources and objectives of a company on global marketing opportunities. Companies engage in global marketing for two reasons: to take advantage of opportunities for growth and expansion and to survive. Companies that fail to pursue global opportunities are likely to eventually lose their domestic markets because they will be pushed aside by stronger and more competitive global competitors. This book presents the theory and practice of applying the universal discipline of marketing to the global opportunities found in world markets.

The basic goals of marketing are to create customer value and competitive advantage by maintaining focus. Company management can be classified in terms of its orientation toward the world: ethnocentric, polycentric, regiocentric, or geocentric. An ethnocentric orientation characterizes domestic and international companies; international companies pursue marketing opportunities outside the home market by extending various elements of the marketing mix. A polycentric world view predominates at a multinational company, where the marketing mix is adapted by local managers operating autonomously. Managers at global and transnational companies are regiocentric or geocentric in their orientation and pursue both extension and adaptation strategies in global markets.

Global marketing's importance today is shaped by the dynamic interplay of several driving and restraining forces. The former include regional trade agreements, market needs and wants, technology, transportation and communication improvements, costs, quality, world economic growth, and a recognition of opportunities to develop leverage by operating globally. Restraining forces include management myopia, organizational culture, and national controls.

DISCUSSION QUESTIONS

1. What are the basic goals of marketing? Are these goals relevant to global marketing?
2. What is meant by "global localization"? Is Coca-Cola a global product? Explain.
3. Describe some of the global marketing strategies available to companies. Give examples of companies using the different strategies.
4. How do the global marketing strategies of Harley-Davidson and Toyota differ?
5. Describe the difference between ethnocentric, polycentric, regiocentric, and geocentric management orientations.
6. Identify and briefly describe some of the forces that have resulted in increased global integration and the growing importance of global marketing.
7. Define *leverage* and explain the different types of leverage utilized by companies with global operations.

BIBLIOGRAPHY

Books

Barnet, Richard J., and John Cavanagh. *Global Dreams: Imperial Corporations and the New World Order*. New York: Simon & Schuster, 1994.

Miller, L. K. *Transnational Corporations: A Selective Bibliography, 1991–1992*. New York: United Nations, 1992.

Ohmae, Kenichi. *The End of the Nation State: The Rise of Regional Economies*. New York: Free Press, 1995.

Ohmae. *The Borderless World: Power and Strategy in the Interlinked Economy*. New York: HarperPerennial, 1991.

Reich, Robert B. *The Work of Nations*. New York: Vintage Books, 1992.

Stahl, M. J., and G. M. Bounds. *Competing Globally through Customer Value: The Management of Strategic Suprasystems*. Westport, CT: Quorum Books, 1991.

Wendt, Henry. *Global Embrace: Corporate Challenges in a Transnational World*. New York: HarperBusiness, 1993.

Articles

Bannister, Geoffrey, C. A. Primo Braga, and Joe Petry. "Transnational Corporations, the Neo-Liberal Agenda and Regional Integration: Establishing a Policy Framework." *Quarterly Review of Economics & Finance* 34 (Summer 1994), pp. 77–99.

Bassiry, G. R., and R. Hrair Dekmejian. "America's Global Companies: A Leadership Profile." *Business Horizons* 36, no. 1 (January–February 1993), pp. 47–53.

Collins, Robert S., and William A. Fischer. "American Manufacturing Competitiveness: The View from Europe." *Business Horizons* 35, no. 4 (July–August 1992), pp. 15–23.

Franko, Lawrence G. "Global Corporate Competition II: Is the Large American Firm an Endangered Species?" *Business Horizons* 34, no. 6 (November-December 1991), pp. 14–22.

Halal, William E. "Global Strategic Management in a New World Order." *Business Horizons* 36, no. 6 (November-December 1993), pp. 5–10.

Hu, Tao-Su. "Global or Stateless Corporations are National Firms with International Operations." *California Management Review* 34, no. 2 (Winter 1992), pp. 107–126.

Kogut, Bruce, and Udo Zander. "Knowledge of the Firm and the Evolutionary Theory of the Multinational Corporation." *Journal of International Business Studies* 24, no. 4 (Fourth Quarter 1993), pp. 625–646.

Li, Jiatao, and Stephen Guisinger. "How Well Do Foreign Firms Compete in the United States?" *Business Horizons* 34, no. 6 (November–December 1991), pp. 49–53.

Malnight, T. W. "Globalization of an Ethnocentric Firm: An Evolutionary Perspective." *Strategic Management Journal* 16, no. 2 (February 1995), pp. 119–141.

Miles, Gregory L. "Tailoring a Global Product." *International Business* (March 1995), pp. 50–52.

Morrison, Allen J., David A. Ricks, and Kendall Roth. "Globalization Versus Regionalization: Which Way for the Multinational?" *Organizational Dynamics* (Winter 1991), pp. 17–29.

Rao, T. R., and G. M. Naidu. "Are the Stages of Internationalization Empirically Supportable?" *Journal of Global Marketing* 1, no. 2 (1992), pp. 147–170.

Reid, David McHardy. "Perspectives for International Marketers on the Japanese Market." *Journal of International Marketing* 3, no. 1 (1995), pp. 63–84.

Smith, Paul M., and Cynthia D. West. "The Globalization of Furniture Industries/Markets." *Journal of Global Marketing* 7, no. 3 (1994), pp. 103–132.

Tahija, Julius. "Swapping Business Skills for Oil." *Harvard Business Review* 71, no. 5 (September 1993), pp. 64–77.

Tiglao, Rigoberto. "Is This the Next Nestlé?" *Far Eastern Economic Review* 157, no. 1 (Dec. 30, 1993), pp. 54–55.

McDonald's, a fast-food legend known for quality and service, is pursuing a global expansion strategy that has brought the famous Golden Arches to 68 different countries. Why go abroad when the company already has more than 9,700 restaurants in the United States and serves up nearly one-third of the hamburgers that Americans consume? With annual advertising and promotion expenditures of $1 billion, McDonald's is the single most advertised brand in the United States. But the company's domestic growth has slowed in recent years. At the same time, annual growth rates for the American fast-food industry as a whole have declined—from an average of 7.1 percent in the 1970s to less than 5 percent in the 1980s.

For example, while U.S. sales grew only 4 percent in 1989, sales at company-owned restaurants outside the United States increased 19 percent. McDonald's has responded by stepping up its rate of new unit opening. In 1991, the company had 3,355 units in 53 countries; by the end of 1994, more than 5,400 overseas restaurants were in operation. Although these non-U.S. restaurants comprised only about one-third of the total (in all, there were 15,205 units worldwide in 1994), they account for about 43 percent of sales. In dollar terms, $11 billion of McDonald's $25.7 billion in 1994 systemwide sales came from outside the United States.

On January 31, 1990, after 14 years of negotiation and preparation, the first "Bolshoi Mac" went on sale in what was then the Soviet Union. The Moscow McDonald's is located on Pushkin Square just four blocks from the Kremlin. It has 700 indoor seats and another 200 outside. It boasts 800 employees and features a 70-foot counter with 27 cash registers—equivalent to 20 ordinary McDonald's rolled into one. The restaurant serves up 18,000 orders of fries, 12,000 Big Macs, and 11,000 apple pies every day. To ensure a steady supply of raw materials, the company built a huge processing facility on the outskirts of Moscow and worked closely with local farmers. Despite the turmoil stemming from the dissolution of the Soviet Union and the political upheaval in the fall of 1993, to date more than 50 million sandwiches have been sold at the Pushkin Square location. Meanwhile, two more McDonald's restaurants were opened in Moscow in 1993. By 1995, the three stores were serving a total of 70,000 customers each day. McDonald's has also set its sights on Central Europe, where 350 new restaurants will be opened in Croatia, Slovakia, Romania, and other countries.

The menu in Moscow—where "meat and potatoes" are staples—has the same basic offerings as in the United States. In other countries, however, McDonald's has adapted its fare in response to local tastes. The varied offerings include teriyaki burgers in Japan, banana fruit pies in Latin America, kiwi burgers (served with beet root sauce) in New Zealand, beer in Germany, McSpaghetti noodles in the Philippines, and chili sauce to go with fries in Singapore. In some countries, McDonald's has been forced to change its food preparation methods as well; in Singapore and Malaysia, for example, the beef that goes into Halal burgers must be slaughtered according to Muslim law.

Having successfully begun to develop the Russian market, McDonald's has set its sights on China and India. China is now home to the world's largest McDonald's. The first Chinese restaurant opened in mid-1992 in central Beijing, a few blocks from the infamous Tiananmen Square. By mid-1995, McDonald's had a total of 12 restaurants in the Chinese capital and 40 throughout the rest of the country. The restaurants get 95 percent of their supplies—including lettuce—from within China. Despite the fact that McDonald's signed a 20-year lease for its central Beijing location, the company found itself in the middle of a dispute between the central government and Beijing's city government. City officials decided to build a new $1.2 billion commercial complex in the city center and demanded that McDonald's vacate the site. However, central government officials had not approved the city's plans.

McDonald's plans for India call for opening restaurants in New Delhi and Bombay in 1996. However, the company must first develop a substitute ingredient for its sandwiches because the Hindu religion prohibits eating beef. A "McMutton" lamb sandwich is a possible alternative. (PepsiCo beat McDonald's into India with the June 1995 opening of a Kentucky Fried Chicken restaurant in Bangalore.)

Despite McDonald's international success, the company has occasionally stumbled in its efforts to promote fast food around the world. A poster that was displayed in 66 Dutch restaurants in October 1991 caused a furor in France, where the first McDonald's opened in 1979. The poster featured a photo of five chefs examining a batch of dressed chickens; the caption indicated that the chefs were actually dreaming of Big Macs. The poster caused an uproar for two reasons. One of the people in the photo was Paul Bocuse, a legendary three-star French chef. Also, the chickens were identified as being from a French region renowned for its poultry. All in all, the posters were taken as an insult to French *haut cuisine*. In a letter of apology to Bocuse, McDonald's only made matters worse by attributing the error in part to the fact that Bocuse is not well known in the Netherlands.

Despite such international *faux pas*, McDonald's is moving forward with its expansion plans. McDonald's International is divided into four regions: Europe/Africa, which currently accounts for approximately two-thirds of international sales; the Pacific Rim, with 23 percent; Latin America, with 6 percent; and Canada, with 2 percent. McDonald's recent strategy included a unified global advertising campaign—a first for the company—used during the 1994 World Cup soccer playoffs. In the words of one market analyst, "McDonald's is similar to Coca-Cola ten years ago. It's on the verge of becoming an international giant, with the United States as a major market, but overseas as the driving force."

DISCUSSION QUESTIONS

1. Why has McDonald's increased its emphasis on markets outside the United States? What criteria appear to be guiding the company in its selection of target markets?
2. Does McDonald's success outside the United States provide support for Professor Levitt's views about the global marketplace?
3. Do you think a company like McDonald's is welcome in developing countries like Russia, China, and India? Why or why not?
4. How can McDonald's avoid future international incidents like the one in France?

Sources: Andrew E. Serwer, "McDonald's Conquers the World," *Fortune* (Oct. 17, 1994) pp. 103–104.
Harlan S. Byrne, "Welcome to McWorld," *Barron's* (Aug. 29, 1994), pp. 25–28.
Steven Greenhouse, "McDonald's Tries Paris, Again," *The New York Times* (June 12, 1988), sec. 3, pp. 1, 17.
Robert Johnson, "Fast Food Leader: McDonald's Combines a Dead Man's Advice with Lively Strategy," *The Wall Street Journal* (Dec. 18, 1987), p. A1.
Barbara Dietrich, "Cohon Launches 'Big Mac Attack' on USSR," *Drake University Update* (Summer 1990), p. 13.
Roger Cohen, "Faux Pas by McDonald's in Europe," *The New York Times* (Feb. 18, 1992), p. C1.
Eben Shapiro, "Overseas Sizzle for McDonald's," *The New York Times* (Apr 17, 1992), p. C1.
Valerie Reitman, "India Anticipates the Arrival of the Beefless Big Mac," *The Wall Street Journal* (Oct. 20, 1993), p. B1.

APPENDIX I

THE STRATEGIC MARKETING PLUS 2000 CONCEPTUAL FRAMEWORK FOR COMPETITIVE AUDIT, STRATEGY FORMULATION AND CAPABILITY ENHANCEMENT

In early 1996, Hermawan Kartajaya, leading service officer of MarkPlus Professional Service, decided that he needed to set down in writing exactly what he meant when he talked about the marketing concept. Indonesia was the fourth-largest country in the world in population and home to one of the fastest-growing economies in which average income was approaching the magic number of $1,000 GNP per capita. It was a remarkable time for Indonesia and for MarkPlus, the firm that Mr. Kartajaya founded to help Indonesian and East Asian firms compete more effectively in a globalizing world economy. The statement which follows is Mr. Kartajaya's marketing manifesto.

INTRODUCTION

The following conceptual framework can be used as a basis for:

- Comparing the actual state of an organization with the competitive setting (*competitive audit*)
- Formulating an appropriate competitive strategy based on the results of the competitive audit (*strategy formulation*)
- Enhancing the organization's ability to compete, in line with the formulated strategy (*capability enhancement*)

Although the model limits itself to the concept of changing one's marketing approach to reflect an increasingly intense competitive setting, the model may also be used as a "practical tool" for analyzing marketing in general.

FUNDAMENTAL CONCEPTS OF MARKETING

From time to time, marketing is redefined to adapt to a highly decisive variable, namely the competitive setting.

Broadly speaking, it can be assumed that:

- At a time when there is not yet any competition, or the competitive setting is not intense, marketing is either not yet needed or not yet too important to a company.
- As the competitive setting intensifies, marketing becomes increasingly important to the company.
- By the time the competitive setting is highly intense, unpredictable and chaotic, marketing must become the "heart and soul" of everyone in the company.

As a result, marketing, as an adaptive concept, will in the future be based on the following philosophy.

Vision: Marketing must be a strategic business concept, aimed at assuring sustainable satisfaction—not momentary satisfaction—to the three main stakeholders in any company: The customers, the people in the organization and the shareholders.

Mission: Marketing will be the soul—not just "one part of the body"—of an organization, and therefore everyone in the company will be a marketer. This means that marketing will no longer be the monopoly of the marketing department, but the basis by which all people make decisions.

Values: Three principal values will be held by the company:

- Brand is more valuable to the customer than product.
- Shareholders must treat their business, whatever it is, as a service business.
- Everyone in the organization must belong to the customer-satisfying process either directly or indirectly, and not to a specific function.

The relationship between these three principal values and the ongoing satisfaction of customers, employees and shareholders is depicted in Figure 1. The sequence of activities is depicted as an anti-clockwise circle and a clockwise circle, neither of which may be broken.

The shareholders of a profitable company must reward the employees appropriately, by treating them as complete human

FIGURE 1

A FRAMEWORK FOR THE
SUCCESS OF INDONESIAN
BUSINESS

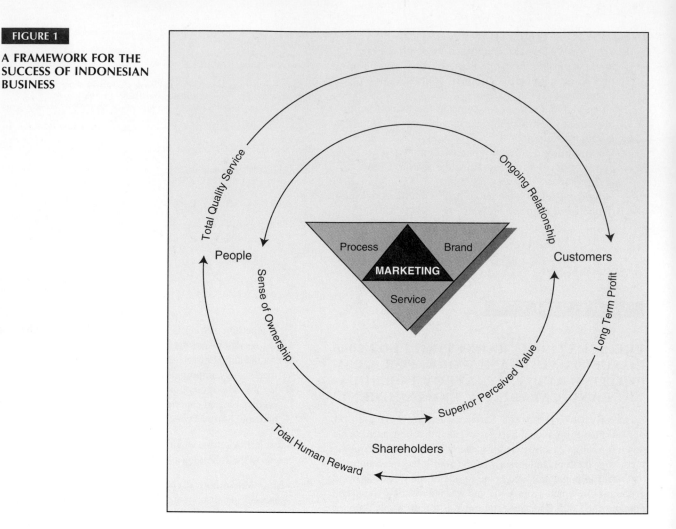

beings. In other words, the employees must be treated as "internal customers" who must be satisfied. Employees who are treated in this way are expected to feel a sense of ownership of the company and therefore to deliver total quality service which fully satisfies its customers. In turn, the satisfied customers will continue their relationship with the employees who satisfied them, and in this way will ensure the long-term profitability of the company concerned.

For the above to happen, in managing their business, the owners of the company must always strive to deliver a product or service of superior value to the customers, compared to the product or service delivered by the competitors.

If the sequence of the above activities is broken at any point, the satisfaction of all three parties will be disturbed, and the company will be unable to win against its competition.

This concept of marketing, if completely and correctly implemented, will guarantee that the above sequence of activities will continue in a whole and mutual fashion.

THE MAIN COMPONENTS OF MARKETING

Figure 2 shows the main components of marketing, which are depicted as three cycles.

1. An inner cycle, which shows the competitive state of a company within its business environment.
2. A middle cycle which depicts marketing strategy, tactics, and value.
3. An outer cycle which shows the three most important question words that must be answered precisely when implementing a marketing program.

The interaction between marketing strategy, tactics, and value is shown in the middle cycle. All three of these factors have an influence on the other two.

At the time of formulating marketing strategy and tactics, marketing value should be the basis of all thought. However, it is quite possible that after the marketing strategy and tactics have been decided, marketing value will have to be adjusted. There will be a similar interaction between marketing strategy and tactics at the time that they are determined, with each influencing and compensating for the other.

Within each of the three circles (strategy, tactics, and value) in the middle cycle, there are three elements which interact with and influence each other, as follows:

1. *The Competitive Strategy Circle* (S)

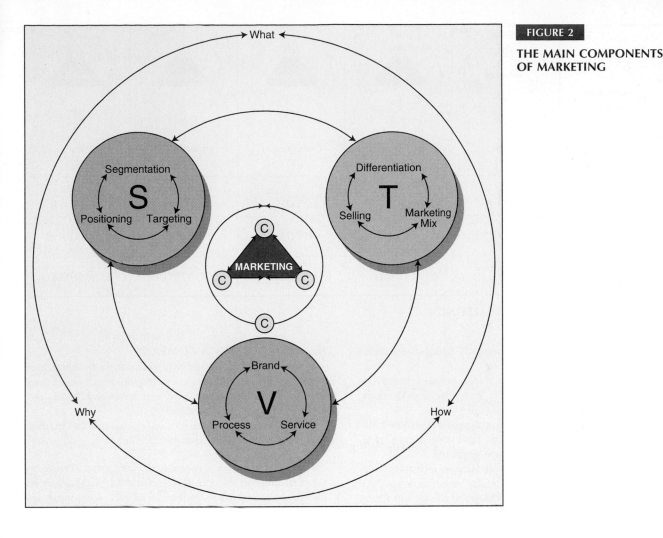

FIGURE 2

THE MAIN COMPONENTS OF MARKETING

- *Segmentation:* The way of dividing the market on the basis of particular variables.
- *Targeting:* Choosing one or more market segments as a target market.
- *Positioning:* The position which is desired within the mind of the consumer.

2. *The Marketing Tactics Circle* (T)

- *Differentiation:* Realizing the marketing strategy with regard to all of the interrelated factors that differentiate one company from another.
- *Marketing Mix:* Determining the combination of product, price, place and promotion in line with the marketing strategy.
- *Selling:* Efforts to induce the consumer to buy what the company has to offer, set in line with the marketing strategy.

3. *The Marketing Value Circle* (V)

- *Brand:* Encompassing the company's principles in increasing brand-equity.
- *Service:* The company's principles for increasing the quality of service delivered to its customers.
- *Process:* The company's principles for involving every employee in the customer satisfaction process, both directly and indirectly.

THE SHIFTING COMPETITIVE SETTING

The cycle in Figure 3 shows the competitive setting, which ranges from a minimum of 2C to a maximum of 4C based on the condition of each of the following 4 Cs:

C1: Customer
C2: Company
C3: Competitor
C4: Change

In Figure 3, one can clearly see the shift which occurs from a stable situation to an interrupted, complicated, sophisticated and finally chaotic state. This transition is outlined below:

The 2C state occurs if a company has no competitors in serving its customers. Additionally, there is no meaningful change in the business environment. In a situation like this, the customer is treated merely as a buyer within a transaction. Because he has no other choice, the buyer is in an extremely weak position, to the extent that he must accept whatever product or service the

Competitive Setting	Stable (2C)	Interrupted (2.5C)	Complicated (3C)	Sophisticated (3.5C)	Chaos (4C)
Customer (C1)	BUYER	CONSUMER	CUSTOMER	CLIENT	PARTNER
Competitor (C3)	NONE	MILD	STRONG	WILD	INVISIBLE
Change (C4)	NONE	GRADUAL	CONTINUOUS	DISCONTINUOUS	SURPRISING

FIGURE 3 THE COMPETITIVE SETTING

company produces. This is the "extreme left" situation, one which can be characterized as a monopoly.

The competitive setting will be shifted to the right towards the 4C state by increasing competition, from none, to mild, strong, wild and finally invisible.

The competitive setting's shift to the right will also be influenced by changes in the environment, from none, through gradual, continuous, and discontinuous, to surprising.

At the same time, customers will become increasingly demanding and therefore, from being treated simply as buyers, will have to be treated as consumers, customers, clients, and finally partners.

At the 4C state, which is the chaotic "extreme right" competitive setting, a company's competitors will become increasingly invisible due to:

- The abundance of new competitors which are considered indirect competitors.
- The abundance of marketing strategies which do not utilize the mass media. The abundance of global competitions which present more and more choices to the buyer in a variety of ways, by using advanced telecommunications and information.

In this state, unexpected and often shocking changes to the environment can occur. At this moment, the customer is highly enlightened, empowered and informed. Sophisticated customers like these demand to be treated as partners.

In reality, the competitive setting can be at a state anywhere between the two extreme states (2C and 4C). The interrupted (2.5C), complicated (3C), and sophisticated (3.5C) states are simply intermediate points between these two extremes.

Measurement of the current state of the competitive setting can be best achieved by conducting a more detailed evaluation of factors that influence and bring about changes in the customer, competitor, and change itself.

THE EVOLUTION OF A COMPANY

Figure 4 shows both the stages of a company's evolution, from production-oriented, through selling-oriented, marketing-oriented and market driven to customer driven and the key success factors in force at each stage.

The fundamental characteristics and emphasis of the first three types of company can be explained as follows:

- *Production-oriented company* (2C company): A company that emphasizes operational efficiency, standardization, products and mass distribution. In a 2C competitive setting, such a company can succeed due to the total absence of competitors and change in the environment. The buyer is forced to accept standard products at locations decided by the company.
- *Selling-oriented company* (2.5C company): A company that emphasizes persuasive selling methods, improvement of products and mass promotion. In a 2.5C competitive setting, this type of company can succeed because the competitors' position is still weak and changes in the business environment, while present, are still inconsequential.

  Consumers are convinced to buy in a potentially win/lose manner by the company's sales force, tempted by unceasing mass promotion and advertising, which claims that the company's own products are better than those of the competitors'.
- *Marketing-oriented company* (3C company): A company at this state does not sell to the entire market, but chooses the segments of the market which it can most effectively serve. Besides this, the company does not merely produce a superior product, but more importantly is able to differentiate its product from other products in line with its customers' needs. Furthermore, promotion is conducted in a balanced manner both towards the end users and to the traders of the product.

Company (C2)	☺ PRODUCER	☺ SELLER	☹ MARKETER	☺ SPECIALIST	☺ SERVICE-PROVIDER
Type of Company	Production Oriented	Selling Oriented	Marketing Oriented	Market Driven	Customer Driven
Key Successful Factors	• Operational Efficiency. • Product Standardization. • Mass Distribution.	• Persuasive Selling. • Product Featuring. • Mass Promotion.	• Market Effectiveness. • Product Differentiation. • Balanced Promotion.	• Niche Selectivity. • Product Specialization. • Integrated Communication.	• Database Accountability. • Product Customization. • Interactive Communication.

FIGURE 4   STAGES OF COMPANY EVOLUTION

In a 3C competitive setting, competition is strong, changes to the business environment are continuous, and customers have numerous choices due to the abundance and openness of available information.

In the above three company types, production is first replaced by selling, which is in turn replaced by marketing as the dominant function within the organization.

The next two company types are market-driven companies and customer-driven companies. In both of these types, the company pays attention not only to the needs and wants, but also to the expectations of its customers, who play an active role in communicating them to the company. The differences between these two company types are as follows:

- *Market-driven company* (3.5C company): This company specializes in serving one or several market fragments. Thus, the key to its success is its ability to provide specialized products. In this state, the customer is treated as a client who is served in a special way. If the same product is to be marketed to several market fragments, the various marketing elements are tailored to each specific fragment.
- *Customer-driven company* (4C company): This type of company gives special service to each individual customer through products which are adjusted to the needs of each individual. A continuously updated data base is an important tool for this kind of relationship marketing.

Interactive two-way communication is employed to continuously exchange information. This is necessary if the company wishes to succeed in the chaotic competitive setting, where competitors are often invisible and change is often shocking.

All 4C level businesses are considered service businesses. Thus, the company considers itself a service provider which serves its partners.

Figure 5 further elaborates the shifting of the nine marketing elements present in strategy, tactics and value (the middle cycle).

COMPONENTS OF STRATEGY
Segmentation

The variable used to divide the market shifts from geographics to demographics, psychographics and behavior to the individual. At the 4C position, the market is considered a collection of individuals who are different from one another. Conversely, companies at the 2C position considered it sufficient to divide the market into geographical areas and to treat everyone as if their needs and wants were the same. There are three other ways to divide the market: Division based on demographic variables, which are concerned with who will buy; psychographic variables, which relate to why they buy and behavioral variables, which pertain to how they buy and focus on actual, concrete buying behavior.

Targeting

A 2C company considers everyone (without exception) as its target market. On the other hand, a 2.5C company selects suitable people (suitable ones) who are believed to be able to buy the company's products. A 3C company chooses people only within market segments considered most effective as target markets. A 3.5C company chooses relatively few people (a few good ones) within one market fragment, especially those which have not yet been well served by the company. However, it is quite possible for such a company to service several fragments at the same time, but in different ways. A 4C company considers every customer as someone who is important to the company, thus requiring individualized service.

Positioning

A 2C company is positioned on its own as the only company in the industry concerned. Conversely, a 4C company occupies a different position for each of its customers. Between these two extremes, the company can position itself as any of the following: Better than other companies, different from other companies, or holding a different position in each different market fragment.

TACTICAL COMPONENTS
Differentiation

2C companies arrange all aspects within the organization for their own benefit. At the other extreme, 4C companies organize all aspects of the company so that they are able to deliver customized service to each individual customer. Between these two

Type of Marketing	No Marketing	Mass Marketing	Segmented Marketing	Niche Marketing	Individualized Marketing
STRATEGY Segmentation	Geographics	Demographics	Psychographics	Behavioral	Individualized
Targeting	Everyone	Suitable Ones	Chosen Ones	A Few Good Ones	Someone
Positioning	The Only One	The Better One	One Statement	Different Ones	One on One
TACTIC Differentiation	Good for Company	Better than Competitor	Preferred by Customer	Specialized for Niches	Customized for Individuals
Marketing Mix	4A Assortment Affordable Available Announcement	4B Best Bargaining Buffer-Stocking Bombarding	4P Product Price Place Promotion	4V Variety Value Venue Voice	4C Customer Solution Cost Convenience Communication
Selling	Informing about Product	Feature Selling	Benefit Selling	Solution Selling	Interacting for Success
VALUE Brand	Just-a-Name	Brand Awareness	Brand Association	Perceived Quality	Brand Loyalty
Service	One Business Category	Value-Added Business	Value-in-Use Business	Customer Satisfying Business	The Only Business Category
Process	System & Procedure Implementation	Interfunctional Team Work	Functional Streamlining	Total Delivery Reengineering	Extended Value Chain

FIGURE 5 HOW THE ELEMENTS OF STRATEGY, TACTICS, AND VALUE SHIFT

extremes, the company can organize all aspects of its operation in line with any of the following: to make a better product than the competition, to be liked by the customers or to tailor its product and/or services to suit one or many market fragments.

Marketing Mix

The marketing mix comprises *product*, *price*, *place* and *promotion* and is thus referred to as 4P In the 2C state, the marketing mix is referred to as 4A, because the company has provided a sufficient choice of products (*assortment*), which do not necessarily match the needs and wants of the customers. More importantly, the product is *affordable* and *available*, and its availability is publicized through simple *announcements*.

In the 2.5C state, the marketing mix can be called 4B, because usually at this state companies are either racing to produce a better product than their competitors' or sufficiently confident to declare their product the *best*. The price is set as high as possible, but is still susceptible to increases or decreases if *bargaining* comes into play. The distribution channels (both distributors and retailers) are "forced" to carry a *buffer* stock through various "push incentives," and the mind of the consumer is *bombarded* by advertisements to create "pull incentives."

In the 3C state, the four Ps of the marketing mix are integrally set in line with the pre-determined marketing strategy.

In the 3.5C state, the marketing mix can be called 4V, because in this state there are many types of products for the *various* heterogeneous market fragments. In determining the price, the actual *value* received by the buyer must be taken into account. A special place must be used for selling to each market fragment (*venue*), and the *voice* of the customer must be given due attention.

In the 4C state, the marketing mix may be called 4C, because a product has no use if it is not a *customer solution*. The products of any given company must be supplemented with an element of service, or if necessary with even the products of other companies, so that they become genuine solutions to particular customer problems. The price set by the company is only one component of the cost to the consumer. Thus, the company must think from the point of view of the buyer and consider the actual total *cost* to the consumer in buying the product. The locations chosen by the company for the sale of the product or delivery of service must be comfortable and *convenient* for the buyer. If not, all efforts will be meaningless. In this situation, promotion, which is one-way and resembles brainwashing, has been supplanted by interactive two-way *communication*.

Selling

Selling also shifts from one form to another form, as follows. At the 2C state, selling, in the sense of convincing someone to buy, is not necessary; it is sufficient for the company to inform the public that its products are available. Since there is only one source, the buyer will make a purchase without any further incentives. At higher states, the nature of selling shifts from selling features of a product and benefits to the buyer, to finally solutions for the buyer. At the 4C state, consumers are sophisticated and knowledgeable and therefore no longer want to "be sold." In fact, the most effective way to sell at this stage is through interacting with the customers for the mutual success of the company and the customers in a genuine win/win climate.

THE VALUE COMPONENT
Brand

At the 2C state, the company employs its brand merely to differentiate its products from those of other companies. Here, brand is just a name. There is not yet any effort to transform the brand into company equity. At subsequent states, the company endeavors to make its brand more widely known (increase brand awareness), to give it a particular association in the mind of the consumer (brand association), and to ensure it is perceived as a symbol of quality (brand quality). Finally, at the 4C state, the company strives to ensure that the buyers are completely satisfied with and loyal to the brand (brand loyalty). In this way, the brand will possess considerable brand equity for the company.

Service

In the 2C state, a new company considers service simply as one category of business from the dichotomy of "service and product" businesses. A company which makes products does not consider itself a service business. In subsequent states, the company feels the need to add or improve service capacity as part of its value-added drive. Further along the line, the company will strive to add value strictly in line with what is actually required by the consumer (value in use). At the next state, the company endeavors to give service that will satisfy the customer and finally at the 4C extreme, the company considers itself a service business regardless of the nature of its business.

Process

At the 2C state, all employees work based on the systems and procedures in force according to their own specific descriptions. The most popular company structure at this stage is the pyramid organization (system and procedure implementation). At subsequent states, cooperation between functions increases, resulting in smoother processes (interfunctional teamwork). Next, if the competitive setting further intensifies, the company will continuously enhance processes by redesigning the company, either by flattening the hierarchy or by employing a matrix organization (functional streamlining). At the next stage, the company will conduct a total rethinking of the processes which occur and transform the organization of the company into a horizontal structure (total delivery reengineering). At the 4C state, the company has formed strategic alliances with related companies, particularly with dealers and suppliers, for the benefit of both parties (extended value chain).

WHAT–WHY–HOW

Figure 6 elaborates the outer cycle of Figure 2. It shows what a company must do at the time of implementing its marketing strategy and tactics in a particular competitive setting.

Information

A 2C company only processes production and distribution data. At subsequent states, the processed data encompasses information on products and promotion (2.5C) and on customers, competitors and the market (3C). At the 3.5C state, the company has collected data on the expectations of particular niches in the market (niche expectation) and the sensitivity of the niche to a proposed marketing mix (mix sensitivity). Meanwhile, 4C companies have researched what is needed by the consumer (customer value package) and the expected total value of purchases by consumers throughout their lifetime (lifetime value). To collect such data, it is necessary to employ market research techniques and consumer behavior concepts.

Analysis

A 2C company conducts analysis using only internal variance methods. Further along the line, a 2.5C company conducts analysis to compare expenditure with the accompanying benefits (cost benefit analysis). A 3C company conducts analyses by comparing itself with the external situation. The analysis conducted by 3.5C companies stresses measurement of market responses, and finally, a 4C company analyses the types of value which are most important to the customer.

Quality Management

The company's attitude towards quality management reflects the extent to which the company cares about its customers. Accordingly, there are considerable differences in the attention companies pay to quality management in implementing their marketing management.

2C companies usually consider their products to be satisfactory, all the time, because buyers have no other alternatives (the

FIGURE 6 THE "WHAT, WHY, AND HOW" OF IMPLEMENTING MARKETING STRATEGY

	2C	2.5C	3C	3.5C	4C
WHAT (Type of information)	Production Distribution	Product Promotion	Market Customer Competitor	Niche Expectation Mix Sensitivity	Customer Value Package Lifetime Value
WHY (Type of Analysis)	Internal Variance	Cost- Benefit	External Competitive	Market Response	Customer Value
HOW (Quality Management)	OK	QC	QA	TQM	TQS

'OK' method of quality management!). 2.5C companies feel the need to implement some sort of quality control (QC), because of the emergence of competitors. 3C companies have gone a step further by implementing QA (quality assurance). 3.5C companies have integrated management totally with efforts to increase quality, cost and delivery (QCD) through total quality management (TQM). 4C companies are still more advanced, focusing on TQS (total quality service) by measuring in advance the value expected by the customer, formulating a service strategy and making all people within the organization aware of it, reviewing service processes and constantly monitoring their results.

CONCLUSION

This conceptual framework has been created not as an academic exercise, but as a practical model for understanding marketing, which is developing rapidly in response to the competitive climate. It has been drawn up based on the results of the varied research, studies, observations and experiences of MarkPlus Professional Service in their capacity as marketing consultants assisting numerous clients, both private companies and state-owned corporations, of various sizes, in the service and manufacturing sectors.

DISCUSSION QUESTIONS

1. What do you think of the Marketing Plus conceptual framework? How does it compare to the marketing concepts and framework that you learned in your basic marketing course or that you have acquired via professional experience as a marketer?
2. Is marketing a universal discipline? Is there any difference in the kind of marketing that has to be practiced in Indonesia as compared to, say, the United States or Tanzania? Explain your answer.

Source: This model is the conceptual framework used by MarkPlus Professional Service, Indonesia's leading marketing consultancy. The firm has offices in Jakarta and Surababy, Indonesia, and Singapore. The framework is the brainchild of Hermawan Kartajaya, leading service office of MarkPlus, a firm which is at the forefront in helping Indonesian and Southeast Asian firms formulate and implement winning local and global marketing strategies. The firm is associated with Ries & Ries of Great Neck, New York, and affiliated with Warren Keegan Associates, Inc., of

The Global Economic Environment

The official dissolution of the Soviet Union on December 31, 1991, signaled the dawning of a new economic era in Central and Eastern Europe. Some industrial products companies, including Komatsu, Hitachi, and Fiat, had successfully conducted business for decades in the Soviet Union under communism. Philip Morris, PepsiCo, and McDonald's were among the consumer products companies with a foothold in the Soviet Union. Now scores of companies from all over the world are vying for position in Russia and the other former Soviet republics. They are lured by the prospect of a fledgling market economy in which tens of millions of consumers—150 million in Russia alone—can finally indulge their pent-up demand for packaged goods, electronics equipment, designer fashions, and other items. Companies new to Russia frequently discover that it is a difficult place in which to do business. Some problems, such as the mafia, have received widespread coverage in the media. Other challenges aren't front-page news, but they do have important business implications. For example, Goskomstat, the Russian government agency that measures the economy, generates mountains of misleading statistics. Real gross domestic product may be 40 percent higher than the official numbers, because much of the economic activity in Russia's transitional economy takes place "underground" and "off the books" due to high taxes and confusing laws.[1]

The situation in Russia is just one example of the diversity of economic environments in which global marketing activities are conducted today. Fortunately for the global marketer, a substantial body of data is available that charts the nature of the economic environment on a country-by-country basis. Each country has national accounts data indicating estimates of gross national product, gross domestic product, consumption, investment, government expenditures, and price levels. Demographic data indicating the population size, distribution of population by age category, and rates of population growth are also available.

National accounts and demographic reports do not exhaust the types of economic data available. A single source, *The Statistical Yearbook of the United Nations*, contains global data on agriculture, mining, manufacturing,

---

[1]Claudia Rosett, "Figures Never Lie, but They Seldom Tell the Truth about the Russian Economy," *The Wall Street Journal* (July 1, 1994), p. A6.

construction, energy production and consumption, internal and external trade, railroad and air transport, wages and prices, health, housing, education, communication infrastructure (mail, telegraph, and telephone), and mass communications. These data are available for all high-income countries. As the situation in Russia illustrates, the less developed a country is, the harder it is to obtain complete economic data. When researching low-income countries, one cannot be certain of obtaining anything more than basic national accounts, demographic figures, and external trade data. Nevertheless, in considering the world economic environment, the marketer's problem is not one of an absence of data but rather of an abundance. This chapter will identify the most salient characteristics of the world economic environment, including a survey of economic system types, stages of market development, and the location of income and population. Other topics covered include the relationship between marketing and economic development, the importance of a country's balance of payments, and patterns of merchandise and services trade.

THE WORLD ECONOMY—AN OVERVIEW[2]

Luxury cars are commonplace in Moscow, an indication that at least some Russians can afford cars that cost hundreds of thousands of dollars. (Photo Swersey-Liaison, courtesy of Gamma-Liaison, Inc.)

The world economy has changed profoundly since World War II. Perhaps the most fundamental change is the emergence of global markets; responding to new opportunities, global competitors have steadily displaced local ones. Concurrently, the integration of the world economy has increased significantly. Economic integration stood at 10 percent at the beginning of the 20th century; today, it is approximately 50 percent. Integration is particularly striking in two regions, the European Union (formerly the European Community) and the North American Free Trade Area.

Just 25 years ago, the world was far less integrated than it is today.[3] As a young man working in Europe and Africa in the 1960s, one of the authors was struck by how *different* everything was. There were many companies, many products, and great differentiation. As evidence of the changes that have taken place, consider the automobile. Cars with European nameplates such as Renault, Citroen, Peugeot, Morris, Volvo, and others were radically different from the American Chevrolet, Ford, or Plymouth, or Japanese models from Toyota or Nissan. These were local cars built by local companies, mostly destined for local or regional markets. Today, the world car is a reality for Toyota, Nissan, Honda, and Ford. Product changes reflect organizational changes as well: The world's largest automakers have, for the most part, evolved into global companies.

Within the past decade, there have been several remarkable changes in the world economy that hold important implications for business. The likelihood of business success is

[2]See Peter F. Drucker's excellent article "The Changed World Economy," *Foreign Affairs* (Spring 1986), and various issues of *The Economist*. For example, "The European Community—Survey," *The Economist* (July 11, 1992), or "When China Wakes," *The Economist* (Nov. 28, 1992).

[3]As economist Paul Krugman points out, the trend toward global integration that began in the 1970s is actually the second of the century; the first ended with the outbreak of World War I. Krugman has written extensively expressing a contrarian view of the extent of global integration. See, for example, "A Global Economy Is Not the Wave of the Future," *Financial Executive* (March–April 1992), pp. 10–13.

■ MEASURING THE RUSSIAN ECONOMY

*I*n today's Russia, average citizens aren't the only ones struggling to keep pace with rapid and revolutionary economic change; government statisticians can't even keep up. The result is that economic information and statistics coming from Russia are inaccurate, inadequate, distorted, and biased.

Russia's main source of economic statistics is an agency called Goskomstat, or the Russian State Statistical Committee. The inherent problem with the statistics generated by Goskomstat is one of original intent: Historically, Goskomstat measured the state economy of the Soviet Union; the purpose of the statistics that are still used for economic measurement today doesn't exist anymore because of the change from a planned economy to a market economy.

Goskomstat continues to collect data and measure production in the least productive sectors, namely industries that have not been privatized and farms still owned by the state. If those statistics were somewhat balanced by equivalent numbers from the private sector, Russian GNP might not be so severely underestimated. However, Goskomstat is not at all aggressive about counting the growing private sector in the Russian economy. The growth in Russian joint ventures, retail and service trade, and private banking has been well documented in the press, but not by Goskomstat.

The problem of gathering data from start-up businesses in the emerging private sector is compounded by the fact that those enterprises are reluctant to be included because of potential tax implications. Also, because of inadequate survey techniques, thousands of sole proprietorships, entrepreneurial and barter trade enterprises, as well as informal black and gray markets are all outside the reach of Goskomstat's reckoning.

Even the data generated from the fading state sector are inadequate because organizations on the government dole are not motivated to report any increased production. Those enterprises could stand to lose government subsidies if production is up. Ironically, in the Soviet era, managers of state-owned businesses were inclined to inflate production numbers in order to reach goals set by state planners.

So what is the impact of the skewed numbers put forth by Goskomstat? The faulty numbers create a ripple effect worldwide. Other agencies that rely on this imperfect source for economic data include the World Bank, the International Monetary Fund, the U.S. Department of Commerce, the CIA, plus countless banks, and industrial and investment analysts. At the very least, statistics severely understate production, especially in the growing private economy. The estimated amount of underreported production ranges from 25 percent to 60 percent, with most experts estimating a 45 percent undercount to be closest to reality. One consequence for the Russian economy is slowed growth, because nervous investors may be reluctant to enter a market depicted by such bleak numbers.

Sources: S. Frederick Starr, "The 'Glass Is Half Full' Case for Russia," *The International Economy* (March-April 1995), pp. 46+.
Judy Shelton, *The Coming Soviet Crash: Gorbachev's Desperate Pursuit of Credit in Western Financial Markets* (New York: Free Press, 1989).

much greater when plans and strategies are based on the new realities of the changed world economy:

- Capital movements rather than trade have become the driving force of the world economy.
- Production has become "uncoupled" from employment.
- The world economy dominates the scene. The macroeconomics of individual countries no longer control economic outcomes.
- The 75-year struggle between capitalism and socialism is over.

The first change is the increased volume of capital movements. The dollar value of world trade is greater than ever before. Trade in goods and services is running at roughly $4 trillion per year. But the London Eurodollar market turns over $400 billion each working day.[4] That totals $100 trillion per year—25 times the dollar value of world trade. In addition, foreign exchange transactions are running at approximately $1 trillion per day worldwide, which is $250 trillion per year—40 times the volume of world trade in goods and services (Shapiro 1996, 137). There is an inescapable conclusion in these data: Global capital movements far exceed the volume of global merchandise and services trade. This explains the bizarre combination of U.S. trade deficits and a continually rising dollar during the first half of the 1980s. Previously, when a country ran a deficit on its trade ac-

---

[4]A Eurodollar is a U.S. dollar held outside the United States. U.S. dollars are subject to U.S. banking regulations; Eurodollars are not.

counts, its currency would depreciate in value. Today, it is capital movements and trade that determine currency value.

The second change concerns the relationship between productivity and employment. Although employment in manufacturing remains steady or has declined, productivity continues to grow. The pattern is especially clear in American agriculture, where fewer farm employees produce more output. In the United States, manufacturing holds a steady 23 to 24 percent of GNP. This is true of all the other major industrial economies as well. Manufacturing is not in decline—it is *employment* in manufacturing that is in decline.[5] Countries like the United Kingdom, which have tried to maintain blue-collar employment in manufacturing, have lost both production and jobs for their efforts.

The third major change is the emergence of the world economy as the dominant economic unit. Company executives and national leaders who recognize this have the greatest chance of success. Those who do not recognize this fact will suffer decline and bankruptcy (in business) or overthrow (in politics). The real secret of the economic success of Germany and Japan is the fact that business leaders and policy makers focus on the world economy and world markets; a top priority for government and business in both Japan and Germany has been their competitive position in the world. In contrast, many other countries, including the United States, have focused upon domestic objectives and priorities to the exclusion of their global competitive position.

The last change is the end of the Cold War. The demise of communism as an economic and political system can be explained in a straightforward manner. Communism is not an effective system. The overwhelmingly superior performance of the world's market economies has led socialist countries to renounce their ideology. A key policy change in such countries has been the abandonment of futile attempts to manage national economies with a single central plan. The different types of economic systems are contrasted in the next section.

ECONOMIC SYSTEMS

There are three types of economic systems: capitalist, socialist, and mixed. This classification is based on the dominant method of resource allocation: market allocation, command or central plan allocation, and mixed allocation, respectively.

Market Allocation

A *market allocation* system is one that relies upon consumers to allocate resources. Consumers "write" the economic plan by deciding what will be produced by whom. The market system is an economic democracy—citizens have the right to vote with their pocketbooks for the goods of their choice. The role of the state in a market economy is to promote competition and ensure consumer protection. The United States, most Western European countries, and Japan—the Triad countries that account for three-quarters of gross world product—are examples of predominantly market economies. The clear superiority of the market allocation system in delivering the goods and services that people need and want has led to its adoption in many formerly socialist countries.

Command Allocation

In a *command allocation* system, the state has broad powers to serve the public interest. These include deciding which products to make and how to make them. Consumers are free to spend their money on what is available, but decisions about what is produced and, therefore, what is available are made by state planners. Because demand exceeds supply, the elements of the marketing mix are not used as strategic variables (Golden et al. 1995). There

[5]Some companies have cut employment by outsourcing or subcontracting nonmanufacturing activities such as data processing, housekeeping, and food service.

is little reliance on product differentiation, advertising, and promotion; distribution is handled by the government to cut out "exploitation" by intermediaries. Three of the most populous countries in the world, China, the former Soviet Union, and India relied upon command allocation systems for decades. All three countries are now engaged in economic reforms directed at shifting to market allocation systems. The prediction made by India's Jawaharlal Nehru nearly a half century ago regarding the imminent demise of capitalism has been refuted. Market reforms and nascent capitalism in many parts of the world are creating opportunities for large-scale investments by global companies. Indeed, Coca-Cola returned to India in 1994, two decades after being forced out by the government. A new law allowing 100 percent foreign ownership of enterprises helped pave the way. By contrast, Cuba stands as one of the last bastions of the command allocation approach.

Mixed Allocation

There are, in reality, no pure market or command allocation systems among the world's economies. All market systems have a command sector, and all command systems have a market sector; in other words, they are "mixed." In a market economy, the command allocation sector is the proportion of GDP that is taxed and spent by government. For the 24 member countries of the Organization for Economic Cooperation and Development (OECD), this proportion ranges from 32 percent of GDP in the United States to 64 percent in Sweden.[6] In Sweden, therefore, where 64 percent of all expenditures are controlled

TABLE 2-1 INDEX OF ECONOMIC FREEDOM

Free	26. Belize	52. Zambia	79. Tanzania
1. Hong Kong	27. Colombia	53. Israel	80. Zimbabwe
2. Singapore	28. Panama	54. Algeria	81. Albania
3. Bahrain	29. Paraguay	55. Honduras	82. Romania
4. USA	30. Slovak Rep.	56. Nigeria	83. Belarus
5. Japan	31. Greece	57. Pakistan	84. Yemen
6. Taiwan	32. Hungary	58. Bolivia	85. Guyana
7. U.K.	33. Jamaica	59. Ecuador	86. India
Mostly Free	34. Portugal	60. Ivory Coast	87. China
8. Canada	35. Sri Lanka	61. Malta	88. Ethiopia
9. Germany	36. Argentina	62. Poland	89. Bangladesh
10. Austria	37. Tunisia	63. Brazil	90. Congo
11. Bahamas	38. Costa Rica	64. Fiji	91. Nicaragua
12. Czech Rep.	39. Jordan	65. Ghana	92. Ukraine
13. S. Korea	40. Morocco	66. Philippines	93. Sierra Leone
14. Malaysia	41. Swaziland	67. Mongolia	**Repressed**
15. Australia	42. Uruguay	68. Guinea	94. Moldova
16. Ireland	43. Uganda	69. Indonesia	95. Haiti
17. Estonia	**Mostly Unfree**	70. Dominican R.	96. Sudan
18. France	44. S. Africa	71. Malawi	97. Angola
19. Thailand	45. Turkey	72. Peru	98. Mozambique
20. Chile	46. Venezuela	73. Russia	99. Vietnam
21. Italy	47. Botswana	74. Bulgaria	100. Cuba
22. Spain	48. Gabon	75. Cameroon	101. N. Korea
23. El Salvador	49. Guatemala	76. Egypt	
24. Oman	50. Kenya	77. Madagascar	
25. Sweden	51. Mexico	78. Mali	

Source: Kim R. Holmes, "In Search of Free Markets," *The Wall Street Journal* (Dec. 12, 1994), p. A17.

[6]Organization for Economic Cooperation and Development, *OECD Economic Outlook*, No. 50 (Paris: OECD, 1991), p. 206.

by government, the economic system is more "command" than "market." The reverse is true in the United States. Similarly, farmers in most socialist countries were traditionally permitted to offer part of their production in a free market. China has given considerable freedom to businesses and individuals in the Guangdong Province to operate within a market system. Still, China's private sector only constitutes 1 to 2 percent of national output.[7]

A recent report by the Washington, D.C.–based Heritage Foundation ranked more than 100 countries by degree of economic freedom. Ten key economic variables were considered: trade policy, taxation policy, government consumption of economic output, monetary policy, capital flows and foreign investment, banking policy, wage and price controls, property rights, regulations, and the black market. The rankings form a continuum from "Free" to "Repressed," with "Mostly Free" and "Mostly Unfree" in between. Hong Kong is ranked number one in terms of economic freedom; Cuba and North Korea are ranked lowest. The report's findings are summarized in Table 2–1.

STAGES OF MARKET DEVELOPMENT

Global country markets are at different stages of development. GNP per capita provides a very useful way of grouping these countries. Using GNP as a base, we have divided global markets into five categories. Although the income definition for each of the stages is arbitrary, countries in the five categories have similar characteristics. Thus, the stages provide a useful basis for global market segmentation and target marketing. The categories are shown in Table 2–2.

Low-Income Countries

Low-income countries, also known as preindustrial countries, are those with GNP per capita of less than $500. The characteristics shared by countries at this income level are:

1. Limited industrialization and a high percentage of the population engaged in agriculture and subsistence farming
2. High birth rates
3. Low literacy rates
4. Heavy reliance on foreign aid
5. Political instability and unrest
6. Concentration in Africa south of the Sahara

In general, these countries represent limited markets for all products and are not significant locations for competitive threats. Still, there are exceptions; for example, in Bangladesh, where per capita GNP is slightly over $200, a growing garment industry has enjoyed burgeoning exports. The dollar value of finished clothing exports recently surpassed that of jute, tea, and other agricultural exports.[8]

Lower-Middle-Income Countries

Lower-middle-income countries (also known as less-developed countries or LDCs) are those with GNP per capita of more than $500 and less than $2,500. These countries are at the early stages of industrialization. Factories supply a growing domestic market with such items as clothing, batteries, tires, building materials, and packaged foods.

Consumer markets in these countries are expanding. LDCs represent an increasing competitive threat as they mobilize their relatively cheap—and often highly motivated—labor force to serve target markets in the rest of the world. LDCs have a major competitive ad-

[7]Jack Goldstone, "The Coming Chinese Collapse," *Foreign Policy* (Summer 1995), pp. 35–52.
[8]Marcus W. Brauchli, "Garment Industry Booms in Bangladesh," *The Wall Street Journal* (Aug. 6, 1991), p. A9.

TABLE 2–2 **STAGES OF MARKET DEVELOPMENT**

Income Group by GNP per Capita	1995 GNP ($ million)	1995 GNP per Capita ($)	% of World GNP	1995 Population (millions)
High-Income Countries				
GNP per capita > $14,000	$17,623.0	$24,500	79.55	814
Upper-Middle-Income Countries				
GNP per capita > $2,500 but < $14,000	3,503.5	4,397	8.92	509
Lower-Middle-Income Countries				
GNP per capita > $500 but < $2,500	2,403.3	1,001	9.58	2,401
Low-Income Countries				
GNP per capita < $500	491.4	300	1.96	1,640
Basket Cases	not available	not available	not available	450

vantage in mature, standardized, labor-intensive industries such as toymaking and apparel. Indonesia, the largest noncommunist country in Southeast Asia, is a good example of an LDC on the move: Per capita GNP has risen from $250 in 1985 to more than $800 in 1995. Several factories there produce athletic shoes under contract for Nike.

Upper-Middle-Income Countries

Upper-middle-income countries, also known as industrializing countries, are those with GNP per capita between $2,500 and $14,000. In these countries, the percentage of population engaged in agriculture drops sharply as people move to the industrial sector and the degree of urbanization increases. Many of the countries in this stage—Malaysia, for example—are rapidly industrializing. They have rising wages and high rates of literacy and advanced education, but they still have significantly lower wage costs than the advanced countries. Countries in this stage of development frequently become formidable competitors and experience rapid, export-driven economic growth.

High-Income Countries

High income countries, also known as advanced, industrialized, postindustrial, or First World countries, are those with GNP per capita above $14,000. With the exception of a few oil-rich nations, the countries in this category reached their present income level through a process of sustained economic growth.

The phrase "postindustrial countries" was first used by Daniel Bell of Harvard to describe the United States, Sweden, Japan, and other advanced, high-income societies. Bell suggests that there is a difference between the industrial and the postindustrial societies that goes beyond mere measures of income. Bell's thesis is that the sources of innovation in postindustrial societies are derived increasingly from the codification of theoretical knowledge rather than from "random" inventions. Other characteristics are the importance of the service sector (more than 50 percent of GNP); the crucial importance of information processing and exchange; and the ascendancy of knowledge over capital as the key strategic resource, of intellectual technology over machine technology, of scientists and professionals over engineers and semiskilled workers. Other aspects of the postindustrial society are an orientation toward the future and the importance of interpersonal relationships in the functioning of society.

Product and market opportunities in a postindustrial society are more heavily dependent upon new products and innovations than in industrial societies. Ownership levels for basic products are extremely high in most households. Organizations seeking to grow often face a difficult task if they attempt to expand share of existing markets. Alternatively, they can endeavor to create new markets. For example, in the 1990s, global companies in a range of communication-related industries are seeking to create new markets for multimedia, interactive forms of electronic communication.

Basket Cases

A basket case is a country with economic, social, and political problems that are so serious they make the country unattractive for investment and operations. Some basket cases are low-income, no-growth countries such as Ethiopia and Mozambique that lurch from one disaster to the next. Others are once growing and successful countries that have become divided by political struggles. The result is civil strife, declining income, and, often, considerable danger to residents. In the mid-1990s, the former Yugoslavia is a case in point. Basket cases embroiled in civil wars are dangerous areas; most companies find it prudent to avoid these countries during active conflict.

The newly independent countries of the former Soviet Union present an interesting situation: Income is declining and there is considerable economic hardship. The potential for disruption is certainly high. Are these nations basket cases? Or, are they attractive opportunities with good potential for moving into the high-income category? These countries present an interesting risk/reward trade-off; while many companies have "taken the plunge," many others are still assessing whether or not to take the risk. The stages of market development described previously can serve as a guide to marketers in evaluating **product saturation levels,** or the percentage of potential buyers or households who own a particular product. In countries with low per-capita income, product saturation levels for many products are low. In India, for example, ownership of private telephones is limited to about 1 percent of the population. In China, saturation levels of private cars and personal computers are at similarly low levels; there is only one car for every 20,000 people, and only one PC for every 6,000 people.

THE PRODUCT TRADE CYCLE MODEL

The **international product trade cycle** model describes the relationships among product life cycle (PLC), trade, and investment. The model served as an accurate description of the way sequential international market development impacted trade patterns and the location of production in textiles, consumer electronics, and other industries from 1950 to the mid-1970s. Simply stated, high-income, mass-consumption countries such as Japan and the United States were initially exporters, but ultimately become importers. A second tier of advanced countries initially imported and, in time, exported the product. Later, a third tier of low-income countries initiated manufacturing operations and then exhibited the same shift from importing to exporting. These shifts corresponded to the introduction, growth, and maturity stages of the product life cycle: the high-income countries were exporters during the introduction phase, the middle-income countries were exporters during the growth phase, and the low-income countries were exporters during the mature phase.

The history of the VCR illustrates several aspects of the model. Starting in the mid-1970s, Sony, JVC, and other Japanese companies produced VCRs for the domestic consumer market and for export. Customers in the United States and Europe who bought Beta- and VHS-format VCRs were buying Japanese-made goods, even if they carried local brand names such as RCA and Zenith. Exports grew to a steady stream as the VCR entered the growth phase of the PLC. South Korean companies such as Goldstar and Samsung were quick to note the opportunity. In short order, they initiated production to take advantage of lower labor and factor costs; production outside of Japan marked the begin-

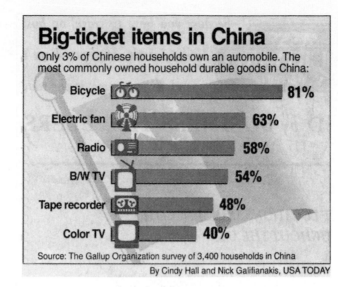

Big-ticket items in China

Only 3% of Chinese households own an automobile. The most commonly owned household durable goods in China:

Bicycle	81%
Electric fan	63%
Radio	58%
B/W TV	54%
Tape recorder	48%
Color TV	40%

Source: The Gallup Organization survey of 3,400 households in China

By Cindy Hall and Nick Galifianakis, USA TODAY

ning of Phase 2 of the trade cycle. During the growth phase of the PLC, exports from both Japan and South Korea supplied the United States and other high-income markets. In the mid-1980s, VCRs matured as design, technology, and demand stabilized.

In Phase 3, production sources in low-income countries displaced production sources in high-income countries. By the early 1990s, for example, American consumers could buy South Korean-built VCRs for $99.00. South Korea and other lower-income countries reached high production volumes based on domestic and export markets and, thanks to lower factory costs, achieved the status of low-cost producers. The cycle was complete, and companies in Japan that had at one time had a monopoly in VCR production found themselves facing stiff foreign competition in their key markets. Their best hope was to create new products and launch the cycle again and again (see Figure 2–1). This is exactly what Sony and other Japanese companies intended to do with products such as portable personal stereos and video camcorders.

The international product trade cycle is an empirical record of trade patterns. It reflects the behavior of many U.S. and European firms in consumer electronics and other industries. The firms have abandoned the investment and effort necessary to maintain world-class production facilities in their home country because they faced the challenge of high wages and other costs. In the United States, for example, many executives faced with quality and cost problems at home made the strategic choice to shift production to lower-cost countries or to give up market share to low-cost producers in other countries. Unfortunately, such an approach may have put the focus of strategy on the wrong dimension. The companies that shifted production to low-wage countries did, indeed, gain a one-time advantage. All other things being equal, they lowered their labor costs. However, a company that focuses too obsessively on getting costs down by moving production to low-income countries may, in the long run, trail its competitors in innovation, product features, manufacturability, and quality.

The product trade cycle model represents a potential trap for global marketers: Unconsciously, many executives in high-income countries have acted as if the shifting cycle of consumption, trade, and investment were inevitable. Under this assumption, companies in advanced countries are forced to discover and introduce new products constantly because they cannot compete with the lower-wage competitors in mature, established products. However, *the cycle is inevitable only if the product does not change.* Innovations in existing products and manufacturing processes enable companies in high-income countries to thrive and prosper in global industries. Innovators can, in effect, make an end run

FIGURE 2-1

**INTERNATIONAL PROD-
UCT TRADE CYCLE**

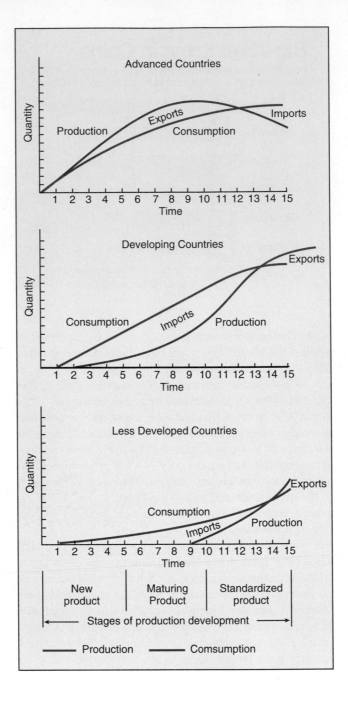

around the international trade cycle. Innovative global companies do not leave an opening for competitors with low-income country production. Rather, innovators make the strategic choice to keep manufacturing facilities close to home-country customers, the better to give those customers what they want.

Market Development and Consumption in the 21st Century

The international trade cycle model reflected a *trickle-down* or *waterfall* pattern of market development shown in Figure 2–2. As the 21st century approaches, global marketers need strategies based on a different pattern of market development and consumption. One

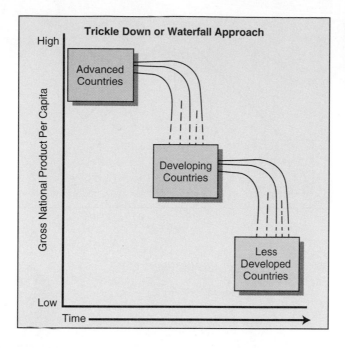

strategy is to develop a product and simultaneously introduce it in world markets (a *shower* instead of a trickle). Gillette used this approach, illustrated in Figure 2–3, for the global launch of its Sensor razor in 1989. Gillette had spent $200 million over a ten-year period to develop Sensor. Similarly, in 1996, Toshiba, Matsushita, Sony, and other consumer electronics companies launched a new home entertainment product, the Digital Video Disc (DVD), that they hope will be the successor to the VCR. Worldwide sales of DVD are expected to pass the billion-dollar level. As the Sensor and DVD examples show, managerial assumptions about the nature of world markets will influence the planning process and the market approach chosen. Strategies based on the waterfall view reflect the assumption that markets develop sequentially over time. Strategies based on the shower approach acknowledge that we live in a global village where market opportunities frequently emerge simultaneously on a regional or global basis.

INCOME AND PURCHASING POWER PARITY AROUND THE GLOBE

When a company charts a plan for global market expansion, it often finds that, for most products, income is the single most valuable economic variable. After all, a market can be defined as a group of people willing and able to buy a particular product. For some products, particularly those that have a very low unit cost—cigarettes, for example—population is a more valuable predictor of market potential than income. Nevertheless, for the vast range of industrial and consumer products in international markets today, the single most valuable and important indicator of potential is income.

Ideally, GNP and other measures of national income converted to U.S. dollars should be calculated on the basis of purchasing power parities (i.e., what the currency will buy in the country of issue) or through direct comparisons of actual prices for a given product. This would provide an actual comparison of the standards of living in the countries of the world. Unfortunately, these data are not available in regular statistical reports. Throughout this book we use, instead, conversion of local currency measured at the yearend U.S. dollar foreign exchange rate. The reader must remember that exchange rates

FIGURE 2–3

**INTERNATIONAL PROD-
UCT LIFE CYCLE—
SHOWER APPROACH**

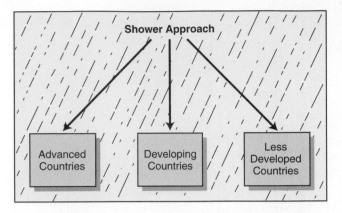

Sharp's innovative consumer electronics products such as the camcorder shown here enjoy worldwide popularity. (Sharp Electronics Corp./Griffin Bacal Inc. Awarded an EFFIE in 1995.)

TABLE 2–3   1995 PER CAPITA INCOME

1995 Per Capita Income		1995 Income Adjusted for Purchasing Power	
1. Luxembourg	$37,794	1. Luxembourg	$31,125
2. Switzerland	36,921	2. USA	25,345
3. Japan	33,748	3. Hong Kong	24,028
4. Denmark	27,095	4. Switzerland	23,952
5. Norway	26,603	5. United Arab Emirates	23,624
6. USA	25,345	6. Singapore	23,044
7. Sweden	24,877	7. Japan	22,636
8. Germany	24,459	8. Qatar	22,590
9. Austria	24,098	9. Germany	21,785
10. Kuwait	23,740	10. Canada	20,574

Source: Warren Keegan Associates, Inc., *Global Income and Population: 1995 and Projections to 2020*, 1995.

equate, at best, the prices of internationally traded goods and services. They often bear little relationship to the prices of those goods and services not traded internationally, which form the bulk of the national product in most countries. Agricultural output and services, in particular, are often priced lower in relation to industrial output in developing countries than in industrial countries. Furthermore, agriculture typically accounts for the largest share of output in developing countries. Thus, the use of exchange rates tends to exaggerate differences in real income between countries at different stages of economic development. Table 2–3 ranks the top 10 countries in terms of 1995 per capita income, then gives the ranking adjusted for purchasing power parity. While the United States ranks seventh in income, its standard of living—as measured by what money can buy—is second only to Luxembourg's.

Beyond the exchange distortion illustrated in Table 2–3, there is the distortion of money itself as an indicator of a nation's welfare and standard of living. A visit to a mud house in Tanzania will reveal many of the things that money can buy: radios, an iron bed frame, a corrugated metal roof, beer and soft drinks, bicycles, shoes, photographs, and razor blades. What Tanzania's per capita income of $250 does not reflect is the fact that instead of utility bills, Tanzanians have the local well and the sun. Instead of nursing homes, tradition and custom ensure families will take care of the elderly at home. Instead of expensive doctors and hospitals, villagers may turn to witch doctors and healers. In industrialized countries, a significant portion of national income is generated by taking goods and services that would be free in a poor country and putting a price on them. Thus, the standard of living in many low-income countries is often higher than income data might suggest.

A striking fact about the world economic environment is the concentration of income in the "Triad"—the United States and Canada, the European Union, and Japan. The Triad accounted for 77 percent of global income but only 14 percent of global population in 1995. The concentration of wealth in a handful of large industrialized countries is the most striking characteristic of the global economic environment. The United States is, of course, a colossus in North America, as is the former Soviet Union in Central and Eastern Europe. In 1992, these countries accounted for 91 percent and 70 percent, respectively, of their region's GDP. In Western Europe, three countries—France, West Germany, and the United Kingdom—accounted for almost 65 percent of that region's GDP. Japan accounted for 62 percent of Asia's GDP; in fact, Japan's GDP alone is nearly twice the size of all other Asia-Pacific countries' GDPs combined. In South America, Argentina, Brazil, Uruguay, and Paraguay account for 70 percent of GDP.

With the exception of China and Brazil, the top 10 countries in GNP in 1995 are all

TABLE 2–4 TOP 10 NATIONS RANKED BY GNP, 1995

Country	GNP ($ millions)
1. USA	$6,658,785.8
2. Japan	4,247,084.1
3. Germany	1,999,334.1
4. France	1,351,860.9
5. Italy	1,183,149.7
6. U.K.	1,076,333.3
7. China	676,550.9
8. Canada	594,596.2
9. Spain	569,810.6
10. Brazil	484,329

Source: Warren Keegan Associates, Inc., *Global Income and Population: 1995 and Projections to 2020*, 1995.

located in the Triad (see Table 2–4). The United States, the world's largest economy, is larger than the rest of the world, excluding the eight other countries in the top 10. No one knows what the future will bring, but an extrapolation of the growth of the period 1985–1993 to the year 2020 produces interesting results, shown in Table 2–5. The United States and Japan remain in the number one and two positions. China overtakes Germany; Brazil and Canada are no longer on the list. Taiwan appears on the list for the first time. These extrapolation results suggest that China, with its combination of high real income growth and relatively low population growth, is a strong candidate to become a leading world economic power.

An examination of the distribution of wealth within countries also reveals patterns of income concentration, particularly in the less-developed countries outside the former communist bloc. Adelman and Morris found that, in less-developed countries, the average share of GNP accruing to the poorest 20 percent of the population was 5.6 percent as compared with 56.0 percent going to the top 20 percent. The income of the bottom 20 percent was about one-fourth what it would have been had income been distributed uni-

TABLE 2–5 TOP 10 NATIONS RANKED BY GNP, 2020 PROJECTIONS

Country	GNP ($ millions)
1. USA	$11,195,374
2. Japan	10,036,900
3. China	4,125,837
4. Germany	3,706,654
5. France	2,445,856
6. South Korea	2,183,938
7. Italy	1,989,222
8. Taiwan	1,824,831
9. U.K.	1,600,625
10. Spain	1,283,035

Source: Warren Keegan Associates, Inc., *Global Income and Population: 1995 and Projections to 2020*, 1995.

formly throughout the population. This study suggests that the relationship between the share of income at the lowest 20 percent and economic development varies with the level of development. Economic development is associated with increases in the share of income of the bottom 20 percent only after relatively high levels of socioeconomic development have been attained. At the early stages of the development process, economic development works to the *relative* disadvantage of the lowest income groups. Brazil, for example, has become one of the world's most unequal societies, with the top 20 percent of the country's population earning some 65 percent of national income and the bottom 20 percent earning less than 3 percent. This is the most extreme income inequality that the World Bank has measured—worse than Bangladesh's.[9] China is experiencing the same type of inequality. As one politician noted, "Economic reform not only changes economic systems but is also a revolution in ideas."[10]

Throughout the ages, people have spent most of their energy finding food, clothing, and shelter. An old Armenian folk saying, "Making a living is like taking food out of a lion's mouth," captures this reality. Although the problem of poverty has not been eliminated in all the industrialized countries, those countries with homogeneous populations and an advanced collective social conscience have indeed greatly reduced poverty within their borders.

The actual conditions of life for the masses in the richest and the poorest countries was not significantly different in the 1850s. This is in sharp contrast to the conditions today where the gap between the living standard of the majority in the high-income countries is vastly different from that of the majority in the low-income countries. This growing gap between the richest and the poorest countries is a tremendous incentive to people in poor countries to move to a high-income country to seek economic opportunity and a higher standard of living.

Since 1850, the distribution of population between the industrial and the preindustrial countries has not changed significantly. But between 1850 and 1992, the industrial countries' share of world income increased from 39 percent to 75 percent. During this period, annual compound rates of growth of 2.7 percent in total output and 1.8 percent in per capita output profoundly altered the world's distribution of income. The magnitude of change, as compared with the previous 6,000 years of our civilized existence, is enormous; over one-third of the real income and about two-thirds of the industrial output produced by people throughout recorded history were generated in the industrialized countries in the last century. Note that *relatively small average annual rates of growth have transformed the economic geography of the world*. What the industrial countries have done is to systematize economic growth. Put another way, they have established a process of continuous, gradual change.

One researcher has calculated that India, one of the poorest countries in the world, could reach U.S. income levels by growing at an average annual rate of 5 to 6 percent in real terms for 40 to 50 years. This is no more than the lifetime of an average Indian, and about half the lifetime of an average American. Japan was the first country with a non-European heritage to achieve high-income status. This was the result of sustained high growth and the ability to acquire knowledge and know-how, first making copies of products and then making improvements. As Japan has dramatically demonstrated, this is a potent formula for catching up and achieving economic leadership.

Today, much more than was true 2,000 years ago, wealth and income are concentrated regionally, nationally, and within nations. The implications of this reality are crucial for the global marketer. A company that decides to diversify geographically can accomplish this objective by establishing operations in a handful of national markets.

---

[9] Jim Rohwer, "Empurrar Com a Barriga," *The Economist* (Dec. 7, 1991), pp. S6–S7.
[10] Marcus W. Brauchli, "Great Wall: As the Rich Grow Richer, the Poor Are Growing Resentful," *The Wall Street Journal* (Jan. 4, 1994), p. A1.

THE LOCATION OF POPULATION

We have already noted the concentration of 77 percent of world income in the Triad (North America, the EU, and Japan). In 1995, the 10 most populous countries in the world accounted for 52.5 percent of world income, and the 5 most populous account for 47.5 percent (see Table 2–6). The concentration of income in the high-income and large-population countries means that a company can be global—derive a significant proportion of its income from countries at different stages of development—while operating in 10 or fewer countries.

As noted before, for products whose price is low enough, population is a more important variable than income in determining market potential. Although population is not as concentrated as income, there is, in terms of size of nations, a pattern of considerable concentration. The 10 most populous countries in the world account for roughly 60 percent of the world's population today.

People have inhabited the earth for over 2.5 million years. The number of human beings has been small during most of this period. In Christ's lifetime there were approximately 300 million people on earth, one-quarter of the number of people on mainland China today. World population increased tremendously during the 18th and 19th centuries, reaching 1 billion by 1850. Between 1850 and 1925, global population doubled, to 2 billion, and from 1925 to 1960 it increased to 3 billion. World population is now approximately 5.7 billion; at the present rate of growth, it will reach 10 billion by the middle of the next century. Simply put, global population will probably double during the lifetime of many students using this textbook (see Figure 2–4).

There is a negative correlation between country population growth rate and income per capita level. The higher the population growth rate, the lower the income per capita. According to a recent United Nations report, 97 percent of the world's population growth is likely to come from developing and undeveloped countries.[11]

---

[11]James Cook, "The Ghosts of Christmas Yet to Come," *Forbes* (June 22, 1992), pp. 92–95.

TABLE 2–6   **THE 10 MOST POPULOUS COUNTRIES, 1995 AND 2020 PROJECTIONS**

Country	1995 Population (thousands)	% of World Population	2020 Projected Population (thousands)	1995 GNP ($ millions)	Per Capita Income	% of World GNP
WORLD TOTAL	5,712,966	100.0	9,131,830	$25,096,757		100.00
1. China	1,208,499	20.8	1,710,785	676,551	$ 560	2.70
2. India	938,763	16.1	1,578,336	290,300	309	1.16
3. USA	262,729	4.5	328,691	6,658,786	25,345	26.53
4. Indonesia	193,949	3.3	302,958	155,671	803	.62
5. Brazil	162,406	2.8	259,990	484,329	2,982	1.93
6. Russia	149,728	2.6	165,442	317,096	2,118	1.26
7. Pakistan	130,562	2.2	280,082	58,262	446	.23
8. Japan	125,846	2.2	139,053	4,247,084	33,748	16.92
9. Bangladesh	121,893	2.1	210,016	27,994	230	.11
10. Nigeria	111,055	1.91	226,966	37,135	334	.15

Source: Warren Keegan Associates, Inc., *Global Income and Population: 1995 and Projections to 2020*, 1995.

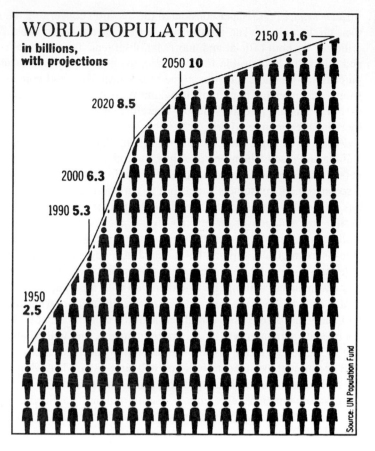

WORLD POPULATION
in billions,
with projections

2150 **11.6**
2050 **10**
2020 **8.5**
2000 **6.3**
1990 **5.3**
1950
2.5

Source: UN Population Fund

MARKETING AND ECONOMIC DEVELOPMENT

An important concern in marketing is whether or not it has any relevance to the process of economic development. Some people believe the field of marketing is relevant only to the conditions that apply in affluent, industrialized countries where the major problem is one of directing society's resources into ever-changing output or production to satisfy a dynamic marketplace. In the less-developed country, the argument goes, the major problem is the allocation of scarce resources toward obvious production needs. Efforts should focus on production and how to increase output, not on customer needs and wants.

Conversely, it can be argued that the marketing process of focusing an organization's resources on environmental opportunities is a process of universal relevance. The role of marketing—to identify people's needs and wants, and to focus individual and organizational efforts to respond to these needs and wants—is the same in both low- and high-income countries. For example, pursuing alternative sources of energy such as wind and solar power is important for two reasons: the lack of coal reserves in many countries and concerns that over-reliance on fossil fuels will contribute to global warming. These concerns have led to the development of solar-powered lanterns that are used in villages in India. Similarly, solar water heaters have been installed in Gaborone, the capital of Botswana, eliminating as much as 40 percent of the energy requirements for thousands of families.

The economics literature places a great deal of emphasis on "the role of marketing in economic development" when marketing is defined as distribution. In his book *West*

African Trade, P. T. Bauer considered the question concerning the number of traders and their productivity.[12] The number and variety of traders in West Africa had been much criticized by both official and unofficial observers. Traders were condemned as wasteful and said to be responsible for wide margins both in the sale of merchandise and in the purchase of produce. Bauer examined these criticisms and concluded that they stemmed from a misunderstanding. In his view, the West African system economized in capital and used a redundant resource—labor. Therefore, Bauer argued, it was a productive system by rational economic criteria.

A simple example illustrates Bauer's point. A trader buys a package of cigarettes for 1 shilling and resells them one at a time for 2 cents each, or a total of 2 shillings. Has this person exploited society to the tune of 1 shilling, or has he provided a useful service? In a society where consumers can afford to purchase only one cigarette at a time, the trader has provided a useful service in substituting labor for capital. In this case, capital would be the accumulation of an inventory of cigarettes by a consumer. The possession of a shilling is the critical first obstacle to this accumulation. However, even if a consumer were able to accumulate a shilling, his standard of living would not allow him to smoke the 20 cigarettes fast enough to prevent them from going stale. Thus, even if he were able to save and accumulate a shilling, he would end up with a package of stale cigarettes. The trader in this case, by breaking bulk, serves the useful function of making available a product in a quantity that a consumer can afford and in a condition that is attractive. As income levels rise, the purchaser will smoke more frequently and will be able to buy an entire package of cigarettes. In the process the amount of local resources consumed by distribution will decline and the standard of living will have risen. Meanwhile, in less-developed countries where labor is redundant and cheap and where capital is scarce, the availability of this distribution function represents a useful, rational application of society's resources. Moreover, experience in distribution is valuable because it generates a pool of entrepreneurial talent in a society where alternatives for such training are scarce.

BALANCE OF PAYMENTS

The *balance of payments* is a record of all economic transactions between the residents of a country and the rest of the world. The U.S. and Japanese balance of payments statistics for the period 1990–1993 are shown in Tables 2–7 and 2–8. The format used closely mirrors that used by the International Monetary Fund in its *Balance of Payments Statistics Yearbook*, which summarizes economic activity for all the countries of the world.[13]

The balance of payments is divided into so-called "current" and "capital" accounts. The current account is a record of all recurring trade in merchandise and service, private gifts, and public aid transactions between countries. The capital account is a record of all long-term direct investment, portfolio investment, and other short- and long-term capital flows. The minus signs signify outflows of cash; for example, in Table 2–7, line 2 shows an outflow of $589 billion in 1993 that represents payment for U.S. merchandise imports. The changes in net errors and omissions, foreign liabilities, and reserves (lines D, F, and G in the tables) are the entries that make the balance of payments balance. In general, a country accumulates reserves when the net of its current and capital account transactions shows a surplus; it gives up reserves when the net shows a deficit. The important fact to recognize about the overall balance of payments is that it is always in balance. Imbalances occur in subsets of the overall balance. For example, a commonly reported balance is the merchandise trade balance (line 3 in the tables).

[12]Peter T. Bauer, *West African Trade* (London: Routledge and K. Paul, 1963).
[13]Balance of payments data are available from a number of different sources, each of which may show slightly different figures for a given line item.

TABLE 2-7   U.S. BALANCE OF PAYMENTS, 1990–1993 (US$ BILLIONS)

	1990	1991	1992	1993
A. Current Account (excl. Group E)	**−91.74**	**−6.91**	**−67.85**	**−103.94**
1. Merchandise: Export FOB	389.31	416.92	440.36	456.87
2. Merchandise: Import FOB	−498.33	−490.98	−536.46	−589.44
3. Trade balance	−109.02	−74.06	−96.10	−132.57
4. Services: Credit	130.47	144.99	156.50	164.21
5. Services: Debit	−112.73	−112.35	−114.66	−121.79
6. Private Unrequited Transfers	−13.04	−13.82	−13.29	−13.72
7. Official Unrequited Transfers	−20.63	−20.48	−18.75	−18.40
B. Direct Investment and Other Long-Term Capital	**7.51**	**17.03**	**−14.04**	**−49.73**
8. Direct Investment	17.97	−5.21	−31.12	−36.51
9. Portfolio Investment	−33.00	8.55	16.63	−17.55
10. Other Long-Term Capital	26.25	19.17	−.07	5.53
Total, Groups A, B	**−84.22**	**10.12**	**−81.89**	**−153.66**
C. Short-Term Capital	**14.44**	**7.83**	**56.90**	**63.87**
D. Net Errors and Omissions	**39.98**	**−39.73**	**−17.20**	**21.14**
E. Exceptional Financing	—	—	—	—
Total, Groups A through E	**−29.81**	**−21.78**	**−42.20**	**−68.65**
F. Liabilities (foreign auth. res.)	**32.04**	**16.02**	**38.27**	**70.02**
G. Reserves	**−2.23**	**5.76**	**3.92**	**−1.37**

Source: Adapted from International Monetary Fund, *Balance of Payments Statistics Yearbook, 1994*, p. 744.

TABLE 2-8   JAPANESE BALANCE OF PAYMENTS, 1990–1993 (US$ BILLIONS)

	1990	1991	1992	1993
A. Current Account (excl. Group E)	**35.87**	**72.91**	**117.64**	**131.51**
1. Merchandise: Export FOB	280.35	306.58	330.87	351.31
2. Merchandise: Import FOB	−216.77	−203.49	−198.47	−209.74
3. Trade balance	63.58	103.09	132.40	141.57
4. Services: Credit	40.83	44.65	48.31	51.51
5. Services: Debit	−81.97	−85.04	−89.73	−92.77
6. Private Unrequited Transfers	−1.01	−.66	−1.31	−2.25
7. Official Unrequited Transfers	−4.51	−11.84	−3.31	−3.84
B. Direct Investment and Other Long-Term Capital	**−53.08**	**31.39**	**−30.78**	**−81.36**
8. Direct Investment	−46.29	−29.37	−14.52	−13.64
9. Portfolio Investment	−14.49	35.45	−28.41	−65.71
10. Other Long-Term Capital	7.7	25.31	12.15	−2.01
Total, Groups A, B	**−17.21**	**104.30**	**86.86**	**50.15**
C. Short-Term Capital	**31.54**	**−103.24**	**−75.77**	**−22.24**
D. Net Errors and Omissions	**−20.92**	**−7.68**	**−10.46**	**−.25**
E. Exceptional Financing	—	—	—	—
Total, Groups A through E	**−6.59**	**−6.63**	**.63**	**27.66**
F. Liabilities (foreign auth. res.)	—	—	—	—
G. Reserves	**6.59**	**6.63**	**−.63**	**−27.66**

Source: Adapted from International Monetary Fund, *Balance of Payments Statistics Yearbook, 1994*, p. 365.

Tables 2–7 and 2–8 show that, between 1990 and 1993, Japan enjoyed a growing surplus in both its current account and its merchandise trade balances. Conversely, in the same period, the United States showed deficits in both balances. The United States's overall trade deficit has continued to surprise observers, given the dollar's weakness relative to the currencies of trading partners such as Germany and Japan. A comparison of lines 4 and 5 in the two tables shows a bright spot, from the U.S. perspective: The United States has maintained a surplus in services traded while Japan shows a deficit. The total of lettered lines A through E is the actual balance of payments figure. Note that in 1993 the United States had a large balance of payments deficit ($69 billion), while Japan had a fairly large surplus ($28 billion). Overall, Japan offsets its trade surplus with an outflow of capital, while the United States offsets its trade deficit with an inflow of capital (line C in Table 2–7 shows short-term capital inflows into the United States; line F shows U.S. liabilities to foreign authorities). As trading partners, the United States owns an increasing quantity of Japanese products, while Japan owns more U.S. land, real estate, and government securities.

TRADE PATTERNS

Since the end of World War II, world merchandise trade has grown faster than world production. In other words, import and export growth has outpaced the rate of increase in GNP. Moreover, since 1983, foreign direct investment has grown five times faster than world trade and 10 times faster than GNP.[14] The structure of world trade is summarized in Figure 2–5. The importance of the Triad countries is quite pronounced: North America, the EU, and Japan accounted for two-thirds of world exports and imports. Industrialized nations have increased their share of world trade by trading more among themselves and less with the rest of the world.

Merchandise Trade

Table 2–9 shows trade patterns for the world. In 1994, the dollar value of world trade was approximately $4.1 trillion. Seventy-five percent of world exports was generated by industrialized countries and 25 percent by developing countries. The EU accounted for

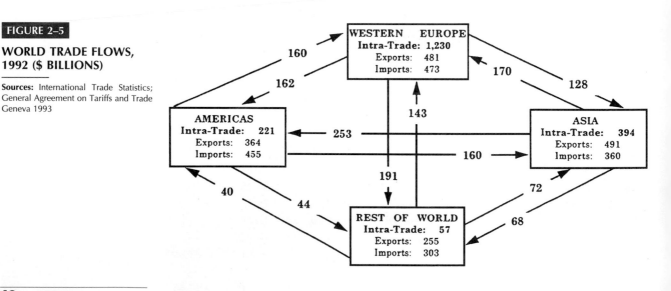

FIGURE 2–5

WORLD TRADE FLOWS, 1992 ($ BILLIONS)

Sources: International Trade Statistics; General Agreement on Tariffs and Trade Geneva 1993

[14]"Who Wants to Be a Giant?" Survey, *The Economist* (June 24, 1995), p. 1.

TABLE 2-9 WORLD MERCHANDISE EXPORTS AND IMPORTS, 1994 (US$ BILLIONS)

Areas	Exports To	Imports From
Direction of Trade WORLD TOTAL	$4,140.10	$4,298.50
Industrial countries	2,730.30	2,878.90
Developing countries	1,348.49	1,366.04
Africa	81.16	86.09
Asia	134.87	756.00
Europe	183.19	186.47
Middle East	130.26	138.84
Western Hemisphere	219.01	198.63

Source: International Monetary Fund, *Direction of Trade Statistics* (Washington, D.C.: IMF, 1994).

40 percent, the United States and Canada for 18 percent, and Japan for 9 percent. If the EU were considered a single country, its share of world exports would be slightly less than that of the United States. Trade growth outside industrialized countries has been slow.

The top 20 exporting and importing countries of the world (as reported by the International Monetary Fund) are shown in Table 2–10. Among Asian exporters, China and South Korea both showed growth exceeding 20 percent from 1993 to 1994, evidence of economic strength. In the Western Hemisphere, Mexico's export growth of 20.73 per-

TABLE 2-10 TWENTY LEADING EXPORTERS AND IMPORTERS IN WORLD MERCHANDISE TRADE, 1994 (US$ BILLIONS)

Leading Exporters	1994	Percent Change '94/'93	Leading Importers	1994	Percent Change '94/'93
1. USA	547.21	12.21	1. USA	662.92	13.76
2. Japan	420.55	8.04	2. Germany	353.01	8.23
3. Germany	403.70	12.13	3. Japan	242.48	12.25
4. France	234.25	13.13	4. France	217.00	9.56
5. U.K.	194.67	13.70	5. U.K.	216.80	8.48
6. China	189.47	21.94	6. Canada	153.34	13.29
7. Italy	182.32	15.23	7. Italy	149.50	12.21
8. Canada	167.26	14.68	8. Netherlands	142.98	8.15
9. Netherlands	133.45	10.13	9. Hong Kong	140.68	21.74
10. Belgium/Luxem.	116.51	12.49	10. Belgium/Luxem.	125.77	10.76
11. South Korea	92.06	24.12	11. China	122.27	12.22
12. Switzerland	77.97	7.27	12. Singapore	93.71	15.86
13. Singapore	73.43	18.34	13. South Korea	88.15	22.27
14. Spain	70.85	22.96	14. Spain	83.57	14.95
15. Malaysia	64.62	16.34	15. Switzerland	72.94	8.96
16. Russia	63.27	48.59	16. Mexico	71.35	19.19
17. Hong Kong	63.06	16.36	17. Austria	53.00	9.18
18. Mexico	61.90	20.73	18. Australia	48.31	16.63
19. Sweden	61.35	17.23	19. Thailand	46.96	15.77
20. Saudi Arabia	49.31	−3.01	20. Sweden	46.31	16.82

Source: Adapted from International Monetary Fund, *Direction of Trade Statistics*, (Washington, D.C.: IMF, June 1995), pp. 2–3.

FIGURE 2–6

U.S. TRADE BALANCE ON SERVICES AND ON MERCHANDISE TRADE ($ BILLIONS)

Source: *Business America* (June 1995), p. 28. U.S. Government Printing Office.

cent shows the impact of NAFTA; by comparison, in 1992–1993, Mexico's exports grew only 9 percent. Perhaps the most surprising statistic in Table 2–10 is the nearly 50 percent increase in Russia's 1994 exports resulting from privatization of major industry sectors and increased emphasis on exports.

Services Trade

Probably the fastest-growing sector of world trade is trade in services. Services include travel and entertainment, education, business services such as engineering, accounting, and legal services, and payments of royalties and license fees. Unfortunately, the statistics and data on trade in services are not as comprehensive as those for merchandise trade. For example, many countries (especially low-income countries) are lax in enforcing international copyrights protecting intellectual property and patent laws. As a result, countries that export service products like software and video entertainment suffer a loss of income. According to the Software Publishers Association, annual worldwide losses due to software piracy amount to $8 billion. In China and the countries of the former Soviet Union, more than 95 percent of the personal computer software in use is believed to be pirated.

As shown in Figure 2–6, in 1994, U.S. services exports totaled $195 billion, partially offsetting the merchandise trade deficit. In 1994, the services surplus—services exports minus imports—stood at $60 billion. American Express, Walt Disney, and Texas Instruments are a few of the U.S. companies currently enjoying rapid growth in demand for their services around the world, fueled in part by the weak dollar.[15]

SUMMARY

The economic environment is a major determinant of global market potential and opportunity. The world's economies can be categorized as market allocation systems, command allocation systems, and mixed allocation systems. A major trend in recent years has been the transition toward market economies in many countries that had been centrally controlled. Countries can be categorized in terms of their stage of economic development: low income, lower middle income, upper middle income, high income, and basket cases. It is possible to identify distinct stages and formulate general estimates about the type of demand associated with a particular stage of development. Since, for

many products, the single most important indicator of market potential is income, the first step in determining the potential of a country or region is to identify the total and per capita income.

Market potential for a product can be evaluated by determining product saturation levels in the light of income levels. In general, it is appropriate to compare the saturation levels of countries or of consumer segments with similar income levels. Balance of payments issues are also important economic considerations. The U.S. merchandise trade deficit has passed the $100 billion mark several times in recent years; the United States is thus a debtor; Japan enjoys a trade surplus and serves as a creditor nation.

[15]Ralph T. King, Jr., "Quiet Boom: U.S. Service Exports Are Growing Rapidly, but Almost Unnoticed," *The Wall Street Journal* (Apr. 21, 1993), p. A1.

1. Explain the difference between a market allocation system and a command allocation system.
2. What are the stages of national market development, and what percentage of world income is found in each of the stages?
3. What is the pattern of income distribution in the world today? How do developing countries' markets compare with high-income countries' markets in the proportion of income going to the bottom and top 20 percent of the population?
4. A manufacturer of satellite dishes is assessing the world market potential for his products. He asks you if he should consider developing countries as potential markets. How would you advise him?
5. Are income and standard of living the same thing? What is meant by the term "standard of living"?
6. A friend tells you that the United States' merchandise trade deficit hit a record $166 billion in 1994. You want to cheer your friend up by demonstrating that the trade picture is not as bleak as it sounds. What do you say?

BIBLIOGRAPHY

Books

Galbraith, John Kenneth. *The Nature of Mass Poverty*. Cambridge: Harvard University Press, 1979.

Gilder, George F. *Microcosm: The Quantum Revolution in Economics and Technology*. New York: Simon and Schuster, 1989.

Isaak, Robert A. *Managing World Economic Change*. Upper Saddle River, N.J.: Prentice Hall, 1995.

Kennedy, Paul. *The Rise and Fall of Great Powers*. New York: Random House, 1987.

Porter, Michael E. *The Competitive Advantage of Nations*. New York: The Free Press, 1990.

Shapiro, Alan C. *Multinational Financial Management*. 5th ed. Upper Saddle River, NJ: Prentice Hall, Inc., 1996.

Thurow, Lester. *Head to Head: The Coming Economic Battle among Japan, Europe, and America*. New York: William Morrow and Company, 1992.

Articles

Ardrey, William J., Anthony Pecotich, and Clifford J. Schultz. "American Involvement in Vietnam, Part II: Prospects for U.S. Business in a New Era." *Business Horizons* 38, no. 2 (March–April 1995), pp. 21–27.

Drucker, Peter F. "Marketing and Economic Development." *Journal of Marketing* (January 1958), pp. 252–259.

"The European Community" Survey. *The Economist* (July 11, 1992), pp. 5–30.

Golden, Peggy A., Patricia M. Doney, Denise M. Johnson, and Jerald R. Smith. "The Dynamics of a Marketing Orientation in Transition Economies: A Study of Russian Firms." *Journal of International Marketing* 3, no. 2 (1995), pp. 29–49.

Prowse, Michael. "Is America in Decline?" *Harvard Business Review* 70, no. 4 (July–August 1992), pp. 36–37.

Yan, Rick. "To Reach China's Consumers, Adapt to *Guo Qing*." *Harvard Business Review* 72, no. 5 (September–October 1994), pp. 66–74.

On February 3, 1994, President Bill Clinton ended America's 19-year economic embargo of Vietnam. The President's move opened the door for U.S. companies to target a market of 72 million people. A number of U.S. companies immediately seized the opportunity. As Brian Watson, a Hong Kong–based deputy regional director for the McCann-Erickson advertising agency, said, "Vietnam is the next great frontier. There is an enormous amount of interest among clients. Every meeting starts with a question about going into Vietnam."

In fact, a wide range of global companies had preceded the Americans into Vietnam, including Daewoo, Sony, Toshiba, Honda, Peugeot, and British Petroleum. Carrier was among the first U.S. companies to legally market in Vietnam; the company's window air conditioners appeared in stores in Hanoi and Ho Chi Minh City. Gillette began shipping razor blades and disposable razors, and AT&T began selling home and office telephone products through a distributor in Taiwan. Mobil began exploring for oil, Caterpillar set up equipment-leasing operations, and the Otis Elevator division of United Technologies joined in the construction boom. Three advertising agencies—J. Walter Thompson, Ogilvy & Mather, and Backer Spielvogel Bates Worldwide—became the first Western ad agencies to open liaison offices in Vietnam.

Since 60 percent of Vietnam's population is under the age of 25, it is no surprise that PepsiCo and the Coca-Cola Company were also quick to make moves in Vietnam. In fact, at the time of the official announcement about ending the embargo, McCann-Erickson had already produced a TV commercial for Coca-Cola that included the global slogan "Always"; Ogilvy & Mather had a Pepsi ad ready for TV. Coca-Cola is building a $20 million bottling plant outside of Hanoi, but was denied permission to build in Ho Chi Minh City (formerly Saigon). PepsiCo's joint venture with a Vietnamese firm in Ho Chi Minh City is bottling Pepsi; local production began within hours of President Clinton's announcement. To supply the market in the south, Coca-Cola must import canned soda from Singapore. As a result, a can of Coke costs twice as much as a bottle of Pepsi.

Experts agree that the Vietnamese market holds tremendous potential over the long term. It may be two decades before Vietnam reaches the level of economic development found in Thailand today. Meanwhile, the country's location in the heart of Asia and the presence of an ample low-wage workforce are powerful magnets for foreign companies. Initially, U.S. investment in Vietnam lagged well behind other countries; in early 1994, Hong Kong ranked first, with more than 200 projects valued at nearly $2 billion, followed by Taiwan and South Korea. By mid-1994, the United States had 14 investment projects. One U.S. banker said, "The figures speak for themselves. They indicate that American companies start slowly. But I think they are picking up steam." By 1995, the United States had moved up to eighth place, with investments passing the $500 billion mark.

There are many challenges for investors in Vietnam. The population is very poor, with annual per capita income of only $200. The infrastructure is undeveloped: Only 10 percent of roads are paved, electricity sources are unreliable, there is less than one telephone per 100 people, and the banking system is undeveloped. The Communist Party of Vietnam (CPV) is struggling to adapt to the principles of a market economy, and the layers of bureaucracy built up over decades of communist rule slow the pace of change. A key agency is the State Committee for Cooperation and Investment; as Vu Tien Phuc, a deputy director of the agency, explained, "Every authority would like to have the last say. We have to improve the investment climate." William Ratliff, an analyst with the Hoover Institute, points out that the question for Vietnam is "whether it's possible to carry on free-market reforms and maintain absolute political power."

Yvonne Gupwell, a business consultant who was born in Vietnam, believes that "The biggest mistake companies make is they think because the Vietnamese are so polite, they're a little bit dim. The Vietnamese are poor, but they are not mentally poor at all." Statistics support this view; for example, adult literacy is nearly 90 percent. In fact, an emerging entrepreneurial class has developed a taste for expensive products such as Nikon cameras and Ray Ban sunglasses—both of which are available in stores. Notes Do Duc Dinh of the Institute on the World Economy, "There is a huge unofficial economy. For most people, we can live only 5 days or 10 days a month on our salary. But people build houses. Where does the money come from? Even in government ministries, there are two sets of books—one for the official money and one for unofficial."

On July 11, 1995, President Clinton provided a further boost to business by reestablishing diplomatic relations with Vietnam. In the absence of diplomatic relations, Vietnamese exports to the United States would face prohibitive tariffs, and U.S. businesses would not qualify for U.S. government loan guarantees. Vietnam must also demonstrate that it complies with international laws concerning workers' rights before the Overseas Private Investment Corporation (OPIC) will provide financial assistance for Americans investing in Vietnam. The CPV's adherence to Marxist-Leninist principles means Vietnam does not qualify for Export-Import Bank financing. A further political step would be granting Vietnam "most-favored nation" status, which would allow Vietnamese imports into the United States to carry the same low-tariff privileges enjoyed by other trading partners.

Meanwhile, Eugene Matthews is proceeding with plans

to establish Vietnam's biggest dairy by importing Holstein cattle from the United States. After working for many years as a consultant to companies doing business in Vietnam, Matthews has a feel for the place. "I don't want to look at anything the Government doesn't regard as a priority. In this case dairy is a priority, so people are nice to you. They want to get this done." However, he notes, "It's still Vietnam. It's still a complicated place. It's still bureaucratic. But there is a system and it does work."

DISCUSSION QUESTIONS

1. Assess the market opportunities in Vietnam.
2. Conduct library research to determine which nation currently leads in foreign direct investment in Vietnam. What is the explanation for the ranking?
3. Some critics have argued that Cuba is more deserving of diplomatic and trade relations with the United States than Vietnam. What are some of the factors behind this argument?

Sources: "Vietnam" Survey, *The Economist* (July 8, 1995), pp. 1–18.
William J. Ardrey, Anthony Pecotich, and Clifford J. Schultz, "American Involvement in Vietnam, Part II: Prospects for U.S. Business in a New Era," *Business Horizons* 38, no. 2 (March–April 1995), pp. 21–27.
Edward A. Gargan, "For U.S. Business, a Hard Road to Vietnam," *The New York Times* (July 14, 1995), p. C1.
Marilyn Greene, "Very Soon, Vietnam Will Be Very Good," *USA Today* (Apr. 1, 1994), p. 8A.
Robert Keatley, "Vietnam, Despite Promise, Faces Climb," *The Wall Street Journal* (Aug. 18, 1994), p. A8.
Philip Shenon, "Vietnam: Behind a Red-Tape Curtain," *The New York Times* (Nov. 13, 1994), Sec. 3, p. 6.
James Cox, "Vietnamese Look Forward to Trade, Jobs," *USA Today* (July 12, 1995), pp. 1A, 2A.
Kevin Goldman, "Agencies Get Ready for Vietnam Business," *The Wall Street Journal* (Feb. 7, 1994), p. B10.

Regional Market Characteristics

"The Chinese leadership is trying to demonstrate that a country can have a powerful modern economy without allowing its people the individual freedoms that the Western world calls 'human rights.' The entire Asian model is based on a variant of this proposition: that it is possible to become as strong as the Western world without embracing its permissive ways." [1]

—James Fallows, Author

The developing regions of the world have attracted a great deal of attention from global companies in the 1990s. Many countries in Asia, Central Europe, and Latin America are experiencing economic growth rates higher than those found in industrial countries. In Latin America, for example, Argentina and Chile are projected to grow more than 6 percent in 1996. Even Cuba—Fidel Castro's communist outpost in the Caribbean where "Socialism or Death" is the national motto—is attracting foreign investment. By mid-1995, foreign commitments in Cuba totaled more than half a billion dollars. Cuba desperately needs investment, in part to compensate for the end of subsidies following the demise of the Soviet Union. U.S. companies are playing a very limited role in Cuba, however; for three decades, the United States has maintained a trade embargo with the tiny island nation. Many American executives are concerned that lucrative opportunities will be lost as Spain, Mexico, Italy, Canada, and other countries move aggressively in Cuba. Anticipating a softening in the U.S. government's stance, representatives from more than 100 U.S. companies have visited Cuba to meet with officials from state businesses.

The growing number of business trips to Cuba reflects the realization among businesspersons of Cuba's growing importance on the world trade scene. While global marketers should be well versed in the characteristics of regional markets most relevant to their business or industry, one need not be an expert on every country in the world. Hopefully, anyone engaged in global marketing will have expertise and experience in one or more regions or countries outside the home market. Obviously, in-depth market and country knowledge must be applied to the country marketing effort by members of the business team; the latter may include local agents, representatives, or employees. For global marketers, the ability to work with other team members and leverage their expertise is just as important as possessing country or regional knowledge oneself. This chapter presents a broad overview of the markets of the world on a regional basis. The first half of the chapter outlines economic cooperation and preferential trade arrangements. The second half describes the characteristics of the major regional markets and includes an extended analysis of the Japanese market.

---

[1] James M. Fallows, *Looking at the Sun: The Rise of the New East Asian Economic and Political System.* New York: Vintage Books, 1995.

ECONOMIC COOPERATION AND PREFERENTIAL TRADE ARRANGEMENTS

Since World War II there has been a tremendous interest among nations in economic cooperation. This interest has been stimulated by the success of the European Community (now the European Union), which was itself inspired by the U.S. economy. There are many degrees of economic cooperation, ranging from agreement among two or more nations to reductions of barriers to trade, to the full-scale economic integration of two or more national economies. The best-known preferential arrangement of the 20th century was the British Commonwealth preference system. This system provided a foundation for trade between the United Kingdom, Canada, Australia, New Zealand, India, and certain other former British colonies in Africa, Asia, and the Middle East. The decision by the United Kingdom to join the European Economic Community resulted in the demise of this system and illustrates the constantly evolving nature of international economic cooperation.

The World Trade Organization and GATT

The General Agreement on Tariffs and Trade (GATT) is a treaty between 125 nations whose governments agreed, at least in principle, to promote trade among members. GATT was intended to be a multilateral, global initiative, and GATT negotiators did indeed succeed in liberalizing world merchandise trade. GATT was also an organization that handled 300 trade disputes—many involving food—during its half century of existence. GATT itself had no enforcement power (the losing party in a dispute was entitled to ignore the ruling), and the process of dealing with disputes sometimes stretched on for years.

(Copyright 1995, *USA TODAY.* Reprinted with permission.)

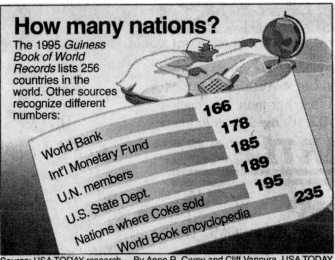

How many nations?

The 1995 *Guiness Book of World Records* lists 256 countries in the world. Other sources recognize different numbers:

World Bank — 166
Int'l Monetary Fund — 178
U.N. members — 185
U.S. State Dept. — 189
Nations where Coke sold — 195
World Book encyclopedia — 235

Source: USA TODAY research   By Anne R. Carey and Cliff Vancura, USA TODAY

The successor to GATT, the World Trade Organization (WTO), came into existence on January 1, 1995. From its base in Geneva, the WTO will provide a forum for trade-related negotiations. One of the WTO's first major tasks was hosting negotiations on the General Agreement on Trade in Services, in which 76 signatories made binding market access commitments in banking, securities, and insurance. The WTO's staff of neutral trade experts will also serve as mediators in global trade disputes. The WTO faced its first real test when representatives from the United States and Japan met to try and resolve a dispute over U.S. claims that the Japanese engaged in unfair trade practices that limited imports of U.S. car parts. The Clinton administration was responding to the fact that one-third of the U.S. merchandise trade deficit—$66 billion in 1994 alone—was with Japan. Moreover, cars and auto parts accounted for approximately two-thirds of that $66 billion.

In the spring of 1995, the United States threatened to slap 100 percent tariffs on 13 models of Japanese cars imported into the United States. Japan formally filed a complaint with the WTO objecting to the tariffs; although a trade war was narrowly averted at the last moment, trade-related tensions between the two countries continue to simmer.[2]

Since 1947, the member countries of GATT completed eight rounds of multilateral trade negotiations. Tariffs have been reduced from an average of 40 percent in 1945 to 5 percent today. The result has been a tremendous growth in trade: Between 1945 and 1975,

---

[2]Lawrence Ingrassia, "Wake Up, Everyone! This Is a Lot Bigger than a Sardine Feud!" *The Wall Street Journal* (May 19, 1995), pp. A1, A4.

A major issue in the recent GATT negotiations was European concern that a flood of entertainment from Hollywood would crowd out local productions. (Copyright Jean-Pierre Arnet, SYGMA.)

the volume of world trade expanded by roughly 500 percent.[3] The seventh round of negotiations was launched in Tokyo and ran from 1973 to 1979. These talks succeeded in cutting duties on industrial products valued at $150 billion by another 30 percent so that the remaining tariffs averaged about 6 percent. In terms of agricultural trade, there was a major clash between the United States and protectionist European and Japanese markets. The clash pitted the American farmer—the world's most efficient producer—against the high-cost, but politically powerful, farmers of Europe and Japan. These deep-rooted differences resulted in little change in the agricultural area during the Tokyo Round. The most notable feature of the Tokyo Round was not the duty cuts, but rather a series of nine new agreements on nontariff trade barriers.

GATT officials also devoted considerable attention to the services industry, addressing market-entry barriers in banking, insurance, telecommunications, and other sectors. The services issue was so volatile that the opening of the Uruguay Round was delayed from 1982 until 1986. In addition to trade in services, these negotiations focused on the above-mentioned nontariff measures that restrict or distort trade, including agricultural trade policy, intellectual property protection, and restrictions on foreign investment.[4]

Agricultural subsidies and quotas that have developed outside the multilateral framework also proved to be another divisive issue. Affluent countries protect and subsidize farm production. While home-market consumers pay high prices, surplus output is sold abroad at artificially low prices. For example, France—where agriculture is a matter of national pride—is intent on preserving its agricultural subsidies. In 1992 alone, these amounted to $44 billion in government expenditures plus an additional $85 billion in outlays by consumers for higher-priced food products.[5] According to the OECD, the total cost of these subsidies to rich-country taxpayers and consumers is more than $200 billion a year. Poor countries (including those in Eastern Europe) are denied their natural path out of poverty, namely food exports.[6] The Uruguay negotiations were suspended in

[3]"GATT's Last Gasp," The Economist (Dec. 1, 1990), p. 16.
[4]Joseph A. McKinney, "How Multilateral Trade Talks Affect the U.S.," Baylor Business Review (Fall 1991), pp. 24–25.
[5]Bob Davis, "Squeaky Wheels: GATT Talks Resume, with France and India Calling Many of the Shots," The Wall Street Journal (Jan. 31, 1992), pp. A1, A13.
[6]"Free Trade's Fading Champion," The Economist (Apr. 11, 1992), p. 65.

THE REST OF THE STORY

■ CUBA

As noted in the chapter introduction, Cuba remains officially off limits to all but a handful of U.S. companies. Some telecommunications and financial services are allowed; AT&T, Sprint, and other companies have offered direct-dial service between the United States and Cuba since 1994. Also, one charter flight is available each day between Miami and Havana.

At a recent State Department briefing for business executives, Assistant Secretary of State for Inter-American Affairs Alexander Watson told his audience, "The Europeans and the Asians are knocking on the door in Latin America. The game is on and we can compete effectively, but it will be a big mistake if we leave the game to others." Secretary Watson was asked whether his comments on free trade applied to Cuba. "No, no. That simply can't be, not for now," Watson replied. "Cuba is a special case. This administration will maintain the embargo until major democratic changes take place in Cuba."

Within the United States, the government's stance toward Cuba has both supporters and opponents. Senator Jesse Helms would like a tougher embargo; he has sponsored a bill in Congress that would penalize foreign countries and companies for doing business with Cuba. The Cuban-American National Foundation actively engages in anti-Cuba

and anti-Castro lobbying. Companies that have openly spoken out against the embargo include Carlson Companies, owner of the Radisson Hotel chain, grain-processing giant Archer Daniels Midland, and the Otis Elevator division of United Technologies. A spokesperson for Carlson noted, "We see Cuba as an exciting new opportunity—the forbidden fruit of the Caribbean." A number of executives, including Ron Perelman, whose corporate holdings include Revlon and Consolidated Cigar Corporation, are optimistic that the embargo will be lifted within a few years.

Meanwhile, not everyone agrees with the view that the embargo is costing U.S. companies once-in-a-lifetime opportunities. Some observers argue that many European and Latin American investments in Cuba are short-term, high-risk propositions that would not create barriers to U.S. companies. The opponents of the embargo, however, point out that some investments are substantial. Three thousand new hotel rooms have been added by Spain's Grupo Sol Melia and Germany's LTI International Hotels. Both companies are taking advantage of the Cuban government's goal to increase tourism. Moreover, contracts to overhaul the country's telecommunications infrastructure are going to Italian and Mexican companies. Wayne Andreas, chairman of Archer Daniels Midland, summed up the views of many American executives when he said, "Our embargo has been a total failure for 30 years. We ought to have all the Americans in Cuba doing all the business they can. It's time for a change."

Sources: Gail DeGeorge, "U.S. Business Isn't Afraid to Shout *Cuba Si!" Business Week* (Nov. 6, 1995), p. 39.
Jose de Cordoba, "Cuba's Business Law Puts Off Foreigners," *The Wall Street Journal* (Oct. 10, 1995), p. A14.
Sam Dillon, "Companies Press Clinton to Lift Embargo on Cuba," *The New York Times* (Aug. 27, 1995), pp. 1, 4.
Thomas T. Vogel, Jr., "Havana Headaches: Investors Find Cuba Tantalizing yet Murky in Financial Matters," *The Wall Street Journal* (Aug. 7, 1995), pp. A1, A4.

December 1990 after 30,000 French farmers took to the streets of Brussels to protest a proposed 30 percent cut in agricultural export subsidies. Negotiations resumed a few months later against the background of the united Western war effort in the Persian Gulf. Negotiators finally reached an agreement by the December 15, 1993, deadline. A stalemate over agricultural subsidies was broken, with France and the EU nations agreeing to reductions. The U.S. Congress voted in favor of GATT at the end of 1994.

Competitive companies will benefit as tariffs are cut or eliminated entirely. The Triad nations agreed to end tariffs in pharmaceuticals, construction and agricultural equipment, Scotch whisky, furniture, paper, steel, and medical equipment. Also, U.S. restrictions on textile and apparel imports from Third World countries will be phased out over a 10-year period. Major issues remain unresolved in the entertainment industry; France has insisted on preferences and subsidies for French producers of television programming and motion pictures in order to limit what they feel is "cultural imperialism." Efforts to reduce European broadcast restrictions on U.S.-produced movies and television programming were unsuccessful.[7]

Free Trade Area

A **free trade area** (FTA) is a group of countries that have agreed to abolish all internal barriers to trade among themselves. Countries that belong to a free trade area can and do maintain independent trade policies vis-à-vis third countries. A system of certificates of origin is used to avoid trade diversion in favor of low-tariff members. The system dis-

---

[7]Bob Davis and Lawrence Ingrassia, "Trade Acceptance: After Years of Talks, GATT Is at Last Ready to Sign Off on a Pact," *The Wall Street Journal* (Dec. 15, 1993), pp. A1, A7.

courages importing goods into the member country with the lowest tariff for transshipment to countries within the area with higher external tariffs; customs inspectors police the borders between members. The European Economic Area is a free trade area that includes the 15-nation European Union and Norway, Liechtenstein, and Iceland. The Canada–U.S. Free Trade Area formally came into existence in 1989. On August 12, 1992, representatives from the United States, Canada, and Mexico concluded negotiations for the North American Free Trade Agreement (NAFTA). The agreement was approved by both houses of the U.S. Congress and became effective on January 1, 1994.

Customs Unions

A **customs union** represents the logical evolution of a free trade area. In addition to eliminating the internal barriers to trade, members of a customs union agree to the establishment of common external barriers. On January 1, 1996, the European Union and Turkey initiated a customs union in an effort to boost two-way trade above the current annual level of $20 billion. The arrangement called for elimination of tariffs averaging 14 percent that added $1.5 billion each year to the cost of European goods imported by Turkey.

Common Market

A **common market** is the next step in the spectrum of economic integration. In addition to the removal of internal barriers to trade and the establishment of common external barriers, the common market allows for free movement of factors of production, including, labor, capital, and information. Examples include the Central American Common Market, the Southern Cone Common Market, and the Andean Group.

Economic Unions

An **economic union** builds upon the elimination of the internal tariff barriers and the establishment of common external barriers. It seeks to coordinate economic and social policy within the union to allow free flow of capital and labor from country to country. An economic union is a common marketplace not only for goods but also for services and capital. For example, if professional people are going to be able to work anywhere in the EU, the members must harmonize their practice licensing so that a doctor or lawyer qualified in one country may practice in any other. The full evolution of an economic union would involve the creation of a unified central bank, the use of a single currency, and common policies on agriculture, social services and welfare, regional development, transport, taxation, competition, and mergers. A fully developed economic union requires extensive political unity, which makes it similar to a nation. The further integration of nations that were members of fully developed economic unions would be the formation of a central government that would bring together independent political states into a single political framework. The European Union is approaching its target of completing most of the steps required to become a full economic union. The various forms of economic integration are compared in Table 3–1.

TABLE 3–1 FORMS OF REGIONAL ECONOMIC INTEGRATION

Stage of Integration	Elimination of Tariffs and Quotes Among Members	Common Tariff and Quota System	Elimination of Restrictions on Factor Movements	Harmonization and Unification of Economic Policies and Institutions
Free trade area	Yes	No	No	No
Customs union	Yes	Yes	No	No
Common market	Yes	Yes	Yes	No
Economic union	Yes	Yes	Yes	Yes

Source: Franklin R. Root, *International Trade and Investment,* Cincinnati Ohio: South Western Publishing Company, 1992, p. 254.

REGIONAL ECONOMIC ORGANIZATIONS

In addition to the multilateral initiative of GATT, countries in each of the world's regions are seeking to lower barriers to trade within their regions. The following section describes the major regional economic cooperation agreements. We begin in North America, then move south into Central and South America.

North American Free Trade Agreement (NAFTA)

In 1988 the United States signed a free trade agreement with Canada (U.S.–Canada Free Trade Agreement or CFTA), the scope of which was enlarged in 1993 to include Mexico. The resulting free trade area had a 1995 population of 381 million and a GNP of $7.6 trillion.

All three governments will promote economic growth through expanded trade and investment. The benefits of continental free trade will enable all three countries to meet the economic challenges of the decades to come. The gradual elimination of barriers to the flow of goods, services, and investment, coupled with strong intellectual property rights protection (patents, trademarks, and copyrights), will benefit businesses, workers, farmers, and consumers.

Canada and Mexico rank first and third as the United States's most important trading partners (Japan ranks second). In 1994, U.S. exports to Canada totaled $114.4 billion; U.S. exports to Mexico were $50.8 billion. U.S. merchandise imports from Canada in 1994 totaled $128.9 billion; imports from Mexico amounted to $49.5 billion. Combined three-way trade in 1990 amounted to $237 billion; the 1994 figures show NAFTA's impact on trade among the three nations. The NAFTA countries are shown in Figure 3–1.

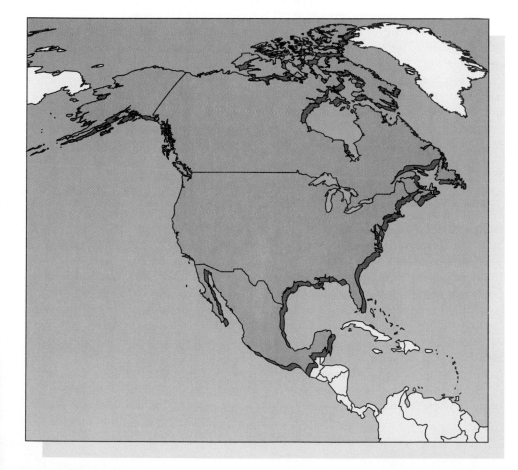

FIGURE 3–1

NAFTA COUNTRIES

FIGURE 3–2

CACM COUNTRIES

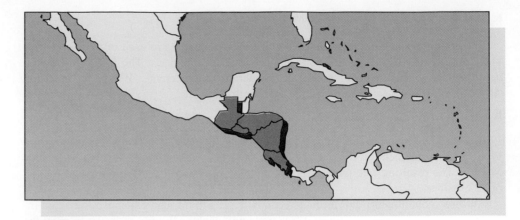

Central American Common Market (CACM)

Central America is trying to revive its common market, which was set up in the 1960s. It collapsed in 1969 when war broke out between Honduras and El Salvador after a riot at a soccer match between teams from the two countries. The five members, El Salvador, Honduras, Guatemala, Nicaragua, and Costa Rica, decided in July 1991 to reestablish the common market by 1994.

The Secretariat for Central American Economic Integration (SIECA), headquartered in Guatemala City, is comprised of ministers responsible for economic integration and regional development. SIECA is charged with helping to coordinate the movement toward a Central American common market. It has been serving as secretariat for a group of customs experts who are in the process of revising the Central American Customs Duty. Effective April 1, 1993, all CACM countries conformed to a common external tariff (CET) of 5 percent to 20 percent for most goods; many tariffs had previously exceeded 100 percent. There was some resistance to this change; for example, the Costa Rican government had previously benefited from the revenues generated by triple-digit tariffs on automobiles imported from Japan and elsewhere. Lower tariffs are expected to result in improved export prospects for U.S. companies. Common rules of origin were also adopted, allowing for free movement of goods among CACM countries. The CACM group is shown in Figure 3–2.

Andean Group

The Andean Group (see Figure 3–3) was formed in 1969 to accelerate development of its member states—Bolivia, Colombia, Ecuador, Peru, and Venezuela—through economic and social integration. Members agreed to lower tariffs on intra-group trade and work together to decide what products each country should produce. At the same time, foreign goods and companies were kept out as much as possible. One Bolivian described the unfortunate result of this lack of competition in the following way: "We had agreed, 'You buy our overpriced goods and we'll buy yours.' "[8]

In 1988, the group members decided to get a fresh start. Beginning in 1992, the Andean Pact signatories agreed to form Latin America's first operating subregional free trade zone. More than 100 million consumers would be affected by the pact, which abolished all foreign exchange, financial and fiscal incentives, and export subsidies at the end of 1992. Common external tariffs were established, marking the transition to a true customs union. A high-level commission will look into any alleged unfair trade practices among countries. The new approach seems to be working; for example, Peru now boasts one of the

[8]"NAFTA Is Not Alone," *The Economist* (June 18, 1994), pp. 47–48.

fastest-growing economies in the region. However, nationalism could still threaten free trade in the region, as evidenced by a recent flareup of hostilities between Peru and Ecuador over a small stretch of border.

Southern Cone Common Market (Mercosur)

Argentina, Brazil, Paraguay, and Uruguay—with a combined population of 200 million people and a GNP of $650 billion—agreed in March 1991 to form the Southern Cone Common Market (in Spanish, *Mercado del Sur*, or Mercosur) (see Figure 3–3). On August 5, 1994, the presidents of the four countries agreed to begin phasing in tariff reform on January 1, 1995. Internal tariffs were eliminated, and external common tariffs of up to 20 percent were established. Goods, services, and factors of production can move freely throughout the four countries. About 15 percent of trade, including advanced electronics and capital goods, is not covered by the agreement.[9] Intra-regional trade has grown 250 percent since 1990.

One immediate result of the tariff reform was that prices of many consumer goods fell overnight in Argentina and Brazil. This, in turn, directly impacted commerce in Paraguay, which had long been a low-tariff haven where cigarette, electronics equipment, and liquor prices were 40 percent lower than in the rest of South America. Historically, bargain seek-

FIGURE 3–3

THE ANDEAN GROUP
AND MERCOSUR
COUNTRIES

Andean Group

Mercosur

---

[9]"Four into One Might Go," *The Economist* (Aug. 13, 1994), pp. 57–58.

ers—and smugglers—swarmed across the Paraguayan border to shop at Ciudad del Este, where annual merchandise sales reached $13 billion in 1994. Now many Paraguayan entrepreneurs who engaged in "import-export" activities will have to seek other sources of income.[10]

Much depends on the successful outcome of this experiment in regional cooperation. If Brazil and Argentina can work well together, hopes for an integrated Latin America will rise significantly. Brazil has a population of 162 million, the strongest economy (in terms of both GDP and exports), and the richest reserves of natural resources in the hemisphere; Argentina has the fourth-largest population and third-largest economy. A major impediment to integration is the lack of economic and political discipline and responsibility, a situation reflected in the volatility of currencies in the Mercosur countries. For example, Brazil devalued its currency in early 1995, much to the dismay of the other three Mercosur members. Then, in June, Brazil announced it was limiting car imports to 100,000 units through the end of 1995. Argentina in particular stood firm against the use of quotas and devaluation to address trade deficits and budgetary imbalances. Mercosur may eventually expand to include Chile (which had been negotiating for inclusion in NAFTA); some observers expect Mercosur and the Andean Group to merge.

Caribbean Community and Common Market (CARICOM)

CARICOM was formed in 1973 as a movement toward unity in the Caribbean. It replaced the Caribbean Free Trade Association (CARIFTA) founded in 1965. The members are Antigua and Barbuda, Bahamas, Barbados, Belize, Dominica, Grenada, Guyana, Jamaica, Montserrat, St. Kitts and Nevis, St. Lucia, St. Vincent and the Grenadines, and Trinidad and Tobago. The population of the entire 13-member CARICOM is 6 million.

CARICOM's main activity is economic integration by means of a Caribbean common market. During the 1980s, the economic difficulties of member states hindered the development of interregional trade. Another problem concerned applying rules of origin to verify that imported goods genuinely come from within the community. As a result, CARICOM has been largely stagnant since it was founded, but at a July 1991 meeting the group agreed to speed integration.

The CARICOM bloc of English-speaking Caribbean states is also concerned with defending its privileged trading position with the United States. That status dates to the Caribbean Basin Initiative (CBI) of 1984, which promoted "nontraditional" export production through duty-free access to the U.S. market. Unfortunately for CARICOM, the Enterprise for the Americas Initiative—with the Mexican free trade agreement as its centerpiece—has overtaken the CBI as the U.S. trade policy flagship in the area. In response to the situation, the CBI members are requesting that the CBI be expanded and its members granted the same trade privileges available to Mexico.[11] CARICOM is shown in Figure 3–4.

Association of Southeast Asian Nations (ASEAN)

ASEAN is an organization for economic, political, social, and cultural cooperation whose six original member countries were Brunei, Indonesia, Malaysia, the Philippines, Singapore, and Thailand (see Figure 3–5). ASEAN (pronounced 'OZZIE-on') was established in 1967 with the signing of the Bangkok Declaration.

Today the ASEAN group has 400 million people and a GNP of $350 billion. Per capita GNPs among ASEAN's original members in 1995 ranged from $21,700 in Singapore to $800 for Indonesia. Vietnam became the first communist nation in the group when it was

[10]Matt Moffett, "Attention, Shoppers! Paraguay's Bargains May Be Going Fast," *The Wall Street Journal* (May 30, 1995), pp. A1, A10.
[11]Ian Walker, "Caribbean Finds Itself in the U.S. Trade Deal Slow Lane," *Financial Times* (Feb. 11, 1992), p. 4.

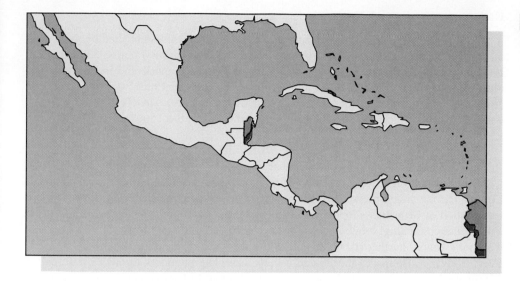

FIGURE 3–4

CARICOM COUNTRIES

admitted to ASEAN in July 1995. ASEAN is the United States' sixth-largest trading partner. Two-way trade between the United States and ASEAN totaled $83.8 billion in 1994.

There is a growing realization among ASEAN officials that broad common goals and perceptions are not enough to keep the association alive. A constant problem is the strict need for consensus among all members before proceeding with any form of cooperative effort. Although the ASEAN member countries are geographically close, they have historically been divided in many respects. One of the reasons the association remained in existence is because it did almost nothing. The situation is changing today, however; in 1994, economic ministers from the member nations agreed to implement an ASEAN Free Trade Area (AFTA) by 2003, five years earlier than previously discussed. Under the agreement, tariffs of 20 percent or more will be reduced to 0 percent to 5 percent.[12]

[12]"ASEAN Economic Ministers Agree to Accelerate AFTA," *ASEAN Business Report* 5, no. 9 (September 1994), pp. 1, 6.

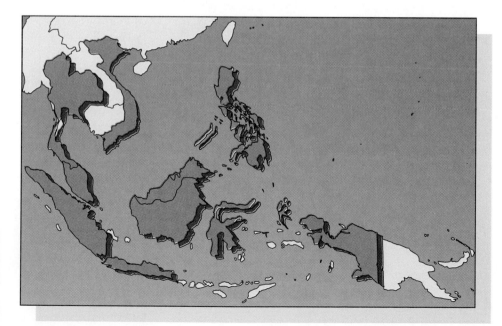

FIGURE 3–5

ASEAN COUNTRIES

European Union (EU)

The EU (formerly known as the European Community) was established by the Treaty of Rome in January 1958. The six original members were Belgium, France, Holland, Italy, Luxembourg, and West Germany. In 1973, Great Britain, Denmark, and Ireland were admitted, followed by Greece in 1981 and Spain and Portugal in 1986. Effective January 1, 1995, the three newest members are Finland, Sweden, and Austria. (In November 1994, voters in Norway rejected a membership proposal.) Today, the 15 nations of the EU represent 372 million people, a combined GNP of $7.6 trillion, and a 39 percent share of world exports. The map in Figure 3–6 shows the EU membership.

Beginning in 1987, the 12 countries that were EC members at that time set about the difficult task of creating a genuine single market in goods, services, and capital. Completing the single-market program by yearend 1992 was a major EC achievement; the Council of Ministers adopted 282 pieces of legislation and regulations to make the single market a reality. Now citizens of the 15 countries are able to freely cross borders within the Union. Further EU enlargement has become a major issue. In December 1991, Czechoslovakia, Hungary, and Poland became associate members through the so-called "European Agreements." The Baltic countries—Latvia, Lithuania, and Estonia—are also hoping to join and thus lower their vulnerability to Russia.

Under provisions of the Maastricht Treaty, the EU is working to create an economic and monetary union (EMU) that will include a European central bank and, possibly, a single European currency. Implementation of the EMU will require working out the ex-

FIGURE 3–6

EU COUNTRIES

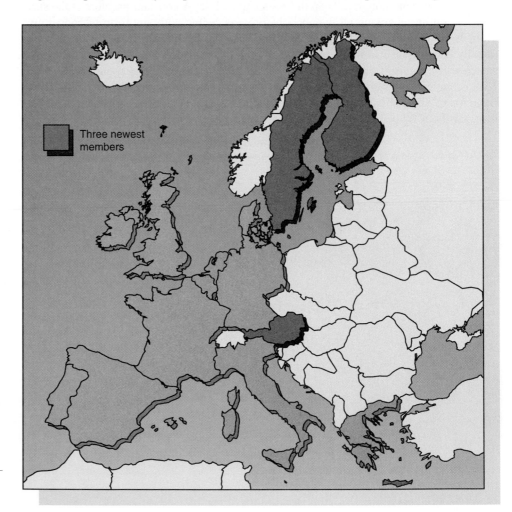

Three newest members

tent to which countries sharing a currency need to coordinate taxes and budgets. A single currency would eliminate costs associated with currency conversion and exchange rate uncertainty. Many obstacles must be overcome, however. For example, many Germans fear that a common European currency will be less stable than the strong Deutsche mark, the bedrock of Germany's economic success. France, Belgium, the Netherlands, and Luxembourg round out a core of five nations with solid monetary policies. Barring the unexpected, if 8 out of 15 members maintain stable exchange rates for two years, reduce public debt to less than 60 percent of GDP, and otherwise bring their economies in line with the standards required to introduce a single currency, the EMU could be implemented as early as January 1997. Otherwise, it will start automatically on January 1, 1999.[13]

European Economic Area (EEA)

In October 1991, after 14 months of negotiations, then-EC and the seven-nation European Free Trade Association (EFTA) reached agreement on the creation of the European Economic Area beginning January 1993. While the goal was to achieve the free movement of goods, services, capital, and labor between the two groups, the EEA is a free trade area, not a customs union with common external tariffs. With Austria, Finland, and Sweden now members of the EU, Norway, Iceland, and Liechtenstein are the only remaining EFTA countries that are not EU members (Switzerland voted not to be part of the EEA). The EEA will be the world's largest trading bloc, with 384 million consumers, $8 trillion combined GDP, and nearly 50 percent of world trade. The three non-EU members of the EEA are expected to adopt all the EU's single-market legislation.[14]

The Lomé Convention

The EU maintains an accord with 70 countries in Africa, the Caribbean and the Pacific (ACP). The Lomé Convention was designed to promote trade and provide poor countries with financial assistance from a European Development Fund. Recently, budget pressures at home have prompted some EU nations to push for cuts in Lomé aid.

Central European Free Trade Association (CEFTA)

The transition in Central and Eastern Europe from command to market economies led to the demise, in June 1991, of the Council for Mutual Economic Assistance. COMECON (or CMEA, as it was also known) was a group of communist bloc countries allied with the Soviet Union. In the post-COMECON era, a number of proposals for multilateral cooperation have been advanced, including the creation of a successor body to be called the Organization for International Economic Cooperation (OIEC). Ultimately, most proposals were blocked by potential member states whose representatives feared that a membership in a new regional bloc would hinder their chances of joining the EU. In December 1992, Hungary, Poland, and Czechoslovakia signed an agreement creating the Central European Free Trade Association (CEFTA). The signatories pledged cooperation in a number of areas, including infrastructure and telecommunications, subregional projects, inter-enterprise cooperation, and tourism and retail trade (Jessop 1995). Meanwhile, within the Commonwealth of Independent States, formal economic integration between the former Soviet republics is proceeding slowly. In May 1995, the governments of Russia and Belarus agreed to form a customs union and remove border posts between their two countries.

---

[13]Christopher Taylor, "EMU: The State of Play," *The World Today* (Apr. 1995), pp. 75–78. See also Kevin Dowd, "European Monetary Reform: Pitfalls of Central Planning," *USA Today* (March 1995), pp. 70–73; and "A Funny New EMU," *The Economist* (Mar. 4, 1995), pp. 49–50.
[14]"European Economic Area: *E Pluribus Unum*," *The Economist* (Jan. 8, 1994), pp. 49–50.

Cooperation Council for the Arab States of the Gulf

The organization generally known as the Gulf Cooperation Council (GCC) was established in 1981 by six Arab states—Bahrain, Kuwait, Oman, Qatar, Saudi Arabia, and the United Arab Emirates (see Figure 3–7).

The organization provides a means of realizing coordination, integration, and cooperation in all economic, social, and cultural affairs. Gulf finance ministers drew up an economic cooperation agreement covering investment, petroleum, the abolition of customs duties, harmonization of banking regulations, and financial and monetary coordination. GCC committees coordinate trade development in the region, industrial strategy, agricultural policy, and uniform petroleum policies and prices.

The GCC is one of three newer regional organizations. In 1989, two other organizations were established. Morocco, Algeria, Mauritania, Tunisia, and Libya banded together in the Arab Maghreb Union (AMU), while Egypt, Iraq, Jordan, and North Yemen created the Arab Cooperation Council (ACC). Many Arabs see their new regional groups—the GCC, ACC, and AMU—as embryonic economic communities which will foster the development of inter-Arab trade and investment. The newer organizations are more promising than the Arab League, which consists of 21 member states and has a constitution that requires unanimous decisions.[15]

Economic Community of West African States (ECOWAS)

The Treaty of Lagos establishing ECOWAS was signed in May 1975 by 16 states with the object of promoting trade, cooperation, and self-reliance in West Africa. The members are Benin, Burkina Faso, Cape Verde, The Gambia, Ghana, Guinea, Guinea-Bissau, Ivory

[15]"A Survey of the Arab World," *The Economist* (May 12, 1990), pp. 3, 19.

FIGURE 3–7

GCC COUNTRIES

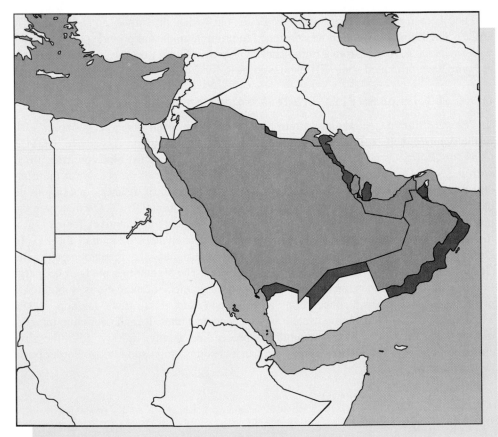

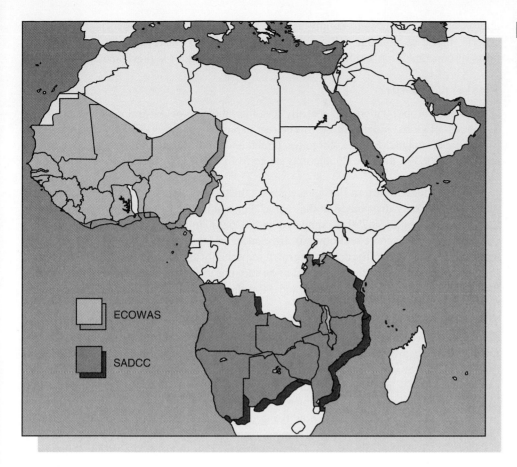

FIGURE 3–8

**ECOWAS AND SADCC
COUNTRIES**

ECOWAS

SADCC

Coast, Liberia, Mali, Mauritania, Niger, Nigeria, Senegal, Sierra Leone, and Togo (see Figure 3–8).

In 1980, the member countries agreed to establish a free trade area for unprocessed agricultural products and handicrafts. Tariffs on industrial goods were also to be abolished; however, there were implementation delays. By January 1990, tariffs on 25 items manufactured in ECOWAS member states had been eliminated. The organization installed a computer system to process customs and trade statistics and to calculate the loss of revenue resulting from the liberalization of intercommunity trade. In June 1990, ECOWAS adopted measures that would create a single monetary zone in the region by 1994.

South African Development Coordination Conference (SADCC)

SADCC was set up in 1980 by the region's black-ruled states to promote trade and cooperation. The members are Angola, Botswana, Lesotho, Malawi, Mozambique, Namibia, Swaziland, Tanzania, Zambia, and Zimbabwe (see Figure 3–8). The real impediment to trade has been SADCC's poverty. The World Bank *Atlas* indicates that combined 1993 GNP for the 10 member nations amounted to less than $25 billion, a figure that represents one-third of Greece's GNP and a fifth of South Africa's.

REGIONAL MARKET CHARACTERISTICS

There are various ways of dividing the countries of the world into different regional markets. In effect, defining regional markets is an exercise in clustering countries so that similarities within clusters and differences between clusters will be maximized. A simple approach to clustering is to simply use one's judgment regarding important or relevant criteria. In the section that follows, national markets are clustered judgmentally on the basis of geographic proximity. A brief survey of each region is presented.

Western Europe

Western Europe, which is physically less than the size of Australia, generated nearly 32 percent of global income in 1995. The region has 23 countries (18 EEA countries, plus Switzerland, Channel Islands, Gibralter, Greenland, and Malta) and a total population of approximately 377 million. Populations range from 270,000 in Iceland to 81.7 million in Germany.

The countries of Western Europe are among the most prosperous in the world, although income is unevenly distributed in the region. For example, the average per capita annual income in Portugal is $8,700 as compared with $36,900 in Switzerland. Even though there are differences in income and obvious differences in language and culture, the once-varied societies of Western Europe have grown remarkably alike. While there are differences in family and work patterns, they tend to be moving in the same direction. For example, the proportion of women between 25 and 34 in the labor force has doubled in the past 30 to 40 years.

The objective of the EU member countries is to harmonize national laws and regulations so that goods, services, people, and eventually money can flow freely across national boundaries. December 31, 1992, marked the dawn of the new economic era in Europe as the Single Market was officially ushered in. The EU is attempting to shake up Europe's cartel mentality by handing down rules of competition patterned after U.S. antitrust law. The EU is encouraging the development of a community-wide labor pool; improvements to highway and rail networks are now being coordinated. A European Monetary System (EMS) is already operating with a European Currency Unit (ECU) as its basis. The ECU exists on paper and in computers, based on a basket of "weighted" currencies. Some companies price their EU supplies and products in the ECU, thereby saving the time and cost of exchange transactions.

Table 3–2 summarizes the changes that will affect marketers in this region. The marketing challenge is to develop strategies to take advantage of opportunities in one of the largest, most stable, and wealthiest markets in the world. Corporations must determine to what extent they can treat the region as one entity and how to change organization structures to best take advantage of a unified Europe. Table 3–3 shows how the *Fortune* Global 500 companies are distributed in various industries in the Triad.

Eastern and Central Europe

Eastern and Central Europe includes the Balkan countries (Albania, Bosnia-Hercegovina, Bulgaria, Croatia, Macedonia, Montenegro, Rumania, Slovenia, and Yugoslavia), the Baltic states (Estonia, Latvia, and Lithuania), the Commonwealth of Independent States (the former Soviet Union), the Czech and Slovak Republics, Hungary, and Poland. In the early 1990s, extraordinary political and economic reforms swept the region and focused attention on a new 430-million–person market. The former Soviet bloc countries accounted for 6.9 percent of world GDP in 1990, and per capita GNP was $3,665. With wage rates much lower than those in Spain, Portugal, and Greece, Eastern and Central Europe represent both important markets and also attractive locations for low-cost manufacturing. As indicated in Table 3–4, to date, the United States is the biggest investor in the Czech Republic, Hungary, and Poland.

Marketing is undoubtedly a key to promoting the economic development of countries in Central and Eastern Europe. It may take several decades for marketing to reach a level of sophistication comparable to Western Europe. The people must "unlearn" the past ways of life and then learn about democracy and capitalism. Countries in these regions need to develop

TABLE 3–2 MARKETING STRATEGIES IN THE EUROPEAN COMMUNITY, 1992

	Changes Affecting Strategies	Threats to Marketers' Planning	Management's Strategic Options
Product Strategies	Harmonization in product standards, testing, and certification process	Untimeliness of directives	Consolidate production
		Rules of origin	Obtain marketing economies
	Common patenting and branding	Local content rules	Shift from brand to benefit segmentation
	Harmonization in packaging, labeling, and processing requirements	Differences in marketing research	Standardize packaging and labeling where possible
Pricing Strategies	More competitive environment	Parallel importing	Exploit different excise and value-added taxes
	Withdrawal of restrictions to foreign products	Different taxation of goods	Understand price elasticity of consumer demand
		Less freedom in setting transfer prices	
	Anti-monopoly measures		Emphasize high-margin products
	Widening of the public procurement market		Introduce visible low-cost brand
Promotion Strategies	Common guidelines on TV broad-casting	Restrictions on alcohol and tobacco advertising	Coordinate components of promotional mix
	Deregulation of national broad-casting monopolies	Limits on foreign TV production	Exploit advantage of pan-European media
	Uniform standards for TV commercials	Differences in permitted promotional techniques	Position the product according to local markets
Distribution Strategies	Simplification of transit documents and procedures	Increase in distributors' margins	Consolidate manu-facturing facilities
	Elimination of customs formalities	Lack of direct marketing infrastructure	Centralize distribution
		Restrictions in the use of computer databases	Develop nontraditional channels (direct mar-keting, telemarketing)

Source: G. Guido, "Implementing a Pan-European Marketing Strategy," *Long Range Planning* (October 1991), p. 32.

TABLE 3–3 **DISTRIBUTION OF FORTUNE GLOBAL 500 COMPANIES IN THE TRIAD**

Industry	Europe	North America	Japan
Aerospace	4	11	—
Apparel	—	3	—
Beverages	6	5	4
Building materials	8	4	5
Chemicals	18	13	12
Computers*	2	10	6
Electronics	10	16	15
Food	15	19	11
Forest products	6	12	3
Furniture	—	—	—
Industrial and farm equipment	9	7	10
Jewelry, silverware	—	—	2
Metal products	6	5	8
Metals	4	6	9
Mining, crude oil production	3	—	—
Motor vehicles/parts	15	8	18
Petroleum refining	12	16	8
Pharmaceuticals	10	11	5
Publishing, printing	4	5	2
Rubber and plastic products	4	3	3
Scientific and photographic equipment	2	6	2
Soaps and cosmetics	4	3	3
Textiles	2	—	6
Tobacco	1	3	1
Toys, sporting goods	—	—	2
Transportation equipment	2	—	—
Total	157	166	135

*Includes office equipment.
Source: *Fortune* (July 25, 1994), pp. 164+.

TABLE 3–4 **CUMULATIVE FOREIGN DIRECT INVESTMENT IN THE CZECH REPUBLIC, HUNGARY, AND POLAND, 1990 THROUGH SEPTEMBER 1994**

Country	(Investment $ millions)	% Share
USA	$2,866	27.0
Germany	2,217	20.9
Austria	890	8.4
France	888	8.4
Italy	535	5.0
U.K.	487	4.6
Netherlands	472	4.5
Switzerland	430	4.1
Belgium	424	4.0
Sweden	311	2.9
Other	1,084	10.2
Total	10,604	100.0

Source: Anjana Shrivastava, "Smaller Firms Lead German Push East; History Forces Low Profile on Investment," *The Wall Street Journal* (June 14, 1995), p. A9.

their infrastructures and move beyond capricious legal and contractual frameworks. A business culture needs to be developed as well as a mechanism for forecasting demand.[16]

Consumer products require minimal adaptation for sales in Eastern European markets. Many Eastern bloc consumers are familiar with Western brand names and view them as being of higher quality than domestic products. Unfortunately, the distribution infrastructure in Eastern and Central Europe is weak. Wholesalers are underdeveloped. Insufficient and unattractive retail space, the absence of self-service, and the three-line system (to select, pay for, and pick up merchandise) make shopping time-consuming and frustrating.[17]

North America

The North American market is a distinctive world regional market. The United States represents a concentration of wealth and income in a single national economic and political environment that presents unique marketing characteristics. The United States, with 262 million people, had a per capita GNP of $25,340 in 1995. The U.S. market offers the combination of high per capita income, large population, vast space, and plentiful natural resources. High product ownership levels are associated with a high income and relatively high receptivity to innovations and new ideas both in consumer and industrial products. The United States is the home country of more global industry leaders than any other country in the world. For example, U.S. companies are the dominant producers in the computer, software, aerospace, entertainment, medical equipment, and jet engines industries.

Foreign companies are attracted to this gigantic market. The U.S. market is as large as all of Western Europe, and is twice as large as the Japanese market. Another distinctive feature is the arm's-length relationship between business and government. This results in greater opportunities for market access than is true in most other countries of the world. Elsewhere, closer partnerships between government and business often hamper the marketing efforts of foreign suppliers.

Canada, with a population of 28.5 million and a 1995 per capita GNP of $20,800, is moving ahead in cooperation with the private sector to create a national industrial policy. Canada's smokestack industries are just beginning to cope with the restructuring that U.S. companies have been going through for more than a decade. Exports represent over 25 percent of Canada's GNP, more than those of any other major industrial country except Germany. The bulk of Canada's exports are unprocessed natural resources, which are vulnerable to low-cost Latin American rivals. An effort is underway to develop innovation-based competitive advantages. The federal and provincial governments will need to align their policies to support this strategic objective.

Nearly $250 billion per year in goods and services flows between Canada and the United States—the biggest trading relationship between any two nations. Canada takes 20 percent of U.S. exports, and the United States buys nearly 80 percent of Canada's exports. Table 3–5 summarizes the top five U.S. trade partners. Americans have more invested in Canada than any other foreign land. Many U.S. companies, including GE and IBM, use their Canadian operations as major global suppliers for some product lines. The auto market enables U.S. automakers to gain greater economies of scale in North America. The U.S.-Canadian Free Trade Agreement, which will be fully implemented in January 1998, is creating a continental market for most other products.

Asia/Pacific

The 23-country Pacific Rim region is a colossus, with 56 percent of the world's population. The region accounted for 28 percent of global income in 1995. Three-fourths of the region's income was concentrated in Japan, which has only 4 percent of the region's

---

[16]Allan C. Reddy, "The Role of Marketing in the Economic Development of Eastern European Countries," *Journal of Applied Business Research* 7, no. 3 (Summer 1991), pp. 104, 106–107.
[17]John A. Quelch, Erich Joachimsthaler, and Jose Luis Nueno, "After the Wall: Marketing Guidelines for Eastern Europe," *Sloan Management Review* (Winter 1991), pp. 90–91.

TABLE 3–5 U.S. TRADE PARTNERS (US$ BILLIONS, YEAR ENDING AUGUST 31)

	1990	1994
Import Sources		
Canada	$91.5	$128.9
Japan	91.5	119.1
Mexico	28.5	49.5
Germany	27.8	31.7
Taiwan	24.5	38.8
Export Markets		
Canada	$81.9	$114.4
Japan	46.7	53.5
Mexico	26.9	50.8
U. K.	22.7	26.8
Germany	18.3	19.2

Source: U.S. Department of Commerce.

population. Four Asian countries—South Korea, Taiwan, Singapore, and Hong Kong—are sometimes referred to as "tigers" or "newly industrializing economies" (NIEs). Fueled by foreign investment and export-driven industrial development, these four countries have achieved stunning rates of economic growth. Four other countries—Thailand, Malaysia, Indonesia, and China—are getting close to the point of industrial take-off. China, with a population of 1.2 billion potential consumers, is a country no marketer can afford to ignore. Table 3–6 contains statistics on Asia/Pacific countries; note in particular the GNP growth rates of the "tigers."

JAPAN • Population density and geographic isolation are the two crucial, immutable factors that cannot be overstated when discussing Japan as a world market. It is interesting that while Japan's territory occupies only 0.28 percent of the world total and its popula-

TABLE 3–6 ASIA/PACIFIC POPULATION AND GNP DATA, 1995

Country	Population (millions)	GNP ($ billions)	GNP per Capita ($)	GNP Growth Rate, 1985–1993 (%)
Japan	125	$4,247	$33,700	4.0
Singapore	3	64	21,700	8.0
Hong Kong	19	118	19,800	6.2
Australia	18	326	17,900	2.6
New Zealand	3	45	13,000	1.0
Taiwan	21	266	12,453	10.5
South Korea	45	402	8,900	9.1
Malaysia	20	70	3,500	8.1
Thailand	61	145	2,400	10.0
Indonesia	194	155	800	6.6
China	1,208	676	560	7.9
India	939	290	309	5.1

Source: Warren J. Keegan, *Global Income and Population: 1995 and Projections to 2020,* 1995.

tion makes up only 2.16 percent of the world total, Japan generates 16.9 percent of the world's GNP. Japan's 1995 per capita GNP totaled $33,700, compared with China's $560.

Seventy-two percent of Japan's land area is mountainous, the residential area represents only 3 percent, and the industrial area is only 1.4 percent. Not surprisingly, land prices are astronomically high. Japan is experiencing an acute shortage of workers due to the steady decline in the birthrate since 1974. As a result, more women and older people are entering the workforce.

Mastering the Japanese market takes flexibility, ambition, and a long-term commitment. Japan has changed from being a closed market to one that's just tough. There are barriers in Japan in terms of attitudes, not laws (see Table 3–7). Any organization wishing to compete in Japan must be committed to providing top-quality products and services. In many cases, products and marketing must be tailored to local tastes. Countless visits and socializing with distributors are necessary to build trust. Marketers must also master the *keiretsu* system of tightly knit corporate alliances. All of these factors served as a backdrop to the trade dispute between Japan and the United States that escalated in mid-1995. In an effort to pry open Japan's market for auto parts, the United States threatened to impose stiff tariffs on Japanese luxury car imports.

SINGAPORE • In fewer than three decades, Singapore has transformed itself from a British colony to a vibrant, 240-square-mile industrial power. Singapore has an extremely

TABLE 3–7 COMPARISONS AND CONTRASTS IN CULTURE, TRADITION, AND BEHAVIOR BETWEEN JAPAN AND THE UNITED STATES*

	Japan	USA
Myth/Hero Emphasis	Group	Individual
Attitude	Self-denial, dependence	Self-expression, independence
Emphasis	Obligations	Rights
Style	Cooperation	Competition
Assumptions	Interdependence	Independence
View of Self	Organization man	Individual with a skill
Cultural Attitude 1	We are unique	Everyone is just like us
Cultural Attitude 2	Willing to borrow/ adopt/adapt	"Not invented here" syndrome
Organizational Goal 1 (Jobs/Employment)	Share of market	Profitability, financial success
Organizational Goal 2	World markets	National markets
Organizational Goal 3	Quality, customer value	Production, financial return
Worker Identification	Company	Craft, function
Management	Generalist	Specialist
Trust In	Feeling	Thinking
Government/Business Relations	Cooperation	Separation
Financial Structure (Debt : Equity)	80 : 20	40 : 60
Key Stakeholders	Employees	Stockholders
Key Values and Goals	Perfection, harmony, consensus	Freedom, success, winning

*The authors are indebted to Chikara Higashi, member of the Japanese Diet and president, Recia, Tokyo, for assistance in preparing this table.

efficient infrastructure—the Port of Singapore is the world's second-largest container port (Hong Kong's ranks first)—and a standard of living second only to Japan's in the region. Singapore's 3 million citizens have played a critical role in the country's economic achievements by readily accepting the notion that "the country with the most knowledge will win" in global competition. Excellent training programs and a 97 percent literacy rate help explain why Singapore has more engineers per capita than the United States. Singapore's Economic Development Board has also actively recruited business interest in the nation. AT&T, Hewlett-Packard, IBM, Philips, and Apple Computer are among the manufacturing companies that have been attracted to Singapore; in all, 3,000 companies have operations or investments in Singapore. Singapore alone accounts for more than one-third of U.S. trading activities with ASEAN countries; U.S. exports to Singapore in 1994 totaled $13 billion, while imports totaled $15.4 billion. Singapore is closely tied with its neighbors; more than 32 percent of imports are reexported to other Asian countries. Singapore's efforts to fashion a civil society have gained the country some notoriety; crime is nearly nonexistent, thanks to the government's severe treatment of criminals. Some people in the United States objected after an American youth living in Singapore was sentenced to a caning after being arrested and convicted of vandalism. Singaporeans believe the United States has given individuals too many liberties while imprisoning American society.

INDIA • In contrast to Singapore, India's population exceeds 900 million people and its per capita GNP is the lowest in the region. As the decade of the 1990s began, India was in the throes of economic crisis: Inflation was high, and foreign exchange reserves were low. Following the assassination of Rajiv Gandhi and the election of P.V. Narasimha Rao to the office of prime minister in 1991, Monmohan Singh was placed in charge of India's economy. Singh, former governor of the Indian central bank and finance minister, noted that, "For years, India has been taking the wrong road."[18] Accordingly, he set about dismantling the planned economy. Changes included the elimination of import licensing requirements for many products, tariff reductions, eased restrictions on foreign investment, and a liberalization of the rupee. The results have been impressive: Foreign exchange reserves jumped to $13 billion in 1993 from $1 billion in 1991. Foreign capital flows and indirect investment were $3 billion in 1993—more than all previous investment since 1947.

GE has established a joint venture with Wipro, Ltd., to make medical devices such as CAT scanners and ultrasound equipment. Some products are being designed especially for the local market. For example, GE has developed a portable ultrasound machine that squeezes 75 percent of the functions of a conventional design into a 20-pound unit that will allow doctors to provide prenatal care in rural areas.[19] Several automakers—including Mitsubishi, Honda, and Ford—are studying the market. Other companies currently investing in India are BMW, DuPont, General Motors, Fujitsu, IBM, and Coca-Cola. PepsiCo plans to invest $80 million in scores of new Pizza Hut and Kentucky Fried Chicken outlets during the next few years. During 1995, there were several ominous reminders that the political environment is still unstable and hostile to foreigners. The government of Maharashtra (a state in western India) abruptly canceled a $2.9 billion power project with the Houston-based Enron Corporation.[20] It was the single largest private investment deal in India since 1991, and the cancellation prompted Enron to sue for $300 million in compensation. The nationalistic Bharativa Janata Party (BJP) has emerged as a vocal and powerful opponent of reform; in New Delhi, pressure from the BJP led to the temporary closing of one of India's first KFC restaurants.

[18]John Burns, "Unlikely Reformer Coaxes India Towards a Market Economy," *The New York Times* (May 8, 1994), Sec. 3, p. 5.
[19]Pete Enguardio, "An Ultrasound Foothold in Asia," *Business Week* (Nov. 8, 1993), pp. 68–69.
[20]See Sharon Moshavi, "India's Pols May Be Turning Against Foreign Business," *Business Week* (Aug. 21, 1995), p. 44; Moshavi, "Get the 'Foreign Devils'," *Business Week* (Oct. 23, 1995), pp. 48, 50.

OCEANIA • Australia and New Zealand are island economies in the Asian region that were originally settled by Europeans. The two countries have a special relationship; however, there is no apparent desire in either country to merge governments. Although the two countries cooperate closely in many areas, there are also many differences in outlook, culture, and character. Citizens of each country do move freely into the other. There are no barriers or border restrictions on trade between the two countries. The combined population is 21 million, or 0.4 percent of the world total. The income level in both countries is relatively high at approximately $16,900 per capita. The region accounts for 1.7 percent of global income. The real rate of growth in Australia, which has been stimulated by the enormous mineral resources of the continent, averaged 2.6 percent in the period 1985–1993.

Australia has a population of 18 million. The country's midsized economy ($326 billion in 1995) is very dependent on trading conditions in world markets for its major exports of low-value-added agricultural and mineral products. In 1992–1993, imports and exports each totaled approximately $60 billion. The ratio of exports to GNP is 18 percent, the same as imports. Asia is Australia's largest market; 25 percent of exports go to Japan and approximately 14 percent to the ASEAN countries.

The domestic marketing environment in Australia is characterized by product and marketing mix strategies comparable to those found in Triad markets. A major challenge facing all marketers in Australia is the fact that the eight major markets are widely dispersed across a vast continent. This presents distribution and communication considerations which tend to increase national marketing costs.

New Zealand is a small, developed country with a population of 3.5 million and a land area approximately the size of Japan or the United Kingdom. Only 40 years ago, the country had the world's third-highest standard of living as measured by per capita GNP. New Zealand now stands at number 35, passed in the last decade by Hong Kong, Singapore, Spain, and other growing countries. The principal cause of the decline in the relative wealth of New Zealand was the country's failure to respond quickly enough to the decline in prices for agricultural commodities, which make up 62 percent of its exports.

Latin America

Latin America, with 5.6 percent of the world's wealth and 8.4 percent of its population, is a developing region. Average per capita income was $3,074 in 1995. The region includes the Caribbean and Central and South America, and Mexico. Latin America is home to 480 million people—a population greater than Western Europe or the combined regions of Central and Eastern Europe. The allure of the Latin American market has been its considerable size and huge resource base.

After a decade of no growth, crippling inflation, increasing foreign debt, protectionism, and bloated government payrolls, the countries of Latin America have shown a startling change. Balanced budgets are a priority, and privatization is underway. All of the countries of Latin America, except Cuba, now have democratically elected governments. Free markets, open economies, and deregulation have begun to replace the policies of the past. In 1994, Peru was the fastest growing country in the world, with an increase in GNP of 12.6 percent. Chile and Mexico have experienced excellent growth in recent years; Brazil, Argentina, Colombia, Bolivia, and Ecuador are also improving. Uruguay and Venezuela lag behind. Venezuelan president Rafael Caldera has begun to reverse the course of economic reforms begun by his predecessor, Carlos Andres Perez.

Latin America is rapidly moving to eliminate barriers to trade and investment. In many countries, tariffs that sometimes reached as much as 100 percent or more have been lowered to 10 to 20 percent. As noted earlier in the chapter, Latin American countries have also focused on developing subregional common markets. These initiatives are seen as precursors to freer trade with the United States and the rest of the world. Many observers envision a free trade area throughout the hemisphere.

Chile's export-driven success makes it a role model for the rest of Latin America as well as Central and Eastern Europe. The world-class wines produced in Chile's vineyards enjoy favor among price-conscious consumers around the world, and Chilean sea bass can be found in fish markets in Europe, Asia, and North America. With inflation held to single digits, unemployment hovering at about 5 percent, and a modest budget surplus, Chile is pointing the way toward changes in economic thinking in other emerging markets. Chile also boasts an impressive record in privatization, and it pioneered debt-for-equity swaps as a way of retiring part of its foreign debt. Long-term foreign investment in 1995 totaled an enviable $5 billion. In fact, government leaders have opted not to join Mercosur on the grounds that such a move might slow Chile's economic progress.

When adjusted for population growth, the Mexican economy grew at an average rate of −0.9 percent per year during the 1980s. This net growth rate increased to about 4.0 percent in the early 1990s. Inflation dropped from a high of 160 percent per year to less than 20 percent. Since the mid-1980s, more than three-quarters of Mexico's state-owned companies have been privatized. Prior to the peso's devaluation at the end of 1994, Mexico's 90 million consumers—40 percent of whom are under age 40—were enjoying the highest level of purchasing power in a decade.

Companies that want to manufacture in Mexico can set up a wholly owned subsidiary, a joint venture, or a maquiladora program. The **maquiladora** allows manufacturing, assembly, or processing plants to import materials, components, and equipment duty-free; in return, they use Mexican labor. When the completed product is exported to the United States, the manufacturer pays duty only on the value added in Mexico.

Latin American reforms show a broad shift away from the policy of protectionism toward recognition of the benefits of market forces and the advantages of participating fully in the global economy. Global corporations are watching developments closely. They are encouraged by import liberalization, the prospects for lower tariffs within subregional trading groups, and the potential for establishing more efficient regional production.

Middle East

The Middle East includes 17 countries: Afghanistan, Cyprus, Bahrain, Egypt, Iran, Iraq, Israel, Jordan, Kuwait, Lebanon, Oman, Qatar, Saudi Arabia, Syria, the United Arab Emirates, and the two Republics of Yemen. The region accounted for 1.5 percent of 1995 world GNP. The Middle East has a total population of approximately 299 million and an annual per capita income of $2,690.

The majority of the population is Arab, followed by a large percentage of Persians and a small percentage of Israelis. Persians and Arabs share the same religion, beliefs, and Islamic traditions, making the population 95 percent Muslim and 5 percent Christian and Jewish. Despite this apparent homogeneity, diversity exists within each country and within religious groups.

Business in the Middle East is driven by the price of oil. Seven of the countries have high oil revenues: Bahrain, Iraq, Iran, Kuwait, Oman, Qatar, and Saudi Arabia hold more than 75 percent of the free world oil reserves. Oil revenues have widened the gap between poor and rich nations in the Middle East, and the disparities contribute to political and social instability in the area. Saudi Arabia remains the most important market in this region. The country is a monarchy with 16 million people. Saudi Arabia has 25 percent of the world's known oil reserves.

In the past, the region was characterized by pan-Arabism, a form of nationalism and loyalty that transcended borders and amounted to anti-Western dogma. During the Persian Gulf War, this pan-Arabism weakened somewhat. To defeat Iraq, the Gulf Arabs and their allies broke many of their unwritten rules including accepting help from the United States, a traditional ally of Israel. Some observers interpret this change as a harbinger of new market opportunities in the region. Another positive sign was the July 1994 peace declaration by Israel and Jordan that may pave the way for a free trade area in the Middle East.

The Middle East does not have a single societal type with a typical belief, behavior, and tradition. Each capital and major city in the Middle East has a variety of social groups that can be differentiated on the basis of religion, social class, educational field, and degree of wealth. In general, Middle Easterners are warm, friendly, and clannish. Tribal pride and generosity toward guests are basic beliefs. Decision making is by consensus, and seniority has more weight than educational expertise. Life of the individual centers on the family. Authority comes with age, and power is related to family size and seniority. In business relations, Middle Easterners prefer to act through trusted third parties, and they also prefer oral communications.

"Connection" is a key word in conducting business. Well-connected people find their progress is made much faster. Bargaining is a Middle Eastern art, and the visiting businessperson must be prepared for some old-fashioned haggling. Establishing personal rapport, mutual trust, and respect are essentially the most important factors leading to a successful business relationship. Decisions are usually not made by correspondence or telephone. The Arab businessperson does business with the individual, not with the company. Most social customs are based on the Arab male-dominated society. Women are usually not part of the business or entertainment scene for traditional Muslim Arabs.

Some conversation subjects be avoided, as they are considered an invasion of privacy. For example:

- Avoid bringing up subjects of business before getting to know your Arab host. This is considered rude.
- It is taboo to ask questions or make comments concerning a man's wife or female children.
- Avoid pursuing the subjects of politics or religion.
- Avoid any discussion of Israel.[21]

Africa

The African continent is an enormous land mass; the United States would fit into Africa about three and one-half times. It is not really possible to treat Africa as a single economic unit. The continent is divided into three distinct areas: the Republic of South Africa, North Africa, and Black Africa located between the Sahara Desert in the north and the Zambezi River in the south. The market is large with 658 million people. Africa, with 1.4 percent of the world's wealth and 11.3 percent of its population, is a developing region with an annual per capita income of $700.

The Republic of South Africa has a GNP per capita of $2,800. South Africa suffers from the same problems as the rest of the continent: slow growth, big families, and low investment. The gold mines, which generate half of South Africa's exports, are winding down. Unemployment is close to 50 percent. Sanctions, official and unofficial, restricted South African growth for years. With the elimination of apartheid and the removal of sanctions in 1992, trade and tourism should improve. Foreign banks are expected to start lending again.

In North Africa, the 78 million Arabs are differentiated politically and economically. They are richer and more developed, with many of the states benefiting from large oil resources. The Arab states have been independent for a longer period than have the Black African nations.

Nigeria is the largest nation of Africa, with a population of 111 million in 1995 and a GNP of $37.1 million. Nigeria was the second-leading supplier of crude petroleum to the United States in 1989, with sales of $5 billion. Only Saudi Arabia supplied more. The stability of Nigeria's general economic situation is highly dependent on the international oil market. Per capita income in 1995 was $334.

---

[21]Philip R. Harris and Robert T. Moran, *Managing Cultural Differences*, 3d. ed. (Houston: Gulf Publishing Co., 1991), p. 506.

The challenge to marketing in the low-income markets of Africa is not to stimulate demand for products but to identify the most important needs of the society and develop products that fit these needs. There is much opportunity for creativity in developing unique products that fit the needs of the people of the developing countries.

MARKETING IN LESS-DEVELOPED COUNTRIES

The shortage of goods and services is the central problem of developing countries and the most pressing need is to expand production. Marketing is a discipline that guides the process of identifying and fulfilling the needs and wants of people. Clearly, marketing is needed in less-developed countries (LDCs).

Long-term opportunities can be nurtured in LDCs. Today, Nike produces and sells only a small portion of its output in China, but when the firm refers to China as a "two-billion-foot market," it clearly has the future in mind. Greater competitive pressures will force firms to reevaluate their strategies and look for new markets in LDCs. Even some fast-growing LDCs are initiating business in countries that lag behind them. Emerging markets can be lost through indifference and preemptive foreign competition. In deciding whether to enter an LDC, one study suggested the following:

- Look beyond per capita GNP. The per capita figures may hide the existence of a sizable middle class in that market. India, for example, has a huge middle class market that is hidden by the country's average statistics.
- Consider LDCs collectively rather than singly. One market may not be appealing; however, there may be broader possibilities with neighboring countries.
- Weigh the benefits and costs of being the first firm to offer a product or service in an LDC. Governments of LDCs often bestow tax subsidies or other special treatment on companies that set up operations. Entering a growing LDC is an opportunity to get in on the ground floor of a significant market opportunity.
- Set realistic deadlines for results. Due to different legal, political, or social forces, events may move slowly.[22]

Despite the serious economic difficulties now facing LDCs in Southeast Asia, Latin America, Africa, and Eastern Europe, many of these nations will evolve into attractive markets. Marketing's role in the LDCs is to focus resources on the task of creating and delivering products that best serve the needs of the people. Basic marketing concepts can be applied so that products are designed that fit the needs and incomes in the LDC market. Appropriate marketing communications techniques can also be applied to accelerate acceptance of these products. Marketing can be the link that relates resources to opportunity and facilitates need satisfaction on the consumer's terms.

SUMMARY

One of the ways of dealing with the complexity of a world with more than 200 national markets is to focus upon economic cooperation agreements. The General Agreement on Tariffs and Trade concerns multilateral trade among 125 signatories. The North American Free Trade Agreement has created a free trade area encompassing Canada, the United States, and Mexico. The Central American Common Market, the Andean Group, the Southern Cone Common Market, and the Caribbean Community are the four main economic cooperation agreements in Central and South America. In the Asia/Pacific region, the Association of Southeast Asian Nations is the basis for cooperation. The European Union and the European Economic Area are bringing down trade barriers in Europe. In the Middle East, the Cooperation Council for the Arab States of the Gulf has six members. In Africa, the two main cooperation agreement are the Economic Community of West African States and the South African Development Coordination Conference.

[22]Donald G. Halper and H. Chang Moon, "Striving for First-Rate Markets in Third-World Nations," *Management Review* (May 1990), pp. 20–21.

It is also possible to examine the world in terms of geographic regions. Each country in the world is sovereign and unique, but there are similarities among countries in the same region that make a regional approach to marketing planning a sound approach. In this chapter, the organization of material is around geographic regions. It could just as well be organized around stage of economic development or some other criterion. It is important for marketers to have a broad overview of the nature of world regions so that they will not make serious oversights in developing the marketing plan.

DISCUSSION QUESTIONS

1. Explain the role of the World Trade Organization.
2. Describe the similarities and differences between a free trade area, a customs union, a common market, and an economic union. Give an example of each.
3. Identify a regional economic organization or agreement in each of the following areas: Latin America, Asia/Pacific, Western Europe, Central Europe, the Middle East, and Africa.
4. Compare and contrast the United States and Japan in terms of traditions and organizational behavior and norms.

BIBLIOGRAPHY

Books

Abegurin, Olayiwola. *Economic Dependence and Regional Cooperation in Southern Africa: SADCC and South Africa in Confrontation.* Lewiston, N.Y.: Edwin Mellen Press, 1990.

Anderson, Kym, and Richard Blackhurst, Eds. *Regional Integration and the Global Trading System.* New York: Harvester/Wheatsheaf, 1993.

Axline, W. Andrew. *The Political Economy of Regional Cooperation.* London: Pinter, 1994.

De Melo, Jaime, and Arvind Panagariya. *New Dimensions in Regional Integration.* Oxford: Oxford University Press, 1993.

Fallows, James M. *Looking at the Sun: The Rise of the New Fast Asian Economic and Political System.* New York: Vintage Books, 1995.

Ohmae, Kenichi. *The End of the Nation State: The Rise of Regional Economies.* New York: Free Press, 1995.

Shaw, Timothy M., and Julius Emeka Okolo, Eds. *The Political Economy of Foreign Policy in ECOWAS.* London: Macmillan/St. Martin's Press, 1994.

Articles

Aho, C. Michael. " 'Fortress Europe': Will the EU Isolate Itself from North America and Asia?" *Columbia Journal of World Business* 29, no. 3 (Fall 1994), pp. 32–39.

Atkinson, Glenn, and Ted Oleson. "Europe 1992: From Customs Union to Economic Community." *Journal of Economic Issues* 28, no. 4 (December 1994), pp. 977–995.

Bakos, Gabor. "After COMECON: A Free Trade Area in Central Europe?" *Europe-Asia Studies* 45, no. 6 (1993), pp. 1025–1044.

Banks, Philip. "India: The New Asian Tiger?" *Business Horizons* 38, no. 3 (May 1995), pp. 47–50.

Bernal, Richard L. "From NAFTA to Hemispheric Free Trade." *Columbia Journal of World Business* 29, no. 3 (Fall 1994), pp. 22–31.

Cosgrove, Carol. "Has the Lomé Convention Failed ACP Trade?" *Journal of International Affairs* 48, no. 1 (Summer 1994), pp. 223–249.

Curry, Robert L., Jr. "A Case for Further Collaboration between the EU and ASEAN." *ASEAN Economic Bulletin* 11, no. 2 (November 1994), pp. 150–157.

Czinkota, Michael R. "The World Trade Organization—Perspectives and Prospects." *Journal of International Marketing* 3, no. 1 (1995), pp. 85–91.

Granell, Francisco. "The European Union's Enlargement Negotiations with Austria, Finland, Norway and Sweden." *Journal of Common Market Studies* 33, no. 1 (March 1995), pp. 117–141.

Healey, Nigel M. "The Transition Economies of Central and Eastern Europe: A Political, Economic, Social and Technological Analysis." *Columbia Journal of World Business* 29, no. 1 (Spring 1994), pp. 62–70.

Jessop, Bob. "Regional Economic Blocs, Cross-Border Cooperation, and Local Economic Strategies in Postsocialism." *American Behavioral Scientist* 38, no. 5 (March 1995), pp. 674–715.

Koch-Weser, Caio. "Economic Reform and Regional Cooperation: A Development Agenda for the Middle East and North Africa." *Middle East Policy* 2, no. 2 (1993), pp. 28–36.

Krum, James R., and Pradeep A. Rau. "Organizational Responses of U.S. Multinationals to EC–1992: An Empirical Study." *Journal of International Marketing* 1, no. 2 (1993), pp. 49–70.

Kurus, Bilson. "The ASEAN Triad: National Interest, Consensus-Seeking, and Economic Cooperation." *Contemporary Southeast Asia* 16, no. 4 (March 1995), pp. 404–420.

Lee, Helen D. "CACM: Reforms and Integration Spur Growth of Market." *Business America* 114, no. 8 (Apr. 19, 1993), pp. 10–11.

Miyoshi, Masao. "A Borderless World? From Colonialism to Transnationalism and the Decline of the Nation-State." *Critical Inquiry* 19, no. 4 (Summer 1993), pp. 726–751.

Paine, George, and Raphael Craig. "ASEAN Nations Look to Trade and Technology to Maintain High Growth." *Business America* 115, no. 11 (November 1994), pp. 14–17.

Paribatra, Sukhumbhand. "From ASEAN Six to ASEAN Ten: Issues and Prospects." *Contemporary Southeast Asia* 16, no. 3 (December 1994), pp. 243–258.

Robson, Peter, and Ian Wooton. "The Transnational Enterprise and Regional Economic Integration." *Journal of Common Market Studies* 31, no. 1 (March 1993), pp. 71–90.

Tuan, Hoang Anh. "Vietnam's Membership in ASEAN: Economic, Political, and Security Implications." *Contemporary Southeast Asia* 16, no. 3 (December 1994), pp. 243–258.

Tyler, Gus. "The Nation-State vs. the Global Economy." *Challenge* 36, no. 2 (March 1993), pp. 26–32.

Wu, Friedrich. "The ASEAN Economies in the 1990s and Singapore's Regional Role." *California Management Review* 34, no. 1 (Fall 1991), pp. 103–114.

*E*ach November, representatives of 18 countries that border on the Pacific Ocean meet formally to discuss prospects for liberalizing trade. Collectively, the countries that make up the Asia-Pacific Economic Cooperation (APEC) forum account for about 40 percent of world trade, 38 percent of world population, and 52 percent of world economic output. APEC provides a chance for annual discussions by people at various levels: academics and business executives, ministers, and heads of state. Some small Asian countries view APEC as a welcome means of using the United States to counterbalance the dominance of Japan and China in the region. And, as noted in *The Economist,* "Not so long ago, the thought of South Korea or Indonesia, let alone China, having anything to do with even a 'vision' of free trade would have been fantastic."

APEC MEMBER COUNTRIES

Australia (1989)	Malaysia (1989)
Brunei (1989)	Mexico (1993)
Canada (1989)	New Zealand (1989)
Chile (1994)	Papua New Guinea (1993)
China (1991)	Philippines (1989)
Hong Kong (1991)	Singapore (1989)
Indonesia (1989)	Taiwan (1991)
Japan (1989)	Thailand (1989)
South Korea (1989)	United States (1989)

U.S. President Bill Clinton put APEC at the center of his administration's Asian trade strategy. In 1993, when President Clinton convened the fifth APEC forum in Seattle, Washington, the United States hoped to boost trade with fast-growing Asian Pacific Rim nations by cutting tariffs, reaching agreement on competition policies, and eliminating subsidies. In fact, after the heads of government met in a special leadership summit convened by President Clinton, an announcement was made regarding commitment to a "vision" of free trade. Washington's efforts came at a time when the Asian nations had increased the share of overall trade that stays within Asia to about 65 percent, up from 58 percent in 1980. Meanwhile, Asian imports from the United States have fallen from 41 percent of overall trade in 1980 to 34 percent of overall trade in 1992. During the decade of the 1980s, the economies of Southeast Asian countries grew twice as fast as the rest of the world; international trade in the region grew at twice the rate experienced in Europe and North America. Observers note that the U.S. role in the 1993 forum provided political momentum in Washington that helped convince the U.S. Congress to approve NAFTA and GATT despite growing protectionist sentiment in some circles.

At APEC's 1994 meeting in Bogor, Indonesia, 10 separate working groups began preparing plans to transform the vision into practice by reducing country differences in such

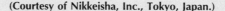

WHERE WERE YOU WHEN THE PACIFIC CENTURY BEGAN?

The "Pacific Century." It's already beginning. It's beginning as nations and peoples around the Pacific open their borders and their minds to each other. An exciting sign of that beginning is emerging under the name *Asia-Pacific Economic Cooperation*—APEC.

Diversity and Tolerance
APEC presently has 18 members. They are fantastically diverse. They speak hundreds of languages and dialects. They comprise scores of ethnic groups. They include highly industrialized economies and up-and-coming economies. They span half the surface of the earth and are home to two-fifths of the world's population.

Diversity is a source of vitality in the Asia-Pacific region. That vitality can help invigorate the entire global economy. But sustaining that vitality will require tolerance. Leaders in all the APEC members recognize the importance of free-market principles in economic development. And each member is beginning to progress at its own pace toward the common, long-term goal of free and open trade and investment.

Initiative
Japan has an important role to fulfill as a force for growth and stability in the Asia-Pacific. And it is the chair of APEC this year. It will host the APEC Ministerial Meeting and Economic Leaders Meeting in November. As this year's chair and host, Japan is taking the initiative in moves to give genuine and lasting meaning to the goals that the APEC leaders agreed on at their meetings last year in Indonesia. It is coordinating efforts to translate those goals into concrete guidelines as the "Action Agenda" for economic liberalization and cooperation.

Open to the world
APEC is an open forum where member economies can come to terms with each other. In the same spirit, the APEC members need to work together to keep the Asia-Pacific open to the whole world. Then, they will be strengthening the world's system for free and multilateral trade. They will be demonstrating that APEC is an idea whose time has come.

JAPAN WELCOMES THE ASIA-PACIFIC TO OSAKA
NOVEMBER 1995

GOVERNMENT OF JAPAN

(Courtesy of Nikkeisha, Inc., Tokyo, Japan.)

areas as customs, product quality standards, and telecommunications. Cabinet ministers arrived at a set of nonbinding principles regarding foreign investment. Included were proposals to minimize performance requirements such as local content laws and export quotas, guidelines pertaining to equal treatment for foreign and domestic investors, and improved clarity in laws. Some of the agenda items had not been addressed by the Uruguay Round of GATT negotiations. For example, APEC members hoped to address investment rules for service providers (GATT dealt with investments by manufacturers); moreover, GATT left opportunities open for countries to insist that local managers be hired and technology be transferred by any company wishing to invest.

Much debate among APEC members has centered on whether all trade barriers in Asia can be eliminated, without exception, by the year 2020. It has become apparent that policy makers and farmers in South Korea, China, and Japan still support agricultural subsidies. Agricultural producers in the United States, Canada, and Australia want to sell more food products in Asia. Although the Japanese government took action in 1993 to end an outright ban on imports of foreign rice, market access is still restricted to outsiders. Australian farmers have worked particularly hard to develop varieties of rice that will appeal to finicky Japanese consumers. Notes a member of an Australian rice growers cooperative, "Japanese are connoisseurs of rice. If we can sell our product in Japan, we can sell it anywhere. All we need is the market to open up."

Besides agriculture, other divisive issues are Washington's annual review of China's most-favored-nation trading status and the Clinton administration's firm stand on human rights. Some in attendence at the 1995 APEC meeting in Osaka, Japan, worried that special interest groups lobbying for "sensitive sectors" in individual countries could derail APEC. Japan's rice farmers, for example, wield a great deal of political clout. Warned one U.S. trade official, "Australia will pull motor vehicles off the list, and we'll pull textiles. The only thing left to talk about will be widgets." President Clinton was unable to attend the Osaka meeting because of a budget battle in Washington; some observers took his non-appearance as a sign that U.S. commitment to Asia was diminishing.

One lesson from the 1995 APEC meeting was that compromise seemed to be inevitable; for example, countries might be allowed to reduce agricultural subsidies gradually. Some trade ministers showed a propensity for using vague phrases such as "economic cooperation" instead of talking "opening trade." Despite concerns that compromise would slow the pace of trade liberalization, some countries in the region have already made progress toward freer trade. At the Osaka meeting, Chinese President Jiang Zemin announced that China would lower tariffs by 30 percent overall beginning in 1996. Indonesia recently announced tariff reductions of up to 35 percent on 6,000 manufactured and agricultural products. In addition, some telecommunications monopolies are being opened to foreign investment. South Korea's president pledged to open 200 types of businesses to foreign investment and simplify customs procedures for imports and exports. As a result of these and other successes, expectations were running high as the 1996 APEC meeting in the Phillipines approached.

DISCUSSION QUESTIONS

1. What are the implications of APEC for global companies?
2. What are the biggest barriers to achieving improved trade conditions under the APEC framework?
3. The Japanese government uses tariffs to protect rice farmers from imports. Why?
4. Go to the library and look up articles concerning the most recent APEC forum. Have any of the issues identified in this case been resolved? What new issues have emerged?

Sources: Jonathan Clark, "APEC as a Semi-Solution," *Orbis* 39, no. 1 (Winter 1995), pp. 81–95.
Martin Rudner, "APEC: The Challenges of Asia Pacific Economic Cooperation," *Modern Asian Studies* 29, no. 2 (1995), pp. 403–437.
Peter Engardio, "Free-Trade Showdown," *Business Week* (Nov. 20, 1995), pp. 60–61.
"Australian, Japanese Ways Differ," *Associated Press* (Nov. 12, 1995).
Helene Cooper and Michael Williams, "U.S. Limits APEC-Summit Expectations," *The Wall Street Journal* (Nov. 16, 1995), p. A12.
Douglas Harbrecht and Amy Borus, "Marching toward Free Trade in Asia?" *Business Week* (Nov. 14, 1994), p. 52–53.
"The Opening of Asia," *The Economist* (Nov. 13, 1995), pp. 23+.
Robert S. Greenberger and Marcus W. Brauchli, "U.S. Has Lost Some of Its Clout in Asia," *The Wall Street Journal* (Nov. 11, 1994), p. A10.

Social and Cultural Environments

In Europe, where scones, croissants, and strudel have long been the pride of bakers and pastry chefs, trend-conscious consumers have started gobbling up American-style baked goods. It seems the Europeans are discovering what Americans have known all along: In addition to being tasty, brownies, muffins, and cookies are perfectly suited to on-the-go lifestyles that include snacking while traveling on the metro or riding a bicycle. Also, American baked goods have a shelf life of more than one day, unlike many traditional European baked goods such as fresh cream tarts. European bakers, many of whom regard pastries from across the Atlantic as inferior, had to make some adjustments to accommodate changing taste buds. As Bernard M. Schapiro, of Millie's Foods Ltd. in Britain, recalls, "It wasn't an easy sell. Here biscuits [cookies] are hard, and you don't find soft cookies. The perception was that it was underbaked."

U.S. companies have also experienced some culture shock. While British consumers snapped up soft, moist Otis Spunkmeyer muffins, the American company's managers soon discovered one of the syllables is slang for "semen" in Great Britain and other countries. After the disk jockey of a national radio show asked on the air, "Who's going to eat a product with a name like that?" the company sent him a free sample. The result was favorable publicity in the form of an on-air endorsement for the goodies. Now some bakeries that sell the muffins put stickers reading "American Muffin" over the offending word. In the final analysis, as Heather McEvoy of the Colorado Cookie Company points out, "A good pastry is a good pastry no matter where it comes from and no matter what country it's sold in. Any company making good pastries will have a market in Europe."[1]

The warm reception in Europe for American baked goods shows that many products can achieve success outside the home-country cultural environment. This chapter focuses on the social and cultural forces that shape and affect individual and corporate behavior in the marketplace. The conceptual orientation of this chapter and this book is that the cultures of the world are characterized by both differences and similarities. Thus, the task of the global marketer is twofold. Marketers must be prepared to recognize and understand the differences between cultures and then incorporate this un-

---

[1]"The Perils of Being Spunky," *Dow Jones*, (Aug. 7, 1995).

derstanding into the marketing planning process so that strategies and marketing programs are adapted when necessary. At the same time, marketers should take advantage of shared cultural characteristics and avoid unneeded and costly adaptations of the marketing mix.

This chapter provides a general discussion of cultural universals and other social and cultural global marketing considerations. To help marketers better understand social and cultural dynamics in the global marketplace, several useful analytical approaches are explained. These include Maslow's hierarchy, Hofstede's cultural typology, the self-reference criterion, and diffusion theory. Next is a discussion of specific examples of the impact of culture and society on the marketing of both industrial and consumer products. The chapter ends with suggested solutions to cross-cultural difficulties and a review of cross-cultural training procedures currently being used in global companies.

BASIC ASPECTS OF SOCIETY AND CULTURE

Anthropologists and sociologists define **culture** as "ways of living, built up by a group of human beings, that are transmitted from one generation to another." A culture acts out its ways of living in the context of social institutions, including family, educational, religious, governmental, and business institutions. Culture includes both conscious and unconscious values, ideas, attitudes, and symbols that shape human behavior *and that are transmitted from one generation to the next*. In this sense, culture does not include one-time solutions to unique problems, or passing fads and styles. As defined by organizational anthropologist Geert Hofstede, culture is "the collective programming of the mind that distinguishes the members of one category of people from those of another" (Hofstede and Bond 1988, 5).

In addition to agreeing that culture is learned, not innate, most anthropologists share two additional views. First, all facets of culture are interrelated: Influence or change one aspect of a culture and everything else is affected. Second, because it is shared by the members of a group, culture defines the boundaries between different groups (Hall 1976, 16).

Culture consists of learned responses to recurring situations. The earlier these responses are learned, the more difficult they are to change. Taste and preferences for food and drink, for example, represent learned responses that are highly variable from culture to culture and can have a major impact on consumer behavior. Preference for color is culturally influenced as well. For example, while green is a highly regarded color in Moslem countries, it is associated with disease in some Asian countries. White, usually associated with purity and cleanliness in the West, can signify death in Asian countries. Red is a popular color in most parts of the world (often associated with full flavor, passion, or virility); it is poorly received in some African countries.[2] Of course, there is no inherent attribute to any color of the spectrum; all associations and perceptions regarding color arise from culture.

Attitudes toward whole classes of products can also be a function of culture. For example, in the United States, consumers have a cultural predisposition for product innovations that have a "gadgety" quality. Thus, the electric knife, the electric toothbrush, the Water-Pik, and a host of other "labor-saving" small appliances find ready market acceptance even though many are purchased, used for a while, and then quietly put away and

---

[2]Richard R. Still and John S. Hill, "Multinational Product Planning: A Meta Market Analysis," *International Marketing Review* (Spring 1985), p. 60.

never used again. There is unquestionably a lesser predisposition to purchase such products in other developed markets such as Europe.

A reasonable hypothesis is that this difference is partially a result of cultural differences. As we noted in the last chapter, income levels also influence consumer behavior and attitudes around the world. Indeed, a basic question that must be answered by marketers who want to understand or predict behavior is, "How much do social and cultural factors influence behavior independent of income levels?" Sometimes the influence is strong. For example, U.S. companies introduced fluffy frosted cake mixes in the United Kingdom where cake is eaten at tea time with the fingers rather than as a dessert with a fork. Green Giant Foods attempted to market corn in Europe where the prevailing attitude is that corn is a grain fed to hogs, not people. In both instances, cultural differences resulted in market failures. Nevertheless, widespread shared preference for convenience foods, disposable products, popular music, and movies in the United States, Europe, and Asia suggests that many consumer products have broad, even universal, appeal. As we saw in the McDonald's case in Chapter 1, the Japanese are consuming increasing quantities of beef and less fish. As cultural differences become less relevant, such products will be purchased in any country when consumer disposable income is high enough. This implies that an important characteristic of culture—that it defines boundaries between people—is gradually disappearing.

THE SEARCH FOR CULTURAL UNIVERSALS

An important quest for the global marketer is to discover cultural universals. A universal is a mode of behavior existing in all cultures. Universal aspects of the cultural environment represent opportunities for global marketers to standardize some or all elements of a marketing program. A partial list of cultural universals, taken from cultural anthropologist's George P. Murdock's classic study, includes the following: athletic sports, body adornment, cooking, courtship, dancing, decorative art, education, ethics, etiquette, family feasting, food taboos, language, marriage, mealtime, medicine, mourning, music, property rights, religious rituals, residence rules, status differentiation, and trade.[3] The astute global marketer often discovers that much of the apparent cultural diversity in the world turns out to be different ways of accomplishing the same thing.

Music provides one example of how these universals apply to marketing. Music is part of all cultures, accepted as a form of artistic expression and source of entertainment. However, music is also an art form characterized by widely varying styles. Therefore, while background music can be used effectively in broadcast commercials, the type of music appropriate for a commercial in one part of the world may not be acceptable or effective in another part. A jingle might utilize a bossa nova rhythm for Latin America, a rock rhythm for North America, and "high life" for Africa. Music, then, is a cultural universal that global marketers can adapt to cultural preferences in different countries or regions.

Increasing travel and improving communications mean that many national attitudes toward style in clothing, color, music, food, and drink are converging. The globalization of culture has been capitalized upon, and even significantly accelerated, by companies that have seized opportunities to find customers around the world. Coca-Cola, PepsiCo, Levi Strauss, McDonald's, IBM, Heineken, and Bertelsmann Music Group are some of the companies breaking down cultural barriers as they expand into new markets with their products.

Similarly, new laws and changing attitudes toward the use of credit are providing huge global opportunities for financial service providers such as American Express, Visa, and

[3]George P. Murdock, "The Common Denominator of Culture," in *The Science of Man in the World Crisis,* ed. Ralph Linton (New York: Columbia University Press, 1945), p. 145.

MasterCard International. According to one estimate, the volume of global credit card sales will double, to $2 trillion, by the year 2000.[4] To reach such a level, however, the credit card companies will have to use communications efforts to persuade large numbers of people to use the cards, because the propensity to "pay with plastic" is currently much lower in other cultures than in the United States.

THE ANTHROPOLOGIST'S STANDPOINT

As Ruth Benedict points out in her classic *The Chrysanthemum and the Sword*, the way a person thinks, feels, and acts has some relation to his or her experience of the world. It doesn't matter if (normal) actions and opinions are thought of as bizarre by outsiders. Successful global marketers must understand human experience from the local point of view—and become insiders with cultural empathy in the process—if they are to understand the dynamics of markets outside the home country.

Any systematic study of a new geographic market requires a combination of tough-mindedness and generosity. The appreciation of another way of life cannot develop when one is defensive about one's own way of life; it is necessary to be secure in one's own convictions and traditions. In addition, generosity is required to appreciate the integrity and value of other ways of life and points of view—to overcome the prejudices that are a natural result of the human tendency toward ethnocentricity. When people from other countries complain that Americans are haughty, patronizing, or arrogant, American ethnocentricity is probably contributing to the problem. Global marketers need to develop an objective standpoint that recognizes diversity and seeks to understand its origins. There are many paths to the same end in life. The global marketer knows this and rejoices in life's rich diversity.

HIGH- AND LOW-CONTEXT CULTURES

Edward T. Hall has suggested the concept of high and low context as a way of understanding different cultural orientations.[5] In a **low-context culture**, messages are explicit; words carry most of the information in communication. In a **high-context culture**, less information is contained in the verbal part of a message. Much more information resides in the context of communication, including the background, associations, and basic values of the communicators. In general, high-context cultures function with much less legal paperwork than is deemed essential in low-context cultures. Japan, Saudi Arabia, and other high-context cultures place a great deal of emphasis on a person's values and position or place in society. In such cultures, a business loan is more likely to be based upon who you are than upon formal analysis of pro forma financial documents. In a low-context culture such as the United States, Switzerland, or Germany, deals are made with much less information about the character, background, and values of the participants. Much more reliance is placed upon the words and numbers in the loan application.

In a high-context culture, a person's word is his or her bond. There is less need to anticipate contingencies and provide for external legal sanctions since the culture emphasizes obligations and trust as important values. In these cultures, shared feelings of obligation and honor take the place of impersonal legal sanctions. This helps explain the importance of long and protracted negotiations that never seem to "get to the point." Part of the purpose of negotiating, for a person from a high-context culture, is to get to know the potential partner.

For example, insisting on competitive bidding can cause complications in low-context

---

[4]Steven Lipin, "Pick a Card: Visa, American Express and MasterCard Vie in Overseas Strategies," *The Wall Street Journal* (Feb. 5, 1994), p. A1.
[5]See Hall. 1976, and "How Cultures Collide," *Psychology Today* (July 1976), pp. 66–97.

cultures. In a high-context culture, the job is given to the person who will do the best work and whom you can trust and control. In a low-context culture, one tries to make the specifications so precise that a builder is forced by the threat of legal sanction to do a good job. According to Hall, a builder in Japan is likely to say, "What has that piece of paper got to do with the situation? If we can't trust each other enough to go ahead without it, why bother?"

Although countries can be classified as high- or low-context cultures in their overall tendency, there are exceptions to the general tendency. These exceptions are found in subcultures. The United States, for example, is a low-context culture with subcultures that operate in the high-context mode. Charles A. Coombs, senior vice president of the Federal Reserve Bank of New York in charge of foreign exchange operations, provides such an example in his book *The Arena of International Finance*. The world of the central banker, as he describes it, is a "gentleman's" world, that is, a high-context culture. Even during the most hectic days in the foreign exchange markets, a central banker's word is sufficient for him to borrow millions of dollars.

During the rioting and political upheavals in France in 1968, the confidence of central bankers in one another was dramatically demonstrated. Except for telephones, all communications between France and the United States were cut off. Consequently, the New York Fed agreed that it would follow instructions received by telephone from the Bank of France for intervening on its behalf in support of the franc. Within eight days, the New York Fed had bought more than $50 million of francs without a single written confirmation for any part of the purchase. The Fed was far out on a limb. A couple of weeks later, the daughter of the governor of the Bank of France came to New York on personal business. She brought written confirmations with her. "Our legal department heaved a sigh of relief," Coombs remembers. The legal department was operating in a low-context culture, with all the assumptions—e.g., everything must be spelled out and confirmed in writing—that go with this culture. The central bankers, who were obviously much more relaxed about the matter, were operating within a high-context subculture in which a person's word is his or her bond. Another high-context subculture in the United States is the Mafia, which has imported the high-context culture of Sicily to the United States and has maintained this culture with language, ritual, and a strong sense of distinct identity.

These examples illustrate the ways of a high-context culture in which there is trust, a sense of fair play, and a widespread acceptance of the rules of the game as it is played. Table 4-1 summarizes some of the ways in which high- and low-context cultures differ.

One of the clearest and most painful instances of the failure of one culture to perceive another culture's motivations and behaviors dates back to the beginnings of World War II. Throughout the war and even to this day, the United States encountered great difficulties in attempting to understand the Empire of Japan, its enemy. In response to the obstacles the United States faced, studies of Japanese culture were commissioned, focusing on Japan's history, tradition, national character, social life and customs, family, personality, and mind. The result is such great works as Benedict's *The Chrysanthemum and the Sword*. Since the end of World War II, Japan has emerged as the leading competitor of the United States; thus, the body of studies and publications has continued to grow over the last 50 years, with the focus shifting somewhat from an emphasis on societal and individual values and motivations to business and corporate culture.

It would be easy to get paranoid about the hazards of doing business across cultures, but in fact, the main obstacle is attitude. If you are sincere and truly want to learn about a culture, you will find that people respond to your sincerity and interest and will help you acquire the knowledge you need to be effective. If you are arrogant and insincere and believe that you are right and "they" are wrong, you can expect a full measure of trouble and misunderstanding. The best antidote to the problem of misperceiving a situation is constant vigilance and an awareness that there are many opportunities to err. This should

TABLE 4–1 HIGH- AND LOW-CONTEXT CULTURES

Factors/Dimensions	High Context	Low Context
Lawyers	Less important	Very important
A person's word	Is his or her bond	Is not to be relied upon; "get it in writing"
Responsibility for organizational error	Taken by highest level	Pushed to lowest level
Space	People breathe on each other	People maintain a bubble of private space and resent intrusions
Time	Polychronic—Everything in life must be dealt with in terms of its own time.	Monochronic—Time is money. Linear—One thing at a time.
Negotiations	Are lengthy—A major purpose is to allow the parties to get to know each other.	Proceed quickly
Competitive bidding	Infrequent	Common
Country/regional examples	Japan, Middle East	United States, Northern Europe

create an attitude of openness to see what is so. Every global marketer should strive to suspend judgment and simply listen, observe, perceive, and take in the facts.

COMMUNICATION AND NEGOTIATION

The ability to communicate in one's own language is, as most of us have learned, not an easy task. Whenever languages and culture change, additional communication challenges will present themselves. For example, "yes" and "no" are used in an entirely different way in Japanese than in Western languages. This has caused much confusion and misunderstanding. In English, the answer "yes" or "no" to a question is based on whether the answer is affirmative or negative. In Japanese, this is not so. The answer "yes" or "no" may indicate whether or not the answer affirms or negates the question. For example, in Japanese the question, "Don't you like meat?" would be answered "yes" if the answer is negative, as in, "Yes, I don't like meat." As another instance, the word *wakarimashita* means both "I understand" and "I agree." To avoid misunderstandings, Westerners must learn to distinguish which interpretation is correct in terms of the entire context of the conversation.

The challenges presented by nonverbal communication are perhaps even more formidable. For example, Westerners doing business in the Middle East must be careful not to reveal the soles of their shoes to hosts or pass documents with the left hand. In Japan, bowing is an important form of nonverbal communication that has many nuances. People who grow up in the West tend to be verbal, while those from the East are more nonverbal. Not surprisingly, there is a greater expectation in the East that people will pick up nonverbal cues and understand intuitively without being told.[6] Westerners must pay close attention not only to what they hear, but also to what they see when conducting business in such cultures.

---

[6]See Anthony C. diBenedetto, Miriko Tamate, and Rajan Chandran, "Developing Strategy for the Japanese Marketplace," *Journal of Advertising Research* (January–February 1992), pp. 39–48.

Knowledge and understanding of cross-cultural differences is crucial during negotiations. Negotiations put global marketers face-to-face with counterparts from diverse cultural backgrounds, challenging both sides to surmount verbal and nonverbal communications barriers.

Americans bring their cultural ethnocentrism to the negotiating table. According to two experts on international negotiations, there are 10 uniquely American tactics that frequently emerge during negotiations. These tactics may be effective with other Americans, but when used with people from other cultural backgrounds, they require modification. The approaches and the corrections required are:

1. "I can go it alone." Americans are typically outnumbered in negotiations.
   Solution: Greater reliance on teamwork and division of negotiating labor.
2. "Just call me John." Americans place a high value on informality and equality of participants in negotiations. This may conflict with the customs and class structures of foreign cultures.
   Solution: Respect the customs and class structure of other cultures. Obtain information from self-study and local agents on local attitudes and values.
3. "That's Greek to me." Americans are culturally monolingual.
   Solution: Forget what "everybody says" about how difficult it is to learn a foreign language and accept that you already have a talent for language (assuming that you read, speak, and write English). If you are going to be regularly doing business with a particular country, take the time, make the effort, and learn their language. If your contact with a culture is too limited to justify the time and effort required to learn their language, make sure that you select and develop a good working relationship with a competent interpreter.
4. "Get to the point." Americans are, in comparison to people from other cultures, blunt and impatient.
   Solution: Understand that people from other cultures need to develop a sense of connection and personal trust in order to feel comfortable about doing business. This takes time. Take time to get to know your negotiating partner.
5. "Lay your cards on the table." Americans like to state the case up front, and are not accustomed to "feeling out" prospective partners.
   Solution: Slow down, and recognize the need to ask the same question in different ways. Prepare to spend double the time you think is needed to get the information you desire.
6. "Don't just sit there, speak up." Americans are uncomfortable with silence during negotiations and often deal with their discomfort by "running at the mouth."
   Solution: Recognize that silence is golden in many cultures. It is not necessary—indeed, it can be detrimental—to keep up a constant stream of chatter. If there is silence, let it be. Reflect. Take in information that comes from body posture and facial expression. Reflect on the words that have been spoken and on your own objectives and values. In other words, *value* the silence. Take advantage of it.
7. "Don't take 'no' for an answer." Persistence and the "hard sell" are highly valued in the United States.
   Solution: If the answer is "no," stop selling and find out why. Respond to the reasons for the answer "no."
8. "One thing at a time." Americans favor a linear, organized, "left-brain" style of negotiating. "Point One, Point Two, and so on" is not a universal approach.
   Solution: Recognize your own right-brain capability. Embrace a more holistic approach toward negotiations.
9. "A deal is a deal." This is a projection of an expectation which may not be shared.

Solution: Accept a more gradual, supplemental view of negotiations and joint effort.

10. "I am what I am."

Solution: Adopt a more flexible standpoint. Be willing to change your mind and manner and to adapt to your opposite.[7]

ANALYTICAL APPROACHES TO CULTURAL FACTORS

The reason cultural factors are a challenge to global marketers is that they are hidden from view. Because culture is learned behavior passed on from generation to generation, it is difficult for the inexperienced or untrained outsider to fathom. Becoming a global manager means learning how to let go of cultural assumptions. Failure to do so will hinder accurate understanding of the meaning and significance of the statements and behaviors of business associates from a different culture.

For example, a person from a culture that encourages responsibility and initiative could experience misunderstandings with a client or boss from a culture that encourages bosses to remain in personal control of all activities. Such a boss would expect to be kept advised in detail of a subordinate's actions; the subordinate might be taking initiative on the mistaken assumption that the boss would appreciate the willingness to assume responsibility.

To transcend ethnocentricity and cultural myopia, managers must make the effort to learn and internalize cultural differences. There are several guidelines that will improve one's ability to learn about other cultures:

1. The beginning of wisdom is to accept that we will never fully understand ourselves or others. People are far too complex to be "understood." As Carl Jung pointed out, "There are no misunderstandings in nature . . . misunderstandings are found only in the realm of what we call 'understanding.' "[8]

2. Our perceptual systems are extremely limited. We "see" almost nothing. Our nervous systems are organized on the principle of negative feedback. That is, the only time our control system is brought into play is when input signals deviate from what we have learned to expect.

3. We spend most of our energy managing perceptual inputs.

4. When we do not understand the beliefs and values of a particular cultural system and society, things that we observe and experience may seem "bizarre."

5. If we want to be effective in another culture, we must attempt to understand that culture's beliefs, motives, and values. This requires an open attitude that allows us to transcend perceptual limitations based on our own culture.

Maslow's Hierarchy of Needs

The late A. H. Maslow developed an extremely useful theory of human motivation that helps explain cultural universals.[9] Maslow's theory is a staple in introductory sociology, psychology, and marketing classes. He hypothesized that people's desires can be arranged into a hierarchy of five needs. As an individual fulfills needs at each level, he or she progresses to higher levels (see Figure 4-1). Once physiological, safety, and social needs have been satisfied, two higher needs become dominant. First is a need for esteem. This is the

---

[7]This section is adapted from John L. Graham and Roy A. Heberger, Jr., "Negotiators Abroad—Don't Shoot from the Hip," *Harvard Business Review* (July–August 1983), pp. 160–168.

[8]C. G. Jung, *Critique of Psychoanalysis*, Bollingen Series XX (Princeton, N.J.: Princeton University Press, 1975), p. 228.

[9]A. H. Maslow, "A Theory of Human Motivation," in *Readings in Managerial Psychology*, ed. Harold J. Levitt and Louis R. Pondy (Chicago: University of Chicago Press, 1964), pp. 6–24.

FIGURE 4–1

MASLOW'S HIERARCHY
OF NEEDS

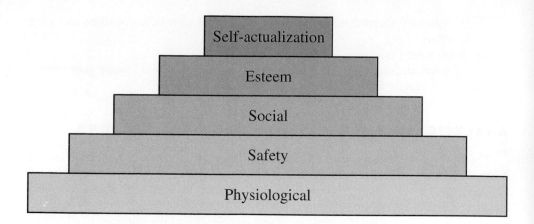

desire for self-respect, self-esteem, and the esteem of others, and is a powerful drive creating demand for status-improving goods. The status symbol cuts across the stages of country development described in Chapter 3. Alfred Zeien, chairman of the Gillette Company, understands this. Marketers in Gillette's Parker Pen subsidiary assume that shoppers in Malaysia and Singapore wishing to give an upscale gift will buy the same Parker pen as Americans shopping at Neiman Marcus. "We are not going to come out with a special product for Malaysia," Zeien says.[10] In East Africa, women who owned bras always wore them with straps exposed to show the world that they owned a bra. In Asia today, young women are taking up smoking—and showing a preference for Western brands—as a symbol of their improved status and increased affluence.

The final stage in the need hierarchy is self-actualization. When all the needs for food, safety, security, friendship, and the esteem of others are satisfied, discontent and restlessness will develop unless one is doing what one is fit for. A musician must make music, an artist must create, a poet must write, a builder must build, and so on.

Maslow's hierarchy of needs is, of course, a simplification of complex human behavior. Other researchers have shown that a person's needs do not progress neatly from one stage of a hierarchy to another. For example, an irony of modern times is the emergence of the need for safety in the United States, one of the richest countries in the world. Indeed, the high incidence of violence in the United States may leave Americans with a lower level of satisfaction of this need than in many so-called "poor" countries. Nevertheless, the hierarchy does suggest a way for relating consumption patterns and levels to basic human need–fulfilling behavior. The usefulness of Maslow's hierarchy is its universality. The model implies that, as countries progress through the stages of economic development, more and more members of society are operating at the esteem need level and higher, having satisfied physiological, safety, and social needs. It appears that self-actualization needs begin to affect consumer behavior as well. For example, there is a growing tendency in the United States to reject material objects as "status symbols." The automobile is no longer the classic American status symbol it once was, and many younger consumers are turning away from material possessions. This trend toward rejection of materialism is not so advanced in other leading industrialized countries. For example, in Germany today, the automobile remains a supreme status symbol. Germans give their automobiles loving care, even going so far as to travel to distant locations on weekends to wash their cars in pure spring water.

[10]Louis Uchitelle, "Gillette's World View: One Blade Fits All," *The New York Times* (Jan. 3, 1994), p. C3.

THE **REST** OF THE **STORY**

■ GETTING LOST IN TRANSLATION

*T*he slang rendering of Otis Spunkmeyer's name described at the beginning of this chapter is hardly unique, but it underscores the importance of language and translation for persons and companies doing business across national boundaries. In Eastern Europe, translation problems often arise because the meanings of many Western business terms are not widely known or are difficult to translate.

Sometimes, translation errors result in bloopers that are harmless but funny. Consider this assortment of hotel signs from around the world translated into English: Paris: "Please leave your values at the front desk." Japan: "You are invited to take advantage of the chambermaid." Zurich: "Because of the impropriety of entertaining guests of the opposite sex in the bedroom, it is suggested that the lobby be used for this purpose." Finally, the following sign appeared in a hotel in Romania: "The lift is being fixed for the next day. During that time we regret that you will be unbearable."

In Japan, many consumer packaged goods—including some that are not imported—have English, French, or German on the labels to suggest a stylish image and Western look. A Westerner may wonder, however, what point the copywriters are actually trying to get across. For example, English on the label of City Original Coffee proclaims "Ease Your Bosoms. This coffee has carefully selected high quality beans and roasted by our all the experience." The intended message: Drinking the coffee provides a relaxing break and "takes a load off your chest." Other products, such as casual wear and sports apparel, are also emblazened with fractured messages. These words appeared on the back of a jacket: "Vigorous throw up. Go on a journey." A sports bag bore the message, "A drop of sweat is the precious gift for your guts."

Finally, consider the message printed on the cover of a notebook: "Be a man I recommend it with confidence as like a most intelligent stationary of basic design." One expert on "Japanese English" believes messages like these highlight basic differences between Japanese and other languages. Many Western languages lack exact equivalents for the rich variety of Japanese words that convey feelings. This presents difficulties for copywriters trying to render feelings in a language other than Japanese. The message on the black notebook was supposed to convey manliness. As the English-speaking Japanese copywriter explained, "I wanted to say I'm proud to present the product to the consumer because it's got a simple, masculine image." While a Westerner might argue whether the copywriter succeeded, Japanese retailers do not seem at all concerned that the messages are gibberish. As one retailer explained, the point is that a message in English, French, or German can convey hipness and help sell a product. "I don't expect people to *read* it," she said.

Sources: Yumiko Ono, "A Little Bad English Goes a Long Way in Japan's Boutiques," *The Wall Street Journal* (May 20, 1992), pp. A1, A6.
Charles Goldsmith, "Look See! Anyone Do Read This and It Will Make You Laughable," *The Wall Street Journal* (Nov. 19, 1992), p. B1.

Hofstede's Cultural Typology[11]

Organizational anthropologist Geerte Hofstede has argued that the cultures of different nations can be compared in terms of four dimensions. The first, *power distance*, is the extent to which the less powerful members of a society accept—even expect—power to be distributed unequally. To paraphrase Orwell, all societies are unequal, but some are more unequal than others. The second dimension is a reflection of the degree to which individuals in a society are integrated into groups. In *individualist cultures*, each member of society is primarily concerned with his or her own interest and those of the immediate family. In *collectivist cultures*, all of society's members are integrated into cohesive in-groups. *Masculinity*, the third dimension, describes a society in which men are expected to be assertive, competitive, and concerned with material success, while women fulfill the role of nurturer and are concerned with issues such as the welfare of children. *Femininity* on the other hand, describes a society in which the social roles of men and women overlap, with neither gender exhibiting overly ambitious or competitive behavior. Hofstede notes that these first three dimensions refer to expected social behavior; the fourth dimension is concerned with, in Hofstede's words, "man's search for Truth." *Uncertainty avoidance* is the extent to which the members of a society are uncomfortable with unclear, ambiguous, or unstructured situations. Some cultures express strong uncertainty

---
[11]Hofstede and Bond 1988.

avoidance with aggressive, emotional, intolerant behavior; they are characterized by a belief in absolute Truth. The manifestation of low uncertainty avoidance is behavior that is more contemplative, relativistic, and tolerant.

Hofstede's research convinced him that, although the four dimensions yielded interesting and useful interpretations, they did not provide any insight into possible cultural bases for economic growth. Hofstede was also disturbed by the fact that the surveys used in the research had been developed by Western social scientists. Because many economists had failed to predict the explosive economic development of Japan and the "tigers," i.e., South Korea, Taiwan, Hong Kong, and Singapore, Hofstede surmised that some cultural dimensions in Asia were eluding the researchers. This methodological problem was remedied by a Chinese Value Survey (CVS) developed by Chinese social scientists. The CVS data supported the first three "social behavior" dimensions of culture identified previously, i.e., power distance, individualism/collectivism, and masculinity/femininity. Uncertainty avoidance, however, did not show up in the CVS. Instead, the CVS revealed a dimension that had eluded Western researchers. Moreover, this dimension—which Hofstede calls "Confucian Dynamism"—concerns several aspects of culture that appear to be strongly linked to economic growth. Hofstede explains that these aspects concern "a society's search for virtue," rather than a search for truth. *Persistence* (perseverance) is a general tenacity in the pursuit of a goal. *Ordering relationships* by status reflects the presence of societal hierarchies, and *observing this order* indicates the acceptance of complementary relations. *Thrift* manifests itself in high savings rates. Finally, *a sense of shame* leads to sensitivity in social contacts. Hofstede notes that these values are widely held within the high-performing countries, but that the presence of these values by themselves is not sufficient to lead to economic growth. Two other conditions are necessary: the existence of a market and a supportive political context.

The Self-Reference Criterion and Perception

As we have shown, a person's perception of market needs is framed by his or her own cultural experience. A framework for systematically reducing perceptual blockage and distortion was developed by James Lee and published in *Harvard Business Review* in 1966. Lee termed the unconscious reference to one's own cultural values the **self-reference criterion,** or SRC. To address this problem and eliminate or reduce cultural myopia, he proposed a systematic four-step framework.

1. Define the problem or goal in terms of home-country cultural traits, habits, and norms.
2. Define the problem or goal in terms of host-country cultural traits, habits, and norms. Make no value judgments.
3. Isolate the SRC influence and examine it carefully to see how it complicates the problem.
4. Redefine the problem without the SRC influence and solve for the host-country market situation.[12]

The Euro Disney case at the end of this chapter provides an excellent vehicle for understanding SRC. As they planned their entry into the French market, how might Disney executives have done things differently?

Step 1. Disney executives believe there is virtually unlimited demand for American cultural exports around the world. Evidence includes the success of McDonald's,

[12]James A. Lee, "Cultural Analysis in Overseas Operations," *Harvard Business Review* (March–April 1966), pp. 106–114.

Coca-Cola, Hollywood movies, and American rock music. Disney has a stellar track record in exporting its American management system and business style. Tokyo Disneyland, a virtual carbon copy of the park in Anaheim, California, has been a runaway success. Disney policies prohibit sale or consumption of alcohol inside its theme parks.

Step 2. Europeans in general, and the French in particular, are sensitive about American cultural imperialism. Consuming wine with the midday meal is a long-established custom. Europeans have their own real castles, and many popular Disney characters come from European folk tales.

Step 3. The significant differences revealed by comparing the findings in steps 1 and 2 suggest strongly that the needs upon which the American and Japanese Disney theme parks were based did not exist in France. A modification of this design was needed for European success.

Step 4. This would require the design of a theme park that is more in keeping with French and European cultural norms. Allow the French to put their own identity on the park.

The lesson that the SRC teaches is that a vital, critical skill of the global marketer is unbiased perception, the ability to see what is so in a culture. Although this skill is as valuable at home as it is abroad, it is critical to the global marketer because of the wide-spread tendency toward ethnocentrism and use of the self-reference criterion. The SRC can be a powerful negative force in global business, and forgetting to check for it can lead to misunderstanding and failure. While planning Euro Disney, chairman Michael Eisner and other company executives were blindsided by a lethal combination of their own prior success and ethnocentrism. Avoiding the SRC requires a person to suspend assumptions based on prior experience and success and be prepared to acquire new knowledge about human behavior and motivation.

ENVIRONMENTAL SENSITIVITY

Environmental sensitivity is the extent to which products must be adapted to the cul-ture-specific needs of different national markets. A useful approach is to view products on a continuum of environmental sensitivity. At one end of the continuum are environ-mentally insensitive products that do not require significant adaptation to the environ-ments of various world markets. At the other end of the continuum are products that are highly sensitive to different environmental factors. A company with environmentally in-sensitive products will spend relatively less time determining the specific and unique con-ditions of local markets because the product is basically universal. The greater a product's

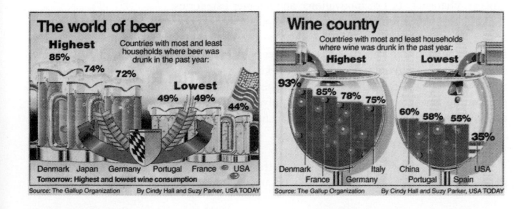

Source: The Gallup Organization   By Cindy Hall and Suzy Parker, USA TODAY

(Copyright 1995, *USA TODAY*. Reprinted with permission.)

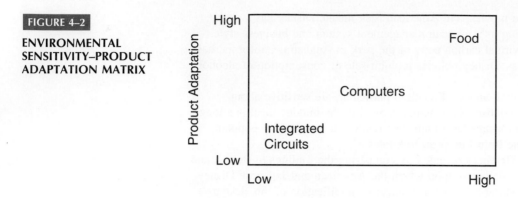

FIGURE 4–2

ENVIRONMENTAL
SENSITIVITY–PRODUCT
ADAPTATION MATRIX

environmental sensitivity, the greater the need for managers to address country-specific economic, regulatory, technological, social, and cultural environmental conditions.

The sensitivity of products can be represented on a two-dimensional scale as shown in Figure 4-2. The horizontal axis shows environmental sensitivity, the vertical axis the degree for product adaptation needed. Any product exhibiting low levels of environmental sensitivity—integrated circuits, for example—belongs in the lower left of the figure. Intel has sold more than 100 million microprocessors, because a chip is a chip anywhere around the world. Moving to the right on the horizontal axis, the level of sensitivity increases, as does the amount of adaptation. Computers are characterized by moderate levels of environmental sensitivity; variations in country voltage requirements require some adaptation. In addition, the computer's software documentation should be in the local language. At the upper right of Figure 4-2 are products with high environmental sensitivity. Food sometimes falls into this category because it is sensitive to climate and culture. As we saw in the McDonald's case at the end of Chapter 1, the fast-food giant has achieved great success outside the United States by adapting its menu items to local tastes. GE's turbine generating equipment may also appear on the high-sensitivity end of the continuum; in many countries, local equipment manufacturers receive preferential treatment when bidding on national projects.

DIFFUSION THEORY[13]

Hundreds of studies have described the process by which an individual adopts a new idea. Sociologist Everett Rogers reviewed these studies and discovered a pattern of remarkably similar findings. In his book *Diffusion of Innovations*, Rogers distilled the research into three concepts that are extremely useful to global marketers: the adoption process, characteristics of innovations, and adopter categories.

An innovation is something new. When applied to a product, "new" can mean different things. In an absolute sense, once a product has been introduced anywhere in the world, it is no longer an innovation because it is no longer new to the world. Relatively speaking, however, a product already introduced in one market may be an innovation elsewhere because it is new and different for the market being targeted. Global marketing often entails just such product introductions. Managers find themselves marketing products that may be, simultaneously, innovations in some markets and mature or declining products in other markets.

The Adoption Process

One of the basic elements of Rogers' diffusion theory is the concept of an **adoption process**—the mental stages through which an individual passes from the time of his or

[13]This section draws from Everett M. Rogers, *Diffusion of Innovations* (New York: Free Press, 1962).

■ "SINCERELY"

While it may be true that "brevity is the soul of wit," when it comes to signing a business letter, the French go far beyond the simple "Sincerely" that often suffices for anyone writing in English. Below are the "top 10" ways to close a business letter in French.

1. Nous vous prions d'agréer, Monsieur, l'expression de nos sentiments dévoués.

   Literally: *"We beg you to receive, Sir, the expression of our devoted sentiments."*

2. Agréez, Monsieur, l'assurance de mes meilleurs sentiments.

   "Accept, sir, the assurance of my best sentiments."

3. Je vous prie d'agréer, Monsieur le Directeur, mes meilleures salutations.

   "I beg you to accept, Mr. Director, my best greetings."

4. Je vous prie d'agréer, Madame la Directrice, mes meilleures salutations.

   "I beg you to accept, Ms. Director, my best greetings."

5. Veuillez, croire, Messieurs, à l'assurance de ma haute considération.

   "Please believe, Gentlemen, the assurance of my highest consideration."

6. Recevez, Messieurs, mes sincères salutations.

   "Receive, Gentlemen, my sincere greetings."

7. Je vous prie d'agréer, Monsieur, l'expression de mes sentiments les meilleurs.

   "I beg you to accept, Sir, the expression of my best sentiments."

8. Je vous prie d'agréer, Mademoiselle, mes respectueuses salutations.

   "I beg you to accept, Miss, my respectful greetings."

9. Veuillez agréer, Monsieur, l'expression de mes sentiments distingués.

   "Please accept, Sir, the expression of my distinguished sentiments."

10. Je vous prie d'agréer, Messieurs, avec mes remerciements anticipés, l'expression de mes sentiments distingués.

    "I beg you to accept, Gentlemen, with my anticipated thanks, the expression of my distinguished sentiments."

---

her first knowledge of an innovation to the time of product adoption or purchase. Rogers suggests that an individual passes through five different stages in proceeding from first knowledge of a product to the final adoption or purchase of that product: awareness, interest, evaluation, trial, and adoption.

1. *Awareness.* In the first stage, the customer becomes aware for the first time of the product or innovation. Studies have shown that at this stage impersonal sources of information such as mass media advertising are most important. An important early communication objective in global marketing is to create awareness of a new product through general exposure to advertising messages.

2. *Interest.* During this stage, the customer is interested enough to learn more. The customer has focused his or her attention on communications relating to the product, and will engage in research activities and seek out additional information.

3. *Evaluation.* In this stage, the individual mentally assesses the product's benefits in relation to present and anticipated future needs and, based on this judgment, decides whether or not to try it.

4. *Trial.* Most customers will not purchase expensive products without the "hands-on" experience marketers call "trial." A good example of a product trial that does not involve purchase is the automobile test drive. For health care products and other inexpensive consumer packaged goods, trial often involves actual purchase. Marketers frequently induce trial by distributing free samples. For inexpensive products, an initial single purchase is defined as trial.

5. *Adoption.* At this point, the individual either makes an initial purchase (in the case of the more expensive product) or continues to purchase—adopts and exhibits brand loyalty to—the less expensive product. Studies show that, as a person moves from the evaluation through trial to adoption, personal sources of

THIS... IS CNN

Global Coverage Available To Over Half-A-Billion People Every Day

GLOBAL VISION
- AVAILABLE TO OVER 160 MILLION HOUSEHOLDS
- WATCHED IN OVER 210 COUNTRIES & TERRITORIES
- 15 SATELLITES COVERING SIX CONTINENTS

GLOBAL RESOURCES
- OVER 600 BROADCAST AFFILIATES WORLDWIDE
- NEARLY 3,000 NEWS PROFESSIONALS
- 30 NEWS BUREAUS AROUND THE WORLD

GLOBAL COMMITMENT
- CNN
- HEADLINE NEWS
- CNN INTERNATIONAL
- CNNfn
- CNN AIRPORT NETWORK
- CNN INTERACTIVE

CNN
THE WORLD'S NEWS LEADER
Access CNN on the World Wide Web at cnn.com

(Courtesy of CNN®.)

information are more important than impersonal sources. It is during these stages that sales representatives and word of mouth become major persuasive forces affecting the decision to buy.

Characteristics of Innovations

In addition to describing the product adoption process, Rogers also identifies five major factors affecting the rate at which innovations are adopted: relative advantage, compatibility, complexity, divisibility, and communicability.

1. *Relative advantage:* How a new product compares with existing products or methods in the eyes of customers. The perceived relative advantage of a new product versus existing products is a major influence on the rate of adoption. If a product has a substantial relative advantage vis-à-vis the competition, it is likely to gain quick acceptance. When compact disc players were first introduced in the early 1980s, industry observers predicted that only audiophiles would care enough about digital sound—and have the money—to purchase them. However, the sonic advantages of CDs compared to LPs were obvious to the mass market; as prices for CD players plummeted, the 12-inch black vinyl LP was rendered virtually extinct in less than a decade.

2. *Compatibility:* The extent to which a product is consistent with existing values and past experiences of adopters. The history of innovations in international marketing is replete with failures caused by the lack of compatibility of new products in the target market. For example, the first consumer VCR, the Sony Betamax, ultimately failed because it could only record for one hour. Most buyers wanted to record movies and sports events; they shunned the Betamax in favor of VHS-format VCRs that could record four hours of programming.

3. *Complexity:* The degree to which an innovation or new product is difficult to understand and use. Product complexity is a factor that can slow down the rate of adoption, particularly in developing country markets with low rates of literacy. In the 1990s, dozens of global companies are developing new interactive multimedia consumer electronics products. Complexity is a key design issue; it is a standing joke that in most households, VCR clocks flash 12:00 because users don't know how to set them. To achieve mass success, new products will have to be as simple to use as slipping a prerecorded videocassette into a VCR.

4. *Divisibility:* The ability of a product to be tried and used on a limited basis without great expense. Wide discrepancies in income levels around the globe result in major differences in preferred purchase quantities, serving sizes, and product portions. CPC International's Hellmann's mayonnaise was simply not selling in U.S.-size jars in Latin America. Sales took off after the company placed the mayonnaise in small plastic packets. The plastic packets were within the food budgets of local consumers, and they required no refrigeration—another plus.

5. *Communicability:* The degree to which benefits of an innovation or the value of a product can be communicated to a potential market. A new digital cassette recorder from Philips is off to a slow start, in part because advertisements have failed to clearly communicate the fact that the product can make CD-quality recordings using new cassette technology while still playing older analog tapes.

Adopter Categories

Adopter categories are classifications of individuals within a market on the basis of their innovativeness. Hundreds of studies of the diffusion of innovation demonstrate that adoption is a social phenomenon that is characterized by a normal distribution curve as shown in Figure 4-3.

Five categories have been assigned to the segments of this normal distribution. The first 2.5 percent of people to purchase a product are defined as innovators. The next 13.5 percent are defined as early adopters, the next 34 percent as the early majority, the next 34 percent as the late majority, and the final 16 percent as laggards. Studies show that innovators tend to be venturesome, more cosmopolitan in their social relationships, and wealthier than those who adopt later. Earlier adopters are the most influential people in their communities, even more than the innovators. Thus the earlier adopters are a critical group in the adoption process, and they have a great influence on the early and late majority, who make up the bulk of the adopters of any product. Several characteristics of

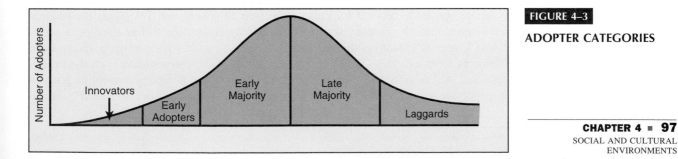

FIGURE 4–3

ADOPTER CATEGORIES

earlier adopters stand out. First, they tend to be younger, have higher social status, and are in a more favorable financial position than later adopters. They must be responsive to mass-media information sources and must learn about innovations from these sources because they cannot simply copy the behavior of some earlier adopters.

One of the major reasons for the normal distribution of adopter categories is the *interaction effect*, that is, the process through which individuals who have adopted an innovation influence others. Adoption of a new idea or product is the result of human interaction in a social system. If the first adopter of an innovation or new product discusses it with two other people, and each of these two adopters passes the new idea along to two other people, and so on, the resulting distribution yields a normal bell shape when plotted.

From the point of view of the marketing manager, steps taken to persuade innovators and early adopters to purchase a product are critical. These groups must make the first move and are the basis for the eventual penetration of a product into a new market because, over time, the majority copy their behavior.

Diffusion of Innovations in Pacific Rim Countries

In a recent cross-national comparison of the United States, Japan, South Korea, and Taiwan, Takada and Jain present evidence that different country characteristics—in particular, culture and communication patterns—affect diffusion processes for room air conditioners, washing machines, and calculators.[14] Proceeding from the observation that Japan, South Korea, and Taiwan are high-context cultures with relatively homogeneous populations while the United States is a low-context, heterogeneous culture, Takada and Jain surmised that faster rates of diffusion would be found in Asia than in the United States. A second hypothesis supported by the research was that adoption would proceed more quickly in markets where innovations were introduced relatively late. Presumably, the lag time would give potential consumers more opportunity to assess the relative advantages, compatibility, and other product attributes. Takada and Jain's research has important marketing implications. They note:

> If a marketing manager plans to enter the newly industrializing countries (NICs) or other Asia markets with a product that has proved to be successful in the home market, the product's diffusion processes are likely to be much faster than in the home market.

SOCIAL AND CULTURAL ENVIRONMENTS: IMPACT ON MARKETING INDUSTRIAL PRODUCTS

The various cultural factors described earlier can exert important influences on industrial products marketing around the globe. They must be recognized in formulating a global marketing plan. Recall that some industrial products may exhibit either low levels of environmental sensitivity, as in the case of computer chips, for example, or high levels, as in the case of turbine generators when "buy national" government policy puts foreign bidders at a disadvantage.

Motorola's growth strategy in the 1980s called for entering the Japanese market. The company wanted to become a supplier to Nippon Telephone and Telegraph, the national telecommunications company that was a monopoly at the time (it has since been privatized). Company executives showed considerable savvy as they pursued the business. First, Motorola hired a former U.S. government assistant trade representative with the experience and skill to guide the company's effort. Motorola had a strong competitive position in pagers; to secure NTT's business, the company invested in a special assembly line to

[14]Hirokazu Takada and Dipak Jain, "Cross-National Analysis of Diffusion of Consumer Durable Goods in Pacific Rim Countries," *Journal of Marketing* 55 (April 1991), pp. 48–53.

build pagers to NTT's specifications. Next, Motorola sought certification to supply mobile telephone equipment. Getting certification in Japan is a difficult process that usually takes at least 18 months. Because of the time and money involved, it is crucial for a company to know what it is doing and why it is doing it. Motorola's understanding of the required approach and persistence paid off; the company was granted the all-important required certification.[15]

SOCIAL AND CULTURAL ENVIRONMENTS: IMPACT ON MARKETING CONSUMER PRODUCTS

Research studies show that, independent of social class and income, culture is a significant influence on consumption behavior and durable goods ownership.[16] Consumer products are probably more sensitive to cultural difference than are industrial products. Hunger is a basic physiological need in Maslow's hierarchy; everyone needs to eat, but what we want to eat can be strongly influenced by culture. Evidence from the front lines of the marketing wars suggests that food is probably the most sensitive category of consumer products. CPC International failed to win popularity for Knorr dehydrated soups among Americans. The U.S. soup market was dominated by Campbell Soup Company; 90 percent of the soup consumed by households was canned. Knorr was a Swiss company acquired by CPC that had a major share of the European prepared food market, where bouillon and dehydrated soups account for 80 percent of consumer soup sales. Despite CPC's failure to change the soup-eating habits of Americans, the company has achieved great success as a global marketer; sales outside the United States constitute 63 percent of its revenues from food lines.

At Campbell, by contrast, the figures are reversed: 63 percent of food revenues are generated in the United States, 27 percent from global markets. Despite the fact that Campbell is one of the world's best-known brand names, the company has discovered that the attitude of homemakers toward food preparation is a major cultural factor in marketing prepared foods. Recall that cooking was one of the cultural universals identified by Murdock. However, cooking habits and customs vary from country to country. Campbell's research revealed that Italian housewives devote approximately 4.5 hours per day to food preparation, versus 60 minutes a day spent by their U.S. counterparts. The difference reflects cultural norms regarding the kitchen as well as the fact that a higher percentage of American women work outside the home.

Campbell discovered a strong negative opinion toward convenience food in Italy. A panel of randomly selected Italian housewives was asked: "Would you want your son to marry a canned soup user?" The response to this question was sobering: All but a small fraction of a percent of the respondents answered, "No." Increased incomes as well as product innovations may have an impact on Italian attitudes toward time and convenience, with a corresponding positive effect on the market for convenience foods. Already, taste improvements in frozen pizza have boosted sales in Italy.

Campbell CEO David Johnson recently acquired a majority stake in Arnotts, Australia's leading biscuit company. Johnson is setting his sights on the $1 billion Asian cracker market, which he expects to triple or quadruple in size by the year 2000. Will consumers in Beijing and Bangkok clamor for Australian baked goods? Only time will tell, but Johnson—a native of Australia—is relying on sophisticated market research to guide the company's product adaptation effort.[17] Other Campbell executives share Johnson's global vision. As C. David Clark, CEO of Campbell Canada, noted, "The strategy for North

[15]"Motorola Hurdles a Japanese Barrier," *Business Week* (June 7, 1982), p. 33.
[16]Charles M. Schaninger, Jacques C. Bourgeois, and Christian W. Buss, "French-English Canadian Subcultural Consumption Differences," *Journal of Marketing* 49 (Spring 1985), pp. 82–92.
[17]Stephen W. Quickel, "Can Campbell Survive the Global Food Wars? M'm! M'm! Maybe!" *CFO* (February 1994), p. 26.

America is very simple. You market locally, manufacture regionally, and resource globally—with common technology, knowledge, and supplies."[18]

Thirst also shows how needs differ from wants. Liquid intake is a universal physiological need. As is the case with food and cooking, however, the particular beverages people *want* to drink can be strongly influenced by culture. Coffee is a beverage category that illustrates the point. In the United Kingdom, instant coffee has 90 percent of the total coffee market, as compared with only 15 percent in Sweden. The other European countries fall between these two extreme points. Instant coffee's large share of the British market can be traced to the fact that, in the hot beverage category, Britain has historically been a nation of tea drinkers. Only in recent times have the British been persuaded to take up coffee drinking. Instant coffee is more like tea in its preparation than brewed coffee. Not surprisingly, when the British did begin to drink coffee, they opted for instant since its preparation was compatible with past experience. Another reason for the popularity of instant coffee in Britain is the practice of drinking coffee with a large quantity of milk, so that the coffee flavor is masked. Differences in the coffee flavor are thus hidden, so that a "better cup" of coffee is not really important. In Sweden, on the other hand, coffee is the hot beverage of choice. Swedes consume coffee without large quantities of milk, and therefore the coffee flavor is not masked and brewed coffee is preferred.

Soft drink consumption patterns also show conspicuous differences around the globe. The Coca-Cola Company reported that, in 1994, per capita consumption of its soft drink products stood at 310 8-ounce servings in the United States, 191 servings in Germany, 94 servings in Italy, and 65 servings in France.[19] Differences in soft drink consumption are associated in part with much higher per capita consumption of other kinds of beverages in Europe. In France and Italy, for example, 30 to 40 times as much wine is consumed as in America on a per capita basis; the French also prefer mineral water to soft drinks. The converse is true in America, where soft drink consumption surpasses that of water. Germany far exceeds the United States in per capita consumption of beer. Does culture alone account for the difference between the popularity of soft drinks in Western Europe and the United States? No, in fact. Several variables—including culture—are responsible for the differences, as portrayed in the following equation:

$$C = f(A, B, C, D, E, F, G)$$

where

C = consumption of soft drinks
f = function of
A = influences of other beverages' relative prices, quality, and taste
B = advertising expenditure and effectiveness (all beverage categories)
C = availability of products in distribution channels
D = cultural elements, tradition, custom, habit
E = availability of raw materials (particularly of water)
F = climatic conditions, temperature, and relative humidity
G = income levels

To be sure, culture affects the demand for soft drinks. Note, however, that it is only one of several variables. Therefore, culture is an influencing, rather than a determining, factor. If a soft drink marketer in Western Europe launches an aggressive marketing program (including lower prices, more intensive distribution, and heavy advertising), consumption can be expected to increase. However, it is also clear that any effort to convert Europeans to soft drinks will run up against cultural tradition, custom, and competition from widely available alternative beverages. Culture in this case is a restraining force, but, because culture is changing so rapidly, it is a restraint that can be overcome. For ex-

[18]Bill Saporito, "Campbell Soup Gets Piping Hot," *Fortune* (Sept. 9, 1991), p. 143.
[19]The Coca-Cola Company, *1994 Annual Report,* p. 30.

ample, Coca-Cola used promotion and a massive sampling effort to increase 1992 unit case volume of Coke Light in Italy by 73 percent over that of 1991. In Germany, Coke's third-largest global market, 1992 unit case volume increased by 6 percent over that of 1991, despite a recession and dislocations due to unification; unit case volume in the former East Germany grew 20 percent. In France, the 1992 marketing effort focused on availability and greater consumer acceptance, resulting in a 6 percent increase in unit case volume.[20]

The penetration of the U.S. beverage market by bottled water producers is another excellent example of the impact of an effective creative strategy on a firmly entrenched cultural tradition. Prior to the 1980s, drinking bottled water was not an important part of American culture. The general attitude in the United States was, "Why pay for something that is free?" Source Perrier SA, the French bottled water firm, decided to take aim at the U.S. market. It hired Bruce Nevin, an experienced American marketing executive, and gave him a free hand to formulate a creative strategy.

Nevin decided to reposition Perrier from an expensive, imported bottled water (which no sane, red-blooded American would touch) to a competitively priced, low-calorie beverage in the soft drink market. To back up this positioning, Nevin launched a major consumer advertising campaign, lowered prices, and moved the product from the gourmet section of the supermarket to the soft drink section. The strategy boiled down to significant adjustment of three marketing mix elements: price, promotion, and place. Only the product was left unchanged.

The campaign succeeded beyond even the most optimistic expectations, essentially creating an entirely new market. By the mid-1980s, the $2.2 billion bottled water category had become the fastest-growing segment of the U.S. beverage industry. Perrier's annual U.S. sales grew from about $40 million to $800 million, and Perrier commanded 80 percent of the U.S. bottled water market. The success of this strategy was rooted in two undisputable facts: Americans were ready for bottled water, and the tactics were brilliantly executed. The results illustrate how the restraining force of culture can be changed by a creative marketing strategy grounded in market possibilities.[21]

CROSS-CULTURAL COMPLICATIONS AND SUGGESTED SOLUTIONS

As we have seen in this chapter and the last, global marketing activities are conducted in an ever-changing environment that blends economic, cultural, and social forces. Stepping out of the global perspective for a moment, we should acknowledge one thing: Even when the parties to a commercial transaction belong to the *same* low-context society—the United States, for example—and the terms of the deal are spelled out "in black and white," different understandings of the respective obligations of the parties will often occur.

Business relationships between parties of *different* cultures and/or nationalities are subject to additional challenges. Parties from different countries may have trouble coming to contract terms because of differences in the laws governing their respective activities and problems of enforcement across international boundaries. No matter what is stated in a contract, taking another party to court for breach of contract will probably require a suit in the defendant's own home turf, which may be an insurmountable advantage for the home-country participant.

When a party from a high-context culture takes part in a business understanding, the proceedings are likely to be even further complicated by very different beliefs about the

---

[20]The Coca-Cola Company, *1992 Annual Report*, p. 32.
[21]Unfortunately, Perrier's poor handling of a public relations crisis in 1990 led to a 50 percent decrease in U.S. sales of Perrier, from which the company has yet to fully recover.

According to the Taoist notion of *feng shui* (winds/water), properly positioned buildings and furniture can bring prosperity and happiness. (Drawing by D. Reilly, copyright 1995 *The New Yorker Magazine, Inc.*)

"A million two does seem a bit heavy for a one-bedroom at first, but this unit has the best feng-shui in the building."

significance of formal business understandings and the ongoing obligations of all parties. The business environment in many countries outside the Triad markets can be characterized by all manner of "hostile" elements: natural and human-induced catastrophes, political problems, foreign exchange inconvertibility, widely fluctuating exchange rates, depressions, and changes in national economic priorities and tariff schedules. One cannot predict precisely how the most carefully laid plans will go awry, only that they will. Marketing executives and managers with dealings outside the home market must build mutual trust, rapport, and empathy with business contacts; all are required to sustain enduring relationships. Appointing a host-country national to a position as sales representative will not automatically guarantee success. If a corporation constantly shuffles its international staff, it risks impeding the formation of what we might call "high-context subcultures" between home-office personnel and host nationals. This diminishes the company's chances of effectively dealing with the business crises that will inevitably occur.

In 1986, Mexico's government imposed severe foreign exchange restrictions. Companies that had sold products or services to Mexican parties on terms other than "confirmed irrevocable international letter of credit" learned that they would have a lengthy wait before receiving payment in U.S. dollars or other "hard" currencies. Mexican companies dependent on essential ingredients, spare parts, and other critical foreign supplies had to deal with a rationed supply of foreign exchange to pay for new orders. In this situation, personal relationships superseded contractual obligations. In some instances, government officials needed to be convinced that a certain transaction deserved a priority allocation of foreign exchange. Some foreign sellers had to accept payment in Mexican products or in pesos that had to be invested in Mexico. Such contingencies arise routinely as companies conduct business around the globe. Solutions often result from individual initiative; personal ties create opportunites for both sides to keep a business relationship alive.

India is an important supplier of crude and processed agricultural and forest product raw materials to world markets. Small family-owned enterprises collect, process, and sell these materials. Typically, months before the crop is in, sellers are required to contract with foreign buyers for later delivery of these products. The buyers, in turn, make long-term contractual commitments to their own customers. It is not possible for the Indian firms to hedge reliably by making forward crop purchases; there are no regulated commodity exchanges for these products. Nor do the farmers and forest product collectors have the resources to cover their sales if the crop fails. There are major problems during most growing seasons: Natural disaster or insufficient plantings result in short crops; strikes, protracted power shortages, or the lack of spare parts result in excessive shipment delays and reduced capacity. Business downturns or unexpected changes in required inventory levels may prompt buyers to request—or even insist—that shipments be held back or prices be reduced. Of course, such actions will cause the supplier severe financial hardship. Sometimes the supplier is unable to comply precisely with the terms of the contract and therefore provides a substitute order (usually without advance notice). The hope is that the buyer will inadvertently pay before discovering the switch and then reluctantly accept the merchandise with only minor adjustment.

Ongoing business between India and its global customers is, of course, perpetuated by mutual interest, but personal relationships are what make it possible. False rumors, supplier defaults, and customer cancellations are prevalent. Therefore, the greatest importance is assigned to contacts and business associates who can be fully trusted and whose culture-influenced perceptions are understood and predictable. Indian society is at least as ethnically and culturally diverse as that in Europe, and business practices are probably even more varied than in Europe.

TRAINING IN CROSS-CULTURAL COMPETENCY

Personal relationships are an essential ingredient for the international businessperson. One-third of a Peace Corps volunteer's training is devoted to learning about ways things are done in the host country (particularly personal relationships). The international businessperson should have comparable preparation and a willingness to at least consider the merits of accommodating to the host culture's ways of doing business. The stakes are high: Experts estimate that between $2 and $2.5 billion worth of business is lost each year because of employee mistakes that occur in other cultures.[22]

Samsung, GE, AT&T, and other large companies that are globalizing are taking steps to train managers and sensitize them to other ways of thinking, feeling, and acting. The goal is to improve their ability to deal effectively with customers, suppliers, bosses, and employees from other countries and regions. Managers must learn to question their own beliefs, to overcome the SRC, and to adapt the way they communicate, solve problems, and even make decisions. Multicultural managers must learn to question and to reevaluate their feelings concerning such rudimentary management issues as leadership, motivation, and teamwork; this means an examination of some extremely fundamental and personal systems of belief. Lastly, managers must learn to overcome stereotypes they hold

---

[22]Joann S. Lublin, "Companies Use Cross-Cultural Training to Help Their Employees Adjust Abroad," *The Wall Street Journal* (Aug. 4, 1992), p. B1.

regarding individuals of various races and religions from other countries; managers must also diplomatically deal with stereotypes others may have about them.

Samsung Group, South Korea's largest company, recently launched an internationalization campaign. Prior to departing for overseas assignments, managers attend a month-long "boot camp," where the topics range from Western table manners to sexual harassment. Hundreds of promising Samsung junior managers spend a year in Western countries pursuing an unusual assignment: goofing off. Notes one Korean management theorist, "International exposure is important, but you have to develop international taste. You have to do more than visit. You have to goof off at the mall, watch people and develop international tastes." Park Kwang Moo, an employee at Samsung's trading subsidiary, didn't get to spend time in malls: His assignment was to visit the former Soviet Union. He spent his first six months immersed in language study, then traveled to all 15 former Soviet republics. Park's superiors were delighted with the 80-page report he filed upon his return, despite the fact that there was very little in it about business issues per se. A director at the trading company noted that the report was mostly about Russians' drinking habits and idiosyncrasies. "But," he noted, "in 20 years, if this man is representing Samsung in Moscow, he will have friends and he will be able to communicate, and then we will get the payoff."[23]

Another widely used approach to accomplish sensitization is the use of workshops, incorporating case studies, role playing, and other exercises designed to permit participants to confront a relevant situation, contemplate what their own thoughts and actions would be in such a situation, and analyze and learn from the results. Participants must be able to understand and evaluate their motivations and approaches. Often, role-playing will bring out thoughts and feelings that otherwise might go unexamined or even unacknowledged. A variety of other techniques have been used for cross-cultural training; the common goal is to teach members of one culture ways of interacting effectively in another culture.

SUMMARY

Culture, a society's "programming of the mind," has both a pervasive and changing influence on each national market environment. Global marketers must recognize the influence of culture and be prepared to either respond to it or change it. Human behavior is a function of both a person's own unique personality and that person's interaction with the collective forces of the particular society and culture in which he or she has lived. A number of concepts can help guide anyone seeking insight into cultural issues. Nations can be classified as high- and low-context cultures; communication and negotiation styles can differ from country to country. Maslow's hierarchy, Hofstede's typology, and the self-reference criterion can provide clues about cultural differences and similarities. An awareness of environmental sensitivity can help marketers determine whether products must be adapted to the needs of various markets. Rogers' research on the diffusion of innovations helps explain how products are adopted by the members of a society.

Global marketing has played an important—even leading—role in influencing the rate of cultural change around the world. This is particularly true of food, but it includes virtually every industry, particularly in consumer products. Soap and detergent manufacturers have changed washing habits, the electronics industry has changed entertainment patterns, clothing marketers have changed styles, and so on. While culture can also affect characteristics of industrial products, it is more important as an influence on the marketing process, particularly in the way business is conducted. Global marketers have learned to rely upon people who know and understand local customs and attitudes for marketing expertise. Even so, many persons doing business in a new culture avail themselves of training opportunities to help avoid potential cross-cultural complications.

DISCUSSION QUESTIONS

1. What is a cultural universal?
2. What is the difference between a low-context culture and a high-context culture? Give an example of a country that is an example of each type, and provide evidence for your answer.
3. How can Hofstede's cultural typologies help Western marketers better understand Asian culture?

[23]"Sensitivity Kick: Korea's Biggest Firm Teaches Junior Execs Strange Foreign Ways," *The Wall Street Journal* (Dec. 30, 1992), p. A1.

4. Explain the self-reference criterion. Go to the library and find examples of product failures that might have been avoided through the application of the SRC.

5. Briefly explain the social research of Everett Rogers regarding diffusion of innovations, characteristics of innovations, and adopter categories. What significance does each concept have for global marketing?

6. Consider the equation $C = f(A, B, C, D, E, F, G)$, where C stands for consumption of soft drinks and D is the variable for cultural elements. How would this equation help a soft drink marketer understand demand for soft drinks in global markets?

BIBLIOGRAPHY

Books

Abegglen, James C., and George Stalk, Jr. *Kaisha, The Japanese Corporation.* New York: Basic Books, Inc., 1985.

Benedict, Ruth. *Patterns of Culture.* Boston: Houghton Mifflin, 1959.

———. *The Chrysanthemum and the Sword.* Rutland, Vt.: Charles E. Tuttle, 1972.

Dale, Peter N. *The Myth of Japanese Uniqueness.* New York: St. Martin's Press, 1986.

de Tocqueville, Alexis. *Democracy In America.* New York: New American Library, 1956.

Fields, George. *From Bonsai to Levis.* New York: Mentor, New American Library, 1983, 1985.

———. *Gucci on the Ginza.* Tokyo and New York: Kodansha International, 1989.

Hagen, E. *On the Theory of Social Change.* Homewood, Ill.: Dorsey Press, 1962.

Hall, Edward T. *Beyond Culture.* Garden City, N.Y.: Anchor Press Doubleday, 1976.

Hall, Edward T., and Mildred Reed Hall. *Hidden Differences: Doing Business with the Japanese.* New York: Doubleday, 1990.

Harris, Philip R., and Robert T. Moran. *Managing Cultural Differences: High Performance Strategies for a New World of Business*, 3d. ed. Houston: Gulf Publishing Company, 1991.

Hofstede, Geert. *Cultures and Organizations: Software of the Mind.* New York: McGraw-Hill, 1991.

McClelland, D. *The Achieving Society.* New York: Van Nostrand, 1961.

Moran, R., and W. Stripp. *Dynamics of Successful International Business Negotiations.* Houston: Gulf Publishing Company, 1991.

Reischauer, Edwin O. *The Japanese.* Cambridge, Mass.: The Belknap Press of Harvard University Press, 1977.

Articles

Clark, Terry. "International Marketing and National Character: A Review and Proposal for an Integrative Theory." *Journal of Marketing* 54, no. 4 (October 1990), pp. 66–79.

Dulek, Ronald E., John S. Fielden, and John S. Hill. "International Communications: An Executive Primer." *Business Horizons* 34, no. 1 (January/February 1991), pp. 20–25.

Fedor, Kenneth J., and William B. Werther, Jr. "Making Sense of Cultural Factors in International Alliances." *Organizational Dynamics* 24, no. 4 (Spring 1995), pp. 33–48.

Ford, John B., and Earl D. Honeycutt, Jr. "Japanese National Culture as a Basis for Understanding Japanese Business Practices." *Business Horizons* 35, no. 6 (November/December 1992), pp. 27–34.

Guptara, Prabhu. "Multicultural Aspects of Managing Multinationals." *Management Japan* 26, no. 1 (Spring 1993), pp. 7–14.

Hampden-Turner, Charless Tom Peters, and Jay Kaijumar. "The Boundaries of Business: Commentaries from the Experts." *Harvard Business Review* 69, no. 5 (September–October 1991), pp. 93–101.

Herbig, Paul A., and Hugh E. Kramer. "Do's and Don'ts of Cross-Cultural Negotiations." *Industrial Marketing Management* 21, no. 4 (November 1992), pp. 287–298.

Hill, David. "Negotiating with the Japanese: Tips for the Uninitiated—Learning from the Successes (and Mistakes) of Others." *East Asian Executive Reports* 15, no. 12 (Dec. 15, 1993), pp. 8, 14.

Hofstede, Geert, and Michael Harris Bond. "The Confucius Connection: From Cultural Roots to Economic Growth." *Organizational Dynamics* (Spring 1988), pp. 5–21.

Jacobs, Laurence, Charles Keown, Regimal Worthley, and Kyung-Il Ghymn. "Cross-Cultural Colour Comparisons—Global Marketers Beware!" *International Marketing Review* 8, no. 3 (1991), pp. 21–30.

Kvint, Vladimir. "Don't Give Up on Russia." *Harvard Business Review* 72, no. 2 (March–April 1994), pp. 62–74.

Lin, Carolyn A. "Cultural Differences in Message Strategies: A Comparison between American and Japanese Commercials." *Journal of Advertising Research* 33, no. 4 (July/August 1993), pp. 40–48.

Mintu, Alma, T., and Roger J. Calantone. "A Comparative Approach to International Marketing Negotiation." *Journal of Applied Business Research* 7, no. 4 (Fall 1991), pp. 90–97.

Miracle, Gorden E., Kyu Yeol Chang, and Charles R. Taylor. "Culture and Advertising Executions: A Comparison of Selected Characteristics of Korean and U.S. Television Commercials." *International Marketing Review* 9, no. 4 (1992), pp. 5–17.

Reardon, Kathleen Kelley, and Robert E. Spekman. "Starting Out Right: Negotiating Lessons for Domestic and Cross-Cultural Business Alliances." *Business Horizons* 37, no. 1 (January/February 1994), pp. 71–79.

Schneider, Susan C., and Arnoud de Meyer. "Interpreting and Responding to Strategic Issues: The Impact of National Culture." *Strategic Management Journal* 12, no. 4 (May 1991), pp. 307–320.

Stening, Bruce W., and Mitchell R. Hammer. "Cultural Baggage and the Adaption of Expatriate American and Japanese Managers." *Management International Review* 32, no. 1 (First Quarter 1992), pp. 77–89.

Sugiura, Hideo. "How Honda Localizes Its Global Strategy." *Sloan Management Review* 32, no. 1 (Fall 1990), pp. 77–82.

Tung, Rosalie L. "Handshakes across the Sea: Cross-Cultural Negotiating for Business Success." *Organizational Dynamics* 19, no. 3 (Winter 1991), pp. 30–40.

Usunier, Jean-Claude G. "Business Time Perception and National Cultures: A Comparative Survey." *Management International Review* 31, no. 3 (Third Quarter 1991), pp. 197–217.

*E*xecutives at Walt Disney Company found themselves working frantically to keep the new Euro Disney in Marne-la-Vallée, France, from drowning in a sea of red ink just two years after the theme park's April 1992 grand opening. Despite the fact that Euro Disney achieved target attendance objectives of 11 million guests in just over a year of operation, cumulative losses at the end of 1993 exceeded $1 billion, and the park was losing $1 million a day. The $4.4 billion, 5,000-acre park represented the second-largest construction project in Europe's history, after the building of the Chunnel, the tunnel beneath the English Channel connecting England and France. Unfortunately, a number of basic assumptions and forecasts made during the planning of Euro Disney turned out to be faulty or misguided.

For example, in their quest for European-style grandeur and perfection, Disney executives spared no expense in building the park and adjacent hotels. The plan called for some of the hotels to be sold at a handsome profit after the park was opened. Disney appointed Robert Fitzpatrick to be the head Euro Disney SCA; although American, he had traveled extensively in Europe, spoke French, and had a French wife. Disney anticipated that the French would, in fact, represent the park's core clientele. An effort was made to ensure that Euro Disney's cast members would be able to speak with guests in French. (Disney uses the words "cast member" and "guest" instead of "employee" and "visitor," respectively.) French food was widely available in restaurants, and characters such as Snow White and Pinocchio from European fairy tales were emphasized rather than Bambi or Dumbo.

Unfortunately, Disney planners failed to anticipate major changes in Europe's economy. The Paris real estate market slumped, making it impossible to sell any of the hotels. Moreover, Europe was heading into a recession at the time

the park opened, and the adult admission to the park, the equivalent of about $43, was out of sync with the times. To make matters worse, currency devaluations in Great Britain and Italy reduced the purchasing power of guests from those countries.

Unanticipated cultural issues compounded the financial problems. Many in the French establishment were vocal critics of the park. For example, the literary critic for the newspaper *Le Figaro* wrote, "Euro Disney is the very symbol of the process by which people's cultural standards are lowered and money becomes all-conquering." When Disney chairman Michael Eisner dismissed such criticism, he and others in his management team were accused of arrogance. Despite negative publicity in the local press, most of the guests were, indeed, from France. However, their numbers were lower than expected; visitors from Great Britain and Germany, taken together, outnumbered the French. Thus, although the hosts of various attractions such as Buffalo Bill's Wild West Show were prepared to speak to guests in French, on any given night the audience could be predominantly from Germany or Spain.

Other embarrassing cross-cultural blunders occurred and were widely, even gleefully, reported in the press. For example, prior to opening the park, Disney insisted that employees comply with a detailed written code regarding clothing, jewelry, and other aspects of personal appearance. Women were expected to wear "appropriate undergarments" and keep their fingernails short. Disney defended its move, noting that similar codes were used in its other parks. The goal was to ensure that guests receive the kind of experience associated with the Disney name. Despite such statements, the French considered the code to be an insult to French culture, individualism, and privacy.

There were other missteps as well. Disney had mistakenly assumed that European parents would readily take their kids out of school in midsemester for short family sojourns to a Disney theme park as Americans often do. Also, in designing hotel restaurants, Disney officials assumed that Europeans don't eat breakfast. The restaurants were scaled down as a result. In reality, most guests wanted to eat a morning meal of more than just a continental breakfast of coffee and pastry, resulting in long lines and disgruntled guests. A similar problem occurred inside the park at lunchtime. The United States is a nation of snackers, and the Disney team assumed that Europeans would be content to "graze" and then eat in shifts. It turned out that at 1 p.m. each day, the park's restaurants were inundated with hungry patrons. To make matters worse, the extension of Disney's standard "no alcohol" policy meant that wine was not available at Euro Disney. This, too, was deemed inappropriate in a country renowned for production and consumption of wine.

A number of changes were made to remedy some of these problems and revitalize Euro Disney. Fitzpatrick left his po-

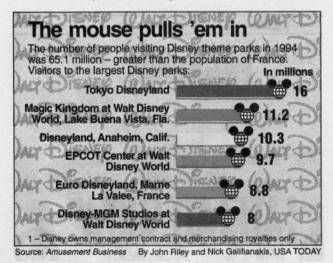

The mouse pulls 'em in

The number of people visiting Disney theme parks in 1994 was 65.1 million – greater than the population of France. Visitors to the largest Disney parks:

	In millions
Tokyo Disneyland	16
Magic Kingdom at Walt Disney World, Lake Buena Vista, Fla.	11.2
Disneyland, Anaheim, Calif.	10.3
EPCOT Center at Walt Disney World	9.7
Euro Disneyland, Marne La Valee, France	8.8
Disney-MGM Studios at Walt Disney World	8

1 – Disney owns management contract and merchandising royalties only

Source: *Amusement Business*   By John Riley and Nick Galifianakis, USA TODAY

(Copyright 1995, *USA TODAY*. Reprinted with permission.)

sition as head of Euro Disney and was replaced by a French national, Philippe Bourguignon. The theme park's official name was changed to Disneyland Paris. A new program called Challenge 1994 was implemented, with efficiency and economy as its hallmarks. To reduce costs, nearly 2,000 full- and part-time employees were dismissed. The number of different souvenirs in the park's shops—30,000 at first—was cut in half. In the hotel restaurants, the selection of food items was reduced from 5,400 to 2,000. Reductions in admission prices after 5 p.m. were introduced to encourage people to visit the park in the evening. Training programs for Euro Disney's cast members used the Mary Poppins character to promote a better service attitude. In an attempt to increase revenue, new flexible job descriptions allowed employees to shift from selling tickets in the morning to selling souvenirs in the afternoon. On September 30, 1995, when Euro Disney closed the books on its fiscal year, the park had finally turned a profit.

DISCUSSION QUESTIONS

1. What issues are at the heart of Euro Disney's problems? Why?
2. How could Disney have avoided some of the problems with the new theme park?
3. Do you predict that Disneyland Paris will continue to be profitable? Why or why not?

Sources: "A Disney Dress Code Chafes in the Land of Haute Couture," *The New York Times* (Dec. 25, 1991), pp. 1, 22.
Martin Parker, "Selling Mickey by the Pound," *New Statement and Policy* (Jan. 5, 1990), pp. 46–47.
Peter Gumbel and David J. Jefferson, "Disney Continues Drive to Expand World-Wide," *The Wall Street Journal* (Nov. 20, 1992), p. B5.
Roger Cohen, "When You Wish Upon a Deficit," *The New York Times* (July 18, 1993), Sec. pp. 2, 1, 18, 19.
Peter Gumbel, "Euro Disney Calls In Mary Poppins To Tidy Up Mess at Resort in France," *The Wall Street Journal* (Feb. 22, 1994), p. A13.
Peter Gumbel and Richard Turner, "Mouse Trap: Fans Like Euro Disney but Its Parent's Goofs Weigh the Park Down," *The Wall Street Journal* (Mar. 10, 1994), pp. A1, A12.

MARKETING AN INDUSTRIAL PRODUCT IN LATIN AMERICA

A Latin American republic had decided to modernize one of its communication networks at a cost of several million dollars. Because of its reputation for quality, the government approached U.S. company Y.

Company management, having been sounded out informally, considered the size of the order and decided to bypass its regular Latin American representative and send its sales manager instead. The following describes what took place.

The sales manager arrived and checked into the leading hotel. He immediately had some difficulty pinning down just who was his business contact. After several days without results, he called at the U.S. Embassy, where he found that the commercial attaché had the necessary up-to-the-minute information. The commercial attaché listened to his story. The attaché realized that the sales manager had already made a number of mistakes, but, figuring that the Latins were used to American blundering, he reasoned that all was not lost. The attaché informed the sales manager that the Minister of Communications was the key man and that whoever got the nod from him would get the contract. He also briefed the sales manager on methods of conducting business in Latin America and offered some pointers about dealing with the minister.

The attaché's advice ran somewhat as follows:

1. "You don't do business here the way you do in the States; it is necessary to spend much more time. You have to get to know your man, and vice versa."
2. "You must meet with him several times before you talk business. I will tell you at what point you can bring up the subject. Take your cues from me." (At this point, our American sales manager made a few observations to himself about "cookie pushers" and wondered how many payrolls had been met by the commercial attaché.)
3. "Take that price list and put it in your pocket. Don't get it out until I tell you to. Down here price is only one of many things taken into account before closing a deal. In the United States, your past experience will prompt you to act according to a certain set of principles, but many of these principles will not work here. Every time you feel the urge to act or to say something, look at me. Suppress the urge and take your cues from me. This is very important."
4. "Down here people like to do business with people who are somebody. 'Being somebody' means having written a book, lectured at a university, or developed your intellect in some way. The man you are going to see is a poet. He has published several volumes of poetry. Like many Latin Americans, he prizes poetry highly. You will find that he will spend a good deal of business time quoting his poetry to you, and he will take great pleasure in this."

5. "You will also note that the people here are very proud of their past and of their Spanish blood, but they are also exceedingly proud of their liberation from Spain and their independence. The fact that they are a democracy, that they are free, and also that they are no longer a colony is very, very important to them. They are warm and friendly and enthusiastic if they like you. If they don't, they are cold and withdrawn."
6. "And another thing, time down here means something different. It works in a different way. You know how it is back in the States when a certain type blurts out whatever is on his mind without waiting to see if the situation is right. He is considered an impatient bore and somewhat egocentric. Well, down here you have to wait much, much longer, and I really mean much, *much* longer, before you can begin to talk about the reason for your visit."
7. "There is another point I want to caution you about. At home, the one who sells takes the initiative. Here, *they* tell you when they are ready to do business. But most of all, don't discuss price until you are asked, and don't rush things."

The Pitch

The next day, the commercial attaché introduced the sales manager to the Minister of Communications. First, there was a long wait in the outer office while people went in and out. The sales manager looked at his watch, fidgeted, and finally asked whether the minister was really expecting him. The reply he received was scarcely reassuring, "Oh yes, he is expecting you but several things have come up that require his attention. Besides, one gets used to waiting down here." The sales manager irritably replied, "But doesn't he know I flew all the way down here from the United States to see him, and I have already spent over a week of my valuable time trying to find him?" "Yes, I know," was the answer, "but things just move much more slowly here."

At the end of about 30 minutes, the minister emerged from the office, greeted the commercial attaché with a double abrazo, throwing his arms around him and patting him on the back as though they were long-lost brothers. Now, turning and smiling, the minister extended his hand to the sales manager, who, by this time, was feeling rather miffed because he had been kept in the outer office so long.

After what seemed to be an all-too-short chat, the minister rose, suggesting a well-known cafe where they might meet for dinner the next evening. The sales manager had expected that, considering the nature of their business and the size of the order, he might be taken to the minister's home, not realizing that the Latin home is reserved for family and very close friends.

Until now, nothing at all had been said about the reason for the sales manager's visit, a fact which bothered him somewhat. The whole setup seemed wrong; nor did he like the idea of wasting another day in town. He had told the home office before he left that he would be gone for a week or ten days at most, and had made a mental note that he would clean this order up in three days and enjoy a few days in Acapulco or Mexico City. Now the week had already gone and he would be lucky if he made it home in ten days.

Voicing his misgivings to the commercial attaché, he wanted to know if the minister really meant business, and if he did, why could they not get together and talk about it? The commercial attaché by now was beginning to show the strain of having to constantly reassure the sales manager. Nevertheless, he tried again: "What you don't realize is that part of the time we were waiting, the minister was rearranging a very tight schedule so that he could spend tomorrow night with you. You see, down here they don't delegate responsibility the way we do in the States. They exercise much tighter control than we do. As a consequence, this man spends up to 15 hours a day at his desk. It may not look like it to you, but I assure you he really means business. He wants to give your company the order; if you play your cards right, you will get it."

The next evening was more of the same. Much conversation about food and music, about many people the sales manager had never heard of. They went to a night club, where the sales manager brightened up and began to think that perhaps he and the minister might have something in common after all. It bothered him, however, that the principal reason for his visit had not even been alluded to tangentially. But every time he started to talk about electronics, the commercial attaché would nudge him and proceed to change the subject.

The next meeting was to be held over morning coffee at a café. By now the sales manager was having difficulty hiding his impatience. To make matters worse, the minister had a mannerism that he did not like. When they talked, the minister was likely to put his hand on him; he would take hold of his arm and get so close that he nearly spit in his face. Consequently, the sales manager kept trying to dodge and put more distance between himself and the minister.

Following coffee, they walked in a nearby park. The minister expounded on the shrubs, the birds, and the beauties of nature. At one spot he stopped to point at a statue, and said: "There is a statue of the world's greatest hero, the liberator of mankind!" At this point, the worst happened, for the sales manager asked who the statue was of and, when told the name of a famous Latin American patriot, said, "I never heard of him," and walked on. After this meeting, the American sales manager was never able to see the minister again. The order went to a Swedish concern.

DISCUSSION QUESTIONS

1. What impression do you think the sales manager made on the minister?
2. How would you critique the quality of the communication between all parties in this case?
3. Is a high-context culture or a low-context culture at work in this case? Explain your answer.

Sources: Edward T. Hall, "The Silent Language in Overseas Business," *Harvard Business Review* (May–June 1960), pp. 93–96. Philip R. Harris and Robert T. Moran. *Managing Cultural Differences: High Performance Strategies for a New World of Business* 3d. ed. (Houston: Gulf Publishing Company, 1991), Chapter 14, "Doing Business With Latin Americans—Mexico, Central & South America," pp. 371–392. Paul Leppert, *Doing Business with Mexico* (Fremont, CA: Jain Publishing Company, 1995). Lawrence Tuller, *Doing Business in Latin America and the Caribbean* (Chicago: Amacom, 1993).

The Political, Legal, and Regulatory Environments

"Today the significance of geopolitical alliances and even of national boundaries is diminishing. Change is so profound that even the historical foundation of the world political order—the concept of the sovereign nation-state—is being shaken strenuously."

—Richard H. Stanley,
President, The Stanley
Foundation

While governments in many countries are studying environmental issues, particularly recycling, Germany already has a packaging ordinance that has shifted the cost burden for waste material disposal onto industry. The German government hopes that the law, known as *Verpackungsverordung*, will create a "closed-loop economy." The goal is to force manufacturers to eliminate nonessential materials that cannot be recycled and adopt other innovative approaches to producing and packaging products. Despite the costs associated with compliance, industry appears to be making significant progress toward creating the closed-loop economy. Companies are developing new packaging that uses less material and includes more recycled content. More than 1,900 non-German companies are currently participating in the program.

The German packaging law is just one example of the impact political, legal, and regulatory environments can have on marketing activities. Each of the world's national governments regulates trade and commerce with other countries and attempts to control the access of outside enterprises to national resources. Every country has its own unique legal and regulatory system that impacts the operations and activities of the global enterprise, including the global marketer's ability to address market opportunities. Laws and regulations constrain the cross-border movement of products, services, people, money, and know-how. The global marketer must attempt to comply with each set of national—and in some instances, regional—constraints. These efforts are hampered by the fact that laws and regulations are frequently ambiguous and continually changing.

In this chapter we consider the basic elements of the political, legal, and regulatory environments of global marketing, including the most pressing current issues and some suggested approaches for dealing with those issues. Some specific topics, such as rules for exporting and importing industrial and consumer products, standards for health and safety, and regulations regarding packaging, labeling, advertising, and promotion, are covered in later chapters devoted to individual marketing mix elements.

THE POLITICAL ENVIRONMENT

Global marketing activities take place within the political environment of governmental institutions, political parties, and organizations through which a country's people and rulers exercise power. Any company doing business outside its home country should carefully study the government structure in the target country and analyze salient issues arising from the political environment. These include the governing party's attitude toward sovereignty, political risk, taxes, the threat of equity dilution, and expropriation.

Nation-States and Sovereignty

Sovereignty can be defined as supreme and independent political authority. A century ago, U.S. Supreme Court Chief Justice Fuller said, "Every sovereign state is bound to respect the independence of every other sovereign state, and the courts in one country will not sit in judgment on the acts of government of another done within its territory." More recently, Richard Stanley, president of The Stanley Foundation, offered the following concise description:

> A sovereign state was considered free and independent. It regulated trade, managed the flow of people into and out of its boundaries, and exercised undivided jurisdiction over all persons and property within its territory. It had the right, authority, and ability to conduct its domestic affairs without outside interference and to use its international power and influence with full discretion.[1]

Government actions taken in the name of sovereignty occur in the context of two important criteria: a country's stage of development and the political and economic system in place in the country.

As outlined in Chapter 2, the economies of individual nations may be classified as industrialized, newly industrializing, or developing. Many governments in developing countries exercise control over their nations' economic development by passing protectionist laws and regulations. Their objective is to encourage economic development by protecting emerging or strategic industries. Conversely, when many nations reach advanced stages of economic development, their governments declare that (in theory, at least) any practice or policy that restrains free trade is illegal. Antitrust laws and regulations are established to promote fair competition. Advanced country laws often define and preserve a nation's social order; laws may extend to political, cultural, and even intellectual activities and social conduct. In France, for example, laws forbid the use of foreign words such as *le weekend* or *le marketing* in official documents. To counteract the exposure of its young citizens to American-style fast foods, the French National Council of Culinary Arts designed a course on French cuisine and "good taste" for elementary school students.[2]

Although, as noted in Chapter 2, most of the world's economies combine elements of command and market systems, the sovereign political power of a government in a predominantly command economy reaches quite far into the economic life of a country. By contrast, in a capitalist, market-oriented democracy, that power tends to be much more constrained. A current global phenomenon in both command and market structures is the trend toward privatization, that is, government actions designed to reduce direct governmental involvement in an economy as a supplier of goods and services. In essence, each act of privatization dilutes the command portion of a mixed economic system. The trend is clearly evident in Mexico, where, at one time, the government controlled over 1,000 "parastatals." Most of them have been sold, including the two Mexican airlines, mines, banks, and other enterprises. In 1990, the government of Mexico proceeded with plans to sell its 54 percent stake—valued at $5 to $6 billion—in the nation's telephone monopoly.

---

[1]See *Changing Concepts of Sovereignty: Can the United Nations Keep Pace?* (Muscatine, Iowa: The Stanley Foundation, 1992), p. 7.
[2]Judith Valente, "The Land of Cuisine Sees Taste Besieged by 'Le Big Mac,' " *The Wall Street Journal* (May 25, 1994), p. A1.

Privatization in Mexico and elsewhere is evidence that national governments are changing how they exercise sovereign power.

Some observers believe global market integration is eroding national economic sovereignty. Economic consultant Neal Soss notes, "The ultimate resource of a government is power, and we've seen repeatedly that the willpower of governments can be overcome by persistent attacks from the marketplace."[3] Is this a disturbing trend? If the issue is framed in terms of marketing, the concept of the exchange comes to the fore: Nations may be willing to give up sovereignty in return for something of value. If countries can increase their share of world trade and increase national income, perhaps they will be willing to cede some sovereignty. In Europe, the EU countries are giving up individual rights—to set their own product standards, for example—in exchange for improved market access.

Political Risk

Political risk—the risk of a change in government policy that would adversely impact a company's ability to operate effectively and profitably—can deter a company from investing abroad. When the perceived level of political risk is lower, a country is more likely to attract investment. The level of political risk is inversely proportional to a country's stage of economic development: All other things being equal, the less developed a country, the greater the political risk. The political risk of the Triad countries, for example, is quite limited as compared with a country in an earlier stage of development in Africa, Latin America, or Asia.

The recent rapid changes in Central and Eastern Europe and the dissolution of the Soviet Union clearly demonstrate the risks and opportunities resulting from political upheavals. The current political climate of Eastern Europe is characterized by a high degree of uncertainty. Having just thrown off the shackles of communism, this region is subject to substantial political risk; political forces could drastically change the business environment with little advance notice. Because of the potential for such volatility, businesspersons need to stay apprised of the formation and evolution of political parties in Russia, particularly those with an ultra-nationalist (i.e., anti-Western) orientation. While some companies have concluded that political risk in Russia and the CIS is too high to justify investment at present, diligent attention to risk assessment should be ongoing to determine when the risk has decreased to acceptable levels.[4]

Taxes

It is not uncommon for a company to be incorporated in one place, do business in another, and maintain its corporate headquarters in a third. This type of diverse geographical activity requires special attention to tax laws. Many companies make efforts to minimize their tax liability by shifting the location of income. For example, it has been estimated that tax avoidance by foreign companies doing business in the United States costs the U.S. government $3 billion each year in lost revenue. In one approach, called "earnings stripping," foreign companies reduce earnings by making loans to U.S. affiliates rather than using direct investment to finance U.S. activities. The U.S. subsidiary can deduct the interest it pays on such loans, thereby reducing its tax burden.

There are no universal international laws governing the levy of taxes on companies that do business across national boundaries. To provide fair treatment, many governments have negotiated bilateral tax treaties to provide tax credits for taxes paid abroad. The United States has dozens of such agreements in place. In 1977, the Organization for Economic Cooperation and Development (OECD) passed the Model Double Taxation Convention on Income and Capital to help guide countries in bilateral negotiations.

[3]Cited in Karen Pennar, "Is the Nation-State Obsolete in a Global Economy?" *Business Week* (July 17, 1995), p. 80.
[4]A thoughtful, detailed discussion of potential political scenarios in Russia can be found in Daniel Yergin and Thane Gustafson, *Russia 2010 and What It Means for the World* (New York: Vintage Books, 1995).

BEHIND THE SCENES

■ NATIONAL CONTROLS CREATE BARRIERS FOR GLOBAL MARKETING

Many countries attempt to exercise control over the transfer of goods, services, money, people, technology, and rights across their borders. Historically, an important control motive was economic: The goal was to generate revenue by levying tariffs and duties. Today, policymakers have additional motives for controlling cross-border flows, including protection of local industry and fostering the development of local enterprise. Such policies are known as protectionism, or economic nationalism.

Differing economic and political goals and different value systems are the primary reasons for protectionism. The barriers that exist between the United States and Cuba, for example, exist because of major differences between the values and objectives of the two countries. Many barriers based upon different political systems have come down with the end of the Cold War. However, barriers based upon different value systems continue. The world's farmers—be they Japanese, European, or American—are committed to getting as much protection as possible from their respective governments. Because of the political influence of the farm lobby in every country, and in spite of the efforts of trade negotiators to open up agricultural markets, controls on trade in agricultural products continue to distort economic efficiency. Such controls work against the driving forces of economic integration.

The price of protection can be very high, for two basic reasons. The first is the cost to consumers: When foreign producers are presented with barriers rather than free access to a market, the result is higher prices for domestic consumers and a reduction in their standard of living. The second cost is the impact on the competitiveness of domestic companies. Companies that are protected from competition may lack the motivation to create and sustain world-class competitive advantage. One of the greatest stimuli to competitiveness is the open market. When a company faces world competition it must figure out how to serve a niche market better than any company in the world, or it must figure out how to compete in face-to-face competition.

Generally, foreign companies are taxed by the host nation up to the level imposed in the home country, an approach that does not increase the total tax burden to the company.

Dilution of Equity Control[5]

Political pressure for national control of foreign-owned companies is a part of the environment of global business in lower-income countries. The foremost goal of national governance is to protect the right of national sovereignty, especially in all aspects of domestic business activity. Host-nation governments sometimes attempt to control ownership of foreign-owned companies operating within their borders. In underdeveloped countries, political pressures frequently cause companies to take in local partners.

Legislation that requires companies to dilute their equity is never popular in the boardroom, yet the consequences of such legislation are often surprisingly favorable. Dennis Encarnation and Sushil Vachani examined corporate responses to India's 1973 Foreign Exchange Regulation Act (FERA), which restricted foreign equity participation in local projects to 40 percent. The researchers identified four options available to companies faced with the threat of dilution:

1. Follow the law to the letter. Colgate Palmolive (India) took this course, became an Indian company, and maintained its dominant position in a growing market.
2. Leave the country. This was IBM's response after several years of negotiations. IBM concluded that it would lose more in shared control than it would gain from continued operations under the new rules.
3. Negotiate under the law. Some companies used the equity dilution requirement to raise funds for growth and diversification. In most cases this was done by issuing fresh equity to local investors. Ciba-Geigy increased its equity base 27

---

[5]This section is based on Dennis J. Encarnation and Sushil Vachani, "Foreign Ownership: When Hosts Change the Rules," *Harvard Business Review* (September–October 1985), pp. 152–160.

◼ THINKING "GREEN" IN GERMANY

As noted in the introduction to this chapter, one of the goals of Germany's packaging laws is to reduce packaging waste. Several types of materials are covered by the regulations. Transport packaging, including pallets and crates that retailers accumulate, constitute one-third of all packaging by weight. Most manufacturers pay a fee to retailers, who in turn arrange for the material to be collected and recycled. Paper, plastic, cardboard, and other so-called primary packaging account for about two-thirds of all German packaging. These materials—milk cartons, soup cans, and other packaging that consumers take home with them—fall under an ordinance known as Der Grüne Punkt ("the Green Dot").

The Green Dot Ordinance originally specified two separate mechanisms for reclaiming primary packaging. First, retailers were required to take back boxes, cartons, and similar primary packaging materials; the success of the "take back" effort depended on voluntary consumer cooperation. Second, the ordinance mandated that consumers pay refundable deposits on nonrefillable beverage, detergent, and paint containers. German legislators left the door open for alternative proposals, however; German businesses re-

sponded by establishing a nonprofit organization, Duales System Deutschland (DSD), that is responsible for collecting and recycling the materials. Retailers pay DSD a licensing fee in exchange for the right to display the green dot on packaging. This arrangement eliminates the need for consumers to pay deposits. DSD provides designated drop-off areas as well as curbside pickup for Green Dot packaging.

Response to the program was so enthusiastic that the amount of material collected exceeded Germany's recycling capacity. In its first two years alone, the Green Dot program reduced the amount of packaging waste by 600 million tons. Many retailers refuse to stock products that do not display the green dot. Ironically, the success of the Green Dot program has resulted in costs hundreds of millions of dollars more than DSD expected. As a result, fee structures have been adjusted to reflect the true costs of handling different types of packaging material. Notes Horst-Henning Wolf, head of BMW's recycling project, "There is no such thing as 'free of charge.' Someone always pays." Still, Clemens Stroetmann, Germany's state secretary for the environment, says, "It is indisputable that this is a sensible idea. Germany has no more room for landfills and almost no natural resources left, so we need the increasingly precious resources we have."

Sources: Gene Bylinsky, "Manufacturing for Reuse," *Fortune* (Feb. 6, 1995), pp. 102+.

Ada S. Rousso and Shvetank P. Shaw, "Packaging Taxes and Recycling Incentives: The German Green Dot Program," *National Tax Journal*, 47, no. 3 (September 1994), pp. 689–701.

Bette K. Fishbein, *Germany, Garbage, and the Green Dot: Challenging the Throwaway Society* (New York: Inform, 1994).

Ferdinand Protzman, "Germany's Push to Expand the Scope of Recycling," *The New York Times* (July 4, 1993), Sec. 3, p. 8.

Lester B. Lave, Chris Hendrickson, and Francis C. McMichael, "Recycling Decisions and Green." *ES&T*, Vol. 28, No. 1, pp. 18A–24A.

percent to $17.7 million, for example, and also negotiated an increase in production that doubled the sales of Hindustan Ciba-Geigy.

4. Take preemptive action. Some foreign firms initiated defensive strategies well before FERA's passage. These included proactive diversification to take advantage of investment incentives, gradual "Indianization" of the company, and continuously updating technology and maintaining export sales.

Encarnation and Vachani's study offers some important lessons.

1. First, look at the range of possibilities. There is no single best solution, and each company should look at itself and at the country situation to decide on strategy.

2. Companies should use the law to achieve their own objectives. The experiences of many companies demonstrate that by satisfying government demands, it is possible to take advantage of government concessions, subsidies, and market protection.

3. Anticipate government policy changes. Create a win-win situation. Companies that take initiatives are prepared to act when the opportunity arises. It takes time to implement changes; the sooner a company identifies possible government directions and initiatives, the sooner it will be in a position to propose its own plan to help the country achieve its objectives.

4. Listen to country managers. Country managers should be encouraged to anticipate government initiatives and to propose company strategy for taking advantage of opportunities created by government policy. Local managers often have the best understanding of the political environment. Experience suggests that they are in the best position to know when issues are arising and how to turn potential adversity into opportunity through creative responses.

The threat of equity dilution has caused some companies to operate in host nations via joint ventures or strategic alliances. These alternatives create special legal problems; there should be clauses in the joint venture or alliance agreement regarding its subsequent dissolution, as well as for the ownership of patents, trademarks, or technology realized from the joint effort.

Expropriation

The ultimate threat a government can pose toward a company is expropriation. *Expropriation* refers to governmental action to dispossess a company or investor. Compensation is generally provided to foreign investors, although not often in the "prompt, effective, and adequate" manner provided for by international standard. *Nationalization* occurs if ownership of the property or assets in question is transferred to the host government. If no compensation is provided, the action is referred to as *confiscation* (Root 1994, 154).

Short of outright expropriation or nationalization, the phrase "creeping expropriation" has been applied to severe limitations on economic activities of foreign firms in certain developing countries. These have included limitations on repatriation of profits, dividends, royalties, or technical assistance fees from local investments or technology arrangements. Other issues are increased local content requirements, quotas for hiring local nationals, price controls, and other restrictions affecting return on investment. Global companies have also suffered discriminatory tariffs and nontariff barriers that limit market entry of certain industrial and consumer goods, as well as discriminatory laws on patents and trademarks. Intellectual property restrictions have had the practical effect of eliminating or drastically reducing protection of pharmaceutical products.

For example, in the mid-1970s, Johnson & Johnson and other foreign investors had to submit to a host of regulations in India to retain majority equity positions in companies already established. Many of these rules were later copied in whole or in part by Malaysia, Indonesia, the Philippines, Nigeria, Brazil, and many other developing countries. By the late 1980s, after a "lost decade" in Latin America characterized by debt crises and low GNP growth, lawmakers reversed many of these restrictive and discriminatory laws. The goal was to again attract foreign direct investment and badly needed Western technology. The end of the Cold War and restructuring of political allegiances contributed significantly to these changes.

When governments expropriate foreign property, there are impediments to action to reclaim that property. For example, according to the U.S. Act of State Doctrine, if the government of a foreign state is involved in a specific act, the U.S. court will not get involved. Representatives of expropriated companies may seek recourse through arbitration at the World Bank Investment Dispute Settlement Center. It is also possible to buy expropriation insurance, either from a private company or the U.S. government's Overseas Private Investment Corporation (OPIC). The expropriation of copper companies operating in Chile in 1970–1971 shows the impact that companies can have on their own fate. Companies that strenuously resisted government efforts to introduce home-country nationals into the company management were expropriated outright; other companies that made genuine efforts to follow Chilean guidelines were allowed to remain under joint Chilean–U.S. management.

INTERNATIONAL LAW

International law may be defined as the rules and principles that nation-states consider binding upon themselves. International law pertains to property, trade, immigration, and other areas that have traditionally been under the jurisdiction of individual nations. International law applies only to the extent that countries are willing to assume all rights and obligations in these areas. The roots of modern international law can be traced back to the 17th century Peace of Westphalia. Early international law was concerned with waging war, establishing peace, and other political issues such as diplomatic recognition of new national entities and governments. While elaborate international rules gradually emerged—covering, for example, the status of neutral nations—the creation of laws governing commerce proceeded on a state-by-state basis in the 19th century. International law still has the function of upholding order, although in a broader sense than dealing with problems arising from war. At first, international law was essentially an amalgam of treaties, convenants, codes, and agreements. As trade grew among nations, order in commercial affairs assumed increasing importance. While the law had originally dealt only with nations as entities, a growing body of law rejected the idea that only states can be subject to international law.

Paralleling the expanding body of international case law in the 20th century, new international judiciary organizations have contributed to the creation of an established rule of international law. These include: the Permanent Court of International Justice (1920–1945); the International Court of Justice (ICJ), the judicial arm of the United Nations, founded in 1946; and the International Law Commission, established by the United States in 1947. Disputes arising between nations are issues of *public international law*, and they may be taken before the World Court, located in the Hague, or the ICJ. Article 38 of the ICJ Statute identifies recognized sources of public international law. As described in the supplemental documents to the United Nations Charter, article 38 of the ICJ Statute concerns international law:

> The Court, whose function is to decide in accordance with international law such disputes as are submitted to it, shall apply:
> a. international conventions, whether general or particular, establishing rules expressly recognized by the contesting states;
> b. international custom, as evidence of a general practice accepted as law;
> c. the general principles of law recognized by civilized nations;
> d. subject to the provisions of Article 59, judicial decisions and the teachings of the most highly qualified publicists of the various nations, as subsidiary means for the determination of rules of law.

What happens if a nation has allowed a case against it to be brought before the ICJ and then refuses to accept a judgment against it? The plaintiff nation can seek recourse through the United Nations Security Council, which can use its full range of powers to enforce the judgment.

Common Law versus Civil Law[6]

Private international law is the body of law that applies to disputes arising from commercial transactions between companies of different nations. As noted, laws governing commerce emerged gradually, leading to a major split in legal systems between various countries. The story of law in the Western World can be traced to two sources: Rome, from which the continental European civil law tradition originated, and English common law, from which the U.S. legal system originated. A civil-law country is one in which the legal system reflects the structural concepts and principles of the Roman Empire in the sixth century.

> For complex historical reasons, Roman law was received differently and at vastly different times in various regions of Europe, and in the nineteenth century each European country made a new start and adopted its own set of national private-law codes, for which the *Code Napoleon* of 1804 was the prototype. But the new national codes drew largely on Roman law in conceptual structure and substantive content. In civil-law countries, the codes in which private law is cast are formulated in broad general terms and

[6]Much of the material in this section is adapted from Kelso and Kelso, 1984, Chapter 2.

are thought of as completely comprehensive, that is, as the all-inclusive source of authority by reference to which every disputed case must be referred for decision.[7]

In common-law countries, on the other hand, many disputes are decided by reliance on the authority of past judicial decisions (cases). Although much of contemporary American and English law is legislative in origin, the law inferred from past judicial decisions is equal in importance to the law set down in codes. Common-law countries often rely on codification in certain areas—the U.S. Uniform Commercial Code is one example—but these codes are not the all-inclusive, systematic statements found in civil-law countries.

The Uniform Commercial Code, fully adopted by 49 U.S. states, codifies a body of specifically designed rules covering commercial conduct. (Louisiana has adopted parts of the UCC, but its laws are still heavily influenced by French civil code.) The host country's legal system—that is, common or civil law—directly affects the form a legal business entity will take. In common-law countries, companies are legally incorporated by state authority. In civil-law countries, companies are formed by contract between two or more parties who are fully liable for the actions of the company.

The United States, nine of Canada's ten provinces, and other former colonies with an Anglo-Saxon history founded their systems on common law. Historically, much of continental Europe was influenced by Roman law and, later, the Napoleonic Code. Asian countries are split: India, Pakistan, Malaysia, Singapore, and Hong Kong are common-law jurisdictions; Japan, Korea, Thailand, Indochina, Taiwan, Indonesia, and China are civil law jurisdictions. The legal systems in Scandanavia are mixed, displaying some civil-law attributes and some common-law attributes. Today, the majority of countries have legal systems based on civil law traditions.

As various countries in Eastern and Central Europe wrestle with establishing legal systems in the postcommunist era, a struggle of sorts has broken out, with consultants representing both common-law and civil-law countries trying to influence the process. In much of Central Europe, including Poland, Hungary, and the Czech Republic, the German tradition prevails. As a result, banks not only take deposits and make loans, but also engage in the buying and selling of securities. In Eastern Europe—particularly Russia—the United States has had greater influence. Germany has accused the United States of promoting a system so complex that it requires legions of lawyers. The United States has responded that the German system is outdated.[8] In any event, the constant stream of laws and decrees issued by President Boris Yeltsin creates an unpredictable, evolving legal environment. Specialized publications such as *The Russian and Commonwealth Business Law Report* are important resources for anyone doing business in Russia or the CIS.

Islamic Law[9]

The legal system in many Middle Eastern countries is identified with the laws of Islam, which are associated with "the one and only one God, the Almighty." In Islamic law, the *sharia* is a comprehensive code governing Moslem conduct in all areas of life, including business. The code is derived from two sources. First is the Koran, the Holy Book written in Arabic that is a record of the revelations made to the Prophet Mohammed by Allah. The second source is the Hadith, which is based on the life, sayings, and practices of Muhammad. The orders and instructions found in the Koran are analogous to code laws; the guidelines of the Hadith correspond to common law. Any Westerner doing business in the Middle East should have, at minimum, a rudimentary understanding of Islamic law and its implications for commercial activities.

---

[7]Harry Jones, "Our Uncommon Common Law," *Tennessee Law Review* 30 (1975), p. 447.
[8]Mark M. Nelson, "Two Styles of Business Vie in East Europe," *The Wall Street Journal* (Apr. 3, 1995), p. A14.
[9]This section is adapted from Mushtaq Luqmani, Ugur Yavas, and Zahir Quraeshi, "Advertising in Saudi Arabia: Content and Regulation," *International Marketing Review* 6, no. 1 (1989), pp. 61–63.

SIDESTEPPING LEGAL PROBLEMS: IMPORTANT BUSINESS ISSUES

Clearly, the global legal environment is very dynamic and complex. Therefore, the best course to follow is to get expert legal help. However, the astute, proactive marketer can do a great deal to prevent conflicts from arising in the first place, especially concerning issues such as establishment, jurisdiction, patents and trademarks, antitrust, licensing and trade secrets, and bribery.

Establishment

Under what conditions can trade be established? To transact business, citizens of one country must be assured that they will be treated fairly in another country. In Western Europe, for example, the creation of the Single Market now ensures that citizens from member nations get fair treatment with regard to business and economic activities carried out within the Common Market. The formulation of the governance rules for trade, business, and economic activities in the EU will provide additional substance to international law.

The United States has signed treaties of friendship, commerce, and navigation with more than 40 countries. These agreements provide U.S. citizens the right to nondiscriminatory treatment in trade, the reciprocal right to establish a business and, particularly, to invest. Commercial treaties provide one with the privilege, not the right, to engage in business activities in other than one's own country (Robock & Simmonds 1989, 171). This can create problems for business managers who may still be under the jurisdiction of their own laws even when they are out of their native country. U.S. citizens, for example, are forbidden by the Foreign Corrupt Practices Act to give bribes to an official of a foreign government or political party, even if bribes are customary for conducting business in that country.

Jurisdiction

Company personnel working abroad should understand the extent to which they are subject to the jurisdiction of host-country courts. Employees of foreign companies working in the United States must understand that courts have jurisdiction to the extent that the company can be demonstrated to be "doing business" in the state in which the court sits. The court may examine whether the foreign company maintains an office, solicits business, maintains bank accounts or other property, or has agents or other employees in the state in question. In a recent case, Revlon Inc. sued United Overseas Ltd. (UOL) in U.S. District Court for the Southern District of New York. Revlon charged the British company with breach of contract, contending that UOL had failed to purchase some specialty shampoos as agreed. UOL, claiming lack of jurisdiction, asked the court to dismiss the complaint. Revlon countered with the argument that UOL was, in fact, subject to the court's jurisdiction; Revlon cited the presence of a UOL sign above the entrance to the offices of a New York company in which UOL had a 50 percent ownership interest. The court denied UOL's motion to dismiss (Ortego & Kardisch 1994, C2).

Normally, all economic activity within a nation is governed by that nation's laws. But when a transaction crosses boundaries, which nation's laws apply? If the national laws of country Q pertaining to a simple export transaction differ from those of country P, which country's law applies to the export contract? And which apply to the letter of credit opened to finance the export transaction? The parties involved must reach agreement on such issues, and the nation whose law applies should be specified in a jurisdictional clause. There are several alternatives to choose from: the law of the domicile or principal place of business of one of the parties, the law of the place where the contract was entered, or the law of the place of performance of the contract. If a dispute arises under such a contract, it must be heard and determined by a neutral party such as a court or an arbitration panel. If the parties fail to specify which nation's laws apply, a fairly complex set of rules governing the "conflict of laws" will be applied by the court or arbitration tribunal. Sometimes the result will be determined with the help of "the scales of justice," with each party's criteria stacked on different sides of the scale.

Intellectual Property: Patents and Trademarks

Patents and trademarks that are protected in one country are not necessarily protected in another, so global marketers must ensure that patents and trademarks are registered in each country where business is conducted. In the United States, where patents, trademarks, and copyrights are registered with the Federal Patent Office, the patent holder retains all rights for the life of the patent even if the product is not produced or sold. Patent and trademark protection in the United States is very good, and U.S. law relies on the precedent of previously decided court cases for guidance. Table 5–1 ranks the 10 companies that received the most U.S. patents in 1994. Note that 6 of the 10 are Japanese companies.

Companies sometimes find ways to exploit loopholes or other unique opportunities offered by patent and trademark laws in individual nations. In France, designer Yves Saint Laurent was barred from marketing a new luxury perfume called Champagne because French laws only allow the name to be applied to sparkling wines produced in the Champagne region. Saint Laurent proceeded to launch Champagne in the United States, Great Britain, Germany, and Belgium; "Champagne" and other geographic names are not protected trademarks in the United States. In France, the perfume is sold without a name.[10] In 1992, Germany's Bayer AG received permission from Russia's patent office to register "aspirin" as a trademark in that country. Rival pharmaceutical companies, such as France's Laboratoire UPSA, were infuriated because the ruling meant that they would effectively be shut out of the Russian market of 150 million people. According to a spokesperson for the French company, "The word never should have been registered in the first place. It's a universally accepted generic name." The issue, which is considered critical to Russia's evolving system of patent law, is under appeal.[11]

Trademark and copyright infringement is a critical problem in global marketing and

| TABLE 5–1 | COMPANIES RECEIVING THE MOST U.S. PATENTS, 1994 |

Company	No. of Patents
1. IBM	1,298
2. Canon	1,096
3. Hitachi	976
4. General Electric	970
5. Mitsubishi Electric	970
6. Toshiba	968
7. NEC	897
8. Kodak	888
9. Motorola	837
10. Matsushita Electric	771

Source: U.S. Department of Commerce.

[10]Karla Vermeulen, "Champagne Perfume Launched in United States but Barred in France," *Wine Spectator* (Oct. 31, 1994), p. 9.
[11]Marya Fogel, "Bayer Trademarks the Word 'Aspirin' in Russia, Leaving Rivals Apoplectic," *The Wall Street Journal* (Oct. 29, 1993), p. A13.

one that can take a variety of forms. *Counterfeiting* is the unauthorized copying and production of a product. An *associative counterfeit*, or *imitation*, uses a product name that differs slightly from a well-known brand but is close enough that consumers will associate it with the genuine product. A third type of counterfeiting is *piracy*, the unauthorized publication or reproduction of copyrighted work. Piracy is particularly damaging to the entertainment and software industries; computer programs, videotapes, cassettes, and CDs are particularly easy to duplicate illegally. The case at the end of this chapter describes some of the problems companies encounter trying to enforce trademarks around the world.

Of the many separate international patent agreements, the most important is the International Convention for the Protection of Industrial Property. Also known as the Paris Union, the convention dates to 1883 and is now honored by nearly 100 countries. This treaty facilitates multicountry patent registrations by ensuring that, once a company files in a signatory country, it will be afforded a "right of priority" in other countries for one year from the date of the original filing. U.S. companies wishing to obtain foreign patent rights must apply to the Paris Union within one year of filing in the United States or risk a permanent loss of patent rights abroad (Root 1994, 113).

Two other treaties deserve mention. The Patent Cooperation Treaty (PCT) has 39 signatories, including Australia, Brazil, France, Germany, Japan, North Korea, South Korea, the Netherlands, Switzerland, the former Soviet Union, and the United States. The members constitute a union that provides certain technical services and cooperates in the filing, searching, and examination of patent applications in all member countries. On January 1, 1994, China became an official signatory of the PCT. The European Patent Office administers applications for the European Patent Convention, which is effective in the EU and Switzerland. An applicant can file a single patent application covering all of the convention states; the advantage is that the application will be subject to only one procedure of grant. While national patent laws remain effective under this system, approved patents are effective in all member countries for a period of 20 years from the filing date.

In the United States, trademarks are covered by the Trademark Act of 1946, also known as the Lanham Act. President Reagan signed the Trademark Law Revision Act into law in November 1988. The law makes it easier for companies to register new trademarks; as a result, the number of filings has increased dramatically. Table 5–2 shows that foreign trademark filings in the United States have increased dramatically since 1988. The U.S. Patent and Trademark Office has focused efforts recently on improving the patent environment in Japan. After years of discussion, the United States and Japan have agreed to make changes in their respective systems; Japan has promised to speed up patent examinations, eliminate challenges to patent submissions, and allow patent applications to be filed in English. Effective June 7, 1995, in accordance with GATT, new U.S. patents are

TABLE 5–2	FOREIGN COMPANY TRADEMARK FILINGS IN THE UNITED STATES FOR SELECTED COUNTRIES		
Country	**1988**	**1990**	**1994**
Belgium	111	200	177
Canada	2,447	3,701	4,330
Germany	1,400	1,846	1,912
Hong Kong	168	285	396
Israel	45	130	242
Japan	1,010	2,412	1,642
Mexico	126	244	435
South Korea	131	200	376
U.K.	1,392	2,265	2,129

Source: U.S. Patent and Trademark Office.

granted for a period of 20 years from the filing date. Previously, patents had been valid for a 17-year term effective after being granted. Thus, U.S. patent laws now harmonize with those in the EU as well as Japan. Even with the changes, however, patents in Japan are narrower than those in the United States. As a result, companies such as Caterpillar have been unable to protect critical innovations in Japan because products very similar to those made by U.S. companies can be patented without fear of infringement.[12]

Antitrust

Antitrust laws in the United States and other countries are designed to combat restrictive business practices and to encourage competition. The Sherman Act of 1890 prohibits certain restrictive business practices, including fixing prices, limiting production, allocating markets, or any other scheme designed to limit or avoid competition. The law applies to foreign companies conducting business in the United States and extends to the activities of U.S. companies outside U.S. boundaries as well.

U.S. antitrust laws are a legacy of the 19th century "trust-busting" era and are intended to maintain free competition by limiting the concentration of economic power. Similar laws are taking on increasing importance outside the United States as well. In Europe, the European Commission prohibits agreements and practices that prevent, restrict, and distort competition. The interstate trade clause of the Treaty of Rome applies to trade with third countries, so that a company must be aware of the conduct of its affiliates. The Commission also exempts certain cartels from Articles 85 and 86 of the Treaty in an effort to encourage the growth of important businesses. The intent is to allow European companies to compete on an equal footing with Japan and the United States.

In some instances, individual country laws in Europe apply to specific marketing mix elements. For example, some countries permit selective or exclusive product distribution. However, European Community law can take precedence. In one case, Consten, a French company, had exclusive French rights to import and distribute consumer electronics products from the German Grundig company. Consten sued another French firm, charging the latter with bringing "parallel imports" into France illegally. That is, Consten charged that the competitor bought Grundig products from various foreign suppliers without Consten's knowledge and was selling them in France. Although Consten's complaint was upheld by two French courts, the Paris Court of Appeals suspended the judgment pending a ruling by the European Commission on whether the Grundig–Consten arrangement violated Articles 85 and 86 of the Treaty of Rome. The Commission ruled against Consten on the grounds that "territorial protection proved to be particularly damaging to the realization of the Common Market" (Vagts 1986, 285–291).

A major antitrust case involving a U.S.-based global company pitted the European Community against IBM during the 1970s and 1980s. IBM was the European market leader in mainframe computers such as the powerful System/370, with 55 percent unit share in 1983. The company's operations were especially strong in Great Britain, France, and West Germany. IBM was charged with four specific violations of Article 86: failure to supply competitors with timely information about interfaces; selling computers without including memory capacity in the price; selling computers without software necessary to operate them; and refusing to supply IBM software to companies that used competing brands of computers. Coincidentally, the U.S. Justice Department had also filed an antitrust case against IBM in the United States with the aim of breaking up the company (the suit was dropped in 1982 after 14 years of litigation). The EC action, however, was an attempt to force IBM to disclose proprietary designs and other trade secrets of benefit to European companies that were IBM suppliers.[13] More recently, Microsoft was the object of antitrust investigations in both the United States and Europe.

---

[12]John Carey, "Inching toward a Border-less Patent," *Business Week* (Sept. 5, 1994), p. 35.
[13]David Sanger, "I.B.M.'s European Accord: Concessions End a Decade of Debate," *The New York Times* (Aug. 3, 1984), p. 38.

Licensing and Trade Secrets

Licensing is a contractual agreement in which a licensor allows a licensee to use patents, trademarks, trade secrets, technology, or other intangible assets in return for royalty payments or other forms of compensation. U.S. laws do not regulate the licensing process per se as do technology transfer laws in the European Union, Australia, Japan, and many developing countries. The duration of the licensing agreement and the amount of royalties a company can receive are considered a matter of commercial negotiation between licensor and licensee, and there are no government restrictions on remittances of royalties abroad. Important considerations in licensing include analysis of what assets a firm may offer for license, how to price the assets, and whether to grant only the right to "make" the product or to grant the rights to "use" and to "sell" the product as well. The right to sublicense is another important issue. As with distribution agreements, decisions must also be made regarding exclusive or nonexclusive arrangements and the size of the licensee's territory.

To prevent the licensor from using the licensed technology to compete directly with the licensee, the latter may try to limit the licensee to selling only in its home country. The licensor may also seek to contractually bind the licensee to discontinue use of the technology after the contract has expired. In practice, host-government laws, and even U.S. antitrust laws, may make such agreements impossible to obtain. Licensing is a potentially dangerous action: It may be instrumental in creating a competitor. Therefore, licensors should be careful to ensure that their own competitive position remains advantageous. This requires constant innovation.

As noted, licensing agreements can come under antitrust scrutiny. In one recent case, Bayer AG granted an exclusive patent license for a new household insecticide to S.C. Johnson & Sons. The German firm's decision to license was based in part on the time required for EPA approval, which had stretched to three years. Bayer decided it made better business sense to let the U.S. firm deal with regulatory authorities in return for a 5 percent royalty on sales. However, a class action suit was filed against the companies alleging that the licensing deal would allow Johnson to monopolize the $450 million home insecticide market. Then the U.S. Justice Department stepped in, calling the licensing agreement anticompetitive. In a statement, Anne Bingaman, head of the Justice Department's antitrust unit, said, "The cozy arrangement that Bayer and Johnson maintained is unacceptable in a highly concentrated market." Bayer agreed to offer licenses to any interested company on better terms than the original contract with Johnson. Johnson agreed to notify the U.S. government of any future pending exclusive licensing agreements for household insecticides. If Bayer is party to any such agreements, the Justice Department has the right to veto them. Not surprisingly, the reaction from the legal community has been negative. One Washington lawyer who specializes in intellectual property law noted that the case "really attacks traditional licensing practices." As Melvin Jager, president of the Licensing Executives Society, explained, "An exclusive license is a very valuable tool to promote intellectual property and get it out into the marketplace."[14]

What happens if a licensee gains knowledge of the licensor's trade secrets? *Trade secrets* are confidential information or knowledge that has commercial value and is not in the public domain, for which steps have been taken to keep it secret. Trade secrets include manufacturing processes, formulas, designs, and customer lists. To prevent disclosure, the licensing of unpatented trade secrets should be linked to confidentiality contracts with each employee who has access to the protected information. In the United States, trade secrets are protected by state law rather than federal statute; most states have adopted the Uniform Trade Secrets Act (UTSA). U.S. law provides trade secret liability against

[14]Brigid McMenamin, "Eroding Patent Rights," *Forbes* (Oct. 24, 1994), p. 92.

third parties that obtain confidential information through an intermediary. Remedies include damages and other forms of relief.

The 1990s have seen widespread improvements in laws pertaining to trade secrets. Several countries have recently adopted trade secret statutes for the first time. Mexico's first statute protecting trade secrets became effective on June 28, 1991; China's first trade secret law took effect December 1, 1993. In both countries, the new laws were part of broader revisions of intellectual property laws. Japan and South Korea have also recently amended their intellectual property laws to include trade secrets. Many countries in Central and Eastern Europe have also enacted laws to protect trade secrets. When NAFTA became effective on January 1, 1994, it marked the first international trade agreement with provisions for protecting trade secrets. This milestone was quickly followed by the Agreement on Trade-Related Aspects of Intellectual Property Rights (TRIPs) that resulted from the Uruguay Round of GATT negotiations. The TRIPs agreement requires signatory countries to protect against acquisition, disclosure, or use of trade secrets "in a manner contrary to honest commercial practices" (Katsch & Dierks 1995, C12). Despite these formal legal developments, in practice, enforcement is the key issue. Companies transferring trade secrets across borders should apprise themselves not only of the existence of legal protection but also of the risks associated with lax enforcement.

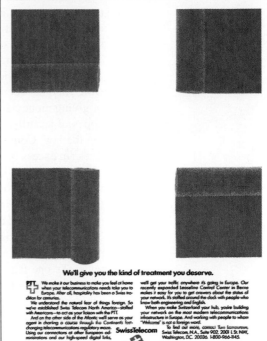

Swiss Telecom promises to help customers deal with a tangle of telecommunications regulations in the European Union. (Courtesy of Swiss Telecom North America.)

Bribery and Corruption: Legal and Ethical Issues[15]

History does not record a burst of international outrage when Charles M. Schwab, head of Bethlehem Steel at the beginning of the 20th century, presented a $200,000 diamond and pearl necklace to the mistress of Czar Alexander III's nephew. In return for that consideration, Bethlehem Steel won the contract to supply the rails for the Trans-Siberian railroad. Today, in the post-Soviet era, Western companies are again being lured by emerging opportunities in Eastern Europe. Here, as in the Middle East and other parts of the world, they are finding that bribery is a way of life, and that corruption is widespread. U.S. companies in particular are constrained in their responses to such a situation by U.S. government policies of the post-Watergate age.

The Foreign Corrupt Practices Act (FCPA) is a legacy of the Watergate scandal during Richard Nixon's presidency. In the course of his investigation, the Watergate special prosecutor discovered that more than 300 U.S. companies had made undisclosed payments to foreign officials totaling hundreds of millions of dollars. The act was unanimously passed by Congress and signed into law by President Jimmy Carter on December 17, 1977. Administered by the Department of Justice and the Securities and Exchange Commission, the act was concerned with disclosure and prohibition. The disclosure part of the act required publicly held companies to institute internal accounting controls that would record all transactions. The prohibition part made it a crime for U.S. corporations to bribe an official of a foreign government or political party to obtain or retain business. Payments to third parties were also prohibited when

---

[15]Much of the material in this section is adapted from Pines 1994.

the company had reason to believe part or all of the money would be channeled to foreign officials.

The U.S. business community immediately began lobbying for changes to the act, complaining that the statute was too vague and so broad in scope that it threatened to severely curtail U.S. business activities abroad. Amendments to the statutes were signed into law by Ronald Reagan in 1988 as part of the Omnibus Trade and Competitiveness Act. Among the changes were exclusions for "grease" payments to low-level officials to cut red tape and expedite "routine governmental actions" such as clearing shipments through customs, securing permits, or getting airport passport clearance to leave a country.

Although several well-known U.S. companies have pleaded guilty to violations of the antibribery provisions, enforcement of the act has generally been lax. A total of 23 cases were filed between 1977 and 1988. In a recent case, a business executive was convicted of giving money and honeymoon airplane tickets to a Nigerian government official in the hopes of securing a contract (Albright & Won 1993). There are stiff penalties for violating the law: Convictions carry severe jail sentences (in excess of 1 to 5 years) and heavy fines (in excess of $1 million). Fines cannot be paid or reimbursed by the company, under the theory that individuals commit such crimes. It has also been made clear that the law will not let a person do indirectly (e.g., through an "agent," joint venture partner, or other third party) what it prohibits directly.

Some critics of the FCPA decry it as a regrettable display of moral imperialism. At issue is the extraterritorial sovereignty of U.S. law. It is wrong, according to these critics, to impose U.S. laws, standards, values, and mores on American companies and citizens worldwide. As one legal expert points out, however, this criticism has one fundamental flaw: There is no nation in which the letter of the law condones bribery of government officials. Thus, the standard set by the FCPA is shared by other nations (Pines 1994, 205).

A second criticism of the FCPA is that it puts U.S. companies in a difficult position vis-à-vis foreign competitors, especially those in Japan and Europe. Several opinion polls and surveys of the business community have revealed the widespread perception that the act adversely affects U.S. businesses overseas. Some academic researchers have concluded that the FCPA has not negatively affected the export performance of U.S. industry. However, a commerce department report prepared with the help of U.S. intelligence services indicated that in 1994 alone, bribes offered by non-U.S. companies were a factor in 100 business deals valued at $45 billion. Foreign companies prevailed in 80 percent of those deals.[16]

When companies operate abroad in the absence of home-country legal constraints, they face a continuum of choices concerning company ethics. At one extreme, they can maintain home-country ethics worldwide with absolutely no adjustment or adaptation to local practice. At the other extreme, they can abandon any attempt to maintain company ethics and adapt entirely to local conditions and circumstances as they are perceived by company managers in each local environment. Between these extremes, one approach that companies may select is to utilize varying degrees of extension of home-country ethics. Alternatively, they may adapt in varying degrees to local customs and practices.

The existence of bribery as a fact of life in world markets will not change because it is condemned by the U.S. Congress. What should a U.S. company do if competitors are willing to offer a bribe? Two alternative courses of action are possible. One is to ignore bribery and act as if it does not exist. The other is to recognize the existence of bribery and evaluate its effect on the customer's purchase decision as if it were just another element of the marketing mix.

The overall value of a company's offer must be as good as, or better than, the competitor's overall offering, bribe included. It may be possible to offer a lower price, a bet-

THE POLITICAL, LEGAL, AND
REGULATORY ENVIRONMENTS

[16]Amy Borrus, "Inside the World of Greased Palms," *Business Week* (Nov. 6, 1995), pp. 36–38.

ter product, better distribution, or better advertising to offset the value added by the bribe. The best line of defense is to have a product that is clearly superior to that of the competition. In such a case a bribe should not sway the purchase decision. Alternatively, clear superiority in service and in local representation may tip the scales.

CONFLICT RESOLUTION, DISPUTE SETTLEMENT, AND LITIGATION

The degree of legal cooperation and harmony in the EU is unique, and stems in part from the existence of civil law as a common bond. Other regional organizations have made far less progress toward harmonization. Countries vary in their approach toward conflict resolution. Table 5–3 shows the number of practicing lawyers per 100,000 in population in selected countries. The United States has more lawyers than any other country in the world and is arguably the most litigious nation on earth. In part, this is a reflection of the low-context nature of American culture, a spirit of confrontational competitiveness, and the absence of one important principle of civil law: The loser pays all court costs for all parties.

Conflicts will inevitably arise in business anywhere, especially when different cultures come together to buy, sell, establish joint ventures, compete, and cooperate in global markets. For U.S. companies, the dispute with a foreign party is frequently in the home-country jurisdiction. The issue can be litigated in the United States, where the company and its attorneys might be said to enjoy "home court" advantage. Litigation in foreign courts, however, becomes vastly more complex. This is due in part to differences in language, legal systems, currencies, and traditional business customs and patterns. In addition, problems arise from differences in procedures relating to discovery. In essence, *discovery* is the process of obtaining evidence to prove claims and determining which evidence may be admissible in which countries under which conditions. A further complication is the fact that judgments handed down in courts in another country may not be enforceable in the home country. For all these reasons, many companies prefer to pursue arbitration before proceeding to litigate.

Alternatives to Litigation for Dispute Settlement

Extrajudicial, alternative approaches often provide a faster, easier, and less expensive way to resolve commercial disputes than litigation. Indeed, alternative approaches have a tradition that is centuries old. Chambers of trade and commerce first began to

| TABLE 5–3 | LAWYERS: AN INTERNATIONAL COMPARISON, 1990 |

Country	Lawyers per 100,000 People
USA	227.0
Germany	199.4
Australia	157.2
U.K.	121.4
France	99.2
Hungary	73.9
Japan	11.4
South Korea	4.7

Source: Shoza Ota and Kahei Rokumoto, "Issues of the Lawyer Population: Japan," *Case Western Reserve Journal of International Law* (Spring 1993).

hear and resolve disputes as trade developed between different tribes or nations. Settlement of modern trade disputes takes various forms and occurs in many locations. Formal arbitration is one means of settling international business disputes outside the courtroom. Arbitration generally involves a hearing of all parties before a three-member panel. The result is usually a decision that the parties agree in advance to abide by. Courts of arbitration have long existed in London and Zurich. For decades, business arbitration has also been promoted through the Paris-based International Chamber of Commerce (ICC). The ICC recently modernized some of its older rules. However, because it is the best-known international business organization, it has the biggest backlog of cases. Thus, the ICC has gained a reputation for being slower, more expensive, and more cumbersome than some alternatives. The United Nations Convention on the Recognition and Enforcement of Foreign Arbitral Awards (also known as the New York Convention) has 107 signatory countries, including China. The New York Convention facilitates arbitration when disputes arise, and signatories agree to uphold international arbitration awards.

Some firms and lawyers inexperienced in the practice of international commercial arbitration have used standard "boilerplate" arbitration clauses in contracts that cover merger, severability, choice of law, and other issues. U.S. companies may stipulate that the arbitration take place in the United States; companies in other countries may choose Paris. Arbitration can be a minefield due to the number of issues that must be addressed. For example, if the parties to a patent licensing agreement agree in the arbitration clause that the validity of the patent cannot be contested, such a provision may not be enforceable in some countries. And which country's laws will be used as the standard for invalidity? Pursuing such an issue on a country-by-country basis would be inordinately time-consuming. In addition, there is the issue of acceptance; by law, U.S. courts must accept an arbitrator's decision in patent disputes; in other countries, however, there is no general rule of acceptance. To reduce delays relating to such issues, one expert suggests drafting arbitration clauses with as much specificity as possible. To the extent possible, for example, patent policies in various countries should be addressed; arbitration clauses may also include provision that all foreign patent issues will be judged according to the standard of home-country law. Another provision could forbid the parties from commencing separate legal actions in other countries. The goal is to help the arbitration tribunal zero in on the express intentions of the parties.[17]

As U.S. involvement in global commerce grew dramatically during the post–World War II period, the American Arbitration Association (AAA) became recognized as a very effective institution within which to resolve disputes. Each year, the AAA uses mediation to help resolve thousands of disputes. The AAA has entered into cooperation agreements with the ICC and other global organizations to promote the use of alternative dispute resolution methods; it serves as the agent to administer arbitrations in the United States under ICC auspices. In 1992, the AAA signed a cooperation agreement with China's Beijing Conciliation Center.

Other agencies for settling disputes include the Swedish Arbitration Institute of the Stockholm Chamber of Commerce. This agency frequently administered disputes between Western and Socialist countries, and has gained credibility for its evenhanded administration. Other alternatives have proliferated in recent years. In addition to those mentioned, active centers for arbitration exist in Vancouver, Hong Kong, Cairo, Kuala Lumpur, Singapore, Buenos Aires, Bogota, and Mexico City. A World Arbitration Institute was established in New York; in the United Kingdom, the Advisory, Conciliation and

---

[17]Bruce Londa, "An Agreement to Arbitrate Disputes Isn't the Same in Every Language," *Brandweek* (Sept. 26, 1994), p. 18. See also John M. Allen, Jr., and Bruce G. Merritt, "Drafters of Arbitration Clauses Face a Variety of Unforeseen Perils," *National Law Journal* 17, no. 33 (Apr. 17, 1995), pp. C6–C7.

Arbitration Service (ACAS) has achieved great success at handling industrial disputes. An International Council for Commercial Arbitration (ICCA) was established to coordinate the far-flung activities of arbitration organizations. The ICCA meets in different locations around the world every four years.

The United Nations Conference on International Trade Law (UNCITRAL) has also been a significant force in the area of arbitration. UNCITRAL rules have become more or less standard, as many of the organizations named previously have adopted them with some modifications. Many developing countries, for example, long held prejudices against the ICC, AAA, and other developed country organizations. Representatives of developing nations assumed that such organizations would be biased in favor of multinational corporations. Developing nations insisted on settlement in national courts, which was unacceptable to the multinational firms. This was especially true in Latin America, where the Calvo Doctrine required disputes arising with foreign investors to be resolved in national courts under national laws. The growing influence of the ICCA and UNCITRAL rules, coupled with the proliferation of regional arbitration centers, have contributed to changing attitudes in developing countries and resulted in the increased use of arbitration around the world.

THE REGULATORY ENVIRONMENT

The regulatory environment of global marketing consists of a variety of agencies, both governmental and nongovernmental, that enforce laws or set guidelines for conducting business. A number of regulatory agencies (sometimes referred to as "international economic organizations," or IEOs) are identified in Table 5–4; they address a wide range of marketing issues, including the following: price control, valuation of imports and exports, trade practices, labeling, food and drug regulations, employment conditions, collective bargaining, advertising content, and competitive practices. The decisions of IEOs are binding and are carried out by the member states (Voitovich 1990).

The influence of regulatory agencies is pervasive, and an understanding of how they operate is essential to protect business interests and advance new programs. For example, in the United States, the International Trade Commission administers the Tariff Act of 1930. Section 337 prohibits "unfair methods of competition" if the effect of this competition is to destroy or substantially injure an industry. To seek relief or defend access to the U.S. market if challenged under this act, a company should retain the services of specialized legal talent, supported by technical expertise in patents and in global marketing. It is useful to call on the assistance of home-country diplomatic staff to assist and support the effort to obtain a favorable ruling.

Regional Economic Organizations: The EU Example

The global regulatory environment includes a number of governmental and nongovernmental regional and international economic organizations. A partial listing is shown in Table 5–4. The overall importance of regional organizations such as the European Union (EU) was discussed in Chapter 3. The legal dimensions are important, however, and will be briefly mentioned here. The Treaty of Rome established the European Community (EC), the precursor to the European Union. The treaty contains hundreds of articles, several of which are directly applicable to global companies and global marketers. Articles 30–36 establish the general policy referred to as "Free Flow of Goods, People, Capital and Technology" among the member states. Articles 85–86 contain competition rules, as amended by various directives of the EU Commission. These articles and directives constitute community law, which is somewhat analogous to U.S. federal law.

The European Court of Justice, based in Luxembourg, hears disputes that arise among the 15 EU member nations on trade issues such as mergers, monopolies, and trade barri-

TABLE 5–4　LIST OF INTERNATIONAL ECONOMIC ORGANIZATIONS

Abbreviation	Full Name
APPA	African Petroleum Producers' Association
ATPC	Association of Tin Producing Countries
CAEU	Council of Arab Economic Unity
CARICOM	Caribbean Community
CCASG	Cooperation Council for the Arab States of the Gulf
EC	European Community (formerly the EEC, now the EU)
ECCAS	Economic Community of Central African States
EEC	European Economic Community (replaced by EC and, subsequently, EU)
EEA	European Economic Area
EFTA	European Free Trade Association
EU	European Union (formerly the EC)
FAO	Food and Agricultural Organization
GATT	General Agreement on Tariffs and Trade (now the WTO)
IBRD	International Bank for Reconstruction and Development (World Bank)
ICAO	International Civil Aviation Organization
IDA	International Development Agency
IEA	International Energy Agency
IFC	International Finance Corporation
IMF	International Monetary Fund
ITPA	International Tea Promotion Association
MIGA	Multilateral Investment Guarantee Agency
OECD	Organization for Economic Cooperation and Development
OPEC	Organization of Petroleum Exporting Countries
UNCTAD	United Nations Conference on Trade and Development
UNIDO	United Nations Industrial Development Organization
UNITAR	United Nations Institute for Training and Research
WACU	West African Customs Union
WHO	World Health Organization
WMO	World Meteorological Organization
WTO	World Trade Organization (successor to GATT)

Source: Adapted from Voitovich 1990.

ers. The Court is also empowered to resolve conflicts between national law and EU law. In most cases, the latter supersedes national laws of individual European countries. Marketers must be aware, however, that national laws should always be consulted. National laws may be *more* strict than community law, especially in such areas as competition and antitrust. Community law is intended to harmonize, to the extent possible, national laws to promote the purposes defined in Articles 30–36. The goal is to bring the "lax" laws of some member states up to designated minimum standards. However, more restrictive positions may still exist in some national laws.

A recent case from Germany helps illustrate the point. A West German court ruled that Pronuptia, a French wedding dressmaker and retailer, couldn't require its German franchisees to buy all their goods from the parent company. Pronuptia took its case to the European Court of Appeals, the EU's main forum for arbitration that makes recommendations to the Court of Justice. Had the German court's ruling been upheld on antitrust grounds, *all* franchisors doing business in Europe—including such well-known companies as McDonald's, Midas Muffler, and PepsiCo's Kentucky Fried Chicken and Pizza Hut units—would have been stripped of their ability to operate U.S.-style franchises in Europe. Key policies, including the right to dictate corporate logos, store designs, and outside suppliers, would have been nullified. After intense lobbying by the International Franchising Association, the Court issued a ruling that was generally favorable to franchisors. Still, the new regulations prohibit franchisors from requiring franchisees to sell specific branded products from outside suppliers. Thus, while McDonald's retains the right to designate suppliers for commodities such as meat and potatoes, it can't force franchisees to conform to the U.S. policy that calls for selling only Coca-Cola beverages at its restaurants.[18]

The 1987 Single European Act amended the Treaty of Rome and provided strong impetus for the creation of a Single Market by December 31, 1992. While technically the target was not completely met, approximately 85 percent of the new recommendations were implemented into national law by most member states by the target date, resulting in substantial harmonization.

The World Trade Organization (WTO)

The World Trade Organization (formerly GATT) is the regulatory body with the broadest impact on global marketing activities. More than 120 governments signed the GATT treaty in an effort to create order and predictability in international trade relations. The WTO is based on three principles. The first concerns *nondiscrimination*: Each member country must treat the trade of all other member countries equally. The second principle is *open markets*, which are encouraged by the WTO through a prohibition of all forms of protection except customs tariffs. *Fair trade* is the third principle, which prohibits export subsidies on manufactured products and limits the use of export subsidies on primary products. In reality, none of these principles is fully realized as yet, although much progress was made during the Uruguay Round. Nontariff barriers, protection of intellectual property rights, and government subsidies remain major stumbling blocks.

[18]Philip Revzin, "European Bureaucrats Are Writing the Rules Americans Live By," *The Wall Street Journal* (May 17, 1989), pp. A1, A12.

SUMMARY

The political environment of global marketing is the set of governmental institutions, political parties, and organizations that are the expression of the people in the nations of the world. In particular, anyone engaged in global marketing should have an overall understanding of the importance of sovereignty to national governments. The political environment varies from country to country, and risk assessment is crucial. It is also important to understand a particular government's actions with respect to taxes, dilution of equity control, and expropriation. The legal environment consists of laws, courts, attorneys, legal customs, and practices. The countries of the world can be broadly categorized in terms of common-law system or civil-law system. The United States and Canada are common-law countries; most other countries are based on civil law. Some of the most important legal issues pertain to establishment, jurisdiction, patents and trademarks, licensing, antitrust, and bribery. When legal conflicts arise, companies can pursue the matter in court or use arbitration. The regulatory environment consists of agencies, both governmental and nongovernmental, that enforce laws or set guidelines for conducting business. Global marketing activities can be affected by a number of international or regional economic organizations; in Europe, for example, the European Union makes laws governing member states. The World Trade Organization will have broad impact on global marketing activities in the years to come. Although these three environments are complex, astute marketers plan ahead to avoid situations that might result in conflict, misunderstanding, or outright violation of national laws.

DISCUSSION QUESTIONS

1. What is "sovereignty"? Why is it an important consideration in the political environment of global marketing?
2. Briefly describe some of the differences between the legal environment of a country that embraces common law and one that observes civil law.
3. Global marketers can avoid legal conflicts by understanding the reasons conflicts arise in the first place.

Identify and describe several legal issues that relate to global commerce.

4. You are an American traveling on business in the Middle East. As you are leaving country X, the passport control officer at the airport tells you there will be a passport "processing" delay of 12 hours. You explain that your plane leaves in 30 minutes, and the official suggests that a contribution of $50 would probably speed things up. If you comply with the suggestion, have you violated U.S. law? Explain.

5. "See you in court" is one way to respond when legal issues arise. What other approaches are possible?

6. Should a company operating internationally adhere to a single standard of conduct, or should it adapt to local conditions? Why?

BIBLIOGRAPHY
Books

Chukwumerige, Okezie. *Choice of Law in International Commercial Arbitration.* Westport, Conn.: Quorum Books, 1994.

Fishbein, Bette K. *Germany, Garbage, and the Green Dot: Challenging the Throwaway Society.* New York: Inform, 1994.

Jacoby, Neil H., Peter Nehmenkis, and Richard Eells. *Bribery and Extortion in World Business.* New York: MacMillan, 1977.

Kelso, R. Randall, and Charles D. Kelso. *Studying Law: An Introduction.* St. Paul, Minn.: West Publishing, 1984.

Ohmae, Kenichi. *The Borderless World.* New York: Harper Perennial, 1991.

Robock, Stefan H., and Kenneth Simmonds. *International Business and Multinational Enterprises.* Homewood, Ill.: Irwin, 1989.

Root, Franklin R. *Entry Strategies for International Markets.* New York: Lexington Books, 1994.

Samuels, Barbara C. *Managing Risk in Developing Countries: National Demands and Multinational Response.* Princeton, N.J.: Princeton University Press, 1990.

Slomanson, William R. *Fundamental Perspectives on International Law.* St. Paul, Minn.: West Publishing, 1990.

Sohn, Louis B., ed. *Basic Documents of the United Nations.* New York: Foundations Press, 1968.

Vagts, Detlev. *Transnational Business Problems.* Mineola, N.Y.: Foundations Press, 1986.

Articles

Akhter, Syed H., and Yusuf A. Choudhry. "Forced Withdrawal from a Country Market: Managing Political Risk." *Business Horizons* (May–June 1993), pp. 47–54.

Albright, Katherine, and Grace Won. "Foreign Corrupt Practices Act." *American Criminal Law Review* 30 (Spring 1993), p. 787.

Bagley, Jennifer M., Stephanie S. Glickman, and Elizabeth B. Wyatt. "Intellectual Property." *American Criminal Law Review* 32, no. 2 (Winter 1995), pp. 457–479.

Bradley, David G. "Managing against Expropriation." *Harvard Business Review* (July–August 1977).

Braithwaite, John. "Transnational Regulation of the Pharmaceutical Industry." *Annals of the American Academy of Political & Social Science* 525 (January 1993), pp. 12–30.

Cleveland, Harlan. "Rethinking International Governance." *The Futurist* 25, no. 3 (May 1991), p. 204.

Gillespie, Kate. "Middle East Response to the U.S. Foreign Corrupt Practices Act." *California Management Review*, Vol. 29 (1987).

Graham, John L. "The Foreign Corrupt Practices Act: A New Perspective." *Journal of International Business Studies* (Winter 1984), pp. 107–121.

Hawkins, Robert B., Norman Mintz, and Michael Provissoiero. "Government Takeovers of U.S. Foreign Affiliates." *Journal of International Business Studies* (Spring 1976).

Kaikati, Jack, and Wayne A. Label. "The Foreign Antibribery Law: Friend or Foe?" *Columbia Journal of World Business* (Spring 1980), pp. 46–51.

Katsh, Salem M., and Michael P. Dierks. "Globally, Trade Secrets Laws Are All Over the Map." *National Law Journal* 17, no. 36 (May 8, 1995), pp. C12–C14.

Nash, Marian Leich. "Contemporary Practice of the United States Relating to International Law." *American Journal of International Law* 88, no. 4 (October 1994), pp. 719–765.

Ortego, Joseph, and Josh Kardisch. "Foreign Companies Can Limit the Risk of Being Subject to U.S. Courts." *National Law Journal* 17, no. 3 (Sept. 19, 1994), pp. C2+.

Pines, Daniel. "Amending the Foreign Corrupt Practices Act To Include a Private Right of Action." *California Law Review* (January 1994), pp. 185–229.

Rodgers, Frank A. "The War Is Won, but Peace Is Not." *Vital Speeches of the Day* (May 14, 1991), pp. 430–432.

Roessler, Frieder. "The Scope, Limits and Function of the GATT Legal System." *World Economy* (September 1985), pp. 287–298.

Spero, Donald M. "Patent Protection or Piracy: A CEO Views Japan." *Harvard Business Review* (September–October 1990), pp. 58–62.

Vernon, Raymond. "The World Trade Organization: A New Stage in International Trade and Development." *Harvard International Law Journal* 36, no. 2 (Spring 1995), pp. 329–340.

Vogel, David. "The Globalization of Business Ethics: Why America Remains Distinctive." *California Management Review* 35, no. 1 (Fall 1992), pp. 30–49.

Voitovich, Sergei A. "Normative Acts of International Economic Organizations in International Law Making." *Journal of World Trade* (Aug. 4, 1990), pp. 21–38.

*I*n many parts of the world, particularly Southeast Asia, well-known global companies are frequently the victims of trademark violations and product counterfeiting. The scale of the problem is so vast that it costs companies billions of dollars in lost sales each year. In South Korea, for example, chewing gum called Juicy & Fresh has the same yellow wrapper, black lettering, and package shape as Wrigley's Juicy Fruit. Other imitations in South Korea include Tie detergent in orange boxes that resemble Procter & Gamble's Tide. Italy's Benetton S.p.A. has also been imitated: A Korean fashion retailer sells brightly colored casual clothes in a chain of stores called Paselton. The store's logo features the same typeface as Benetton's, including the distinctive design of the letter "t." Similar products abound in China, where consumers can pick up a tube of "Cologate" toothpaste in a bright red box and "Kongalu" Corn Strips whose box is emblazoned with the distinctive signature of Kellogg's cereals. The issue extends far beyond consumer packaged goods, however; Chrysler Corporation has even discovered sport utility vehicles on the streets of Beijing that were nearly identical to Jeep Cherokees.

The garment and fashion industries have also been hard hit. Levi Strauss has faced an uphill battle trying to stop counterfeit sales of its popular jeans in more than 30 countries. The problem is especially acute in Europe, where Levis are a status symbol. The company can't keep up with demand, so counterfeiters take up the slack. The fake jeans are such close copies that, a Levi spokesperson says, "The typical consumer would not be able to detect that they are buying counterfeits." After a few washings, however, the bogus jeans deteriorate quickly; colors fade, seams come apart, and rivets begin to rust. Many of the counterfeits now come from China, where factories produce jeans for about

$5 per pair and sell them to people who falsely claim to be legitimate Levi representatives. To disguise their Asian origins, the jeans may be shipped through the Panama Canal and then across the Mexican border; jeans bound for Europe are often shipped overland through the former Soviet bloc countries.

There are various explanations for why counterfeiting and piracy are so widespread. The reasons are partially cultural. One U.S. trade official noted that, in South Korea, there is the notion that "the thoughts of one man should benefit all." Another reason is the "hands-off" policy of local law enforcement agencies. Even though the South Korean government passed trademark, patent, and copyright protection laws in the late 1980s, enforcement is lax. Steven M. Weinberg, an attorney who is also executive editor of a newsletter on trademarks, says, "It's one thing to have a law on the books. It's another thing to have cultural values and views change in order to accommodate, particularly, the interests of people who are from outside the country or region."

The issue of intellectual property rights is especially problematic in China. In 1994, the Clinton administration considered launching an investigation to determine whether U.S. companies had been hurt by piracy and trademark infringements. Under Section 301 of the U.S. trade act, findings of harm could lead to trade sanctions. To head off such confrontation, China has passed stringent laws on counterfeiting. According to lawyer David Buxbaum, "It's quite clear that in terms of a comprehensive legal framework, China has done an excellent job." However, he notes, "It's only beginning to dawn on people that copyrights and trademarks are property." A lot is at stake: The International Intellectual Property Alliance estimates that Chinese counterfeiting of copyrighted material alone costs U.S. companies $800 million annually; the figure would be much higher if trademark and patent infringement were added.

In fall 1994, Universal Pictures, Twentieth Century Fox, and six other U.S. movie companies filed a joint suit against a Chinese video distributor. The filmmakers asked the Beijing Intermediate Peoples Court to stop distributors from selling illegal laser disc copies of "Rocky," "The Godfather," and other hit movies. Each of the eight studios joining in the suit asked for 50,000 yuan ($5,882) in damages as well as legal costs. The suit was filed in the midst of ongoing talks between U.S. and Chinese trade officials. The United States wanted the Chinese government to close the more than two dozen CD plants that produce pirated music and movie discs. The piracy issue threatened to diminish China's chances of joining the World Trade Organization.

There are other ways to deal with the video piracy problem. The Motion Picture Export Association of America hired Richard O'Neill, a Green Beret and Vietnam veteran. Using guerrilla tactics, O'Neill raided hundreds of South Korea's

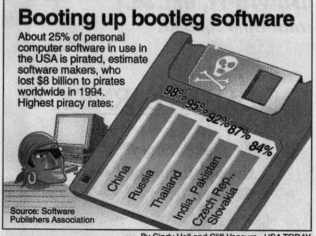

Booting up bootleg software

About 25% of personal computer software in use in the USA is pirated, estimate software makers, who lost $8 billion to pirates worldwide in 1994.
Highest piracy rates:

China 98%
Russia 95%
Thailand 92%
India, Pakistan 87%
Czech Rep., Slovakia 84%

Source: Software Publishers Association

By Cindy Hall and Cliff Vancura , USA TODAY

30,000 video stores. His efforts have helped reduce the number of stores selling pirated videos from 85 percent to below 20 percent.

DISCUSSION QUESTIONS

1. What legal woes might befall a businessperson from a common-law country hoping to protect intellectual property in a civil-law country?
2. Identify the different types of trademark infringement described in the case.
3. What would you do in South Korea if you were Benetton?
4. If you were an executive responsible for protecting your company's intellectual property rights, what would you do to address the piracy problem in China? in Africa and the Middle East? in the CIS? in Southeast Asia?

Sources: Marcus W. Brauchli, "Chinese Blatantly Copy Trademarks of Foreigners," *The Wall Street Journal* (June 20, 1994), pp. B1, B5.
Junda Woo and Richard Borsuk, "Asian Trademark Litigation Continues," *The Wall Street Journal* (Feb. 16, 1994), p. B10.
Marcus W. Brauchli, "Fake CDs Are a Growth Industry in China," *The Wall Street Journal* (Feb. 11, 1994), pp. B1, B10.
Damon Darlin, "Copycat Crime: Video Pirates Abroad Face a Swashbuckler Worthy of Hollywood," *The Wall Street Journal* (Jan. 28, 1992), pp. A1, A8.
Thomas C. O'Donnell and Elizabeth Weiner, "The Counterfeit Trade," *Business Week* (Dec. 16, 1985), pp. 64+.
Damon Darlin, "Where Trademarks Are Up for Grabs," *The Wall Street Journal* (Dec. 5, 1989), pp. B1, B8.
Carrie Dolan, "Levi Tries To Round Up Counterfeiters," *The Wall Street Journal* (Feb. 19, 1992), p. B1.
Joshua Levine and Nancy Rotenier, "Seller Beware," *Forbes* (Oct. 25, 1993), pp. 170, 174.

The Global Financial Environment and Foreign Exchange Decisions

"Imagine if the Texas dollar suddenly devalued massively against the New York dollar. That's approximately what we have in Europe today."[1]

—George Jolles, President, Union of Textile Industries, France

On December 20, 1994, the Bank of Mexico embarked on a course of action that sent shock waves around the world. A combination of circumstances, including a $28 billion current-account deficit, dwindling reserves, the murder of presidential candidate Donaldo Colosio, and eroding investor confidence, forced the Bank of Mexico to devalue the peso. The Clinton administration quickly arranged $20 billion in loans and loan guarantees, secured in part by some of Mexico's $7 billion in annual oil export revenues. Opponents of NAFTA—notably Ross Perot—seized the opportunity to denounce both the loans and the trade agreement itself. The devalued peso, critics predicted, would make U.S. exports to Mexico more expensive and reduce the $2 billion trade surplus that the United States enjoys with Mexico. NAFTA opponents also noted that increased imports of Mexican goods into the United States would constitute a new threat to U.S. jobs.

In the months following the peso crisis, the global financial environment and foreign exchange were widely covered in the news media. Several related themes were reinforced in the reporting: Foreign exchange makes it possible to do business across the boundary of a national currency. *However, foreign exchange is an aspect of global marketing that involves certain financial risks, decisions, and activities that are completely different than those facing a domestic marketer.* Moreover, those risks can be even higher in an emerging market such as Mexico. When a company conducts business within a single country, with domestic customers and suppliers paying in the domestic currency, there is no exchange risk. All prices, payments, receipts, assets, and liabilities are in the national currency. However, when a company conducts business across boundaries it is thrust into the turbulent world of exchange risk. Foreign exchange issues can directly impact a company's market opportunities, financial resources, and pricing strategy. Therefore, every student of global marketing should understand the financial considerations of global marketing decisions. While Chapter 2 described the economic environment *within* the countries and regions of the world, this chapter explores the institutions, factors, and forces that affect trade relations and marketing opportunities *between* countries. To be sure, the

---

[1]Thomas Kamm, "Monetary Chaos Precedes Europe's Single Market," *The Wall Street Journal* (July 28, 1995), p. A6.

driving force of the successful company must be marketing. However, marketing personnel must maintain a high level of global awareness by monitoring and understanding their company's financial environment—especially foreign exchange—if marketing objectives are to be achieved.

FOREIGN EXCHANGE

What is foreign exchange? Is the U.S. dollar foreign exchange? Is the French franc foreign exchange? The answer, of course, is that it depends. If the U.S. dollar is used in the United States, it is not foreign exchange. If it is traded for another currency, it becomes, in that transaction, foreign exchange. Similarly, the French franc in France, or for that matter anywhere else in the world, is still a French franc. It becomes foreign exchange when it is traded for any other currency and is held by foreign persons or institutions.

What is the foreign exchange market? All the people and institutions who buy and sell currencies make up the foreign exchange market. Tourists who sell dollars to a Russian on the street in Moscow have created a retail foreign exchange market right at the moment of the transaction. This is a real foreign exchange market, but it is retail and represents a minute percentage of the total annual trade in foreign exchange. In terms of volume, the "real" foreign exchange market is a wholesale market between banks and institutional foreign exchange traders. Professional traders at trading desks are in contact with each other via telephone and on-line, real-time monitors that track transactions and bid and offer prices for various currencies. To meet customer requirements, traders engage in transactions with their counterparts in banks and foreign exchange trading houses around the world. Foreign exchange trading takes place during normal business hours in every world time zone, with the result that foreign exchange trading activity is being conducted on a 24-hour basis every day of the year. When traders in Europe conclude their work at the end of a business day, currency trading prices for the following working day will be established in the United States, then Australia and Japan while they are sleeping.

Traders at Citicorp participate in the trillion-dollar currency market. (George Rose, Gamma-Liaison.)

The principal players in the foreign exchange market are major banks such as Citicorp, Bankers Trust, and J.P. Morgan, whose trading activities comprise nearly 80 percent of foreign exchange transactions. Other players include: the International Monetary Market (IMM) of the Chicago Mercantile Exchange, which trades currency futures; the London International Financial Futures Exchange (LIFFE); and the Philadelphia Stock Exchange (PSE), which specializes in currency options.

The volume of trading in the foreign exchange market is enormous. According to studies by the Bank for International Settlements, daily turnover exceeds $1 trillion, making foreign exchange the world's largest financial market. This figure is so huge it is hard to get a handle on. One trillion dollars represents one-seventh of the United States' GDP, one-fourth of Japan's GDP, and half of Germany's GDP. In any two weeks, foreign exchange traders do as much business as importers and exporters of goods and services do in a year. Put differently, it takes the New York Stock Exchange two months to ring up a dollar volume equivalent to the value of foreign exchange transactions recorded in a single day.[2] The dollar is the most heavily traded currency, accounting for 80 percent of transactions. In 1995, London was the leading foreign exchange market, with 30 percent of average daily foreign exchange turnover (see Table 6–1). Each market has its own focus: London is dollars per pound sterling (£), New York is dollars per Deutsche mark (DM), and Tokyo is dollars per yen (¥).

In sum, the foreign exchange market consists literally of a buyer's and a seller's market where currencies are traded for both spot and future delivery on a continuous basis. The *spot* market is for immediate delivery; the market for future delivery is called the *forward* market. This is a true market, where prices are based on the combined forces of supply and demand that come into play at the moment of any transaction. A currency in this market is worth what people are willing to pay for it; put another way, it is worth what people are prepared to sell it for. It is a commodity.

Managed Dirty Float with SDRs

Today's global financial system can be described as a "managed dirty float with SDRs." What does this mean? *Managed* refers to the specific use of fiscal and monetary policy by governments to influence exchange rates. The peso devaluation in Mexico is a recent example; devaluation occurs when a country's central bank decrees a reduction in the value of the local currency against other currencies. *Dirty* refers to the fact that, besides currency traders, central banks buy and sell currencies in the foreign exchange market in an effort to influence exchange rates. Such interventions may be intended to dampen the fluctuations in foreign exchange rates, or they may represent attempts to influence the actual exchange rate over the short and medium term. In 1995, news stories with headlines such as "Dollar Surges as Central Banks Intervene" were quite common; they reflected the widely publicized efforts of the central banks of Germany, Japan, and the United States to prop up the dollar. Finally, *float* refers to the system of fluctuating exchange rates. As currency trader Andrew Krieger notes, in this system currencies are "up for auction," with rates "floating" or adjusting in the foreign exchange market subject to all the forces of supply and demand. In other words, the buying and selling activities of currency traders partially determine a specific currency's value on a given day.

Special drawing rights (SDRs) were created by the International Monetary Fund (IMF) to supplement the dollar and gold as reserves. The IMF's lendable resources are largely derived from quotas paid by each member in accordance with economic size. SDRs create liquidity and thus facilitate trade among nations; the SDR Department of the IMF allocates reserves to member countries according to a formula which takes into account

TABLE 6–1

LEADING FOREIGN EXCHANGE MARKETS BY PERCENT OF AVERAGE DAILY TURNOVER, 1995

City	Percent
London	30
New York	16
Tokyo	10
Singapore	7
Hong Kong	6
Zurich	5
Frankfurt	5
Paris	4

Source: Bank for International Settlements.

[2]George Anders, "Answers to Commonly Asked Questions about Currency Trading in a Wild Week," *The Wall Street Journal* (Sept. 17, 1992), p. A7.

BEHIND THE SCENES

■ A BRIEF HISTORY OF THE INTERNATIONAL FINANCIAL SYSTEM, 1944–1971

*I*n 1944, finance ministers and other representatives of the Allied powers met at Bretton Woods, New Hampshire, to create an international financial framework that would encourage and support postwar reconstruction and economic growth. In addition to providing for currency convertibility, the architects of the postwar system intended to stimulate trade and investment via orderly adjustment of currency values. Their goal was to maintain ongoing equilibrium in exchange rate values. British economist John Maynard Keynes advocated the creation of a single international currency, the bancor. The value of world currencies would be established relative to this new international reserve asset, the supply of which would expand in tandem with global economic development. Keynes envisioned the bancor as replacing gold (supplies of which were relatively fixed) and supplementing each nation's individual currency.

Lord Keynes' specific recommendation concerning the bancor was not adopted; the world was apparently not yet ready for "paper gold." There would indeed be a new international reserve asset, but it would consist of gold and various currencies. However, Lord Keynes' broader vision—the creation of a world lending organization—was realized. Two new institutions comprised the cornerstone for the new financial system that emerged from Bretton Woods. The International Bank for Reconstruction and Development (or IBRD, also known as the World Bank, with headquarters in Washington, D.C.) was chartered to promote economic development and reconstruction by making loans to war-torn countries. The International Monetary Fund (IMF) was chartered to oversee the management of the international financial system and make currency adjustments. The main elements of the system were: fixed or pegged rates for all currencies; tight bands of fluctuation around the pegged rates; a dollar that was both defined in terms of its gold value and exchangeable for gold; and controlled adjustment of fixed exchange values.

In 1971, the old system collapsed under the weight of U.S. balance-of-payments deficits. As production increased throughout Europe, U.S. imports increased. The result was an accumulation of dollars in exporting countries, and official reserves held by central banks around the world far exceeded the U.S. supply of gold (which, as Keynes had warned, was relatively fixed). Meanwhile, the United States was waging a very expensive war in Vietnam. It was clear that the United States—with some $11 billion of gold in official reserves and a liability of over $47 billion to foreign holders of official dollars—could not honor its commitment to redeem official dollars for gold. President Nixon announced that the United States was unilaterally withdrawing its promise to redeem official dollars for gold. This signaled the collapse of the old system of reserve currencies, and the world moved to a new system: a foreign exchange market of floating exchange rates.

---

such factors as share of gross world product and share of world trade. Participants in the IMF with a balance-of-payments need can use SDRs to obtain currency from other participants designated by the fund. The value of one SDR represents a weighted average of five currencies: the U.S. dollar, the German mark, the French franc, the Japanese yen, and the British pound. In fact, some countries—Burma, Jordan, and Libya, for example—pursue an exchange rate policy of pegging the value of their currencies to SDRs.

As of August 31, 1994, quotas totaling 144.9 billion SDRs (equivalent to $210 billon) had been paid by IMF members; 29.7 billion SDRs have, in turn, been lent. Besides mandating the use of SDRs to help countries deal with balance-of-payments deficits, the IMF also permits a variety of additional uses among participants including settlement of financial obligations, swaps, donations, and security for performance of financial obligations.

Today, 179 countries—including many from the former communist bloc—are IMF members; all 15 republics of the former Soviet Union have recently joined. The IMF oversees the operation of the international monetary system; exercises surveillance over the exchange rate policies of members; monitors developments in the field of international liquidity and manages the SDR system; provides temporary balance-of-payments assistance to members in external difficulties; and performs a variety of other functions, including technical assistance, designed to promote effective cooperation in international financial relations.

TABLE 6–2 EXCHANGE RISKS AND GAINS IN FOREIGN TRANSACTIONS

Foreign Exchange Rates	$1,000,000 Contract		DM 1.750,000 Contract	
	U.S. Seller Receives	German Buyer Pays	U.S. Seller Receives	German Buyer Pays
DM2 = $1	$1,000,000	DM2,000,000	$875,000	DM1,750,000
DM1.75 = $1	$1,000,000	DM1,750,000	$1,000,000	DM1,750,000
DM1.5 = $1	$1,000,000	DM1,500,000	$1,160,000	DM1,750,000
DM1.25 = $1	$1,000,000	DM1,250,000	$1,400,000	DM1,750,000

Foreign Exchange Market Dynamics

Some of the trading in the foreign exchange market represents supply and demand of each of the world's traded currencies derived from actual trade in goods and services. To the extent that a country sells more than it buys, there will be a greater demand for its currency and a tendency for it to *appreciate* in value. The strength of the Japanese yen in the mid-1990s is a case in point. If the foreign exchange market were influenced only by purchases and sales to settle accounts for merchandise and services trade, it would be a fairly simple matter to forecast foreign exchange rates. However, short- and long-term capital flows and speculative purchases and sales are a major source of supply and demand for foreign exchange. Short-term capital is sensitive to interest rates, long-term capital to return expectations, and both are sensitive to perceptions of risk. Today, currency speculators appear to wield more power to move currency markets than government central bankers.[3]

Table 6–2 shows how fluctuating currency values can affect financial risk, depending on the terms of payment specified in the contract. Suppose that, at the time a deal is made, the exchange rate is DM1.75 = $1. What happens to a U.S. exporter if the dollar strengthens against the mark—trades at DM2 = $1—and the contract specifies payment in dollars? What happens if the dollar weakens (DM1.5 = $1)? Conversely, what if the German buyer contracts to pay in marks rather than dollars?

FORECASTING FOREIGN EXCHANGE RATES

Foreign exchange rate forecasting is a tricky task largely because there are a multitude of factors and forces which determine rates, and many of these factors and forces are not quantifiable. Any forecast of exchange rates is necessarily a combination of economic analysis and judgment.

Purchasing Power Parity

An important economic fundamental that must be considered in forecasting foreign exchange rates is purchasing power parity (PPP). This concept was first introduced in Chapter 2 in the context of adjustments in per capita income statistics to reflect a nation's standard of living. Purchasing power parity can also be used to explain how, from an equilibrium exchange rate, a change in the relationship between domestic and foreign price levels will require an adjustment in the currency exchange rate to offset the difference in price levels. According to PPP, if inflation causes price levels to go up in country A while prices remain the same in country B, the currency in country A should be devalued relative to the currency in country B. In plain English, PPP means that, if country A experiences inflation while country B does not, one unit of currency A will no longer buy the

---

[3]This issue has also been widely covered in the business press. For example, see Randall Smith, "The Big Casino: How Currency Traders Play for High Stakes against Central Banks," *The Wall Street Journal* (Sept. 18, 1992), pp. A1, A5.

goods and services in equivalent amounts in country B unless the currency in country B increases in value by the same percentage amount as the rate of inflation in country A.

The lower a country's rate of inflation as compared to the world's, the greater will be the PPP effect. If prices in local currency rise faster or more slowly than prices in the rest of the world, an equal adjustment of the exchange value of the currency in the opposite direction will restore equilibrium to correct relative price levels. For example, if a Mercedes 190 carries a sticker price of DM40,000 and the exchange rate is DM2 = $1, the equivalent price will be $20,000 in the United States. If there is a zero rate of inflation in Germany and a 20 percent rate of inflation in the United States, an exchange rate of DM1.67 = $1 would restore equilibrium. This is because inflation would result in the Mercedes 190 costing $24,000 ($20,000 × 120 percent—the U.S. rate of inflation); and at the new exchange rate, $24,000 is still equal to DM40,000 (24,000 × 1.67 = 40,000). Since the U.S. money supply would have expanded by 20 percent, the new exchange value of the DM would ensure that 1.2 units of the depreciated dollar would buy the same amount of goods that 1 unit of the preinflationary dollar could purchase—e.g., the Mercedes that left the factory in Germany with a sticker price of DM40,000. In other words, PPP is the mechanism whereby, theoretically, $24,000 still buys the Mercedes 190. This is irrespective of whether, say, an American businessperson buys the car in the United States or travels to Germany, converts dollars to marks, and then buys the 190.

A simpler approach to purchasing power parity compares world prices for a single well-known product: McDonald's Big Mac hamburger. The so-called Big Mac Index is a "quick and dirty" way of determining which of the world's currencies are too weak or strong. The underlying assumption is that the price of a Big Mac in any world currency should, after being converted to dollars, equal the price of a Big Mac in the United States. A country's currency would be overvalued if the Big Mac price (converted to dollars) is higher than the U.S. price. Conversely, a country's currency would be undervalued if the converted Big Mac price was lower than the U.S. price.

Table 6–3 shows the Big Mac Index for selected countries in 1994. The first column of figures shows the price of a Big Mac in the local currency. The second column shows the implied PPP of the dollar, obtained by dividing the local currency price by the dollar price. Thus, for example, in Japan a Big Mac costs ¥ 391, yielding a Big Mac PPP of 169 (391 ÷ 2.32). Note that the yen/dollar exchange rate at the time was only 84.20 to 1, meaning that $2.32 would be the equivalent of ¥ 195.34—not enough to buy a Big Mac in Tokyo! Thus, we can see that the yen is overvalued against the dollar by about 100 percent. In other words, based on the U.S. price for a Big Mac, the yen/dollar exchange rate ought to be 169 to 1, not 84.20 to 1.

If foreign exchange transactions were concluded solely to provide exchange for purchases of goods and services (i.e., the current account of the balance of payments) and if rates of inflation were easily predictable, PPP would be a reliable and useful predictor of the foreign exchange rate. To forecast exchange rates, one would need only to forecast

| TABLE 6–3 | THE BIG MAC INDEX |

Country	Big Mac Price in Local Currency	Exchange Rate Implied by PPP	Actual Official Exchange Rate	Over/Undervaluation of Local Currency (%)
France	FFr18.50	7.97/$1	4.80/$1	+66
Switzerland	SwFr5.90	2.54/$1	1.13/$1	+124
Canada	C$2.77	1.19/$1	1.39/$1	−14
Japan	¥391	169/$1	84.20/$1	+100
Russia	Ruble 8,100	3,491/$1	4,985/$1	−30
USA	$2.32	—	—	—

Source: Adapted from "Big MacCurrencies," *The Economist* (Apr. 15, 1995), p. 74.

differential rates of price inflation. Unfortunately, the current account of the balance of payments is not the sole measure of demand and supply of foreign exchange, and rates of inflation are not easy to predict.

This was illustrated in the United States between 1980 and 1985 when, in spite of growing deficits in the current account of the balance of payments, the U.S. dollar continued to soar in value in foreign exchange markets. The strong demand for dollars was due in part to demand for oil, which is priced in dollars on world markets. However, the dollar's strength contradicted PPP theory, and foreign exchange traders who based their purchases on PPP suffered major losses. During this period, it was a case of the tail (capital movements) wagging the dog (current account of the balance of payments). According to PPP, the dog is the current account of the balance of payments, and the tail is the capital account.

Other Influences on Foreign Exchange

As noted earlier, there are a host of factors besides PPP that impact the foreign exchange rate of currency, including economic factors related to a country's fiscal, monetary, and economic policies. Economic policy and performance that create a rate of economic growth higher than the world average will, over the long run, increase the exchange value of a country's currency. The best examples of currencies reflecting this fact are the Japanese yen and the German mark. Although it is not yet apparent, this fundamental economic law will be reflected in the exchange value of the Korean won, the Taiwan dollar, and the currency of any other country that is growing in real terms faster than the world average.

Another important economic factor is a country's interest rate as compared to world averages. In a situation where a country's real rate of interest—the nominal rate of interest minus the rate of inflation—is higher than interest rates in comparable countries, capital will be attracted. This creates demand for the country's currency and puts upward pressure on the currency value in the foreign exchange market. This was exactly the case in the fall of 1992, when Germany's Bundesbank raised interest rates to finance the unification of East and West Germany without sparking inflation. The strength of the German mark led to chaos in the currency trading world. The central banks of Italy and Great Britain **devalued**—cut the value of—their countries' respective currencies and withdrew from the Exchange Rate Mechanism.

A key currency such as the U.S. dollar is less subject to economic laws such as PPP because it is held by individuals, companies, and countries for many purposes. The willingness to hold the dollar creates a demand source that impacts its exchange market value. Political factors are important determinants of currency value. These include the country's political situation, especially the philosophy of the party in power and the proximity of elections. In the short run, perhaps the single most important factor impacting currency value is a psychological one, namely, what analysts and traders believe and expect is going to happen. Indeed, currency market movements can be driven by what analysts and traders believe *other* analysts and traders are thinking. This is illustrated by the impact currency speculators had on the Exchange Rate Mechanism in 1992. Traders believe that all information about the value of a currency can be read on their computer screens. Thus, while bureaucrats proclaimed an improved, unified Europe, speculators were concerned with two questions: When would the European Monetary System fall apart, and what size bet should they place (Millman 1995, 64)?

Notwithstanding the short-run factors and the attitudes of traders that influence exchange rates, the fundamentals cannot be avoided. A country's ability to purchase foreign goods and services is based on its ability to earn foreign exchange. If that ability is limited, its ability to maintain its exchange value will be limited.

Following is a partial list of factors that impact foreign exchange rates. The bottom line for all the factors is that foreign exchange rates are determined by transactions which reflect the sum total of all of the motives, reasoning, and beliefs behind currency supply and demand. The intersection of the supply and the demand *is* the rate.

Economic Factors

1. Balance of payments:
   a. Current account: Trade surplus or deficit for goods, services, investment income and payments, and so on
   b. Capital account: Surplus or deficit of demand for short- and long-term financial instruments

2. Nominal and real interest rates
3. Domestic inflation
4. Monetary and fiscal policies
5. Estimate of international competitiveness, present and future
6. Foreign exchange reserves
7. Attractiveness of country currency and assets, both financial and real
8. Government controls and incentives
9. Importance of currency in world finance and trade (the dollar, mark, and yen are the most important today)

Political Factors

10. Philosophies of political party and leaders
11. Proximity of elections or change in leadership
12. Political turmoil (war, insurrection, or civil unrest)

Sources: Craig Torres, "Headed South: Mexico's Devaluation Stuns Latin America—and U.S. Investors," *The Wall Street Journal* (Dec. 22, 1994), pp. A1, A12.
"Ford Lifts Prices, Avon Tries to Calm Holders, Dina Estimates Loss as Peso Fallout Continues," *The Wall Street Journal* (Jan. 13, 1995).
Michael Clements and Bill Montague, "Will Peso's Fall Prove Perot Right?" *USA Today* (Jan. 17, 1995), pp. B1, B2.

■ THE PESO CRISIS

*T*he Bank of Mexico's decision to devalue the peso meant that the Mexican currency declined nearly 40 percent relative to key currencies such as the dollar, the mark, and the yen. One immediate effect of the devaluation was a sharp decline in Mexican purchases of U.S. imports. For example, Westinghouse and Lennox had been aggressively selling air conditioners after NAFTA reduced tariffs; sales quickly slowed down after the devaluation. McDonald's, Kentucky Fried Chicken, Dunkin' Donuts, and other U.S. restaurant chains were also hard hit as they were forced to raise prices. Many franchisees had contracted to pay rent for their facilities in dollars; after the devaluation, franchisees who couldn't pay the rent were forced to shut down. Simply put, the purchasing power of Mexican consumers was cut nearly in half. To reduce the risk of inflation, the Mexican government pledged to cut spending and allow interest rates to rise. Meanwhile, investors who had poured money into Mexico since the late 1980s—lured by the promise of low inflation and a stable currency—faced huge declines in the value of their holdings.

For many manufacturing companies, the weaker peso wreaked havoc with 1995 sales forecasts. GM, for example,

had hoped to export 15,000 vehicles to Mexico in 1995, a goal rendered unattainable by the financial crisis. Ford raised vehicle prices in Mexico; the increases applied to vehicles built in Mexico as well as those imported from Canada and the United States. Shares of Avon Products, whose Mexican sales comprise 11 percent of the company's $4 billion in annual revenue, declined sharply on Wall Street. Hoping to calm investors' fears, company executives predicted that a decline in Mexican sales would be offset in 1995 by gains in Brazil and other countries.

Supporters and opponents of NAFTA debated the long-term effects of the devaluation. Harley Shaiken, a labor professor at the University of California and NAFTA critic, noted, "It will have a dual impact: It will diminish the market for U.S. goods in Mexico, but the more sizable impact will be the transfer of production to Mexico. It's going to make Mexico less desirable as a place to sell things and far more desirable as a place to make things." Persons holding opposing views acknowledged that the devaluation cut Mexican wages in dollar terms. However, NAFTA supporters have pointed out that labor's percentage of total cost in autos and auto parts—which constitute Mexico's largest export sector—is relatively low. Thus, despite the devaluation, NAFTA supporters deny that there will be a "giant sucking sound" caused by an exodus of U.S. jobs south of the border.

Psychological Factors

13. Expectations and opinions of analysts, traders, bankers, economists, and business people
14. Forward exchange market prices

EXCHANGE RATE EXPOSURE[4]

Exchange rate exposure (sometimes called exchange rate risk exposure) refers to the degree to which a company is affected by exchange rate changes. There are two categories of exposure: translation exposure (also known as accounting exposure) and economic exposure (also known as operating exposure).

Translation (Accounting) Exposure[5]

Translation exposure is the degree to which exchange rate fluctuations affect a company's book value when financial statements of global operations are consolidated and stated in the company's home currency. Translation exposure occurs because of an accounting fundamental: Balance sheet accounts must balance. Owner's equity is the key to keeping liabilities in balance with assets. If the foreign currency has weakened between the date reflected on the foreign balance sheet and the date the foreign balance sheet is consolidated with home-country financial documents, the value of every item listed as an asset decreases; owner's equity must decrease as well to keep the accounts in balance. This means a decrease in the book value of the company in terms of home-country financial statements. Of course, the converse is also true: If the foreign currency strengthens relative to the home-country currency, owner's equity—and therefore book value—will increase. Table 6–4 shows the situation for a hypothetical U.S. company and its French subsidiary when the franc weakens against the dollar. The U.S. financial statements show assets and liabilities balancing at $2,750,000 when the French statements are translated at an exchange rate of FFr4 = $1 on June 30, 1995. However, if the French franc weakens on July 1, the U.S. financial statements will have to reflect the adjustment; the new figure of $2,200,000 reflects the drop in book value due to exchange rate fluctuations.[6]

It is important to remember that translation exposure simply reflects accounting reports of the value of foreign operations. Book value, however, does not really say anything about a company's future cash flows. Cash flow issues that stem from fluctuating currencies have a direct influence on company investment decisions, as well as decisions regarding markets and production.

Economic (Operating) Exposure

The degree to which exchange rates affect a company's market value as measured by its stock price is known as *economic*, or operating, *exposure* (recall that translation exposure impacts a company's book value rather than its market value). Economic exposure refers to the impact of currency fluctuations on the present value—hence the purchasing power—of a company's expected future cash flows. As noted earlier, Mexican sales account for 11 percent of Avon Products' annual sales; thus, Avon had a great deal

---

[4]This section draws heavily on Chapters 8–11 in Shapiro 1996.

[5]For further examples and more detailed discussion, see Schweikart 1992.

[6]Currency translations by U.S. firms must adhere to generally accepted accounting principles. Of particular relevance is FASB–52, a standard issued in 1981 by the Financial Accounting Standards Board (FASB). According to FASB–52, foreign country balance sheet accounts in the local currency must be translated at the currency exchange rates prevailing on the date reflected on the home-country balance sheet. In some instances, a functional currency other than the local currency can be established. In Brazil, for example, where foreign currency statements become meaningless due to inflation, the dollar can be the functional currency. This is an FASB–8 conversion, and changes are run through the income statement rather than through equity as shown in Table 6–4. Monetary assets and liabilities are converted at current rates; inventory is converted at historical dollar rates.

TABLE 6-4	BALANCE SHEET OF MYCORP INTERNATIONAL—FRANCE, JUNE 30, 1995		
Cash	FFr1,000,000	Debt	FFr5,000,000
Accounts receivable	3,000,000	Equity	6,000,000
Plant & equipment	5,000,000		
Inventory	2,000,000		
	FFr11,000,000		FFr11,000,000
Dollar translation on June 30, 1995: FFr4 = $1			
Cash	$ 250,000	Debt	$1,250,000
Accounts receivable	750,000	Equity	1,500,000
Plant & equipment	1,250,000		
Inventory	500,000		
	$2,750,000		$2,750,000
Dollar translation on July 1, 1995: FFr5 = $1			
Cash	$ 200,000	Debt	$1,000,000
Accounts receivable	600,000	Equity	1,500,000
Plant & equipment	1,000,000		
Inventory	400,000	Cumulative translation adjustment	(300,000)
	$2,200,000		$2,200,000

Source: Adapted from Michael Melvin, *International Money and Finance*, 2d. ed. (New York: Harper & Row, 1989), pp. 100–101.

of economic exposure to the peso's devaluation. The extent of the exposure prompted many investors to sell Avon stock.

Economic exposure can be further divided into two categories: transaction exposure and real operating exposure. *Transaction exposure* arises when the company's activities result in sales or purchases denominated in foreign currencies. For example, in the mid-1980s, a third of Eastman Kodak's revenues were generated from non-U.S. sales; according to company estimates, the strength of the dollar in the early 1980s resulted in lost profits totaling $500 million over a 4-year period. This loss occurred despite the fact that Kodak's foreign exchange trading team bought and sold $10 billion worth of currencies on foreign exchange markets every year to protect the company's $1.5 billion transaction exposure.[7] The importance of transaction exposure is directly proportional to the amount of business a company conducts outside the home market. Table 6–5 shows a sampling of companies with more than $3 billion in annual sales that derive 50 percent or more of those sales outside the home country. Note that Kodak generated 52 percent of 1994 revenues outside the United States, so its potential exposure has increased during the past decade. Obviously, currency exposure is a critical issue for Nestlè, with 98 percent of annual sales taking place outside Switzerland. By contrast, GE generated 83 percent of 1994 revenues in the United States, so the relative extent of GE's exposure is much less than that of the companies shown in the table.

Transaction exposure may vary among a company's business units. For example, Daimler-Benz's aircraft group, Daimler-Benz Aerospace AG (Dasa), accounts for 16 percent of the parent company's annual revenue. However, world prices for aircraft are denominated in dollars, and 75 percent of Dasa's revenues are in dollars. This has grave implications in view of the mark's strength. Compounding the problem is the fact that most of Dasa's employees are paid in marks. Dasa's net losses for 1992–1994 totaled nearly 1.5 billion marks. Company executives simply misforecast how far the dollar would fall against the mark. Budgets for 1995 were based on an exchange rate of 1.6 marks to the dollar, but by mid-1995 the actual rate was 1.38 to 1.[8]

Real operating exposure arises when currency fluctuations, together with price changes,

[7]Michael Sesit, "Avoiding Losses: By Trading Currencies, Kodak's Eric R. Nelson Saves the Firm Millions," *The Wall Street Journal* (Mar. 5, 1985), p. 1.
[8]Brian Coleman, "Daimler Aerospace Comes Down to Earth," *The Wall Street Journal* (July 27, 1995), p. A7.

THE GLOBAL FINANCIAL ENVIRONMENT AND FOREIGN EXCHANGE DECISIONS

TABLE 6–5 SOME COMPANIES THAT DERIVE OVER 50% OF REVENUES OUTSIDE THE HOME COUNTRY

Company	Home Country	Revenues, 1994 (billions)	Percent of Revenues outside Home Country
Nestlè	Switzerland	SwFr56.9	98.1
Philips	Netherlands	guilders 60.9	95.0
Unilever	U.K./Netherlands	guilders 82.5	85.0*
Colgate	USA	$7.6	79.0**
Sony	Japan	¥3,983	72.6
Gillette	USA	$6.0	67.9
Canon	Japan	¥1,993	67.1
Coca-Cola	USA	$13.9	67.0
IBM	USA	$64.0	63.0
Kodak	USA	$13.5	52.0
3M	USA	$15.0	50.0

*Estimate based on company reports.
**Excludes Hills Pet food subsidiary.
Source: Company reports.

alter a company's future revenues and costs. According to this definition, the firms that face operating exposure include not only those that have overseas operations but also those whose manufacturing plan calls for sourcing goods abroad. Economic exposure arises whenever companies commit to setting up new product development centers and distribution systems, getting foreign supply, or installing foreign production facilities.

In dealing with the economic exposure introduced by currency fluctuations, a key issue is whether the company can use price as a strategic tool for maintaining its profit margins. Can the company adjust prices in response to a rise or fall in foreign exchange rates in various markets? That depends on the price elasticity of demand. The less price-sensitive the demand, the greater the flexibility a company has in responding to exchange rate changes. Price elasticity, in turn, depends on the degree of competition and the location of the competitors. As noted earlier, Ford managers believed a 10 percent price increase following the peso devaluation in Mexico was feasible. In the case of Daimler-Benz's Dasa unit, the presence of numerous regional competitors constrains the company's ability to push through price increases. As a result, Dasa executives will likely have to resort to more drastic measures, such as cutting jobs and rethinking supplier agreements. Dasa currently buys only 25 percent of its parts outside Germany, so one option would be to switch to suppliers in the United States or other countries with relatively weak currencies. Another option is to persuade German suppliers to "share the pain" by accepting payment in dollars. Finally, Dasa may be forced to exit some segments of the industry.

MANAGING EXCHANGE RATE EXPOSURE

As the Dasa example illustrates, it is very difficult to accurately forecast the movement of exchange rates. Over the years, the search for other ways of managing cash flows to eliminate or reduce exchange rate risks has resulted in development of numerous techniques. For example, it may be desirable to sell products in the company's home-country currency. When this is not possible, two categories of approaches are available: techniques to reduce transaction and translation exposure and techniques for reducing real operating exposure. Because translation exposure management issues are more properly the domain

THE GLOBAL FINANCIAL
ENVIRONMENT AND FOREIGN
EXCHANGE DECISIONS

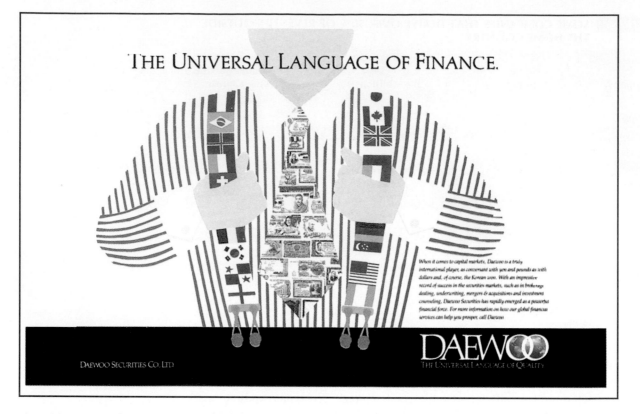

This ad for South Korea's Daewoo explains that finance is a universal language that knows no national borders. (Courtesy of Daewoo Securities Co. Ltd.)

of finance rather than marketing, the following discussion will focus on hedging techniques for managing transaction and operating exposure.

Hedging

Hedging exchange rate exposure involves establishing an offsetting currency position such that the loss or gain of one currency position is offset by a corresponding gain or loss in some other currency. A basic rule of thumb is this: If company forecasts indicate that the value of the foreign currency will weaken against the home currency, a hedge to protect against potential transaction losses is a prudent course of action. Conversely, for predictions that the foreign currency will appreciate (strengthen) against the home currency, then a gain, rather than a loss, can be expected on foreign transactions when revenues are converted into the home currency. Given this situation, the best decision may be not to hedge at all.

External hedging methods for managing both transaction and translation exposure call for participating in the foreign currency market. Specific hedging tools include forward contracts and currency options. Internal hedging methods include price adjustment clauses and intra-corporate borrowing or lending in foreign currencies. The accompanying sidebar illustrates how internal hedging has helped Sun Microsystems reduce its transaction exposure.

FORWARD CONTRACTS • The **forward market** is a mechanism for buying and selling currencies at a preset price for future delivery. If it is known that a certain amount of foreign currency is going to be paid out or received at some future date, a company can insure itself against exchange loss by buying or selling forward. With a forward contract, the company can lock in a specific fixed exchange rate for a future date and thus immunize itself from the loss (or gain) caused by the exchange rate fluctuation. By consulting

TABLE 6–6 DOLLAR VALUE OF DM-DENOMINATED CONTRACT FOR DELIVERY OF GOODS

	Exchange Rate	Value of DM100M Contract
January 1984 Actual	DM2.7458 = $1	$36.4 million
December 1984 Actual	DM3.1570 = $1	31.7 million
December 1984 Future	DM2.6450 = $1	37.8 million

any published source (*The Wall Street Journal*'s foreign exchange page is in its Section 3), it is possible to determine exchange rates on a given day. In addition to spot prices, 30-, 60-, and 180-day forward prices are quoted for dozens of world currencies.

In the first half of the 1980s, the dollar rose in value against the world's currencies. Consider, for example, the case of a U.S. exporter selling in West Germany. At the beginning of 1984, the Deutsch mark/dollar exchange rate was 2.7458 to 1. If the U.S. exporter anticipated receiving DM100 million by the end of 1984, the dollar value of the deal would have been $36.4 million (see Table 6–6). However, by the end of 1984 the dollar had strengthened against the mark, to DM3.1570/$1. Thus, those DM100 million were only worth $31.7 million, and the exporter would have faced a $4.7 million transaction loss. Ideally, the exporter would have turned to the forward market at the beginning of 1984 to hedge the dollar value of the German receivables due at year's end. He or she could have locked in a rate of DM2.6450/$1, a rate which reflected the predictions of many forecasters that the dollar would fall in 1984 (which, in fact, it did not do). Note that at the prevailing forward rate in January 1984, our exporter would have done better than simply covering potential losses from a weaker mark. The exporter would have received $37.8 million for the DM100 million, a price that was actually $1.4 million *more* than the dollar amount originally expected.[9]

OPTIONS • Companies use the forward market when the currency exposure is known in advance, e.g.,when a firm contract of sale exists. In some situations, however, companies are not certain about the future foreign currency cash inflow or outflow. Consider the risk

[9]Sesit, p. 1.

Source: Adapted from Jonathan Fuerbringer, "Learning to Dance with a Bouncy Dollar," *The New York Times* (Sept. 8, 1991), Sec. 3, pp. 1, 6.

■ HEDGING AT SUN MICROSYSTEMS

BEHIND THE SCENES

*W*hen Robert J. Prantis left Beatrice Corporation in Chicago and joined Sun Microsystems in Silicon Valley, the move symbolized the increasing sophistication of dealing with dollar volatility of U.S. corporations competing in the global marketplace. More than 50 percent of Sun's sales are overseas, and transactions involve 20 different currencies.

Mr. Prantis's first task was to identify Sun's exposure to foreign exchange risk. This task was complicated by the slow pace of information flow in the growing company with a decentralized structure. Thomas J. Meredith, treasurer at Sun, noted, "In a place like the United States, that is tied to the quarterly earnings report, foreign exchange is more and more a driving force. Sun has to be vigilant month to month and has to identify all the exposures."

Mr. Prantis and Mr. Meredith discovered that Sun's Japanese subsidiary was buying computer work stations from headquarters for dollars and selling them back in Japan for yen even as headquarters was buying yen for dollars to pay for work station components that it sourced in Japan. Thus, the company was experiencing transaction exposure from both the yen/dollar and the dollar/yen sides. To insulate the company from this exposure, headquarters instituted a policy whereby its Japanese subsidiary would pay for work stations with yen; the same yen would be used by headquarters to pay Japanese component suppliers. This natural hedge, estimates Mr. Meredith, saved Sun about $1 million in its first year. The losers, of course, were the Japanese banks that lost Sun's foreign currency business.

Citibank can boast of being a leader in both global and local financial services. (Courtesy of Citicorp.)

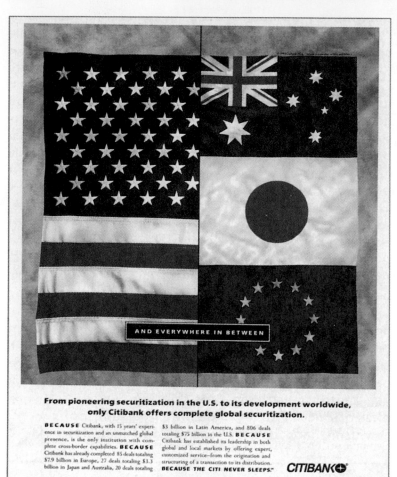

From pioneering securitization in the U.S. to its development worldwide, only Citibank offers complete global securitization.

BECAUSE Citibank, with 15 years' experience in securitization and an unmatched global presence, is the only institution with complete cross-border capabilities. **BECAUSE** Citibank has already completed 85 deals totaling $7.9 billion in Europe, 27 deals totaling $3.3 billion in Japan and Australia, 20 deals totaling $3 billion in Latin America, and 806 deals totaling $75 billion in the U.S. **BECAUSE** Citibank has established its leadership in both global and local markets by offering expert, customized service—from the origination and structuring of a transaction to its distribution. **BECAUSE THE CITI NEVER SLEEPS.** CITIBANK

AND EVERYWHERE IN BETWEEN

exposure of a U.S. company that bids for a foreign project but won't know if the project will be granted until sometime later. The company needs to protect the dollar value of the contract by hedging the *potential* foreign currency cash inflow that will be generated if the company turns out to be the winning bidder. In such an instance, forward contracts are not the appropriate hedging tool.

A foreign currency **option** is best for such situations. A **put option** gives the buyer the right, not the obligation, to sell a specified number of foreign currency units at a fixed price, up to the option's expiration date. (Conversely, a **call option** is the right, but not the obligation, to buy the foreign currency). In the example of bidding the foreign project, the company can take out a put to sell the foreign currency for dollars at a set price in the future. In other words, the U.S. company locks in the value of the contract in dollars. Thus, if the project is granted, the future foreign currency cash inflow has been hedged by means of the put option. If the project is *not* granted, the company can trade the put option in the options market without exercising it; remember, options are rights, not obligations. The only money the company stands to lose is the difference between what it paid for the option and what it receives upon selling it.

A company may choose to manage its foreign exchange exposure in either one or both directions. At Avon Products, for example, CFO Edward J. Robinson mapped out two strategies. The first calls for using forward contracts to cover not only the amount to be expatriated from the United Kingdom, Japan, Germany, and other markets, but also a certain portion of profits forecast for the coming year. The second strategy calls for hedging half of the exposure in the forward market and half with options.[10]

Financial officers of global firms can avoid transaction exposure altogether by demanding a particular currency as the payment for its foreign sales. As noted, a U.S-based company might demand U.S. dollars as the payment currency for its foreign sales. This, however, does not eliminate currency risk; it simply shifts that risk to the customers. In common practice, companies typically attempt to invoice exports (receivables) in strong currencies and imports (payables) in weak currencies. However, in today's highly competitive world market, such a practice may reduce a company's competitive edge.

Pricing Strategies for Managing Economic Exposure

Economic exposure to exchange rate risk is based on the sensitivity of a company's projected currency inflows and outflows over a specified time period to the combination of exchange rate changes and inflation. Price adjustments can sometimes be used to off-

THE GLOBAL FINANCIAL ENVIRONMENT AND FOREIGN EXCHANGE DECISIONS

[10]Stephen J. Govoni, "Creating Avon's New Look," *CFO* (May 1992), p. 42.

set exchange-related losses. Managers responsible for factoring exchange rate changes into companies' pricing strategies need to answer two key questions: (1) Should market share or profit maximization be emphasized? and (2) How frequently should prices be adjusted?

MARKET SHARE VERSUS PROFIT MARGIN • Export price adjustments in response to exchange rate movements on products bound for specific country destinations are sometimes known as *pricing to market* (PTM). Consider the situation faced by Japanese automobile manufacturers vis-à-vis the Big Three U.S. automakers when the dollar began to decline relative to the yen and other currencies in 1985. The price advantage of Japanese imports associated with the strong dollar disappeared; by the end of 1986, the yen had appreciated nearly 50 percent against the dollar. Carmakers such as Toyota, Honda, and Nissan raised U.S. prices by 15 percent and absorbed the rest of the currency exposure in lower profits.[11] This would have been an ideal opportunity for the Big Three to hold the line on prices and increase market share. In fact, Ford, GM, and Chrysler raised their prices in step with Japan, as a result of which U.S. corporate profits soared in the late 1980s and the Japanese share of the U.S. car market *increased*, rather than decreased.[12]

The auto industry example shows what commonly happens following an appreciation of one country's currency relative to the currency of an important trading partner. Companies based in the strong-currency country—Japanese producers, for example—may have to consider increasing prices in dollars or other currencies to offset exchange rate losses. But, producers based in the country with the relatively weaker currency now have a cost advantage over exporters based in countries with strong currencies. By holding the line on prices, local producers can use that advantage to expand market share at home—unless they are greedy. Thus it is unlikely that the exporting company (for example, a Japanese automaker) will be able to raise its product prices by the full extent of the foreign currency devaluation or depreciation. When competitors based in the weak-currency country hold the line on prices, exporters will be forced to absorb a percentage of the reduction in home-currency revenues to maintain market share.

In the situation of home-currency devaluation or depreciation, exporters can gain a competitive price advantage in world markets by reducing prices and expanding market share. Some U.S. manufacturers were concerned that some Mexican manufacturers would do precisely that following the peso devaluation in December 1994. Note that companies do not *have* to reduce or increase export prices by the full amount of the decrease or increase in the home currency's value. A recent study comparing price adjustments of automobile exports from the United States, Japan, and Germany yielded some interesting results. Although Japan and Germany are both strong-currency countries, German exporters to the United States tended to pass along more of the exchange rate change (in the form of price increases) than Japanese exporters. However, price adjustments by German manufacturers varied by vehicle size; for example, BMW's markup on its smallest sedan amounted to only 20 percent of the mark's appreciation, while Mercedes raised the dollar price of its station wagon to almost completely offset the stronger mark (Gagnon & Knetter 1995, 302).

FREQUENCY OF PRICE ADJUSTMENTS • Factors influencing PTM decisions include the persistence of the exchange rate changes, economies of scale, price elasticity of product demand, and the likelihood of attracting competition if high unit profitability is obvious. The frequency of price adjustments depends on the length of time that the real foreign exchange rate change is expected to persist. A general rule of thumb is that move-

[11]Paul Ingrassia and Damon Darlin, "Tokyo's Troubles: Japanese Auto Makers Find the Going Tough because of Yen's Climb," *The Wall Street Journal* (Dec. 15, 1986), p. 1.
[12]John Bussey, "Fateful Choice: Did U.S. Car Makers Err by Raising Prices When the Yen Rose?" *The Wall Street Journal* (Apr. 18, 1988), p. A1.

ments in the exchange rate toward equilibrium of PPP are likely to be longer lasting than the movements away from equilibrium.

While companies can adjust prices in response to the exchange rate changes, ability and willingness to adjust prices are two different things. Many companies view the stability of prices over a period of time as a good way to maintain loyalty of their distributors and customers. For companies that are selling through catalogs, it is essential to keep prices stable because of the long lead time required to prepare and distribute catalogs.

Advance planning in adjusting prices is particularly important if price controls are expected to follow a currency devaluation. One way to deal with price controls without risking loss of market share is to raise list prices but continue selling at existing prices, or selling at a discount of raised list prices. Price control can be avoided by eliminating part or all of the discount. Another way of avoiding price controls is to develop alternative products that are only slightly different from existing products and sell them at the higher prices. For example, the Model 86B could be replaced with the Model 88TX. The two products could be functionally identical, but the newer model, with a different name, catalog number, and designation, could be priced differently than its predecessor.

SUMMARY

The international financial system is continually evolving. The gold standard system devised at Bretton Woods following World War II collapsed in the early 1970s. Today's system is based on floating exchange rates where exchange values are established by the market forces of supply and demand. The volume of foreign exchange trading is $1 trillion per day—a figure that far outstrips the value of global merchandise and services trading. The concept of purchasing power parity can help global marketers understand how relative rates of inflation and exchange values can theoretically create price equilibrium in different national markets. Even with such conceptual tools, forecasting foreign exchange value is extremely difficult in today's volatile financial environment.

Today's global financial resources represent an excellent example of the principle of infinite supply. Any company that has a sound marketing strategy and plan should be able to obtain the financial resources needed to implement them. Companies that wish to protect themselves from currency fluctuations can, in effect, sell off the risk by using various hedging techniques. It is possible to hedge exchange rate exposure, operating exposure, and transaction exposure. Forward market contracts, put options, and call options are some of the tools available. Companies must also make strategic decisions regarding market share versus profit margin, as well as how frequently to make price adjustments.

DISCUSSION QUESTIONS

1. What causes foreign exchange rates to change? Are exchange rates predictable? Why?
2. *The Economist* magazine's 1994 Big Mac index indicated that the average price for a Big Mac in the United States and Mexico were $2.30 and 8.10 pesos, respectively. The actual peso/dollar exchange rate in April 1994 was 3.36 to 1. Based on this data, what can you say about the peso's devaluation in December 1994? Does the Big Mac Index indicate that the peso was overvalued? Explain.
3. If, over the course of a year, prices rise 100 percent in Argentina and 1 percent in Germany, what would you expect to happen to the value of the mark and the Argentine peso, all other things being equal?
4. In your own words, what does purchasing power parity mean?
5. What is hedging? What are the different choices available for hedging transaction exposure, and when should each be used?

BIBLIOGRAPHY

Books

Eiteman, David K., Arthur I. Stonehill, and Michael H. Moffett. *Multinational Business Finance*, 6th ed. Reading, Mass.: Addison-Wesley Publishing Company, 1992.

Krieger, Andrew. *The Money Bazaar: Inside the Trillion-Dollar World of Currency Trading*. New York: Times Books, 1992.

Millman, Gregory J. *The Vandals' Crown: How Rebel Currency Traders Overthrew the World's Central Banks*. New York: Free Press, 1995.

Rodriguez, Rita M., and E. Eugene Carter. *International Financial Management*, 5th ed. Upper Saddle River, N.J.: Prentice Hall, 1984.

Shapiro, Alan C. *Multinational Financial Management*, 5th ed. Upper Saddle River, N.J.: Prentice Hall, 1996.

Shelton, Judy. *Money Meltdown: Restoring Order to the Global Currency System*. New York: Free Press, 1994.

Smith, Roy C., and Ingo Walter. *Global Financial Services*. New York: Harper & Row, 1990.

Volcker, Paul, and Toyoo Gyohten. *Changing Fortunes: The World's Money and the Threat to American Leadership*. New York: Times Books, 1992.

Articles

Cheung, Yin-Wong, Hung-Gay Fung, Kon S. Kai, and Wai-chung Lo, "Purchasing Power Parity under the European Monetary System," *Journal of International Money and Finance* 14, no. 2 (1995), pp. 179–189.

Froot, Kenneth A., David S. Scharfstein, and Jeremy C. Stein. "A Framework for Risk Management." *Harvard Business Review* 72, no. 6 (November–December 1994), pp. 91–102.

Gagnon, Joseph E., and Michael M. Knetter. "Markup Adjustment and Exchange Rate Fluctuations: Evidence from Panel Data on Automobile Exports." *Journal of International Money and Finance* 14, no. 2 (1995), pp. 289–310.

Glassgall, William, and Bill Javetski. "Borderless Finance: Fuel for Growth." *Business Week* (Nov. 18, 1994), pp. 40+.

Lessard, Donald, and John B. Lightstone. "Volatile Exchange Rates Can Put Operations at Risk." *Harvard Business Review* 64, no. 4 (July–August 1986), pp. 107–114.

Schweikart, James A. "Teaching Foreign Currency Translation and Its Effect on Financial Statement Analysis: A Spreadsheet Approach." *Journal of Teaching in International Business* 3, no. 4 (1992), pp. 23–43.

When leaders of the European Union member nations met in the Netherlands in 1991, they drafted a Maastricht Treaty on European Union to create an "economic and monetary union" (also known as "European Monetary Union"). Creating the EMU would require member nations to put control of monetary policy in the hands of a European central bank. Implementation of the EMU would also create a single European currency, thus eliminating costs associated with currency conversion and exchange rate uncertainty. In addition, an EU study noted that the single Euro currency would "permit a genuine comparison of the prices of goods and services across frontiers." The EU also hoped that the new currency would be a strong head-to-head contender with the dollar in international finance. Governments would no longer be able to use currency devaluations or revaluations as economic adjustment mechanisms.

Meeting in Madrid in December 1995, EU representatives hoped to finalize details of the plan for a new European economic order. It was agreed that the EMU would be implemented in two stages. Starting January 1, 1999, governments and the European central bank would begin using the new currency, whose exchange rate value would be fixed as of that date. Other financial institutions and private companies would be allowed nearly four years to convert to the new currency. Thus, each participating country could have two parallel currencies in circulation during the transition period. Individual shop owners might be required to reprogram their cash registers, accept cash and make change in two currencies, and maintain a separate bank account for each currency. The open-ended nature of the two-stage schedule has prompted criticism; for example, Graham Bishop of the Salomon Brothers investment firm warned, "The longer the changeover, the greater the risk of some shock." Some observers predicted that, during a year-long Intergovernmental Conference (IGC) of EU nations scheduled to run from March 1996 to March 1997, the final implementation date would be pushed ahead.

Representatives of the European Commission insist that it is important to adhere to the original timetable even if only two countries meet the stringent economic criteria. To qualify for inclusion in the EMU, the Maastricht Treaty specifies that a country's leaders must maintain stable exchange rates for two years and reduce public debt to less than 60 percent of GDP. Germany, France, the Netherlands, Belgium, Luxembourg, and Austria are expected to qualify. Many obstacles must be overcome, however. Britain and Denmark retain the right to exclude themselves from the EMU if concerns about national independence are not resolved. Several countries—in particular, Italy, Greece, Portugal, and Spain—are unlikely to qualify because of high national debt levels and other economic difficulties.

In Germany, there is much concern over the impending EMU. Many Germans fear that a common European currency will be less stable than the strong Deutsche mark, the bedrock of Germany's economic success. A poll published in Germany's *DM* business magazine in mid-1995 indicated that nearly two-thirds of the country's population opposed the EMU currency plan. (In a separate poll published by the EU, only 51 percent of EU citizens showed support for the single currency.) Many Germans fear that the value of their savings will be cut when the new currency is introduced. German investors helped drive up the Swiss franc more than 12 percent as they shifted holdings to the Swiss currency and purchased Swiss bonds rather than German ones. The Swiss franc's appreciation, in turn, is driving up prices of Swiss exports of industrial products such as precision machine tools and consumer products such as popular Swatch watches.

Most observers agree that Italy is unlikely to meet the EMU criteria. Government debt stands at 122 percent of GDP—twice as high as the Maastrict limit; annual inflation exceeds 5 percent. The situation in Italy presents a dilemma for the EU. If Italy is excluded from the EMU, some observers fear that it would have an advantage compared to much of Europe because its government would not have to adhere to stringent monetary rules. On the other hand, Italy's inclusion could make the single Euro currency rather weak. The situation with Italy, Britain, and Denmark has prompted some observers to question whether the EMU can function properly if some major countries are not included.

On a more personal level, the EMU would eliminate currencies that are closely associated with individual countries, such as the German mark, the French franc, and the Italian lira. This has sparked an emotional concern in individual countries even among persons who acknowledge that a single currency could be the cornerstone of a united Europe. As one retired French businesswoman said, "I am for the French franc, for the national money. I am not for the European money. The franc is part of the spirit of the country, its vigor, its weaknesses. It seems France will lose a bit of its personality. The money of a country is something personal. It is more than a tool of a market."

DISCUSSION QUESTIONS

1. How will Europe benefit from a single currency?
2. What, if any, pricing adjustments will companies marketing in all EU countries have to make if the EMU is implemented?

3. How might a Swiss company attempt to deal with exchange-rate losses caused by a strong Swiss franc?
4. What do you think will be the biggest impediments to successful implementation of the EMU? What will be the major forces behind successful implementation?
5. Go to the library and research the Intergovernmental Conference. Has the IGC addressed any issues pertaining to Maastrict's single currency provisions?

Sources: "Worries about Identity, Values," *Associated Press* (Nov. 18, 1995).
Jay Branegan, "With E.U. Countries Struggling to Qualify on Time, Economic and Monetary Union May Be Delayed," *Time International* (December 1995).
Peter Gumbel, "Germans Fret about Currency Union," *The Wall Street Journal* (July 25, 1995), p. A11.
Christopher Taylor, "EMU: The State of Play," *The World Today* (April 1995), pp. 75–78.
Kevin Dowd, "European Monetary Reform: Pitfalls of Central Planning," *USA Today* (March 1995), pp. 70–73.
"A Funny New EMU," *The Economist* (Mar. 4, 1995), pp. 49–50.

Global Marketing Information Systems and Research

> *"To survive in this new globally competitive world, we had to modernize. Information technology is the glue for everything we do."*
>
> —James Wogsland,
> Vice Chairman, Caterpillar

Club Med, the French-based travel and leisure company that offers "the antidote for civilization," has attempted to reposition itself away from the sexy, swinging-singles image that was integral to its early success. In particular, the company has tried to increase its appeal to Americans, who make up about 20 percent of the club's total guests. The most elusive prospect is a traveler who has never taken a Club Med vacation. Club Med's creative advertising generates a high volume of telephone inquiries to the company's tollfree telephone reservation center in Scottsdale, Arizona. Names, addresses, and telephone numbers of all the callers become part of the database. For years, however, unless a caller actually took a Club Med vacation, the information was not put to further use.

In 1991, Club Med executives realized that the 150,000 "hot prospects" in its information system represented a potential gold mine. These prospects were people who had responded to ads and requested promotional material and information in the past five years but who had never actually tried Club Med. These prospects were regarded as having high potential to actually book a vacation. The company decided to hire an outside firm, Gannett TeleMarketing, to call these households and obtain several pieces of important information, including family profiles, a list of activities the family enjoyed, and an indication of what activities the family would like Club Med to offer.

As the Club Med example shows, information is the raw material of executive and managerial action. Club Med's actions combine elements of a marketing information system with market research. In general, global marketers must know where to go to obtain information, what information and subject areas to look for, the different ways information can be acquired, and the various analysis approaches used to provide marketing intelligence. This chapter presents an information acquisition model for global marketing as well as an outline of the global marketing research process. Once acquired, information must be processed in an efficient and effective way. The chapter concludes with a discussion of how to manage the marketing information collection system and the marketing research effort.

OVERVIEW OF GLOBAL MARKET INFORMATION SYSTEMS

One purpose of a marketing information system (MIS) is to provide managers and other decision makers with a continuous flow of information about company operations. A company's MIS should provide a means for gathering, analyzing, classifying, storing, retrieving, and reporting relevant data. A company's MIS should also cover important aspects of a company's external environment, including customers and competitors. As suggested by the quote from James Wogsland of Caterpillar at the beginning of this chapter, global competition intensifies the need for an effective MIS. In addition to Caterpillar, Federal Express, Grand Metropolitan PLC, Ford, and Texas Instruments are among the companies with global operations that have invested in sophisticated electronic data interchange (EDI) systems to improve intra-company information sharing.

Poor operating results can often be traced to insufficient data and information about events both inside and outside the company. For example, when a new management team was installed at the U.S. unit of Adidas AG, the German athletic shoe marketer, data were not even available on normal inventory turnover rates. A new reporting system revealed that arch-rivals Reebok and Nike turned inventories five times a year, compared with twice a year at Adidas. This information was used to tighten the marketing focus on the best-selling Adidas products. Benetton SpA's use of MIS as a strategic competitive tool is described in the sidebar on p. 160.

Colgate-Palmolive recently succeeded in standardizing its disparate and frequently incompatible electronic mail systems at locations around the globe. The process was tedious, but Colgate executives realized that a global messaging system would increase employee productivity. As a result, employees in 165 countries can now easily exchange messages and files; electronic mail traffic almost doubled in a 3-year period after the system was fully implemented. An undertaking of this magnitude required the full support of senior management inside and outside the marketing function and integration into the strategic planning process.

Indeed, it is no easy task to organize, implement, and monitor global marketing information and research strategies and programs. Moreover, these are not simply marketing issues; they are organizational imperatives. These tasks must be coordinated in a coherent manner that contributes to the overall strategic direction of the organization. The marketing information system and research function must provide relevant information in a timely, cost-efficient, and actionable manner.

The past few years have seen dramatic changes in worldwide political and economic events. Increased global economic integration between countries, the demise of communism, volatile currency exchange rates, and other factors are driving the demand for access to credible worldwide business and political information. Today's economic and political environments require worldwide news information on a daily basis. Geocentric, global companies generally have intelligence systems that meet these challenges. Typically, the strategic planning or market research departments staff these systems. They distribute information to senior management and to managers throughout the organization.

A more detailed discussion of the workings of an intra-company MIS is beyond the scope of this book. The discussion that follows focuses on the subject agenda, scanning modes, and information sources characteristic of a global information system that is oriented toward the external environment.

Information Subject Agenda

A starting point for a global marketing information system is a list of subjects about which information is desired. The resulting "subject agenda" should be tailored to the specific needs and objectives of the company. The general framework suggested in Table

TABLE 7–1   SIX SUBJECT AGENDA CATEGORIES FOR A GLOBAL MARKETING INFORMATION SYSTEM

Category	Coverage
1. Market Potential	Demand estimates, consumer behavior, review of products, channels, communication media
2. Competitor Information	Corporate, business, functional strategies
3. Foreign Exchange	Balance of payments, interest rates, attractiveness of country currency, expectations of analysts
4. Prescriptive Information	Laws, regulations, rulings concerning taxes, earnings, dividends in both host and home countries
5. Resource Information	Availability of human, financial, information, physical resources
6. General Conditions	Overall review of sociocultural, political, technological environments

7–1 consists of six broad information areas. The framework satisfies two essential criteria. First, it comprises all the information subject areas relevant to a company with global operations. Second, the categories in the framework are mutually exclusive; any kind of information encompassed by the framework can be correctly placed in one and only one category. The basic elements of the external environment outlined in the last four chapters—economic, social and cultural, legal/regulatory, and financial factors—will undoubtedly be on the information agenda of most companies, as shown in the table.

Scanning Modes: Surveillance and Search

Once the subject agenda has been determined, the next step is the actual collection of information. This can be accomplished using either surveillance or search.

In the *surveillance* mode, the marketer engages in informal information gathering.

Sources: Martin Everett, "Extra! Extra! Gannett Helps Club Med Mine Its Database," *Sales & Marketing Management* (October 1992), pp. 120, 122.
James R. Rosenfield, "In the Mail," *Direct Marketing* (February 1992), pp. 15–17.
Edwin McDowell, "Club Med Is Developing Luxury Resort in China," *The New York Times* (June 10, 1993), p. C4.
Joshua Levine, "You've Got To Be Perfect, but not Plastic Perfect," *Forbes* (Sept. 30, 1991), pp. 152–154.

■ CLUB MED

*A*s noted in the chapter introduction, Club Med turned to a specialist for help with its information and research needs. Gannett's staff was specially trained to treat prospects as valued customers. Gannett was also able to offer automated dialing and sophisticated voice recognition; by eliminating the chore of dialing, telemarketers were able to concentrate on talking with the prospect. The telemarketers assigned to the Club Med account were chosen on the basis of their superior conversational skills; preference was also given to those who had themselves taken a cruise or a Club Med vacation or had families. The calling campaign was started in time for the summer 1991 vacation season.

The name of any person who expressed an interest in booking a vacation was immediately conveyed to the Scottsdale reservation center. Other leads were referred to Club Med's own in-house telemarketing staff. Paul Link, vice president of operations for Gannett, was particularly impressed by the quality of Club Med's database. In many cases 90 telephone numbers must be dialed each hour to reach 30 households; the Club Med list required only 55 to 66 calls to reach 27 people each hour. The first year of the new approach yielded an increase in the number of multiple bookings with as many as a dozen people.

In the second year, Club Med and Gannett divided the original database into two segments of about 10,000 names. Rather than call prospects whose original contact had occurred as much as five years before, the telemarketers focused on leads who had just placed a call to Club Med. The system was also capable of classifying prospects according to whether they learned about Club Med from TV or a print ad, the season they preferred for vacations, and whether or not they had taken a Club Med cruise.

Globally oriented marketers are constantly on the lookout for information about potential opportunities and threats in various parts of the world. They want to know everything about the industry, the business, the marketplace, and consumers. This passion shows up in the way they keep their ears and eyes tuned for clues, rumors, nuggets of information, and insights from other peoples' experiences. Browsing through newspapers and magazines is one way to ensure exposure to information on a regular basis. Global marketers may also develop a habit of watching news programs from around the world via satellite. This type of general exposure to information is known as *viewing*. If a particular news story has special relevance for a company—for example, renewal of China's most-favored-nation status or the dollar's decline against major world currencies—the marketer will pay special attention, tracking the story as it develops. This is known as *monitoring*.

The *search* mode is characterized by more formal activity. Search is characterized by the deliberate seeking out of specific information. Search often involves *investigation*, a relatively limited and informal type of search. Investigation often involves seeking out books or articles in trade publications on a particular topic or issue. Search may also consist of *research*, a formally organized effort to acquire specific information for a specific purpose. This type of formal, organized research is described later in the chapter.

One study found that nearly 75 percent of the information acquired by headquarters executives at U.S. global companies comes from surveillance as opposed to search. However, the viewing mode generated only 13 percent of important external information, while monitoring generated 60 percent. Two factors contribute to the paucity of information generated by viewing. One is the limited extent to which executives are exposed to information that is not included in a clearly defined subject agenda. The other is the limited receptivity of the typical executive to information outside this agenda. Every executive limits his or her exposure to information that will not have a high probability of being relevant to the job or company. This is rational; a person can absorb only a minute fraction of the data available to him or her. Exposure to and retention of information stimuli must be selective.

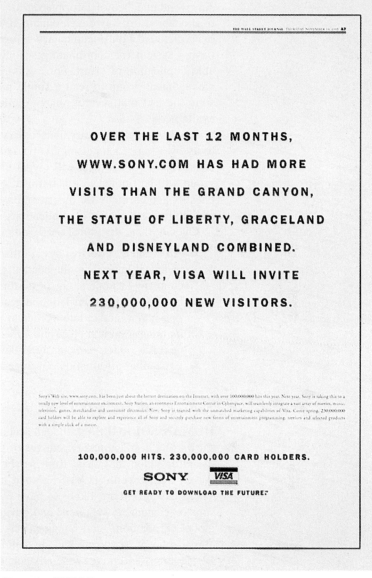

(Courtesy of SONY.)

Nevertheless, it is vital that the organization as a whole be receptive to information not explicitly recognized as important. To be effective, a scanning system must ensure that the organization is viewing areas where developments that could be important to the company might occur. Innovations in information technology have increased the speed with which information is transmitted and simultaneously shortened the life of its usefulness to the company. Advances in technology have also placed new demands on the global firm in terms of shrinking reaction times to information acquired. In some instances, the creation of a full-time scanning unit with explicit responsibility for acquiring and disseminating strategic information may be required.

Of all the changes in recent years affecting the availability of information, perhaps none is more apparent than the explosion of documentary and electronic information. An overabundance of information has created a major problem for anyone attempting to stay abreast of key developments in multiple national markets. Today, executives are overwhelmed with documentary information. However, too few companies employ a formal system for coordinating scanning activities. This situation results in considerable duplication of effort. For example, it is not uncommon for members of an entire management group to read a single publication covering a particular subject area despite the fact that several other excellent publications covering the same area may be available.

The best way to identify unnecessary duplication is to carry out an audit of reading activity by asking each person involved to list the publications he or she reads regularly. A consolidation of the lists will reveal the surveillance coverage. Often, the scope of the group will be limited to a handful of publications to the exclusion of other worthwhile ones. A good remedy for this situation is consultation with outside experts regarding the availability and quality of publications in relevant fields or subject areas.

Overall, then, the global organization is faced with the following needs:

■ An efficient, effective system that will scan and digest published sources and technical journals in the headquarters country as well as countries in which the company has operations or customers.
■ Daily scanning, translating, digesting, abstracting, and electronic input of information into a market intelligence system. Despite the advances in global information, its translation and electronic input is mostly manual. This will continue for the next few years, particularly in developing countries.
■ Expanding information coverage to other regions of the world.

Sources of Market Information

HUMAN SOURCES • Although scanning is a vital source of information, research has shown that headquarters executives of global companies obtain as much as two-thirds of the information they need from personal sources. A great deal of external information comes from executives based abroad in company subsidiaries, affiliates, and branches. These executives are likely to have established communication with distributors, consumers, customers, suppliers, and government officials. Indeed, a striking feature of the global corporation—and a major source of competitive strength—is the role executives abroad play in acquiring and disseminating information about the world environment. Headquarters executives generally acknowledge that company executives overseas are the people who know best what is going on in their areas. The following is a typical comment of headquarters executives:

> Our principal sources are internal. We have a very well-informed and able overseas establishment. The local people have a double advantage. They know the local scene and they know our business. Therefore, they are an excellent source. They know what we are interested in learning, and because of their local knowledge they are able to effectively cover available information from all sources.

The information issue exposes one of the key weaknesses of a domestic company: Although more attractive opportunities may be present outside existing areas of operation, they will likely go unnoticed by inside sources in a domestic company because the scanning horizon tends to end at the home-country border. Similarly, a company with only limited geographical operations may be at risk because internal sources abroad tend to scan only information about their own countries or regions.

Other important information sources are friends, acquaintances, professional colleagues, consultants, and prospective new employees. The latter are particularly important if they have worked for competitors. Sometimes information-related ethical and legal issues arise when a person changes jobs. In 1993, J. Ignacio Lopez de Arriortua, head of purchasing at General Motors, accepted a job as production chief with Volkswagen. GM charged that Mr. Lopez had taken important documents and computer files when he moved to Volkswagen. The resulting publicity has been an ongoing source of embarrassment to Volkswagen.

As noted in Chapter 4, it is hard to overstate the importance of travel and contact for building rapport and personal relationships. Moreover, one study found that three-quarters of the information acquired from human sources is gained in face-to-face conversation. Why? Some information is too sensitive to transmit in any other way. For example, highly placed government employees could find their careers compromised if they are identified as information sources. In such cases the most secure way of transmitting information is face-to-face rather than in writing. Information that includes estimates of future developments or even appraisals of the significance of current happenings is often considered too uncertain to commit to writing. Commenting upon this point, one executive said:

> People are reluctant to commit themselves in writing to highly "iffy" things. They are not cowards or overly cautious; they simply know that you are bound to be wrong in trying to predict the future, and they prefer to not have their names associated with documents that will someday look foolish.

The great importance of face-to-face communication lies also in the dynamics of personal interaction. Personal contact provides an occasion for executives to get together for a long-enough time to permit communication in some depth. Face-to-face discussion also exposes highly significant forms of nonverbal communication, as discussed in Chapter 4. One executive described the value of face-to-face contact in these terms:

> If you really want to find out about an area, you must see people personally. There is no comparison between written reports and actually sitting down with a man and talking. A personal meeting is worth four thousand written reports.

DIRECT PERCEPTION • Direct sensory perception provides a vital background for the information that comes from human and documentary sources. Direct perception gets all the senses involved. It means seeing, feeling, hearing, smelling, or tasting for oneself to find out what is going on in a particular country, rather than getting secondhand information by hearing or reading about a particular issue. Some information is easily available from other sources but requires sensory experience to sink in. Often, the background information or context one gets from observing a situation can help fill in the "big picture." For example, David Becker, a sales manager for a U.S. industrial supplies company, regularly visits accounts in Latin America. On a trip to Mexico, Becker realized that potential customers were intimidated because they had to speak English when placing orders by telephone. The company added telephone lines staffed by Spanish-speaking order takers and translated catalog indexes into Spanish. Telephone order volume from Mexico increased dramatically as a result.[1]

The chief executive of a small U.S. company that manufactures an electronic device for controlling corrosion had a similar experience. After spending much time in Japan,

---

[1]Tracey Tomashpol, "Off the Beaten Path," *International Business* (July 1994), p. 64.

the executive managed to book several orders for the device. Following an initial burst of success, Japanese orders dropped off; for one thing, the executive was told the packaging was too plain. "We couldn't understand why we needed a five-color label and a custom-made box for this device, which goes under the hood of a car or in the boiler room of a utility company," the executive said. While waiting for the bullet train in Japan one day, the executive's local distributor purchased a cheap watch at the station and had it elegantly wrapped. The distributor asked the American executive to guess the value of the watch based on the packaging. Despite everything he had heard and read about the Japanese obsession with quality, it was the first time the American understood that in Japan, "a book is judged by its cover." As a result, the company revamped its packaging, seeing to such details as ensuring that strips of tape used to seal the boxes were cut to precisely the same length.[2]

Toyota relied heavily on direct perception when redesigning its flagship luxury car, the Lexus LS 400, for the 1995 model year. The chief engineer of Lexus and a five-person team came to the United States in 1991. They stayed in luxury hotels to gain an understanding of the level of service Lexus customers demanded. Design team members visited customers' homes and took notes on preferences for such things as furniture, paintings—even briefcases. As Ron Brown, a U.S.-based product planning manager for Lexus, recalled, "It's like if you just bought a new washer-dryer, and the Kenmore people called and said they wanted to bring a bunch of people out to watch you wash your clothes." One thing the team discovered was that the coat hooks in the first-generation LS 400 were too small. The Japanese thought a coat hook was, literally, for hanging a coat. In reality, Lexus owners regularly hang their dry-cleaning in the car. The hook has been redesigned for 1995. "You can get five coat hangers on it. But now it's big enough that you wouldn't want it out all the time, so it retracts," says Brown.[3]

As these examples show, cultural and language differences require firsthand visits to important markets to "get the lay of the land." Travel should be seen not only as a tool for management control of existing operations but also as a vital and indispensable tool in information scanning.

FORMAL MARKET RESEARCH

Information is a critical ingredient in formulating and implementing a successful marketing strategy. As described earlier, a marketing information system should produce a continuous flow of information. Marketing research, on the other hand, is the project-specific, systematic gathering of data in the search scanning mode. Michael Czinkota and Illka Ronkainen note that the objectives of international market research are the same as the objectives of domestic research. However, the authors have identified four specific environmental factors that may require that international research efforts be conducted differently than domestic research. First, researchers must be prepared for new parameters of doing business. Not only will there be different requirements, but the ways in which rules are applied may differ as well. Second, "cultural megashock" may occur as company personnel come to grips with a new set of culture-based assumptions about conducting business. Third, a company entering more than one new geographic market faces a burgeoning network of interacting factors; research may help prevent psychological overload. Fourth, company researchers may have to broaden the definition of competitors in international markets to include competitive pressures that would not be present in the domestic market (Czinkota and Ronkainen 1994, 22–24).

There are two ways to conduct marketing research. One is to design and implement a

[2]Nilly Landau, "Face to Face Marketing Is Best," *International Business* (June 1994), p. 64.
[3]James R. Healy, "Toyota Strives for New Look, Same Edge," *USA Today* (Oct. 13, 1994), pp. 1B–2B.

TABLE 7–2 RESEARCH COMPANIES RANKED BY NON-U.S. REVENUE, 1993

Company (Home Country)	Non-U.S. Research Revenues (millions)	Percent of Total Revenues
1. Nielsen/IMS International (USA/Switzerland)	$1,158.0	62.0
2. Video Research Limited	132.0	100.0
3. Research International Group (U.K.)	124.3	84.6
4. MRB Group (U.K.)	69.0	66.3
5. Walsh International (USA)	54.0	42.9
6. Global Market Research (U.K.)	51.1	96.9
7. Information Resources Inc. (USA)	50.2	15.0
8. Millward Brown (USA)	46.7	61.4
9. Gallup Organization (USA)	27.0	26.2
10. Louis Harris & Associates (USA)	18.0	62.1

Source: Adapted from "Research: Special Report," *Advertising Age* (Nov. 28, 1994), p. 30.

study with in-house staff. The other is to use an outside firm specializing in marketing research. The importance of the global market to research firms has increased considerably in recent years. For example, A.C. Nielsen Co.'s 1993 revenues from non-U.S. research totaled $1.1 billion, nearly two-thirds of total revenue. (Market research companies are ranked in Table 7–2 according to revenues generated outside the United States.) With offices in Poland, the Czech Republic, the Slovak Republic, and Hungary, Nielsen is spearheading the move into Eastern Europe.

The process of collecting data and converting it into useful information can be divided into five basic steps: identifying the research problem, developing a research plan, collecting data, analyzing data, and presenting the research findings. Each step is discussed subsequently.

Step 1: Identifying the Research Problem

The following story illustrates the first step in the formal marketing research process.

The vice presidents of finance and marketing of a shoe company were traveling around the world to estimate the market potential for their products. They arrived in a very poor country and both immediately noticed that none of the local citizens were wearing shoes. The vice president of finance said, "We might as well get back on the plane. There is no market for shoes in this country." The vice president of marketing replied, "What an opportunity! Everyone in this country is a potential customer!"

The potential market for shoes was enormous in the eyes of the marketing executive. To formally confirm her instinct, some research would be required. As this story shows, research is often undertaken after a problem or opportunity has presented itself. Perhaps a competitor is making inroads in one or more important markets around the world. Or, as in the story recounted above, a company may wish to determine whether a particular country or regional market provides good growth potential. It is a truism of market research that "a problem well defined is a problem half solved." Thus, regardless of what situation sets the research effort in motion, the first two questions a marketer should ask are, "What information do I need?" and "Why do I need this information?"

The research problem often involves assessing the nature of the market opportunity. This, in turn, depends in part on whether the market that is the focus of the research effort can be classified as existing or potential. *Existing* markets are those in which customer needs are already being served by one or more companies. In many countries, data

■ BENETTON'S INFORMATION SYSTEM

*I*n the fashion business, the company that gets preferred styles and colors to market in the shortest length of time gains an edge over competitors. Luciano Benetton, founder of the Italian company that bears his name, notes that "Benetton's market is, for reasons of product and target, very dynamic, evolving rapidly." The company's information system includes relational databases and a network for electronic data interchange. Benetton managers rely heavily on inbound data generated at the point of purchase; data about each sales transaction are instantly transmitted via satellite to headquarters from thousands of cash registers around the world. Analysts sift through the data to identify trends, which are conveyed to manufacturing.

Most of Benetton's knitwear is produced as undyed "gray goods"; garments are dyed in batches in accordance with the fashion trends identified by the MIS. Benetton's system helps cut inventory carrying costs and reduce the number of slow-selling items that must be marked down. The company's staff of field agents uses a tracking system to follow the movement of outbound merchandise. The system shows whether a particular item is in production, in a warehouse, or in transit. In Benetton's state-of-the-art, $57 million distribution center, computer-controlled robots sort, store, and retrieve up to 12,000 bar-coded boxes of merchandise each day.

The MIS even helps the designer team work more efficiently. Before the MIS was installed, designers had to personally visit the warehouse to review samples of clothing from previous seasons. With the new system, all clothing items are photographed and the images digitized and stored on a laser disc connected to a personal computer. A designer sitting at the computer can request any item from seasonal collections dating back several years and it will be displayed on screen.

Taken as a whole, Benetton's MIS has slashed the amount of time required to design and ship knitwear from six months to a matter of weeks. Still, Luciano Benetton is not satisfied. He hopes to go beyond data processing and use information technology as a tool for motivating employees. Explains MIS manager Bruno Zuccaro, "He says it's not enough to know what we sold, but we need to know what we should have sold and that we lost X dollars by not realizing our potential."

Source: Janette Martin, "Benetton's IS Instinct," *Datamation* (July 1, 1989), pp. 68-15–68-16.

about the size of existing markets—in terms of dollar volume and unit sales—are readily available. In the United States, for example, Information Resources Inc. and Nielsen Marketing Research compile exhaustive amounts of data about sales in various product categories. Data about the Asian market is available from the Hong Kong–based Survey Research Group. In countries where such data are not available, a company focusing on existing markets must first estimate the market size, the level of demand, or the rate of product purchase or consumption. A second research objective in existing markets may be assessment of the company's overall competitiveness in terms of product appeal, price, distribution, and promotional coverage and effectiveness. Researchers may be able to pinpoint a weakness in the competitor's product or identify an unserved market segment.

The 35mm camera category is a good illustration of the opportunity that can be presented by an existing market. Prior to 1960, German companies dominated the world market for 35mm cameras with their range finder design. Then, Japanese companies introduced a superior design, the single lens reflex. In addition to offering high overall quality and an innovative design, the Japanese made sure that prices were relatively low, distribution was intensive, and communication strategies focused on the superiority of the SLR design. The results of the Japanese strategy were dramatic. In 1960, Germany exported $42 million in 35mm cameras, more than double the value of Japan's $16 million in exports. By 1970, the market positions of the two countries were reversed: The value of 35mm cameras exported from Japan was nearly triple that of German camera exports. The Japanese have continued innovating in such areas as optics, motor miniaturization, and microprocessor control, and today they virtually monopolize the market.

Potential markets can be further subdivided into latent and incipient markets. A *latent* market is, in essence, an undiscovered segment. It is a market in which demand would materialize *if* an appropriate product were made available. In a latent market, demand is zero before the product is offered. In the case of existing markets, the main research challenge is to understand the extent to which competition fully meets customer needs. With latent markets, initial success is not based on a company's competitiveness. Rather, it depends on the prime mover advantage—a company's ability to uncover the opportunity and launch a marketing program that taps the latent demand. Sometimes, traditional marketing research is not an effective means for doing this. As Peter Drucker has pointed out, the failure of U.S. companies to successfully commercialize fax machines—an American innovation—can be traced to research that indicated no potential demand for such a product. The problem, in Drucker's view, stems from the typical survey question for a product targeted at a latent market. Suppose a researcher asks, "Would you buy a telephone accessory that costs upwards of $1,500 and enables you to send, for $1 a page, the same letter the post office delivers for 25 cents?" On the basis of economics alone, the respondent most likely will answer "no."

Drucker explains that the reason Japanese companies are the leading sellers of fax machines today is that their understanding of the market was not based on survey research. Instead, they reviewed the early days of mainframe computers, photocopy machines, cellular telephones, and other information and communications products. The companies realized that, judging only by the initial economics of buying and using these new products, the prospects of market acceptance were low. Yet, each of these products had become a huge success after people began to use them. This realization prompted the Japanese to focus on the market for the *benefits* provided by fax machines, rather than the market for the machines themselves. By looking at the success of courier services such as Federal Express, the Japanese realized that, in essence, the fax machine market already existed.[4]

An *incipient* market is a market that will emerge if a particular economic, political, or sociocultural trend continues. If a company offers a product in an incipient market before the trends have taken root, it will have little market response. After the trends have had a chance to unfold, the incipient market will become latent, and later, existing. This can be illustrated by the impact of rising income on demand for automobiles and other expensive consumer durables. As per capita income rises in a country, the demand for automobiles will also rise. Therefore, if a company can predict a country's future rate of income growth, it can also predict the growth rate of its automobile market. China's rapid growth has encouraged several Western automakers, including Volkswagen, Peugot, and Chrysler, to set up in-country Chinese manufacturing operations. In 1992, GM announced a $100 million joint venture to assemble pickup trucks in the city of Shenyang. There was even incipient demand in China for exotic cars; in early 1994, Ferrari opened its first showroom in Beijing. The company has sold several cars, including a Testarossa that cost $700,000 after the 150 percent import tax had been added. The first buyers were entrepreneurs who had profited from China's increasing openness to Western-style marketing and capitalism.

Step 2: Developing a Research Plan

After defining the problem to be studied or the question to be answered, the marketer must address a new set of questions. What is this information worth to us in dollars (or yen, etc.)? What will we gain by collecting this data? What would be the cost of not getting the data that could be converted into useful information? Research requires the investment of both money and managerial time, and it is necessary to perform a cost/benefit analysis before proceeding further.

In some instances, a company may pursue the same course of action no matter what the research reveals. Even when more information is needed to ensure a high-quality decision, a realistic estimate of a formal study may reveal that the cost to perform research

---

[4]Peter F. Drucker, "Marketing 101 for a Fast-Changing Decade," *The Wall Street Journal* (Nov. 20, 1990), p. A17.

is simply too high. As discussed in the next section, a great deal of potentially useful data already exists; utilizing such data instead of commissioning a major study can result in significant savings. In any event, during the planning step, methodologies, budgets, and time parameters are all spelled out. Only when the plan is completed should the next step be undertaken.

Step 3: Collecting Data

Are data available in company files, a library, industry or trade journals, or on-line? When is the information needed? Marketers must address these issues as they proceed to the data collection step of the research. Using data that are readily available saves both money and time. A formal market study can cost hundreds of thousands of dollars and take many months to complete.

SECONDARY DATA • A low-cost approach to market research and data collection begins with desk research. Personal files, company or public libraries, on-line databases, government census records, and trade associations are just a few of the data sources that can be tapped with minimal effort and cost. Data from these sources already exist. Such data are known as *secondary* data because they were not gathered for the specific project at hand. *Statistical Abstract of the United States* is just one of the annual publications issued by the U.S. government that contains myriad data about international markets. Many market research reports are contained in the National Trade Data Base (NTDB), a CD-ROM resource published by the U.S. Department of Commerce. Syndicated studies published by research companies are another source of secondary data and information. The Cambridge Information Group publishes Findex, a directory of more than 13,000 reports and studies covering 90 industries. One information services company, FIND/SVP, sells reports on a wide range of global business sectors, including: retailing, personal-care products, packaging, food, beverages, health care, energy, transportation, and telecommunications. A sampling of reports available from FIND/SVP is shown in Table 7–3; the cost of a single report can run into thousands of dollars.

PRIMARY DATA AND SURVEY RESEARCH • When data are not available through published statistics or studies, direct collection is necessary. *Primary data* are gathered through original research pertaining to the particular problem identified in step 1. Survey

TABLE 7–3   **GLOBAL MARKET RESEARCH REPORTS FROM FIND/SVP**

Title of Study	Length (pages)	Price
Grocery Retailing in Europe	490	$5,995
50 Leading Cosmetics and Toiletries Companies in Europe	1,088	9,800
Statistical Review of European Packaging Markets	1,400	5,600
Dairy Products—The International Market	120	2,395
Soft Drink Markets and the European Consumer	360	7,995
World Therapeutic and Surgical Equipment	273	1,895
Oil Refining and Petrol Distribution in Eastern Europe and the U.S.S.R.	350	2,500
Worldwide Automobile Industry	153	1,000
Pacific Rim Telecommunications	300	1,495

research, interviews, and focus groups are some of the tools used to collect primary market data. Personal interviews—with individuals or groups—allow researchers to ask "why" and then explore answers. A focus group is a group interview led by a trained moderator who facilitates discussion of a product concept, advertisement, social trend, or other topic. For example, the Coca-Cola Company recently convened focus groups in Japan, England, and the United States to explore potential consumer reaction to a prototype 12-ounce contoured aluminum soft drink can. Coca-Cola is particularly anxious to counteract competition from private-label colas in key markets. In England, for example, Sainsbury's store-brand cola has an 18 percent market share.[5]

In some instances, product characteristics dictate a particular country location for primary data collection. For example, Case Corporation recently needed input from farmers about cab design on a new generation of tractors. Case markets tractors in North America, Europe, and Australia, but the prototypes it had developed were too expensive and fragile to ship. Working in conjunction with Jefferson Davis Associates, an Iowa-based market research company, Case invited 40 farmers to an engineering facility near Chicago for interviews and reactions to instrument and control mock-ups. The visiting farmers were also asked to examine tractors made by Case's competitors and evaluate them on more than 100 different design elements. Case personnel from France and Germany were on hand to assist as interpreters.[6]

Survey research often involves obtaining data from customers or some other designated group by means of a questionnaire. Surveys can be designed to generate quantitative data ("How often would you buy?"), qualitative data ("Why would you buy?"), or both. Survey research generally involves administering a questionnaire by mail, by telephone, or in person. Many good marketing research textbooks provide details on questionnaire design and administration. A good questionnaire has three main characteristics:

1. It is simple.
2. It is easy for respondents to answer and for the interviewer to record.
3. It keeps the interview to the point and obtains desired information.

An important survey issue in global marketing is potential bias due to the cultural background of the persons designing the questionnaire. For example, a survey designed and administered in the United States may be inappropriate in non-Western cultures, even if it is carefully translated.[7] This is especially true if the person designing the questionnaire is not aware of the self-reference criterion. A technique known as *back translation* can help increase comprehension and validity; the technique requires that, after a questionnaire or survey instrument is translated into a particular "target language," it be translated once again into the original by a different translator. For even greater accuracy, *parallel translations*—that is, two versions by different translators—can be used as input to the back translation process. The same techniques can be used to ensure that advertising copy is accurately translated into different languages. Sometimes bias is introduced when a survey is sponsored by a company with a financial stake in the outcome that plans to publicize the results. For example, American Express joined with the French tourist bureau in producing a study that, among other things, covered the personality of the French people. The report ostensibly showed that, contrary to a longstanding stereotype, the French are not "unfriendly" to foreigners. However, the survey respondents were people who already

[5]Karen Benezra, "Coke Queries on Contour Can," *Brandweek* (Nov. 7, 1994), p. 4.
[6]Jonathan Reed, "Unique Approach to International Research," *Agri Marketing* (March 1995), pp. 10–13.
[7]Geert Hofstede and Michael Harris Bond, "The Confucius Connection: From Cultural Roots to Economic Growth," *Organizational Dynamics* (Spring 1988), p. 15.

A market researcher interviews an Australian cotton grower to gauge his reaction to a new tractor from Case Corporation. (Photo courtesy of Case Corporation and Jefferson Davis Associates, Inc.)

had traveled to France on pleasure trips in the previous two years—a fact that likely biased the result.[8]

SAMPLING • When collecting data, researchers generally cannot administer a survey to every possible person in the designated group. A *sample* is a selected subset of a population that is representative of the entire population. The two best-known types of samples are *probability samples* and *nonprobability samples*. A probability sample is generated by following statistical rules that ensure that each member of the population under study has an equal chance—or probability—of being included in the sample. The results of a probability sample can be projected to the entire population with statistical reliability reflecting sampling error, degree of confidence, and standard deviation.

[8]Cynthia Crossen, "Margin of Error: Studies Galore Support Products and Positions, but Are They Reliable?" *The Wall Street Journal* (Nov. 4, 1991), pp. A1, A7.

The results of a nonprobability sample cannot be projected with statistical reliability. One form of nonprobability sample is a *convenience sample*. As the name implies, researchers select people who are easy to reach. For example, in one study comparing consumer shopping attitudes in the United States, Jordan, Singapore, and Turkey, data for the latter three countries were gathered from convenience samples recruited by an acquaintance of the researcher. While data gathered in this way are not subject to statistical inference, they may be adequate to address the problem defined in step 1. In this study, for example, the researchers were able to identify a clear trend toward cultural convergence in shopping attitudes and customs that cut across modern industrial countries, emerging industrial countries, and developing countries.[9]

To obtain a *quota sample*, the researcher divides the population under study into categories; a sample is taken from each category. The term "quota" refers to the need to make sure that enough people are chosen in each category to reflect the overall makeup of the population. For example, assume that a country's population may be divided into six categories according to monthly income as follows:

Percent of population	10%	15%	25%	25%	15%	10%
Earnings per month	0–9	10–19	20–39	40–59	60–69	70–100

If it is assumed that income is the characteristic that adequately differentiates the population for study purposes, then a quota sample would include respondents of different income levels in the same proportion as they occurred in the population, that is, 15 percent with monthly earnings from 10 to 19, and so on.

Step 4: Analyzing Data

DEMAND PATTERN ANALYSIS • Industrial growth patterns provide an insight into market demand. Because they generally reveal consumption patterns, production patterns are helpful in assessing market opportunities. Additionally, trends in manufacturing production indicate potential markets for companies that supply manufacturing inputs. At the early stages of growth in a country, when per capita incomes are low, manufacturing centers on such necessities as food and beverages, textiles, and other forms of light industry. As incomes rise, the relative importance of these industries declines as heavy industry begins to develop (Moyer 1968).

INCOME ELASTICITY MEASUREMENTS • Income elasticity describes the relationship between demand for a good and changes in income. Income elasticity studies of consumer products show that necessities such as food and clothing are characterized by inelastic demand. Stated differently, expenditures on products in these categories increase but at a slower percentage rate than do increases in income. This is the corollary of Engel's law, which states that as incomes rise, smaller proportions of total income are spent on food. Demand for durable consumer goods such as furniture and appliances tends to be income elastic, increasing relatively faster than increases in income.

MARKET ESTIMATION BY ANALOGY • Estimating market size with available data presents challenging analytical tasks. Global marketers often find that certain types of desired data are unavailable. If this is the case, it is sometimes possible to estimate market size by analogy. Drawing an analogy is simply stating a partial resemblance. For example, while Russia and the United States are very different, each country has a basic monetary unit that can be divided into 100 subunits. In the United States, 100 cents equals one dollar, and in Russia, 100 kopecks equals one ruble. Thus, one cent is to one dollar

---

[9]Eugene H. Fram and Riad Ajami, "Globalization of Markets and Shopping Stress: Cross-Country Comparisons," *Business Horizons* (January–February 1994), pp. 17–23.

in the United States as one kopeck is to one ruble in Russia. By stating the relationship in the form of an analogy, it is possible to show a level of analysis at which the U.S. and Russian currency systems resemble each other.

Time-series displacement is an analogy technique based on the assumption that an analogy between markets exists in different time periods. Displacing time is a useful form of market analysis when data are available for two markets at different levels of development. The time displacement method requires a marketer to estimate when two markets are at similar stages of development. For example, the market for Polaroid instant cameras in Russia in the mid-1990s is comparable to the instant camera market in the United States in the mid-1960s. By obtaining data on the factors associated with demand for instant cameras in the United States in 1964 and in Russia in 1994, as well as actual U.S. demand in 1964, one could estimate potential in Russia at the present time.

Several issues should be kept in mind in using estimation by analogy:

1. Are the two countries for which the analogy is assumed really similar? To answer this question with regard to a consumer product, the analyst must understand the similarities and differences in the cultural systems in the two countries. If the market for an industrial product is under study, an understanding of the respective national technology bases is required.
2. Have technological and social developments resulted in a situation where demand for a particular product or commodity will leapfrog previous patterns, skipping entire growth patterns that occurred in more-developed countries? For example, washing machine sales in Europe leapfrogged the pattern of sales in the United States. In the United States, washing evolved from hand-washing methods to nonautomatic washing machines and then, when reliable units were finally available, to semiautomatic and fully automatic machines. In Europe, many consumers are skipping the nonautomatic and semiautomatic stages and moving from hand-washing to fully automatic equipment. A simple analogy between the growth in sales for manual, semiautomatic, and automatic machines does not exist between the United States and Europe. Nevertheless, the market analyst might combine sales of nonautomatic and semiautomatic equipment in the U.S. market and use this growth pattern in an analogy-based estimation of potential demand in Europe.
3. If there are differences among the availability, price, quality, and other variables associated with the product in the two markets, potential demand in a target market will not develop into actual sales of a product because the market conditions are not comparable.

COMPARATIVE ANALYSIS • One of the unique opportunities in global marketing analysis is to conduct comparisons of market potential and marketing performance in different country markets at the same point in time. One form of comparative analysis is the intra-company cross-national comparison. For example, general market conditions in country X (as measured by income or stage of industrialization) may be similar to those in country Y. If there is a significant discrepancy between per capita sales of a given product in the two countries, the marketer might reasonably wonder about it and determine what actions need to be taken. Soon after George Fisher became CEO of Kodak, he asked for a review of market share in color film on a country-by-country basis. Fisher was shocked to learn that Kodak's market share in Japan was only 7 percent, compared with 40 percent in most other countries. The situation prompted Fisher to lodge a petition with the U.S. trade representative seeking removal of alleged anticompetitive barriers in Japan.[10]

A second form of comparative analysis looks at national and subnational markets. Table

[10]Wendy Bounds, "George Fisher Pushes Kodak into Digital Era," *The Wall Street Journal* (June 8, 1995), p. B1.

TABLE 7–4   NATIONAL/SUBNATIONAL MARKET COMPARISONS, 1992

	France	California
Gross product	$1.15 trillion	$800 billion
Gross product per capita	$20,000	$26,000
Population	56,910,000	30,867,000
Population growth (1980–1990)	.5%	25.7%
Population density (1993; per square mile)	273	197.9
Principal city	Paris	Los Angeles
Population of principal city	8,589,000	10,072,000
Motor vehicle registrations (1990)	28,500,000	21,926,000

Source: Data from U.S. Bureau of the Census, *Statistical Abstract of the United States: 1993* (113th ed.), Washington D.C., 1993. Table prepared by author.

7–4 is a comparison between France, a national market, and California, a subnational market. The two markets are substantially different in terms of total population and total income. France's population is nearly double that of California, although it was growing much more slowly. French GNP is double California's gross state product. Despite these differences, there are striking similarities in the consumption of many products. Indeed, for many products, such as microwave ovens and dishwashers, California—a subnational market—is a bigger market than is France.

CLUSTER ANALYSIS • The objective of cluster analysis is to group variables into clusters that maximize within-group similarities and between-group differences. Cluster analysis is well suited to global marketing research because similarities and differences can be established between local, national, and regional markets of the world. For example, Claritas/NPDC uses geodemographic data to cluster neighborhoods into types. Claritas has begun matching some U.S. cities to "twins" in Canada.[11]

Step 5: Presenting the Findings

The report based on the market research must be useful to managers as input to the decision-making process. Whether the report is presented in written form, orally, or electronically via videotape, it must relate clearly to the problem or opportunity identified in step 1. Many managers are uncomfortable with research jargon and complex quantitative analysis. Results should be clearly stated and provide a basis for managerial action. Otherwise, the report may end up on the shelf where it will gather dust and serve as a reminder of wasted time and money. As the data provided by a corporate information system and market research become increasingly available on a worldwide basis, it becomes possible to analyze marketing expenditure effectiveness across national boundaries. Managers can then decide where they are achieving the greatest marginal effectiveness for their marketing expenditures and can adjust expenditures accordingly.

CURRENT ISSUES IN GLOBAL MARKETING RESEARCH

Marketers engaged in global research face special problems and conditions that differentiate their task from that of the domestic market researcher. First, instead of analyzing a single national market, the global market researcher must analyze many national markets, each of which has unique characteristics that must be recognized in analysis. As noted earlier, for many countries the availability of data is limited.

---

[11]Claudi Montague, "Is Calgary Denver's Long-Lost Twin?" *American Demographics* (June 1993), pp. 12–13.

Second, the small markets around the world pose a special problem for the researcher. The relatively low profit potential in smaller markets justifies only a modest marketing research expenditure. Therefore, the global researcher must devise techniques and methods that keep expenditures in line with the market's profit potential. In smaller markets, there is pressure on the researcher to discover economic and demographic relationships that permit estimates of demand based on a minimum of information. It may also be necessary to use inexpensive survey research that sacrifices some elegance or statistical rigor to achieve results within the constraints of the smaller market research budget.

Another frequently encountered problem in developing countries is that data may be inflated or deflated, either inadvertently or for political expediency. For example, a Middle Eastern country deliberately revised its balance of trade in a chemical product by adding 1,000 tons to its consumption statistics in an attempt to encourage foreign investors to install domestic production facilities. In Russia, Goskomstat, the state agency that measures the economy, generates mountains of misleading statistics. Real GDP may be 40 percent higher than the official numbers, because much of the economic activity in Russia's transitional economy is "off the books" due to high taxes and confusing laws.[12]

Another problem is that the comparability of international statistics varies greatly. An absence of standard data-gathering techniques contributes to the problem. In Germany, for example, consumer expenditures are estimated largely on the basis of turnover tax receipts, whereas in the United Kingdom data from tax receipts are used in conjunction with data from household surveys and production sources.

Even with standard data-gathering techniques, definitions differ around the world. In some cases, these differences are minor; in others, they are quite significant. Germany, for example, classifies television set purchases as expenditures for "recreation and entertainment," whereas the same expenditure falls into the "furniture, furnishings, and household equipment" classification in the United States.

Survey data have similar comparability problems. When PepsiCo International, a typical user of global research, reviewed its data, it found a considerable lack of comparability in a number of major areas. Table 7–5 shows how age categories were developed in seven countries surveyed by PepsiCo. PepsiCo's headquarters marketing research group pointed out that findings in one country could only be compared with those in another if data were reported in standard five-year intervals. Without this standardization, comparability was not possible. The marketing research group recommended, therefore, that standard five-year intervals be required in all reporting to headquarters, but that any other intervals deemed useful for local purposes be allowed. Thus, for the purposes of local analysis, ages 14 to 19 might be a pertinent "youth" classification in one country, whereas ages 14 to 24 might be a more useful definition of the same segment in another country.

PepsiCo also found that local market definitions of consumption differed so greatly that it was unable to make intermarket comparisons of brand share figures. Representative definitions of consumption are shown in Table 7–6.

[12]Claudia Rosett, "Figures Never Lie, but They Seldom Tell the Truth about the Russian Economy," *The Wall Street Journal* (July 1, 1994), p. A6.

TABLE 7–5 AGE CLASSIFICATIONS FROM CONSUMER SURVEYS, MAJOR MARKETS

Mexico	Venezuela	Argentina	Germany	Spain	Italy	Philippines
14–18	10–14	14–18	14–19	15–24	13–20	14–18
19–25	15–24	19–24	20–29	25–34	21–25	19–25
26–35	25–34	25–34	30–39	35–44	26–35	26–35
36–45	35–44	35–44	40–49	45–54	36–45	36–50
46+	45+	45–65	50+	55–64	46–60	
				65+		

Source: Pepsico International.

TABLE 7-6 **DEFINITION OF CONSUMPTION USED BY PEPSICO MARKET RESEARCHER**

Mexico	Count of number of occasions product was consumed on day prior to interview.
Venezuela	Count of number of occasions product was consumed on day prior to interview.
Argentina	Count of number of drinks consumed on day prior to interview.
Germany	Count of number of respondents consuming "daily or almost daily."
Spain	Count of number of drinks consumed "at least once a week."
Italy	Count of number of respondents consuming product on day prior to interview.
Philippines	Count of number of glasses of product consumed on day prior to interview.

Source: PepsiCo International.

Finally, global consumer research is inhibited by people's reluctance to talk to strangers, greater difficulty in locating people, and fewer telephones. Both industrial and consumer research services are less developed, although the cost of these services is much lower than in a high-wage country.

Headquarters Control of Global Marketing Research

An important issue for the global company is where to locate control of the organization's research capability. The difference between a multinational, polycentric company and a global, geocentric company on this issue is significant. In the multinational company responsibility for research is delegated to the operating subsidiary. The global company delegates responsibility for research to operating subsidiaries but retains overall responsibility and control of research as a headquarters function. In practice, this means that the global company will, as in the PepsiCo example cited above, ensure that research is designed and executed so as to yield comparable data.

Comparability requires that scales, questions, and research methodology be standardized. To achieve this, the company must inject a level of control and review of marketing research at the global level. The director of worldwide marketing research must respond to local conditions as he or she searches for a research program that can be implemented on a global basis. It is most likely that the marketing director will end up with a number of marketing programs tailored to clusters of countries that exhibit within-group similarities. The agenda of a coordinated worldwide research program might look like that in Table 7-7.

The director of worldwide research should not simply direct the efforts of country research managers. His or her job is to ensure that the corporation achieves maximum results worldwide from the total allocation of its research resources. Achieving this requires that personnel in each country are aware of research being carried out in the rest of the world and are involved in influencing the design of their own in-country research as well as the overall research program. Ultimately, the director of worldwide research must be responsible for the overall research design and program. It is his or her job to take inputs

TABLE 7-7 **WORLDWIDE MARKETING RESEARCH PLAN**

Research Objective	Country Cluster A	Country Cluster B	Country Cluster C
Identify market potential			X
Appraise competitive intentions		X	X
Evaluate product appeal	X	X	X
Study market response to price	X		
Appraise distribution channels	X	X	X

from the entire world and produce a coordinated research strategy that generates the information needed to achieve global sales and profit objectives.

The Marketing Information System as a Strategic Asset

The advent of the transnational enterprise means that boundaries between the firm and the outside world are dissolving. Marketing has historically been responsible for managing many of the relationships across that boundary. The boundary between marketing and other functions is also dissolving, implying that the traditional notion of marketing as a distinct functional area within the firm is giving way to a new model. The process of marketing decision making is also changing. This is due largely to the changing role of information: from a support tool to information as a wealth-generating, strategic asset. Earlier in the chapter we saw how Club Med is tapping long-neglected customer information in its database to increase sales.

Some firms are experimenting with "flatter" organizational structures, with less hierarchical, less centralized decision-making structures. Such organizations facilitate the exchange and flow of information between otherwise noncommunicative departments. The more information-intensive the firm, the greater the degree to which marketing is involved in activities traditionally associated with other functional areas. In such firms there is "parallel" processing of information.

Information intensity in the firm impacts market attractiveness, competitive position, and organizational structure. The greater a company's information intensity, the more the traditional product/market boundaries shift. In essence, companies increasingly face new sources of competition from other firms in historically noncompetitive industries, particularly if those firms are also information intensive. The most obvious and dramatic example is the emergence of the "superindustry" combining telecommunications, computers, financial services, and retailing into what is essentially an information industry. Such diverse firms as AT&T, IBM, Merrill Lynch, Citicorp, and Sears now find themselves in direct competition with each other. They offer essentially the same products, although not as a result of diversification. Rather, the new competition reflects a natural extension and redefinition of traditional product lines and marketing activities. Today, when a company speaks of "value added," it is less likely to be referring to unique product features. Rather, the emphasis is on the information exchanged as part of customer transactions—much of which cuts across traditional product lines.

AN INTEGRATED APPROACH TO INFORMATION COLLECTION[13]

Coordinated organization activity is required to maintain surveillance of those aspects of the environment about which the organization wishes to stay informed. The goal of this activity, which may be termed *organized intelligence*, is to systematize the collection and analysis of competitive intelligence to serve the needs of the organization as a whole. Organizing for intelligence requires more than gathering and disseminating good intelligence. Many companies that simply assign an analyst the task of gathering, analyzing, and disseminating intelligence encounter problems in getting managers to use the output, gaining credibility for the output and its function, and establishing the relevance of the output for users.

The role of organized competitive intelligence in shaping strategy will depend on its ability to supplement, rather than replace, the informal activities of employees, especially top management. One obstacle to a fully integrated MIS encompassing both formal and

[13]This section is adapted from Gilad 1989.

informal information-gathering techniques is that monitoring activities are not usually fully integrated with the decision-making process. If the information isn't used, the monitoring effort will invariably fail to increase a company's competitiveness. Michael Porter's influential work on competitive strategy, together with increasing global competitive pressures and loss of market dominance by many U.S. companies, has helped bring environmental scanning into a new focus. The emphasis has been on competitive intelligence rather than on broader environmental scanning. When considering the possibility of establishing an organized intelligence system, a company may want to review the following questions:

1. Are top executives well informed about the competitive conditions in the market, or do they typically grumble about lack of sufficient knowledge?
2. Do proposals and presentations by middle management show an intimate knowledge of competitors and other industry players? Do these managers seem to know more than what has been published in trade literature?
3. Do managers in one department/division know of intelligence activities in other units? Do they share intelligence regularly?
4. How many times during the last 6 months was management surprised by developments in the marketplace? How many decisions yielded less-than-satisfactory results, and what percentage was caused by lack of accurate assessment of competitive response?
5. Has competitive pressure increased in the industry in question? Does management feel comfortable about its state of familiarity with foreign competitors?
6. How much does the company spend on on-line databases? How many users know about the availability of the system and how to access it?
7. Do users of information suffer from overload of data but underload of good analysis and estimates of implications to the company?

SUMMARY

Information is one of the most basic ingredients of a successful marketing strategy. The global marketer must scan the world for information about opportunities and threats and make information available via a management information system. Scanning can be accomplished by keeping in touch with an area of information via surveillance or by actively seeking out information via search. Information can be obtained from human and documentary sources or from direct perception.

Formal research is often required before decisions can be made regarding specific problems or opportunities. After developing a research plan, data are collected using either primary or secondary sources. A number of techniques are available for analyzing data, including demand pattern analysis, income elasticity measurements, estimation by analogy, comparative analysis, and cluster analysis. Research findings must be presented clearly in order to facilitate decision making. Global marketing research presents a number of challenges. First is the simple fact that research on a number of markets may be required, some of which are so small that only modest research expenditures can be made. Secondary data from some countries may be distorted; also, comparability may be an issue. A final issue is how much control headquarters will have over research and the overall management of the organization's information system.

DISCUSSION QUESTIONS

1. What is the major source of information for headquarters executives of global companies?
2. What are the different modes of information acquisition? Which is the most important for gathering strategic information?
3. Assume that you have been asked by the president of your organization to devise a systematic approach to scanning. The president does not want to be surprised by major market or competitive developments. What would you recommend?
4. Outline the basic steps of the market research process.
5. What is the difference between existing, latent, and incipient demand? How might these differences affect the design of a marketing research project?
6. Describe some of the analytical techniques used by global marketers. When is it appropriate to use each technique?

BIBLIOGRAPHY

Books

Crossen, Cynthia. *Tainted Truth: The Manipulation of Fact in America*. Upper Saddle River, N.J.: Prentice-Hall, 1994.

Douglas, Susan P., and C. Samuel Craig. *International Marketing Research*. Upper Saddle River, N.J.: Prentice-Hall, 1983.

Heath, Daniel, and Oxford Analytica. *America in Perspective: Major Trends in the United States through the 1990s*. Boston: Houghton Mifflin, 1986.

Jaffe, Eugene D. *Grouping: A Strategy for International Marketing*. New York: AMA, 1974.

Kelly, John M. *How To Check Out Your Competition: A Complete Plan for Investigating Your Market*. New York: Wiley, 1987.

Keyes, Jessica. *Infotrends: The Competitive Use of Information*. New York: McGraw-Hill, 1993.

Kiplinger, Austin H., and Knight A. Kiplinger. *America in the Global 90's: The Shape of the Future—How You Can Profit From It*. Washington, D.C.: Kiplinger Books, 1989.

Kravis, Irving B., Zoltan Kenessey, Alan Heston, and Robert Summers. *A System of International Comparisons of Gross Product and Purchasing Power*. Baltimore: Johns Hopkins University Press, 1975.

Krugman, Paul R. *The Age of Diminished Expectations: U.S. Economic Policy in the 1990s*. Cambridge, Mass.: MIT Press, 1990.

Porter, Michael E. *Competitive Strategy*. New York: Free Press, 1980.

Weekly, James K., and Mark K. Cary. *Information for International Marketing: An Annotated Guide to Sources*. New York: Greenwood Press, 1986.

Articles

Adler, Lee. "Managing Marketing Research in the Diversified Multinational Corporation." In *Marketing in Turbulent Times; and Marketing: The Challenges and Opportunities—Combined Proceedings*, ed. Edward M. Mazze. Chicago: American Marketing Association, 1975, pp. 305–308.

Cavusgil, S. Tamer. "Qualitative Insights into Company Experiences in International Marketing Research." *Journal of Business and Industrial Marketing* (Summer 1987), pp. 41–54.

Czinkota, M. R., and I. A. Ronkainen. "Market Research for Your Export Operations, Part I—Using Secondary Sources of Research." *International Trade Forum* 30, no. 3 (1994), pp. 22–33.

———. "Market Research for Your Export Operations, Part II—Conducting Primary Market Research." *International Trade Forum* 31, no. 1 (1995), pp. 16+.

Davenport, Thomas H., Michael Hammer, and Tauno J. Metsisto. "How Executives Can Shape Their Company's Information Systems." *Harvard Business Review* 67, no. 2 (March–April 1989), pp. 130–134.

Davidson, Lawrence S. "Knowing the Unknowable." *Business Horizons* 32, no. 5 (September–October 1989), pp. 2–8.

Douglas, Susan P., C. Samuel Craig, and Warren J. Keegan. "Approaches to Assessing International Marketing Opportunities for Small- and Medium-sized Companies." *Columbia Journal of World Business* 17, no. 3 (Fall 1982), pp. 2–30.

Gilad, Benjamin. "The Role of Organized Competitive Intelligence in Corporate Strategy." *Columbia Journal of World Business* 24, no. 4 (Winter 1989), pp. 29–36.

Glazer, Rashi. "Marketing in an Information-Intensive Environment: Strategic Implications of Knowledge as an Asset." *Journal of Marketing* (October 1991), pp. 1–19.

Green, Robert, and Eric Langeard. "A Cross-National Comparison of Consumer Habits and Innovator Characteristics." *Journal of Marketing* (July 1975), pp. 34–41.

Keegan, Warren J. "Scanning the International Business Environment: A Study of the Informational Acquisition Process," Doctoral Dissertation, Harvard Business School, 1967.

King, W. R., and V. Sethi. "Developing Transnational Information Systems: A Case Study." *Omega* (January 1993), pp. 53–59.

Lindberg, Bertil C. "International Comparison of Growth in Demand for a New Durable Consumer Product." *Journal of Marketing Research* (August 1982), pp. 364–371.

Moyer, Reed. "International Market Analysis." *Journal of Marketing Research* (November 1968).

Naumann, Earl, Donald W. Jackson, Jr., and William G. Wolfe. "Comparing U.S. and Japanese Market Research Firms." *California Management Review* 36, no. 4 (Summer 1994), pp. 49–69.

Sethi, S. Prakash. "Comparative Cluster Analysis for World Markets." *Journal of Marketing Research* 8 (August 1971), p. 350.

Sharer, Kevin. "Top Management's Intelligence Needs: An Executive's View of Competitive Intelligence." *Competitive Intelligence Review* (Spring 1991), pp. 3–5.

Stanat, Ruth. "Tracking Your Global Competition." *Competitive Intelligence Review* (Spring 1991), pp. 17–19.

Vogel, R. H. "Uses of Managerial Perceptions in Clustering Countries." *Journal of International Business Studies* (Spring 1976), pp. 91–100.

Wasilewski, Nikolai. "Dimensions of Environmental Scanning Systems in Multinational Enterprises." Pace University, Working Papers no. 3 (May 1993).

RESEARCH POINTS WHIRLPOOL TOWARD GLOBAL MARKET

The Whirlpool Corporation, headquartered in Benton Harbor, Michigan, is the number one appliance company in the United States. The company sells $7 billion worth of "white goods" each year, and its share of the U.S. appliance market is 34 percent. Its success has been achieved in part by offering products in three different price ranges: top-of-the-line Kitchen Aid appliances, the medium-priced Whirlpool and Sears Kenmore lines, and Roper and Estate at the low end. Faced with a slow-growing, mature domestic market, Whirlpool has been aggressively pursuing overseas expansion plans. The company has been in Latin America since 1957; today it is the market share leader in that region. Whirlpool moved into the number three position in Europe by acquiring Philips Electronics' European appliance business for $1 billion. Now Whirlpool is also targeting Japan and the developing nations in Asia in an effort to achieve growth.

In Europe, the presence of more than one hundred competitors makes the appliance industry highly fragmented—and highly competitive. AB Electrolux, a Swedish company, and Germany's Bosch-Siemens Hausgerate GmbH are the number one and number two companies. Whirlpool executives are aiming for 10 percent operating profit margins; margins in Europe are currently 5.6 percent. To reach this goal, the company has streamlined its European organization. Four regional sales offices have replaced sales organizations in 17 separate countries. Hank Bowman, president of Whirlpool Europe BV, has trimmed the number of warehouses from 30 to 16, and hopes eventually to have as few as 5 or 6. A global parts sourcing strategy has helped reduce the number of suppliers by 40 percent. Over the next several years, Whirlpool will invest hundreds of millions of dollars in new product development. It has already begun marketing a new dryer designed to operate more efficiently and provide higher quality despite containing fewer parts.

Bowman seems convinced that a global market segmentation approach is the key to success in Europe. Whirlpool relies heavily on market research to maintain its leadership in the United States; listening to consumers is also important in Europe. "Research tells us that the trends, preferences and biases of consumers, country by country, are reducing as opposed to increasing," Bowman said recently. He believes that European homemakers fall into distinct "Euro-segments"—"traditionalists" and "aspirers," for example—allowing Whirlpool to duplicate the three-tiered approach to brands that has worked so well in the United States. Thus, the Baukneckt brand will be positioned at the high end of the market, with Whirlpool in the middle and Ignis at the lower end. To the extent possible, the brands will be marketed on a pan-European basis. In 1990, Whirlpool became the first appliance manufacturer to launch a pan-European ad campaign.

Bowman's global approach does not ignore regional preferences. For example, research data showed that fewer than one-third of European households had microwave ovens; the research also indicated that more Europeans might buy microwave ovens that functioned more like conventional ovens. The findings were based in part on data gathered at the company's Usability Lab in Italy, where customers are paid to come in and experiment with various appliances. In response, Whirlpool introduced the VIP Crisp microwave with a broiler coil to brown meat on the top and an attachment that sizzles the bottom of food as it cooks. The new features ensure that microwaved bacon comes out crisp on top while pizza crust is crisp, not soggy, on the bottom. Today the VIP is the top-selling microwave in Europe. The company is backing up its products with advertising expenditures of more than $100 million each year.

Having built a solid foundation in Europe, CEO David Whitwam is now setting his sights on Asia. "Our success as a global company rests on our ability to position Whirlpool in Asia," he says. To achieve that success, Whirlpool will invest in five Asian manufacturing facilities over the next five years. Already, Whirlpool has established Asian headquarters in Tokyo and a regional office in Hong Kong; a design center has been set up in Singapore. The company's actions met with approval by many industry observers. Notes Jerry Herman, an analyst with Kemper Securities, "Whirlpool gets very high marks in its global strategy. They are outpacing the industry dramatically." Still, the company faces a number of challenges in the region. For one thing, Whirlpool faces stiff competition from Japanese companies. Not surprisingly, such companies as Matsushita, Sharp, and Toshiba have a strong presence in the region; back home in the United States, Japanese companies are not a factor in major appliances. Also, four U.S. companies—Whirlpool, GE, Frigidaire, and Maytag—control 93 percent of the U.S. market. In Asia, the situation is reversed: Asian companies have 98 percent share.

Whirlpool hopes that a global approach will work as well in Asia as it did in Europe. The Whirlpool brand will be used throughout the region, with attention to local preferences. Thus, bright red refrigerators and green top-loading washers are available in several Asian countries. China symbolizes the market opportunity in the region: Only 10 percent of Chinese households currently have refrigerators. Whitwam concludes, "Five years ago we were essentially a domestic company. Today about 40 percent of our revenues are overseas, and by the latter part of this decade, a majority will be."

DISCUSSION QUESTIONS

1. Summarize the role of market research in Whirlpool's globalization effort.
2. Describe Whirlpool's global marketing strategy.
3. What do you think are the requirements for market success in Japan, which accounts for one-third of major appliance sales in Asia?

Sources: Patrick Oster, "Call It Worldpool," *Business Week* (Nov. 28, 1994), pp. 98–99.
Robert L. Rose, "Whirlpool Is Expanding in Europe Despite the Slump," *The Wall Street Journal* (Jan. 27, 1994), p. B4.
David Woodruff, "Whirlpool Goes Off on a World Tour," *Business Week* (June 3, 1991) pp. 99–100.
Barry Rehfield, "Where Whirlpool Flies, and Maytag Sputters," *The New York Times* (Jan. 3, 1993), Sec. 3, p. 5.
Sally Solo, "Whirlpool: How to Listen to Consumers," *Fortune* (Jan. 11, 1993), pp. 77, 79.
Gregory E. David, "Spin Dry: Asia Is the Last Phase in Whirlpool's Global Wash Cycle," *Financial World* (Oct. 26, 1993), pp. 30–31.

Going Global: Segmentation, Targeting, and Sourcing Decisions

Cigarettes are the most widely distributed and profitable global consumer product.[1] However, as the number of smokers in many industrialized countries declines due to heightened antismoking sentiment and health concerns, tobacco industry giants such as Britain's B.A.T Industries PLC and the U.S. Philip Morris Company have set their sights on new market opportunities. In particular, tobacco companies are targeting smokers in industrializing countries such as China, South Korea, Thailand, India, and Russia. These are nations in which a combination of forces—relatively high economic growth, smoking's fashionableness, and the status assigned to Western cigarette brands—may interact. Moreover, because many women in these countries view smoking as a symbol of their improving status in society, the tobacco companies are aggressively targeting women.

The actions taken by managers at Philip Morris, B.A.T, and other tobacco companies are examples of market segmentation and targeting. *Market segmentation* represents an effort to identify and categorize groups of customers and countries according to common characteristics. *Targeting* is the process of evaluating the segments and focusing marketing efforts on a country, region, or group of people that has significant potential to respond. Such targeting reflects the reality that a company should identify those consumers it can reach most effectively and efficiently. A company must also find a source for the product that will best meet customer needs. This may require a decision on whether a company should manufacture the product itself or buy it from an outside source. A related decision concerns *where* to make or buy the product—i.e., inside or outside the home country. Both aspects of sourcing should provide a combination of quality and cost considerations that maximizes both customer benefits and company profits. Segmentation, targeting, and sourcing are all examined in this chapter.

---

[1]Richard J. Barnet and John Cavanagh, *Global Dreams: Imperial Corporations and the New World Order* (New York: Simon & Schuster, 1994), p. 184.

GLOBAL MARKET SEGMENTATION

Global market segmentation has been defined as "the process of identifying specific segments—whether they be country groups or individual consumer groups—of potential customers with homogeneous attributes who are likely to exhibit similar buying behavior."[2] Interest in global market segmentation dates back several decades. In the late 1960s, one observer suggested that the European market could be divided into three broad categories—international sophisticate, semisophisticate, and provincial—solely on the basis of consumers' presumed receptivity to a common advertising approach.[3] Another writer suggested that some themes—for example, the desire to be beautiful, the desire to be healthy and free of pain, the love of mother and child—were universal and could be used in advertising around the globe.[4]

As noted in earlier chapters, in the 1980s, Professor Theodore Levitt advanced the thesis that consumers in different countries increasingly seek variety, and that the same new segments are likely to show up in multiple national markets. Thus, ethnic or regional foods such as sushi, Greek salad, or hamburgers might be in demand anywhere in the world. Levitt described this trend as the "pluralization of consumption" and "segment simultaneity" that provides an opportunity for marketers to pursue a segment on a global scale.

Today, global companies (and the advertising agencies that serve them) are likely to segment world markets according to one or more key criteria: demographics (including national income and size of population), psychographics (values, attitudes, and lifestyles), behavioral characteristics, and benefits sought. It is also possible to cluster different national markets in terms of their environments—e.g., the presence or absence of government regulation in a particular industry—to establish groupings.

Demographic Segmentation

Demographic segmentation is based on measurable characteristics of populations such as age, gender, income, education, and occupation. A number of demographic trends—fewer married couples, fewer children, changing roles of women, higher incomes and living standards—suggest the emergence of global segments.[5]

For most consumer and industrial products, national income is the single most important segmentation variable and indicator of market potential. Annual per capita income varies widely in world markets, from a low of $71 in Mozambique to a high of $50,000 in the Falkland Islands. A traditional approach to demographic segmentation involved clustering countries into segments of high, middle, and low income; companies simply targeted those with the highest income levels.

The U.S. market, with per capita income of $25,000, more than $6.6 trillion in 1995 national income, and a population of more than 260 million, is enormous. Little wonder, then, that Americans are a favorite target market! Despite having comparable per capita incomes, other industrialized countries are nevertheless quite small in terms of total annual income. In Sweden, for example, per capita GNP is $26,300; however, Sweden's smaller population—8.6 million—means that annual national income is only about $227 billion. About 75 percent of world GNP is located in the Triad. Thus, by segmenting in terms of a single demographic variable—income—a company could reach the most affluent markets by targeting three regions: the European Union, North America, and Japan.

Many global companies realize that for products with a low enough price—for example, cigarettes, soft drinks, and some packaged goods—population is a more important

[2] Salah S. Hassan and Lea Prevel Katsanis, "Identification of Global Consumer Segments: A Behavioral Framework," *Journal of International Consumer Marketing* 3, no. 2 (1992), p. 17.

[3] John K. Ryans, Jr., "Is It Too Soon To Put a Tiger in Every Tank?" *Columbia Journal of World Business* (March–April 1969), p. 73.

[4] Arther C. Fatt, "The Danger of 'Local' International Advertising," *Journal of Marketing* (January 1967).

[5] Teresa J. Domzal and Lynette Unger, "Emerging Positioning Strategies in Global Marketing," *Journal of Consumer Marketing* 4, no. 4 (Fall 1987), pp. 26–27.

GOING GLOBAL: SEGMENTATION, TARGETING, AND SOURCING DECISIONS

This scene at a Bangkok luxury car dealership suggests that an upper-income segment of consumers in Asian countries has a great deal of purchasing power. (Photo by Adrian Bradshaw, courtesy of SABA Press Photos, Inc.)

segmentation variable than income. Thus, China and India, with respective populations of 1.2 billion and 900 million, might represent attractive target markets. In a country like China, where per capita GNP is only $430, the marketing challenge is to successfully serve the existing mass market for inexpensive consumer products. Procter & Gamble, Unilever, Kao, Johnson & Johnson, and other packaged goods companies are targeting and developing the China market, lured in part by the possibility that as many as 100 million Chinese customers are affluent enough to spend, say, 14 cents for a single-use pouch of shampoo.[6]

Segmenting decisions can be complicated by the fact that the national income figures such as those cited above for China and India are averages. There are also large, fast-growing, high-income segments in both of these countries. In India, for example, 100 million people can be classified as "upper-middle class," with average incomes of more than $1,400. Pinning down a demographic segment may require additional information. India's middle class has been estimated to be 250 to 300 million people. However, if middle class is defined as "persons who own a refrigerator," the figure would be 30 million people. If television ownership were used as the benchmark, the middle class would be 100 to 125 million people.[7] The lesson is to guard against being blinded by averages.

Note also that the average income figures quoted above do not reflect the standard of living in these countries. In order to really understand the standard of living in a country, it is necessary to determine the purchasing power of the local currency. In low-income countries, the *actual* purchasing power of the local currency is much higher than that implied by exchange values. In other words, the per capita income average for China of $430 equals 3,569 Chinese Renminbi (8.3 Renminbi = U.S.$1.00), and 3,569 Renminbi will buy much more in China than $430 will buy in the United States.

Age is another useful demographic variable. One global segment based on demo-

---

[6]Valerie Reitman, "Enticed by Visions of Enormous Numbers, More Western Marketers Move into China," *The Wall Street Journal* (July 12, 1993), pp. B1, B6.

[7]John Bussey, "India's Market Reform Requires Perspective," *The Wall Street Journal* (May 8, 1994), p. A1. See also Miriam Jordan, "In India, Luxury Is within Reach of Many," *The Wall Street Journal* (Oct. 17, 1995), p. A1.

graphics is global teenagers—young people between the ages of 12 and 19.[8] Teens, by virtue of their interest in fashion, music, and a youthful lifestyle, exhibit consumption behavior that is remarkably consistent across borders. Young consumers may not yet have conformed to cultural norms—indeed, they may be rebelling against them. This fact, combined with shared universal needs, desires, and fantasies (for name brands, novelty, entertainment, trendy and image-oriented products), make it possible to reach the global teen segment with a unified marketing program. This segment is attractive both in terms of its size (about 1.3 billion) and its multibillion dollar purchasing power. Coca-Cola, Benetton, Swatch, and Sony are some of the companies pursuing the global teenage segment. The global telecommunications revolution is a critical driving force behind the emergence of this segment. Global media such as MTV are perfect vehicles for reaching this segment. Satellites such as AsiaSatI are beaming Western programming and commercials to millions of viewers in China, India, and other countries.

Another global segment is the so-called elite: older, more affluent consumers who are well traveled and have the money to spend on prestigious products with an image of exclusivity. This segment's needs and wants are spread over various product categories: durable goods (luxury automobiles such as Mercedes Benz), nondurables (upscale beverages such as Perrier mineral water or Chivas Regal scotch), and financial services (American Express Gold and Platinum cards). Technological change in telecommunications makes it easier to reach the global elite segment. Global telemarketing is a viable option today as AT&T International 800 services are available in more than 40 countries. Increased reliance on catalog marketing by upscale retailers such as Harrods, Laura Ashley, and Ferragamo has also yielded impressive results.

Psychographic Segmentation

Psychographic segmentation involves grouping people in terms of their attitudes, values, and lifestyles. Data are obtained from questionnaires that require respondents to indicate the extent to which they agree or disagree with a series of statements. In the United States, psychographics is primarily associated with SRI International, a market research organization whose original VALS and updated VALS 2 analyses of U.S. consumers are widely known.

Porsche AG, the German sports car maker, turned to psychographics after watching worldwide sales decline from 50,000 units in 1986 to about 14,000 units in 1993. Its U.S. subsidiary, Porsche Cars North America, already had a clear demographic profile of its typical customer: a 40-plus-year-old, male college graduate whose annual income exceeded $200,000. A psychographic study showed that, demographics aside, Porsche buyers could be divided into five distinct categories (see Table 8–1). Top Guns, for example, buy Porsches and expected to be noticed; for Proud Patrons and Fantasists, on the other hand, such conspicuous consumption is irrelevant. Porsche is using the profiles to develop advertising tailored to each type. Notes Richard Ford, Porsche vice president of sales and marketing, "We were selling to people whose profiles were diametrically opposed. You wouldn't want to tell an Elitist how good he looks in the car or how fast he could go." Results have been promising; Porsche's U.S. sales improved nearly 50 percent in 1994.[9]

One early application of psychographics outside the United States focused on value orientations of consumers in the United Kingdom, France, and Germany. Although the study was limited in scope, the researcher concluded that "the underlying values structures in each country appeared to bear sufficient similarity to warrant a common overall

[8]Marcus W. Brauchli, "Star Struck: A Satellite TV System Is Quickly Moving Asia into the Global Village," *The Wall Street Journal* (May 10, 1993), pp. A1, A8.
[9]Alex Taylor III, "Porsche Slices Up Its Buyers," *Fortune* (Jan. 16, 1995), p. 24.

TABLE 8–1 PSYCHOGRAPHIC PROFILES OF PORSCHE'S AMERICAN CUSTOMERS

Category	Percent of All Owners	Description
Top Guns	27	Driven and ambitious. Care about power and control. Expect to be noticed.
Elitists	24	Old-money. A car—even an expensive one—is just a car, not an extension of one's personality.
Proud Patrons	23	Ownership is what counts. A car is a trophy, a reward for working hard. Being noticed doesn't matter.
Bon Vivants	17	Cosmopolitan jet setters and thrill seekers. Car heightens excitement.
Fantasists	9	Car represents a form of escape. Don't care about impressing others; may even feel guilty about owning car.

Source: Alex Taylor III, "Porsche Slices Up Its Buyers," *Fortune* (Jan. 16, 1995), p. 24.

communications strategy."[10] SRI International has recently conducted psychographic analyses of the Japanese market; broader-scope studies have been undertaken by several global advertising agencies, including Backer Spielvogel & Bates Worldwide (BSB), D'arcy Massius Benton & Bowles (DMBB), and Young & Rubicam (Y&R). The following analyses offer a detailed understanding of various segments, including the global teenager and global elite discussed previously.[11]

BSB'S GLOBAL SCAN • Global Scan is a study that encompasses 18 countries, mostly located in the Triad. To identify attitudes that could help explain and predict purchase behavior for different product categories, the researchers studied consumer attitudes and values, as well as media viewership/readership, buying patterns, and product use. The survey attempts to identify both country-specific and global attitudinal attributes; sample statements are "The harder you push, the farther you get," and "I never have enough time or money."

Combining all the country data yielded a segmentation study known as TARGET SCAN, a description of five global psychographic segments that BSB claims represent 95 percent of the adult populations in the 18 countries surveyed (see Figure 8–1). BSB has labeled the segments Strivers, Achievers, Pressured, Adapters, and Traditionals.

Strivers (26 percent). This segment consists of young people with a median age of 31 who live hectic, on-the-go lives. Driven to achieve success, they are materialistic pleasure seekers for whom time and money are in short supply.

Achievers (22 percent). Older than the Strivers, the affluent, assertive Achievers are upwardly mobile and already have attained a good measure of success. Achievers are status-conscious consumers for whom quality is important.

Pressured (13 percent). The Pressured segment, largely comprised of women, cuts across age groups and is characterized by constant financial and family pressures.

---

[10]Alfred S. Boote, "Psychographic Segmentation in Europe," *Journal of Advertising Research* 22, no. 6 (December 1982–January 1983), p. 25.
[11]The following discussion is adapted from Piirto 1991.

Adapters (18 percent). This segment is comprised of older people who are content with their lives and who manage to maintain their values while keeping open minds when faced with change.

Traditionals (16 percent). This segment is "rooted to the past" and clings to the country's heritage and cultural values.

While Global Scan is a helpful tool for identifying consumer similarities across national boundaries, it can also help to highlight differences *between* segments in different countries. For example, in the United States, the 75 million baby boomers help swell the ranks of Strivers and Achievers to nearly half the population. In Germany, on the other hand, the Striver segment is older and comprises a smaller proportion of the population. Global Scan has also pinpointed important differences between Americans and Canadians, who are often considered to be part of the same geographic segment of North America.

Similarly, Global Scan revealed marked differences between the circumstances in which Strivers find themselves in different countries. In the United States, Strivers are chronically short of both time and money, while Japanese Strivers have ample monetary resources. These differences translate directly into different preferences: Whereas U.S. Strivers buy cars that are fun, stylish, and represent a good value, Japanese Strivers view cars as an extension of their homes and will accessorize them with lavish features—curtains and high-end stereo systems, for example. This implies that different advertising appeals would be necessary when targeting Strivers in the two countries.

DMBB'S EUROCONSUMER STUDY • DMBB's research team focused on Europe and produced a 15-country study titled "The Euroconsumer: Marketing Myth or Cultural Certainty?" The researchers identified four lifestyle groups: Successful Idealists, Affluent Materialists, Comfortable Belongers, and Disaffected Survivors. The first two groups represent the elite, the latter two, mainstream European consumers.

Successful Idealists. Comprising from 5 to 20 percent of the population, this segment consists of persons who have achieved professional and material success while maintaining commitment to abstract or socially responsible ideals.

Affluent Materialists. These status-conscious "up-and-comers"—many of whom are business professionals—use conspicuous consumption to communicate their success to others.

Comfortable Belongers. Comprising one-fourth to one-half of a country's population, this group, like Global Scan's Adapters and Traditionals, is conservative and most comfortable with the familiar. Belongers are content with the comfort of home, family, friends, and community.

Disaffected Survivors. Lacking power and affluence, this segment harbors little hope for upward mobility and tends to be either resentful or resigned. This segment is concentrated in high-crime, inner-city neighborhoods. Despite Disaffecteds' lack of societal status, their attitudes nevertheless tend to affect the rest of society.

DMBB has also recently completed a psychographic profile of the Russian market. The

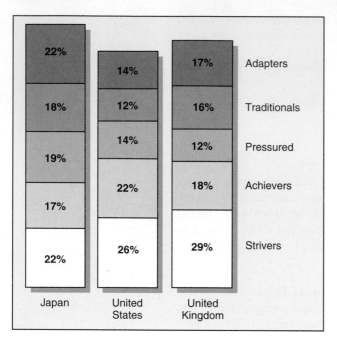

FIGURE 8–1

GLOBAL SCAN SEGMENTATION STUDY

study divides Russians into five categories, based on their outlook, behavior, and openness to Western products. The categories include *kuptsy*, Cossacks, students, business executives, and Russian Souls. Members of the largest group, the *kuptsy* (the label comes from the Russian word for "merchant"), theoretically prefer Russian products but look down on mass-produced goods of inferior quality. *Kuptsy* are most likely to admire automobiles and stereo equipment from countries with good reputations for engineering, such as Germany and Scandanavia. Nigel Clarke, the author of the study, notes that segmentation and targeting are appropriate in Russia, despite the fact that its broad consumer market is still in its infancy. "If you're dealing with a market as different as Russia is, even if you want to go 'broad,' it's best to think: 'Which group would go most for my brand? Where is my natural center of gravity?' "[12]

Y&R's CROSS-CULTURAL CONSUMER CHARACTERIZATIONS (4CS) • 4Cs is a 20-country psychographic segmentation study focusing on goals, motivations, and values that help to determine consumer choice. The research is based on the assumption that "there are underlying psychological processes involved in human behavior that are culture-free and so basic that they can be found all over the globe" (Piirto 1991, 161).

Three overall groupings can be further subdivided into a total of seven segments: Constrained (Resigned Poor and Struggling Poor), Middle Majority (Mainstreamers, Aspirers, and Succeeders), and Innovators (Transitionals and Reformers). The goals, motivation, and values of these segments range from "survival," "given up," and "subsistance" (Resigned Poor) to "social betterment," "social conscience," and "social altruism" (Reformers). Table 8–2 shows some of the attitudinal, work, lifestyle, and purchase behavior characteristics of the seven groups.

Combining the 4Cs data for a particular country with other data permits Y&R to predict product and category purchase behavior for the various segments. Yet, as noted previously in the discussion of Global Scan, marketers at global companies that are Y&R clients are cautioned not to assume they can develop one strategy or one commercial to be used to reach a particular segment across cultures. As a Y&R staffer notes, "As you get closer to the executional level, you need to be acutely sensitive to cultural differences. But at the origin, it's of enormous benefit to be able to think about people who share common values across cultures."

Behavior Segmentation

Behavior segmentation focuses on whether people buy and use a product, as well as how often and how much they use it. Consumers can be categorized in terms of **usage rates**—for example, heavy, medium, light, and nonuser. Consumers can also be segmented according to **user status:** potential users, nonusers, ex-users, regulars, first-timers, and users of competitors' products. Campbell Soup Company has targeted China for the simple reason that the Chinese have the highest per capita consumption of soup in the world.[13] Similarly, the tobacco companies are targeting China because the Chinese are heavy smokers.

In 1993, Tambrands Inc., marketers of Tampax brand tampons, launched a $20 million global advertising effort in North America, Eastern and Western Europe, Latin America, and the Pacific Rim. The campaign had two strategic purposes directly related to usage rates and user status. One ad was designed to show women new times and ways to use tampons; it included advice from gynecologists that tampons can be worn safely

---

[12]Stuart Elliot, "Figuring Out the Russian Consumer," *The New York Times* (Apr. 1, 1992), pp. C1, C19.
[13]Adam Heller, "A Recipe for Success?" *China Business Review* (July–August 1993), p. 30.

TABLE 8–2   **Y&R'S 4CS STUDY BEHAVIOR CHARACTERISTICS**

Group	Attitudes	Work	Lifestyle	Purchase Behavior
Resigned Poor	Unhappy Distrustful	Labor Unskilled	Shut-in Television	Staples Price
Struggling Poor	Unhappy Dissatisfied	Labor Craftsmen	Sports Television	Price Discount Stores
Mainstreamers	Happy Belong	Craftsmen Teaching	Family Gardening	Habit Brand loyal
Aspirers	Unhappy Ambitious	Sales White collar	Trendy sports Fashion magazines	Conspicuous consumption Credit
Succeeders	Happy Industrious	Managerial Professional	Travel Dining out	Luxury Quality
Transitionals	Rebellious Liberal	Student Health field	Arts/crafts Special interest magazines	Impulse Unique products
Reformers	Inner growth Improve world	Professional Entrepreneur	Reading Cultural events	Ecology Homemade/grown

overnight, a creative appeal reflecting research showing that two-thirds of tampon users don't use them at night. Other creative executions featured stylish women who scoff at sanitary pads—which Tambrands doesn't make. This message may be particularly effective in reaching nonusers in overseas markets, where tampon use is not as high as in the United States.[14]

Benefit Segmentation

Global benefit segmentation focuses on the numerator of the value equation—the B in $V = B/P$. This approach can achieve excellent results by virtue of marketers' superior understanding of the problem a product solves or the benefit it offers, regardless of geography. For example, Nestlè discovered that cat owners' attitudes toward feeding their pets are the same everywhere. In response, a pan-European campaign was created for Friskies

[14]Laura Bird, "Tambrands Plans Global Ad Campaign," *The Wall Street Journal* (June 22, 1993), p. B8. See also Dyan Machan, "Will the Chinese Use Tampons?" *Forbes* (Jan. 16, 1995), pp. 86–87; Pam Weisz, "Turning Around Tambrands," *Brand Week* (May 1, 1995), pp. 32+.

Doonesbury Flashbacks

BY GARRY TRUDEAU

■ SMOKING IN THE FREE WORLD

*I*n 1994, 575 billion cigarettes—including local brands—were sold in Eastern Europe and the former Soviet Union; total U.S. sales were 490 billion cigarettes. Philip Morris, whose Marlboro brand is smoked throughout the world, was the market leader in Eastern Europe with sales of 90 billion cigarettes. R.J. Reynolds Tobacco ranked second with 65 billion, and British American Tobacco sold 40 billion cigarettes. One reason for the success of Western brands is that "American-blend" cigarettes are milder than domestic cigarettes. Also, notes RJR's Andre Benoit, "There's a perception that locally made products are of lower quality. One of the biggest challenges is destroying that myth." Currently, top brands such as Marlboro, Camel, Lucky Strike, and HB are imported; all three Western companies are investing in factories with the intention of boosting local production in the near future.

Today, cigarettes constitute a $28 billion market in Japan, the country widely believed to have the highest smoking rate in the world. Sixty percent of Japanese men smoke, and, overall, smokers comprise about 36 percent of the population. Cigarette advertising on television is permitted late at night. Japan also has half a million cigarette vending machines. Nevertheless, sales of foreign cigarettes still represent only 17 percent of the market. The reason is simple: Japan Tobacco Inc. is a government monopoly. Taxes make up 60 percent of the price of a pack of cigarettes; Japan Tobacco generates $15 billion in tax revenues each year. Thus, the government's attitude of tolerance stands in stark contrast to much of the industrialized world. Indeed, the warning on cigarette packs says only, "For the sake of health, don't smoke too much."

A great deal of the cigarette advertising in Asia—for both local and Western brands—targets women. The shift in focus of the global tobacco giants—both in terms of geography and gender—is alarming to many observers. Officials at the World Health Organization accuse the tobacco companies of exploiting increased prosperity in emerging economies by pushing an addictive product linked to serious health problems. Moreover, observers note that the Western invasion is forcing local cigarette companies to step up their promotional activities. For example, a cigarette company in the Phillippines distributed wall calenders with a portrait of the Virgin Mary juxtaposed with logos of its brands.

Dry Cat Food. The appeal was that dry cat food better suits a cat's universally recognized independent nature.

Sources: Neela Banerjee, "Western Cigarettes Are Smoking in Russia," *The Wall Street Journal* (Aug. 14, 1995), p. A8.
Richard J. Barnet and John Cavanagh, *Global Dreams: Imperial Corporations and the New World Order* (New York: Simon & Schuster, 1994).
Philip Shenon, "Asia's Having One Big Nicotine Fit," *The New York Times* (May 15 , 1994), Sec. 4, p. 1.
James Sterngold, "When Smoking Is a Patriotic Duty," *The New York Times* (Oct. 17, 1993), Sec. 3, pp. 1, 6.
Peter Schmeisser, "Pushing Cigarettes Overseas," *The New York Times Magazine* (July 10, 1988).

GLOBAL TARGETING

As discussed previously, segmenting is the process by which marketers identify groups of consumers with similar wants and needs. Targeting is the act of evaluating and comparing the identified groups and then selecting one or more of them as the prospect(s) with the highest potential. A marketing mix is then devised that will provide the organization with the best return on sales while simultaneously creating the maximum amount of value to consumers.

Criteria for Targeting

The three basic criteria for assessing opportunity in global target markets are the same as in single-country targeting: current size of the segment and anticipated growth potential, competition, and compatibility with the company's overall objectives and the feasibility of successfully reaching a designated target.

CURRENT SEGMENT SIZE AND GROWTH POTENTIAL • Is the market segment currently large enough that it presents a company with the opportunity to make a profit? If it is not large enough or profitable enough today, does it have high growth potential so that it is attractive in terms of a company's long-term strategy? Indeed, one of the advantages of targeting a market segment globally is that, while the segment in a single-country market might be too small, even a narrow segment can be served profitably with a standardized product if the segment exists in several countries.[15] The billion-plus members of the global "MTV Generation" constitute a huge market, that, by virtue of its size, is extremely attractive to many companies.

China represents an individual geographic market that offers attractive opportunities in many industries. Consider the growth opportunity in financial services, for example. There are currently only about 3 million credit cards in circulation, mostly used by businesses. Low product saturation levels are also found for personal computers; there is one PC for every 6,000 people. The ratio in the United States is one computer for every four people. The opportunity for automobile manufacturers is even greater. China has 1.2 million passenger cars, one car for every 20,000 Chinese. Only 60,000 of those cars are owned by private citizens.

The sport utility vehicle segment of the U.S. auto market is a textbook example of a growth segment. SUV sales grew by nearly 35 percent between 1990 and 1994; analysts predict the same level of growth between 1994 and 1996. Reacting to high demand for the Jeep Cherokee, Ford Explorer, and Chevy Blazer, manufacturers from outside the United States are struggling to keep up with demand. In addition to the Big Three U.S. automakers, competitors from Japan (Toyota, Nissan, and Isuzu) and Great Britain (Land Rover) are already in the market; both BMW and Mercedes are developing new products that will target upscale SUV buyers. At the low end, South Korea's Kia launched its $20,000 Sportage at the end of 1994; China is even exporting a revamped military vehicle to the United States that it intends to sell for $10,000.[16] The SUV segment is growing outside the United States as well; Chrysler builds a right-seat-drive Jeep Cherokee for the Japanese market. The strong yen has enabled Chrysler to cut prices in Japan by 30 percent; the current price is the equivalent of $36,000. In 1994, Chrysler sold 10,000 Cherokees in Japan, more than double the number in 1993.[17]

---

[15]Michael E. Porter, "The Strategic Role of International Marketing," *Journal of Consumer Marketing* 3, no. 2 (Spring 1986), p. 21.

[16]Sarah Lubman, "Do the Chinese Have a Word for Edsel? Maybe It's GongStar," *The Wall Street Journal* (July 5, 1995), p. A1.

[17]Andrew Pollack, "Jeep Is Giving Chrysler a Success Story in Japan," *The New York Times* (Apr. 26, 1994), p. C1.

Range Rover is riding a crest of popularity for sport utility vehicles. Range Rover dealerships in the United States are decorated like upscale boutiques with a safari theme. (Courtesy of Land Rover North America, Inc.)

POTENTIAL COMPETITION • A market or market segment characterized by strong competition may be a segment to avoid. However, Kodak's position as the undisputed leader in the $2.4 billion U.S. color film market did not deter Fuji from launching a competitive offensive. In addition to offering traditional types of 35mm film at prices below Kodak's, Fuji quickly made inroads by introducing a number of new film products targeted at the "advanced amateur" segment that Kodak had neglected. Despite its early successes, after nearly two decades of effort, Fuji's U.S. market share has been only in the 10 to 12 percent range. Part of the problem is Kodak's distribution clout: Kodak is well entrenched in supermarket and drugstore chains, where Fuji must also jostle with other newcomers such as Konica and Polaroid. In addition, Kodak has agreements with dozens of U.S. amusement parks guaranteeing that only Kodak film will be sold on the premises. For these reasons, Fuji has shifted its attention from the U.S. market to Europe, where Kodak commands "only" 40 percent of the color film market. Fuji currently enjoys 25 percent of the European market, compared with 10 percent a decade ago. Meanwhile, Kodak has spent half a billion dollars in Japan, the world's second-largest market for photographic supplies; its market share there currently stands at about 7 percent.[18]

COMPATIBILITY AND FEASIBILITY • If a global target market is judged to be large enough, and if strong competitors are either absent or not deemed to represent insurmountable obstacles, then the final consideration is whether a company can and should target that market. In many cases, reaching global market segments requires considerable resources such as expenditures for distribution and travel by company personnel. Another question is whether the pursuit of a particular segment is compatible with the company's overall goals and established sources of competitive advantage. L'Oreal, the French cosmetics giant, has proceeded with plans to roll out its Biotherm line in the United States despite the fact that Estee Lauder's Clinique line is firmly entrenched. L'Oreal fortunately has a $1 billion "war chest" at its disposal to help finance the effort. Chairman Lindsay Owen-Jones believes that an expanded presence in the U.S. market is critical if L'Oreal is to sustain double-digit growth.[19] At the end of 1995, L'Oreal made an even bigger commitment to the U.S. market with the announcement that it would acquire Maybelline for $508 million. The acquisition propelled L'Oreal from fourth place to second place in the U.S. cosmetics market.

Selecting a Global Target Market Strategy

If, after evaluating the identified segments in terms of the three criteria presented above, a decision is made to proceed, an appropriate targeting strategy must be developed. There are three basic categories of target marketing strategies: standardized marketing, concentrated marketing, and differentiated marketing.

STANDARDIZED GLOBAL MARKETING • Standardized global marketing is analogous to mass marketing in a single country. Strictly speaking, it involves creating the same marketing mix for a broad mass market of potential buyers. This strategy calls for extensive distribution in the maximum number of retail outlets. The appeal of standardized global marketing is clear: lower production costs. The same is true of standardized global communications.

Executives at Revlon International recently adopted a standardized strategy when they announced their intention of making Revlon a global name. President Paul Block declared,

---

[18]Clare Ansberry, "Uphill Battle: Eastman Kodak Co. Has Arduous Struggle To Regain Lost Edge," *The Wall Street Journal* (Apr. 2, 1987), pp. 1, 12.
[19]Toy Stewart, "Can the Queen of Cosmetics Keep Her Crown?" *Business Week* (Jan. 17, 1994), pp. 90–92.

"All Revlon North American advertising for all products, whether they are cosmetics, skincare, haircare, or Almay, will now be used worldwide."[20] The global theme was keyed to a "Shake Your Body" campaign. Revlon's strategy calls for developing the huge consumer markets emerging in Central and Eastern Europe, including Hungary and the former Soviet republics.

CONCENTRATED GLOBAL MARKETING • The second global targeting strategy involves devising a marketing mix to reach a single segment of the global market. In cosmetics, this approach has been used successfully by House of Lauder, Chanel, and other cosmetics houses that target the upscale, prestige segment of the market.

DIFFERENTIATED GLOBAL MARKETING • The third target marketing strategy, differentiated global marketing, represents a more ambitious approach than concentrated target marketing. It entails targeting two or more distinct market segments with multiple marketing mix offerings. This strategy allows a company to achieve wider market coverage. For example, in the SUV segment described previously, Land Rover has a $50,000 Range Rover at the high end of the market; a scaled-down version, the Land Rover Discovery, is priced at under $35,000 and competes directly with the Jeep Grand Cherokee.

In the cosmetics industry, Unilever NV and Cosmair Inc. pursue differentiated global marketing strategies by targeting both ends of the perfume market. Unilever targets the luxury market with Calvin Klein and Elizabeth Taylor's Passion; Wind Song and Brut are its mass-market brands. Cosmair sells Tresnor and Giorgio Armani Gio to the upper end of the market and Gloria Vanderbilt to the lower end. Mass marketer Procter & Gamble, known for its Old Spice and Incognito brands, also embarked upon this strategy with its 1991 acquisition of Revlon's EuroCos, marketer of Hugo Boss for men and Laura Biagiotti's Roma perfume. Now P&G is launching a new prestige fragrance, Venezia, in the United States and nine European countries.[21]

SOURCING

In global marketing, the issue of customer value is inextricably tied to the sourcing decision. If customers are nationalistic, they may put a positive value on the feature "made in the home country." Such preferences must be identified using market research and factored in to solve for V in the value equation $V = B/P$. Those global companies located outside the United States that have achieved the greatest success in the U.S. market have done so by convincing American customers that their products offer higher quality and superior value than competing products from U.S. companies.

Another key variable in the location decision is the vision and values of company leadership. Some chief executives are obsessed with manufacturing in their home country. Nicolas Hayek is head of Swiss Corporation for Microelectronics and Watchmaking (SMH), the company best known for its line of inexpensive Swatch watches. SMH's chief executive has presided over a spectacular comeback—the revitalization of the Swiss watch industry. Swatch has become a pop culture phenomenon, and in 1992, SMH sold 27 million watches. The flagship brand on the high end is Omega, whose models carry prices ranging from $700 to $20,000. SMH recently acquired Blancpain, a niche producer of luxury mechanical watches that retail for $200,000 and up. Hayek has demonstrated that, by embracing the fantasy and imagination of childhood and youth, a person can build

[20]Pat Sloan, "Revlon Eyes Global Image; Picks Y & R," *Advertising Age* (Jan. 1, 1993), p. 1.
[21]Gabriella Stern, "Procter Senses Opportunity in Posh Perfume," *The Wall Street Journal* (July 9, 1993), pp. B1, B5.

■ TARGETING ADVENTURE SEEKERS WITH AN AMERICAN CLASSIC

Over the past decade, savvy export marketing has enabled Harley-Davidson to dramatically increase worldwide sales of its heavyweight motorcycles. Export sales increased from 3,000 motorcycles in 1983 to 15,000 units for the 1990 model year. By 1993, non-U.S. sales neared the $300 million mark, up from $115 million in 1989. From Australia to Germany to Mexico City, Harley enthusiasts are paying the equivalent of up to $25,000 to own an American-built classic. In many countries, dealers must put would-be buyers on a six-month waiting list because of high demand.

Harley's international success comes after years of neglecting overseas markets. Early on the company was basically involved in export selling, symbolized by its underdeveloped dealer network. Moreover, print advertising simply used word-for-word translations of the U.S. ads. By the late 1980s, after recruiting dealers in the important Japanese and European markets, company executives discovered a basic principle of global marketing. "As the saying goes, we needed to think global but act local," said Jerry G. Wilke, vice president for worldwide marketing. Harley began to adapt its international marketing, making it more responsive to local conditions.

In Japan, for example, Harley's rugged image and high quality helped make it the best-selling imported motorcycle. Still, Toshifumi Okui, president of Harley's Japanese division, was not satisfied. He worried that the tag line from the U.S. ads, "One steady constant in an increasingly screwed-up world," didn't connect with Japanese riders. Okui finally convinced Milwaukee to allow him to launch a Japan-only advertising campaign juxtaposing images from both Japan and the United States, such as American motorcyclists passing a rickshaw carrying a geisha. After learning that riders in Tokyo consider fashion and customized bikes to be essential, Harley opened two stores specializing in clothes and bike accessories.

In Europe, Harley discovered that an "evening out" means something different than it does in America. The company sponsored a rally in France, where beer and live rock music were available until midnight. Recalls Wilke, "People asked us why we were ending the rally just as the evening was starting. So I had to go persuade the band to keep playing and reopen the bar until 3 or 4 a.m." Still, rallies are less common in Europe than in the United States, so Harley encourages its dealers to hold open houses at their dealerships.

While biking through Europe, Wilke also learned that German bikers often travel at speeds exceeding 100 miles per hour. Now the company is investigating design changes to create a smoother ride at Autobahn speeds. Harley's German marketing effort may also begin focusing on accessories to increase rider protection.

Despite high levels of demand, the company intentionally limits production increases in order to uphold Harley's recent improvements in quality and to keep the product supply limited in relation to demand. Harley is still careful to make home-country customers a higher priority than those living abroad; thus, only 30 percent of its production goes outside the United States. The Harley shortage seems to suit company executives just fine. Notes Harley's James H. Patterson, "Enough motorcycles is too many motorcycles."

---

mass-market products in countries like Switzerland or the United States. The Swatch story is a triumph of engineering as well as a triumph of the imagination.

The sourcing decision highlights three roles for marketing in a global competitive strategy. The first relates to the configuration of marketing. While many marketing activities must be performed in every country, advantage can be gained by concentrating some of the marketing activities in a single location. Service, for example, must be dispersed to every country. Training, however, might be at least partially concentrated in a single location for the world. A second role for marketing is the coordination of marketing activities across countries to leverage a company's know-how. This integration can take many forms, including the transfer of relevant experience across national boundaries in areas such as global account management, and the use of similar approaches or methods for marketing research, product positioning, or other marketing activities. A third critical role of marketing is its role in tapping opportunities for product development and R&D. The development of Canon's AE–l camera is a case in point. Research provided the information on market requirements that enabled Canon to develop a "world" product. Canon was able to develop a physically uniform product that required fewer parts, far less engineering, lower inventories, and longer production runs. Such advantages would have been

Sources: Kevin Kelly and Karen Lowry Miller, "The Rumble Heard Round the World: Harleys," *Business Week* (May 24, 1993), pp. 58, 60.

Robert L. Rose, "Vrooming Back: After Nearly Stalling, Harley-Davidson Finds New Crowd of Riders," *The Wall Street Journal* (Aug. 31, 1990), pp. A1, A6.

John Holusha, "How Harley Outfoxed Japan with Exports," *The New York Times* (Aug. 12, 1990), p. F5.

Robert C. Reid, "How Harley Beat Back the Japanese," *Fortune* (Sept. 25, 1989), pp. 155+.

lacking if Canon had developed separate camera models that were adapted to the unique conditions in each national market.

Sourcing Decision Criteria

There are no simple rules to guide sourcing decisions. Indeed, the sourcing decision is one of the most complex and important decisions faced by a global company. Six factors must be taken into account in the sourcing decision:

1. Factor costs and conditions
2. Logistics (time required to fill orders, security and safety, and transportation costs)
3. Country infrastructure
4. Political risk
5. Market access (tariff and nontariff barriers to trade)
6. Exchange rate, availability, and convertibility of local money

FACTOR COSTS AND CONDITIONS • Factor costs are land, labor, materials, and capital costs (remember Economics 101!). Labor includes the cost of workers at every level: manufacturing and production, professional and technical, and management. Basic manufacturing direct labor costs today range from $0.50 per hour in the typical less-developed country to $6 to $12 per hour in the typical developed country. In certain industries in the United States, direct labor costs in manufacturing exceed $20 per hour without benefits. The latter can equal the hourly rate (see Table 8–3).

Notice in Table 8–3 that German hourly compensations costs for production workers in manufacturing are 160 percent of those in the United States, while those in Mexico are only 15 percent of those in the United States. For Volkswagen, the wage differential between Mexico and Germany, combined with the strength of the mark, dictate a Mexican manufacturing facility that builds Golf and Jetta models destined for the United States. Do lower wage rates demand that a company relocate its manufacturing to the low-wage country? Hardly. In Germany, VW Chairman Ferdinand Piech is trying to improve his company's competitiveness by convincing unions to allow flexible work schedules. For example, during peak demand, employees would work six-day weeks; when demand slows, factories would produce cars only three days per week.

Moreover, wages are only one of the costs of production. Many other considerations enter into the sourcing decision, such as management's aspirations. For example, SMH assembles all of the watches it sells, and it builds most of the components for the watches it assembles. It manufactures in Switzerland, the highest-income country in the world. SMH's Hayek decided that he wanted to manufacture in Switzerland in spite of the fact that a secretary in Switzerland makes more money than a chief engineer in Thailand. He did this by making a commitment to drive wage costs down to less than 10% of total costs. At this level, wage rates are no longer a significant factor in competitiveness. As Hayek puts it, he does not care if his competitor's workers work for free! He will still win in a competitive marketplace because his value is so much greater (Taylor 1993).

The other factors of production are land, materials, and capital. The cost of these factors depends upon their availability and relative abundance. Often, the differences in factor costs will offset each other so that, on balance, companies have a "level field" in the competitive arena. For example, the United States has abundant land and Japan has abundant capital. These advantages partially offset each other. When this is the case, the critical factor is management, professional, and worker team effectiveness.

World factor costs that affect manufacturing can be divided into three tiers. The first tier consists of the industrialized countries where factor costs are tending to equalize. The second tier consists of the industrializing countries—for example, Singapore and other Pacific Rim countries—that offer significant factor cost savings as well as an increasingly

TABLE 8-3 MANUFACTURING HOURLY WAGE RATES FOR SELECTED COUNTRIES, 1980–1992

Area or Country	United States = 100					
	1980	1985	1989	1990	1991	1992
United States	100	100	100	100	100	100
Total[1]	71	55	83	90	92	96
OECD[2]	84	65	97	105	107	111
Europe[3]	103	63	102	119	118	126
Asian newly industrializing economies[4]	12	12	23	25	27	30
Canada	88	84	104	107	110	105
Mexico	22	12	10	11	13	15
Australia	85	63	86	86	86	80
Hong Kong[5]	15	13	19	21	23	24
Israel	38	31	54	57	56	(NA)
Japan	56	49	87	85	93	100
South Korea	10	10	23	26	28	30
New Zealand	54	34	54	56	54	49
Singapore	15	19	22	25	28	31
Sri Lanka	2	2	2	2	(NA)	(NA)
China: Taiwan	10	12	25	26	28	32
Austria[6]	87	56	95	114	111	122
Belgium	133	69	108	129	127	136
Denmark	110	62	101	120	117	124
Finland[7]	83	63	116	139	132	116
France	91	58	88	102	98	104
Germany[6,8]	125	74	124	147	145	160
Greece	38	28	38	45	44	(NA)
Ireland	60	46	67	79	77	82
Italy	83	59	101	117	117	120
Luxembourg	121	59	95	110	(NA)	(NA)
Netherlands	122	67	105	123	118	128
Norway	117	80	128	144	139	143
Portugal	21	12	20	25	27	31
Spain	60	36	62	76	78	83
Sweden	127	74	122	140	142	150
Switzerland	112	74	117	140	139	144
United Kingdom	77	48	74	85	88	91

NA Not available.

[1]The 25 foreign economies for which 1992 data are available.

[2]Canada, Australia, Japan, New Zealand, and the 16 European countries for which 1992 data are available.

[3]The 16 European countries for which 1992 data are available.

[4]Hong Kong, South Korea, Singapore, and China: Taiwan.

[5]Average of selected manufacturing industries.

[6]Excludes workers in establishments considered handicraft manufacturers (including all printing and publishing and miscellaneous manufacturing in Austria).

[7]Includes workers in mining and electrical power plants.

[8]Former West Germany (prior to unification).

developed infrastructure and political stability, making them extremely attractive manufacturing locations. The third tier includes Russia and other countries that have not yet become significant locations for manufacturing activity. Third-tier countries present the combination of lower factor costs (especially wages) offset by limited infrastructure development and greater political uncertainty.

The application of advanced computer controls and other new manufacturing technologies has reduced the proportion of labor relative to capital for many businesses. In formulating a sourcing strategy, company managers and executives should also recognize the declining importance of direct manufacturing labor as a percentage of total product cost. The most advanced global companies are no longer blindly chasing cheap labor manufacturing locations, because direct labor cost may be a very small percentage of the total. As a result, it may not be worthwhile to incur the costs and risks of establishing a manufacturing activity in a distant location. For example, Greg Petsch, senior vice president of manufacturing at Compaq, had to decide whether to close plants in Houston and Scotland and contract out assembly work to the Far East. After determining that the human labor content in a PC is only about 15 minutes, he opted to run Compaq's existing Houston factory 24 hours a day. Another decision was whether to source motherboards from a vendor in Asia. Petsch calculated that Compaq could produce the boards—which account for 40 percent of the cost of a PC—for $25 less than suppliers in the Far East. Manufacturing in Houston also saved two weeks in shipping time, which translated into inventory savings.[22]

The experience of the Arrow Shirt Company also illustrates several issues relating to factor costs. During the 1980s, Arrow sourced 15 percent of its dress shirts from the Far East at a cost savings of $15 per dozen compared to U.S.-manufactured shirts. Arrow decided to phase out imports after spending $15 million to automate its U.S. plants. Productivity increased 25 percent, and Arrow is no longer at the mercy of a 12-month lead time between ordering and delivery; U.S.-sourced shirts can be ordered a mere three months in advance—a critical issue in the fashion industry. Interestingly, the Arrow experience illustrates how the decision to source at home rather than abroad does not automatically defuse the political issue of "exporting jobs": After automating, Arrow laid off 400 U.S. workers and closed four factories.[23]

Many companies have been chagrined to discover that today's cheap factor costs can disappear as the law of supply and demand drives up wages and land prices. Shirtmakers like Arrow began sourcing in Japan in the 1950s. As wages and real estate costs increased, production was shifted to Hong Kong, then to Taiwan and Korea. During the 1970s and 1980s, production kept shifting, to China, Indonesia, Thailand, Malaysia, Bangladesh, and Singapore. In recent years, shirt production has shifted from the Far East to Costa Rica, the Dominican Republic, Guatemala, Honduras, and Puerto Rico. In addition to low wages, these countries offer tax incentives under the 1983 Caribbean Basin Initiative agreement.[24]

LOGISTICS • In general, the greater the distance between the product source and the target market, the greater the time delay for delivery and the higher the transportation cost. However, innovation and new transportation technologies are cutting both time and dollar costs. To facilitate global delivery, transportation companies such as CSX Corporation are forming alliances and becoming an important part of industry value systems. Manufacturers can take advantage of intermodal services that allow containers to be transferred between rail, boat, air, and truck carriers. Today, transportation expenses for U.S. exports and imports represent approximately 5 percent of total costs. In Europe,

[22]Doron P. Levin, "Compaq Storms the PC Heights from Its Factory Floor," *The New York Times* (Nov. 4, 1994), Sec. 3, p. 5.
[23]Cynthia Mitchell, "Coming Home: Some Firms Resume Manufacturing in U.S. after Foreign Fiascoes," *The Wall Street Journal* (Oct. 14, 1986), p. 1.
[24]Peter C. T. Elsworth, "Can Colors and Stripes Rescue Shirt Makers from a Slump?" *The New York Times* (Mar. 17, 1991), Sec. 3, p. 5.

the advent of the single market means fewer border controls, which greatly speeds up delivery times and lowers costs.

Memorex Telex provides an excellent illustration of how companies can reconfigure inbound logistics in the value chain to support an overseas sourcing strategy. Memorex, which manufactures computer peripherals in Raleigh, North Carolina, sources components in Asia. The company originally shipped by water from Taiwan, through the Panama Canal, and on to the Port of Norfolk. A short trip by truck to Raleigh completed the journey. In the late 1980s, Memorex switched to ship-and-train intermodal transport; using Long Beach as the port of entry cut 10 days off the water route and saved $400 to $800 per container. In 1992, Memorex began using long-haul trucks instead of trains, resulting in additional savings of more than $1,000 per container (Miles 1993).

COUNTRY INFRASTRUCTURE • In order to present an attractive setting for a manufacturing operation, it is important that the country's infrastructure be sufficiently developed to support a manufacturing operation. The required infrastructure will vary from company to company, but minimally, it will include power, transportation and roads, communications, service and component suppliers, a labor pool, civil order, and effective governance. In addition, a country must offer reliable access to foreign exchange for the purchase of necessary material and components from abroad as well as a physically secure setting where work can be done and product can be shipped to customers.

A country may have cheap labor, but does it have the necessary supporting services or infrastructure to support a manufacturing activity? Many countries offer these conditions, including Hong Kong, Taiwan, and Singapore. There are many other countries that do not, such as Lebanon, Uganda, and El Salvador. One of the challenges of doing business in the new Russian market is an infrastructure that is woefully inadequate to handle the increased volume of shipments. The Mexican government, anticipating much heavier trade volume because of NAFTA, has committed $14 billion for infrastructure improvements.

POLITICAL RISK • Political risk, or the risk of a change in government policy that would adversely impact a company's ability to operate effectively and profitably, is a deterrent to investment in local sourcing. Conversely, the lower the level of political risk, the less likely it is that an investor will avoid a country or market. The difficulty of assessing political risk is inversely proportional to a country's stage of economic development: All other things being equal, the less developed a country, the more difficult it is to predict political risk. The political risk of the Triad countries, for example, is quite limited as compared to that of a less-developed, pre-industrial country in Africa, Latin America, or Asia.

The recent rapid changes in Central and Eastern Europe and the dissolution of the Soviet Union have very clearly demonstrated the risks *and* opportunities resulting from political upheavals.

MARKET ACCESS • A key factor in locating production facilities is market access. If a country or a region limits market access because of local content laws, balance-of-payments problems, or any other reason, it may be necessary to establish a production facility within the country itself. The Japanese automobile companies invested in U.S. plant capacity because of concerns about market access. By producing cars in the United States, they have a source of supply that is not exposed to the threat of tariff or nontariff barriers. In the 1950s and 1960s, U.S. companies created production capacity abroad to ensure continued access to markets that had been established with supply exported from U.S. plants.

The U.S. tax laws provide incentives for U.S. companies to locate manufacturing in the Caribbean because production from Caribbean plants has full access to the U.S. market, including the military procurement market, which is subject to security clearances.

FOREIGN EXCHANGE RATES • In deciding where to locate a manufacturing activity, the cost of production supplied by a country source will be determined in part by the prevailing foreign exchange rate for the country's currency. Exchange rates are so volatile today that many companies pursue global sourcing strategies as a way of limiting exchange-related risk. At any point in time, what has been an attractive location for production may become much less attractive due to exchange rate fluctuation. For example, the exchange value of the U.S. dollar declined more than 50 percent vis-à-vis the Japanese yen between 1985 and the present. Of course, the flip side of this adjustment is that the yen appreciated more than 100 percent in the same period. The prudent company will incorporate exchange volatility into its planning assumptions and be prepared to prosper under a variety of exchange rate relationships.

The dramatic shifts in price levels of commodities and currencies are a major characteristic of the world economy today. Such volatility argues for a sourcing strategy that provides alternative country options for supplying markets. Thus, if the dollar or the yen or the mark becomes seriously overvalued, a company with production capacity in other locations can achieve competitive advantage by shifting production among different sites. For example, in mid-1993, Bridgestone Corp. increased the production of European- and U.S.-made tires carrying the Bridgestone brand name in the face of a strong yen.

SUMMARY

The global environment must be analyzed before a company pursues expansion into new geographic markets. Through global market segmentation, the similarities and differences of potential buying customers can be identified and grouped. Demographics, psychographics, behavioral characteristics, and benefits sought are common attributes used to segment world markets. After marketers have identified segments, the next step is targeting. The identified groups are evaluated and compared; the prospect(s) with the greatest potential is selected from them. The groups are evaluated on the basis of several factors: segment size and growth potential, competition, and compatibility and feasibility. After evaluating the identified segments, marketers must decide on an appropriate targeting strategy. The three basic categories of global target marketing strategies are: standardized marketing, concentrated marketing, and differentiated marketing.

Sourcing is the what, where, and how of production to create the greatest possible value for the customers targeted in the marketing plan. Marketing can play a strategic role in the sourcing decision. Some activities may be concentrated in a single location, with appropriate coordination to leverage knowledge. Marketing can also tap opportunities for advantage in design and product development.

The ultimate objective of any sourcing decision is to supply customers with the highest quality at the lowest cost. Quality and cost are affected by factor costs, logistics, country infrastructure, political risk, market access, and exchange rates. The declining proportion of direct labor as a cost element for most products is reducing the importance of wage rates in the sourcing decision. There is no simple formula for arriving at a sourcing decision. A global approach to sourcing takes into account all of the variables that have an impact on the company's ability to create and deliver value to customers over the long term. Because many of the variables are subject to change, companies are advised to devise flexible sourcing plans that will permit customer needs to be met under a variety of conditions.

DISCUSSION QUESTIONS

1. Identify the five basic segmentation strategies. Give an example of a company that has used each one.
2. Explain the difference between segmenting and targeting.
3. Compare and contrast standardized, concentrated, and differentiated global marketing.
4. What are the three criteria that guide a company in its targeting decision?
5. Why does sourcing represent a critical issue in global marketing?
6. Identify and describe several sourcing criteria.

BIBLIOGRAPHY

Books

Hassan, Salah S., and Roger D. Blackwell. *Global Marketing*. Orlando, Fla.: The Dryden Press, 1994.

Hickman, Bert. *International Productivity and Competitiveness*. New York: Oxford University Press, 1992.

Miller, Jeffrey G., Arnoud De Meyer, and Jinichiro Nakane. *Benchmarking Global Manufacturing: Understanding International Suppliers, Customers and Competitors*. Homewood, Ill.: Business One Irwin, 1992.

Ohmae, Kenichi. *Triad Power*. New York: Free Press, 1985.

Piirto, Rebecca. *Beyond Mind Games: The Marketing Power of Psychographics*. Ithaca, N.Y.: American Demographics Books, 1991.

Porter, Michael E. *Competitive Advantage: Creating and Sustaining Superior Performance*. New York: Free Press, 1985.

———. *Competition in Global Industries*. Boston: Harvard Business School Press, 1986.

————. *The Competitive Advantage of Nations*. New York: Free Press, 1990.

Root, Franklin R. *Entry Strategies for International Markets*. Lexington, Mass.: Lexington Books, 1987.

Sonnenberg, Frank K. *Marketing to Win: Strategies for Building Competitive Advantage in Service Industries*. New York: Harper Business, 1990.

Womack, James P., Daniel T. Jones, and Daniel Roos. *The Machine That Changed The World*. New York: HarperCollins, 1990.

Articles

Akhter, Syed H., and Yusuf A. Choudhry. "Forced Withdrawal from a Country Market: Managing Political Risk." *Business Horizons* (May–June 1993), pp. 47–54.

Alster, Judith, and Holly Gallo. "Corporate Strategies for Global Competitive Advantage." Reader's Digest Association Conference Board, Working Papers No. 996 (1992).

Davis, Edward W. "Global Outsourcing: Have U.S. Managers Thrown the Baby Out with the Bath Water?" *Business Horizons* 35, no. 4 (July–August 1992), pp. 58–65.

Fagan, Mark L. "A Guide to Global Sourcing." *Journal of Business Strategy*, 12, no. 2 (March–April 1991), pp. 21–25.

Faltermayer, Edmund. "Is 'Made in the U.S.A.' Fading Away?" *Fortune* (Sept. 24, 1990), pp. 62–73.

Garland, Barbara C., and Marti J. Rhea. "American Consumers: Profile of an Import Preference Segment." *Akron Business and Economic Review* 19, no. 2 (1988), pp. 20–29.

Green, Paul E., and Abba M. Krieger. "Segmenting Markets with Conjoint Analysis." *Journal of Marketing*, 55, no. 4 (October 1991), pp. 20–31.

Hout, Thomas, Michael E. Porter, Eileen Rudden. "How Global Companies Win Out." *Harvard Business Review* 60, no. 5, (September–October 1982), pp. 98–108.

Kotabe, Masaaki. "Patterns and Technological Implications of Global Sourcing Strategies: A Study of European and Japanese Multinational Firms." *Journal of International Marketing* 1, no. 1 (1993), pp. 26–43.

Kotabe, Masaaki, and K. Scott Swan. "Offshore Sourcing: Reaction, Maturation, and Consolidation of U.S. Multinationals." *Journal of International Business Studies* 25, no. 1 (First Quarter 1994), pp. 115–140.

MacCormack, Alan David, Lawrence James Newman III, and Donald B.

Rosenfield. "The New Dynamics of Global Manufacturing Site Locations." *Sloan Management Review* 35, no. 4 (Summer 1994), pp. 69–80.

McClenahen, John S. "Sources of Frustration." *Industry Week* (Oct. 1, 1990), pp. 74–81.

McGrath, Michael E., and Richard W. Hoole. "Manufacturing's New Economies of Scale." *Harvard Business Review* 70, no. 3 (May–June 1992), pp. 94–102.

McMillan, John. "Managing Suppliers: Incentive Systems in Japanese and U.S. Industry." *California Management Review* 32, no. 4 (Summer 1990), pp. 38–55.

Miles, Gregory L. "Think Global, Go Intermodal." *International Business* (March 1993), pp. 61+.

Morwitz, Vicki G., and David Schmittlein. "Using Segmentation To Improve Sales Forecasts Based on Purchase Intent: Which 'Intenders' Actually Buy?" *Journal of Marketing Research* 29, no. 4 (November 1992), pp. 391–405.

Murray, Janet Y., Masaaki Kotabe, and Albert R. Wildt. "Strategic and Financial Performance Implications of Global Sourcing Strategy: A Contingency Analysis." *Journal of International Business Studies* 26, no. 1 (First Quarter 1995), pp. 181–202.

Pascarella, Perry. "The Seamless Company." *Industry Week* (Sept. 18, 1989), p. 5.

Quinn, James Brian, and Frederick G. Hilmer. "Strategic Outsourcing." *Sloan Management Review* 35, no. 4 (Summer 1994), pp. 43–56.

Rohan, Thomas. "Supplies Customer Links Multiplying." *Industry Week* (Apr. 17, 1989), p. 20.

Rosewater, Amy. "Letter from Mexico: More than 'Screwdriver' Shops." *Electronics* (December 1990), pp. 13–15.

Sheridan, John. "World-Class Manufacturing." *Industry Week* (July 2, 1990), pp. 36–46.

Taylor, William. "Message and Muscle: An Interview with Swatch Titan Nicolas Hayek." *Harvard Business Review* 71 no. 2 (March–April 1993), pp. 99–110.

Venkatesan, Ravi. "Strategic Sourcing: To Make or Not To Make." *Harvard Business Review* 70, no. 6 (November–December 1992), pp. 98–107.

Wolfe, Bonnie Heineman. "Finding the International Niche: A "How To" for American Small Business." *Business Horizons* 34, no. 2 (March–April 1991), pp. 13–17.

HARPERCOLLINS—IS THE "GLOBAL BOOK" A REALITY?

HarperCollins Publishers had a banner year in 1995, with revenues up 10 percent to $1 billion, compared with 1994. The company's best-selling titles for adults included John Gray's *Men Are from Mars, Women Are from Venus*, as well as a book by Newt Gingrich. Sales increased in other categories as well, including audio books and children's books. The revenue growth provided evidence that a global strategy undertaken several years ago was paying off.

In May 1990, the U.S. publisher Harper & Row merged with the British publisher William Collins & Sons. Both companies had come under the ownership of Rupert Murdoch's News Corporation, and HarperCollins Publishers instantly became the largest English-language publisher in the world in an industry with $13 billion in worldwide sales. *The New York Times* once described Harper—which published John F. Kennedy's *Profiles in Courage*—as the embodiment of the American establishment publisher. Harper's strength was in trade books, which are hardcover and paperback books sold in bookstores. Collins, whose authors included Agatha Christie, was known in Great Britain for its strong commercial instincts, aggressive marketing, and diverse titles. One of its strengths was in mass-market books—standardized in format, less expensive than trade books, and sold on newsstands as well as in bookstores. The symbol of the new company is a blue and red water-and-fire symbol, combining the former corporate symbols of Harper (a torch) and Collins (a fountain).

The rationale for the merger was the increasingly global nature of the publishing industry as evidenced by the worldwide success of such books as Alex Haley's *Roots* and Umberto Eco's *The Name of the Rose*, as well as books by John Le Carré and Gore Vidal. A "global book" is one that achieves worldwide popularity and sales, much like recordings by opera singer Lucianno Pavarotti or pop star Madonna. A recent study by Euromonitor showed that two-thirds of the world's book market is outside the United States; the United States ranks fifth in per capita expenditures on books. According to some observers, the best approach for growth in this global publishing market is the "bigger is better" approach. Theoretically, larger companies—including those resulting from mergers—with higher sales volumes can enjoy economies of scale and reduce costs. Before the merger, George Craig had slashed overhead at Harper & Row by $20 million a year and boosted operating profits at Harper's American business between 1987 and 1989. As the chief executive of HarperCollins, Craig moved quickly to exploit the advantages of global scale in the marketing (especially in distribution) of books.

Craig's actions are consistent with the point of view that publishing companies are actually in the entertainment business—just like major motion picture studios or recording companies, which are also global in scope. In the film and music industries, fixed costs are high, and a few hit movies or recordings pay for a multitude of misses. Thus, the argument goes, a publishing company must be big enough and rich enough to have numerous projects in the production pipeline and to pay multimillion-dollar advances to popular authors whose books are usually hits. For example, Harper paid $1 million for the rights to E.L. Doctorow's *Billy Bathgate*. This side of the argument was recently summarized in the British magazine *The Economist*: "Only a diversified global publisher can grab all the various hardback and paperback profits from its best-sellers around the world." Or, as William Shinker, head of the adult book division until 1994, put it, "Publishing for the world English market simply makes sense."

Some critics, however, believe that Craig's strategy—which also includes the introduction of a new line of mass-

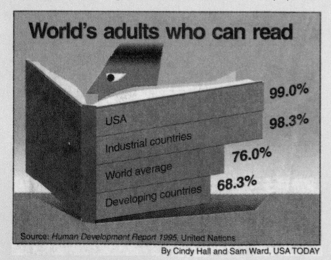

World's adults who can read

USA — 99.0%
Industrial countries — 98.3%
World average — 76.0%
Developing countries — 68.3%

Source: *Human Development Report 1995*, United Nations
By Cindy Hall and Sam Ward, USA TODAY

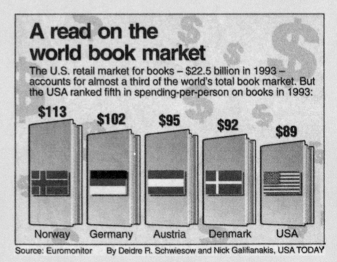

A read on the world book market

The U.S. retail market for books – $22.5 billion in 1993 – accounts for almost a third of the world's total book market. But the USA ranked fifth in spending-per-person on books in 1993:

Norway	Germany	Austria	Denmark	USA
$113	$102	$95	$92	$89

Source: Euromonitor   By Deidre R. Schwiesow and Nick Galifianakis, USA TODAY

market paperbacks—will tarnish the image of the American half of the new company and thus backfire. But, according to Craig, Harper had grown "old-fashioned, a bit dull, very bureaucratic, and it suffered from a lack of direction." Sonia Land, who quit as chief executive of Collins a few months before the merger, had this response to Craig's criticism: "By trying to create the true international publishing conglomerate, all George has done is destroy two great publishing traditions." In her view, both publishers—Harper, with its old-line, establishment American tradition, and Collins, with its more commercial British one—would suffer as a result of the merger. Land's concern is that the HarperCollins name will not be a source of synergy in the global marketplace; it will stand for less, not more. Speaking of HarperCollins' new corporate symbol, Land says that someone should tell Craig that "fire and water do not mix." Land feels that, because it is the foundation on which the company's reputation was built, it is a mistake to change the venerable Collins name. Craig is said to have replied that "we are a world-wide publishing group. International branding is what we're all about."

The controversy over Craig's global ambitions for HarperCollins is perhaps most evident in the area of the children's books published by Harper Junior Books. Children's books represent a $1.5 billion growth segment in an otherwise stagnant industry; in the first half of 1989, sales of hardcover children's books were 15 percent ahead of 1988 sales, and sales of children's paperback books increased 51 percent in the same period. According to Harper Junior Books publisher Elizabeth Gordon, despite the fact that Collins has its own children's department, Craig was unfamiliar with the children's book market in the United States. Libraries and schools buy the titles first; only later do sales of children's books pick up in American bookstores. Moreover, as part of his global plan, Craig intended to copublish children's books. Gordon disagreed: "American children want to read what

they know," she said. "There are books that transcend national boundaries, such as *The Secret Garden*. But the majority tend to be set in the child's very particular world." Dissatisfied with the changes, Gordon resigned.

Many people in the publishing industry agree with Gordon. "The whole idea of global publishing like HarperCollins is crazy," says Roger Straus III of Farrar, Straus & Giroux. "A book is about as personal as deodorant. You can count on one hand the authors who can really be sold globally." Publishing consultant Charles Elbaum agrees: "You can't move ideas, techniques, and technologies from another country and jam them down people's throats." His recommendation for Craig's globalization strategy: Establish semiautonomous operating units and allow them the discretion to customize when necessary.

DISCUSSION QUESTIONS

1. Is trade book publishing a global industry? Why or why not?
2. Why does Ms. Land feel that Mr. Craig is "destroying two great publishing traditions"? Do you agree? Why or why not?
3. Do you agree that there is a global segment for children's books?
4. What recommendations would you make to Mr. Craig?

Sources: John F. Baer, "Reinventing the Book Business," *Publishers Weekly* (Mar. 14, 1994), pp. 36–40.
Roger Cohen, "Birth of a Global Book Giant," *The New York Times* (June 11, 1990), pp. D1, D10.
"The Diseconomies of Scale," *The Economist* (Apr. 7, 1990), pp. 25–28.
Eden Ross Lipson, "The Little Industry That Could," *The New York Times Magazine* (Dec. 3, 1989), pp. 20, 50, 52.
Meg Cox, "Murdoch Puts Global Imprint on Books," *The Wall Street Journal* (May 4, 1990), pp. B1, B5.

Sourcing Strategies: Exporting and Importing

> *"The small business owner in Muncie, Indiana is starting to think, 'If I am using a computer assembled in Taiwan, drinking from a Coca-Cola fountain manufactured in Germany, and writing at a desk designed in Scandinavia—why can't I export my auto parts to someone?'"*
>
> —Bonnie Heineman Wolfe, President, New Venture Development Corporation

In Germany, exporting is a way of life for the *Mittelstand*, 2.5 million small and midsized companies that generate two-thirds of Germany's GNP and account for 30 percent of exports. For companies such as steelmaker J.N. Eberle, machine tool manufacturer Trumpf, and J. Eberspächer, which makes auto exhaust systems, exports account for as much as 40 percent of sales. *Mittelstand* owner-managers target global niche markets and prosper by focusing on quality, innovation, and investing heavily in research and development. For example, the chief executive of G.W. Barth, a company that manufactures cocoa-bean roasting machines, invested nearly $2 million in infrared technology that reduced temperature variances. The company's global market share stands at 70 percent—a threefold increase in a 10-year period—as Ghirardelli Chocolate, Hershey Foods, and other companies have snapped up Barth's roasters. At ABM Baumüller, a $40 million manufacturer of motors and other components for cranes, a major investment in flexible manufacturing technology allows the company to tailor products to customer needs. New automated production equipment was installed—at a cost of $20 million—that allows changeover to different products in a matter of seconds. The story is repeated throughout Germany; as a result, in industry after industry, the *Mittelstand* are world-class exporters.[1]

The success of the *Mittelstand* serves as a reminder of the impact exporting can have on a country's economy. It also demonstrates the difference between *export selling* and *export marketing.* Export selling does not involve tailoring the product, the price, or the promotional material to suit the requirements of global markets. The only marketing mix element that differs is the "place"—i.e., the country where the product is sold. This selling approach may work for some products or services; for unique products with little or no international competition, such an approach is possible. Similarly, companies new to exporting may initially experience success with selling. Even today, the managerial mind-set in many companies still favors export selling. But, as companies mature in the global marketplace or as new competitors enter the picture, it becomes necessary to engage in *export marketing.*

---

[1]Gail E. Schares and John Templeman, "Think Small: The Export Lessons To Be Learned from Germany's Midsize Companies," *Business Week* (Nov. 4, 1994), pp. 58+.

Export marketing targets the customer in the context of the total market environment. The export marketer does not take the domestic product "as is" and simply sell it to international customers. To the export marketer, the product offered in the home market represents a starting point. It is modified as needed to meet the preferences of international target markets. *Mittelstand* companies such as ABM Baumüller exemplify this approach. Similarly, the export marketer sets prices to fit the marketing strategy and does not merely extend home-country pricing to the target market. Charges incurred in export preparation, transportation, and financing must be taken into account in determining prices. Finally, the export marketer also adjusts strategies and plans for communications and distribution to fit the market. In other words, effective communication about product features or uses to buyers in export markets may require creating brochures with different copy, photographs, or artwork. As the vice president of sales and marketing of one manufacturer noted, "We have to approach the international market with *marketing* literature as opposed to *sales* literature."

Export marketing is the integrated marketing of goods and services that are destined for customers in international markets. Export marketing requires:

1. An understanding of the target market environment
2. The use of marketing research and the identification of market potential
3. Decisions concerning product design, pricing, distribution and channels, advertising and communications—the marketing mix.

Items 1 and 2 are covered in preceding chapters. Chapters 13 through 16 are devoted to the marketing mix. The purpose of this chapter is to provide an overview of the issues and problems facing companies engaged in export marketing.

ORGANIZATIONAL EXPORT ACTIVITIES[2]

Exporting is becoming increasingly important as companies in all parts of the world step up efforts to supply and service markets located outside their national boundaries. Research has shown that exporting is essentially a developmental process that can be divided into the following distinct stages:

1. The firm is unwilling to export; it will not even fill an unsolicited export order. This may be due to perceived lack of time ("too busy to fill the order") or to apathy or ignorance.
2. The firm fills unsolicited export orders but does not pursue orders. Such a firm would be an export seller.
3. The firm explores the feasibility of exporting (this stage may bypass stage 2).
4. The firm exports to one or more markets on a trial basis.
5. The firm is an experienced exporter to one or more markets.
6. After this success, the firm pursues country- or region-focused marketing based on certain criteria (e.g., all countries where English is spoken; all countries where it is not necessary to transport by water, etc.).
7. The firm evaluates global market potential before screening for the "best" target markets to include in its marketing strategy and plan. *All* markets—domestic and international—are regarded as equally worthy of consideration.

[2]This section relies heavily on Bilkey 1978. The stages are based on Rogers' adoption process. See Everett M. Rodgers, *Diffusion of Innovations* (New York: Free Press, 1962).

The probability that a firm will advance from one stage to the next depends on different factors. Moving from stage 2 to stage 3 depends on management's attitude toward the attractiveness of exporting and its confidence in the firm's ability to compete internationally. However, *commitment* is the most important aspect of a company's international orientation. Before a firm can reach stage 4, it must receive and respond to unsolicited export orders. The quality and dynamism of management are important factors that can lead to such orders. Success in stage 4 can lead a firm to stages 5 and 6. A company that reaches stage 7 is a mature, geocentric enterprise that is relating global resources to global opportunity. To reach this stage requires management with vision and commitment.

One recent study noted that export procedural expertise and sufficient corporate resources are required for successful exporting. An interesting finding was that even the most experienced exporters express a lack of confidence in their knowledge about shipping arrangements, payment procedures, and regulations. The study also showed that, although profitability is an important expected benefit of exporting, other advantages include increased flexibility and resiliency and improved ability to deal with sales fluctuations in the home market. While research generally supports the proposition that the probability of being an exporter increases with firm size, it is less clear that export intensity—the ratio of export sales to total sales—is positively correlated with firm size. Following are some of the export-related problems that a company typically faces (Kotabe & Czinkota 1992):

Logistics

Arranging transportation
Transport rate determination
Handling documentation
Obtaining financial information
Distribution coordination
Packaging
Obtaining insurance

Legal Procedure

Government red tape
Product liability
Licensing
Customers/duty

Servicing Exports

Providing parts availability
Providing repair service
Providing technical advice
Providing warehousing

Sales Promotion

Advertising
Sales effort
Marketing information

Foreign Market Intelligence

Locating markets
Trade restrictions
Competition overseas

NATIONAL POLICIES GOVERNING EXPORTS AND IMPORTS

It is hard to overstate exporting's importance to national economies around the world. In the United States alone, exports of goods and services reached $640 billion in 1993. The Department of Commerce reports that exports' share of total United States GDP grew from 7.5 percent in 1986 to 10.6 percent in 1992. This increase represents 42.7 percent of real GDP growth during that seven-year period. Between 1986 and 1990, U.S. employment increased by 900,000 in manufacturing companies engaging in merchandise exports. In China, foreign trade represents about 4.7 percent of GDP. China's pace-setting economic growth in the Asia/Pacific region is reflected by trends in both exports and imports. Since 1979, exports from China have grown 16 percent annually, while imports have grown 15 percent.[3]

Despite, or perhaps because of, this importance, national policies toward exports and

[3]"For Richer, For Poorer," *The Economist* (Mar. 18, 1995), p. SS9.

imports can be summarized in one word: schizophrenic. For centuries, the nation-states of the world have combined two opposing policy attitudes toward the movement of goods across national boundaries. Nations take steps to encourage exports by outright subsidy and by indirect measures. The latter include tax rebates and extensive government support programs in the area of promotion and producer education. The flow of goods in the other direction, imports, is generally restricted by national policy. Measures such as tariffs, import control, and a host of nontariff barriers are designed to limit the inward flow of goods. Thus the international situation is a combination of measures designed to simultaneously encourage exports and restrict imports.

U.S. agricultural exports and and imports illustrate this perfectly. On the one hand, the U.S. dairy industry is greatly shielded from imports. Cheese is a protected product through access controls that have the flavor of Catch-22: A company cannot import cheese into the United States unless it has done so in the past; quantities are determined by lottery. On the other hand, the U.S. government is actively pursuing Japan to open its rice markets to U.S. producers; this effort finally met with success in 1993.

To see the tremendous results that can come from a government-encouraged export strategy, consider Japan, Singapore, South Korea, and the so-called "greater China" or "China Triangle" market, which includes Taiwan, Hong Kong, and the People's Republic of China. In the last four decades, Japan totally recovered from the destruction of World War II and became an economic superpower as a direct result of export strategies devised by the Ministry for International Trade and Industry (MITI). The "four tigers"—Singapore, South Korea, Taiwan, and Hong Kong—built upon the Japanese experience and all have export-based economies. China may be a "fifth tiger"; booming along with 6 percent growth and low inflation, China has attracted increased foreign investment from Chrysler, Hewlett-Packard, Daimler-Benz, and other companies setting up production facilities to support local sales as well as exports to world markets.

Government Programs Supporting Exports

Any government concerned with trade deficits or economic development should focus attention on educating uninvolved firms about the potential gains from exporting. This is true at the national, regional, and local government levels. There are three commonly used governmental activities designed to support export activities of national firms. *Tax incentives* treat earnings from export activities preferentially either by applying a lower rate to earnings from these activities or by providing a refund of taxes already paid on income associated with exporting. The tax benefits offered by export-conscious governments include varying degrees of tax exemption or tax deferral on export income, accelerated depreciation of export-related assets, and generous tax treatment of overseas market development activities. Naturally, in many cases, the actual treatment of export-related income is even more favorable than tax statutes would imply. Far Eastern, Latin American, and European trading nations have been particularly generous in providing these kinds of special aids to exporting companies. The major tax incentive under U.S. law since 1985 has been the Foreign Sales Corporation (FSC), through which an exporter can obtain a 15 percent exclusion on earnings from international sales. FSCs must be located outside the United States.

Governments also support export performance by providing outright *subsidies*, which are direct or indirect financial contributions that benefit producers. Export subsidies can severely distort trade patterns when less competitive but subsidized producers displace competitive producers in world markets. Export subsidies to support agricultural trade will be reduced under the WTO.

The third support area is *governmental assistance* to exporters. As noted in the chapter introduction, Germany's *Mittelstand* companies can avail themselves of a great deal of information concerning the location of markets and credit risks. Assistance may also be oriented toward export promotion. Government agencies at various levels often take the lead in setting up trade fairs and trade missions designed to promote sales to foreign customers.

TARIFFS • Before World War II, specific duties were widely used and the tariffs of many countries, particularly those in Europe and Latin America, were extremely complex. Since the war, the trend has been toward the conversion to ad valorem duties—that is, duties expressed as a certain percentage of the value of the goods. Between 1959 and 1988, tariff administration was simplified by the use of the Brussels nomenclature (BTN). This nomenclature was worked out by an international committee of experts under the sponsorship of the Customs Cooperation Council, which in 1955 produced a convention that took effect in 1959.

The rules of this convention were used by most GATT member countries until the Harmonized Tariff System (HTS) went into effect in January 1989. Under this system, importers have to determine the correct import classification number. With the harmonized tariff schedule B, the export classification number for any exported item is now the same as the import classification number. Under the BTN system, these numbers differed. HTS, adopted by more than 65 countries, has standardized a common classification system for all products (Johnson 1991, 201). This makes it easier for buyers and sellers to determine export classifications. Also, exporters must include the harmonized tariff schedule B number on their export documents to facilitate customs clearance. Accuracy—especially in the eyes of customs officials—is essential. For example, if an export administrator of a U.S. company doing business with Mexico puts the wrong schedule B number on a document, the document will be returned for correction.

In spite of the progress made in simplifying tariff procedures, the task of administrating a tariff presents an enormous problem. Persons who work with imports and exports must familiarize themselves with the different classifications and use them accurately. Even a tariff schedule of several thousand items cannot clearly describe every product traded globally. The introduction of new products and new materials used in manufacturing processes creates new problems. Often, determining the rate on a particular article requires assessing how the item is used or determining its main component material. Two or more alternative classifications may have to be considered.

The classification of a product can make a substantial difference in the duty applied. Under the BTN, it was sometimes possible to seek a more favorable classification to minimize the duty levied in the importing country. For example, one U.S. importer of semifinished products was able to secure a lower tariff rate by calling its product a "pump housing"—a casing with some internal components—instead of a pump. Under the HTS, however, "a pump is a pump"; the manufacturer was forced to import the casings with fewer working parts and do more finishing in the U.S. plant to maintain the lower import rates.

NONTARIFF BARRIERS • A **nontariff trade barrier** (NTB) is any measure, other than a tariff, that is a deterrent or obstacle to the sale of products in a foreign market. The five major types of NTBs—or hidden trade barriers, as they are sometimes called—are discussed below.

Quotas and Trade Controls • Quotas are government-imposed limits or restrictions on the number of units or the total value of a particular product or product category that can be imported. The trade distortion caused by a quota is even more severe than a tariff because once the quota has been reached, market price mechanisms are not allowed to operate. The phrase *state trade controls* refers to the practice of monopolizing trade in certain commodities. In the former Soviet Union, all commodities were monopolized; there are also many examples of noncommunist government monopolies. The Swedish government,

OPEN TO DISCUSSION

Many nations export up to 20 percent of their total production; the United States exports only about 10 percent. Businesses in smaller industrialized countries easily exhaust the potential of their home market and are forced to search internationally for expansion opportunities. Meanwhile, their U.S. counterparts appear to have fallen victim to one or more barriers to successful exporting. First, the limited ambition of many American business managers may result in complacency and a lack of export consciousness. A second barrier is lack of knowledge of market opportunities abroad or misperceptions about those markets. Third, the perceived lack of necessary resources—managerial skill, time, financing, and productive capacity—are often cited as reasons for not pursuing export opportunities. Unrealistic fears are a fourth type of barrier to exporting. When weighing export expansion opportunities, managers may express concerns about operating difficulties, environmental differences, credit or other types of risks, and possible strains upon the company. A fifth type of barrier is management inertia—the simple inability of company personnel to overcome export myopia.

U.S. exports have historically been dominated by the large companies of the Fortune 500 (see Table 9–1). As noted at the beginning of the chapter, small businesses in Germany are export powerhouses. Studies have shown that, in the United States, it is smaller-sized businesses rather than the Fortune 500 that are the major source of new jobs. Until recently, relatively few of these smaller companies were involved with exports. Dun & Bradstreet tracks U.S. exports in 70 industries; its figures now show that the majority of companies exporting employ less than 100 people. The U.S. Department of Commerce found that after participating in trade missions in 1987, 3,000 companies (most of which were small) generated $200 million in new export business. Yet, the U.S. Small Business Administration estimates that there are tens of thousands of small companies that could export but do not. For many of these firms, exporting represents a major untapped market opportunity.

Current research generally supports the proposition that the probability of being an exporter increases with firm size. However, it is less clear that the degree of export involvement (as determined by export intensity, i.e., the ratio of export sales to total sales) is positively correlated with firm size. In Italy, for example, a number of very small firms (those with 11 to 20 employees) in several industry sectors exhibit higher-than-average export intensity. One observer has called on the U.S. government to make exporting a top national priority, revise and abolish outdated programs and policies that favor overseas production, and give greater emphasis in trade negotiations to reducing barriers to U.S. exports. Judging by the narrowly averted trade war between Japan and the United States in 1995, it seems that Washington is heeding this advice.

Sources: Christopher M. Korth, "Managerial Barriers to U.S. Exports," *Business Horizons* 34, no. 2 (March–April 1991), pp. 18–26.

Joseph P. Pattison, *Acquiring the Future* (Homewood, Ill.: Dow Jones Irwin, 1990), p. 65.

Stefan H. Robock, "The Export Myopia of U.S. Multinationals: An Overlooked Opportunity for Creating U.S. Manufacturing Jobs," *Columbia Journal of World Business* 28, no. 2 (Summer 1993), pp. 24–32.

for example, controls the import of all alcoholic beverages and tobacco products, and the French government controls all imports of coal.

In the United States there are more than 8,000 different tariff classifications, of which some 3,600 are restricted by quotas and other control mechanisms. For example, there are machine tool agreements with Japan and Taiwan, 20 steel trade agreements, textile quotas for most Southeast Asian and Third World countries, the U.S.–Japan Semiconductor Agreement, and Japanese "voluntary" restraints on the export of cars and TVs to the United States. The United States even has a "Memorandum of Understanding on Softwood Lumber" with Canada, its largest trading partner. The extent of these and other similar agreements on a worldwide basis has led some critics to argue that the United States engages in "managed" trade rather than free trade.

Discriminatory Procurement Policies • These can take the form of government rules and administrative regulations, as well as formal or informal company policies, that discriminate against foreign suppliers. For example, the Buy American Act of 1933 stipulates that U.S. federal agencies must buy articles produced in the United States unless domestically produced goods are not available or the cost is unreasonable, or if purchasing U.S. materials would be inconsistent with the public interest.

Restrictive Customs Procedures • The rules and regulations for classifying and valuing commodities as a basis for levying import duties can be administered in a way that makes compliance difficult and expensive. For example, a product might be classified by the

TABLE 9–1   TOP 50 U.S. EXPORTERS ($ MILLION)

Company	Exports	Company	Exports
1. General Motors	$16,127.1	26. IBP	$1,549.6
2. Ford Motor	11,892.0	27. Weyerhaeuser	1,540.0
3. Boeing	11,844.0	28. Textron	1,441.0
4. Chrysler	9,400.0	29. International Paper	1,421.0
5. General Electric	8,110.0	30. Xerox	1,291.0
6. Motorola	7,370.0	31. Rockwell International	1,280.0
7. IBM	6,336.0	32. Abbott Laboratories	1,231.5
8. Philip Morris	4,942.0	33. Union Carbide	1,198.0
9. Archer Daniels Midland	4,675.0	34. FMC	1,150.0
10. Hewlett-Packard	4,653.0	35. Deere	1,144.0
11. Intel	4,561.0	36. Sun Microsystems	1,123.4
12. Caterpillar	4,510.0	37. Unisys	1,075.6
13. McDonnell Douglas	4,235.0	38. Georgia-Pacific	1,020.0
14. E.I. Du Pont de Nemours	3,635.0	39. Cummins Engine	1,004.0
15. United Technologies	3,108.0	40. Alcoa	988.0
16. Eastman Kodak	2,600.0	41. Dresser Industries	938.7
17. Lockheed	2,079.0	42. Monsanto	900.0
18. Compaq Computer	2,018.0	43. Bristol-Myers Squibb	867.0
19. Raytheon	1,867.0	44. Novell	860.0
20. Digital Equipment	1,830.7	45. Exxon	834.0
21. AlliedSignal	1,818.0	46. Microsoft	787.0
22. 3M	1,755.0	47. Honeywell	780.0
23. Westinghouse Electric	1,613.0	48. Occidental Petroleum	756.0
24. Dow Chemical	1,575.0	49. Ingersoll-Rand	743.0
25. Merck	1,572.0	50. General Dynamics	722.0

Source: Adapted from James Aley, "New Lift for the U.S. Export Boom," *Fortune* (Nov. 13, 1995), pp. 74–76.

U.S. Department of Commerce under a certain harmonized number; Canadian customs may disagree. The U.S. exporter may have to attend a hearing with Canadian customs officials to reach an agreement. Such delays cost time and money for both the importer and exporter.

Selective Monetary Controls and Discriminatory Exchange Rate Policies • Discriminatory exchange rate policies distort trade in much the same way as selective import duties and export subsidies. Selective monetary policies are definite barriers to trade. For example, many countries from time to time require importers to place on deposit— at no interest—an amount equal to the value of imported goods. In effect, these regulations raise the price of foreign goods by the cost of money for the term of the required deposit.

Restrictive Administrative and Technical Regulations • These include antidumping regulations, size regulations, and safety and health regulations. Some of these regulations are intended to keep out foreign goods, while others are directed toward legitimate domestic objectives. For example, the safety and pollution regulations being developed in the United States for automobiles are motivated almost entirely by legitimate concerns about highway safety and pollution. However, an effect of these regulations has been to make it so expensive to comply with U.S. safety requirements that some automakers have

■ GERMANY'S *MITTELSTAND*

*P*art of the *Mittelstand*'s success can be attributed to Germany's export infrastructure. Diplomats, bankers, and other officials around the world are constantly on the lookout for opportunities; information about promising deals is conveyed back to Germany. Meanwhile, representatives from trade associations, export trading companies, and banks assist exporters with documentation and other issues. Some banks have special *Mittelstand* departments to provide export financing and assist companies in obtaining insurance.

The current business environment both outside and inside Germany is presenting difficult challenges to the *Mittelstand*. In response to the 1992–1993 recession in Europe, several countries—notably Great Britain, Italy, and Sweden—devalued their currencies. This move brought down prices on exports from those countries and made Germany's exports correspondingly less price competitive. Meanwhile, German unions have won wage hikes for workers, and the mark's continued strength puts additional upward pressure on export prices. *Mittelstand* owners are taking steps to ensure their own survival, but a lack of organization has limited their political influence in Bonn. Germany's banks have tightened loan terms, resulting in a credit crunch. Many companies are going public to raise capital, but venture capital can be hard to find. Professional managers are being hired to assist the owners. Some companies may even move production out of Germany. Melitta, for example, began assembling home coffeemakers in Portugal in 1995. For companies where money is tight, licensing production is an economical alternative.

Sources: Matt Marshall, "Timid Lending Hits Germany's Exporters," *The Wall Street Journal* (Nov. 21, 1995), p. A14. Karen Lowry Miller, "The *Mittelstand* Takes a Stand," *Business Week* (Apr. 10, 1995), pp. 54–55. Gail E. Schares and John Templeman, "Think Small: The Export Lessons To Be Learned from Germany's Midsize Companies," *Business Week* (Nov. 4, 1994), pp. 58+.

withdrawn certain models from the market. Volkswagen, for example, no longer sells diesel automobiles in the United States for this reason.

Despite a GATT agreement concerning technical barriers to trade, Japan used technical standards unrelated to performance to bar U.S. forest products from its market. In May 1989, these restrictive technical regulations became part of the basis for listing Japan as guilty of unfair trade practices under Section 301 of the 1988 trade act.

Another example of a restrictive technical regulation is found in Germany, which requires that imports of feed meal contain only 5 percent fat. Wellens & Company, a Minneapolis-based firm, produces a feed meal that contains about 10 percent fat, and, according to the company president, "We simply don't sell any to the German corporations. To change the meal's fat content would involve special machinery which would greatly increase production costs; it simply wouldn't be worth it." Wellens expects several other Western European countries to adopt the 5 percent regulation, which the company claims does nothing for animals' health.

As discussed in earlier chapters, there is a growing trend to remove all such restrictive trade barriers on a regional basis. The largest single effort was undertaken by the EU in an effort to create a single market starting January 1, 1993. The intent is to have one standard for all of Europe for such things as automobile safety, drug testing and certification, and food and product quality controls, as well as the development of a single currency, the ECU, to facilitate trade and commerce. Some observers believe that elimination of these intra-European barriers will result in the creation of a so-called Fortress Europe with new external barriers designed to keep out the foreign (e.g., Japanese) competition. The creation of a single North American market consisting of the United States, Canada, and Mexico is another example. President Clinton signed the North American Free Trade Agreement into law in November 1993.

CHOOSING EXPORT MARKETS

The decision to engage in export marketing should be based on a number of criteria, including potential market size, competitor activities, and overall marketing mix issues such as price, distribution, and promotion. The next step is the choice of one or more export markets to target. The selection process should begin with a product-market profile.

Creating a Product-Market Profile

The first step in choosing export markets is to establish the key factors influencing sales and profitability of the product in question. If a company is getting started for the first time in exporting, its product-market profile will have to be based upon its experience in the home market. The basic questions to be answered can be summarized as the nine Ws:

1. Who buys our product?
2. Who does not buy our product?
3. What need or function does our product serve?
4. What problem does our product solve?
5. What are customers currently buying to satisfy the need and/or solve the problem for which our product is targeted?
6. What price are they paying for the product they are currently buying?
7. When is our product purchased?
8. Where is our product purchased?
9. Why is our product purchased?

Any company must answer these critical questions if it is going to be successful in export markets. Each answer provides an input into decisions concerning the four Ps. Remember, the general rule in marketing is that, if a company wants to penetrate an existing market, it must offer more value than competitors—better benefits, lower prices, or both. This applies to export marketing as well as marketing in the home country.

Market Selection Criteria

Once a company has created a product-market profile, the next step in choosing an export market is to appraise possible markets. Six criteria should be assessed: market potential, market access, shipping costs, potential competition, product fit, and service requirements.

Market Potential • What is the basic market potential for the product? To answer this question, the library is a good place to start. In the United States, the federal government has numerous publications available, compiled by the United Nations, the Central Intelligence Agency, and various other agencies and organizations. Market data are also available from export census documents compiled by the Department of Commerce on the basis of shippers' export declarations (known as "ex-decs" or SEDs, these must be filled out for any export valued at $1,500 or more). Another important source of market data is the Foreign Commercial Service.

A number of electronic resources have been developed in recent years. These include the National Trade Data Base, which is available on CD-ROM from the Department of Commerce. The GateWaze company in Manchester, Massachusetts, has developed PC software called "The World Trader" to help small firms find opportunities in export markets. Similarly, the Port Authority of New York developed a program called "Export to Win" to help small business owners learn about exporting. In addition, the Internet and other interactive information services such as Prodigy and America On-Line feature bulletin boards where a great deal of information about various world markets is exchanged.

Whatever source of information is used, the ultimate goal is to determine the major factors affecting demand for a product. Then, using the tools and techniques described in Chapter 7 and available data, it is possible to arrive at a rough estimate of total potential demand for the product in one or more particular international markets. National income is often a good starting indicator on which to base demand estimates. Additional statistical measures will considerably sharpen the estimate of total demand. For example, when estimating the demand for automobile tires, data on the total number of cars registered in any country in the world should be easy to obtain. This data, combined with data on gasoline consumption, should permit estimation of the total mileage driven in the target market. When this figure is combined with tire life predictions, it is a straightforward matter to calculate demand estimates.

Market Access Considerations for Exporters • This aspect of market selection concerns the entire set of national controls that applies to imported merchandise. It includes such items as import duties, import restrictions or quotas, foreign exchange regulations, and preference arrangements. This topic is discussed in more detail in the next main section.

Shipping Costs • Export preparation and shipping costs can affect the market potential for a product. If a similar product is already being manufactured in the target market, shipping costs may render the imported product uncompetitive. It is important to investigate alternative modes of shipping as well as ways to differentiate a product to offset the price disadvantage.

Potential Competition • Discussions with exporters, bankers, and other industry executives are extremely useful in appraising the level and quality of competition in the potential market. Using a country's commercial representatives abroad can also be valuable. When contacting country representatives abroad, it is important to provide as much specific information as possible. If a manufacturer simply says, "I make lawnmowers. Is there a market for them in your territory?" the representative cannot provide much helpful information. If, on the other hand, the manufacturer provides the following information: (1) sizes of lawnmowers manufactured, (2) descriptive brochures indicating features and advantages, and (3) estimated cost including insurance and freight (CIF) and retail price in the target market, then the commercial representative could provide a very useful report assessing the company's product market in terms of needs.

Product Fit • With information on market potential, cost of access to the market, and local competition, the next step is to decide how well a company's product fits the market in question. In general, a product fits a market if it satisfies the following criteria: (1) The product is likely to appeal to customers in the potential market; (2) the product will not require more adaptation than is economically justifiable by the expected sales volume; (3) import restrictions and/or high tariffs do not exclude or make the product so expensive in the target market as to effectively eliminate demand; (4) shipping costs to the target market are in line with the requirements for competitive price; and (5) the cost of assembling sales literature, catalogs, and technical bulletins is feasible in view the market potential. The last factor is particularly important in selling highly technical products.

Service Requirements • If service is required for the product, can it be delivered at a cost that is consistent with the size of the market?

Table 9–2 presents a market selection framework that incorporates the information elements just discussed. Suppose a company has identified China, Russia, and Mexico as potential export markets. The table shows the countries arranged in declining rank by mar-

TABLE 9–2 MARKET SELECTION FRAMEWORK

Market	Market Size		Competitive Advantage Index		Market Potential		Terms of Access Index		Export Potential
China (1.2 billion)	100	×	0.07	=	7	×	.20	=	1.4
Russia (150 million)	50	×	.10	=	5	×	.60	=	3.0
Mexico (94 million)	20	×	.20	=	4	×	.90	=	3.6

ket size. At first glance, China might appear to hold the greatest potential simply on the basis of size. While it is true that population is a major factor in assessing market potential, there are other important issues to be considered.

First, the competitive advantage index of our hypothetical firm is 0.07 in China, 0.10 in Russia, and 0.20 in Mexico. Multiplying the market size by the competitive advantage index yields a market potential of 7 in China, 5 in Russia, and 4 in Mexico.

The next stage in the analysis requires an assessment of the relevant "market access considerations." In Table 9–2, all these conditions or terms are reduced to an index of terms of access, which is .20 for China, .60 for Russia, and .90 for Mexico. In other words, the "market access considerations" are more favorable in Mexico than in Russia, perhaps due to NAFTA. Multiplying the market potential by the terms of access index shows that Mexico, despite its small size, holds greater export potential than China or Russia. In this example, a company with limited resources would want to begin its export marketing program in Mexico because it offers the highest export market potential when a variety of criteria are considered.

Visiting the Potential Market

After the research effort has zeroed in on potential markets, there is no substitute for a personal visit to size up the market firsthand and begin the development of an actual export marketing program. A market visit should do several things. First, it should confirm (or contradict) assumptions regarding market potential. A second major purpose is to gather additional data necessary to reach the final go/no-go decision regarding an export marketing program. There are certain kinds of information that simply cannot be obtained from secondary sources. For example, an export manager or international marketing manager may have a list of potential distributors provided by the U.S. Department of Commerce. He or she may have corresponded with distributors on the list and formed some tentative idea of whether they meet the company's international criteria. It is difficult, however, to negotiate a suitable arrangement with international distributors without actually meeting face to face to allow each side of the contract to appraise the capabilities and character of the other party. A third reason for a visit to the export market is to develop a marketing plan in cooperation with the local agent or distributor. Agreement should be reached on necessary product modifications, pricing, advertising and promotion expenditures, and a distribution plan. If the plan calls for investment, agreement on the allocation of costs must also be reached.

One way to visit a potential market is through a trade show or a federally or state-sponsored trade mission. Hundreds of trade fairs—usually organized around a product, a group of products, or an activity—are held in major markets. For example, U.S. trade centers alone hold 60 product shows annually in major cities abroad.

By attending trade shows and missions, company representatives can conduct market assessment, develop or expand markets, find distributors or agents, or locate potential end users (i.e., engage in direct selling). Perhaps most important, by attending a trade show it is possible to learn a great deal about competitors' technology, pricing, and the depth of their market penetration. For example, while walking around the exhibit hall, one can gather literature about products that often contains strategically useful technological information. Overall, company managers or sales personnel should be able to get a good general impression of competitors in the marketplace while at the same time trying to sell their own company's product.

MARKET ACCESS CONSIDERATIONS

The phrase "market access considerations" refers to all the conditions that apply to the importation of goods manufactured outside of the buyer's country. Four important considerations are tariff systems, preferential tariffs, customs valuation codes, and duties.

Colleen Crowley is an export administrator with a $7 million company that specializes in animal nutrition products and agricultural processing machinery. From its headquarters in the midwestern United States, the company exports machinery to nearly 100 countries; Colleen is responsible for the Latin American market and Russia; the company's other export administrator is responsible for the rest of the world. Colleen's background includes a B.A. degree in international relations from a small liberal arts college in the Midwest. During her senior year, Colleen was awarded a Rotary International scholarship, and following graduation, she spent a year working as a volunteer in Nicaragua on an economic development project. The following year she used her scholarship to study economics at the University of Costa Rica. When her year of study ended, Colleen stayed in Costa Rica and worked at an international investment company.

After three years, Colleen returned to the United States with the intention of finding a job in which she could use her Spanish language skills. When the export administrator opportunity presented itself, Colleen jumped at the chance to get an entry-level job related to global marketing. "The best part of my job is dealing directly with customers," Colleen says. "If you provide good service, and they get to know you, they are appreciative and keep returning to do more business with you." Colleen arrives at work each morning and checks for faxes the way most people check their mail. On any given day, faxes may be from Poland, Russia, Taiwan, or Colombia. Some faxes are inquiries from prospective customers who have just heard about the company's products; others are from established customers requesting replacements parts or technical assistance. Sometimes Colleen responds to faxes on her own; other times, she translates an entire document into English and routes it to the appropriate company specialist.

"People in Latin America prefer to speak with business partners," Colleen explains. "That's why I'll find a fax from Colombia when I arrive in the morning—and I'll also get a telephone call from the same customer later that day. Needless to say, I get to use my Spanish every day. Anything important gets done by phone, not by fax." Colleen says, "All these international calls are expensive—so they had better lead to some business. Exporting sometimes means higher costs compared to selling to a customer in the next state. One of the skills I need is the ability to be congenial—ask my customer about his or her day, for example—but also get to the point so I don't run up a huge phone bill."

A person in Colleen's position must sometimes deal with requests to falsify invoices. For example, a buyer might ask Colleen to submit a bill for a particular item showing a price of $499 instead of, say, $600. Such a request may be prompted by the fact that, in many countries, items invoiced at less than $500 pass through customs more quickly and with lower duties. Colleen's response to such requests is always the same: She explains to the buyer that such an action would not only violate company policy, but it is illegal as well.

Colleen also deals extensively with transportation specialists and freight forwarders. She schedules shipments with steamship companies such as Sea-Land, Hyundai, and Evergreen; she also deals with trucking companies such as Yellow Freight or Contract Freighters. "Surprisingly enough, more than 50 percent of what I ship goes by air," Colleen notes. "It's easier and cheaper in the long run to send 5,000 pounds to Brazil by air than to deal with hassles like port strikes and the inevitable bureaucratic delays." Colleen obtains space, negotiates rates, and makes sure her shipments will get to customers at the right time. When this is done, Colleen conveys this information to the customer, who must obtain the appropriate import permits and advise his or her in-country customs agent about the pending shipment.

After the shipping arrangements have been made, Colleen checks with her bank to make sure the letter of credit documentation is accurate. This means making sure the company names—both the seller's and the buyer's—are spelled identically on both the invoice and the letter of credit. The description of the merchandise, the price, and all other information must be identical on all documents. Any discrepency—a wayward dash, or a missing space between two words—can cost $50 to $100 to correct once the merchandise has arrived at the destination. Even worse, a severe discrepancy can mean the seller doesn't get paid.

As for the future, Colleen hopes to rise to a higher level of management responsibility so that she can broaden her involvement in global marketing. To that end, Colleen plans to pursue MBA studies at a graduate school with a strong international orientation. Colleen says, "I know from experience that international trade benefits both companies and the country markets those companies serve. I want to help my employer make a profit, but I also want to play a role in improving economic conditions in other parts of the world."

A major U.S. objective in the Uruguay Round of GATT negotiations was to improve market access for U.S. companies with major U.S. trading partners. When the round ended in December 1993, the United States had secured reductions or total elimination of tariffs on 11 categories of U.S. goods exported to the EU, Japan, five of the EFTA nations (Austria, Switzerland, Sweden, Finland, and Norway), New Zealand, South Korea, Hong Kong, and Singapore. The categories affected included equipment for the construction, agricultural, medical, and scientific industry sectors, as well as steel, beer, brown distilled spirits, pharmaceuticals, paper, pulp and printed matter, furniture, and toys. In most instances, the tariffs are scheduled to be phased out over a five-year period.

For example, Weyerhaeuser Co. and other exporters of paper products to Europe have been burdened with tariffs of 6 to 9 percent. Scandanavian paper companies, meanwhile, have enjoyed tariff-free access to the European market. While elimination of tariffs means improved market access and new commercial opportunities, the paper industry is unhappy with the 10-year time frame for phasing out current duties. Exports of electronics products to the EU have also been subject to tariff barriers—14 percent for semiconductors and 4 percent for computer components. The Uruguay Round resulted in cuts and elimination of tariffs on these items. Overall, the Commerce Department predicts that enhanced market access conditions could increase U.S. output by more than $1 trillion over the next decade.

Tariff Systems

Tariff systems provide either a single rate of duty for each item applicable to all countries, or two or more rates, applicable to different countries or groups of countries. Tariffs are usually grouped into two classifications.

Single-Column Tariff • The single-column tariff is the simplest type of tariff and consists of a schedule of duties in which the rate applies to imports from all countries on the same basis.

Two-Column Tariff • Under the two-column tariff, the initial single column of duties is supplemented by a second column showing reduced rates as determined through tariff negotiations with other countries. Rates agreed upon by "convention" are supplied to all countries enjoying most-favored-nation (MFN) status within the framework of GATT. Under GATT, nations agree to apply their most favorable tariff or lowest tariff rate to all nations—subject to some exceptions—that are signatories to GATT.

The United States has given MFN status to some 180 countries around the world, so the name is really a misnomer. Only Vietnam, North Korea, Iran, and Libya are excluded, showing that MFN is really a political tool more than an economic one. For example, China has been threatened with the loss of MFN status because of alleged human rights violations. The landed prices of its products would rise by 60 to 100 percent or more, which would price Chinese products out of the market. The loss of MFN status could have a significant impact on its trade with the United States. Table 9–3 illustrates what a change in tariffs could mean to China.

TABLE 9–3 **TARIFF RATES, MFN VS. NON-MFN**

	MFN	Non-MFN
Gold jewelry, such as plated neckchains	6.5%	80%
Screws, lock washers, misc. iron/steel parts	5.8%	35%

Source: U.S. Customs Service.

Preferential Tariff

A preferential tariff is a reduced tariff rate applied to imports from certain countries. GATT prohibits the use of preferential tariffs, with three major exceptions. First are historical preference arrangements such as the British Commonwealth preferences and similar arrangements that existed before GATT. Second, preference schemes that are part of a formal economic integration treaty, such as free trade areas or common markets, are excluded. Third, industrial countries are permitted to grant preferential market access to companies based in less-developed countries.

Customs Valuation Code

The United States is now a signatory to the GATT Customs Valuation Code. U.S. customs value law was amended in 1980 to conform to the GATT valuation standards. Under the code, the primary basis of customs valuation is known as "transaction value." As the name implies, transaction value is defined as the actual individual transaction price paid by the buyer to the seller of the goods being valued. In instances in which the buyer and seller are related parties (for example, when Honda's U.S. manufacturing subsidiaries purchase parts from headquarters in Japan), customs authorities have the right to scrutinize the transfer price to make sure it is a fair reflection of market value. If there is no established transaction value for the good, alternative methods are used to compute the customs value which sometimes results in increased values and, consequently, increased duties. In the late 1980s, the U.S. Treasury Department began a major investigation into the transfer prices charged by the Japanese automakers to their U.S. subsidiaries. It was charged that the Japanese paid virtually no U.S. income taxes because of "losses" on the millions of cars they import into the United States each year.

During the Uruguay Round of GATT negotiations, the United States successfully sought a number of amendments to the Agreement on Customs Valuations. Most importantly, the United States wanted clarification of the rights and obligations of importing and exporting countries in cases in which fraud was suspected. Two overall categories of products were frequently targeted for investigation. The first included exports of textiles, cosmetics, and consumer durables; the second included entertainment software such as videotapes, audiotapes, and compact discs. Such amendments will improve the ability of U.S. exporters to defend their interests if charged with fraudulent practices. The amendments were also designed to encourage nonsignatories—especially developing countries—to become parties to the Agreement.

Types of Duties

CUSTOMS DUTIES • Customs duties are divided into two categories. They may be calculated either as a percentage of the value of the goods (ad valorem duty) or as a specific amount per unit (specific duty) or as a combination of both of these methods.

Ad Valorem Duties • This duty is expressed as a percentage of the value of goods. The definition of customs value varies from country to country. Therefore, an exporter is well advised to secure information about the valuation practices applied to his or her product in the country of destination. A uniform basis for the valuation of goods for customs purposes was elaborated by the Customs Cooperation Council in Brussels and was adopted in 1953. In countries adhering to HTS conventions on customs valuation, the customs value is landed CIF cost at the port of entry. This cost should reflect the arm's-length price of the good at the time the duty becomes payable.

Specific Duties • These duties are expressed as a specific amount of currency per unit of weight, volume, length, or number of other units of measurement, for example, "50 cents

U.S. per pound," "$1.00 U.S. per pair," or "25 cents U.S. per square yard." Specific duties are usually expressed in the currency of the importing country, but there are exceptions, particularly in countries that have experienced sustained inflation.

Alternative Duties • In this case, both ad valorem and specific duties are set out in the custom tariff for a given product. Normally, the applicable rate is the one that yields the higher amount of duty, although there are cases where the lower is specified.

Compound or Mixed Duties • These duties provide for specific, plus ad valorem, rates to be levied on the same articles.

OTHER DUTIES • Antidumping Duties • Dumping, which is the sale of merchandise in export markets at unfair prices, is discussed in detail in Chapter 14. To offset the impact of dumping and to penalize guilty companies, most countries have introduced legislation providing for the imposition of antidumping duties if injury is caused to domestic producers. Such duties take the form of special additional import charges equal to the dumping margin. Antidumping duties are almost invariably applied to articles that are also produced in the importing country. In the United States, antidumping duties are assessed after the Commerce Department finds a foreign company guilty of dumping and the International Trade Commission rules that the dumped products injured U.S. companies.

Countervailing Duties • Countervailing duties (CVDs) are additional duties levied to offset subsidies granted in the exporting country. In the United States, CVD legislation and procedures are very similar to those pertaining to dumping. The Commerce Department and International Trade Commission jointly administer both the CVD and antidumping laws under provisions of the Trade and Tariff Act of 1984. Subsidies and countervailing measures received a great deal of attention during the Uruguay Round of GATT negotiations. In 1996, the ITC and Commerce Department planned to impose both countervailing and antidumping duties on four Italian companies and two Turkish companies that market pasta in the United States. Responding to complaints by Borden, Gooch Foods, and Hershey Foods, the U.S. agencies determined that the Italian and Turkish firms were both receiving export subsidies and selling pasta at less than fair value and harming the American companies.

Other Import Charges

Variable Import Levies • Several countries, including Sweden and some other members of the EU, apply a system of variable import levies to certain categories of imported agricultural products. In instances where the prices of imported products would undercut those of domestic products, the effect of these levies would be to raise the price of imported products to the domestic price level.

Temporary Import Surcharges • Temporary surcharges have been introduced from time to time by certain countries, such as the United Kingdom and the United States, to provide additional protection for local industry and, in particular, in response to balance-of-payments deficits.

Compensatory Import Taxes • In theory these taxes correspond to various internal taxes, such as value-added taxes (VAT's) and sales taxes. Such "border tax adjustments" must not, according to GATT, amount to additional protection for domestic producers or to a subsidy for exports. In practice, one of the major tax inequities today is the fact that manufacturers in Europe's VAT countries do not pay a VAT on sales to non-VAT countries such as the United States, whereas U.S. manufacturers that pay income taxes in the United States must also pay VAT taxes on sales in VAT countries.

ORGANIZING FOR EXPORTING

Manufacturers interested in export marketing have two broad considerations: Organizing in the home country and organizing in the target market country. The issues and approaches that relate to organizing are discussed below.

Organizing in the Manufacturer's Country

Home-country issues involve deciding whether to assign export responsibility inside the company or to work with an external organization specializing in a product or geographic area.

IN-HOUSE EXPORT ORGANIZATION • Most companies handle export operations within their own organization. Depending on the company's size, responsibilities may be incorporated into an employee's domestic job description. Alternatively, these responsibilities may be handled as part of a separate division or organizational structure.

The possible arrangements for handling exports include the following:

1. As a part-time activity performed by domestic employees
2. Through an export partner affiliated with the domestic marketing structure that takes possession of the goods before they leave the country
3. Through an export department that is independent of the domestic marketing structure
4. Through an export department within an international division
5. For multidivisional companies, each of the foregoing possibilities within each division

A company that assigns a sufficiently high priority to its export business will establish an in-house organization. It then faces the question of how to organize effectively. This depends on two things: the company's appraisal of the opportunities in export marketing and its strategy for allocating resources to markets on a global basis. It may be possible for a company to make export responsibility part of a domestic employee's job description. The advantage of this arrangement is obvious: It is a low-cost arrangement requiring no additional personnel. However, this approach can only work under two conditions. First, the domestic employee assigned to the task must be thoroughly competent in terms of product/customer knowledge. Second, that competence must be applicable to the target international market(s). The key issue underlying the second condition is the extent to which the target export market is different from the domestic market. If customer circumstances and characteristics are similar, the requirements for specialized regional knowledge are reduced.

EXTERNAL INDEPENDENT EXPORT ORGANIZATIONS • If a company chooses not to perform its own marketing and promotion in-house, there are numerous export services providers to choose from. These include export trading companies (ETCs), export management companies (EMCs), export merchants, export brokers, combination export managers, manufacturer's export representatives or commission agents, and export distributors. The definitions in Appendix 9-A are provided as guides to current industry usage. However, because these terms and labels may be used inconsistently, the reader is urged to check and confirm the services performed by a particular independent export organization.

In 1982, the United States Congress passed the Export Trading Company Act. This measure was designed to spur the development of ETCs by improving their access to capital, ensuring the availability of products, and improving the international marketing skills of company personnel, while limiting exposure to antitrust considerations. Congress hoped to increase U.S. exports by encouraging more efficient provision of export trade services, and to permit banks to make limited equity investments in ETCs. Findings from one study of the act's effects indicate that the performance of ETCs has been disappointing, in part because of the dollar's strength in the mid-1980s. Banks have demonstrated a reluctance to become involved in exporting, and the act did not provide enough incentive for nonexporting companies to become exporters (Terpstra & Chow-Ming 1992).

A typical ETC acts as the "export department" for several unrelated companies that lack export experience. EMCs perform a variety of services, including marketing research, channel selection, arranging financing and shipping, and documentation. According to one recent survey of U.S.-based EMCs, the most important activities for export success are marketing information gathering, communication with markets, setting prices, and ensuring parts availability. The same survey ranked export activities in terms of degree of difficulty; analyzing political risk, sales force management, setting pricing, and obtaining financial information were deemed most difficult to accomplish. One of the study's conclusions was that the U.S. government should do a better job of helping EMCs and their clients analyze the political risk associated with foreign markets (Howard 1994).

Organizing in the Market Country

In addition to deciding whether to rely on in-house or external export specialists in the home country, a company must also make arrangements to distribute the product in the target market country. The basic decision that every exporting organization faces is: To what extent do we rely upon direct market representation as opposed to representation by independent intermediaries?

DIRECT MARKET REPRESENTATION • There are two major advantages to direct representation in a market: control and communications. Direct representation allows decisions concerning program development, resource allocation, or price changes to be implemented unilaterally. Moreover, when a product is not yet established in a market, special efforts are necessary to achieve sales. The advantage of direct representation is that these special efforts are ensured by the marketer's investment. With indirect or independent representation, such efforts and investment are often not forthcoming; in many cases, there is simply not enough incentive for independents to invest significant time and money in representing a product. The other great advantage to direct representation is that the possibilities for feedback and information from the market are much greater. This information can vastly improve export marketing decisions concerning product, price, communications, and distribution.

Direct representation does not mean that the exporter is selling directly to the consumer or customer. In most cases, direct representation involves selling to wholesalers or retailers. For example, the major automobile exporters in Germany and Japan rely upon direct representation in the U.S. market in the form of their distributing agencies, which are owned and controlled by the manufacturing organization. The distributing agencies sell products to franchised dealers.

INDEPENDENT REPRESENTATION • In smaller markets, it is usually not feasible to establish direct representation because the low sales volume does not justify the cost. Even in larger markets, a small manufacturer usually lacks adequate sales volume to justify the cost of direct representation. Whenever sales volume is small, use of an independent distributor is an effective method of sales distribution. Finding "good" distributors can be the key to export success.

PIGGYBACK MARKETING • *Piggyback marketing*, or the use of a "mother hen" sales force, is an innovation in international distribution that has received much attention in recent years. This is an arrangement whereby one manufacturer obtains distribution of products through another's distribution channels. Both parties can benefit: The active distribution partner makes fuller use of its distribution system capacity and thereby increases the revenues generated by the system. The manufacturer using the piggyback arrangement does so at a cost that is much lower than that required for any direct arrangement. Successful piggyback marketing requires that the combined product lines be complementary. They must appeal to the same customer, and they must not be competitive with each other. If these requirements are met, the piggyback arrangement can be a very effective way of fully utilizing an international channel system to the advantage of both parties. A case in point is the Hawaiian Kauai Kookie Kompany, whose owners observed Japanese tourists stocking up on cookies before returning home from Hawaii. Now the cookies are sold in a piggyback arrangement with travel agencies in Japan. The cookies can be purchased from a catalog after travelers have returned home, thus reducing the amount of baggage.[4]

EXPORT FINANCING/METHODS OF PAYMENT

The decision as to the appropriate method of payment for a given international sale is a basic credit decision. A number of factors must be considered, including currency availability in the buyer's country, creditworthiness of the buyer, and the seller's relationship to the buyer. Finance managers at companies that have never exported often express concern regarding payment. Many CFOs with international experience know that a comparison of international receivables with domestic receivables often demonstrates that there is less problem collecting on international sales than on domestic sales, provided the proper financial instruments are used. The reason is simple: As explained below, a letter of credit can be used to guarantee payment for a product. Domestic sales, on the other hand, are usually conducted on an open-account basis; collecting thus hinges on the creditworthiness of the buyer. After an exporter and importer have established a good working relationship, and the finance managers' level of confidence increases, it may be possible to move to a documentary collection or open-account method of payment. The different methods for arranging payment for export merchandise sales to buyers abroad are explained below.

LETTERS OF CREDIT • Letters of credit (L/C) are widely used as a payment method in international export trade. Excluding advance payment terms, an L/C offers the exporter the best assurance of being paid for products sold internationally. That assurance arises from the fact that the payment obligation under an L/C lies with the buyer's bank and not the buyer.

An L/C is essentially a "letter" by which a bank substitutes its creditworthiness for that of the buyer. An L/C can be considered a conditional guarantee issued by the bank on behalf of the buyer to a seller assuring payment if the seller complies with the terms set forth in the L/C. For importers, however, the letter is more expensive because funds might have to be deposited in their bank to secure the credit line. If an L/C is the method of financing, the exporter ordinarily receives payment at the time shipping documents are presented to the bank negotiating the L/C in the seller's country.

DOCUMENTARY COLLECTIONS (DRAFTS) • A documentary collection is a method of payment using a bill of exchange, also known as a draft. A bill of exchange is a negotiable instrument that is easily transferable from one party to another. In its simplest form, it is a written order by one party directing a second party to pay to the order of a third party.

---

[4]Jack G. Kaikati, "Don't Crack the Japanese Distribution System—Just Circumvent It," *Columbia Journal of World Business* 28, no. 2 (Summer 1993), p. 41.

A documentary draft is an important instrument in an export transaction. With a documentary draft, the documents that are required to clear the goods through customs and convey title, plus other important shipping documents, are sent to a bank in the importer's country. The draft is presented to the importer along with these documents, which are delivered against the importer's honoring of the draft.

CASH IN ADVANCE • There are a number of conditions which may prompt the exporter to request cash payment—in whole or in part—in advance of shipment. Examples include times when credit risks abroad are high, when exchange restrictions within the country of destination may delay return of funds for an unreasonable period, or when, for any other reason, the exporter may be unwilling to sell on credit terms. Because of competition and restrictions against cash payment in many countries, the volume of business handled on a cash-in-advance basis is small.

SALES ON OPEN ACCOUNT • Open-account terms generally prevail in areas where exchange controls are minimal and exporters have had longstanding relations with good buyers in nearby or long-established markets. Open-account terms also prevail when sales are made to branches or subsidiaries of the exporter. The main objection to open-account sales is the absence of a tangible obligation. Normally, if a time draft is drawn and is dishonored after acceptance, it can be used as a basis of legal action, whereas in the case of a dishonored open-account transaction, the legal procedure may be more complicated. Starting in 1995, the Export-Import Bank expanded insurance coverage on open-account transactions to limit the risk for exporters.

SALES ON A CONSIGNMENT BASIS • As in the case of sales on open account, no tangible obligation is created by consignment sales. In countries with free ports or free trade zones, it can be arranged to have consigned merchandise placed under bonded warehouse control in the name of a foreign bank. Sales can then be arranged by the selling agent and arrangements made to release partial lots out of the consigned stock against regular payment terms. The merchandise is not cleared through customs until after the sale has been completed.

COUNTERTRADE[5]

In recent years, many exporters have been forced to finance international transactions by taking full or partial payment in some form other than money. A number of alternative finance methods, known as countertrade, are widely used. In a *countertrade* transaction, a sale results in product flowing in one direction to a buyer; a separate stream of products and services, often flowing in the opposite direction, is also created. Countertrade generally involves a seller from the West and a buyer in a developing country; for example, the countries in the former Soviet bloc have historically relied heavily on countertrade. This approach, which reached a peak in popularity in the mid-1980s, is now used in some 100 countries. Unconfirmed estimates of the countertrade share of world trade volume put it as high as 25 to 30 percent. For East-West trade, the share is estimated to be even higher.

As one expert notes, countertrade flourishes when hard currency is scarce. Exchange controls may prevent a company from expatriating earnings; the company may be forced to spend money in-country for products that are then exported and sold in third-country markets. Perhaps the single most important driving force behind the proliferation of countertrade has been the decreasing ability of developing countries to finance imports through

[5]Many of the examples in the following section are adapted from Schaffer 1989.

bank loans. This trend has resulted in debt-ridden governments pushing for self-financed deals.[6] Two conditions determine the probability that importing nations will demand countertrade: (1) the priority attached to the Western import and (2) the value of the transaction. Overall, the advantages to nonmarket and developing economies are access to Western marketing expertise and technology in the short term, and creation of hard currency export markets in the long term. The U.S. government officially opposes government-mandated countertrade, because it may represent the type of bilateral trade agreement that violates the free trading system established by GATT.

Two categories of countertrade are discussed below. Barter falls into one category; the mixed forms of countertrade, including counterpurchase, offset, compensation trading, and cooperation agreements belong in a separate category. They incorporate a real distinction from barter, because money or credit is involved in the transaction.

SIMPLE BARTER • Also termed *straight*, *classical*, or *pure barter*, this term describes the least complex and oldest form of bilateral, nonmonetized countertrade. Simple barter is a direct exchange of goods or services between two parties. Although no money is involved, both partners construct an approximate shadow price for products flowing in each direction. One contract formalizes simple barter transactions, which are generally for less than one year to avoid problems in price fluctuations. However, for some transactions, the exchange may span months or years, with contract provisions allowing adjustments in the exchange ratio to handle fluctuations in world prices.

Companies sometimes seek outside help from barter specialists. For example, New York–based Atwood Richards Inc. engages in barter in all parts of the world. Generally, however, distribution is direct between trading partners with no middleman included. For example, General Electric sold a turbine generator to Romania in the late 1970s; for payment, GE Trading Company accepted $150 million in chemicals, metals, nails, and other products which it then sold on the world market.

One of the most high-profile companies involved in barter deals is PepsiCo, which has done business in the Soviet and post-Soviet market for more than 20 years. In the Soviet era, PepsiCo bartered soft-drink syrup concentrate for Stolichnaya vodka that was, in turn, exported to the United States by the PepsiCo Wines & Spirits subsidiary and marketed by M. Henri Wines. In the post-Soviet market economy in the CIS, barter is no longer required. Today, Stolichnaya is imported and marketed in the United States by Carillon Importers, a unit of Grand Metropolitan PLC.

COUNTERPURCHASE • This form of countertrade, also termed *parallel trading* or *parallel barter*, is distinguished from other forms in that each delivery in an exchange is paid for in cash. For example, Rockwell International sold a printing press to Zimbabwe for $8 million. The deal only went through, however, after Rockwell agreed to purchase $8 million in ferrochrome and nickel from Zimbabwe, which it subsequently sold on the world market.

The Rockwell-Zimbabwe deal illustrates several aspects of counterpurchase. Generally, products offered by the foreign principal are not related to the Western firm's exports and thus cannot be used directly by the firm. In most counterpurchase transactions, two separate contracts are signed. In one the supplier agrees to sell products for a cash settlement (the original sales contract); in the other, the supplier agrees to purchase and market unrelated products from the buyer (a separate, parallel contract). The dollar value of the counterpurchase generally represents a set percentage—and sometimes the full value—of the products sold to the foreign principal. When the Western supplier sells these goods, the trading cycle is complete.

---

[6]Pompiliu Verzariu, "Trends and Developments in International Countertrade," *Business America* (Nov. 2, 1992), p. 2.

OFFSET • *Offset* is a technique whereby the government in the country of import seeks to recover large sums of hard currency spent on expensive purchases such as military aircraft or telecommunications systems. In effect, the government is saying, "If you want us to spend government money on your exports, you must import products from our country" (Schaffer 1989). On occasion, offset may also involve cooperation in manufacturing or some form of technology transfer. For example, a foreign principal may include requirements to place subcontracts locally and/or to arrange local assembly or manufacturing equal to a certain percentage of the contract value.[7] In the 1980s, General Dynamics sold F-16 fighters to Turkey for $4.2 billion. General Dynamics committed to offsets totaling $1 billion, about 24 percent of the sale's contract value.

Offset may be distinguished from counterpurchase because the latter is characterized by smaller deals over shorter periods of time.[8] Another major distinction between offset and other forms of countertrade is that the agreement is not contractual but reflects a memorandum of understanding that sets out the dollar value of products to be offset and the time period for completing the transaction. In addition, there is no penalty on the supplier for nonperformance. Typically, as in the General Dynamics case, requests range from 20 to 50 percent of the value of the supplier's product. Some highly competitive sales have required offsets exceeding 100 percent of the valuation of the original sale.

COMPENSATION TRADING • This form of countertrade is also called *buyback*, and involves two separate, and parallel, contracts. In one contract, the supplier agrees to build a plant or provide plant equipment, patents or licenses, or technical, managerial, or distribution expertise for a hard-currency downpayment at the time of delivery. In the other contract, the supplier company agrees to take payment in the form of the plant's output equal to its investment (minus interest) for a period of as many as 20 years.

Essentially, the success of compensation trading rests on the willingness of each firm to be both a buyer and a seller. China has used compensation trading extensively. Egypt also used this approach to develop an aluminum plant. A Swiss company, Alusuisse, built the plant and also exports alumina (an oxide of aluminum found in bauxite and clay) to Egypt. Alusuisse takes back a percentage of the finished aluminum produced at the plant as partial payment for building the plant. As this example shows, compensation differs from counterpurchase in that the technology or capital supplied is related to the output produced.[9] In counterpurchase, as noted previously, the goods taken by the supplier typically cannot be used directly in its business activities.

COOPERATION AGREEMENTS • Cooperation agreements meet the needs of Western firms doing business with nonmarket economies, which are reluctant to link selling and buying. What distinguishes these arrangements from other types of countertrade is the specialization of each Western firm for either buying or selling, not both. Each of the three forms of cooperation agreements represents an increasingly complex accommodation to the needs of trading partners. They include cooperation and simple barter (triangular deals); cooperation and counterpurchase; and cooperation, counterpurchase, and credit by a bank. As an example of cooperation and simple barter, the parties to the transaction might be two unrelated Western firms, with a U.S. firm specialized as a seller and a Western European firm as a buyer, and an Eastern European Foreign Trade Organization (FTO). The U.S. firm may perform the selling function by delivering goods to the FTO. In payment for the goods, the FTO might deliver raw materials to the Western European firm, which carries out the buying function. The Western European firm then pays the

---

[7]The commitment to local assembly or manufacturing under the supplier's specifications is commonly termed a *coproduction agreement*, which is tied to the offset but does not, in itself, represent a type of countertrade.
[8]Patricia Daily and S. M. Ghazanfar, "Countertrade: Help or Hindrance to Less-Developed Countries?" *Journal of Social, Political, and Economic Studies* 18, no. 1 (Spring 1993), p. 65.
[9]Ibid., p. 66.

U.S. firm for the raw materials in an amount equivalent to the value of goods originally sent to the Eastern FTO. The advantage to the U.S. firm offering goods is in removing the obligation to buy, and for the Western European firm receiving raw materials in, a considerable reduction in transport costs. Problems associated with these arrangements include finding two Western firms with the appropriate supply-demand fit and the flexibilities to handle time delays in receipt of payment or in delivery of goods.

HYBRID COUNTERTRADE ARRANGEMENTS • Hybrid forms of countertrade are becoming more prevalent in trading arrangements. For example, the investment performance contract in Third World markets is an additional condition of offset arrangements. Countries such as Brazil, Mexico, and even Canada now make official approval of investment proposals contingent on commitments by the investors to export. As a second example, "project accompaniment" typifies an arrangement in which a Western supplier is encouraged to buy a greater volume and/or wider range of products, compared with the countertrade commitment. Project accompaniment has surfaced as a condition to the exchange of industrial goods by the West for oil from Middle Eastern producers.

SWITCH TRADING • Also called *triangular trade* and *swap*, switch trading is a mechanism that can be applied to barter or countertrade. In this arrangement, a professional switch trader, switch trading house, or bank steps into a simple barter or other countertrade arrangement when one of the parties is not willing to accept all the goods received in a transaction. The switching mechanism provides a "secondary market" for countertraded or bartered goods and reduces the inflexibilities inherent in barter and countertrade. Fees charged by switch traders range from 5 percent of market value for commodities to 30 percent for high-technology items. Switch traders develop their own networks of firms and personal contacts and are generally headquartered in Vienna, Amsterdam, Hamburg, and London. If a party anticipates that the products received in a barter or countertrade deal will be sold eventually at discount by a switch trader, the common practice is to price the original products higher or build in "special charges" for port storage or consulting or require shipment by the national carrier.

The advantages of switching are that (1) its multilateral character offers a greater degree of economic efficiency in pricing and in increasing trade, (2) discounted prices can open new markets more rapidly, and (3) Western firms can shed the responsibilities of marketing goods received in countertrade. Disadvantages include (1) disruptions of producers' established markets, when switch dealers offer their products at discount to such markets; (2) products that may be in oversupply or difficult to sell on the world market; (3) the foreign principal assessing the Western firm as uncommitted to a long-term trade relationship, particularly if the foreigner's established markets are threatened by discounted products; and (4) the complex and cumbersome nature of switching transactions. Switch trading's complexity is rooted in the mechanics of the transaction; typically, the switch trader sells a commodity for "soft"—i.e., nonconvertible—currency, uses the soft currency to purchase another commodity, and repeats the process until he or she can purchase a commodity that can be sold for hard currency.

SUMMARY

This chapter provides an overview of export marketing and the decisions company personnel have to make to become successful exporters. Governments exert a strong influence on exports, through support programs, regulations, nontariff barriers, and tariff classifications.

In choosing export markets, companies must assess market potential, market access, shipping costs, potential competition, product fit, and service requirements. It is definitely a good idea to visit a potential market before developing an export program. Market access considerations are particularly important for the exporter and the importer. Exporters must understand how tariffs and duties affect the prices that must be paid by the importers. Successful exporting entails organizational decisions—e.g., regarding internal or external expertise—in both the manufacturer's country and the market country.

Exporters and importers must have a thorough understanding of international financial instruments, especially letters of credit. Exporters and importers must also be familiar with the various forms of barter and countertrade that represent nonmonetary methods of conducting trade with cash-poor countries new to market-driven economies.

DISCUSSION QUESTIONS

1. Why is exporting from the United States dominated by large companies? What, if anything, could be done to increase exports from smaller companies?

2. What six criteria should be assessed when evaluating potential export markets?

3. What are the various types of duties that export marketers should be aware of?

4. What is the difference between barter and countertrade? Why do companies barter?

5. What does it take to be a successful exporter?

6. Why are smaller companies in countries like Germany and Italy so much more active in exporting than similar-sized companies in North America?

BIBLIOGRAPHY

Books

Branch, Alan E. *Elements of Export Marketing Management.* London: Chapman and Hall, 1990.

Gordon, John S. *Profitable Exporting: A Complete Guide to Marketing Your Products Abroad.* New York: Wiley, 1993.

Johnson, Thomas E. *Export/Import Procedure and Documentation.* New York: AMACOM, 1991.

Maggiori, Herman J. *How To Make the World Your Market: The International Sales and Marketing Handbook.* Los Angeles: Burning Gate Press, 1992.

Pattison, Joseph E. *Acquiring the Future: America's Survival and Success in the Global Economy.* Homewood, Ill.: Dow-Jones-Irwin, 1990.

Raynauld, Andre. *Financing Exports to Developing Countries.* Paris: Development Centre of the Organization for Economic Cooperation and Development, 1992.

Rossen, Philip J., and Stan D. Reid, eds. *Managing Export Entry and Expansion.* New York: Praeger, 1987.

Schaffer, Matt. *Winning the Countertrade War: New Export Strategies for America.* New York: John Wiley & Sons, 1989.

U.S. Department of Commerce. *A Basic Guide to Exporting.* Washington, D.C.: U.S. Department of Commerce, 1992.

————. *Toward a National Export Strategy: U.S. Exports = U.S. Jobs: Reports to the United States Congress.* Washington, D.C.: Trade Promotion Coordinating Committee, 1993.

Venedikian, Harry M. *Export-Import Financing.* New York: Wiley, 1992.

Verzariu, Pompiliu. *Countertrade, Barter, and Offsets: New Strategies for Profit in International Trade.* New York: McGraw-Hill, 1985.

Articles

Bilkey, Warren J. "Attempted Integration of the Literature on the Export Behavior of Firms." *Journal of International Business Studies* 8, no. 1 (Spring–Summer 1978), pp. 33–46.

Bonaccorsi, Andrea. "On the Relationship between Firm Size and Export Intensity." *Journal of International Business Studies* 23, no. 4 (Fourth Quarter 1992), pp. 605–636.

————. "What Do We Know about Exporting by Small Italian Exporting Firms?" *Journal of International Marketing* 1, no. 3 (1993), pp. 49–76.

Cavusgil, S. Tamer, and V. H. Kirpalani. "Introducing Products into Export Markets: Success Factors." *Journal of Business Research* 27, no. 1 (May 1993), pp. 1–15.

Cavusgil, S. Tamer, V. H. Kirpalani, Shaoming Zou, and G. M. Naidu. "Product and Promotion Adaptation in Export Ventures: An Empirical Investigation." *Journal of International Business Studies* 24, no. 3 (Third Quarter 1993), pp. 449–464.

Chan, T. S. "Emerging Trends in Export Channel Strategy: An Investigation of Hong Kong and Singaporean Firms." *European Journal of Marketing* 26, no. 3, pp. 18–26.

Davis, Edward W. "Global Outsourcing: Have U.S. Managers Thrown the Baby Out with the Bath Water?" *Business Horizons* 35, no. 4 (July–August 1992). pp. 58–65.

Dominguez, Luis V., and Carlos G. Gequeira. "Strategic Options for LDC Exports to Developed Countries." *International Marketing Review* 8, no. 5 (1991), pp. 27–43.

Howard, Donald G. "The Role of Export Management Companies in Global Marketing." *Journal of Global Marketing* 8, no. 1 (1994), pp. 95–110.

Katsikeas, Constantine S. "Perceived Export Problems and Export Involvement: The Case of Greek Exporting Manufacturers." *Journal of Global Marketing* 7, no. 4 (1994), pp. 29–57.

Katsikeas, Constantine S., and Nigel F. Piercy. "Long-Term Export Stimuli and Firm Characteristics in a European LDC." *Journal of International Marketing* 1, no. 3 (1993), pp. 23–48.

Koh, Anthony C., James Chow, and Sasithorn Smittivate. "The Practice of International Marketing Research by Thai Exporters." *Journal of Global Marketing* 7, no. 2 (1993), pp. 7–26.

Korth, Christopher M. "Managerial Barriers to U.S. Exports." *Business Horizons* 34, no. 2 (March–April 1991), pp. 18–26.

Kostecki, Michel M. "Marketing Strategies between Dumping and Anti-Dumping Action." *European Journal of Marketing* 25, no. 12 (1992), pp. 7–19.

Kotabe, Masaaki, and Michael R. Czinkota. "State Government Promotion of Manufacturing Exports: A Gap Analysis." *Journal of International Business Studies* 23, no. 4 (Fourth Quarter 1992), pp. 637–658.

Larsen, Trina L., and Robert T. Green. "Export Opportunities in a Crumbling Economy: The Soviet Union in 1990." *Journal of International Marketing* 1, no. 4 (1993), pp. 71–90.

Leonidou, Leonidas C. "Empirical Research on Export Barriers: Review, Assessment, and Synthesis." *Journal of International Marketing* 3, no. 1 (1995), pp. 29–44.

Louter, Pieter J., Cok Ouwerkerk, and Ben A. Bakker. "An Inquiry into Successful Exporting." *European Journal of Marketing* 25, no. 6 (1991), pp. 7–23.

Mahone, Charlie E., Jr. "Penetrating Export Markets: The Role of Firm Size." *Journal of Global Marketing* 7, no. 3 (1994), pp. 133–148.

Namiki, Nobuaki. "A Taxonomic Analysis of Export Marketing Strategy: An Exploratory Study of U.S. Exporters of Electronics Products." *Journal of Global Marketing* 8, no. 1 (1994), pp. 27–50.

Parke, David. "U.S. National Security Export Controls: Implications for Global Competitiveness of U.S. High-Tech Firms." *Strategic Management Journal* 13, no. 1 (January 1992), pp. 47–66.

Rao, C. P., M. Krishna Erramilli, and Gopala K. Ganesh. "Impact of Domestic Recession on Export Marketing Behavior." *International Marketing Review* 7, no. 2 (1990), pp. 54–65.

Raven, Peter V., Jim M. McCullough, and Patriya S. Tansuhaj. "Environmental Influences and Decision-Making Uncertainty in Export Channels: Effects on Satisfaction and Performance." *Journal of International Marketing* 2, no. 3 (1994), pp. 37–60.

Reich, Michael R. "Why the Japanese Don't Export More Pharmaceuticals: Health Policy as Industrial Policy." *California Management Review* 32, no. 2 (Winter 1990), pp. 124–150.

Robock, Stefan H. "The Export Myopia of U.S. Multinationals: An Overlooked Opportunity for Creating U.S. Manufacturing Jobs." *Columbia Journal of World Business* 28, no. 2 (Summer 1993), pp. 24–32.

Rynning, Marjo-Riitta, and Otto Andersen. "Structural and Behavioral Predictors of Export Adoption: A Norwegian Study." *Journal of International Marketing* 2, no. 1 (1994), pp. 73–90.

Samiee, Saeed. "Strategic Considerations of the EC 1992 Plan for Small Exporters." *Business Horizons* 22, no. 2 (March–April 1990), pp. 48–52.

Seringhaus, F. H. Rolf. "A Comparison of Export Marketing Behavior of Canadian and Austrian High-Tech Firms." *Journal of International Marketing* 1, no. 4 (1993), pp. 49–70.

———. "Export Promotion in Developing Countries: Status and Prospects." *Journal of Global Marketing* 6, no. 4 (1993), pp. 7–32.

Singer, Thomas Owen, and Michael R. Czinkota. "Factors Associated with Effective Use of Export Assistance." *Journal of International Marketing* 2, no. 1 (1994), pp. 53–72.

Swamidass, Paul M. "Import Sourcing Dynamics: An Integrative Perspective." *Journal of International Business Studies* 24, no. 4 (Fourth Quarter 1993), pp. 671–692.

Terpstra, Vern, and Chow-Ming Joseph Yu. "Export Trading Companies: An American Trade Failure?" *Journal of Global Marketing* 6, no. 3 (1992), pp. 29–54.

CONCERNS ABOUT FACTORY SAFETY AND WORKER EXPLOITATION IN DEVELOPING COUNTRIES

In August 1995, federal agents raided a garment manufacturing facility near Los Angeles. The agents discovered 60 people, all from Thailand, who worked as much as 22 hours per day for $1.60 an hour to repay expenses for travel to the United States. The U.S. Labor Department charged the six Thai nationals believed to be running the sweatshop operation with harboring illegal immigrants and smuggling immigrants. Under the Fair Labor Standards Act, the Labor Department can hold the various manufacturers who bought goods from the sweatshop legally liable for $5 million in worker back pay. The Labor Department also identified a number of retailers—including May Department Stores, Sears, and Venture Stores—that were selling goods that originated in the Los Angeles factory.

The Labor Department's actions shed new light on an issue that had previously focused attention on labor conditions in developing countries. Catastrophic industrial fires in several countries have resulted in extensive loss of life. In Dongguan, China, 80 workers died in a fire at a raincoat factory in 1991. In 1993, 84 people were killed in a handicrafts factory fire in the Chinese city of Shenzhen. The most deadly industrial fire in history broke out on May 10, 1993, in a four-story toy factory near Bangkok, Thailand. Nearly 200 workers—most of whom were women and teenage girls—died in the blaze. The factory was owned by Kader Industrial Toy Company, which supplies toys to well-known U.S. companies such as Fisher-Price, Toys R Us, and Hasbro. One reason so many perished is that several emergency exit doors were locked.

Government support is just one reason companies can rely on farflung manufacturing; 900 million—about 15 percent—of the world's 6 billion people are unemployed. Thus, governments in many countries encourage foreign investment that will create jobs. Moreover, manufacturing companies account for nearly three-fourths of the dollar value of world trade. Improved communications technology allows company headquarters to closely monitor operations throughout the world. As John Cavanagh, a fellow at Washington's Institute for Policy Studies, explains, "Companies can coordinate production in plants scattered all over the world on a real-time, minute-to-minute basis."

Not surprisingly, many U.S. companies are scouring the globe for low-cost sources of labor. As wages have increased in South Korea, Taiwan, and Singapore, offshore assembly and manufacturing has moved to developing countries such as Indonesia, Thailand, India, Mexico, and China. For example, almost half of all the toys sold in the United States are produced in Asia; in 1992, Chinese factories turned out $3.3 billion worth of toys for the United States. The minimum wage in China is about 80 cents per day.

Disturbed by the trend, many U.S. observers characterize factories in developing countries as "sweatshops" where "semislave labor" is forced to work in inhumane, unsafe working conditions for very low wages. These critics suggest that profit-hungry American executives often turn a blind eye to working conditions outside the United States. For their part, executives and industry spokespersons point out that, in many cases, U.S. companies do not own the factories where goods are made. Labor movement representatives in the United States, concerned that U.S. companies are unwilling to support improved working conditions abroad, have even attempted to align with labor movements in developing countries.

Despite the terrible tragedies in Thailand and China, not everyone in the United States agrees with the view that workers in developing countries are being exploited. Although wages in some countries may seem low by U.S. standards, they are relatively high by East Asian standards. These wages represent both an improvement compared to a subsistence, agriculture-based standard of living and an important step forward in terms of economic development. As advocates of global production point out, wages in Japan, Taiwan, and Korea were low in the years after World War II but increased as those countries' economies developed. Some experts predict that business executives are starting to realize that it is simply good business to be concerned with factory conditions. Notes Professor Elliot Schrage of Columbia University, "Many companies are being forced to examine their labor practices around the world by consumer pressure or fear of consumer backlash." Indeed, the U.S. government hoped that publicizing the names of retailers buying from the Los Angeles manufacturers would encourage retailers to improve their social responsibility policies.

Athletic shoe marketers source virtually 100 percent of their shoes in Asia, where contractors are responsible for the production of the shoes. For example, 80 million pairs of Nikes are manufactured each year in dozens of factories outside the United States. During the 1980s, most of Nike's man-

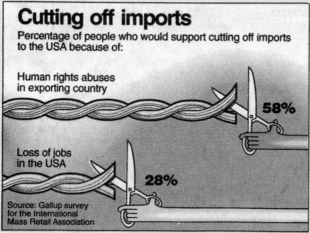

Cutting off imports

Percentage of people who would support cutting off imports to the USA because of:

Human rights abuses in exporting country

58%

Loss of jobs in the USA

28%

Source: Gallup survey for the International Mass Retail Association

By Cindy Hall and Elys A. McLean, USA TODAY

(Copyright 1994, _USA TODAY_. Reprinted with permission.)

ufacturing was located in South Korea and Taiwan. As workers there gained the right to organize and strike, wage rates increased. Nike responded by shifting production to China, Malaysia, Indonesia, and Thailand, leaving 20 closed factories in its wake. In Indonesia, where six factories make shoes for Nike, the nonunion workforce is made up mostly of young women paid wages starting at about $1.35 a day.

Nike's practice of following cheap labor around the globe has made it the target of increasing criticism from the ranks of workers and scholars alike. For example, *Solidarity* magazine, published by the United Auto Workers, recently urged union members to send their "dirty, smelly, worn-out" running shoes to Nike as a way of protesting overseas production. John Cavanagh and others have written numerous articles criticizing Nike for profiting at the expense of low-wage workers. Cavanagh has pointed out that, although 2.5 million people enter the Indonesian job market each year, employment options are so limited that most people can only find work making athletic shoes. Low wages permit only subsistence living in shanties without electricity or plumbing and also result in malnutrition.

Nike's vice president for Asia has said, "We don't know the first thing about manufacturing. We are marketers and designers." When Nike's general manager in Indonesia was asked about problems in the factories, he replied, "I don't know that I need to know." These answers seem at odds with the philosophy expressed by company founder, chairman, and CEO Phil Knight. When asked, "Is social responsibility part of being a marketing-oriented company?" Knight responded that inner-city youth are an important consumer group for the company, even though such young people cannot afford its products. He said, "I've always believed that businesses should be good citizens, which has nothing to do with marketing. But the thing I was missing until recently was the issue of visibility—and that is tied to marketing. It's not enough to do good things. You have to let people know what you're doing."

DISCUSSION QUESTIONS

1. Do you think toy company executives—in Japan, the United States, and elsewhere—should take steps to ensure the safety and welfare of factory workers in developing countries? Why or why not?
2. How have the low wages paid in developing country manufacturing operations impacted the number of manufacturing jobs in the high-wage Triad countries?
3. If higher wages in toy factories led to higher prices in the United States for toys, how would the toy industry be impacted?
4. Should the subject of working conditions be included in international trade agreements?
5. Do you think companies are doing enough to act responsibly and ensure that human rights standards are upheld for workers both inside and outside their home countries?

Young women make up the majority of the workers in Asian toy factories. Concerns about workplace safety in Asia are increasing in the West. (Photo by Mary Beth Camp, Matrix International, Inc.)

Sources: Asra Q. Nomani, "Labor Department Asks $5 million for Alleged Worker Enslavement," *The Wall Street Journal* (Aug. 16, 1995), p. B4.
Lori Ioannou, "Capitalizing on Global Surplus Labor," *International Business* (April 1995), pp. 32+.
G. Pascal Zachary, "Multinationals Can Aid Some Foreign Workers," *The Wall Street Journal* (Apr. 24, 1995), p. A1.
Bob Herbert, "Terror in Toyland," *The New York Times* (Dec. 21, 1994), p. A27.
"102 Dead in Thai Factory Fire; Higher Toll Seen," *The New York Times* (May 11, 1993), p. A3.
"Thai Factory Fire's 200 Victims Were Locked Inside, Guards Say," *The New York Times* (May 12, 1993), p. A5.
Jeffrey Ballinger, "The New Free-Trade Heel," *Harper's Magazine* (August 1992), pp. 46–47.
Geraldine E. Willigan, "High-Performance Marketing: An Interview with Nike's Phil Knight," *Harvard Business Review* (July–August 1992), pp. 91–101.
Richard J. Barnet and John Cavanagh, "Just Undo It: Nike's Exploited Workers," *The New York Times* (Feb. 13, 1994), Sec. 3, p. 11.

APPENDIX I

EXPORT AGENTS AND ORGANIZATIONS: DEFINITIONS OF TERMS

NO ASSIGNMENT OF RESPONSIBILITY FROM CLIENT
Purchasing Agent

Foreign purchasing agents are variously referred to as "buyer for export," "export commission house" or "export confirming house." They operate on behalf of, and are remunerated by, an overseas customer. They generally seek out the U.S. manufacturer whose price and quality match the demands of their overseas principal.

Foreign purchasing agents often represent large users of materials abroad—governments, utilities, and railroads, for example. They do not offer the U.S. manufacturer stable volume except when long-term supply contracts are agreed upon. Purchases may be completed as domestic transactions, with the purchasing agent handling all export packing and shipping details, or the agent may rely on the manufacturer to handle the shipping arrangements.

Export Broker

The export broker receives a fee for bringing together the U.S. seller and the overseas buyer. The fee is usually paid by the seller, but sometimes the buyer pays it. The broker takes no title to the goods and assumes no financial responsibility. A broker usually specializes in a specific commodity, such as grain or cotton, and is less frequently involved in the export of manufactured goods.

Export Merchant

Export merchants are sometimes referred to as "jobbers." They seek out needs in foreign markets and make purchases in the United States to fill these needs. Conversely, they often complement this activity by importing to fill needs in the United States. Export merchants often handle staple, openly traded products, for which brand names or manufacturers' identities are not important.

ASSIGNMENT OF RESPONSIBILITY FROM CLIENT

Export Management Companies

Export management company (EMC) is the term used to designate an independent export firm that acts as the export department for more than one manufacturer. The EMC usually operates in the name of a manufacturer-client for export markets, but it may operate in its own name. It may act as an independent distributor, purchasing and reselling goods at an established price or profit margin, or as a commission representative taking no title and bearing no financial risks in the sale.

Manufacturer's Export Representative

Combination export management companies often refer to themselves as *manufacturer's export representatives* whether they act as export distributors or export commission representatives.

Export Distributor

The export distributor assumes financial risk. The firm usually has exclusive right to sell a manufacturer's products in all or some markets outside the United States. The distributor pays for goods in the United States in a domestic transaction and handles all financial risks in the foreign sale. The firm ordinarily sells at manufacturer's list price abroad, receiving an agreed percentage of list price as remuneration. The distributor may operate in its own name or in the manufacturer's. It handles all shipping details. The export distributor usually represents several manufacturers and hence is a combination EMC.

Export Commission Representative

The export commission representative assumes no financial risk and is sometimes termed an "agent," although this term is generally avoided because of the legal connotations of the term. The commission representative is assigned all or some foreign markets by the manufacturer. The manufacturer carries all accounts, although the representative often provides credit checks and arranges financing. The representative may operate in its own name or in the manufacturer's. Generally, the export commission representative handles several accounts and hence is a combination export management company.

Cooperative Exporter

The cooperative exporter, sometimes called a "mother hen," "piggyback exporter," or "export vendor," is an export organization of a manufacturing company retained by other independent manufacturers to sell their products in some or all foreign markets. Cooperative exporters usually operate as export distributors for other manufacturers, but in special cases they operate as export commission representatives. They are regarded as a form of export management company.

Webb-Pomerene Association

Webb-Pomerene associations are organizations jointly owned, maintained, or supported by competing U.S. manufacturers especially and exclusively for export trade. Special legislation gives them qualified exemption from antitrust laws. They may provide informational services to their members, as well as buy and sell abroad, and may engage in other activities such as setting prices and allocating orders.

Freight Forwarder

Freight forwarders are licensed by the Federal Maritime Commission and are considered an integral part of the U.S. merchant marine. They are specialists in traffic operations, customs clearance, and shipping tariffs and schedules. They assist exporters in determining and paying freight, fees, and insurance charges. Forwarders may also do export packing, when necessary. They usually handle freight from port of export to overseas port of import. They may also move inland freight from factory to port of export and, through affiliates abroad, handle freight from port of import to customer. Freight forwarders also perform consolidation services for air and ocean freight. They contract for blocks of space on a ship or airplane and resell that space to various shippers at a rate lower than that generally available to individual shippers.

A licensed forwarder receives brokerage or rebates from shipping companies for booked space. Some companies and manufacturers engage in freight forwarding or some phase of it on their own, but they may not, under law, receive brokerage from shipping lines.

CHAPTER 10

Global Market Entry Strategies: Licensing, Joint Ventures, and Ownership

"The world is changing and we can't do business the way we used to. We used to be very much a company that didn't look much beyond Germany. But the globalization of the industry has meant that we had to expand into the United States and other parts of the world. There is no choice."[1]

—Chairman Horst Urban, Continental AG

Gerber Products is the undisputed leader in the U.S. baby food market. Despite enjoying a 70 percent market share, Gerber faces a mature market and stagnant growth at home. Since 9 out of 10 of the world's births take place outside the United States, Gerber executives hoped to make international sales a greater part of the company's $1.17 billion in annual revenues. Overall, Gerber's international sales increased 150 percent between 1989 and 1993, from $86.5 million to $216.1 billion.

Still, for two decades Gerber's globalization effort had been slowed by a combination of changing market conditions, management inconsistency, and decisions that didn't pay off. Gerber entered the Latin American market in the 1970s, but then closed down operations in Venezuela in the wake of government-imposed price controls. Management's focus on the U.S. market resulted in a series of diversifications into nonfood categories that were not successful. Meanwhile, management was not willing to sacrifice short-term quarterly earnings growth to finance an international effort. As Michael A. Cipollaro, Gerber's former president of international operations, remarked, "If you are going to sow in the international arena today to reap tomorrow, you couldn't have that [earnings] growth on a regular basis." In the 1980s, Gerber pursued a strategy of licensing the manufacture and distribution of its baby food products to other companies. In France, for example, Gerber selected CPC International as a licensee.

Gerber's global experiences illustrate the fact that every firm, at various points in its history, faces a broad range of strategy alternatives. In far too many cases, companies fail to appreciate the range of alternatives open to them and therefore employ only one strategy—often to their grave disadvantage. The same companies also fail to consider the strategy alternatives open to their competitors and thereby set themselves up to be victims of the dreaded "Titanic" syndrome—the thud in the night that comes without warning, which sinks the ship.

Some companies are making the decision to "go global" for the first time; other companies seek to expand their share of world markets. Companies in either situation face the same basic sourcing issues introduced in the previous chapter. Companies must also address issues of marketing and value

---

[1]Jonathan Hicks, "The Takeover of American Industry," *The New York Times* (May 8, 1989), Sec. 3, p. 8.

chain management before deciding to enter or expand their share of global markets by means of licensing, joint ventures or partial ownership, and majority (or 100%) ownership. The latter decision is affected by issues of investment and control as well as a company's attitude toward risk.

LICENSING

Licensing can be defined as a contractual arrangement whereby one company (the licensor) makes an asset available to another company (the licensee) in exchange for royalties, license fees, or some other form of compensation (Root 1994, 107). The licensed asset may be a patent, trade secret, or company name. Licensing is a global market entry and expansion strategy with considerable appeal. A company with advanced technology, know-how, or a strong brand image can use licensing agreements to supplement its bottom-line profitability with little initial investment. Licensing can offer an attractive return on investment for the life of the agreement, provided that the necessary performance clauses are in the contract. The only cost is the cost of signing the agreement and of policing its implementation.

Trademarks can be an important part of the creation and protection of opportunities for lucrative licenses.[2] Image-oriented U.S. companies such as Coca-Cola and Disney, for example, are licensing their trademarked names and logos to overseas producers of clothing, toys, and watches. In Asia and the Pacific alone, sales of licensed Disney products doubled between 1988 and 1990 and were expected to double again by 1994.[3]

Of course, anything so easily attained has its disadvantages and risks. The principal disadvantage of licensing is that it can be a very limited form of participation. When licensing technology or know-how, what a company doesn't know can put it at risk. Potential returns from marketing and manufacturing may be lost, and the agreement may have a short life if the licensee develops its own know-how and capability to stay abreast of technology in the licensed product area. Even more distressing, licensees have a troublesome way of turning themselves into competitors or industry leaders. This is especially true because licensing enables a company to "borrow"—leverage and exploit—another company's resources. In Japan, for example, Meiji Milk produced and marketed Lady Borden premium ice cream under a licensing agreement with Borden Inc. Meiji learned important skills in dairy product processing and, as the expiration dates of the licensing contracts drew near, rolled out its own premium ice cream brands.[4]

Perhaps the most famous U.S. licensing fiasco dates back to the mid-1950s, when Sony cofounder Masaru Ibuka obtained a licensing agreement for the transistor from AT&T's Bell Laboratories. Ibuka dreamed of using transistors to make small, battery-powered radios. Bell engineers informed Ibuka that it was impossible to manufacture transistors that could handle the high frequencies required for a radio; they advised him to try making hearing aids. Undeterred, Ibuka presented the challenge to his Japanese engineers, who spent many months improving high-frequency output. Sony was not the first company to unveil a transistor radio; a U.S.-built product, the Regency, featured transistors from Texas Instruments and a colorful plastic case. However, it was Sony's high-quality, distinctive approach to styling, and marketing savvy that ultimately translated into worldwide success.

---

[2]Private communication, E. M. Lang, President, REFAC Technology Development Corporation, 122 East 42nd Street, New York, New York.

[3]John Huey, "America's Hottest Export: Pop Culture," *Fortune* (Dec. 31, 1990), p. 58.

[4]Yumiko Ono, "Borden's Breakup with Meiji Milk Shows How a Japanese Partnership Can Curdle," *The Wall Street Journal* (Feb. 21, 1991), p. B1.

As the Borden and transistor stories make clear, companies may find that the upfront easy money obtained from licensing turns out to be a very expensive source of revenue. To prevent a licensor/competitor from gaining unilateral benefit, licensing agreements should provide for a cross-technology exchange between all parties. At the absolute minimum, any company that plans to remain in business must ensure that its license agreements provide for full cross-licensing—i.e., that the licensee shares its developments with the licensor. Overall, the licensing strategy must ensure ongoing competitive advantage. For example, license arrangements can create export market opportunities and open the door to low-risk manufacturing relationships. They can also speed diffusion of new products or technologies.

When companies do decide to license, they should sign agreements that anticipate more extensive market participation in the future. Insofar as is possible, a company should keep options and paths open for other forms of market participation. One path is joint venture with the licensee.

JOINT VENTURES

A joint venture with a local partner represents a more extensive form of participation in foreign markets than either exporting or licensing. The advantages of this strategy, in which partners share ownership, include the sharing of risk and the ability to combine different value chain strengths—for example, international marketing capability and manufacturing. One company might have in-depth knowledge of a local market, an extensive distribution system, or access to low-cost labor or raw materials. Such a company might link up with a foreign partner possessing considerable know-how in the area of technology, manufacturing, and process applications. Companies that lack sufficient capital re-

Sources: Jennifer Reingold, "The Pope of Basel," *Financial World* (July 18, 1995), pp. 36–38.
Margaret Studer, "Sandoz AG Is Foraging for Additional Food Holdings," *The Wall Street Journal* (Feb. 21, 1995), p. B4.
Richard Gibson, "Growth Formula: Gerber Missed the Boat in Quest To Go Global, So It Turned to Sandoz," *The Wall Street Journal* (May 24, 1994), pp. A1, A7.
Leah Rickard and Laurel Wentz, "Sandoz Opens World for Gerber," *Advertising Age* (May 30, 1994), p. 4.
Margaret Studer and Ron Winslow, "Sandoz, Under Pressure, Looks to Gerber for Protection," *The Wall Street Journal* (May 25, 1994), p. B3.

■ GERBER'S GLOBAL STRATEGY

THE REST OF THE STORY

As noted in the chapter introduction, licensing became a cornerstone of Gerber's global expansion strategy in the 1980s and 1990s. Unfortunately, Gerber couldn't force its licensees to make baby food a priority business. In France, for example, baby food represented a meager 2 percent of CPC's European revenues. When CPC closed down its French plant, Gerber had to find another manufacturing source. It bought a stake in a Polish factory, but production was held up for months while quality improvements were made. The delay ended up costing Gerber its market position in France.

Belatedly, Gerber discovered that strong competitors already dominated many markets around the globe. Heinz has about one-third of the $1.5 billion baby food market outside the United States; Gerber's share of the global market is 17 percent. Competitors with less global share than Gerber—including France's BSN Group (15 percent market share) and Switzerland's Nestlè SA (8 percent)—have been aggressively building brand loyalty. In France, for example, parents traveling with infants can get free baby food and diapers through

Nestlè's system of roadside changing stations. Another barrier is that many European mothers think homemade baby food is healthier than food from a jar.

Meanwhile, Gerber's global efforts were interrupted by the resignations of several key executives. Mr. Cipollaro, the chief of international operations, left, as did the vice president for Europe and the international director of business development. Gerber's management team was forced to rethink its strategy: In May 1994, it agreed to be acquired by Sandoz AG, a $10.3 billion Swiss pharmaceutical and chemical company. As market analyst David Adelman noted, "It was very expensive for Gerber to build business internationally. This was one of the driving reasons why Gerber wanted to team up with a larger company."

Some industry analysts expressed doubts about the logic behind the acquisition. London broker Peter Smith said, "I'm sorry: Baby food and anticancer drugs don't really come together." Nevertheless, the deal will give Gerber immediate access to a global marketing and distribution network that is particularly strong in developing countries such as China and India. Sandoz, which faces expiring patents for some of its most profitable drugs, will instantly assume a strong position in the U.S. nutrition market.

GE and Tungsram managers inspect fluorescent bulbs coming off the production line at a joint venture plant in Hungary. (Copyright Tomas Muscionico/Contact Press Images.)

sources might seek partners to jointly finance a project. Finally, a joint venture may be the only way to enter a country or region if government bid award practices routinely favor local companies or if laws prohibit foreign control but permit joint venture.

For example, Lenwest is a joint venture between Germany's Salamander AG, a shoe manufacturer, and the Proletarian Shoe factory in St. Petersburg, Russia. The Russian side brought abundant low-wage labor and plentiful raw materials to the table; the Germans provide machinery and, equally important, the know-how, management techniques, and quality control that are virtually unknown in the former Soviet Union. The joint venture agreement called for both parties to reinvest all profits from the first three years of operation to double production.[5]

Some other recent joint venture alliances are outlined in Table 10–1.

It is possible to use a joint venture as a source of supply for third-country markets. This must be carefully thought out in advance. One of the main reasons for joint venture "divorce" is disagreement about third-country markets where partners face each other as actual or potential competitors. To avoid this, it is essential to work out a plan for approaching third-country markets as part of the venture agreement.

The disadvantages of joint venturing can be significant. Joint venture partners must share rewards as well as risks. The main disadvantage of this global expansion strategy is that a company incurs very significant costs associated with control and coordination issues that arise when working with a partner. Also, as noted previously with licensing, a dynamic joint venture partner can evolve into a stronger competitor. In some instances, country-specific restrictions limit the share of capital help by foreign companies. Cross-

TABLE 10–1	MARKET ENTRY AND EXPANSION BY JOINT VENTURE
Companies Involved	**Purpose of Joint Venture**
GM, Toyota	NUMMI—a jointly operated plant in Freemont, California.
Ford, Mazda	Joint operation of a plant in Flat Rock, Michigan.
AT&T, NEC	AT&T provides CAD technology in exchange for NEC's advanced logic chips.
AT&T, Mitsubishi Electric	AT&T manufactures and markets Mitsubishi's memory chips in exchange for the technology used to design them.
Texas Instruments, Kobe Steel	Joint effort making logic semiconductors in Japan.
IBM, Siemens AG	Joint research in advanced semiconductor chips.
James River Corp., Oy Nokia AB, Cragnotti & Partners Capital Investment	Jamont, a European-based paper products venture.

Source: Adapted from Bernard Wysocki, Jr., "Global Reach: Cross-Border Alliances Become Favorite Way To Crack New Markets," *The Wall Street Journal* (Mar. 26, 1990), pp. A1, A12.

[5]Thomas F. O'Boyle, "Western Ways: How a German Firm Joined with Soviets To Make Good Shoes," *The Wall Street Journal* (Feb. 14, 1989), p. A1.

GLOBAL MARKET ENTRY STRATEGIES: LICENSING, JOINT VENTURES, AND OWNERSHIP

cultural differences in managerial attitudes and behavior can present formidable challenges as well.

James River's European joint venture, Jamont, for example, brought together 13 companies from 10 countries. Major problems included computer systems and measures of production efficiency; Jamont uses committees to solve these and other problems as they arise. For example, agreement had to be reached on a standardized table napkin size; for some country markets, 30 by 30 centimeters was the norm; for others, 35 by 35 centimeters was preferred.[6]

Difficulties such as those outlined above are so serious that, according to one study of 170 multinational firms, more than one-third of 1,100 joint ventures were unstable, ending in divorce or a significant increase in the U.S. firm's power over its partner.[7] Another researcher found that 65 joint ventures with Japanese companies were either liquidated or transferred to the Japanese interest in 1976. This was up from 6 in 1972, a 600 percent increase. The most fundamental problem was the different benefits that each side expected to receive.[8]

As one global marketing expert warns, "In an alliance you have to learn skills of the partner, rather than just see it as a way to get a product to sell while avoiding a big investment." Yet, compared to U.S. and European firms, Japanese and Korean firms seem to excel in their ability to leverage new knowledge that comes out of a joint venture. For example, Toyota learned many new things from its partnership with GM—about U.S. supply and transportation, and managing American workers—that have been subsequently applied at its Camry plant in Kentucky. However, some American managers involved in the venture complained that the manufacturing expertise they gained was not applied broadly throughout GM. To the extent that this complaint has validity, GM has missed opportunities to leverage new learning. Still, many companies have achieved great successes pursuing joint ventures. Gillette, for example, has used this strategy to introduce its shaving products in the Middle East and Africa.

OWNERSHIP

The most extensive form of participation in global markets is 100 percent ownership, which may be achieved by start-up or acquisition. Ownership requires the greatest commitment of capital and managerial effort and offers the fullest means of participating in a market. Companies may move from licensing or joint venture strategies to ownership in order to achieve faster expansion in a market, greater control, or higher profits. In 1991, for example, Ralston Purina ended a 20-year joint venture with a Japanese company to start its own pet food subsidiary. Monsanto Co. and Bayer AG, the German pharmaceutical company, are two other companies that have also recently disbanded partnerships in favor of wholly owned subsidiaries in Japan.[9] In many countries, government restrictions may prevent majority or 100 percent ownership by foreign companies.

Large-scale direct expansion by means of establishing new facilities can be expensive and require a major commitment of managerial time and energy. Alternatively, acquisition is an instantaneous—and sometimes, less expensive—approach to market entry. While full ownership can yield the additional advantage of avoiding communication and con-

[6]James Guyon, "A Joint-Venture Papermaker Casts Net across Europe," *The Wall Street Journal* (Dec. 7, 1992), p. B6.
[7]G. Franko, "Joint Venture Divorce in the Multinational Company," *Columbia Journal of World Business* (May–June 1971), pp. 13–22.
[8]W. Wright, "Joint Venture Problems in Japan," *Columbia Journal of World Business* (Spring 1979), pp. 25–31. See also W. Wright and C. S. Russell, "Joint Venture in Developing Countries: Reality and Responses," *Columbia Journal of World Business* (Summer 1975), pp. 74–80.
[9]Ono 1991, B1.

flict of interest problems that may arise with a joint venture or coproduction partner, acquisitions still present the demanding and challenging task of integrating the acquired company into the worldwide organization and coordinating activities.

Table 10–2 lists some additional examples, grouped by industry, of companies that have pursued global expansion via acquisition. What is the driving force behind many of these acquisitions? It is globalization, as Continental's Horst Urban noted at the beginning of the chapter.

The decision to invest abroad—whether by expansion or acquisition—sometimes clashes with short-term profitability goals. This is an especially important issue for publicly held U.S. companies. Despite these challenges, there is an increasing trend toward foreign investment by U.S. companies. Cumulative U.S. direct investment abroad is projected to exceed $500 billion in 1995.

Several of the advantages of joint venture alliances also apply to ownership, including access to markets and avoidance of tariff or quota barriers. Like joint ventures, ownership also permits important technology experience transfers and provides a company with access to new manufacturing techniques. For example, the Stanley Works, a tool maker with headquarters in New Britain, Connecticut, has bought more than a dozen companies since 1986. Among them: Taiwan's National Hand Tool/Chiro company, a socket wrench manufacturer and developer of a "cold-forming" process that speeds up production and reduces waste. Stanley is now using the technology in the manufacture of other tools. Chairman Richard H. Ayers sees such global cross-fertilization and "blended technology" as a key benefit of globalization.[10]

The alternatives discussed above—licensing, joint ventures, and ownership—are in fact points along a continuum of alternative strategies or tools for global market entry and expansion. There are many possible combinations of these basic alternatives; Jamont, the European paper products company discussed above, utilizes a hybrid joint venture/ownership strategy. The overall design of a company's global strategy may call for combinations of exporting/import, licensing, joint ventures, and ownership among different

TABLE 10–2	MARKET ENTRY AND EXPANSION BY ACQUISITION	
Product Category/Industry	**Acquiring Company**	**Target**
Apparel, personal care, and food products	Sara Lee Corp. (USA)	Douwe Egberts (coffee and tea), Dim (hosiery), and other companies with total sales in excess of $1 billion in seven different countries
	Sandoz AG (Switzerland)	Gerber (1994)
	L'Oreal SA (France)	Maybelline (1995)
Automotive tires	Bridgestone Corporation (Japan)	Firestone Tire and Rubber Company (1988; $2.6 billion)
	Continental AG (Germany)	General Tire (1987)
	Pirelli SpA (Italy)	Armstrong Tire (1988)
	Michelin (France)	Uniroyal/Goodrich (1990; $1.5 billion)
Media and entertainment	Sony	CBS Records (1987; $2 billion); Columbia Pictures (1989; $3.4 billion)
	Matsushita (Japan)	MCA/Universal (1990; $6.59 billion)
Consumer electronics	Thomson SA (France)	GE's consumer electronics business, GE's RCA subsidiary; Telefunken (West Germany)

[10]Louis Uchitelle, "The Stanley Works Goes Global," *The New York Times* (July 23, 1989), Sec. 3, pp. 1, 10.

GLOBAL MARKET ENTRY STRATEGIES: LICENSING, JOINT VENTURES, AND OWNERSHIP

operating units. Such is the case in Japan for Borden Inc.; it is ending licensing and joint venture arrangements for branded food products and setting up its own production, distribution, and marketing capabilities for dairy products. Meanwhile, in nonfood products, Borden has maintained joint venture relationships with Japanese partners in flexible packaging and foundry materials.[11]

A firm may decide to enter into a joint venture or coproduction agreement for purposes of manufacturing and may either market the products manufactured under this agreement in a wholly owned marketing subsidiary or sell the products from the coproduction facility to an outside marketing organization. Joint ventures may be 50 : 50 partnerships or minority or majority partnerships. Majority ownership may range anywhere from 51 percent to 100 percent.

Ericsson is a world-class competitor in the global telecommunications equipment and systems market. (Courtesy of Ericsson Cellular Phones. Reprinted by permission.)

MARKET EXPANSION STRATEGIES[12]

Companies must decide whether to expand by seeking new markets in existing countries or, alternatively, seeking new country markets for already identified and served market segments. These two dimensions in combination produce four strategic options, as shown in Table 10–3. Strategy 1 concentrates on a few segments in a few countries. This is typically a starting point for most companies. It matches company resources and market investment needs. Unless a company is large and endowed with ample resources, this strategy may be the only realistic way to begin.

In strategy 2, country concentration and segment diversification, a company serves

[11]*Annual Report*, Borden, Inc. (1990), p. 13.

[12]This section draws on I. Ayal and J. Zif, "Market Expansion Strategies in Multinational Marketing," *Journal of Marketing* 43 (Spring 1979), pp. 84–94; and "Competitive Market Choice Strategies in Multinational Marketing," *Columbia Journal of World Business* (Fall 1978), pp. 72–81.

TABLE 10-3 MARKET EXPANSION STRATEGIES

| | MARKET | |
COUNTRY	Concentration	Diversification
Concentration	1. Narrow Focus	2. Country Focus
Diversification	3. Country Diversification	4. Global Diversification

many markets in a few countries. This strategy was implemented by many European companies that remained in Europe and sought growth by expanding into new markets. It is also the approach of the U.S. companies that decide to diversify in the U.S. market as opposed to going international with existing products or creating new global products. According to the U.S. Department of Commerce, more than 80 percent of U.S. companies that export limit their sales to five or fewer markets. This means that the majority of U.S. companies are pursuing strategies 1 or 2.

Strategy 3, country diversification and market segment concentration, is the classic global strategy whereby a company seeks out the world market for a product. The appeal of this strategy is that by serving the world customer, a company can achieve a greater accumulated volume and lower costs than any competitor and therefore have an unassailable competitive advantage. This is the strategy of the well-managed business that serves a distinct need and customer category.

Strategy 4, country and segment diversification, is the corporate strategy of a global, multibusiness company such as Matsushita. *Overall*, Matsushita is multicountry in scope, and its various business units and groups serve multiple segments. Thus, at the level of corporate strategy, Matsushita may be said to be pursuing strategy 4. At the operating business level, however, managers of individual units must focus on the needs of the world customer in their particular global market. In Table 10–3, this is strategy 3—country diversification and market segment concentration. An increasing number of companies all over the world are beginning to see the importance of market share not only in the home or domestic market but also in the world market. Success in overseas markets can boost a company's total volume and lower its cost position.

ALTERNATIVE STRATEGIES: STAGES OF DEVELOPMENT MODEL

Below are listed the stages in the evolution of the transnational corporation. As discussed in previous chapters, the differences between the stages can be quite significant. Unfortunately, there is little general agreement about the usage of each term. The terminology suggested here conforms to current usage by leading scholars. However, it should be noted that executives, journalists, and others who are not familiar with the scholarly literature may use the terms in quite different ways.

Stages of Development

1. Domestic
2. International
3. Multinational
4. Global
5. Transnational

Bartlett and Ghoshal[13] provide an excellent discussion of three industries—branded packaged goods, consumer electronics, and telecommunications switching—in which individual competitors have exemplified the different stages at various times in their corporate histories. For example, Procter & Gamble, GE, and Ericsson were stage 2,

[13]See Christopher A. Bartlett and Sumantra Ghoshal, *Managing Across Borders: The Transnational Solution* (Boston: Harvard Business School Press, 1989).

■ FORD BETS BILLIONS ON JAGUAR

*I*n 1989, the Ford Motor Company acquired Jaguar PLC of Coventry, England, for $2.6 billion. L. Lindsay Halstead, chairman of Ford of Europe, called the Jaguar acquisition the fulfillment of "a longtime strategic objective of entering the luxury car market in a significant way." Ford lacked a high-end luxury model for both the U.S. and European markets, and the company was betting it could take a nameplate highly valued for exclusivity and sell it to more people by launching a new, less-expensive line of Jaguars. The challenge: How to accomplish this goal without damaging Jaguar's reputation. The problem, notes Daniel Jones, a professor at the University of Cardiff and an auto industry expert, is that the Ford name is synonymous with bread and butter.

In 1988, its best sales year, Jaguar sold just under 50,000 cars worldwide. Ford set an objective of producing 150,000 cars by the end of the 1990s, two-thirds of which would be the lower-priced sporty sedan. Ford also targeted 1992 as the year Jaguar would show a positive cash flow. Unfortunately, the Jaguar acquisition coincided with the global recession that hurt sales in Japan, Germany, and the United States. To make matters worse, a 10 percent luxury tax imposed in the United States scared off potential buyers. By 1991, Jaguar sales slipped to 25,676 cars. Now, in the face of losses totaling $431 million in 1990 and 1991, Ford has scaled back its original volume target to 100,000 cars.

Ford must also deal with other challenges. Although Jaguar's classy image and racing heritage are prized attributes, the cars are also legendary for their unreliability. Gears sometimes don't shift, headlights don't light, and the brakes have been known to catch fire. Part of the problem can be traced to manufacturing, in that there were 2,500 defects per 100 cars produced in 1990. By 1992, that number had been reduced to 500 defects per 100 cars.

Because Jaguar was arguably one of the world's worst auto manufacturing operations, Ford has been forced to invest heavily to update and upgrade Jaguar's plant facilities and improve productivity. As a benchmark, Ford's manufacturing experts know that German luxury car makers can build a car in 80 hours; the Japanese need only 20 hours. If Jaguar is ever to achieve world-class status, Jaguar's assembly time of 110 hours per car must be drastically reduced.

Ironically, die-hard Jaguar loyalists—customers whose continued support Jaguar desperately needs—are giving the new, improved Jaguars mixed reviews. It seems many Jaguar owners enjoy the misery brought on by an unreliable car. In fact, Jaguar clubs in the United States bestow "Cat Bite" awards on members with the best tales of woe. According to these owners, the new Ford-era cars "lack mystique."

Some observers question the wisdom of Ford's purchase, expressing doubts that Ford will ever break even on its investment. Ford's Japanese competitors, including Honda, Nisson, and Toyota, have allocated their financial resources differently. They made major investments to launch new nameplates and upgrade their dealer organizations. Infiniti, Lexus, and other new luxury sedans are winning new buyers with high quality, high performance, and outstanding dealer service. Publicly, Ford is confident its multibillion dollar bet will pay off. As chairman Halstead said in 1990, "We're happy we made the purchase. It was a long-term vision. We don't expect results overnight."

Sources: Joann S. Lublin and Craig Forman, "Going Upscale: Ford Snares Jaguar, but $2.5 Billion Is High Price for Prestige," *The Wall Street Journal* (Nov. 3, 1989), pp. A1, A4.
Steven Prokesch, "Jaguar Battle at a Turning Point," *The New York Times* (Oct. 29, 1990), p. C1.
Steven Prokesch, "Ford's Jaguar Bet: Payoff Isn't Close," *The New York Times* (Apr. 21, 1992), p. C1.
Robert Johnson, "Jaguar Owners Love Company and Sharing Their Horror Stories," *The Wall Street Journal* (Sept. 28, 1993), p. A1.

international companies. For many years, Unilever, Philips, and ITT were stage 3 multinationals. The stage 4 global companies included in the study were all from Japan: Kao, Matsushita, and NEC.

Figure 10–1 outlines the various orientations of management.

As can be seen in Table 10–4, orientation does not change as a company moves from domestic to international. The difference between the domestic and the international company is that the international is doing business in many countries. Like the domestic company, it is ethnocentric and home-country oriented. However, the stage 2 international company sees extension market opportunities outside the home country and extends marketing programs to exploit those opportunities. The first change in orientation occurs as a company moves to stage 3, multinational. At this point, its orientation shifts from ethnocentric to polycentric. The difference is quite important. The stage 2 ethnocentric company seeks to extend its products and practices to foreign countries. It sees similarities outside the home country but is relatively blind to differences. The stage 3 multinational is the opposite: It sees the differences and is relatively blind to similarities. The focus of the stage 3 multinational is on adapting to what is different in a country.

FIGURE 10–1

ORIENTATION OF
MANAGEMENT AND
COMPANIES

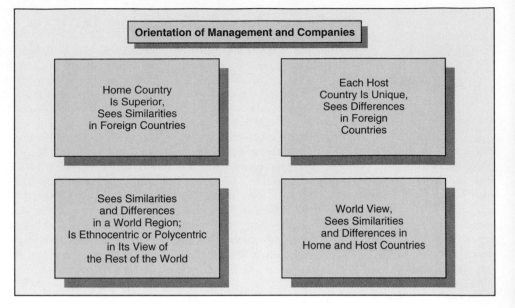

Orientation of Management and Companies

| Home Country Is Superior, Sees Similarities in Foreign Countries | Each Host Country Is Unique, Sees Differences in Foreign Countries |
| Sees Similarities and Differences in a World Region; Is Ethnocentric or Polycentric in Its View of the Rest of the World | World View, Sees Similarities and Differences in Home and Host Countries |

The stage 4 global company is a limited form of the transnational. Management's orientation is either on global markets or global resources, but not on both. For example, Harley-Davidson is focused on global markets, but not on global resources. The company has no interest in conducting R&D, design, engineering, or manufacturing outside of the United States. Until recently, the same was true for BMW and Mercedes. Both companies marketed globally, but limited R&D, engineering, design, and manufacturing activity to Germany. Mercedes now plans to double its purchases from outside suppliers and to build more than 10 percent of its vehicles outside Germany. Notes Mercedes chairman Helmut Werner, "The fundamental problem of German exports is that we are producing in a country with a hard currency and selling in countries with soft currencies."[14] When a company moves from stage 4 to stage 5, its orientation encompasses *both* global markets and global resources.

Table 10–5 illustrates some of the other differences in companies at the different stages. Special mention must be made of some of the distinctive qualities of stage 4 companies that pursue integrated global strategies. Key assets are dispersed, specialized, and interdependent. A transnational automobile company—Toyota, for example—makes engines and transmissions in various countries and ships these components to assembly plants located in each of the world's regions. Specialized design labs might be located in different countries and work together on the same project. The role of country units changes dramatically as a company moves across the stages of development. In the stage 2 inter-

[14]Audrey Choi, "For Mercedes, Going Global Means Being Less German," *The Wall Street Journal* (Apr. 27, 1995), p. B4.

TABLE 10–4 STAGES OF DEVELOPMENT I

	1 Domestic	2 International	3 Multinational	4 Global	5 Transnational
Strategy	Domestic	International	Multidomestic	Global	Global
Model	N.A.	Coordinated federation	Decentralized federation	Centralized hub	Integrated network
View of world	Home country	Extension markets	National markets	Global markets or resources	Global markets and resources
Orientation	Ethnocentric	Ethnocentric	Polycentric	Mixed	Geocentric

TABLE 10–5 STAGES OF DEVELOPMENT II: ORGANIZATION CHARACTERISTICS

	1 Domestic	2 International	3 Multinational	4 Global	5 Transnational
Key Assets	Located in home country	Core centralized, others dispersed	Decentralized and self-sufficient	All in home country except marketing or sourcing	Dispersed, interdependent, and specialized
Role of Country Units	Single country	Adapting and leveraging competencies	Exploiting local opportunities	Marketing or sourcing	Contributions to company worldwide
Knowledge	Home country	Created at center and transferred	Retained within operating units	Marketing or sourcing developed jointly and shared	All functions developed jointly and shared

national company, the role of the country unit is to adapt and leverage the competence of the parent or home-country unit. In the stage 5 transnational, the role of each country is to contribute to the company worldwide. In the international and multinational, the responsibility of the marketing organization is to realize the potential of the individual national markets. In the transnational, the responsibility of the marketing unit is to realize the potential of the national market and, if possible, to contribute to the success of marketing efforts worldwide by sharing successful innovations and ideas with the entire organization.

Each of the stages has its strengths. The international company's strength is its ability to exploit the parent company's knowledge and capabilities outside the home country. In the telecommunications industry, Ericsson gained a competitive edge over NEC and ITT by pursuing this approach. The multinational's strength is its ability to adapt and respond to national differences. Unilever's local responsiveness was well suited to the packaged goods industry. Thus, in many markets, the company outperformed both Kao and Procter & Gamble. The global company leverages internal skills and resources by taking advantage of global markets or global resources. In consumer electronics, Matsushita's ability to serve global markets from world-scale plants caused great woes for Philips and GE. (In fact, GE's Jack Welch decided to exit the business altogether.)[15] The transnational combines the strengths of each of the earlier stages by serving global markets using global resources and leveraging global learning and experience.

In stage 3, the most frequently preferred sourcing arrangement is local manufacture. In stage 5, product sourcing is based on an analysis that takes into account cost, delivery, and all other factors affecting competitiveness and profitability. This analysis produces a sourcing plan that maximizes both competitive effectiveness and profitability. When a company is in stage 2, key jobs go to home-country nationals in both the subsidiaries and the headquarters. In stage 3, key jobs in host countries go to country nationals, whereas headquarters management positions are usually held by home-country nationals. In stage 5, the best people are selected for all management positions regardless of nationality. Research and development in stage 2 is conducted in the home country; in stage 3, R&D becomes decentralized and fragmented. By the time a company reaches stage 5, research is part of an integrated worldwide R&D plan and is typically decentralized. The stage 5

---

[15]For an excellent in-depth treatment of GE, see Noel Tichy and Stratford Sherman, *Control Your Destiny or Someone Else Will* (New York: HarperBusiness, 1994).

TABLE 10–6 THE EVOLUTION OF FLEETGUARD, INC.

Strategic Dimension	Stage 2 International (Years 1–4)	Stage 3 Multinational (Years 5–8)	Stage 5 Emerging Transnational (Years 9–11)
Management assumptions	70% ethnocentrism 30% polycentrism	80% polycentrism 20% ethnocentrism	60% polycentrism 40% geocentrism
Design	Extension	75% decentralized 25% extension	80% integration 20% decentralized
Structure	Regional	Regional	20% matrix 80% regional
Planning process	Bottom-up	Bottom-up	20% interactive 80% bottom-up
Decision making	70% decentralized 30% centralized	80% decentralized 20% centralized	80% decentralized 20% centralized
Marketing process	Not standardized	Partially standardized	Standardized
Marketing programs	Standardized	30% unique 70% standardized	Unique
Product sourcing	Export	Construct plant Export	60% local manufacture 40% export
Human resources Key job nationality:			
Country management	Home country	Host country	Host country
HQ management	NA	Host country	Best person
R&D, product development	Home country	60% home country 40% decentralized	70% integrated 30% decentralized
Control/measurement	50% home standardized 50% decentralized	60% decentralized 40% home standardized	75% decentralized 25% integrated

transnational company can take advantage of resources as well as respond to local aspirations to produce a worldwide decentralized R&D program.

The strengths of companies at each stage in development are as follows:

International. Ability to exploit the parent company's knowledge and capabilities through worldwide diffusion of products.

Multinational. Flexible ability to respond to national differences.

Global. Global market or supplier reach which leverages the home-country organization, skills, and resources.

Transnational. Combines the strengths of each of the previous stages in an integrated network which leverages worldwide learning and experience.

Table 10–6 shows an example of how Fleetguard, Inc., a wholly owned subsidiary of Cummins Engine Company, evolved over an 11-year period.[16]

[16]This example was provided by Jon Adamson.

SUMMARY

Companies can choose from among a wide range of alternatives when deciding how to participate in markets around the world. Exporting, licensing, joint ventures, and ownership each represent distinct advantages and disadvantages.

The choice depends in part on how a firm configures its value chain. Exporting can help a company build volume and achieve scale economies. If a country's currency is weak relative to currencies of trading partners, export sales should be emphasized. Licensing is a good strategy for increasing the bottom line with little investment; it can be a good choice for a company with advanced technology or a strong brand image. Joint ventures, the third strategic alternative, offer companies the opportunity to share risk and combine value chain strengths. Companies considering joint ventures must plan carefully and communicate with partners to avoid "divorce." Ownership, through start-up or acquisition, can require a major commitment of resources. Acquisitions can offer the benefits of full control and an opportunity to blend technologies.

Market expansion strategies can be represented in matrix form to assist managers in thinking through the various alternatives. The options include country and market concentration; country concentration and market diversification; country diversification and market concentration; and country and market diversification. The preferred expansion strategy will be a reflection of a company's stage of development. An international company will use exporting and licensing to exploit headquarters knowledge through worldwide diffusion of products. Multinational companies will respond to local differences using acquisitions and manufacturing start-ups in various countries. Global companies will either export products around the globe from world-scale plants or will rely on the world for resources. The stage 5 transnational combines the strengths of these three stages into an integrated network to leverage worldwide learning.

DISCUSSION QUESTIONS

1. What are the alternative tools or strategies for expanding internationally? What are the major advantages and disadvantages of each strategy?

2. The president of XYZ Manufacturing Company of Buffalo, New York, comes to you with a license offer from a company in Osaka. In return for sharing the company's patents and know-how, the Japanese company will pay a license fee of 5 percent of the ex–factory price of all products sold based on the U.S. company's license. The president wants your advice. What would you tell him?

3. What are the differences between companies at the international, multinational, global, and transnational stages of development? Find examples of companies that fit the characteristics of each of these types.

4. Which strategic options for market entry or expansion would a small company be likely to pursue? A large company?

5. Do you agree with Ford's decision to acquire Jaguar? What was Ford buying, the physical assets or the name?

BIBLIOGRAPHY

Books

Campbell, Dennis, Louis Lafill, and McGeorge School of Law. *Distributorship, Agency and Franchising in an International Arena: Europe, the United States, Japan and Latin America.* Boston: Kluwer Law and Taxation Publishers, 1990.

James, Harvey S., and Murray L. Weidenbaum. *When Businesses Cross International Borders: Strategic Alliances and Their Alternatives.* Westport, Conn.: Praeger, 1993.

Lorange, Peter, and Johan Roos. *Strategic Alliances: Formation, Implementation and Evolution.* Cambridge, Mass.: Blackwell, 1992.

McCaffrey, Roger A., and Thomas A. Meyer. *An Executive's Guide to Licensing.* Homewood, Ill.: Dow Jones Irwin, 1989.

Nadel, Jack. *Cracking the Global Market: How To Do Business around the Corner and around the World.* New York: American Management Association, 1987.

Oster, Sharon. *Modern Competitive Analysis.* New York: Oxford University Press, 1990.

Root, Franklin R. *Entry Strategies for International Markets.* New York: Lexington Books, 1994.

Rosow, Jerome M. *The Global Marketplace.* New York: Facts on File, 1988.

Sherman, Andrew. *Franchising and Licensing: Two Ways To Build Your Business.* New York: American Management Association, 1991.

Treece, David J., ed. *The Competitive Challenge: Strategies for Industrial Innovation and Renewal.* Cambridge, Mass.: Ballinger Publishing, 1987.

Yip, George S. *Total Global Strategy: Managing for Worldwide Competitive Advantage.* Upper Saddle River, N.J.: Prentice Hall, 1992.

Articles

Agarwal, Sanjeev. "Socio-Cultural Distance and the Choice of Joint Venture: A Contingency Perspective." *Journal of International Marketing* 2, no. 2 (1994), pp. 63–80.

Agarwal, Sanjeev, and Sridhar N. Ramaswami. "Choice of Foreign Market Entry Mode: Impact of Ownership, Location and Internalization Factors." *Journal of International Business Studies* 23, no. 1 (First Quarter 1992), pp. 1–27.

Ali, Abbas J., and Robert C. Camp. "The Relevance of Firm Size and International Business Experience to Market Entry Strategies." *Journal of Global Marketing* 6, no. 4 (1993), pp. 91–112.

Atuahene-Gime, Kwaku. "International Licencing of Technology: An Empirical Study of the Differences between Licensee and Non-Licensee Firms." *Journal of International Marketing* 1, no. 2 (1993), pp. 71–88.

Beamish, Paul W. "The Characteristics of Joint Ventures in the People's Republic of China." *Journal of International Marketing* 1, no. 2 (1993), pp. 29–48.

Berlew, F. Kingston. "The Joint Venture—A Way into Foreign Markets." *Harvard Business Review* (July–August 1984), pp. 48–54.

Chan, Peng S., and Robert T. Justis. "Developing a Global Business Strategy Vision for the Next Decade and Beyond." *Journal of Management Development* 10, no. 2, pp. 38–45.

Davidson, Kenneth. "Strategic Investment Theories." *The Journal of Business Studies* 6, no. 1 (Summer 1985), pp. 1–28.

Doz, Yves L. "Strategic Management in Multinational Companies." *Sloan Management Review* (Winter 1980), pp. 27–46.

Doz, Yves L., Christopher A. Bartlett, and C. K. Prahalad. "Global Competitive Pressures and Host Country Demands." *California Management Review* (Spring 1981), pp. 63–73.

Doz, Yves L., and C. K. Prahalad. "How MNC's Cope with Host Government Demands. *Harvard Business Review* 58, no. 2 (March–April 1980), pp. 149–160.

Egelhoff, William G. "Great Strategy or Great Strategy Implementation—Two Ways of Competing in Global Markets." *Sloan Management Review* 34, no. 2 (Winter 1993), pp. 37–50.

Hamel, Gary, and C. K. Prahalad. "Do You Really Have a Global Strategy?" *Harvard Business Review* (July–August 1985). pp. 139–148.

Harrigan, Kathryn Rudie. "Joint Ventures and Global Strategies." *Columbia Journal of World Business* (Summer 1984), pp. 7–16.

Hill, Charles W. L., Peter Hwang, and W. Chan Kim. "An Eclectic Theory of the Choice of International Entry Mode." *Strategic Management Journal* 11, no. 2, pp. 117–128.

Hwang, Peter, Williams P. Burgers, and W. Chan Kim. "Global Diversification Strategy and Corporate Profit Performance." *Strategic Management Journal* 10, no. 1 (January–February 1989), pp. 45–57.

Jatusripitak, Soi'ikid, Liam Fahey, and Philip Kotler. "Strategic Global Marketing: Lessons from the Japanese." *Columbia Journal of World Business* (Spring 1985), pp. 47–53.

Kim, W. Chan, and Peter Hwang. "Global Strategy and Multinationals' Entry Mode Choice." *Journal of International Business Studies* 23, no. 1 (First Quarter 1992), pp. 29–54.

Kogut, Bruce. "Designing Global Strategies: Comparative and Competitive Value-Added Chains." *Sloan Management Review* (Summer 1985), pp. 17–27.

———. "Designing Global Strategies: Profiting from Operational Flexibility." *Sloan Management Review* (Fall 1985), pp. 27–38.

Lee, Chong S., and Yoo S. Yang. "Impact of Export Market Expansion Strategy on Export Performance." *International Marketing Review* 7, no. 4, pp. 41–51.

Madhok, Anoop. "Revisiting Multinational Firms' Tolerance for Joint Ventures: A Trust-Based Approach." *Journal of International Business Studies* 26, no. 1 (First Quarter 1995), pp. 117–138.

McDougall, Patricia. "New Venture Strategies: An Empirical Identification of Eight 'Archetypes' of Competitive Strategies for Entry." *Strategic Management Journal* 11, no. 6 (October 1990), pp. 447–467.

Miller, Danny. "The Generic Strategy Trap." *Journal of Business Strategy* 13, no. 1 (January–February 1992), pp. 37–41.

Morrison, Allen J., and Kendall Roth. "A Taxonomy of Business-Level Strategies in Global Industries." *Strategic Management Journal* 13, no. 6 (September 1992), pp. 399–417.

Negandi, Anant R., and Peter A. Donohue. "It's Time To Explore New Global Trade Options." *Journal of Business Strategy* 10, no. 1 (January–February 1991), pp. 27–31.

O'Reilly, Anthony J. F. "Leading a Global Strategic Charge." *Journal of Business Strategy* 12, no. 4, pp. 10–13.

Osland, Gregory E. "Successful Operating Strategies in the Performance of U.S.-China Joint Ventures." *Journal of International Marketing* 32, no. 4 (1994), pp. 53–78.

Perlmutter, Howard V., and David A. Heenan. "How Multinational Should Your Top Managers Be?" *Harvard Business Review* (November–December 1974), pp. 121–132.

Quelch, John A., and James E. Austin. "Should Multinationals Invest in Africa?" *Sloan Management Review* 4, no. 3 (Spring 1993), pp. 107–119.

Rabstejnek, George. "Let's Go Back to the Basics of Global Strategy." *Journal of Business Strategy* 10, no. 5 (September–October 1989), pp. 32–35.

Schill, Ronald L., and David N. McArthur. "Redefining the Strategic Competitive Unit: Towards a New Global Marketing Paradigm?" *International Marketing Review* 9, no. 3, pp. 5–24.

Schoemaker, Paul J. H. "How To Link Strategic Vision to Core Capabilities." *Sloan Management Review* 34, no. 1 (Fall 1992), pp. 67–81.

Segev, Eli. "A Systematic Comparative Analysis and Synthesis of Two Business-Level Strategic Typologies." *Strategic Management Journal* 10, no. 5 (September–October 1989), pp. 487–505.

Van Fleet, Mark. "Two Sources of Overseas Investment and Export Expertise." *Journal of Business Strategy* 2, no. 6 (November–December 1991), pp. 62–63.

Van Wolferen, Karel G. "The Japan Problem." *Foreign Affairs* (Winter 1986), pp. 288–303.

Wind, Yoram, and Susan Douglas. "International Portfolio Analysis and Strategy: The Challenge of the 80's." *Journal of International Business Studies* (Fall 1981), pp. 69–82.

Wind, Yoram, Susan P. Douglas, and Howard V. Perlmutter. "Guidelines for Developing International Marketing Strategies." *Journal of Marketing* 37, no. 2 (April 1973), pp. 14–23.

Wind, Yoram, and Thomas S. Robertson. "Marketing Strategy: New Directions for Theory and Research." *Journal of Marketing* 47, no. 2 (Spring 1983), pp. 12–25.

Yavas, Ugur, Doran Eroglu, and Sevgin Eroglu. "Sources and Management of Conflict: The Case of Saudi-U.S. Joint Ventures." *Journal of International Marketing* 2, no. 3 (1994), pp. 61–82.

Yip, George S., Pierre M. Loewe, and Michael Y. Yoshino. "How To Take Your Company to the Global Market." *Columbia Journal of World Business* 23, no. 4 (Winter 1988).

*F*ederal Express achieved extraordinary success in the 1970s with a pioneering approach to overnight letter and package distribution in the United States. After many successful years of serving customers with the pledge "When it absolutely, positively has to get there overnight," FedEx's growth in the United States slowed considerably. One problem: arch-competitor United Parcel Service, which started overnight package deliveries in 1982. In addition, the increasing popularity of fax machines began to erode demand for overnight letter delivery. Accordingly, FedEx founder Frederick Smith began to look abroad for new growth opportunities.

International delivery services had been part of Smith's strategic plan since the early 1980s. Between 1983 and 1990, FedEx made more than 20 international acquisitions, including courier services and trucking operations. Unfortunately, strong overseas rivals such as DHL Worldwide Express and TNT, Ltd., were becoming entrenched in Europe at the same time. Another problem was foreign government regulations.

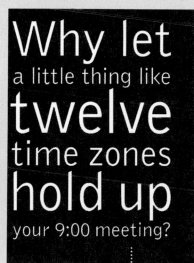

Why let
a little thing like
twelve
time zones
hold up
your 9:00 meeting?

The world of business today is just that, the world. You've got legal documents in Berlin and presentation materials in Hong Kong. And you need them all in your hands by 8:00 tomorrow morning. Sound impossible? Not with the newest worldwide delivery service from UPS. We now offer overnight delivery of packages from around the world to major business centers in the U.S., guaranteed by 8:00 a.m. You'll also feel better knowing that the status of all worldwide shipments is available instantly with our global tracking network. Remember, the world won't wait for you to start the business day. And now you don't have to wait for it.

MOVING at the SPEED of BUSINESS.

UPS is an archrival of FedEx in the global package delivery market. (UPS and UPS shield design are registered trademarks of United Parcel Service of America, Inc. Used with permission.)

For example, Japanese regulators took steps to protect local express companies. It took three years of negotiations before FedEx could get permission to make four flights a week from Memphis to Tokyo. Then, in May 1988, just days before service to Japan was to begin, FedEx was informed that no packages weighing more than 70 pounds could be flown into Tokyo, even if they were en route to other destinations. The result: FedEx lost over a million dollars per month on the Tokyo route for a year.

In December 1988, Smith announced his intention to acquire Tiger International, the world's biggest air heavy-cargo company which included the Flying Tiger Line. FedEx gained delivery routes in North and South America that it could service with its own airplanes plus Flying Tiger's fleet of long-range aircraft for use in the international heavy-freight industry. Tiger also provided FedEx with additional routes in Europe. Although the price tag was steep—$880 million—Smith believed that the acquisition was an important step toward his goal of making FedEx "the largest and best transportation company in the world." This statement said a lot about Smith's ambitions. In fact, *Business Week* magazine concluded that, of all the factors contributing to the success of FedEx, the most important might well be Smith's overwhelming desire to be number one. As Smith confidently proclaimed in 1988: "We consider our international business to be as important as our domestic business."

However, the Tiger acquisition brought with it a number of challenges. First, the move more than doubled FedEx's debt, to $2.1 billion. Second, Tiger's system was designed for slow-moving heavy freight—a sharp contrast to FedEx's high-speed network for handling small packages. A third problem: Competitors such as DHL and Australian-based TNT seemed likely to follow FedEx's lead and make their own acquisitions to expand globally. Finally, and perhaps most importantly, FedEx stood to lose customers that had traditionally used Flying Tiger. Some of these customers, such as UPS and DHL World Airways Inc., were actually FedEx's competitors in the overseas express delivery business. They relied on Tiger for shipping to countries where they had no airport landing rights.

A related issue concerned freight forwarders, companies with no airplanes or trucks that contract with customers to provide door-to-door delivery of shipments anywhere in the world. Freight forwarders booked space in planes and ships, took care of paperwork, hired trucks, and took care of all the "red tape." In the United States, FedEx's door-to-door service put most domestic freight forwarders out of business. In the international markets served by Flying Tiger, however, cultural and political factors helped preserve the freight forwarding industry. Thus, FedEx had to reassure such customers that it would not encroach on their business lest freight forwarders work with another carrier. Some industry observers expected passenger lines like Northwest and

Carrier	% of U.S. shipments	% of U.S. exports	Logistics Services
FedEx	44	30.0	Logistics Division
UPS	27	10.0	UPS Worldwide Logistics
DHL	2	13.5	World Wide Express Logistics
Airborne Express	17	2.0	

Source: Adapted from data in Lisa Coleman, "Overnight Isn't Fast Enough," *Brandweek* (July 31, 1995), pp. 26–27.

American Airlines to seek business from disgruntled freight forwarders.

Despite these hurdles, FedEx had gained the ability to operate in all 12 countries of the European Union and was thus well positioned to take advantage of reduced restrictions on surface transportation companies that were expected in 1992. The acquisition meant that FedEx could seek additional growth overseas faster than if it tried to develop the foreign business on its own, especially in Asia.

Still, FedEx had to change some parts of its formula to meet the needs of its new markets. For example, headquarters designated a 5 p.m. deadline for pickups on the European continent, even though it is customary in Spain for employees to work until 8 p.m. Also, all of FedEx's brochures and shipping bills were available only in English, a situation that has only been recently addressed. In general, overnight delivery has not been nearly as popular in Europe as it has in the United States. One symbol of the European pace: FedEx became owner of a German-based barge business, and barges painted with FedEx's distinctive orange and purple colors could be seen floating down the Rhine carrying salad oil.

By 1992, it became clear that the European market was much harder to crack than Smith had thought. Losses from four years of operations totaled $1.2 billion, forcing a cost-cutting campaign. About 6,600 employees were fired, and FedEx operations in 100 cities across Europe were closed. Some of its delivery business between the United States and Europe was contracted out to other firms. Meanwhile, rivals UPS and DHL began picking up some of FedEx's former customers.

What went wrong? Besides the fierce competitive rivalry, Smith concedes he overestimated the size of the market, expecting daily shipment volume to approach the U.S. level of 3 million units. In anticipation of this growth, Smith set up an operations center in Brussels that duplicated the hub-and-spokes approach that had been at the heart of the company's U.S. success. Unfortunately, the volume of European express shipments leveled off at about 100,000 units per day. Many of the planes in FedEx's fleet flew their routes with partial loads. To address this problem, Smith began to deemphasize the heavy cargo business and focus on the more lucrative small-package overnight business. Also, he replaced some of the company's older 747 cargo jets with smaller, more efficient aircraft; the resulting savings on the Hong Kong–Anchorage route alone could amount to $12 million.

Meanwhile, the nature of the express deliver business was changing. DHL had begun offering "same day" delivery in the late 1980s; FedEx launched a similar service in June 1995. The global opportunities for package delivery and related services were huge; in 1994, the United States accounted for only 5 percent of the market, or a total of 61 million of the 1.1 billion industry shipments. DHL's global strength could be inferred from the fact that only about 25 percent of its 95 million shipments were generated in the United States DHL, FedEx, and UPS all stressed technology as ways to differentiate themselves from each other. All three companies offered PC software that allowed customers to track their packages from desktop computers. In March 1995, FedEx became the first of the three to have a home page on the World Wide Web from which customers could obtain information and order pickups. All three companies offered logistics support to companies seeking assistance with warehousing and mail-order distribution. Noted FedEx vice president Robert Miller, "Our industry has become central to how companies do business, and they are putting within our hands increasingly larger parts of their business."

DISCUSSION QUESTIONS

1. Why did FedEx decide to "go global"? Do you agree with the decision?
2. Evaluate FedEx's European entry strategy. What mistakes did management make?
3. Formulate a new European entry strategy for FedEx.
4. What are FedEx's future prospects around the world?

Sources: Lisa Coleman, "Overnight Isn't Fast Enough," *Brandweek* (July 31, 1995), pp. 26–27.
Donna Rosato, "FedEx Displays Ability To Deliver," *USA Today* (Mar. 16, 1994), p. 3B.
Chuck Hawkins, "FedEx: Europe Nearly Killed the Messenger," *Fortune* (May 25, 1992), pp. 124, 126.
Daniel Pearl, "Innocents Abroad: Federal Express Finds Its Pioneering Formula Falls Flat Overseas," *The Wall Street Journal* (Apr. 15, 1991), p. A1.
Dean Foust, "Mr. Smith Goes Global," *Business Week* (Feb. 13, 1989), pp. 66–69, 72.
Larry C. White, "Federal Express: Managing Ahead for 1992 Is Risky," *Business Month* (August 1989), pp. 32–34.
Rick Christie, "Federal Express Needs a Lift Overseas after Expansion," *The Wall Street Journal* (Mar. 22, 1989), p. A9.
Keith Bradsher, "A Fragile Air Freight Strategy," *The New York Times* (Sept. 6, 1989), p. 29.
Kathryn Graven, "Air Express Firms Battle for Turf in Japan," *The Wall Street Journal* (Dec. 27, 1988), p. A8.

Cooperative Strategies and Global Strategic Partnerships

> *"A partnership is one of the quickest and cheapest ways to develop a global strategy."*[1]
>
> —Roland Smith, Chairman, British Aerospace

otorola thinks the future of telephone communications is up in the air—literally. The company has embarked on an ambitious program called Iridium, at the heart of which is a network of 66 powerful, low-orbit satellites. Starting in 1998, Iridium will allow Motorola to offer global personal communications services that will supplement—and perhaps render obsolete—ground-based wire and cellular telephone service. Iridium's first customers will probably be globetrotting business executives who need to send and receive voice messages and data. But the needs of business travelers may be just the beginning: 90 percent of the world's population lacks access to telephones. Iridium could bring telephone service to rural areas in South America, Africa, and Asia—without wires. With a price tag of $3.4 billion, Iridium is too expensive for Motorola to undertake on its own. Iridium's global reach also requires government cooperation and participation since, in many countries, governments own the telephone systems and rely on them for revenues. Motorola executives project that Iridium will attract 1 million users within three years of the system's launch. Each subscriber is expected to contribute $1,000 per year in net revenues to Iridium.

In previous chapters, we reviewed the range of options—exporting, licensing, joint ventures, and ownership—traditionally used by companies wishing either to enter global markets for the first time or to expand their activities beyond present levels. However, recent changes in the political, economic, sociocultural, and technological environments of the global firm have combined to change the relative importance of those strategies. Trade barriers have fallen, markets have globalized, consumer needs and wants have converged, product life cycles have shortened, and new communications technologies and trends have emerged. While these developments provide unprecedented market opportunities, there are strong strategic implications for the global organization and new challenges for the global marketer. Like Motorola's Iridium program, such strategies will undoubtedly incorporate—or may even be structured around—a variety of collaborations. Once thought of only as joint ventures with the more dominant party reaping most of the benefits (or losses) of the partnership, cross-border alliances are taking on surprising new configurations and even more surprising players.

---

[1] Jeremy Main, "Making Global Alliances Work," *Fortune* (Dec. 17, 1990), p. 121.

Why would any firm—global or otherwise—seek to collaborate with another firm, be it local or foreign? Motorola, for example, has more than 40 percent share of the world market for cellular phones; its share of the global pager market exceeds 50 percent. Why have Motorola executives decided to pursue "competitive collaboration" with other firms, some of which are rivals? As noted, a combination of environmental trends may soon render traditional competitive strategies obsolete. Many firms face a business environment characterized by unprecedented degrees of dynamism, turbulence, and unpredictability. Today's firm must be equipped to respond to mounting economic and political pressures. Reaction time has been sharply cut by advances in technology. Ironically, to succeed in today's global arena, firms can no longer rely on the very technological superiority which brought them past success. The firm of tomorrow must look toward new strategies that will enhance environmental responsiveness. This chapter focuses on global strategic partnerships, the Japanese *keiretsu*, and various other types of cooperation strategies that are important to the success of the global firm.

THE NATURE OF GLOBAL STRATEGIC PARTNERSHIPS

The terminology used to describe the new forms of cooperation strategies varies widely. The phrases **collaborative agreements, strategic alliances, strategic international alliances,** and **global strategic partnerships** (GSPs) are frequently used to refer to linkages between companies to jointly pursue a common goal. A broad spectrum of interfirm agreements, including joint ventures, can be covered by this terminology. However, the strategic alliances discussed in this chapter exhibit three characteristics (see Figure 11–1):[2]

1. The participants remain independent subsequent to the formation of the alliance.
2. The participants share the benefits of the alliance as well as control over the performance of assigned tasks.
3. The participants make ongoing contributions in technology, products, and other key strategic areas.

According to estimates, the number of strategic alliances has been growing at a rate of 20 to 30 percent since the mid-1980s. The upward trend for GSPs comes in part at the expense of traditional cross-border mergers and acquisitions. In 1992, there were about 1,800 of the latter-type linkup, down from about 2,700 in 1989. Meanwhile, according to data compiled by Venture Economics, 2,084 U.S. companies allied with international partners in 1991, up from 1,393 in 1990. By an overwhelming margin, U.S. companies favor GSPs with Japanese partners (Kruytbosch 1993, 92).

Roland Smith, chairman of British Aerospace, offers a straightforward reason why a firm would enter into a GSP: "A partnership is one of the quickest and cheapest ways to develop a global strategy."[3] Like traditional joint ventures, GSPs have some disadvantages. Each partner must be willing to sacrifice some control, and there are potential risks associated with strengthening a competitor from another country. Despite these drawbacks, GSPs are attractive for several reasons. First, high product development costs may force a company to seek partners; this was part of the rationale for Boeing's partnership with a Japanese consortium to develop a new jet aircraft, the 777. Second, the technol-

[2]Michael A. Yoshino and U. Srinivasa Rangan, *Strategic Alliances: An Entrepreneurial Approach to Globalization* (Boston: Harvard Business School Press, 1995) p. 5. For an alternative decription see Riad Ajami and Dara Khambata, "Global Strategic Alliances: The New Transnationals," *Journal of Global Marketing* 5, no.1/2 (1991), pp. 55–59.
[3]Main 1990.

FIGURE 11–1

THREE CHARACTERISTICS
OF STRATEGIC ALLIANCES

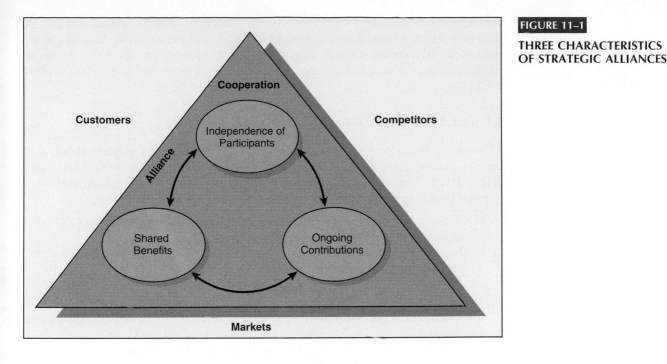

ogy requirements of many contemporary products mean that an individual company may lack the skills, capital, or know-how to go it alone (Ohmae 1989, 145). Third, partnerships may be the best means of securing access to national and regional markets. Fourth, partnerships provide important learning opportunities; in fact, one expert regards GSPs as a "race to learn." Professor Gary Hamel of the London Business School has observed that the partner that proves to be the fastest learner can ultimately dominate the relationship.[4]

As noted earlier, GSPs and joint ventures differ in significant ways. Traditional joint ventures are basically alliances focusing on a single national market or a specific problem. For example, Lenwest, the joint venture described in Chapter 10 between Germany's Salamander AG and the Proletarian Shoe Factory in St. Petersburg, Russia, fits this description; the basic goal is to make shoes for the Russian market. A true global strategic partnership is different; it is distinguished by the following five attributes (Perlmutter & Heenan 1986, 137):

1. Two or more companies develop a joint long-term strategy aimed at achieving world leadership by pursuing cost-leadership, differentiation, or a combination of the two.
2. The relationship is reciprocal. Each partner possesses specific strengths that it shares with the other; learning must take place on both sides.
3. The partners' vision and efforts are truly global, extending beyond home countries and the home regions to the rest of the world.
4. The relationship is organized along horizontal, not vertical, lines. Continual transfer of resources laterally between partners is required, with technology sharing and resource pooling representing norms.
5. When competing in markets excluded from the partnership, the participants retain their national and ideological identities.

The Iridium program described in the chapter introduction embodies several "prerequisites" that experts believe are the hallmarks of good alliances. First, Motorola is forming an alliance to exploit a unique strength, namely, its leadership in wireless

[4]Main 1990, p. 122.

communications. Second, the Iridium alliance partners all possess unique strengths of their own. Third, it is unlikely that any of the partners has the ability or the desire to acquire Motorola's unique strength. Finally, rather than focusing on a particular market or product, Iridium is an alliance based upon skills, know-how, and technology (Robert 1993).

SUCCESS FACTORS

Assuming that a proposed alliance meets the five prerequisites outlined above, it is necessary to consider six basic factors are deemed to have significant impact on the success of GSPs. These are mission, strategy, governance, culture, organization, and management (Perlmutter & Heenan 1986, 137).

1. *Mission.* Successful GSPs create win-win situations, where participants pursue objectives on the basis of mutual need or advantage.
2. *Strategy.* A company may establish separate GSPs with different partners; strategy must be thought out up front to avoid conflicts.
3. *Governance.* Discussion and consensus must be the norms. Partners must be viewed as equals.
4. *Culture.* Personal "chemistry" is important, as is the successful development of a shared set of values. The failure of a partnership between Great Britain's General Electric Company and Siemens AG was blamed in part on the fact that the former was run by finance-oriented executives, the latter by engineers.
5. *Organization.* Innovative structures and designs may be needed to offset the complexity of multicountry management.
6. *Management.* GSPs invariably involve a different type of decision making. Potentially divisive issues must be identified in advance and clear, unitary lines of authority established that will result in commitment by all partners.

Companies forming GSPs must keep these factors in mind. Moreover, successful collaborators will be guided by the following four principles. First, despite the fact that partners are pursuing mutual goals in some areas, partners must remember that they are competitors in others. Second, harmony is not the most important measure of success. some conflict is to be expected. Third, all employees, engineers, and managers must understand where cooperation ends and competitive compromise begins. Finally, as noted earlier, learning from partners is critically important (Hamel, Doz, & Prahalad 1989, 134).

The issue of learning deserves special attention. As one team of researchers notes,

> The challenge is to share enough skills to create advantage vis-à-vis companies outside the alliance while preventing a wholesale transfer of core skills to the partner. This is a very thin line to walk. Companies must carefully select what skills and technologies they pass to their partners. They must develop safeguards against unintended, informal transfers of information. The goal is to limit the transparency of their operations (Hamel, et al., 1989, 136).

Motorola's paging systems are a low-cost communication tool ideally suited to China's booming market. (Ad courtesy of Motorola, Inc.)

Alliances with Asian Competitors

Western companies may find themselves at a disadvantage in GSPs with an Asian competitor, especially if the latter's manufacturing skills are the attractive quality. Unfortunately for Western companies, manufacturing excellence represents a multifac-

■ IRIDIUM

Motorola is partnering with more than a dozen companies from various parts of the world, each with a specific strength. Lockheed, for example, will build the satellites at a cost of $13 million each; subcontractors will include Raytheon, Martin Marietta, and Siemens AG. Some partners will be responsible for connecting calls in specific geographic regions; for example, Vebacom GmbH, a subsidiary of Germany's Veba AG, will provide service in northern and western Europe. Other participants include Krunichev Enterprise, a Russian rocket manufacturer, and Great Wall Industry Corporation, which is affiliated with the Chinese army.

All the participants are betting that the limitations of conventional cellular telephone systems will provide the key to Iridium's success. For example, cellular phone standards are different in Europe and the United States, so a European businessperson's cellular phone unit is rendered inoperable after he or she crosses the Atlantic to the United States. Moreover, callers using cellular systems need to know the geographic location of the party they wish to reach. Iridium's early cus-

tomers will have to pay as much as $3,000 for new telephones, plus charges of $3 per minute.

Industry observers note that Iridium must overcome some major hurdles if it is to succeed. For one thing, Iridium is just one of several telephone and data systems currently in development. Competitors include Globalstar, a satellite system one-third owned by Loral, the U.S. defense contractor. Globalstar's partners include Vodafone of Great Britain, France Telecom, and Deutsche Aerospace. Another competitor, Odyssey, is a satellite venture created by TRW; Teleglobe, a Canadian firm, is a major partner. Hughes Electronics is designing less-expensive regional satellite networks that may be dedicated to specific geographic regions such as Asia and Africa.

Another problem is that the high risks associated with a venture such as Iridium may limit interest from outside investors. In the fall of 1995, Iridium was forced to withdraw a $300 million offering of high-yield "junk" bonds after investors demanded a return of approximately 25 percent. Noted Ira Brodsky, a consultant at Datacomm Research, "There's an issue of high-stakes projects here." Brodsky predicted that Iridium could cost as much as $6 billion. "Can they really make that back?" he asks.

---

eted competence that is not easily transferred. Non-Asian managers and engineers must also learn to be more receptive and attentive—they must overcome the "not-invented-here" syndrome and begin to think of themselves as students, not teachers. At the same time, they must learn to be less eager to show off proprietary lab and engineering successes. To limit transparency, some companies involved in GSPs establish a "collaboration section." Much like a corporate communications department, this department is designed to serve as a gatekeeper through which requests for access to people and information must be channeled. Such gatekeeping serves an important control function that guards against unintended transfers.

A 1991 report by McKinsey and Company sheds additional light on the specific problems of alliances between Western and Japanese firms (Jones & Schill 1991). Often, problems between partners had less to do with objective levels of performance than with a feeling of mutual disillusionment and missed opportunity. The study identifies four common problem areas in alliances gone wrong. The first problem was that each partner had a "different dream"; the Japanese partner saw itself emerging from the alliance as a leader in its business or entering new sectors and building a new basis for the future, while the Western partner sought relatively quick and risk-free financial returns. Said one Japanese manager, "Our partner came in looking for a return. They got it. Now they complain that they didn't build a business. But that isn't what they set out to create."

A second area of concern is the balance between partners. Each must contribute to the alliance and each must depend on the other to a degree that justifies participation in the alliance. The most attractive partner in the short run is likely to be a company that is already established and competent in the business with the need to master, say, some new technological skills. The best long-term partner, however, is likely to be a less competent player or even one from outside the industry.

Another common cause of problems is "frictional loss" caused by differences in man-

Sources: Jeff Cole, "Star Wars: In New Space Race, Companies Are Seeking Dollars from Heaven," *The Wall Street Journal* (Oct. 10, 1995), pp. A1, A12.
Harlan S. Byrne, "Far Out," *Barron's* (June 19, 1995), pp. 31–35.
Joe Flowers, "Iridium, Parts I and II," *Wired* (Fall 1993).
Quentin Hardy, "Iridium Pulls $300 Million Bond Offer; Analysts Cite Concerns about Projects," *The Wall Street Journal* (Sept. 22, 1995), p. B5.
Nancy Hass, "Preemptive Strike," *Financial World* (Sept. 14, 1993), pp. 36–39.
Rob Frieden, "Satellite-based Personal Communications Services," *Telecommunications* (December 1993), pp. 25–28.

agement philosophy, expectations, and approaches. All functions within the alliance may be affected, and performance is likely to suffer as a consequence. Speaking of his Japanese counterpart, a Western businessman said, "Our partner just wanted to go ahead and invest without considering whether there would be a return or not." The Japanese partner stated that "the foreign partner took so long to decide on obvious points that we were always too slow." Such differences often cause much frustration and time-consuming debates, which stifle decision making.

Last, the study found that short-term goals can result in the foreign partner limiting the number of people allocated to the joint venture. Those involved in the venture may only perform two- or three-year assignments. The result is "corporate amnesia"; that is, little or no corporate memory is built up on how to compete in Japan. The original goals of the venture will be lost as each new group of managers takes their turn. When taken collectively, these four problems will almost ensure that the Japanese partner will be the only one in it for the long haul.

GE/Snecma: A Success Story

Commercial Fan Moteur (CFM) International, a partnership between GE's jet engine division and Snecma, a government-owned French aerospace company, is a frequently cited example of a successful GSP. GE was motivated in part by the desire to gain access to the European market so it could sell engines to Airbus Industrie; also, the $800 million in development costs was more than GE could risk on its own. While GE focused on system design and high-tech work, the French side handled fans, boosters, and other components. The partnership resulted in the development of a highly successful new engine that, to date, has generated tens of billions of dollars in sales to 125 different customers.

The alliance got off to a strong start because of the personal chemistry between two top executives, GE's Gerhard Neumann and the late General René Ravaud of Snecma. The partnership thrives despite each side's differing views regarding governance, management, and organization. Brian Rowe, senior vice president of GE's engine group, has noted that the French like to bring in senior executives from outside the industry, while GE prefers to bring in experienced people from within the organization. Also, the French prefer to approach problem solving with copious amounts of data, while Americans may take a more intuitive approach.[5] Still, senior executives from both sides involved in the partnership have been delegated substantial responsibility.

AT&T/Olivetti: A Failure

In theory, the partnership in the mid-1980s between AT&T and Italy's Olivetti appeared to be a winner: The collective mission was to capture a major share of the global market for information processing and communications (Perlmutter & Heenan 1986, 145). Olivetti had what appeared to be a strong presence in the European office equipment market; AT&T executives, having just presided over the divestiture of their company's regional telephone units, had set their sights on overseas growth with Europe as the starting point. AT&T promised its partner $260 million and access to microprocessor and telecommunications technology. The partnership called for AT&T to sell Olivetti's personal computers in the United States; Olivetti, in turn, would sell AT&T computers and switching equipment in Europe. Underpinning the alliance was the expectation that synergies would result from the pairing of companies from different industries—communications and computers.

Unfortunately, that vision was nothing more than a hope: There was no real strength

[5]Bernard Wysocki, "Global Reach: Cross Border Alliances Become Favorite Way to Crack New Markets," *The Wall Street Journal* (Mar. 26, 1990), p. A12.

in Olivetti in the computer market, and Olivetti had no experience or capability in communications equipment. Tensions ran high when sales did not reach expected levels. AT&T group executive Robert Kavner cited communication and cultural differences as being important factors leading to the breakdown of the alliance. "I don't think we or Olivetti spent enough time understanding behavior patterns," Kavner said. "We knew the culture was different but we never really penetrated. We would get angry, and they would get upset."[6] In 1989, AT&T cashed in its Olivetti stake for a share in the parent company Compagnie Industriali Riunite SpA (CIR). In 1993, citing a decline in CIR's value, AT&T sold its remaining stake.

Boeing/Japan: A Controversy

GSPs have been the target of criticism in some circles. Critics warn that employees of a company that becomes reliant on outside suppliers for critical components will lose expertise and experience erosion of their engineering skills. Such criticism is often directed at GSPs involving U.S. and Japanese firms. For example, a proposed alliance between Boeing and a Japanese consortium to build a new fuel-efficient airliner, the 7J7, generated a great deal of controversy. The project's $4 billion price tag was too high for Boeing to shoulder alone. The Japanese were to contribute between $1 billion and $2 billion; in return, they would get a chance to learn manufacturing and marketing techniques from Boeing. Although the 7J7 project was shelved in 1988, a new widebody aircraft, the 777, was developed with about 20 percent of the work subcontracted out to Mitsubishi, Fuji, and Kawasaki.[7]

Critics envision a scenario in which the Japanese use what they learn to build their own aircraft and compete directly with Boeing in the future—a disturbing thought since Boeing is a major exporter to world markets. One team of researchers has developed a framework outlining the stages that a company can go through as it becomes increasingly dependent on partnerships (Lei & Slocum 1992):

Stage 1: Outsourcing of assembly for inexpensive labor
Stage 2: Outsourcing of low-value components to reduce product price
Stage 3: Growing levels of value-added components move abroad
Stage 4: Manufacturing skills, designs, and functionally related technologies move abroad
Stage 5: Disciplines related to quality, precision-manufacturing, testing, and future avenues of product derivatives move abroad
Stage 6: Core skills surrounding components, miniaturization, and complex systems integration move abroad
Stage 7: Competitor learns the entire spectrum of skills related to the underlying core competence.

INTERNATIONAL PARTNERSHIPS IN DEVELOPING COUNTRIES

Central and Eastern Europe, Asia, India, and Mexico offer exciting opportunities for firms seeking to enter gigantic and largely untapped markets. An obvious strategic alternative for entering these markets is the strategic alliance. Like the early joint ventures between U.S. and Japanese firms, potential partners will trade market access for know-how. Assuming that such problems as cash shortages and organized crime can be overcome, joint ventures in Central and Eastern Europe could evolve at a more accelerated pace than did past joint ventures with Asian partners.

---

[6]Ibid.
[7]John Holusha, "Pushing the Envelope at Boeing," *The New York Times* (Nov. 10, 1991), Sec. 3, pp. 1,6.

A number of factors combine to make Russia an excellent location for an alliance. There is a well-educated workforce. Quality is very important to the Russian consumer. And, social, political, and economic problems can be turned to success and new growth opportunities. Conversely, several problems are frequently cited for Western ventures in Russia. They are: flourishing organized crime, supply shortages, and outdated regulatory and legal systems in a constant state of flux.

Who exactly is in Russia now? For the most part, firms actively participating in joint ventures there are small to midsize companies, which can adapt rapidly in a still-unstable environment. One study noted that of the 6,000 joint ventures registered in Russia since 1987, 20 percent are up and running. Most of the joint ventures studied were initiated by the Western partner. The major business activities were evenly divided between services and manufacturing. Some were targeted at Westerners in Russia, for example, hotel, exhibition, and legal services. Others targeted the domestic market in computer software and systems, telecommunications, music recording, architecture, and medicine. Others focused on both markets: engineering, retail distribution, dentistry, security services, business consulting, banking, construction, and the leasing of construction equipment. Most of the manufacturing ventures were initially limited to assembly work but have moved on to producing components in Russia. The activities range from computer manufacturing to fish processing. Some of the joint ventures combined manufacturing and services; for example, there is a camera company that both sells and services the equipment it makes and a roofing company that designs, produces, and installs roofing.

A Central European market with interesting potential is Hungary. Hungary already has the most liberal financial and commercial system in the region. It has also provided investment incentives to Westerners, especially in high-tech industries. Like Russia, this former communist economy has its share of problems. Digital's recent joint venture agreement with the Hungarian Research Institute for Physics and the state-supervised computer systems design firm Szamalk is a case in point. Although the venture was formed so Digital will be able to sell and service its equipment in Hungary, the underlying importance of the venture was to stop cloning of Digital's computers by Central European firms.

The Asian-Pacific market is huge, with half of the world population and one-third of world GNP; besides Japan, Austrialia, and New Zealand, it includes Korea, China, and India. GE has put several of these countries at the center of its growth strategy for the next century. For example, the company has invested $100 million in India and expects sales there to reach $1 billion by the end of the decade.

COOPERATIVE STRATEGIES IN JAPAN: *KEIRETSU*

Japan's *keiretsu* represent a special category of cooperative strategy. A *keiretsu* is an interbusiness alliance or enterprise group that, in the words of one observer, "resembles a fighting clan in which business families join together to vie for market share."[8] *Keiretsu* exist in a broad spectrum of markets, including the capital market, primary goods markets, and component parts markets.[9] *Keiretsu* relationships are often cemented by bank ownership of large blocks of stock as well as cross-ownership of stock between a company and its buyers and nonfinancial suppliers. Further, *keiretsu* executives can legally sit on each other's boards and share information and coordinate prices in closed-door meetings of "presidents' councils." Thus, *keiretsu* are essentially cartels that have the government's blessing.

Some observers have disputed charges that *keiretsu* have an impact on market relationships in Japan, claiming instead that the groups primarily serve a social function.

[8]Robert L. Cutts, "Capitalism in Japan: Cartels and *Keiretsu*," *Harvard Business Review* (July–August 1992), p. 49.
[9]Michael L. Gerlach, "Twilight of the *Keiretsu*? A Critical Assessment," *Journal of Japanese Studies* 18 no. 1 (Winter 1992), p. 79.

Others acknowledge the past significance of preferential trading patterns associated with *keiretsu* but assert that the latter's influence is now weakening. While it is beyond the scope of this chapter to address these issues in detail, there can be no doubt that, for companies competing with the Japanese or wishing to enter the Japanese market, a general understanding of *keiretsu* is crucial. Imagine, for example, what it would mean in the United States if an automaker (e.g., GM), an electrical products company (GE), a steelmaker (USX), and a computer firm (IBM) were interconnected, rather than separate, firms. Global competition in the era of *keiretsu* means that competition exists not only among products, but between different systems of corporate governance and industrial organization.[10]

As the hypothetical example from the United States suggests, some of Japan's biggest and best-known companies are at the center of *keiretsu*. For example, Mitsui Group and Mitsubishi Group are organized around big trading companies. These two, together with the Sumitomo, Fuyo, Sanwa, and DKB groups, make up the "big six" *keiretsu*. Each group strives for a strong position in each major sector of the Japanese economy. Annual revenues in each group are in the hundreds of billions of dollars (Prestowitz 1989, 296). In absolute terms, *keiretsu* constitute less than 0.01 percent of all Japanese companies. However, they account for an astonishing 78 percent of the market valuation of shares on the Tokyo Stock Exchange, a third of Japan's business capital, and approximately a quarter of its sales.[11] These alliances can effectively block foreign suppliers from entering the market and result in higher prices to Japanese consumers, while at the same time resulting in corporate stability, risk sharing, and long-term employment. The Mitsubishi Group's *keiretsu* structure is shown in detail in Figure 11–2.

In addition to the big six, several other *keiretsu* have formed, bringing new configurations to the basic forms described above. Vertical supply and distribution *keiretsu* are alliances between manufacturers and retailers. For example, Matsushita controls a chain of 25,000 National stores in Japan through which it sells its Panasonic, Technics, and Quasar brands. About half of Matsushita's domestic sales are generated through the National chain, 50 to 80 percent of whose inventory consists of Matsushita's brands. Japan's other major consumer electronics manufacturers, including Toshiba and Hitachi, have similar alliances. (Sony's chain of stores is much smaller and weaker by comparison.) All are fierce competitors in the Japanese market.[12]

Another type of manufacturing *keiretsu* outside the big six consists of vertical hierarchical alliances between assembly companies and suppliers and component manufacturers. Intergroup operations and systems are closely integrated, with suppliers receiving long-term contracts. Toyota, for example, has a network of about 175 primary and 4,000 secondary suppliers. One supplier is Koito; Toyota owns about one-fifth of Koito's shares and buys about half of its production. The net result of this arrangement is that Toyota produces about 25 percent of the sales value of its cars, compared with 50 percent for GM. Manufacturing *keiretsu* show the gains that can result from an optimal balance of supplier and buyer power. Because Toyota buys a given component from several suppliers (some are in the *keiretsu*, some are independent), discipline is imposed down the network. Also, because Toyota's suppliers do not work exclusively for Toyota, they have an incentive to be flexible and adaptable.[13]

The practices described above lead to the question of whether or not *keiretsu* violate antitrust laws. As many observers have noted, the Japanese government frequently puts the interests of producers ahead of the interests of consumers. In fact, the *keiretsu* were

---

[10]Ronald J. Gilson and Mark J. Roe, "Understanding the Japanese Keiretsu: Overlaps between Corporate Governance and Industrial Organization," *The Yale Law Journal* 102, no. 4 (January 1993), p. 883.

[11]Carla Rappoport, "Why Japan Keeps On Winning," *Fortune* (July 15, 1991), p.76.

[12]The importance of the chain stores is eroding due to increasing sales at mass merchandisers not under the manufacturers' control.

[13]"Japanology, Inc.—Survey," *The Economist* (Mar. 6, 1993), p. 15.

FIGURE 11–2

MITSUBISHI GROUP'S *KEIRETSU* STRUCTURE

Source: Courtesy of The Mitsubishi Group, from Collins & Doorley *Teaming Up for the '90s,* (Copyright Deloitte & Touche 1991.)

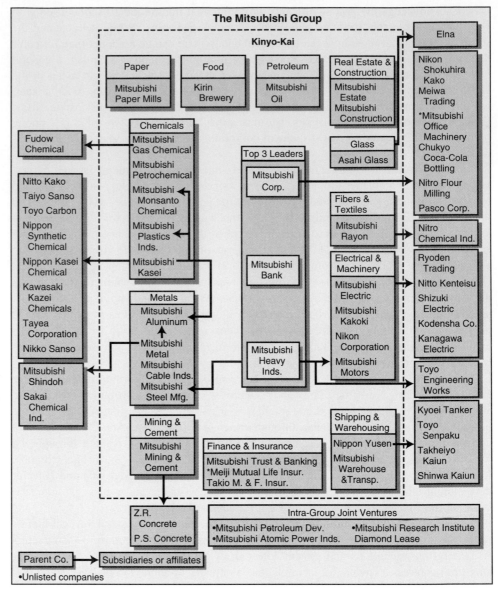

formed in the early 1950s as regroupings of four large conglomerates—*zaibatsu*—that dominated the Japanese economy until 1945. They were dissolved after the occupational forces introduced antitrust as part of the reconstruction. Today, Japan's Fair Trade Commission appears to favor harmony rather than pursuing anticompetitive behavior. As a result, the U.S. Federal Trade Commission has launched several investigations of price fixing, price discrimination, and exclusive supply arrangements. Hitachi, Canon, and other Japanese companies have also been accused of restricting the availability of high-tech products in the U.S. market. The Justice Department has considered prosecuting the U.S. subsidiaries of Japanese companies if the parent company is found guilty of unfair trade practices in the Japanese market.[14]

How *Keiretsu* Affect U.S. Business: Two Examples

Clyde Prestowitz provides the following example to show how *keiretsu* relationships have the potential to impact U.S. businesses. In the early 1980s, Nissan was in the market for a supercomputer to use in car design. Two vendors under consideration were Cray,

[14]Rappoport 1991, p. 84.

the worldwide leader in supercomputers at the time, and Hitachi, which had no functional product to offer. When it appeared that the purchase of a Cray computer was pending, Hitachi executives called for solidarity—both Nissan and Hitachi were members of the same big six *keiretsu*, the Fuyo Group. Hitachi essentially mandated that Nissan show preference to Hitachi, a situation that rankled U.S. trade officials. Meanwhile, a coalition within Nissan was pushing for a Cray computer; ultimately, thanks to U.S. pressure on both Nissan and the Japanese government, the business went to Cray.

Prestowitz describes the Japanese attitude toward this type of business practice:[15]

> . . . It respects mutual obligation by providing a cushion against shocks. Today Nissan may buy a Hitachi computer. Tomorrow it may ask Hitachi to take some of its redundant workers. The slightly lesser performance it may get from the Hitachi computer is balanced against the broader considerations. Moreover, because the decision to buy Hitachi would be a favor, it would bind Hitachi closer and guarantee slavish service and future Hitachi loyalty to Nissan products. . . . This attitude of sticking together is what the Japanese mean by the long-term view; it is what enables them to withstand shocks and to survive over the long term (Prestowitz 1989, 299–300).

U.S. companies have reason to be concerned with *keiretsu* outside the Japanese market as well. *Keiretsu* relationships are crossing the Pacific and directly affecting the U.S. market. According to 1991 data compiled by Dodwell Marketing Consultants, in California alone *keiretsu* own more than half of the Japanese-affiliated manufacturing facilities. But the impact of *keiretsu* extends beyond the West Coast. Illinois-based Tenneco Automotive, a maker of shock absorbers and exhaust systems, does a great deal of worldwide business with the Toyota *keiretsu*. In 1990, however, Mazda dropped Tenneco as a supplier to its U.S. plant in Kentucky. Part of the business was shifted to Tokico Manufacturing, a Japanese transplant and a member of the Mazda *keiretsu*; a non-*keiretsu* Japanese company, KYB Industries, was also made a vendor. A Japanese auto executive explained the rationale behind the change: "First choice is a *keiretsu* company, second choice is a Japanese supplier, third is a local company."[16]

COOPERATIVE STRATEGIES IN THE UNITED STATES: TARGETING THE DIGITAL FUTURE

Increasing numbers of U.S. companies are entering into alliances that resemble *keiretsu*. In fact, the phrase "digital *keiretsu*" is frequently used to describe alliances between companies in several industries—computers, communications, consumer electronics, and entertainment—that are undergoing transformation and convergence. These processes are the result of tremendous advances in the ability to transmit and manipulate vast quantities of audio, video, and data, and the rapidly approaching era of an electronic "superhighway" in the United States composed of fiber optic cable and digital switching equipment.

One U.S. technology alliance, Sematech, is unique in that it is the direct result of government industrial policy. The U.S. government, concerned that key companies in the domestic semiconductor industry were having difficulty competing with Japan, agreed to subsidize a consortium of 14 technology companies beginning in 1987. Sematech was comprised of 700 employees, some permanent, some on loan from IBM, AT&T, Advanced Micro Devices, Intel, and other companies. The task facing the consortium was to save the U.S. chipmaking equipment industry, whose manufacturers were rapidly losing market share in the face of intense competition from Japan. Although initially plagued by attitudinal and cultural differences between different factions, Sematech eventually helped

---

[15]For years, Prestowitz has argued that Japan's industry structure—*keiretsu* included—gives its companies unfair advantages. A more moderate view might be that any business decision must have an economic justification. Thus, a moderate would caution against overstating the effect of *keiretsu*.
[16]Rappoport 1991, p. 80.

chipmakers try new approaches with their equipment vendors. By 1991, the Sematech initiative, along with other factors such as the economic downturn in Japan, reversed the market share slide of the semiconductor equipment industry (Spencer & Grindley 1993).

Although Sematech is not without its critics, its creation heralded a new era in cooperation among technology companies. Motorola's Iridium project is one example. AT&T, as noted earlier, failed in its attempt to form a GSP with Olivetti in the 1980s. Yet, in the 1990s, AT&T has successfully entered into so many multiple relationships with U.S. companies that it represents a digital *keiretsu*. Just since 1991, AT&T has invested in: EO Inc., which makes personal communicators; Spectrum Holobyte, a pioneer in virtual reality; GO Corp., a specialist in handwriting recognition software; General Magic; 3DO, which has developed an interactive multimedia player; Sierra Network, an on-line information service (now called the Imagination Network); and Knowledge Adventure, which develops multimedia education software. AT&T has also formed a partnership with Sega of America to develop technology that will allow video games to be played over telephone lines.[17]

By 1993, Tele-Communications, Inc. (TCI), the largest cable TV operator in the United States, had also developed into a kind of "home-grown" *keiretsu*. TCI had forged agreements with Time Warner to develop hardware and software standards for interactive TV; it owned a portion of Turner Broadcasting, and had alliances with AT&T, U. S. West, and other rival cable companies.[18] In October, TCI CEO John Malone stunned the business community with the announcement that TCI would be acquired by Bell Atlantic Corp., a regional Bell telephone company. The logic behind the deal was similar to that of GSPs discussed previously; noted Bell Atlantic Chairman Raymond W. Smith, "no one cable company or telco or even media company brings to bear all the capabilities we need to capitalize on the premier growth opportunity of the decade."[19] Thus, the new company would combine TCI's programming and high-capacity distribution system with Bell Atlantic's switching technology. There was much speculation about why this proposed merger was canceled. However, it can be said that breaking off an engagement is different than a divorce. The reasons for the attraction to marriage are still there.

The dawn of the digital era is also witnessing the formation of GSPs of the general type described earlier in this chapter. A good example is General Magic, an alliance between six firms: three U.S. (Apple, Motorola, and AT&T), two Japanese (Sony and Matsushita), and one Dutch (Philips). While these companies continue to compete in consumer electronics and wireless communications, they are collaborating to produce a new hand-held personal communicator that provides message exchanging, databases, electronic shopping, and other consumer services.

BEYOND STRATEGIC ALLIANCES

The "relationship enterprise" is said to be the next stage of evolution of the strategic alliance. Groupings of firms in different industries and countries, they will be held together by common goals which encourage them to act almost as a single firm. Cyrus Freidheim, vice chairman of the Booz, Allen & Hamilton consulting firm, recently outlined an alliance that, in his opinion, might be representative of an early relationship enterprise. He suggests that, within the next few decades, Boeing, British Airways, Siemens, TNT, and Snecma might jointly build several new airports in China. As part of the package, British Airways and TNT would be granted preferential routes and landing slots, the

---

[17]Bart Ziegler, "AT&T's Bold Bet," *Business Week* (Aug. 30, 1993), pp. 28–29.
[18]Stephen Kreider Yoder and G. Pascal Zachary, "Vague New World: Digital Media Business Takes Form as a Battle of Complex Alliances," *The Wall Street Journal* (July 14, 1993), pp. A1, A6.
[19]Dennis Kneale, Johnnie L. Robers, and Laura Landro, "Plugging In: Bell Atlantic and TCI Are Poised to Shape New Interactive World," *The Wall Street Journal* (Oct. 14, 1993), p. A15.

Chinese government would contract to buy all its aircraft from Boeing/Snecma, and Siemens would provide air traffic control systems for all the airports.[20]

More than the simple strategic alliances we know today, relationship enterprises will be super-alliances among global giants, with revenues approaching $1 trillion. They would be able to draw on extensive cash resources, circumvent antitrust barriers, and, with home bases in all major markets, enjoy the political advantage of being a "local" firm almost anywhere. This type of alliance is not driven simply by technological change, but by the political necessity of having multiple home bases.

Another perspective on the future of cooperative strategies envisions the emergence of the "virtual corporation." (The term "virtual" is borrowed from computer science; some computers feature "virtual memory" that allows them to function as though they have more storage capacity than is actually built into their memory chips.) As described in a recent *Business Week* cover story, the virtual corporation "will seem to be a single entity with vast capabilities but will really be the result of numerous collaborations assembled only when they're needed."[21]

On a global level, the virtual corporation could combine the twin competencies of cost effectiveness and responsiveness; thus, it could pursue the "think globally, act locally" philosophy with ease. This reflects the trend toward "mass customization." The same forces that are driving the formation of the "digital *keiretsu*" described above—high-speed communication networks, for example—are embodied in the virtual corporation. As noted by William Davidow and Michael Malone in their book *The Virtual Corporation*, "The success of a virtual corporation will depend on its ability to gather and integrate a massive flow of information throughout its organizational components and intelligently act upon that information" (Davidow & Malone 1993, 59).

Why has the virtual corporation suddenly burst onto the scene? Previously, firms lacked the technology to facilitate this type of data management. Today, distributed databases, networks, and open systems make possible the kinds of data flow required for the virtual corporation. In particular, these data flows permit "supply chain management." Ford provides an interesting example of how technology is improving information flows among the farflung operations of a single company. Ford's $6 billion "world car"—known as the Mercury Mystique and Ford Contour in the United States, the Mondeo in Europe—was developed using an international communications network linking computer workstations of designers and engineers on three continents.[22]

One of the hallmarks of the virtual corporation will be the production of "virtual products"—a product that practically exists before it is manufactured. As described by Davidow and Malone, the concept, design, and manufacture of virtual products are stored in the minds of cooperating teams, in computers, and in flexible production lines (Davidow & Malone 1993, 4).

[20]"The Global Firm: R.I.P." *The Economist,* (Feb. 6, 1993), p. 69.
[21]John Byrne, "The Virtual Corporation," *Business Week* (Feb. 8, 1993), p. 103.
[22]Julie Edelson Halpert, "One Car, Worldwide, with Strings Pulled from Michigan," *The New York Times* (Aug. 29, 1993), Sec. 3, p. 7.

SUMMARY

Changes in the political, economic, sociocultural, and technological environments are leading to new strategies in global competition. Cooperative strategies, including global strategic partnerships (GSPs) and the Japanese *keiretsu*, have become more important as companies need to share the high cost of product development, pool skills and know-how, gain access to markets, and find new opportunities for organizational learning. GSPs are distinguished by five attributes: they represent long-term strategies for achieving global leadership; they involve reciprocal relationships; the partners' vision is truly global, extending beyond home markets; they

involve continual lateral transfer of resources; and the partners retain their identities in markets not included in the partnership. Six factors are critical to the success of a GSP: mission, strategy, governance, culture, organization, and management.

In Japan, a unique cooperative strategy in both manufacturing and distribution, known as *keiretsu*, has had enormous significance for the success of Japanese companies, both in Japan and the rest of the world. In the United States, the dawning of the digital age is resulting in *keiretsu*-style alliances among companies in the computer, telecommunications, and entertainment industries. At the same time, some alliances are resulting in the creation of the "virtual corporation," an organization that exists solely in the network of linkages among partners.

DISCUSSION QUESTIONS

1. What are the three key characteristics that distinguish strategic alliances from the broad spectrum of interfirm agreements?

2. What are some of the attributes that distinguish GSPs from traditional joint ventures?
3. What basic factors affect the success of GSPs?
4. What are *keiretsu*? How does this form of industrial structure affect companies that compete with Japan or that are trying to enter the Japanese market?
5. Describe what is meant by a "virtual corporation."

BIBLIOGRAPHY

Books

Bleeke, Joel, and David Ernst. *Collaborating To Compete*. Somerset, N.J.: John Wiley & Sons, 1991.

Carter, John D., Robert Frank Cushman, and C. Scott Hartz. *The Handbook of Joint Venturing*. Homewood, Ill.: Dow Jones Irwin, 1988.

Contractor, Farok, and Peter Lorange. *Cooperative Strategies in International Business*. Cambridge, Mass.: Ballinger, 1987.

Davidow, William H., and Michael S. Malone. *The Virtual Corporation: Structuring and Revitalizing the Corporation for the 21st Century*. New York: HarperBusiness, 1993.

Doorley, Thomas L., III. *Teaming Up for the '90s: A Guide to International Joint Ventures and Strategic Alliances*. New York: Business One Irwin, 1991.

Enen, Jack. *Venturing Abroad: International Business Expansion via Joint Ventures*. Blue Ridge Summit, Penn.: Liberty Hall Press, 1991.

Fruin, Mark. *The Japanese Enterprise System*. Oxford: Oxford University Press, 1992.

Gates, Stephen. *Strategic Alliances: Guidelines for Successful Management*. New York: Conference Board, 1993.

Gerlach, Michael L. *Alliance Capitalism: The Social Organization of Japanese Business*. Berkeley: University of California Press, 1992.

Gillespie, Ian. *Joint Ventures*. London: Eurostudy, 1990.

Lewis, Jordan D. *Partnerships for Profit: Structuring and Managing Strategic Alliances*. New York: Free Press, 1990.

Lindsey, Jennifer. *Joint Ventures and Corporate Partnerships: A Step-by-Step Guide to Forming Strategic Business Alliances*. Chicago: Probus Publishing Co., 1989.

Lynch, Robert. *The Practical Guide to Joint Ventures and Corporate Alliances: How to Form, How to Organize, How to Operate*. New York: Wiley, 1989.

Prestowitz, Clyde V., Jr. *Trading Places: How We Are Giving Our Future to Japan and How to Reclaim It*. New York: Basic Books, 1989.

Robert, Michel. *Strategy Pure and Simple: How Winning CEOs Outthink Their Competition*. New York: McGraw-Hill, 1993.

Starr, Martin Kenneth. *Global Corporate Alliances and the Competitive Edge: Strategies and Tactics for Management*. New York: Quorum Books, 1991.

Articles

Adler, Paul S. "Time-and-Motion Regained," *Harvard Business Review* 71, no. 1 (January–February 1993), pp. 97–108.

Adler, Paul S., and Robert E. Cole. "Designed for Learning: A Tale of Two Auto Plants," *Sloan Management Review* 34, no. 3 (Spring 1993), pp. 85–94.

Ajami, Riad, and Dara Khambata. "Global Strategic Alliances: The New Transnationals." *Journal of Global Marketing* 5, no. 1/2 (1991), pp. 55–69.

Badaracco, Joseph L., Jr. "Alliances Speed Knowledge Transfer." *Planning Review* 19, no. 2 (March–April 1991), pp. 10–16.

Bell, Brian. "Two Separate Teams Should Be Set Up to Facilitate Strategic Alliances." *Journal of Business Strategy* 11, no. 6 (November–December 1990), pp. 63–64.

Bleeke, Joel, and David Ernst. "The Way to Win in Cross-Border Alliances." *Harvard Business Review* 69, no. 6 (November–December 1991), pp. 127–135.

———. "Is Your Strategic Alliance Really a Sale?" *Harvard Business Review* 73, no. 1 (January–February 1995), pp. 97–105.

Blodgett, Linda Longfellow. "Research Notes and Communications Factors in the Instability of International Joint Ventures: An Event Historical Analysis." *Strategic Management Journal* 13, no. 6 (September 1992), pp. 475–481.

Darnall, Robert J. "Inland Steel's Joint Venture from Competitive Gap to Competitive Advantage." *Planning Review* 18, no. 5 (September–October 1990), pp. 10–14.

Erdmann, Peter B. "When Businesses Cross International Borders: Strategic Alliances and Their Alternatives." *Columbia Journal of World Business* 28, no. 2 (Summer 1993), pp. 107–108.

Fedor, Kenneth J., and William B. Werther, Jr. "Making Sense of Cultural Factors in International Alliances." *Organizational Dynamics* 24, no. 4 (Spring 1995), pp. 33–48.

Ferguson, Charles H. "Computers and the Coming of the U.S. *Keiretsu*." *Harvard Business Review* 68, no. 4 (July–August 1990), pp. 55–70.

Flanagan, Patrick. "Strategic Alliances Keep Customers Plugged In." *Management Review* 82, no. 3 (March 1993), pp. 24–26.

Gabor, Andrea. "Rochester Focuses: A Community's Core Competence." *Harvard Business Review* 69, no. 4 (July–August 1991), pp. 116–126.

Gomes-Casseres, Benjamin. "Joint Ventures in the Face of Global Competition." *Sloan Management Review* 30, no. 3 (Spring 1989), pp. 17–26.

Grant, Robert M., R. Krishnan, Abraham B. Shani, and Ron Baer. "Appropriate Manufacturing Technology: A Strategic Approach." *Sloan Management Review* 33, no. 1 (Fall 1991), pp. 43–54.

Haigh, Robert W. "Building a Strategic Alliance—The Hermosillo Experience as a Ford-Mazda Proving Ground." *Columbia Journal of World Business* 27, no. 1 (Spring 1992), pp. 60–74.

Hamel, Gary, Yves L. Doz, and C. K. Prahalad. "Collaborate with Your Competitors—and Win." *Harvard Business Review* 67, no. 1 (January–February 1989), pp. 133–139.

Hamel, Gary, and C. K. Prahalad. "Strategic Alliances: Success or Surrender." Mimeo. London Business School.

Hertzfeld, Jeffrey M. "Joint Ventures: Saving the Soviets from Perestroika." *Harvard Business Review* 69, no. 1 (January–February 1991), pp. 80–91.

Jarillo, J. Carlos, and Howard H. Stevenson. "Co-operative Strategies—The Payoffs and the Pitfalls." *Long Range Planning* 24, no. 1 (February 1991), pp. 64–70.

Johnston, Gerald A. "The Yin and the Yang: Cooperation and Competition in International Business." *Executive Speeches* 7, no. 6 (June–July 1993), pp. 15–17.

Jones, Kevin K., and Walter E. Schill. "Allying for Advantage." *The McKinsey Quarterly* no. 3, pp. 73–101.

Jorde, Thomas M., and David J. Teece. "Competition and Cooperation: Striking the Right Balance." *California Management Review* 31, no. 3 (Spring 1989), pp. 25–37.

Ketelhohn, Werner. "What Do We Mean by Cooperative Advantage?" *European Management Journal* 11, no. 1 (March 1993), pp. 30–37.

Klein, Saul, and Jehiel, Zif. "Global versus Local Strategic Alliances." *Journal of Global Marketing* 8, no. 1 (1994), pp. 51–72.

Kodama, Fumio. "Technology Fusion and the New R&D." *Harvard Business Review* 70, no. 4 (July–August 1992), pp. 70–78.

Kruytbosch, Carla. "Let's Make a Deal." *International Business* 6, no. 3 (March 1993), pp. 92–96.

Lawrence, Paul, and Charalambos Vlachoutsicos. "Joint Ventures in Russia: Put the Locals in Charge." *Harvard Business Review* 71, no. 1 (January–February 1993), pp. 44–51.

Lei, David. "Offensive and Defensive Uses of Alliances." *Long Range Planning* 25, no. 6 (December 1992), pp. 10–17.

Lei, David, and John W. Slocum, Jr. "Global Strategy, Competence-Building and Strategic Alliances." *California Management Review* 35, no. 1 (Fall 1992), pp. 81–97.

Lewis, Jordan D. "Competitive Alliances Redefine Companies." *Management Review* 80, no. 4 (April 1991), pp. 14–18.

———. "The New Power of Strategic Alliances." *Planning Review* 20, no. 5 (September–October 1992), pp. 45–46.

Lodge, George, and Richard Walton. "The American Corporation and Its New Relationships." *California Management Review* 31, no. 3 (Spring 1989), pp. 9–24.

Lorange, Peter, and Johan Roos. "Why Some Strategic Alliances Succeed and Others Fail." *Journal of Business Strategy* 12, no. 1 (January–February 1991), pp. 25–30.

McMillan, John. "Managing Suppliers: Incentive Systems in Japanese and U.S. Industry." *California Management Review* 32, no. 4 (Summer 1990), pp. 38–55.

Michelet, Robert, and Rosemary Remacle. "Forming Successful Strategic Marketing Alliances in Europe." *Journal of European Business* 4, no. 1 (September–October 1992), pp. 11–15.

Mowery, David C., and David J. Teece. "Japan's Growing Capabilities in Industrial Technology: Implications for U.S. Managers and Policymakers." *California Management Review* 35, no. 2 (Winter 1993), pp. 9–34.

Murray, Edwin A., Jr., and John F. Mahon. "Strategic Alliances: Gateway to the New Europe?" *Long Range Planning* 26, no. 4 (August 1993), pp. 102–111.

Niland, Powell. "Case Study—U.S.-Japanese Joint Venture: New United Motor Manufacturing, Inc. (NUMMI)." *Planning Review* 17, no. 1 (January–February 1989), pp. 40–45.

Ohmae, Kenichi. "The Global Logic of Strategic Alliances. *Harvard Business Review* 67, no. 2 (March–April 1989), pp. 143–154.

Olson, Philip D. "Choices for Innovation-Minded Corporations." *Journal of Business Strategy* 11, no. 1 (January–February 1990), pp. 42–46.

Parkhe, Arvind. "Interfirm Diversity, Organizational Learning and Longevity in Global Strategic Alliances." *Journal of International Business Studies* 22, no. 4 (Fourth Quarter 1991), pp. 579–601.

Perlmutter, Howard V., and David A. Heenan. "Cooperate to Compete Globally." *Harvard Business Review* 64, no. 2 (March–April 1986), pp. 136–152.

Robert, Michel. "The Do's and Don'ts of Strategic Alliances." *Journal of Business Strategy* 13, no. 2 (March–April 1992), pp. 50–53.

Rosten, Keith A. "Soviet-U.S. Joint Ventures: Pioneers on a New Frontier." *California Management Review* 33, no. 2 (Winter 1991), pp. 88–108.

Smart, Tim, Pete Engardio, and Geri Smith. "GE's Brave New World," *Business Week* (Nov. 8, 1993), pp. 64–70.

Spencer, William J., and Peter Grindley. "SEMATECH after Five Years: High-Technology Consortia and U.S. Competitiveness." *California Management Review* 35, no. 4 (Summer 1993), pp. 9–35.

Spinks, Stephen O., and Robert C. Stanley. "Joint Ventures under EC Antitrust and Merger Control Rules: Concentrative or Cooperative?" *Journal of European Business* 2, no. 4 (March–April 1991), pp. 29–34.

Thakar, Manab, and Luis Ma. R. Calingo. "Strategic Thinking Is Hip, but Does It Make a Difference?" *Business Horizons* 35, no. 5 (September–October 1992), pp. 47–54.

Voss, Bristol. "Strategic Federations Frequently Falter in Far East. *Journal of Business Strategy* 14, no. 4 (July–August 1993), p. 6.

Wever, Kirsten S., and Christopher S. Allen. "Is Germany a Model for Managers?" *Harvard Business Review* 70, no. 5 (September–October 1992), pp. 36–43.

Yablonsky, Dennis. "The US West/Carnegie Group Strategic Alliance." *Planning Review* 18, no. 5 (September–October 1990), pp. 18–19.

Yoshida, Kosaku. "New Economic Principles in America—Competition and Cooperation: A Comparative Study of the U.S. and Japan. *Columbia Journal of World Business* 26, no. 4 (Winter 1992), pp. 30–44.

*B*eginning January 1, 1997, airline companies based in the EU will be able to fly into more countries and offer lower ticket prices to passengers. The deregulation of air travel is leading to sweeping changes for European carriers such as Lufthansa, British Airways, Alitalia, and KLM. Ownership of many airline companies is shifting from government to private hands as a wave of privatization sweeps across Europe. Also, the carriers are rushing to form strategic alliances as the pace of industry globalization increases. Alliances have been formed between Lufthansa and United, between British Air and USAir, and between Swissair, Delta, and Singapore Air. Some observers expect that within a few years, a handful of mega-carriers will dominate the scene; currently, more than 120 different airlines fly in Europe.

The global strategic alliance between KLM Royal Dutch Airlines and U.S.-based Northwest Airlines is viewed by many as the most successful. The origins of the alliance date back to 1989 when KLM purchased 20 percent of Northwest. Today, combined annual revenues make the alliance partners the third-largest carrier in the world behind American and United. Although only half the size of British Airways and Lufthansa, KLM is now Europe's fastest-growing carrier. KLM's visionary chairman Pieter Bouw has succeeded in cutting costs without firing employees while increasing the percentage of seats filled on each flight. The Dutch government owns only about a third of KLM; the company had a net profit of $298 million in 1994, a year in which government-owned Air France, Alitalia, and Iberia sustained huge losses. For its part, Northwest's $296 million profit in 1994 allowed it to surpass American Airlines in profitability. Meanwhile, the EU has approved billions of dollars in government subsidies to Europe's state-run airlines, including $3.7 billion to Air France in 1994.

Thanks to a 1992 "open-sky" treaty between the United States and the Netherlands, airline companies from both countries have unrestricted rights to fly into each other's markets. The alliance was also granted exemption from U.S. antitrust laws, so the two carriers can set prices jointly. The alliance also allowed Northwest to add seven U.S.–Amsterdam routes on KLM to its schedule. Dozens more KLM routes to Europe, Africa, and Asia are also available to Northwest. For example, Northwest flights are not allowed to land in Rome, but KLM can exercise its privileges as an EU–based company to provide Northwest passengers with service to Rome.

KLM and Northwest also engage in a practice known as "code sharing," whereby each alliance partner can add its two-letter airline identification code to flights operated by the other partner. This can have a significant impact on how international connecting flights are booked, because computer reservation systems are programmed to give higher priority to flights bearing codes from two airlines as opposed to one. Therefore, when booking connections, travel agents

are likely to show preference to alliance partners as opposed to an independent carrier flying the same route. Notes Michael E. Levine, a senior Northwest marketing executive, "We sit down and conspire, we set prices, we share routes— it's wonderful."

Despite the success the KLM-Northwest alliance has enjoyed to date, some industry observers believe some business issues must still be addressed. One airline analyst noted that KLM-Northwest is not widely perceived by the general public as a common entity, something that could be changed with advertising or public relations. Service standards on the two carriers must be harmonized so that passengers are willing to fly on either airline. Due to cultural differences, for example, first-class passengers on KLM receive complimentary Dutch gin in miniature china houses; Northwest passes out rock music CDs. The demeanor of Dutch cabin attendants has been described as "formal," while Northwest's American crews have been described as too "enthusiastic" for European tastes.

There are also objections to the KLM-Northwest alliance on a variety of different grounds. Some object to code sharing. David Schwarte, an attorney for American Airlines, believes the practice may violate antitrust regulations. In his view, code sharing "virtually ensures that the code sharing partner will not launch independent service to compete with the operating partner, and that the two will refrain from lowering fares against one another." Another issue is whether airline companies are rushing into alliances for the wrong reasons. Explains industry consultant Albert DeLauro, "They saw somebody else doing it and got worried about being left out in the cold. Or, they got into it as a hedge. You're seeing people taking shots in the dark."

DISCUSSION QUESTIONS

1. Identify some of the immediate benefits for an American airline company forming an alliance with a European one.
2. How is the global strategic alliance between KLM and Northwest different from a traditional joint venture?
3. Do you think other airlines will follow KLM's example and pursue global alliances of their own?
4. What are some of the internal issues that could yet emerge and threaten to undermine the relationship between KLM and Northwest Airlines?

Sources: Stewart Toy, "Flying High: Why KLM's Global Strategy Is Working," *Business Week* (Feb. 27, 1995), pp. 90–91.
Brian Coleman, "Among European Airlines, the Privatized Soar to the Top," *The Wall Street Journal* (July 21, 1995), p. B4.
Susan Carey, "Flight Patterns: Cross-border Linkups Bring Airlines Range but Uncertain Benefits," *The Wall Street Journal* (June 7, 1995), pp. A1, A5.
Joan M. Feldman, "Cross-border Airline Links: Naughty or Nice?" *Air Transport World* (June 1994), pp. 173–176.
John Tagliabue, "Swissair Plies the Unfriendly Skies of United Europe," *The New York Times* (Sept. 18, 1994), Sec. 3, p. 10.

Strategic Elements of Competitive Advantage

"The only way to gain lasting competitive advantage is to leverage your capabilities around the world so that the company as a whole is greater than the sum of its parts. Being an international company—selling globally, having global brands or operations in different countries—isn't enough."[1]

—CEO David Whitwam, Whirlpool

From its home base in Sweden, Ikea has become a $4 billion global home furnishings powerhouse. With 120 stores in 25 countries, the company's success reflects founder Ingvar Kamprad's vision of selling a wide range of stylish, functional home furnishings at prices so low that the majority of people can afford to buy them. The store exteriors are painted bright blue and yellow—Sweden's national colors. Shoppers view furniture on the main floor in scores of realistic settings arranged throughout the cavernous showrooms. In a departure from standard industry practice, Ikea's furniture bears names such as "Ivar" and "Sten" instead of model numbers. At Ikea, shopping is very much a self-service activity; after browsing and writing down the names of desired items, shoppers can pick up their furniture on the lower level. There they find boxes containing the furniture in kit form; one of the cornerstones of Ikea's strategy is having customers take their purchases home in their own vehicles and assemble the furniture themselves. The lower level of a typical Ikea store also contains a restaurant, a grocery store called the Swede Shop, a supervised play area for children, and a baby care room.

The essence of marketing strategy is successfully relating an organization to its environment. As the horizons of marketers have expanded from domestic to global, so too have the horizons of competitors. The reality in almost every industry today—including home furnishings—is global competition. This fact of life puts an organization under increasing pressure to master techniques for conducting industry analysis and competitor analysis and understanding competitive advantage at both the industry and national levels. These topics are covered in detail in this chapter.

[1]Regina Fazio Maruca, "The Right Way to Go Global: An Interview with Whirlpool CEO David Whitwam," *Harvard Business Review* 72, no. 2 (March–April 1994), p. 135.

INDUSTRY ANALYSIS: FORCES INFLUENCING COMPETITION

A useful way of gaining insight into competitors is through industry analysis. As a working definition, an industry can be defined as a group of firms that produce products that are close substitutes for each other. In any industry, competition works to drive down the rate of return on invested capital toward the rate that would be earned in the economist's "perfectly competitive" industry. Rates of return that are greater than this so-called "competitive" rate will stimulate an inflow of capital either from new entrants or from existing competitors making additional investment. Rates of return below this "competitive" rate will result in withdrawal from the industry and a decline in the levels of activity and competition.

According to Michael E. Porter of Harvard University, a leading theorist of competitive strategy, there are five forces influencing competition in an industry (see Figure 12–1): the threat of new entrants, the threat of substitute products or services, the bargaining power of buyers, the bargaining power of suppliers, and the competitive rivalry between current members of the industry. In industries such as soft drinks, pharmaceuticals, and cosmetics, the favorable nature of the five forces has resulted in attractive returns for competitors. However, pressure from any of the forces can limit profitability, as evidenced by the recent fortunes of some competitors in the personal computer and semiconductor industries. A discussion of each of the five forces follows.

Threat of New Entrants

New entrants to an industry bring new capacity, a desire to gain market share and position, and, very often, new approaches to serving customer needs. The decision to become a new entrant in an industry is often accompanied by a major commitment of resources. New players mean prices will be pushed downward and margins squeezed, resulting in reduced industry profitability in the long run. Porter describes eight major sources of barriers to entry, the presence or absence of which determines the extent of threat of new industry entrants (Porter 1980, 7–33).

The first barrier, **economies of scale,** refers to the decline in per-unit product costs as the absolute volume of production per period increases. Although the concept of scale economies is frequently associated with manufacturing, it is also applicable to R&D, general administration, marketing, and other business functions. Honda's efficiency at engine R&D, for example, results from the wide range of products it produces that feature gasoline-powered engines. When existing firms in an industry achieve significant economies of scale, it becomes difficult for potential new entrants to be competitive.

Product differentiation, the second major entry barrier, is the extent of a product's perceived uniqueness—in other words, whether or not it is a commodity. High levels of

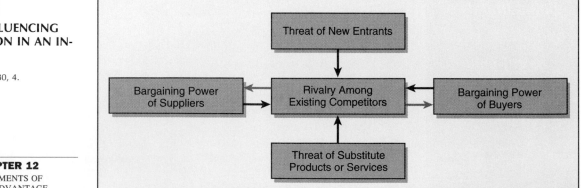

product differentiation and brand loyalty, whether the result of physical product attributes or effective marketing communication, "raise the bar" for would-be industry entrants. For example, managers at Monsanto's G.D. Searle subsidiary achieved differentiation and erected a barrier in the artificial sweetener industry by insisting that the Nutrasweet logo and brand mark—a red and white swirl—appear on diet soft drink cans.[2]

A third entry barrier relates to **capital requirements.** Capital is required not only for manufacturing facilities (fixed capital) but also for financing R&D, advertising, field sales and service, customer credit, and inventories (working capital). The enormous capital requirements in such industries as pharmaceuticals, mainframe computers, chemicals, and mineral extraction present formidable entry barriers.

A fourth barrier to entry involves one-time **switching costs** caused by the need to change suppliers and products. These might include retraining, ancillary equipment costs, the cost of evaluating a new source, and so on. The perceived cost to customers of switching to a new competitor's product may present an insurmountable obstacle preventing industry newcomers from achieving success. For example, Microsoft's huge installed base of PC operating systems and applications presents a formidable entry barrier.

A fifth barrier to entry is access to **distribution channels.** To the extent that channels are full, or unavailable, the cost of entry is substantially increased because a new entrant must create and establish new channels. Some Western companies have encountered this barrier in Japan.

Government policy is frequently a major entry barrier. In some cases, the government will restrict competitive entry. This is true in a number of industries, especially those outside the United States, that have been designated as "national" industries by their respective governments. Japan's postwar industrialization strategy was based on a policy of reserving and protecting national industries in their development and growth phases. The result was a market that proved difficult for non-Japanese competitors to enter, an issue that was targeted by the Clinton administration. American business executives in a wide range of industries urged adoption of a government policy that would reduce some of these barriers and open the Japanese market to more U.S. companies.

Established firms may also enjoy **cost advantages independent of scale economies** that present barriers to entry. Access to raw materials, favorable locations, and government subsidies are several examples.

Finally, expected **competitor response** can be a major entry barrier. If new entrants expect existing competitors to respond strongly to entry, their expectations about the rewards of entry will certainly be affected. A potential competitor's belief that entry into an industry or market will be an unpleasant experience may serve as a strong deterrent. Bruce Henderson, former president of the Boston Consulting Group, used the term "brinkmanship" to describe a recommended approach for deterring competitive entry. Brinkmanship occurs when industry leaders convince potential competitors that any market entry effort will be countered with vigorous and unpleasant responses.

G.D. Searle used brinkmanship—especially price cuts—to deter competitors from entering the low-calorie artificial sweetener market as Nutrasweet's patents expired. At the end of 1989, Systse T. Kuipers, a marketing manager at Holland Sweetener Company, complained that "it is a bloody fight and everybody's losing money. [Nutrasweet managers] go for the last kilo even if they have to give the product away." In Kuipers' view, G.D. Searle's tactic of deep price cuts on Nutrasweet had "the sole intent of chasing competitors out of the marketplace."[3] In fact, several European producers have already abandoned the business, proof that G.D. Searle's policy of brinkmanship was an effective competitive response to the threat of new entrants.

---

[2]Eben Shapiro, "Nutrasweet's Bitter Fight," *The New York Times* (Nov. 19, 1989), p. C4.
[3]Ibid.

Threat of Substitute Products

A second force influencing competition in an industry is the threat of substitute products. The availability of substitute products places limits on the prices market leaders can charge in an industry; high prices may induce buyers to switch to the substitute.

Similarly, G.D. Searle enjoyed near-monopoly profits on sales of its Nutrasweet-brand aspartame sweetener thanks to patent protection and a track record for quality and safety. As patents expired around the world (the U.S. patent expired in December 1992), Nutrasweet was forced to cut prices to preserve market share. Besides facing a threat from makers of generic aspartame, a new generation of artificial sweeteners is waiting in the wings. One product, Johnson & Johnson's sucralose, offers the benefit of longer shelf life compared to aspartame.[4] For the first time, the threat of substitute products represents a significant negative competitive force for Nutrasweet.

Bargaining Power of Buyers

The ultimate aim of industrial customers is to pay the lowest possible price to obtain the products or services that it uses as inputs. Usually, therefore, the buyers' best interests are served if they can drive down profitability in the supplier industry. To accomplish this, the buyers have to gain leverage over firms in the supplier industry. One way they can do this is to purchase in such large quantities that supplier firms depend on the buyers' business for survival. Second, when the suppliers' products are viewed as commodities—that is, as standard or undifferentiated—buyers are likely to bargain hard for low prices, since many firms can meet their needs. Buyers will also bargain hard when the supplier industry's products or services represent a significant portion of the buying firms' costs. A fourth source of buyer power is the willingness and ability to achieve backward integration.

Nutrasweet is affected both positively and negatively by several of the factors associated with buyer bargaining power. Soft drink bottlers such as PepsiCo and Coca-Cola are major buyers of Nutrasweet, which historically was the most expensive ingredient in diet soft drinks. As Nutrasweet's patents expired, the soft drink giants' bargaining power increased as they sought sharply lower prices for this key ingredient. While the soft drink makers buy in large quantities, Nutrasweet is used in more than 5,000 products—a fact that diminishes buyer power by reducing the leverage associated with losing one or a few buyers. Coca-Cola's buyer power is also enhanced because it has developed and patented its own low-calorie sweetener.

Bargaining Power of Suppliers

Supplier power over industry firms is the flip side of the coin of buyer power. If suppliers have enough leverage over industry firms, they can raise prices high enough to significantly influence the profitability of their organizational customers. Suppliers' ability to gain leverage over industry firms is determined by several factors. Suppliers will have the advantage if they are large and relatively few in number. Second, when the suppliers' products or services are important inputs to user firms, are highly differentiated, or carry switching costs, the suppliers will have considerable leverage over buyers. Suppliers will also enjoy bargaining power if their business is not threatened by alternative products. A fourth source of supplier power is the willingness and ability of suppliers to develop their own products and brand names if they are unable to get satisfactory terms from industry buyers.

Rivalry among Competitors

Rivalry among firms refers to all the actions taken by firms in the industry to improve their positions and gain advantage over each other. Rivalry manifests itself in price competition, advertising battles, product positioning, and attempts at differentiation. To the

[4]Eben Shapiro, "Nutrasweet's Race with the Calendar," *The New York Times* (Apr. 8, 1992), p. C1.

extent that rivalry among firms forces companies to rationalize costs, it is a positive force. To the extent that it drives down prices, and therefore profitability, and creates instability in the industry, it is a negative factor. Several factors can create intense rivalry. Once an industry becomes mature, firms focus on market share and how it can be gained at the expense of others. Second, industries characterized by high fixed costs are always under pressure to keep production at full capacity to cover the fixed costs. Once the industry accumulates excess capacity, the drive to fill capacity will push prices—and profitability—down. A third factor affecting rivalry is lack of differentiation or an absence of switching costs, which encourages buyers to treat the products or services as commodities and shop for the best prices. Again, there is downward pressure on prices and profitability. Fourth, firms with high strategic stakes in achieving success in an industry generally are destabilizing because they may be willing to accept unreasonably low profit margins to establish themselves, hold position, or expand.

COMPETITIVE ADVANTAGE

Competitive advantage exists when there is a match between a firm's distinctive competencies and the factors critical for success within its industry. Any superior match between company competencies and customers' needs permits the firm to outperform competitors. There are two basic ways to achieve competitive advantage. First, a firm can pursue a low-cost strategy that enables it to offer products at lower prices than do competitors. Competitive advantage may also be gained by a strategy of differentiating products so that customers perceive unique benefits that justify a premium price. Note that both strategies have the same effect: They increase the perceived benefits that accrue to customers (Porter 1985).

The quality of a firm's strategy is ultimately decided by customer perception. Operating results such as sales and profits are measures that depend on the level of psychological value created for customers: The greater the perceived consumer value, the better the strategy. A firm may market a better mousetrap, but the ultimate success of the product depends on customers deciding for themselves whether to buy it. Value is like beauty—it's in the eye of the beholder. In sum, competitive advantage is achieved by creating more value than does the competition, and value is defined by customer perception.

Two different models of competitive advantage have received considerable attention. The first offers "generic strategies," four routes or paths that organizations choose to offer superior value and achieve competitive advantage. According to the second model, generic strategies alone don't account for the astonishing success of many Japanese companies in recent years. The more recent model, based on the concept of "strategic intent," proposes four different sources of competitive advantage. Both models are discussed subsequently.

Generic Strategies for Creating Competitive Advantage

In addition to the "five forces" model of industry competition, Michael Porter has developed a framework of so-called generic business strategies based on the two types or sources of competitive advantage mentioned previously: *low cost* and *differentiation*. Figure 12–2 on page 260 shows that the combination of these two sources with the scope of the target market served (narrow or broad) or product mix width (narrow or wide) yields four **generic strategies:** cost leadership, product differentiation, cost focus, and focused differentiation.

Generic strategies aiming at the achievement of competitive advantage or superior marketing strategy demand that the firm make choices. The choices concern the **type** of competitive advantage it seeks to attain (based on cost or differentiation) and the **market scope** or **product mix width** within which competitive advantage will be attained (Porter 1985, (12)). The nature of the choice between types of advantage and market scope is a gam-

FIGURE 12–2

GENERIC COMPETITIVE
STRATEGIES

Source: Porter 1990, 39.

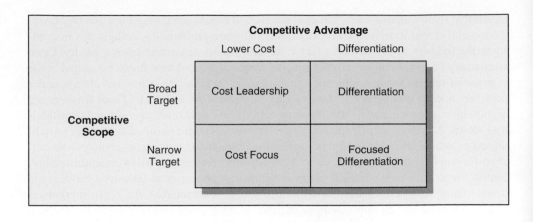

ble, and it is the nature of every gamble that it entails *risk*: By choosing a given generic strategy, a firm always risks making the wrong choice.

BROAD MARKET STRATEGIES: COST LEADERSHIP AND DIFFERENTIATION • **Cost leadership advantage** is based on a firm's position as the industry's low-cost producer, in broadly defined markets or across a wide mix of products. This strategy has become increasingly popular in recent years as a result of the popularization of the experience curve concept. In general, a firm that bases its competitive strategy on overall cost leadership must construct the most efficient facilities (in terms of scale or technology) and obtain the largest share of market so that its cost per unit is the lowest in the industry. These advantages, in turn, give the producer a substantial lead in terms of experience with building the product. Experience then leads to more refinements of the entire process of production, delivery, and service, which leads to further cost reductions.

Whatever its source, cost leadership advantage can be the basis for offering lower prices (and more value) to customers in the late, more-competitive stages of the product life cycle. In Japan, companies in a range of industries—35mm cameras, consumer electronics and entertainment equipment, motorcycles, and automobiles—have achieved cost leadership on a worldwide basis.

Cost leadership, however, is a sustainable source of competitive advantage only if barriers exist that prevent competitors from achieving the same low costs. In an era of increasing technological improvements in manufacturing, manufacturers constantly leapfrog over one another in pursuit of lower costs. At one time, for example, IBM enjoyed the low-cost advantage in the production of computer printers. Then Japanese companies took the same technology and, after reducing production costs and improving product reliability, gained the low-cost advantage. IBM fought back with a highly automated printer plant in North Carolina, where the number of component parts was slashed by more than 50 percent and robots were used to snap many components into place. Despite these changes, IBM ultimately chose to exit the business; the plant was sold.

When a firm's product has an actual or perceived uniqueness in a broad market, it is said to have a **differentiation advantage.** This can be an extremely effective strategy for defending market position and obtaining above-average financial returns; unique products often command premium prices. Examples of successful differentiation include Maytag in large home appliances, Caterpillar in construction equipment, and almost any successful branded consumer product. IBM traditionally has differentiated itself with a strong sales/service organization and the security of the IBM standard in a world of rapid obsolescence. (Unfortunately for IBM, as customer preferences have shifted away from mainframes, IBM's differentiation advantage has eroded.) Among athletic shoe manufacturers, Nike stands out as the technological leader thanks to unique product features found in a wide array of shoes.

NARROW TARGET STRATEGIES: COST FOCUS AND FOCUSED DIFFEREN-TIATION • The preceding discussion of cost leadership and differentiation considered only the impact on broad markets. By contrast, strategies to achieve a narrow focus advantage target a narrowly defined market/customer. This advantage is based on an ability to create more customer value for a narrowly targeted segment and results from a better understanding of customer needs and wants. A narrow-focus strategy can be combined with either cost- or differentiation-advantage strategies. In other words, while a *cost focus* means offering a narrow target market low prices, a firm pursuing *focused differentiation* will offer a narrow target market the perception of product uniqueness at a premium price.

The German *Mittelstand* companies discussed in Chapter 9 have been extremely successful pursuing **focused differentiation** strategies backed by a strong export effort. The world of "high-end" audio equipment offers another example of focused differentiation. A few hundred companies, in the United States and elsewhere, make speakers and amplifiers and related hi-fi gear that cost thousands of dollars per component. While audio components as a whole represent a $21 billion market worldwide, annual sales in the high-end segment are only $1 billion. In Japan alone, discriminating audiophiles purchase $200 million in high-end audio equipment each year—much of it U.S. made. The weak dollar and increases in disposable income in Japan and other Pacific Rim countries have provided opportunities for U.S. consumer electronics companies. Also, the U.S. companies are learning more about their overseas customers and building relationships with distributors outside the United States.[5]

The final strategy is **cost focus,** when a firm's lower cost position enables it to offer a narrow target market lower prices than does the competition. In the shipbuilding industry, for example, Polish and Chinese shipyards offer simple, standard vessel types at low prices that reflect low production costs (Porter 1990, 39). Ikea, the Swedish furniture company described in the chapter introduction, is a perfect example of the cost focus strategy. Notes George Bradley, president of Levitz Furniture in Boca Raton, Florida, "[Ikea] has really made a splash. They're going to capture their niche in every city they go into." Of course, such a strategy can be risky. As Bradley explains, "Their market is finite because it is so narrow. If you don't want contemporary, knock-down furniture, it's not for you. So it takes a certain customer to buy it. And remember, fashions change."[6]

The issue of sustainability is central to this strategy concept. As noted, cost leadership is a sustainable source of competitive advantage only if barriers exist that prevent competitors from achieving the same low costs. Sustained differentiation depends on continued perceived value and the absence of imitation by competitors (Porter 1980, 158). Several factors determine whether focus can be sustained as a source of competitive advantage. First, a cost focus is sustainable if a firm's competitors are defining their target markets more broadly. A focuser doesn't try to be all things to all people: Competitors may diminish their advantage by trying to satisfy the needs of a broader market segment—a strategy that, by definition, means a blunter focus. Second, a firm's differentiation focus advantage is only sustainable if competitors cannot define the segment even more narrowly. Also, focus can be sustained if competitors cannot overcome barriers that prevent imitation of the focus strategy, and if consumers in the target segment do not migrate to other segments that the focuser doesn't serve.

Creating Competitive Advantage via Strategic Intent

An alternative framework for understanding competitive advantage focuses on competitiveness as a function of the pace at which a company implants new advantages deep within its organization. This framework identifies **strategic intent,** growing out of ambi-

---

[5]Jared Sandberg, "High-End Audio Entices Music Lovers," *The Wall Street Journal* (Feb. 12, 1993), p. B1.
[6]Jeffrey A. Trachtenberg, "Home Economics: Ikea Furniture Chain Pleases with Its Prices, not with Its Service," *The Wall Street Journal* (Sept. 17, 1991), pp. A1, A5.

THE REST OF THE STORY

■ IKEA

*I*kea's approach to the furniture business has enabled it to rack up impressive growth in a $30 billion industry where overall sales have been flat. Sourcing furniture from more than 2,300 suppliers in 70 countries helps the company maintain its low-cost position. During the 1990s, Ikea opened several stores in Central and Eastern Europe. Because many consumers in those regions have relatively low purchasing power, the stores offer a smaller selection of goods; some furniture was designed specifically for the cramped living styles typical in former Soviet bloc countries. Throughout Europe, Ikea benefits from the perception that Sweden is the source of high-quality products. The United Kingdom represents the fastest-growing market in Europe; Ikea's London store has achieved annual sales growth of 20 percent. Germany currently accounts for more than one-quarter of Ikea's total revenues; store openings are planned in Berlin, Dresden, Leipzig, and other cities in the former East Germany.

Industry observers predict that the United States will eventually be Ikea's largest market. The company opened its first U.S. store in Philadelphia in 1985; today, Ikea has more than two dozen outlets—most on the East Coast—that generate $500 million in annual sales. Notes Jeff Young, chief operating officer of Lexington Furniture Industries, "Ikea is on the way to becoming the Wal-Mart Stores of the home-furnishing industry. If you're in this business, you'd better take a look." Some American customers, however, are irked to find popular items sometimes out of stock. Another problem is the long lines resulting from the company's no-frills approach. Complained one shopper, "Great idea, poor execution. The quality of much of what they sell is good, but the hassles make you question whether it's worth it."

Goran Carstedt, president of Ikea North America, responds to such criticism by referring to the company's mission. "If we offered more services, our prices would go up," he explains. "Our customers understand our philosophy, which calls for each of us to do a little in order to save a lot. They value our low prices. And almost all of them say they will come back again." To keep them coming back, Ikea is spending between $25 million and $35 million on advertising to get its message across. While it is a common industry practice to rely heavily on newspaper and radio advertising, two-thirds of Ikea's North American advertising budget is allocated for TV. John Sitnik, an executive at Ikea's U.S. Inc., says, "We distanced ourselves from the other furniture stores. We decided TV is something we can own."

Sources: Loretta Roach, "Ikea: Furnishing the World," *Discount Merchandiser* (October 1994), pp. 46, 48.
"Furnishing the World," *The Economist* (Nov. 19, 1994), pp. 79–80.
Jeffrey A. Trachtenberg, "Home Economics: Ikea Furniture Chain Pleases with Its Prices, not with Its Service," *The Wall Street Journal* (Sept. 17, 1991), pp. A1, A5.
Jack Burton, "Rearranging the Furniture," *International Management* (September 1991), pp. 58–61.
Ela Schwartz, "The Swedish Invasion," *Discount Merchandiser* (July 1990), pp. 52, 56.
Lisa Marie Petersen, "The 1992 Client Media All-Stars: John Sitnik, Ikea," *Mediaweek* (Dec. 12, 1992), pp. 25+.

tion and obsession with winning, as the means for achieving competitive advantage. Writing in the *Harvard Business Review*, Gary Hamel and C. K. Prahalad note:

> Few competitive advantages are long lasting. Keeping score of existing advantages is not the same as building new advantages. The essence of strategy lies in creating tomorrow's competitive advantages faster than competitors mimic the ones you possess today. An organization's capacity to improve existing skills and learn new ones is the most defensible competitive advantage of all. (Hamel & Prahalad 1989, 69; see also Hamel & Prahalad 1990, 79–91)

This approach is founded on the principles of W. E. Deming, who stressed that a company must commit itself to continuing improvement in order to be a winner in a competitive struggle. For years, Deming's message fell on deaf ears in the United States, while the Japanese heeded his message and benefited tremendously. Japan's most prestigious business award is named after him. Finally, however, U.S. manufacturers are starting to respond.

The significance of Hamel and Prahalad's framework becomes evident when comparing Caterpillar and Komatsu. As noted earlier, Caterpillar is a classic example of differentiation: The company became the largest manufacturer of earthmoving equipment in the world because it was fanatical about quality and service. Caterpillar's success as a global marketer has enabled it to achieve a 35 percent share of the worldwide market for earthmoving equipment—more than half of which represents sales to developing countries. The differentiation advantage was achieved with product durability, global spare parts service (including guaranteed parts delivery anywhere in the world within 48 hours), and a strong network of loyal dealers.

Caterpillar faced a very challenging set of environmental forces during the past decade. Many of Caterpillar's plants were closed by a lengthy strike in the early 1980s; a world-wide recession at the same time caused a downturn in the construction industry. This hurt companies that were Caterpillar customers. In addition, the strong dollar gave a cost advantage to foreign rivals.

Compounding Caterpillar's problems was a new competitive threat from Japan. Komatsu was the world's number two construction equipment company and had been competing with Caterpillar in the Japanese market for years. Komatsu's products were generally acknowledged to offer a lower level of quality. The rivalry took on a new dimension after Komatsu adopted the slogan "*Maru-c*," meaning "encircle Caterpillar." Emphasizing quality and taking advantage of low labor costs and the strong dollar, Komatsu surpassed Caterpillar as number one in earthmoving equipment in Japan and made serious inroads in the United States and other markets. Yet the company continued to develop new sources of competitive advantage even after it achieved world-class quality. For example, new product development cycles were shortened, and manufacturing was consolidated. Caterpillar struggled to sustain its competitive advantage because many customers found that Komatsu's combination of quality, durability, and lower price created compelling value. Yet even as recession and a strong yen put new pressure on Komatsu, the company sought new opportunities by diversifying into machine tools and robots.[7]

The Komatsu/Caterpillar saga is just one example of how global competitive battles are shaped by more than the pursuit of generic strategies. Many firms have gained competitive advantage by *disadvantaging* rivals through "competitive innovation." Hamel and Prahalad define *competitive innovation* as "the art of containing competitive risks within manageable proportions" and identify four successful approaches utilized by Japanese competitors. These are: building layers of advantage, searching for loose bricks, changing the rules of engagement, and collaborating.

Ikea's management understands that young adults who shop for furniture often bring the family. Child care, strollers, and free diapers are available to Ikea customers. (Courtesy of Ikea U.S., Inc. Photo by Hayden Saunders/*Image*.)

LAYERS OF ADVANTAGE • A company faces less risk in competitive encounters if it has a wide portfolio of advantages. Successful companies steadily build such portfolios by establishing layers of advantage on top of one another. Komatsu is an excellent example of this approach. Another is the TV industry in Japan. By 1970, Japan was not only the world's largest producer of black-and-white TV sets but was also well on its way to becoming the leader in producing color sets. The main competitive advantage for such companies as Matsushita at that time was low labor costs.

Because they realized that their cost advantage could be temporary, the Japanese also added an additional layer of *quality and reliability* advantage by building plants large enough to serve world markets. Much of this output did not carry the manufacturer's brand name. For example, Matsushita Electric sold products to other companies such as RCA that marketed them under their own brand names. Matsushita was pursuing a simple idea: A product sold was a product sold, no matter whose label it carried.[8]

[7]Robert L. Rose and Masayoshi Kanabayashi, "Komatsu Throttles Back on Construction Equipment," *The Wall Street Journal* (May 13, 1992), p. B4.
[8]James Lardner, *Fast Forward: Hollywood, the Japanese, and the VCR Wars* (New York: New American Library, 1987), p. 135.

Caterpillar spent billions of dollars on factory improvements in a successful effort to head off a competitive threat by Komatsu. (Photo courtesy Caterpillar, Inc.)

In order to build the next layer of advantage, Japanese companies spent the 1970s investing heavily in marketing channels and Japanese brand names to gain recognition. This strategy added yet another layer of competitive advantage: the *global brand franchise*—that is, a global customer base. By the late 1970s, channels and brand awareness were established well enough to support the introduction of new products that could benefit from global marketing—VCRs and photocopy machines, for example. Finally, many companies have invested in *regional manufacturing* so their products can be differentiated and better adapted to customer needs in individual markets.

The process of building layers illustrates how a company can move along the value chain to strengthen competitive advantage. The Japanese began with manufacturing (an upstream value activity) and moved on to marketing (a downstream value activity) and then back upstream to basic R&D. All of these sources of competitive advantage represent mutually reinforcing layers that are accumulated over time.

LOOSE BRICKS • A second approach takes advantage of the "loose bricks" left in the defensive walls of competitors whose attention is narrowly focused on a market segment or a geographic area. For example, Caterpillar's attention was focused elsewhere when Komatsu made its first entry into the Eastern Europe market. A similar chain of events occurred in the global motorcycle industry. For many years, Harley-Davidson focused its efforts on large motorcycles. Thus it was not concerned when Honda first entered the U.S. motorcycle market with exports of bikes with small (50cc) engines. Managers at Harley weren't aware of—or didn't appreciate the significance of—Honda's involvement with racing larger bikes in Europe. But Honda used this approach to gain important experience in large-displacement engine design and technology. Harley was caught off guard, and by 1983 Honda had more than 50 percent of the U.S. market share of motorcycles with 700cc or larger engines.

That same year, import quotas were imposed on large motorcycles imported into the United States. Even though the quotas helped save Harley from extinction, Honda was already using its core competence in engines to diversify. It created engines for other products, starting with cars. The first Honda Civic models were powered by overhead cam motorcycle engines. Today, Honda boasts a wide product mix that includes lawnmowers, outboard marine motors, welders, and generators—in short, anything powered by a gasoline engine. This approach, as noted earlier, allows Honda to enjoy significant scale economies in R&D and production. Harley-Davidson eventually reshaped itself by dramatically improving product quality and has successfully won back much of its lost market share.

CHANGING THE RULES • A third approach involves changing the so-called "rules of engagement" and refusing to play by the rules set by industry leaders. For example, in the copier market, IBM and Kodak imitated the marketing strategies used by market leader Xerox. Meanwhile Canon, a Japanese challenger, wrote a new rulebook.

While Xerox built a wide range of copiers, Canon built standardized machines and components, reducing manufacturing costs. While Xerox employed a huge direct sales force, Canon chose to distribute through office product dealers. Canon also designed serviceability, as well as reliability, into its products so that it could rely on dealers for service rather than incurring the expense required to create a national service network. Canon further decided to sell rather than lease its machines, freeing the company from the burden of financing the lease base. In another major departure, Canon targeted its copiers at secretaries and department managers rather than at the heads of corporate duplicating operations (Hamel and Prahalad 1989, 69).

Canon introduced the first full-color copiers and the first copiers with "connectivity"—the ability to print images from such sources as video camcorders and computers. The results have been impressive; in 1994, Canon's share of the U.S color copier market was 64 percent. In both 1988 and 1992, Canon was granted more U.S. patents than any other company in the world. The Canon example shows how an innovative marketing strategy—with fresh approaches to the product, pricing, distribution, and selling— can lead to overall competitive advantage in the marketplace. Canon is not invulnerable, however; in 1991, Tektronix, a *U.S.* company, leapfrogged past Canon in the color copier market by introducing a plain-paper color copier that offered sharper copies at a much lower price.[9]

COLLABORATING • A final source of competitive advantage is using know-how developed by other companies. Such collaboration may take the form of licensing agreements, joint ventures, or partnerships. History has shown that Japanese companies have excelled at using the collaborating strategy to achieve industry leadership. As noted in Chapter 10, one of the legendary licensing agreements of modern business history is Sony's licensing of transistor technology from AT&T's Western Electric subsidiary in the 1950s for $25,000. This agreement gave Sony access to the transistor and allowed the company to become a world leader. Building on its initial successes in the manufacturing and marketing of portable radios, Sony has grown into a superb global marketer whose name is synonymous with a wide assortment of high-quality consumer electronics products.

More recent examples of Japanese collaboration are found in the aircraft industry. Today, Mitsubishi Heavy Industries Ltd. and other Japanese companies manufacture airplanes under license to U.S. firms and also work as subcontractors for aircraft parts and systems. Many observers fear that the future of the U.S. aircraft industry may be jeopar-

---

[9]G. Pascal Zachary, "Color Printer Gives Tektronix Jump on Canon," *The Wall Street Journal* (June 14, 1991), p. B1.

Innovation has enabled U.S.-based Tektronix to succeed in the global color printer and copier market against strong Japanese competitors such as Canon. (Ad reproduced with permission of Tektronix.)

[10] Hamel and Prahalad have continued to refine and develop the concept of strategic intent since it was first introduced in their ground-breaking 1989 article. Recently the authors outlined four broad categories of resource leverage that managers can use to achieve their aspirations: concentrating resources on strategic goals via convergence and focus; accumulating resources more efficiently via extracting and borrowing; complementing one resource with another by blending and balancing; and conserving resources by recycling, co-opting, and shielding. (From Hamel & Prahalad 1993, 75–85)

[11] This section draws heavily on Chapter 3, "Determinants of National Competitive Advantage," and Chapter 4, "The Dynamics of National Advantage," in Porter 1990.

dized as the Japanese gain technological expertise. Various examples of "collaborative advantage" are discussed in detail in the next section.[10]

GLOBAL COMPETITION AND NATIONAL COMPETITIVE ADVANTAGE[11]

An inevitable consequence of the expansion of global marketing activity is the growth of competition on a global basis. In industry after industry, global competition is a critical factor affecting success. In some industries, global companies have virtually excluded all other companies from their markets. An example is the detergent industry where three companies—Colgate, Unilever, and Procter & Gamble—dominate an increasing number of detergent markets in Latin America and the Pacific Rim. Many companies can make a quality detergent, but brand-name muscle and the skills required for quality packaging overwhelm local competition in market after market.[12]

The automobile industry has also become fiercely competitive on a global basis. Part of the reason for the initial success of foreign automakers in the United States was the reluctance—or inability—of U.S. manufacturers to design and manufacture high-quality, inexpensive small cars. The resistance of U.S. manufacturers was based on the economics of car production: the bigger the car, the higher the list price. Under this formula, small cars meant smaller unit profits. Therefore, U.S. manufacturers resisted the increasing preference in the U.S. market for smaller cars—a classic case of ethnocentrism and management myopia. European and Japanese manufacturers' product lines have always included cars smaller than those made in the United States. In Europe and Japan, market conditions were much different than in the United States: less space, high taxes on engine displacement and on fuel, and greater market interest in functional design and engineering innovations. First Volkswagen, then Japanese automakers such as Nissan and Toyota discovered a growing demand for their cars in the U.S. market. It is noteworthy that many significant innovations and technical advances—including radial tires, antilock breaks, and fuel injection—also came from Europe and Japan. Airbags are a notable exception.

The effect of global competition has been highly beneficial to consumers around the world. In the two examples cited—detergents and automobiles—consumers have benefited. In Central America, detergent prices have fallen as a result of global competition. In the United States, foreign companies have provided consumers with the automobile products, performance, and price characteristics they wanted. If smaller, lower-priced imported cars had not been available, it is unlikely that Detroit manufacturers would have provided a comparable product as quickly. What is true for automobiles in the United States is true for every product class around the world. Global competition expands the range of products and increases the likelihood that consumers will get what they want.

The downside of global competition is its impact on the producers of goods and services. Global competition creates value for consumers, but it also has the potential to destroy jobs and profits. When a company offers consumers in other countries a better product at a lower price, this company takes customers away from domestic suppliers. Unless the domestic supplier can create new values and find new customers, the jobs and livelihoods of the domestic supplier's employees are threatened.

This section addresses the following issue: Why is a particular nation a good home base for specific industries? Why, for example, is the United States the home base for the leading competitors in PCs, software, credit cards, and movies? Why is Germany the home of so many world leaders in printing presses, chemicals, and luxury cars? Why are so many leading pharmaceutical, chocolate/confectionery, and trading companies located in Switzerland? Why are the world leaders in consumer electronics home based in Japan?

According to Porter (1990), the presence or absence of particular attributes in individual countries influences industry development, not just the ability of individual firms to create core competencies and competitive advantage. Porter describes these attributes— factor conditions; demand conditions; related and supporting industries; and firm strategy,

[12]See Joseph Kahn, "Cleaning Up: P&G Viewed China as a National Market and Is Conquering It," *The Wall Street Journal* (Sept. 12, 1995), pp. A1, A6.

structure, and rivalry—in terms of a national "diamond" (see Figure 12–3). The diamond shapes the environment in which firms compete.

Factor Conditions

The phrase *factor conditions* refers to a country's endowment with resources. Factor resources may have been created or inherited, and may be divided into five categories: human, physical, knowledge, capital, and infrastructure.

Human Resources • The quantity of workers available, the skills possessed by these workers, the wage levels, and the overall work ethic of the workforce together constitute a nation's human resource factor. Countries with a plentiful supply of low-wage workers have an obvious advantage in the production of labor-intensive products. On the other hand, such countries may be at a *disadvantage* when it comes to the production of sophisticated products requiring highly skilled workers capable of working without extensive supervision.

Physical Resources • The availability, quantity, quality, and cost of land, water, minerals, and other natural resources determine a country's physical resources. A country's size and location are also included in this category, since proximity to markets and sources of supply, as well as transportation costs, are strategic considerations. These factors are obviously important advantages or disadvantages to industries dependent on natural resources.

Knowledge Resources • The availability within a nation of a significant population having scientific, technical, and market-related knowledge means that the nation is endowed with knowledge resources. The presence of this factor is usually a function of the number of research facilities and universities—both government and private—operating in the country. This factor is important to success in sophisticated products and services, and to doing business in sophisticated markets. This factor relates directly to Germany's leadership in chemicals; for some 150 years, Germany has been home to top university chemistry programs, advanced scientific journals, and apprenticeship programs.

Capital Resources • Countries vary in the availability, amount, cost, and types of capital available to the country's industries. The nation's savings rate, interest rates, tax laws,

FIGURE 12–3

DETERMINANTS OF NATIONAL ADVANTAGE

Source: Porter 1990, 72.

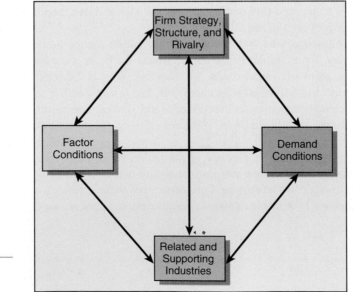

and government deficit all affect the availability of this factor. The advantage enjoyed by industries in countries with low capital costs versus those located in nations with relatively high capital costs is sometimes decisive. Firms paying high capital costs are frequently unable to stay in a market where the competition comes from a nation with low capital costs. The firms with the low cost of capital can keep their prices low and force the firms paying high costs to either accept low returns on investment or leave the industry.

Infrastructure Resources • Infrastructure includes a nation's banking system, health care system, transportation system, communications system, as well as the availability and cost of using these systems. More sophisticated industries are more dependent on advanced infrastructures for success.

Competitive advantage accrues to a nation's industry if the mix of factors available to the industry is such that it facilitates pursuit of a generic strategy: low-cost production or the production of a highly differentiated product or service. Competitive advantage may also be created indirectly by nations that have selective factor *disadvantages*. For example, the absence of suitable labor may force firms to develop forms of mechanization that give the nation's firms an advantage. High transportation costs may motivate firms to develop new materials that are less expensive to transport.

Demand Conditions

The nature of home demand conditions for the firm's or industry's products and services is important because it determines the rate and nature of improvement and innovation by the firms in the nation. These are the factors that either train firms for world-class competition or fail to adequately prepare them to compete in the global marketplace. Four characteristics of home demand are particularly important to creation of competitive advantage: the composition of home demand, the size and pattern of growth of home demand, rapid home market growth, and the means by which a nation's home demand pulls the nation's products and services into foreign markets.

Composition of Home Demand • It is this that determines how firms perceive, interpret, and respond to buyer needs. Competitive advantage can be achieved when the home demand sets the quality standard and gives local firms a better picture of buyer needs, at an earlier time, than is available to foreign rivals. This advantage is enhanced when home buyers pressure the nation's firms to innovate quickly and frequently. The basis for advantage is the fact that the nation's firms can stay ahead of the market when they are more sensitive to and more responsive to home demand, and when that demand, in turn, reflects or anticipates world demand.

Size and Pattern of Growth of Home Demand • These are important only if the composition of the home demand is sophisticated and anticipates foreign demand. Large home markets offer opportunities to achieve economies of scale and learning while dealing with familiar, comfortable markets. There is less apprehension about investing in large-scale production facilities and expensive R&D programs when the home market is sufficient to absorb the increased capacity. If the home demand accurately reflects or anticipates foreign demand, and if the firms do not become content with serving the home market, the existence of large-scale facilities and programs will be an advantage in global competition.

Rapid Home Market Growth • This is another incentive to invest in and adopt new technologies faster, and to build large, efficient facilities. The best example of this is in Japan, where rapid home market growth provided the incentive for Japanese firms to

conditions in the diamond shown in Figure 12–3. The nation with the most favorable diamond, however, will be the one most likely to take advantage of these events and convert them into competitive advantage. For example, Canadian researchers were the first to isolate insulin, but they could not convert this breakthrough into an internationally competitive product. Firms in the United States and Denmark were able to do that because of their respective national diamonds.

Government

Although it is often argued that government is a major determinant of national competitive advantage, the fact is that government is not a determinant, but rather an influence on determinants. Government influences determinants by virtue of its role as a buyer of products and services, and by its role as a maker of policies on labor, education, capital formation, natural resources, and product standards. It also influences determinants by its role as a regulator of commerce, for example, by telling banks and telephone companies what they can and cannot do.

By reinforcing determinants in industries where a nation has competitive advantage, government improves the competitive position of the nation's firms. Governments devise legal systems that influence competitive advantage by means of tariffs and nontariff barriers and laws requiring local content and labor. In the United States, for example, the dollar's decline over the past decade has been due in part to a deliberate policy to enhance U.S. export flows and stem imports. In other words, government can improve or lessen competitive advantage, but it cannot create it.

The System of Determinants of National Competitive Advantage

It is important to view the determinants of national competitive advantage as an interactive system where activity in any one of the four points of the diamond impacts on all the others and vice versa. This interplay between the determinants is depicted in Figures 12–4A and B. The interaction of all the forces is presented in Figure 12–5.

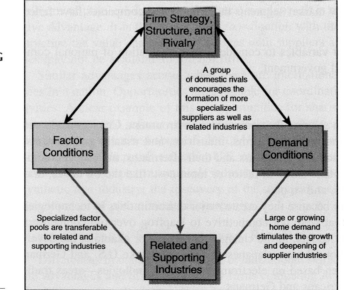

FIGURE 12–4A

INFLUENCES ON THE DEVELOPMENT OF RELATED AND SUPPORTING INDUSTRIES

Source: Porter 1990, 139.

STRATEGIC ELEMENTS OF
COMPETITIVE ADVANTAGE

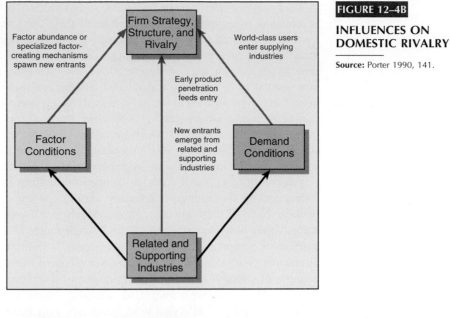

FIGURE 12–4B

INFLUENCES ON
DOMESTIC RIVALRY

Source: Porter 1990, 141.

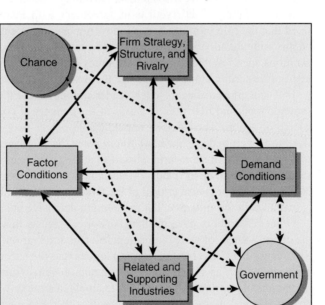

FIGURE 12–5

THE COMPLETE SYSTEM

Source: Porter 1990, 127.

CURRENT ISSUES IN COMPETITIVE ADVANTAGE

Porter's work on national competitive advantage has stimulated a great deal of further research. In a recent book, Dartmouth College professor Richard D'Aveni suggests that the Porter strategy frameworks fail to adequately address the dynamics of competition in the 1990s (D'Aveni 1994). D'Aveni takes a different approach. He notes that, in today's business environment, market stability is undermined by short product life cycles, short product design cycles, new technologies, and globalization. The result is an escalation and acceleration of competitive forces. In light of these changes, D'Aveni believes the goal of strategy has shifted from sustaining to disrupting advantages. The limitation of the Porter models, D'Aveni argues, is that they provide a snapshot of competition at a given point in time. In other words, they are static models. Acknowledging that Hamel and Prahalad broke new ground in recognizing that few advantages are sustainable, D'Aveni aims to build upon their work in order to shape "a truly dynamic approach to the creation and destruction of traditional advantages." D'Aveni uses the term *hypercompetition* to describe a dynamic competitive world in which no action or advantage can be sustained for long. In such a world, D'Aveni argues, "everything changes" because of the dynamic maneuvering and strategic interactions by hypercompetitive firms such as Microsoft and Gillette.

According to D'Aveni's model, competition unfolds in a series of dynamic strategic interactions in four arenas: cost/quality, timing and know-how, entry barriers, and deep pockets. Each of these arenas is "continuously destroyed and recreated by the dynamic maneuvering of hypercompetitive firms." According to D'Aveni, the only source of a truly sustainable competitive advantage is a company's ability to manage its dynamic strategic interactions with competitors by means of frequent movements that maintain a relative position of strength in each of the four arenas. The irony and paradox of this model is that, in order to achieve a sustainable advantage, companies must seek a series of *unsustainable* advantages! D'Aveni is in agreement with Peter Drucker, who has long counseled that the role of marketing is innovation and the creation of new markets. Innovation begins with abandonment of the old and obsolete. In Drucker's words, "Innovative organizations spend neither time nor resources on defending yesterday. Systematic abandonment of yesterday alone can transfer the resources . . . for work on the new."

D'Aveni urges managers to reconsider and reevaluate the use of what he believes are old strategic tools and maxims. He warns of the dangers of commitment to a given strategy or course of action. The flexible, unpredictable player may have an advantage over the inflexible, committed opponent. D'Aveni notes that, in hypercompetition, pursuit of generic strategies results in short-term advantage at best. The winning companies are the ones that successfully move up the ladder of escalating competition, not the ones that lock into a fixed position. D'Aveni is also critical of the five forces model. The best entry barrier, he argues, is maintaining the initiative, not mounting a defensive attempt to exclude new entrants.

Other researchers have challenged Porter's thesis that a firm's home-base country is the main source of core competencies and innovation. For example, Professor Alan Rugman of the University of Toronto argues that the success of companies based in small economies such as Canada and New Zealand stems from the diamonds found in a particular *host* country or countries. For example, a company based in an EU nation may rely on the national diamond of one of the 14 other EU members. Similarly, one impact of NAFTA on Canadian firms is to make the U.S. diamond relevant to competency creation. Rugman argues that, in such cases, the distinction between the home nation and the host nation becomes blurred. He proposes that Canadian managers must look to a "double diamond" and assess the attributes of both Canada and the United States when formulating corporate strategy (Rugman & Verbeke 1993).

SUMMARY

In this chapter we focus on factors helping industries and countries achieve competitive advantage. According to Porter's five forces model, industry competition is a function of the threat of new entrants, the threat of substitutes, the bargaining power of suppliers and buyers, and rivalry among existing competitors. Porter's generic strategies model can be used by managers to conceptualize possible sources of competitive advantage. A company can pursue broad market strategies of low cost and differentiation, or the more targeted approaches of cost focus and focused differentiation. Hamel and Prahalad have proposed an alternative framework for pursuing competitive advantage, growing out of a firm's strategic intent and use of competitive innovation. A firm can build layers of advantage, search for loose bricks in a competitor's defensive walls, change the rules of engagement, or collaborate with competitors and utilize their technology and know-how.

Today, many companies are discovering that industry competition is changing from a purely domestic to a global phenomenon. Thus, competitive analysis must also be carried out on a global scale. Global marketers must also have an understanding of national sources of competitive advantage. Porter has described four determinants of national advantage. Factor conditions include human, physical, knowledge, capital, and infrastructure resources. Demand conditions include the composition, size, and growth pattern of home demand. The rate of home market growth and the means by which a nation's products are pulled into foreign markets also affect demand conditions. The final two determinants are the presence of related and supporting industries and the nature of firm strategy, structure, and rivalry. Porter notes that chance and government also influence a nation's competitive advantage. Porter's work has been the catalyst for promising new research into strategy issues, including D'Aveni's work on hypercompetition and Rugman's new double-diamond framework for national competitive advantage.

DISCUSSION QUESTIONS

1. How can a company measure its competitive advantage? How does a firm know if it is gaining or losing competitive advantage?
2. Outline Porter's five forces model of industry competition. How are the various barriers to entry relevant to global marketing?
3. Give an example of a company that illustrates each of the four generic strategies that can lead to competitive advantage: overall cost leadership, cost focus, differentiation, and differention focus.
4. Briefly describe Hamel and Prahalad's framework for competitive advantage.
5. How can a nation achieve competitive advantage?
6. According to current research on competitive advantage, what are some of the shortcomings of Porter's models?
7. What is the connection, if any, between *national* competitive advantage and *company* competitive advantage? Discuss and explain.

BIBLIOGRAPHY

Books

Abegglen, James C., and George Stalk, Jr. *Kaisha: The Japanese Corporation.* New York: Basic Books, 1985.

Clifford, Donald K., Jr., and Richard E. Cavanagh. *The Winning Performance, How America's High-Growth Midsize Companies Succeed.* New York: Bantam Books, 1985.

D'Aveni, Richard. *Hypercompetition: Managing the Dynamics of Strategic Maneuvering.* New York: Free Press, 1994.

Day, George S. *Market Driven Strategy: Processes for Creating Value.* New York: Free Press, 1990.

Dertouzos, Michael L., Richard K. Lester, and Robert M. Solow. *Made in America: Regaining the Competitive Edge.* New York: HarperCollins, 1989.

Halberstam, David. *The Reckoning.* New York: William Morrow and Company, 1986.

Ohmae, Kenichi. *Triad Power.* New York: Free Press, 1985.

Pattison, Joseph E. *Acquiring the Future: America's Survival and Success in the Global Economy.* Homewood, Ill.: Dow Jones Irwin, 1990.

Porter, Michael E. *Competitive Strategy.* New York: Free Press, 1980.

———. *Competitive Advantage: Creating and Sustaining Superior Performance.* New York: Free Press, 1985.

———. *Competition in Global Industries.* Boston: Harvard Business School Press, 1986.

———. *The Competitive Advantage of Nations.* New York: Free Press, 1990.

Womack, James P., Daniel T. Jones, and Daniel Roos. *The Machine that Changed the World.* New York: HarperCollins, 1990.

Yip, George S. *Total Global Strategy: Managing for Worldwide Competitive Advantage.* Upper Saddle River, N.J.: Prentice Hall, 1995.

Articles

Aharoni, Yair. "The State-Owned Enterprise as a Competitor in International Markets." *Columbia Journal of World Business* 15, no. 1 (Spring 1980), pp. 14–22.

Bartmess, Andrew, and Keith Cerny. "Building Competitive Advantage through a Global Network of Capabilities." *California Management Review* 35, no. 2 (Winter 1993), pp. 78–103.

Brouthers, Lancer Eliot, and Steven Werner. "Are the Japanese Good Global Competitors?" *Columbia Journal of World Business* 25, no. 3 (Fall 1990), pp. 5–11.

Calantone, Roger J., and C. Anthony Di Benedetto. "Defensive Marketing in Globally Competitive Industrial Markets." *Columbia Journal of World Business* 23, no. 3 (Fall 1988), pp. 3–14.

Cravens, David W., H. Kirk Downey, and Paul Lauritano. "Global Competition in the Commercial Aircraft Industry: Positioning for Advantage by the Triad Nations." *Columbia Journal of World Business* 26, no. 4 (Winter 1992), pp. 46–58.

Douglas, Susan B., and C. Samuel Craig. "Examining Performance of U.S. Multinationals in Foreign Markets." *Journal of International Business Studies* (Winter 1983), pp. 51–61.

Egelhoff, William G. "Great Strategy or Great Strategy Implementation—Two Ways of Competing in Global Markets." *Sloan Management Review* 34, no. 2 (Winter 1993), pp. 37–50.

Garsombke, Diane J. "International Competitor Analysis." *Planning Review* 17, no. 3 (May–June 1989), pp. 42–47.

Ghosal, Sumantra, and D. Eleanor Westney. "Organizing Competitor Analysis Systems." *Strategic Management Journal* 12, no. 1 (January 1991), pp. 17–31.

"Global Competition: Confront Your Rivals on Their Home Turf." *Harvard Business Review* 71, no. 3 (May–June 1993), p. 10.

Hamel, Gary, and C. K. Prahalad. "Strategic Intent." *Harvard Business Review* 67 no. 3 (May–June 1989), pp. 63–76.

———. "The Core Competence of the Corporation." *Harvard Business Review* 68 no. 3 (May–June 1990), pp. 79–93.

———. "Strategy as Stretch and Leverage." *Harvard Business Review* 71, no. 2 (March–April 1993), pp. 75–85.

Henzler, Herbert A. "The New Era of Eurocapitalism." *Harvard Business Review* 70, no. 4 (July–August 1992), pp. 57–68.

Hillis, W. Daniel, Daniel F. Burton, Robert B. Costello, Robert M. White, Murray Weidenbaum, Luke Georghiou, Umberto Colombo, Leslie Schneider, Thomas H. Lee, and Julie Fox Gorte. "Technology Policy: Is America on the Right Track?" *Harvard Business Review* 70, no. 3 (May–June 1992), pp. 140–157.

Jacquemin, Alexis. "The International Dimension of European Competition Policy." *Journal of Common Market Studies* 31, no. 1 (March 1993), pp. 91–101.

Li, Jiatao, and Stephen Guisinger. "How Well Do Foreign Firms Compete in the United States?" *Business Horizons*, 34, no. 6 (November–December 1991), pp. 49–53.

Lorange, Peter, and Johan Roos. "Why Some Strategic Alliances Succeed and Others Fail." *Journal of Business Strategy* 12, no. 1 (January–February 1991), pp. 25–30.

Magrath, Allan J. "Marketing's Agenda for the 1990's." *Journal of Business Strategy* 13, no. 4 (July–August 1992), pp. 33–37.

Mascarenhas, Briance. "Order of Entry and Performance in International Markets." *Strategic Management Journal* 13, no. 7 (October 1992), pp. 499–510.

Morrison, Allen J., and Kendall Roth. "A Taxonomy of Business-Level Strategies in Global Industries." *Strategic Management Journal* 13, no. 6 (September 1992), pp. 399–417.

Nees, Danielle B. "Building an International Practice." *Sloan Management Review* 27, (Winter 1986), pp. 15–26.

Pearson, Andrall E. "Corporate Redemption and the Seven Deadly Sins." *Harvard Business Review* 70, no. 3 (May–June 1992), pp. 65–75.

Peters, Tom. "Rethinking Scale." *California Management Review* 35, no. 1 (Fall 1992), pp. 7–29.

Robert, Michel M. "Attack Competitors by Changing the Game Rules." *Journal of Business Strategy* 12, no. 5 (September–October 1991), pp. 53–56.

Rugman, Alan M., and Alain Verbeke. "Foreign Subsidiaries and Multinational Strategic Management: An Extension and Correction of Porter's Single Diamond Framework." *Management International Review* 33, no. 2 (Special Issue 1993/2), pp. 71–84.

Schill, Ronald L., and David N. McArthur. "Redefining the Strategic Competitive Unit: Towards a New Global Marketing Paradigm?" *International Marketing Review* 9, no. 3, 1992, pp. 5–24.

Schoemaker, Paul J. H. "How to Link Strategic Vision to Core Capabilities." *Sloan Management Review* 34, no. 1 (Fall 1992), pp. 67–81.

Shostack, G. Lynn. "Limitation Is the Mother of Innovation." *Journal of Business Strategy* 9, no. 6 (November–December 1988), pp. 51–52.

Wheelwright, Steven C. "Restoring the Competitive Edge in U.S. Manufacturing." *California Management Review* 27, no. 3 (Spring 1985), pp. 26–42.

Williams, Jeffrey R. "How Sustainable Is Your Competitive Advantage?" *California Management Review* 34, no. 3 (Spring 1992), pp. 29–51.

CASE 12-1

Eastman Kodak Co., headquartered in Rochester, New York, has long been synonymous with amateur and professional photography in the United States and around the world. Ranked 43rd in the 1995 *Fortune* 500, Kodak has enjoyed decades of undisputed leadership in the silver-halide chemical processes that formed the basis of the photography industry. Taken together, film and photofinishing represent a $15 billion worldwide market. Sales of Kodak film—packaged in familiar yellow boxes—and easy-to-use "point and shoot" Kodak cameras contributed to the company's domination of photography throughout the 20th century. While profits from camera sales were modest, profits on film were spectacular.

In recent years, Kodak has faced serious challenges to its leadership position. The company's long-entrenched conservative corporate culture, bureaucratic organizational structure, and go-slow approach to innovation resulted in sluggish, ill-fated reactions to changes in the photography market. The company that has been a particular headache for Kodak is Japan's Fuji Photo Film Co. Fuji launched an ambitious attack on the market leader by offering film products that many believed offered better color at lower prices. Kodak's share of the U.S. color-negative film market—in

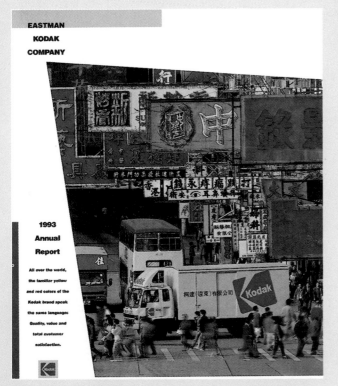

(Reprinted with permission from Eastman Kodak Company.)

which it once enjoyed a near monopoly—slipped to 82 percent by the mid-1980s.

Fuji proved adept at innovating, by launching new products and targeting new segments. In 1982, it was the first to launch color-print film with a speed of 400, which made it the world's fastest film ("faster"—or "higher speed"—film gives superior results under low-light or fast-action conditions). Kodak's fast color film was not introduced until months later. In 1984, Fuji introduced 1600-speed color film; Kodak was not able to match it until 1990. Kodak and Fuji have both introduced new film products targeted at "advanced amateurs"—a new segment midway between the traditional segments of consumer and professional. Fuji also recently introduced a new professional slide film, Velvia, that offers super-saturated colors; although Kodak quickly responded with a competitive product, Velvia has gained wider acceptance.

Fuji's innovations eventually enabled it to achieve more than 10 percent penetration of the U.S. market during the 1980s. Moreover, Fuji scored another important competitive victory when it beat out Kodak for the honor of official photographic sponsor of the 1984 Olympics. Kodak, apparently convinced of its own invulnerability, offered the Olympic committee $1 million plus free film; Fuji bid $7 million, was awarded the sponsorship, and achieved high visibility at the event with its green blimps. Since that time, Fuji's annual sales volume has grown at rates exceeding 20 percent—outpacing growth in the overall market. Chastened by one missed opportunity, Kodak successfully bid $10 million for a sponsorship position at the 1988 Olympics in Seoul, Korea.

Fuji has also demonstrated superiority in operations as well as marketing. Sales per employee at Fuji totaled $380,000 in 1988, compared to Kodak's per-employee sales figure of only $140,000. Fuji also adopted a more innovative approach to distribution: While Kodak, for example, kept warehouses stocked to overflowing with most of its products, Fuji used overnight air shipments to cut inventory costs and delivery times. Fuji also artfully infiltrated Kodak's home turf; it managed to obtain technology licenses from Kodak's patent attorneys, who failed to inform Kodak executives of their actions. According to the manager who first uncovered and then reported this fact, Kodak executives were unresponsive.

Kodak has not been content to sit back and idly watch as Fuji encroaches on its home turf; it has retaliated. Yet, Kodak has enjoyed mixed success in launching a counterattack in Fuji's home market, the world's second-largest photographic market. Each year, amateur Japanese photographers buy 300 million rolls of film. Even though Kodak has invested half a billion dollars in the Japanese market during the past several years, headquarters had a tendency to turn a deaf ear to employee suggestions. Specifically, employees based in Japan urged Kodak to behave more like a Japanese corporation and less like a foreign-based one. For example, Kodak supplied the Japanese with film in boxes with English printing on them until 1985. Kodak also waited until the mid-1980s to open offices in Japan (it currently has 4,500 employees there). When Kodak did open for business in Japan, it imposed its U.S. work policies and procedures; for example, it did not offer its Japanese employees a housing allowance—a common practice among Japanese firms. This approach resulted in high employee turnover and slow acceptance of Kodak in the Japanese market, where consumers show high awareness of the companies behind the brand names.

Although dollar sales of all Kodak products in Japan have increased to $1.3 billion, sales of color-print film have been below expectations. Kodak has only a 7 percent share of the Japanese market—about equivalent to Fuji's share in the United States. Nevertheless, Kodak has been successful with two disposable camera products—one with a wide-angle lens, the other, a disposable underwater model. The Japanese like to take group pictures—on the golf course, for example—and the wide-angle disposable gets everyone in the picture better than a conventional camera. Meanwhile, the underwater disposable has proven to be a big hit with Japanese youth, who are fond of snorkeling. Still, Kodak's disposable cameras have to compete with Fuji's—which reached the market a year earlier and were promoted as "film with lens."

Back in the United States, after a slow start, sales of cardboard "single-use" or "one-time" cameras from both companies have also taken off. Thanks to a name change—from "Fling" to "Funsaver"—and a recycling program, the cameras have overcome objections from environmentalists; Kodak commands about 80 percent of the market. In 1991, Americans bought 15 million one-time cameras, which accounted for all the growth in film sales. Touted as "the perfect second camera" and selling for as little as $9.00, the cameras appeal to vacationers, tourists, and parents who buy them for children to use. In addition to the underwater and wide-angle models, the cameras also are available in flash and telephoto models.

Kodak's final line of defense in the domestic market may well be its distribution clout. Kodak products are well entrenched in supermarket and drugstore chains, where Fuji must jostle with other newcomers such as Konica and Polaroid for shelf space. In addition, Kodak has agreements with 40 of America's largest amusement parks guaranteeing that only Kodak film will be sold on the premises. Kodak is the exclusive supplier to the Air Force Exchange Service, which stocks film at PX stores on military bases. These are some of the reasons Fuji has shifted its attention from the United States to Europe, where Kodak has a 40 percent share

of the film market and Germany's Agfa has about 20 percent. Fuji currently has about a 25 percent share of the European market, compared with 10 percent a decade ago.

The distribution issue was at the center of a trade dispute between Kodak and Fuji that erupted in 1995. George Fisher, Kodak's new CEO, decided to turn up the pressure on Japan. Kodak charged Fuji with unfairly dominating the Japanese photography market and requested that the U.S. government intervene. Fuji responded with similar charges about Kodak's behavior in the United States. One of Kodak's concerns is the fact that Fuji is closely linked with the four biggest film distributors in Japan and holds equity stakes in two of them. Kodak alleges that this arrangement allows Fuji to dissuade distributors from handling other brands of film. Fuji says its Japanese distributors are not prevented from dealing with other suppliers; moreover, it says Kodak's Japanese problems are self-inflicted, the result of poor strategy execution such as concentrating the marketing effort on large cities. Fuji claims that *Kodak* is the film industry's unfair competitor that binds U.S. stores with exclusive arrangements by paying them fees and rebates. A Kodak spokesperson replied to these allegations by noting, "We offer incentives, but retailers are free to carry other brands if they wish. These relationships are completely voluntary."

DISCUSSION QUESTIONS

1. Evaluate Kodak's competitive strategy and give the company a grade for its strategy during the 1980s. Explain the basis of your grade.
2. How has Fuji achieved competitive advantage over Kodak?
3. What must Kodak do to dominate the photography business in the 21st century the way it did in the 20th century?
4. What is your assessment of the trade dispute? Do you think Kodak engages in anticompetitive acts? Fuji?

Sources: Wendy Bounds, "Film Exposures: Fuji, Accused by Kodak of Hogging Markets, Spits Back: 'You Too,'" *The Wall Street Journal* (July 31, 1995).
Joan E. Rigdon, "For Cardboard Cameras, Sales Picture Enlarges and Seems Brighter than Ever," *The Wall Street Journal* (Feb. 11, 1992), p. B1.
Clare Ansberry and Masayoshi Kanabayashi, "Kodak Remains Out of Focus in Japan When It Comes to Key Color Film Market," *The Wall Street Journal* (Dec. 7, 1990), p. B1.
Clare Ansberry, "New Kodak and Fuji Films Target Advanced Amateurs," *The Wall Street Journal* (Mar. 17, 1989), p. B1.
Clare Ansberry and Carol Hymowitz, "Last Chance: Kodak Chief Is Trying, for the Fourth Time, to Trim Firm's Costs," *The Wall Street Journal* (Sept. 19, 1989), pp. A1, A24.
Gale Eisenstodt and Amy Feldman, "Sharply Focused," *Forbes* (Dec. 24, 1990), pp. 50, 53.
Alex Taylor III, "Kodak Scrambles to Refocus," *Fortune* (Mar. 3, 1986), pp. 34+.
"Now for Kodak," *Economist* (July 30, 1988), pp. 67–68.

Product Decisions

Ste. Suisse Microelectronique et d'Horlogerie SA (SMH) is best known as the corporate home of the Swatch wristwatch. A truly global brand, the Swatch name is synonymous with innovative watch designs that, in the early 1980s, virtually reinvented the watch as a moderately priced, durable fashion accessory. Trend-conscious consumers snapped up 100 million of the colorful watches between 1983 and 1993. During the same period, the Swiss share of the global timepiece market rose from 15 percent to more than 50 percent, in large measure because of Swatch.

In 1991, SMH chairman Nicolas Hayek announced the signing of a contract with Volkswagen to develop a battery-powered "Swatch car." At the time, Hayek said his goal was to build "an ecologically inoffensive, high-quality city car for two people" that would sell for about $6,300. Two years later, the alliance with Volkswagen was dissolved; Hayek claimed it was because of disagreement on the concept of the car (Volkswagen officials said low profit projections were the problem). In the spring of 1994, Hayek announced that he had lined up a new joint venture partner. The Mercedes-Benz unit of Daimler-Benz AG would invest 750 million Deutsche marks in a new factory in Hambach-Saargemuend, France. Although a prototype was unveiled in Stuttgart in March, test models were not scheduled to be available until the 1996 Olympics in Atlanta. Swatch is spending $40 million to be an official sponsor of the 1996 games.

The focus of this chapter is the product, probably the most crucial element of a marketing program. To a very important degree, a company's products define its business. Every aspect of the enterprise—including pricing, communication, and distribution policies—must fit the product. A firm's customers and competitors are determined by the products it offers. R&D requirements will depend in part upon the technologies of a company's products and in part—as is clear from the Swatch example—on the vision of its managers and executives. The challenge facing a company with global horizons is to develop product policies and strategies that are sensitive to market needs, competition, and company resources on a global scale. Product policy must strike a balance between the payoff from adapting products to local market preferences and the competitive advantages that come from concentrating company resources on a limited number of standardized products.

This chapter examines the major dimensions of global product decisions. First, basic product concepts are explored. The diversity of preferences and needs in global markets is then underlined by an examination of product saturation levels. Product design criteria are identified, and attitudes toward foreign products are explored. The next section outlines strategic alternatives available to global marketers. The chapter concludes with an examination of new product issues in global marketing.

BASIC CONCEPTS OF PRODUCTS

We begin our introduction to global product decisions by briefly reviewing product concepts typically covered in a basic marketing course. All basic product concepts are fully applicable to global marketing. Additional concepts that apply specifically to global marketing are discussed below.

What is a product? On the surface, this seems like a simple question with an obvious answer. A *product* can be defined in terms of its *tangible*, physical attributes—such things as weight, dimensions, and materials. Thus, an automobile could be defined as 3,000 pounds of metal or plastic, measuring 190 inches long, 75 inches wide, and 59 inches high. However, any description limited to physical attributes gives an incomplete account of the benefits a product provides. At a minimum, car buyers expect an automobile to provide safe, comfortable transportation, which derives from physical features such as air bags and adjustable seats. However, marketers cannot ignore status, mystique, and other *intangible* product attributes that a particular model of automobile may provide. Indeed, major segments of the auto market are developed around these intangible attributes. Similarly, loyal Harley-Davidson riders get much more than basic transportation from their beloved "hogs." A product, then, can be defined as a collection of physical, psychological, service, and symbolic attributes that collectively yield satisfaction, or benefits, to a buyer or user.

A number of frameworks for classifying products have been developed. A frequently used classification is based on users and distinguishes between consumer and industrial goods. Both types of goods, in turn, can be further classified on the basis of other criteria, such as how they are purchased (convenience, preference, shopping, and specialty goods) and their life span (durable, nondurable, and disposable).[1] These and other classification frameworks developed for domestic marketing are fully applicable to global marketing.

LOCAL–INTERNATIONAL–GLOBAL PRODUCTS: A CONTINUUM

Many companies find that, as a result of expanding existing businesses or acquiring a new business, they have a product for sale in a single national market. For example, General Foods at one time found itself in the chewing gum business in France, the ice cream business in Brazil, and the pasta business in Italy. While each of these unrelated businesses was, in isolation, quite profitable, the scale of each was too small to justify heavy expenditures on R&D, let alone marketing, production, and financial management

[1]For a more detailed discussion, see Warren Keegan, Sandra Moriarty, and Thomas Duncan, *Marketing*, 2d ed. (Upper Saddle River, N.J.: Prentice Hall, 1995), Chapter 10.

from international headquarters. *An important question regarding any product is whether it has the potential for expansion into other markets.* The answer will depend upon the company's goals and objectives and upon perceptions of opportunity.

Managers run the risk of committing two types of errors regarding product decisions in global marketing. One error is to fall victim to the "not invented here" (NIH) syndrome, *ignoring* product decisions made by subsidiary or affiliate managers. Managers who behave in this way are essentially abandoning any effort to leverage product policy outside the home-country market. The other error has been to *impose* product decisions policy upon all affiliate companies on the assumption that what is right for customers in the home market must also be right for customers everywhere. German carmaker Volkswagen AG has learned the consequences of this latter error; it has seen its position in the U.S. import market erode from leader to also-ran over the past two decades. While the company once sold more cars in the United States than all other foreign automakers combined, today Volkswagen has less than 2 percent market share in the United States. One industry observer sums up the company's main mistake this way: "Up to now Volkswagen has thought that what works in Germany should work in the United States." Volkswagen recently opened a design studio in Los Angeles, hoping to become better attuned to the tastes of American car buyers.[2]

There are three product categories in the local-to-global continuum: local products, international products, and global products.

Local Products

A local product is one that, in the context of a particular company, is perceived as having potential only in a single national market. Sometimes local products appear when a global company caters to the needs and preferences of particular country markets. For example, Coca-Cola developed a noncarbonated, ginseng-flavored beverage for sale only in Japan. Similarly, Sony and other Japanese consumer electronics companies produce a variety of products that are not sold outside of Japan. The reason? Japanese consumers have a seemingly insatiable appetite for electronic gadgets. One recent example is Casio's 16,000-yen ($155) Can-Tele, a television-in-a-beer-can with a one-inch screen. It is designed to fit in an automobile drink holder. Also, there is Sony's Uka LaLa, a desktop speaker system designed to work with Walkman and Discman portable music players.[3]

Such examples notwithstanding, there are several reasons why local products—even those that are quite profitable—may represent a substantial opportunity cost to a company. First, the existence of a single national business does not provide an opportunity to develop and utilize global leverage from headquarters in marketing, R&D, and production. Second, the local product does not allow for the transfer and application of experience gained in one market to other markets. As noted in Chapter 7, one of the major tools available to the multicountry marketer is comparative analysis. By definition, single-country marketers cannot avail themselves of this tool. A third shortcoming of a single-country product is the lack of transferability of managerial expertise acquired in the single-product area. Managers who gain experience with a local product can only utilize their product experience in the one market where the product is sold. Similarly, any manager coming from outside the market where the single product is sold will not have had any experience in the single-product business. For these reasons, purely local products should generally be viewed as less attractive than products with international or global potential.

[2]Steven Greenhouse, "Carl Hahn's East German Homecoming," *The New York Times* (Sept. 23, 1990), Sec. 3, p. 6.
[3]David P. Hamilton, "Wacky Electronic Gear Again Fills Japanese Stores," *The Wall Street Journal* (May 4, 1994), p. B1.

International Products

International products exhibit potential for extension into a number of national markets. Because industrial products tend to exhibit less environmental sensitivity than do consumer products, industrial manufacturers should be especially alert to extension possibilities. For example, Loctite Corp. is a $500 million U.S.-based manufacturer of industrial adhesives and sealants that are sold in more than 80 countries. In 1991, 60 percent of company sales and 80 percent of profits came from overseas. Loctite's double-digit sales and earnings growth over the past several years can be partially attributed to top management's recognition that the products it had developed for the U.S. market could be sold without adaptation virtually anywhere.[4]

Global Products and Global Brands

Global products are designed to meet the needs of a global market. A global brand, like a national or regional brand, is a symbol about which customers have beliefs or perceptions. A global brand has high recognition levels in world markets. Note that a product is not a brand. For example, personal stereos are a category of global product; Sony is a global brand. Many companies, including Sony, make personal stereos. Sony created the category more than 10 years ago, when it introduced the Walkman. It is important to understand that global brands must be created by marketers; a global brand name can be used as an umbrella for introducing new products. Although Sony, as noted above, markets a number of local products, the company also has a stellar track record both as a global brand and a manufacturer of global products. Sony's latest global product offering is a digital record/playback system called the Minidisc.

Table 13–1 shows two different global brand rankings in the mid-1990s, from a recent Young & Rubicam study that included 23,000 consumers in 16 countries. The first column, labeled "Brand Stature," shows the current strength of leading brands. Not surprisingly, Coca-Cola tops the list. Coke is also at the top of the second column, labeled "Brand Vitality," ranking brands in terms of perceived relevance as well as distinctness. The fact that Nike is not even in the top 25 brands in terms of stature can be explained by its relatively short history as a brand. The vitality rank tells a different story. Notes Jim Williams of Y&R Europe, "Nike is not just another shoe. It stands for an attitude and way of life that people respond to. Nike is seen as a dynamic leader, modern, individual."[5]

When an industry globalizes, companies are under pressure to develop global products. A major driver for the globalization of products is the cost of product R&D. As competition intensifies, companies discover they can reduce the cost of R&D for a product by developing a global product design. Even products like automobiles which must meet national safety and pollution standards are under pressure to become global: With a global product, companies can offer an adaptation of a global design instead of a unique national design in each country.

Mars Inc. confronted the global brand issue with its chocolate-covered caramel bar that sold under a variety of national brand names such as Snickers in the United States and Marathon in the United Kingdom. Mars decided to transform the candy bar—a global product—into a global brand. This decision entailed some risk, such as the possibility that consumers in the United Kingdom would associate the name Snickers with "knickers," the British slang for a woman's undergarment. Mars also changed the name of its successful European chocolate biscuit from Raider to Twix, the same name used in the United States. In both instances, a single brand name gives Mars the opportunity to leverage all of its product communications across national boundaries. In doing this, managers must

---

[4]Tim Smart, "Why Ignore 95% of the World's Market?" *Business Week/ Reinventing America* (1992), p. 64.
[5]Laurel Wentzel, "Upstart Brands Steal Spotlight from Perennials," *Advertising Age* (Sept. 19, 1994), p. I–13.

TABLE 13-1 HOW GLOBAL BRANDS MEASURE UP

Brand Stature (Y&R)	Brand Vitality (Y&R)
1. Coca-Cola	1. Coca-Cola
2. Kodak	2. Nike
3. Sony	3. Adidas
4. Mercedes-Benz	4. Sony
5. Pepsi-Cola	5. Ferrari
6. Nestlé	6. Reebok
7. Gillette	7. Disney
8. Colgate	8. Porsche
9. Adidas	9. Pepsi-Cola
10. Volkswagen	10. Mercedes-Benz
11. Nescafé	11. BMW
12. Ford	12. Kodak
13. Panasonic	13. Rolls-Royce
14. Philips	14. Levi
15. Levi	15. Chanel
16. Honda	16. Nestlé
17. BMW	17. Pierre Cardin
18. Toyota	18. Nescafé
19. Rolls-Royce	19. Christian Dior
20. Fanta	20. Harley-Davidson
21. Disney	21. Jaguar
22. Palmolive	22. McDonald's
23. Lux	23. Polaroid
24. Nivea	24. Volkswagen
25. McDonald's	25. Benetton

Source: Laurel Wentzel, "Upstart Brands Steal Spotlight from Perennials," *Advertising Age* (Sept. 19, 1994), p. I-13.

now think globally about the positioning of Snickers and Twix, something that they were not obliged to do when the candy products were marketed under different national brand names.

Coke is arguably the quintessential global product and global brand. Coke is positioned and marketed the same in all countries; it projects a global image of fun, good times, and enjoyment. The product itself may vary to suit local tastes; for example, Coca-Cola increased the sweetness of its beverages in the Middle East where customers prefer a sweeter drink. Also, prices may vary to suit local competitive conditions, and the channels of distribution may differ. However, the basic underlying strategic principles that guide the management of the brand are the same worldwide. Only an ideologue would insist that a "global product" cannot be adapted to meet local preferences; certainly no company building a global brand needs to limit itself to absolute product uniformity. The issue is not exact uniformity, but rather: Are we offering *essentially* the same product? As discussed in the next few chapters, other elements of the marketing mix—for example, price, communications appeal and media strategy, and distribution channels—may also vary.

Global marketers should systematically identify and assess opportunities for developing global brands. Creating a global brand requires a different type of marketing effort—including up-front creative vision—than that required to create one or more national brands. On the other hand, the ongoing effort to *maintain* brand awareness is less for a leading world brand than it is for a collection of national brands. What criteria do marketers use to decide whether or not to establish global brands? One expert has argued that the decision must be "determined by bottom-up consumer-driven considerations, not by top-down manufacturer-driven business convenience."[6] A major determinant of success will be whether the marketing effort is starting from scratch with a "blank slate," or whether the task is to reposition or rename an existing national brand in an attempt to create a global brand. Starting with a blank slate is vastly easier than repositioning existing brands. Still, Mars and many companies have succeeded in transforming national brands into regional or world brands. Today there are thousands of global brands, and every day the list grows longer.

POSITIONING

Positioning is a communication strategy based on the notion of mental "space": *Positioning* refers to the act of locating a brand in customers' minds over and against other products in terms of product attributes and benefits that the brand does and does not offer. The word, first formally used in 1969 by Al Ries and Jack Trout in an article that appeared in *Industrial Marketing*, describes a strategy for "staking out turf" or "filling a slot" in the mind of target customers.[7]

Several general strategies have been suggested for positioning products: positioning by attribute or benefit, quality/price, and use/user.[8] Two additional strategies, high-tech and high-touch, have been suggested for global products.

The name Mercedes-Benz is synonymous around the world with prestigious vehicles. Mercedes executives hope that new lower-priced models will account for 40 percent of car sales by the year 2000. (Courtesy of Mercedes-Benz Nederland B. B.)

Attribute or Benefit

A frequently used positioning strategy exploits a particular product attribute, benefit, or feature. In global marketing, the fact that a product is "imported" can itself represent a benefit positioning. Economy, reliability, and durability are other frequently used attribute/benefit positions. Volvo automobiles are known for solid construction that offers safety in the event of a crash. In the ongoing credit card wars, Visa's advertising focuses on the benefit of worldwide merchant acceptance.

Quality/Price

This strategy can be thought of in terms of a continuum from high fashion/quality and high price to good value (rather than "low quality") at a low price.[9] The American Express Card, for example, has traditionally been positioned as an upscale card whose prestige justifies higher annual fees than Visa or MasterCard. The Discover card is at the other end of the continuum. Discover's value position results from no annual fee and a cash rebate to cardholders each year.

Marketers of imported vodkas such as Absolut, Finlandia, and Stolichnaya Cristall have successfully positioned their brands as super premium products at double the price of "ordinary" vodka. For example, ads for Cristall vodka hail it as "flawless." Advertising is used to support this image. Vodkas also play up their national origins, demonstrating how quality/price can also be used in conjunction with other positioning strategies such as at-

[6]A. E. Pitcher, "The Role of Branding in International Advertising," *International Journal of Advertising*, no. 4 (1985), p. 244.
[7]Al Ries and Jack Trout, *Positioning: The Battle for Your Mind* (New York: Warner Books, 1982), p. 44.
[8]David A. Aaker and J. Gary Shansby, "Positioning Your Product," *Business Horizons* (May–June 1982), pp. 56–62.
[9]Ibid., p. 57.

DIESEL SHOULD BE SIPPED.

The stuff's aged for millions of years, yet there are engines out there swigging it down like they might never drink again. Perhaps they could all stand a lesson in etiquette from the new Mack E7, a refined, 12-liter engine ...that doesn't slam, gulp or guzzle. Weighing in at 600 to 800 lbs less than the competition's 14-liter   *engines, the trim 250 to 454 horsepower Mack E7s provide a power to weight ratio like no other engine on the road. Plus all the durability and reliability of the diesel-chugging big boys. For information on the fuel efficient E7 engine, call 1-800-922-MACK.* DRIVE ONE AND YOU'LL KNOW.

Humor and brand personality are combined in this business-to-business ad for Mack Trucks stressing the fuel efficiency of the company's diesel engines. (Advertising created by Carmichael Lynch, Minneapolis, MN. Awarded an EFFIE in 1995.)

tribute/benefit. Marketers sometimes use the phrase "transformation advertising" to describe advertising that seeks to change the experience of buying and using a product—in other words, the product benefit.[10] Presumably, the experience of buying and consuming Stolichnaya Cristall is a higher-quality experience than that of buying and consuming a "bar brand" such as Popov.

Use or User

Positioning can also be achieved by describing how a product is used or associating a product with a user or class of users. Marlboro's extraordinary success as a global brand is due in part to the product's association with cowboys—*the* archetypal symbol of freedom—and transformation advertising that targets urban smokers. As Clive Chajet, a corporate and brand identity expert, explains, "The cowboy is as enduring an icon as you can have. And the stronger your brand image, regardless of the environment in which you compete, the better off you are."[11] Why choose Marlboro instead of another brand? Smoking Marlboro is a way of getting in touch with a powerful urge to be free and independent. The message is reinforced in advertising that urges smokers to "join that rugged, independent cowboy in the Old West!" The advertising succeeds because it is very well done and, evidently, addresses a deep, powerful need that is found everywhere around the globe.

---

[10]William Wells, John Burnett, and Sandra Moriarty, *Advertising: Principles and Practices* (Upper Saddle River, N.J.: Prentice Hall, 1989), p. 207.
[11]Stuart Elliott, "Uncle Sam is No Match for the Marlboro Man," *The New York Times* (Aug. 27, 1995), Sec 3, p. 11.

THE REST OF THE STORY

■ SWATCHMOBILE

*T*he Swatchmobile concept is based on Hayek's conviction that consumers become emotionally attached to cars just as they do to watches. Like the Swatch, the Swatchmobile (officially named "Smart") will be affordable, durable, and stylish. Hayek notes that safety will be another key selling point, declaring, "This car will have the crash security of a Mercedes." Composite exterior panels mounted on a cage-like body frame will allow owners to change colors by switching panels. Further, the car will emit almost no pollutants, thanks to its electric engine. The car will also be capable of gasoline-powered operation, using a highly efficient, miniaturized engine capable of achieving speeds of 80 miles per hour. Hayek predicts that worldwide sales will reach 1 million units, with the United States accounting for about half the market.

Some observers attribute the hoopla surrounding the Swatchmobile concept to Mr. Hayek's charismatic personality. Some believe his automotive vision is overly optimistic,

noting that other attempts at extending the Swatch brand name to new categories, including a brightly colored unisex clothing line, had flopped. Other products such as Swatch telephones, pagers, and sunglasses have also met with lukewarm consumer acceptance. Industry observers warn, however, that both the Swatch and Mercedes names could be hurt if the Swatchmobile is plagued by recall or safety problems.

What does Mercedes stand to gain by participating in the joint venture, which is officially known as Micro Compact Car GmBH (MCC)? Its strategy calls for broadening the company's appeal beyond the high end of the automobile market and leveraging its engineering skills. As Mercedes chairman Helmut Werner said, "With the new car, Mercedes wants to combine ecology, emotion and intellect." Approximately 80 percent of the Smart's parts will be components and modules sourced from outside suppliers and subcontractors. The decision to manufacture in France disappointed German labor unions, but Mercedes executives expected to save 500 marks per car. The reason: French workers are on the job 275 days per year, while German workers average only 242; also, overall labor costs are 40 percent lower in France than in Germany.

Sources: William Taylor, "Message and Muscle: An Interview with Swatch Titan Nicolas Hayek," *Harvard Business Review* (March–April 1993), pp. 99–110. Kevin Helliker, "Swiss Movement: Can Wristwatch Whiz Switch Swatch Cachet to an Automobile?" *The Wall Street Journal* (Mar. 4, 1994), pp. A1, A3. Ferdinand Protzman, "Off the Wrist, Onto the Road: A Swatch of Wheels," *The New York Times* (Mar. 4, 1994), p. C1. Daphne Angles, "Swiss Watchmaker Joins the Auto Game," *The New York Times* (July 7, 1991), Sec. 3, p. 10. Mary Lu Carnevale, "BellSouth Unit and Swatch to Introduce Wristwatch Pager, Joint Marketing Plan," *The Wall Street Journal* (Mar. 4, 1992), p. B5.

Honda used the slogan "You meet the nicest people on a Honda" to attract a new segment of first-time American motorcycle buyers in the 1960s. More recently, Harley-Davidson has successfully broadened its image to reach a new class of motorcycle enthusiast: aging baby boomer professionals who wanted to adopt an "outlaw" persona on weekends. An ad for the upscale Range Rover showing the sport utility vehicle on a mountaintop has the headline "The real reason many CEOs are unavailable for comment."

In today's global market environment, many companies find it increasingly important to have a unified global positioning strategy. For example, in 1991, Chase Manhattan Bank launched a $75 million global advertising campaign geared to the theme "Profit from experience." According to Aubrey Hawes, a vice president and corporate director of marketing for the bank, Chase's business and private banking clients "span the globe and travel the globe. They can only know one Chase in their minds, so why should we try to confuse them?"[12]

Some products can be positioned the same way in every market. For example, Benetton uses the same positioning for its clothing when it targets the global youth market. Marlboro cigarettes are positioned around the world as a rugged, virile brand. The Marlboro man symbolizes rugged independence, freedom, and space, an image carefully calculated to appeal to the universal human desire for those things. Lack of freedom and physical space are acutely felt by urban dwellers, whose loyalty to Marlboro may be a reflection of their own sense of "macho-ness" or a symbol of freedom and independence. (Not surprisingly, Marlboro is the most popular cigarette brand in the former Soviet Union.)

Can global positioning work for all products? One study suggests that global positioning is most effective for product categories that approach either end of a "high tech/high touch" continuum.[13] Both ends of the continuum are characterized by high levels of customer involvement and by a shared "language" among consumers.

[12]Gary Levin, "Ads Going Global," *Advertising Age* (July 22, 1991), p. 42.
[13]The following discussion is adapted from Teresa J. Domzal and Lynette Unger, "Emerging Positioning Strategies in Global Marketing," *Journal of Consumer Marketing* 4, no. 4 (Fall 1987), pp. 26–27.

High-Tech

Personal computers, video and stereo equipment, and automobiles are product categories for which high-tech positioning has proven effective. Such products are frequently purchased on the basis of physical product features, although image may also be important. Buyers typically already possess—or wish to acquire—considerable technical information. High-tech products may be divided into three categories: technical products, special-interest products, and demonstrable products.

Computers, chemicals, tires, and financial services are "technical" products in the sense that buyers have specialized needs, require a great deal of product information, and share a common "language." Computer buyers in Russia and the United States are equally knowledgable about Pentium microprocessors, 500-meg hard drives, and software RAM requirements. Marketing communications for high-tech products should be informative and emphasize features. Special-interest products also are characterized by a shared experience and high involvement among users, although they are less technical and more leisure or recreation oriented. Again, the common language and symbols associated with such products can transcend language and cultural barriers. Fuji bicycles, Adidas sports equipment, Canon cameras, and Sega video games are examples of successful global special-interest products. Finally, products that "speak for themselves" in advertising in terms of features and benefits can also travel well.

High-Touch

Marketing of high-touch products requires less emphasis on specialized information and more emphasis on image. Like high-tech products, however, high-touch categories are highly involving for consumers. Buyers of high-touch products also share a common language and set of symbols relating to themes of wealth, materialism, and romance. There are three categories of high-touch products: products that solve a common problem, "global village" products, and products with a universal theme. At the other end of the price spectrum from high-tech, products that can solve a problem often provide benefits linked to "life's little moments." Ads that show friends talking over a cup of coffee in a café or quenching thirst with a soft drink during a day at the beach put the product at the center of everyday life and communicate the benefit offered in a way that is understood worldwide. Upscale fragrances such as Chanel, designer fashions, mineral water, and pizza are all examples of products whose positioning is strongly cosmopolitan in nature. Fragrances and fashions have traveled as a result of growing worldwide interest in high-quality, highly visible, high-price products that often enhance social status. However, the lower-priced food products mentioned show that the "global village" category encompasses a broad price spectrum.[14] Products may have a global appeal by virtue of their country of origin. The "American-ness" of Levis, Marlboro, and Harley-Davidson enhances their appeal to cosmopolitans around the world and offers opportunities for benefit positioning. In consumer electronics, Sony is a name synonymous with vaunted Japanese quality; in automobiles, Mercedes is the embodiment of legendary German engineering.

Some products can be positioned in more than one way, within either the high-tech or high-touch poles of the continuum. Other products may be positioned in a "bipolar" fashion, i.e., as both high-tech and high-touch. For example, Bang & Olufsen consumer electronics products, by virtue of their design elegance, are perceived as both high-tech and high-touch.

---

[14]Domzal & Unger 1987, 31.

AN OCCASION IS SIMPLY A DECISION TO CELEBRATE SOMETHING.

THE WYNNEWOOD CHAMPAGNE FLUTE, LIKE ALL WATERFORD PATTERNS, WILL NEVER BE DISCONTINUED. FOR A BROCHURE, CALL 1-800-523-0009.

WATERFORD
WORTHY OF THE MOMENT
FOR OVER TWO CENTURIES.

FAYERWEATHER'S FIVE PRODUCT CHARACTERISTICS

Another way of looking at a product is to consider its characteristics. John Fayerweather has suggested five important characteristics that are relevant to global marketing product decisions: primary functional purpose, secondary purpose, durability and quality, method of operation, and maintenance.

Primary function is illustrated by the example of the refrigerator as used in industrialized, high-income countries. The primary functions of the refrigerator in these countries are (1) to store frozen foods for a week or more, (2) to preserve perishable food (vegetables, milk, and meat) between car trips to the supermarket, (3) to store products not requiring refrigeration, such as margarine, and (4) to keep bottled drinks cold for short-notice consumption.

In lower-income countries, frozen foods are not widely available. Housewives shop for food on a daily, rather than weekly, basis. Because of lower incomes, people are reluctant to pay for the last two uses of the refrigerator noted above—i.e., refrigerating items that do not actually require refrigeration to prevent spoilage and cooling beverages. These are luxury uses that require high income levels to support. The functions of the refrigerator in a lower-income country are merely (1) to store small quantities of perishable food for one day and (2) to store leftovers for slightly longer periods. Because the needs ful-

A MATTER OF CULTURE

*W*hile many differences separate consumers in different parts of the world, there is one characteristic that consumers everywhere seem to share: a preference for low-priced, high-quality, private-label products, rather than better-known—and more expensive—brands. In some places the move toward private labels is just beginning. In other countries, private labels have been dominant for years.

In some of the world's markets, consumer preference for private labels—often encouraged by local companies—undermines hard-fought efforts by U.S. companies to open markets to imports. In 1992, for example, after prolonged trade negotiations, Dole, Tropicana, and other U.S. beverage makers finally were able to sell their orange juice brands in Japan. At about the same time the American products appeared on store shelves, the Daiei supermarket chain launched its own Savings private-label brand. Daiei's private-label products include: juice made from Brazilian oranges and priced 40 percent cheaper than U.S. brands; pints of premium ice cream that sell for 299 yen, half the price of Lady Borden; and canned-coffee drinks priced 30 percent cheaper than Coca-Cola's Georgia brand. Competitive imitation helps sell the Savings brands; Daiei buys the ice cream from the same supplier as Borden and packages it in rectangular cartons similar to Lady Borden's.

In Great Britain, grocery store operating profit margins are as high as 8 percent—while those in the United States are a meager 1 percent. The reason? Private labels. Moreover, private labels account for 36 percent of total grocery sales in Great Britain, compared with 14 percent in the United States. The success of private labels in Great Britain is due partly to much less national advertising, thereby preventing brand loyalty among consumers. In particular, the BBC's refusal to carry advertising means that TV advertising—a key strategy for building brands and brand loyalty—is much less important than in the United States. Industry structure is also a factor: The grocery business in Great Britain is much less fragmented than in the United States. Great Britain's five largest chains—including J. Sainsbury PLC, Safeway, and Tesco—command nearly two-thirds of the grocery business; in the United States, Safeway and other major chains account for about one-fifth of grocery sales. Well-known brands are feeling the heat: Sainsbury's Gio lemon-lime soft drink competes directly with 7UP and Sprite; its Novon laundry detergent outsells brands from global giants Procter & Gamble and Unilever PLC.

The story is much the same in Canada. In the early 1980s, David A. Nichols, head of the Toronto-based Loblaw Cos. Ltd., created a private-label brand called President's Choice (PC). Today, the upscale PC products are found not only throughout Canada but in many U.S. grocery stores as well. Savvy marketing and advertising helps differentiate the line: Unending puffery and hyperbole ("decadent" cookies, peanut butter that is "too good to be true," "the ultimate" frozen pizza), fancy labels, and exotic names ensure consumer attention and interest. Coca-Cola and PepsiCo are now faced with a soft drink market in Canada in which the share of private labels has grown from 5 percent in 1990 to as high as 25 percent in 1993.

---

filled by the refrigerator are limited in these countries as compared with advanced countries, a much smaller refrigerator is quite adequate.

In some developing countries, refrigerators have an important secondary purpose: They fulfill a need for prestige. In these countries, there is demand for the largest model available, which is prominently displayed in the living room rather than hidden in the kitchen.

Durability and quality are important product characteristics that must be appropriate for the proposed market. The durability and quality of home appliances, for example, must be suited to the availability of service within a market. In lower-income markets, appliances are more likely to be repairable—indeed, a repairable appliance is a quality appliance in these markets. Conversely, in advanced countries, where the cost of labor makes it prohibitively expensive to repair appliances costing less than $40, appliances are designed without the additional "quality" that would allow a repair person to take the appliance apart and repair it. Since the availability of small-appliance repair in advanced countries is either nonexistent or prohibitively expensive, to build reparability into appliances would add nothing of value for the consumer. However, an attempt to sell the high-income product in a low-income market may result in failure; it may be perceived as a *lower*-quality product because of its lack of an important benefit, namely reparability.

The last two product characteristics described by Fayerweather are method of opera-

Sources: E. S. Browning, "Europeans Witness Proliferation of Private Labels," *The Wall Street Journal* (Oct. 20, 1992), p. B1.
Yumiko Ono, "The Rising Sun Shines on Private Labels," *The Wall Street Journal* (Apr. 26, 1993), pp. B1, B6.
Richard Gibson, "Pitch, Panache Buoy Fancy Private Label," *The Wall Street Journal* (Jan. 27, 1994), p. B1.
Eleena De Lisser and Kevin Helliker, "Private Labels Reign in British Groceries," *The Wall Street Journal* (Mar. 3, 1994), p. B4.

In Italy this fine olive oil is only sold by one long established family business. Just like in Britain.

The Archibusacci's have much in common with Sainsbury's.

Both businesses, for example, are run with the sort of care that only comes with generations of tradition.

But while Sainsbury's is 122 years old, the Archibusacci family has been making and selling olive oil since 1700.

Continuing a tradition in the village of Canino near the Tuscan border that dates back to Etruscan times.

The Canino Olive is small and matures slowly. And Sainsbury's Extra Virgin Olive Oil Di Canino comes from olives grown on the thousands of trees surrounding the village. (Some are over 300 years old.) It is made from the first cold pressing of the olives which takes place within 24 hours of picking.

Nothing is added to it at any stage.

It is a rich dark green colour. And intensely fruity in flavour.

Perfect in salad dressings or as a marinade.

The same oil, in fact, that's been enjoyed for hundreds of years by families all over Italy.

Thanks to Sainsbury's, it can now be enjoyed by yours.

Good food costs less at Sainsburys.

tion and maintenance. For example, the voltage and cycle requirements for an electrical appliance or the driving conditions for an automobile are important method-of-operation considerations in determining product design and characteristics. The same principle is true of maintenance, the availability and cost of which vary in different parts of the world. It is especially important that these factors be taken into account when product characteristics and features are being developed.

PRODUCT SATURATION LEVELS IN GLOBAL MARKETS

Many factors determine a product's market potential. In general, product saturation levels, or the percentage of potential buyers or households who own a particular product, increase as national income per capita increases. However, in markets where income is sufficient to enable consumers to buy a particular product, other factors must be considered. For example, the sale of air conditioners is explained by income *and* climate. In a low-income country, many people cannot afford an air conditioner no matter how hot it is. Affluent people in a northern climate can easily afford an air conditioner but have little need for one.

During the 1960s, the ownership of electric vacuum cleaners in the European Common Market ranged from a high of 95 percent of households in the Netherlands to a low of 7 percent of households in Italy. The differences in ownership of this appliance in Europe are explained only partially by income. A much more important factor is the type of floor covering used in the homes of the country. Almost every home in the Netherlands contains rugs, whereas in Italy the use of rugs is uncommon. This illustrates the importance of need in determining the sales potential for a product. Thus, in addition to attitudes toward cleanliness, the presence or absence of a particular *companion product* is very significant for electric vacuum cleaners. If the Italians had more carpets covering their floors, the saturation level for vacuum cleaners would be higher.

The existence of wide disparities in the demand for a product from one market to the next is an indication of the potential for that product in the low-saturation-level market. For example, a major new product category in the United States in the early 1980s was mousse, a hair-grooming product for women that is more flexible than stiff, dry hair spray.

This product, known as gel in France, had been available in France and Europe for 25 years prior to its introduction in the United States. The success of the product in Europe was a clear signal of market potential. Indeed, it is more than likely that this opportunity could have been tapped earlier. Every company should have an active global scanning system to identify potential market opportunities based on demand disparities.

PRODUCT DESIGN CONSIDERATIONS

Product design is a key factor determining success in global marketing. Should a company adapt product design for various national markets or offer a single design to the global market? In some instances, making a design change may increase sales. However, the benefits of such potential sales increases must be weighed against the cost of changing a product's design and testing it in the market. Global marketers need to consider four factors when making product design decisions: preferences, cost, laws and regulations, and compatibility.

Preferences

There are marked and important differences in preferences around the world for factors such as color and taste. Marketers who ignore preferences do so at their own peril. In the 1960s, for example, Italy's Olivetti Corporation had gained considerable distinction in Europe for its award-winning modern consumer typewriter designs; Olivetti typewriters had been displayed at the Museum of Modern Art in New York City. While critically acclaimed, Olivetti's designs did not enjoy commercial success in the United States. The U.S. consumer wanted a heavy, bulky typewriter that was "ugly" by modern European design standards. Bulk and weight were considered prima facie evidence of quality by American consumers, and Olivetti was therefore forced to adapt its award-winning design in the United States.

Sometimes, a product design that is successful in Europe does meet with success in the United States. Ford Motor Company decided to introduce U.S. cars with a European aerodynamic design, first with the Thunderbird, then with the Taurus. Ford's aero design was dramatically different from the boxy designs of most American cars in the early 1980s. The design was an immediate success in the United States and contributed significantly to Ford's huge success in 1986 when company profits exceeded those of GM for the first time since 1923.

Cost

In approaching the issue of product design, company managers must consider cost factors broadly. Of course, the actual cost of producing the product will create a cost floor. Other design-related costs—whether incurred by the manufacturer or the end user—must also be considered. Earlier in this chapter we noted that the cost of repair services varies around the world and has an impact on product design. Another example of how labor cost affects product decisions is seen in the contrasting approaches to aircraft design adopted by the British and the Americans. The British approach, which resulted in the Comet, was to place the engine inside the wing. This design meant lower wind resistance and therefore greater fuel economy. A disadvantage of the design was less-accessible engines than externally mounted ones, meaning they were more time-consuming to maintain and repair. The American approach to the question of engine location was to hang the engines from the wings at the expense of efficiency and fuel economy to gain a more accessible engine and, therefore, to reduce the amount of time required for engine maintenance and repair. Both approaches to engine location were rational. The British approach took into account the relatively lower cost of the labor required for engine repair, and the American approach took into account the relatively high cost of labor for engine repair in the United States.

Laws and Regulations

As we discussed in Chapter 5, compliance with laws and regulations in different countries has a direct impact on product design decisions, frequently leading to product design adaptations that increase costs. This may be seen especially clearly in Europe, where one impetus for the creation of the single market was to dismantle regulatory and legal barriers—particularly in the areas of technical standards and health and safety standards—that prevented pan-European sales of standardized products. In the food industry, for example, there were 200 legal and regulatory barriers to cross-border trade within the EU in 10 food categories. Among these were prohibitions or taxes on products with certain ingredients and different packaging and labeling laws. Experts predict that the removal of such barriers will reduce the need to adapt product designs and will result in the creation of standardized "Euro-products."[15]

Compatibility

The last product design issue that must be addressed by company managers is product compatibility with the environment in which it is used. A simple thing like failing to translate the user's manual into various languages can hurt sales of U.S.-made home appliances outside the United States. Also, electrical systems range from 50 to 230 volts and from 50 to 60 cycles. This means that the design of any product powered by electricity must be compatible with the power system in the country of use.

Manufacturers of televisions and video equipment find that the world is a very incompatible place for reasons besides those related to electricity. Three different TV broadcast and video systems are found in the world today: the U.S. NTSC system, the French SECAM system, and the German PAL system. Companies that are targeting global markets design "multisystem" TVs and VCRs that allow users to simply flip a switch for proper operation with any system. Companies that are not aiming for the global market design products that comply with a single type of technical requirements.

Measuring systems do not demand compatibility, but the absence of compatibility in measuring systems can create product resistance. The lack of compatibility is a particular danger for the United States, which is the only nonmetric country in the world. Products calibrated in inches and pounds are at a competitive disadvantage in metric markets. When companies integrate their worldwide manufacturing and design activity, the metric/English measuring system conflict requires expensive conversion and harmonization efforts.

ATTITUDES TOWARD FOREIGN PRODUCTS

One of the facts of life in global marketing is the existence of stereotyped attitudes toward foreign products. Stereotyped attitudes may either favor or hinder the marketer's efforts. On the positive side, as one marketing expert pointed out, "German is synonymous with quality engineering, Italian is synonymous with style, and French is synonymous with chic."[16] However, no country has a monopoly on a favorable foreign reputation for its products or a universally inferior reputation. Similarly, individual citizens in a given country are likely to differ in terms of both the importance they ascribe to a product's country of origin and their perceptions of different countries. A recent Gallup poll showed that, among Americans, people 61 years of age or older were most likely to determine a product's origin before buying (see Table 13–2).

The manufacturing reputation of a particular country may vary around the world; a particular country's reputation can change over time. Studies conducted during the 1970s

TABLE 13–2

INFLUENCE OF COUNTRY OF MANUFACTURE ON CONSUMER PURCHASE DECISIONS

Age	Percentage
18–30	19
31–45	35
46–60	29
61+	50

Source: Gallup poll conducted for the International Mass Retail Association.

---

[15]John Quelch, Robert Buzzell, and Eric Salama, *The Marketing Challenge of Europe 1992* (Reading, Mass.: Addison-Wesley, 1991), p. 71.
[16]Dana Milbank, "Made in America Becomes a Boast in Europe," *The Wall Street Journal* (Jan. 19, 1994), p. B1.

and 1980s indicated that the "Made in the USA" image lost ground when compared with the "Made in Japan" image. Today, however, a number of U.S. companies and U.S. brands are finding renewed acceptance in Europe, Japan, and elsewhere. For example, Jeep Cherokee sport utility vehicles, Lands End clothing, and even Budweiser beer are being successfully marketed in Europe with strong "USA" themes.

Country stereotyping can present a considerable disadvantage to a competitor in a given market. Because of this, global marketers should consider shifting production locations to exploit country-specific advantages. One recent study investigated the relationship between a product's country of origin and American consumer perceptions of risk. Specifically, the study compared perceptions of two product categories—microwave ovens and blue jeans—produced in the United States, Mexico, and Taiwan. Overall, the study found a significant consumer bias in favor of U.S.-made microwaves and jeans. However, the study also showed no difference in perceived risk between microwave ovens in terms of "Made in the USA" and "Made in Taiwan." On the other hand, respondents indicated a higher perceived risk for jeans manufactured in Taiwan compared with those from the United States. Comparison of the two product categories for the United States and Mexico showed a negative country-of-origin bias for Mexican-made products. Finally, the survey indicated a significantly higher perceived risk for a Mexican microwave oven compared to one made in Taiwan; there was no significant difference between Mexico and Taiwan in terms of perceived risk for jeans.[17]

Of course, customers in Mexico and Taiwan exhibit country-of-origin biases of their own. One new enterprise in Brazil, which supplied a sensitive scientific instrument to the oil-drilling industry, discovered that its Mexican customers would not accept scientific instruments manufactured in Brazil. To overcome the prejudice in Mexico against instruments from Brazil, the company was forced to export the components for its instruments to Switzerland where they were assembled and the finished product stamped "Made in Switzerland." Only then did the company achieve satisfactory sales levels in Mexico.

If a country's manufacturers produce quality products that are nonetheless *perceived* as being of low quality, there are two alternatives. One is to attempt to hide or disguise the foreign origin of the product. Package, label, and product design can minimize evidence of foreign sourcing. A brand policy of using local names will contribute to a domestic identity. The other alternative is to continue the foreign identification of the product and attempt to change consumer or customer attitudes toward the product. Over time, as consumers experience higher quality, the perception will change and adjust. It is a fact of life that perceptions of quality often lag behind reality.

In some market segments, foreign products have a substantial advantage over their domestic counterparts simply because they are foreign. This appears to be the case with beer in the United States. In one study, subjects who were asked to indicate taste preference for beer in a blind test indicated a preference for domestic beers over imports. The same subjects were then asked to indicate preference ratings for beers in an open test with labels attached. In this test, the subjects preferred imported beer. Today, many Americans still seem to have a taste for imported beers; 1993 import sales added up to 9.2 billion barrels—the largest volume in five years. According to *Impact*, a beverage industry newsletter, imports account for 5 percent of U.S. beer sales by volume.

It is a happy situation for the global marketer when foreign origin has a positive influence on perceptions of quality. One way to reinforce foreign preference is by charging a premium price for the foreign product to take advantage of consumer tendencies to associate price and quality. The relative position of imported beer in the U.S. premium-priced beer market is an excellent example of this positioning strategy. Similarly, Anheuser Busch is enjoying great success with its Budweiser brand in Europe. In Great Britain,

---

[17]Jerome Witt and C. P. Rao, "The Impact of Global Sourcing on Consumers: Country-of-Origin Effects on Perceived Risk," *Journal of Global Marketing* 6, no. 3 (1992), pp. 105–128.

where it is positioned as a super-premium beer, a six-pack of Bud sells for the equivalent of $7—about twice the U.S. price.

GEOGRAPHIC EXPANSION: STRATEGIC ALTERNATIVES

Companies can grow in three different ways. The traditional methods of market expansion—further penetration of existing markets to increase market share and extension of the product line into new product market areas in a single national market—are both available. In addition, a company can expand by extending its existing operations into new countries and areas of the world. The latter method, geographical expansion, is one of the major opportunities of international marketing. To pursue geographic expansion effectively, a framework for considering alternatives is required. When a company has a single or multicountry product/market base, it can select from five strategic alternatives to extend this base into other geographic markets.

Strategy 1: Product-Communication Extension (Dual Extension)

Many companies employ product-communication extension as a strategy for pursuing opportunities outside the home market. Under the right conditions, this is the easiest product marketing strategy and, in many instances, the most profitable one as well. U.S. companies pursuing this strategy sell exactly the same product, with the same advertising and promotional appeals used in the United States, in some or all world market countries or segments. Note that this strategy is utilized by companies in stages 2, 4, and 5 as defined in Chapter 10. The critical difference is one of execution and mind-set. In the stage 2 company, the dual extension strategy grows out of an ethnocentric orientation; the stage 2 company is making the *assumption* that all markets are alike. A company in stage 4 or 5 does not fall victim to such assumptions; the company's geocentric orientation allows it to thoroughly understand its markets and consciously take advantage of similarities in world markets.

One of the leading practitioners of this approach is PepsiCo, whose outstanding global performance shows the rewards of this practice. Gillette also recently used this strategy in the worldwide launch of its Sensor razor, using the advertising theme "The Best a Man Can Get."

Some marketers have learned the hard way that the dual extension approach does not work in every market. When Campbell Soup tried to sell its tomato soup in the United Kingdom, it discovered, after substantial losses, that the English prefer a more bitter taste than Americans. Happily, Campbell learned its lesson and subsequently succeeded in Japan by offering seven soup varieties—for example, corn potage—designed specifically for the Japanese markets. Another U.S. company spent several million dollars in an unsuccessful effort to capture the British cake mix market. It offered fancy U.S.-style cake mixes with frosting. After the product was launched, the company discovered that the British consume their cake at tea time. The cake they prefer is dry, spongy, and suitable for being picked up with the left hand while the right manages a cup of tea. A second U.S. company hoping to sell cake mixes in the United Kingdom assembled a panel of housewives and asked them to bake their favorite cake. Having learned about British cake preferences, this company created a dry, spongy cake mix product and acquired a major share of the British market.

Philip Morris once attempted to take advantage of the fact that its U.S. TV advertising reached a sizable Canadian audience in border areas. Canadian smokers prefer a "straight" Virginia cigarette, in contrast to American smokers who prefer cigarettes made from blended tobacco. Philip Morris managers chose to ignore market research indicating that Canadians would not accept a blended cigarette. The managers went ahead with marketing programs designed to extend retail distribution of U.S. blended brands in the

Canadian border areas served by U.S. television. Not surprisingly, the Canadian preference for straight, nonblended cigarettes remained unchanged. American-style cigarettes sold right up to the border but no farther. Philip Morris had to withdraw its U.S. brands.

In the early 1960s, CPC International hoped to pursue a product extension strategy with Knorr dehydrated soups in the United States. Dehydrated soups dominate the soup market in Europe, and CPC managers believed they had a market opportunity in the United States. However, a faulty marketing research design led to erroneous conclusions concerning market potential for this product. CPC based its decision to go ahead with Knorr on reports of taste panel comparisons of Knorr dehydrated soups with popular canned soups. The results of these panel tests indicated a strong preference for the Knorr product. Unfortunately, these taste panel tests did not simulate the actual market environment for soup, which includes not only eating but also preparation. Dry soups require 15 to 20 minutes cooking time, whereas canned soups offer the benefit of "heat and serve." The preparation difference is a critical factor in influencing soup purchases, and it resulted in another failure of the extension strategy. In this case, it was only partial extension: Flavors were adapted, but the basic form of the product was extended. And, the failure was not absolute. The product has been a failure in relation to the original expectations but it has been a success in the United States in its category (dry soups). However, the category market share remains small compared with Europe's.

The product-communication extension strategy has an enormous appeal to global companies because of the cost savings associated with this approach. The two most obvious sources of savings are manufacturing economies of scale and elimination of duplicate product R&D costs. Also important are the substantial economies associated with standardization of marketing communications. For a company with worldwide operations, the cost of preparing separate print and TV ads for each market can be enormous. Although these cost savings are important, they should not distract executives from the more important objective of maximum profit performance, which may require the use of an adaptation or invention strategy. As we have seen, product extension, in spite of its immediate cost savings, may in fact result in market failure.

Strategy 2: Product Extension/Communication Adaptation

When a product fills a different need, appeals to a different segment, or serves a different function under conditions of use that are the same or similar to those in the domestic market, the only adjustment that may be required is in marketing communications. Bicycles and motor scooters are examples of products that have been marketed with this approach. They satisfy recreation needs in the United States but serve as basic transportation in many other countries. Similarly, outboard marine motors are usually sold to a recreation market in the United States, whereas the same motors in many foreign countries are often sold to fishing and transportation fleets. Another example is the U.S. farm machinery company that decided to market its U.S. line of home lawn and garden power equipment in less-developed countries (LDCs) as agricultural implements. The equipment was ideally suited to the needs of farmers in many LDCs. Equally important was the lower price: almost a third less than competing equipment especially designed for small-acreage farming offered by competing foreign manufacturers.

As these examples show, the product extension/communication adaptation strategy—either by design or by accident—results in **product transformation.** The same physical product ends up serving a different function or use than that for which it was originally designed or created. There are many examples of food product transformation. The classic example is Perrier, discussed in earlier chapters; recall that, while mineral water has long been advertised and consumed in Europe as a staple with healthful qualities, Perrier became a success in America only after it was marketed as *the* chic beverage to order in restaurants and bars instead of a cocktail.

The appeal of the product extension/communication adaptation strategy is its relatively low cost of implementation. Since the product in this strategy is unchanged, R&D, tooling, manufacturing setup, and inventory costs associated with additions to the product line are avoided. The only costs of this approach are in identifying different product functions and revising marketing communications (including advertising, sales promotion, and point-of-sale material) around the newly identified function.

Strategy 3: Product Adaptation/Communication Extension

A third approach to global product planning is to extend, without change, the basic home-market communications strategy while adapting the product to local use or preference conditions. Note that this strategy (and the one that follows) may be utilized by both stage 3 and stage 4 companies. The critical difference is, as noted above, one of execution and mindset. In the stage 3 company, the product adaptation strategy grows out of a polycentric orientation; the stage 3 company *assumes* that all markets are different. By contrast, the geocentric orientation of managers and executives in a stage 4, global company has sensitized them to actual, rather than assumed, differences between markets.

Exxon adheres to this third strategy: It adapts its gasoline formulations to meet the weather conditions prevailing in different markets while extending the basic communications appeal, "Put a Tiger in Your Tank" without change. There are many other examples of products that have been adjusted to perform the same function around the globe under different environmental conditions. Soap and detergent manufacturers have adjusted their product formulations to meet local water and washing equipment conditions with no change in their basic communications approach. Household appliances have been scaled to sizes appropriate to different use environments, and clothing has been adapted to meet fashion criteria. Also, food products, by virtue of their potentially high degree of environmental sensitivity, are often adapted. Mueslix, for example, is the name of a mushlike European "health" cereal that is popular in Europe. Kellogg's brought the Mueslix name and product concept to the United States but completely changed the formulation and nature of the product.

Strategy 4: Product-Communication Adaptation (Dual Adaptation)

Sometimes, when comparing a new geographic market to the home market, marketers discover that environmental conditions or consumer preferences differ; the same may be true of the function a product serves or consumer receptivity to advertising appeals. In essence, this is a combination of the market conditions of strategies 2 and 3. In such a situation, a stage 4 or 5 company will utilize the strategy of product and communication adaptation. As is true about strategy 3, stage 3 companies will also use dual adaptation—regardless of whether the strategy is warranted by market conditions, preferences, function, or receptivity.

Unilever's experience with fabric softener in Europe exemplifies the classic multinational road to adaptation. For years, the product was sold in 10 countries under seven different brand names, with different bottles and marketing strategies. Unilever's decentralized structure meant that product and marketing decisions were left to country managers. They chose names that had local-language appeal and selected package designs to fit local tastes. Today, rival Procter & Gamble is introducing competitive products with a pan-European strategy of standardized products with single names, suggesting that the European market is more similar than Unilever assumed. In response, Unilever's European brand managers are attempting to move gradually toward standardization.[18]

Hallmark, American Greetings, and other U.S.-based greeting card manufacturers have faced genuine market condition and preference differences in Europe, where the function

[18]E. S. Browning, "In Pursuit of the Elusive Euroconsumer," *The Wall Street Journal* (Apr. 23, 1992), p. B2.

of a greeting card is to provide a space for the sender to write an individual message. In contrast, U.S. cards contain a prepared message, known in the greeting card industry as a "sentiment." In European stores, cards are handled frequently by customers, a practice that makes it necessary to wrap greeting cards in cellophane. Thus, U.S. manufacturers pursuing an adaptation strategy have changed both their product and their marketing communications in response to this set of environmental differences.

Sometimes, a company will draw upon all four of these strategies simultaneously when marketing a given product in different parts of the world. For example, H.J. Heinz utilizes a mix of strategies in its ketchup marketing. While a dual extension strategy works in England, spicier, hotter formulations are also popular in central Europe and Sweden. Recent ads in France featured a cowboy lassoing a bottle of ketchup and thus reminded consumers of the product's American heritage. Swedish ads conveyed a more cosmopolitan message; by promoting Heinz as "the taste of the big world" and featuring well-known landmarks such as the Eiffel Tower, the ads disguised the product's origins.[19]

Strategy 5: Product Invention

Adaptation strategies are effective approaches to international (stage 2) and multinational (stage 3) marketing, but they may not respond to global market opportunities. Nor do they respond to the situation in markets where customers do not have the purchasing power to buy either the existing or adapted product. This latter situation applies to LDCs of the world which are home to roughly three-quarters of the world's population. When potential customers have limited purchasing power, a company may need to develop an entirely new product designed to satisfy the need or want at a price that is within the reach of the potential customer. Invention is a demanding but potentially rewarding product strategy for reaching mass markets in LDCs.

The winners in global competition are the companies that can develop products offering the most benefits, which in turn create the greatest value for buyers. In some instances, value is not defined in terms of performance, but rather in terms of customer perception. The latter is as important for an expensive perfume or champagne as it is for an inexpensive soft drink. Product quality is essential—indeed, it is frequently a given—but it is also necessary to support the product quality with imaginative, value-creating advertising and marketing communications. Most industry experts believe that a global appeal and a global advertising campaign are more effective in creating the perception of value than are a series of separate national campaigns.

Colgate pursued this strategy in developing Total, a new toothpaste brand whose formulation, imagery, and ultimate consumer appeal were designed from the ground up to translate across national boundaries. The product was tested in six countries, each of which had a different cultural profile: the Philippines, Austrialia, Colombia, Greece, Portugal, and the United Kingdom. Total is now sold in 75 countries and generates $150 million in revenues. According to John Steel, senior vice president for global business development at Colgate, Total's success results from the application of a fundamental marketing principle: Consumers are the ones who make or break brands. "There ain't no consumers at 300 Park Avenue," he says, referring to company headquarters. Steel explains, "You get a lot more benefit and you can do a lot more with a global brand than you can a local brand. You can bring the best advertising talent from the world onto a problem. You can bring the best research brains, the best leverage of your organization onto something that is truly global. Then all your R&D pays off, the huge packaging costs pay off, the advertising pays off, and you can leverage the organization all at once."[20]

---

[19]Gabriella Stern, "Heinz Aims to Export Taste for Ketchup," *The Wall Street Journal* (Nov. 20, 1992), pp. B1, B9.
[20]Pam Weisz, "Border Crossings: Brands Unify Image to Counter Cult of Culture," *Brandweek* (Oct. 31, 1994), p. 24.

TABLE 13–3 GLOBAL PRODUCT/COMMUNICATION MIX: STRATEGIC ALTERNATIVES

Strategy*	Product Function or Need Satisfied	Conditions of Product Use	Ability to Buy Product	Recommended Product Strategy	Recommended Communication Strategy	Product Examples
1	Same	Same	Yes	Extension	Extension	Soft drinks
2	Different	Same	Yes	Extension	Adaptation	Bicycles
3	Same	Different	Yes	Adaptation	Extension	Gasoline
4	Different	Different	Yes	Adaptation	Adaptation	Greeting cards
5	Same	—	No	Invention	New communications	Hand-powered washing machines

*Strategies are as follows:
1 = Dual Extension
2 = Product Extension/Communication Adaptation
3 = Product Adaptation/Communication Extension
4 = Dual Adaptation
5 = Product Invention

How To Choose a Strategy

Most companies seek a product strategy that optimizes company profits over the long term. Which strategy for global markets best achieves this goal? There is, unfortunately, no general answer to this question. Rather, the answer depends upon the specific product-market-company mix.

As noted in Chapter 2, a product's environmental sensitivity may be assessed in terms of a continuum ranging from low to high. Also, recall from Chapter 4 that, in terms of cultural sensitivity, consumer products are more sensitive than industrial products. Another rule of thumb is that food products frequently exhibit the highest degree of cultural sensitivity. What this means to managers is that some products, by their nature, are likely to demand significant adaptation. Others require only partial adaptation, and still others are best left unchanged.

Companies differ in both their willingness and capability to identify and produce profitable product adaptations. Unfortunately, too many stage 1 and 2 companies are oblivious to the issues presented above. One new-product expert has described three stages that a company must go through as follows:

1. *Cave dweller.* The primary motivation behind launching new products internationally is to dispose of excess production or increase plant capacity utilization.
2. *Naive nationalist.* The company recognizes growth opportunities outside the domestic market. It realizes that cultures and markets differ from country to country, and as a result, it sees product adaptation as the only possible alternative.
3. *Globally sensitive.* The company views regions or the entire world as the competitive marketplace. New product opportunities are evaluated across countries, with some standardization planned as well as some differentiation to accommodate cultural variances. New product planning processes and control systems are reasonably standardized.[21]

To sum up, the choice of product and communication strategy in international marketing is a function of three key factors: (1) the product itself, defined in terms of the function or need it serves; (2) the market, defined in terms of the conditions under which the product is used, the preferences of potential customers, and the ability to buy the products in question; and (3) the costs of adaptation and manufacture to the company considering these product-communication approaches. Only after analysis of the product/market fit and of company capabilities and costs can executives choose the most profitable international strategy. The alternatives are outlined in Table 13–3.

[21]Thomas D. Kuczmarski, *Managing New Products: The Power of Innovation* (Upper Saddle River, N.J.: Prentice Hall, 1992), p. 254.

NEW PRODUCTS IN GLOBAL MARKETING

In today's dynamic, competitive market environment, many companies realize that continuous development and introduction of new products are keys to survival and growth. Which companies excel at these activities? Gary Reiner, a new product specialist with the Boston Consulting Group, has compiled the following list: Honda, Compaq, Motorola, Canon, Boeing, Merck, Microsoft, Intel, and Toyota. One common characteristic: They are global companies that pursue opportunities in global markets where competition is fierce, thus ensuring that new products will be world class. Other characteristics noted by Reiner are:

1. They focus on one or only a few businesses.
2. Senior management is actively involved in defining and improving the product development process.
3. They have the ability to recruit and retain "the best and the brightest" people in their fields.
4. They understand that speed in bringing new products to market reinforces product quality.[22]

What is a new product? Newness can be assessed in the context of the product itself, the organization, and the market. The product may be an entirely new invention or innovation—for example, the VCR or the compact disc. It may be a line extension (a modification of an existing product) such as Diet Coke. Newness may also be organizational, as when a company acquires an already existing product with which it has no previous experience. Finally, an existing product that is not new to a company may be new to a particular market.

Identifying New Product Ideas

The starting point for an effective worldwide new product program is an information system that seeks new product ideas from all potentially useful sources and channels these ideas to relevant screening and decision centers within the organization. There are many sources of new product ideas, including customers, suppliers, competitors, company salespeople, distributors and agents, subsidiary executives, headquarters executives, documentary sources (for example, information service reports and publications), and, finally, actual firsthand observation of the market environment.

The value of firsthand market observation as a source of new product ideas is illustrated by troll dolls, which were originally popular in the United States during the 1960s. While traveling in Denmark in 1982, Steven Stark, a U.S. marketing executive, discovered that trolls had never gone out of style in that country. Stark and his wife licensed the Danish designs and began to manufacture them in the United States; by 1992, company sales had reached the $150 million mark.[23]

The International New Product Department

As noted above, a high volume of information flow is required to scan adequately for new product opportunities, and considerable effort is subsequently required to screen these opportunities to identify candidates for product development. The best organizational design for addressing these requirements is a new product department.[24] The function of such a department would be fourfold: (1) to ensure that all relevant information sources are continuously tapped for new product ideas; (2) to screen these ideas to identify candidates for investigation; (3) to investigate and analyze selected new product ideas; and (4) to ensure that the organization commits resources to the most likely new product candidates and is continuously involved in an orderly program of new product introduction and development on a worldwide basis.

With the enormous number of possible new products, most companies establish screen-

[22]Gary Reiner, "Lessons from the World's Best Product Developers," *The Wall Street Journal* (Apr. 4, 1990), p. A12.
[23]Anne Underwood, "Daddy, Can I Have One?" *Newsweek* (Nov. 2, 1992), p. 74.
[24]See, for example, "Introducing a New Product in a Foreign Market," Management Monograph No. 33 (New York: Business International 1966), p. 7.

ing grids in order to focus on those ideas that are most appropriate for investigation. The following questions are relevant to this task:

1. How big is the market for this product at various prices?
2. What are the likely competitive moves in response to our activity with this product?
3. Can we market the product through our existing structure? If not, what changes and what costs will be required to make the changes?
4. Given estimates of potential demand for this product at specified prices with estimated levels of competition, can we source the product at a cost that will yield an adequate profit?
5. Does this product fit our strategic development plan? (a) Is the product consistent with our overall goals and objectives? (b) Is the product consistent with our available resources? (c) Is the product consistent with our management structure? (d) Does the product have adequate global potential?

Testing New Products in National Markets

The major lesson of new product introduction outside the home market has been that whenever a product interacts with human, mechanical, or chemical elements, there is the potential for a surprising and unexpected incompatibility. Since virtually *every* product matches this description, it is important to test a product under actual market conditions before proceeding with full-scale introduction. A test does not necessarily involve a full-scale test-marketing effort. It may simply involve observing the actual use of the product in the target market.

Failure to assess actual use conditions can lead to big surprises, as in the case of Singer sewing machines sold in African markets. These machines, manufactured in Scotland by Singer, were slightly redesigned by Scottish engineers. The location of a small bolt on the product's base was changed; the change had no effect on product performance but did save a few pennies per unit in manufacturing costs. Unfortunately, when the modified machine reached Africa, it was discovered that this small change was disastrous for product sales. The Scottish engineers did not take into account the fact that in Africa, it is customary for women to transport any bundle or load—including sewing machines—on their heads. The relocated bolt was positioned at exactly the place where head met machine for proper balance; since the sewing machines were no longer transportable, demand decreased substantially.

SUMMARY

The product is the most important element of a marketing program. Global marketers face the challenge of formulating a coherent global product strategy for their companies. Product strategy requires an evaluation of the basic needs and conditions of use in the company's existing and proposed markets. Whenever possible, opportunities to market global products should be given precedence over opportunities to market local or international products. Companies must plan a way to reach their chosen target market(s) by determining the best positioning for its product offerings. Here marketers devise an appropriate marketing mix to fix the product in the mind of the potential buyers in the target market. High-tech and high-touch positioning are two strategies that can work well for a global product. The same positioning and marketing approaches can be used with global brands such as Coca-Cola.

Marketers must consider four factors when designing products for global markets: preferences, cost, regulations, and compatibility. Attitudes toward a product's country of origin must also be taken into account. Five strategic alternatives are open to companies pursuing geographic expansion: product-communication extension, product extension/communication adaptation, product adaptation/communication extension, product-communication adaptation, and product invention. Global competition has created pressure on companies to excel at product development. While there are different definitions of what constitutes a "new" product, the most difficult type of new product launch is clearly one involving an entirely new product in a market where a company has little or no experience. Successful global product launch requires leverage. An organization must accumulate and disseminate knowledge concerning past practices—both successful and unsuccessful. Opportunities for comparative analysis further enhance the effectiveness of marketing planning activities within the global system.

DISCUSSION QUESTIONS

1. What is the difference between a product and a brand?
2. What are the differences among a local, an international, and a global product or brand? Cite examples.
3. What criteria should global marketers consider when making product design decisions?
4. How can buyer attitudes about a product's country of origin affect marketing strategy?
5. Identify several global brands. What are some of the reasons for the global success of the brands you chose?
6. Briefly describe various combinations of product-communication strategies available to global marketers. When is it appropriate to use each?

BIBLIOGRAPHY

Books

Keegan, Warren J., Sandra Moriarty and Tom Duncan. *Marketing*, 2nd. ed. Upper Saddle River, N.J.: Prentice Hall, 1995.

Kuczmarski, Thomas D. *Managing New Products: The Power of Innovation.* Upper Saddle River, N.J.: Prentice-Hall, 1992.

Macrae, Chris. *World Class Brands*. Reading, Mass.: Addison-Wesley, 1991.

Papadopoulos, Nicolas, and Louise A. Heslop. *Product-Country Images: Impact and Role in International Marketing.* New York: International Business Press, 1993.

Quelch, John A., Robert Buzzell, and Eric Salama. *The Marketing Challenge of Europe 1992.* Reading, Mass.: Addison-Wesley, 1991.

Rosenthal, Stephen R. *Effective Product Design and Development: How to Cut Lead Time and Increase Customer Satisfaction.* Homewood, Ill.: Business One Irwin, 1992.

Articles

Ayers, Robert U., and Wilbur A. Steger. "Rejuvenating the Life Cycle Concept." *Journal of Business Strategy* 6, no. 1 (Summer 1985), pp. 6–76.

Carpano, Claudio, and James J. Chrisman. "Performance Implications of International Product Strategies and the Integration of Marketing Activities." *Journal of International Marketing* 3, no. 1 (1995), pp. 9–28.

Chao, Paul. "Partitioning Country of Origin Effects: Consumer Evaluations of a Hybrid Product." *Journal of International Business Studies* 24, no. 2 (Second Quarter 1993), pp. 291–306.

Cordell, Victor V. "Effects of Consumer Preferences for Foreign Sourced Products." *Journal of International Business Studies* 23, no. 2 (Second Quarter 1992), pp. 251–270.

Domzal, Teresa J., and Lynette Unger. "Emerging Positioning Strategies in Global Marketing." *Journal of Consumer Marketing* 4, no. 4 (Fall 1987), pp. 27–37.

Du Preez, Johann P., Adamantios Diamantopoulos, and Bodo B. Schlegelmilch. "Product Standardization and Attribute Saliency: A Three-Product Empirical Comparison." *Journal of International Marketing* 2, no. 1 (1994), pp. 7–28.

Elliott, Gregory R., and Ross C. Cameron. "Consumer Perception of Product Quality and the Country-of-Origin Effect." *Journal of International Marketing* 2, no. 2 (1994), pp. 49–62.

Faulds, David J., Orlen Grunewald, and Denise Johnson. "A Cross-National Investigation of the Relationship Between the Price and Quality of Consumer Products: 1970–1990." *Journal of Global Marketing* 8, no. 1 (1994), pp. 7–26.

Grune, George V. "Global Marketing." *Vital Speeches* 55, no. 19 (July 15, 1989), pp. 580–582.

Hansotia, Behran J., and Muzaffar A. Shaikh. "The Strategic Determinancy Approach to Brand Management." *Business Marketing* 70 (February 1985), pp. 66–82.

Hill, John S., and William L. James. "Product and Promotion Transfers in Consumer Goods Multinationals." *International Marketing Review* 8, no. 2, pp. 6–17.

Hill, John S., and Up Kwon. "Product Mixes in U.S. Multinationals: An Empirical Study." *Journal of Global Marketing* 6, no. 3 (1992), pp. 55–73.

Johansson, Johny K., Susan P. Douglas, and Ikuiiro Nonaka. "Assessing the Impact of Country of Origin on Product Evaluations: A New Methodologic Prospective." *Journal of Marketing Research* 22, no. 4 (November 1985), pp. 388–396.

Johansson, Johny K., and Hans B. Thorelli. "International Product Positioning." *Journal of International Business Studies* 16, no. 3 (Fall 1985), pp. 57–76.

Johansson, Johny K., Ilkka A. Ronkainen, and Michael R. Czinkota. "Negative Country-of-Origin Effects: The Case of the New Russia." *Journal of International Business Studies* 25, no. 1 (First Quarter 1994), pp. 157–176.

Kotabe, Masaaki. "Corporate Product Policy and Innovative Behavior of European and Japanese Multinational: An Empirical Investigation." *Journal of Marketing* 54, no. 2 (April 1990), pp. 19–33.

Moskowitz, Howard R., and Samuel Rabino. "Sensory Segmentation: An Organizing Principle for International Product Concept Generation." *Journal of Global Marketing* 8, no. 1 (1994), pp. 73–94.

Ogbuehi, Alphonso O., and Ralph A. Jr. Bellas. "Decentralized R&D for Global Product Development: Strategic Implications for the Multinational Corporation." *International Marketing Review* 9, no. 5, pp. 60–70.

Prasad, V. Kanti, and G.M. Naidu. "Perspectives and Preparedness Regarding ISO-9000 International Quality Standards." *Journal of International Marketing* 2, no. 2 (1994), pp. 81–98.

Robinson, William T., and Claes Fornell. "Sources of Market Pioneer Advantages in Consumer Goods Industries." *Journal of Marketing Research* 22, no. 3 August 1985 pp. 305–317.

Roth, Martin S., and Jean B. Romeo. "Matching Product Category and Country Image Perceptions: A Framework for Managing Country-of-Origin Effects." *Journal of International Business Studies* 23, no. 3 (Third Quarter 1992), pp. 477–498.

Samiee, Saeed. "Customer Evaluation of Products in a Global Market." *Journal of International Business Studies* 25, no. 3 (Third Quarter 1994), pp. 579–604.

Tse, David K., and Gerald Gorn. "An Experiment on the Salience of Country-of-Origin in the Era of Global Brands." *Journal of International Marketing* 1, no. 1 (1993), pp. 57–76.

Tse, David K., and Wei-na Lee. "Removing Negative Country Images: Effects of Decomposition, Branding, and Product Experience." *Journal of International Marketing* 1, no. 4 (1993), pp. 25–48.

Ulgado, Francis M. and Moonku Lee. "Consumer Evaluations of Bi-National Products in the Global Market." *Journal of International Marketing* 1, no. 3 (1993), pp. 5–22.

Walters, Peter G.P., and Brian Toyne. "Product Modification and Standardization in International Markets: Strategic Options and Facilitating Policies." *Columbia Journal of World Business* 24, no. 4 (Winter 1989), pp. 37–44.

Witt, Jerome, and C.P. Rao. "The Impact of Global Sourcing on Consumers: Country-of-Origin Effects on Perceived Risk." *Journal of Global Marketing* 6, no. 3 (1992), pp. 105–128.

PHILIPS ELECTRONICS NV: A SLEEPING GIANT WAKES TO DISCOVER MARKETING

Philips Electronics NV is a giant $32 billion consumer electronics company headquartered in the Netherlands. Philips manufactures a vast array of products. The company's Domestic Appliance and Personal Care unit sells 40 million household appliances and related items each year. Philips Lighting is the largest manufacturer of lightbulbs the world; in Western Europe alone, the Philips brand commands a 36 percent share of the lightbulb market. Other divisions include Consumer Electronics, Industrial Electronics, Semiconductors, Medical Systems, and Polygram records. Twenty-five percent of Philips's sales come from the United States, where its hi-fi and television products are sold under both the Magnavox and Philips brand names.

Philips, one of only two non-Japanese firms among the top 10 global consumer electronics companies, faces a number of difficult problems. For one thing, profit margins are only 2 percent—half of what most Japanese companies enjoy and especially meager when compared to GE's 9 percent. Even worse, in 1990, the Dutch newspaper *Financieel Dagblad* reported that Japanese competitors were twice as efficient as Philips. For example, sales per employee for Matsushita totaled $190,390; the figure at Philips was $94,436.

Compounding these difficulties is the fact that Philips has not been adept at capitalizing on innovations resulting from its own R&D efforts. A major problem has been the glorification of academic, laboratory-based advances rather than marketing, consumer-based achievements. Quite simply, Philips has succeeded brilliantly in developing technically superior products but has failed to *market* them well. Indeed, it has been reported that researchers at some eight Philips R&D centers around the world touted most highly those discoveries that did not lead to commercial products.

Such attitudes have left Philips playing catch-up behind more marketing-minded competitors. For example, when Philips invented the audiocassette in 1962, it envisioned using the technology only for such professional purposes as dictaphones. Japanese companies, however, spotted the *consumer* potential of the same technology and quickly developed audiocassette decks for home use. Philips entered the consumer market much later, and today commands a meager 2 percent of the market for consumer tape decks.

The same story was repeated with videocassette recorders. Philips first developed a product for broadcast and professional use in 1972, ignoring the possibility of marketing a videocassette recorder for home use. Although the Philips recorder enjoyed some success in Europe as an alternative to Sony's U-matic professional VCR, Sony and other Japanese companies ultimately set their sights on home users. While Sony's Beta and Matsushita's VHS VCRs—each representing incompatible technologies—thus battled it out for dominance in the home market, Philips belatedly offered a home VCR with technology that represented yet a *third* incompatible approach. Tapes recorded on Philips's system could not be played back on Japanese VCRs, and vice versa. Even though experts considered Philips's V-2000 system superior to the Japanese designs, it arrived on the market too late to prevent Japanese domination of the worldwide VCR industry. In the end, the VHS format became the dominant home standard.

Philips fared somewhat better with a third innovation—the compact disc player. In order to avoid a repeat of the incompatibility problems that plagued the development of its VCRs, Philips shared its research on disc players with Sony. As a result of the successful collaboration, CD players, introduced in the early 1980s, became a worldwide success. However, Sony's advertisements left many people with the impression that Sony, rather than Philips, was the inventor of the CD player. Nevertheless, Philips has 20 percent of the market for CD players and receives licensing fees from other manufacturers that use its technology.

In order to help achieve similar successes in the future, Philips has reorganized and put marketers in closer touch with researchers. Now a marketing staffer is assigned to each research effort during the final stages of laboratory development. Moreover, the company's budget for basic research—as opposed to research applied to specific product or technology-related issues—has been cut in half, to 10 percent of total R&D. Says Keith Fuller of Philips's lab in Redhill, England, "The researcher wants to keep on researching." Now, however, he notes that Philips is "trying to put time and cost limits on our work." In addition, researchers who have put in five to eight years of service in laboratory work are being rotated into marketing and other departments to promote better working relationships between the different functional areas. In the words of another Philips representative, "We have found out that our own picture of the company was different from the impression the outside world had of us. . . . We have found out that we were not as good as we thought we were."

This newfound attitude came not a moment too soon. In 1990, Philips's problems cost president C. J. van der Klugt his job after company profits plunged. The new president, Jan D. Timmer, immediately embarked upon a program to make Philips a leaner organization. In July 1990, he cut nearly 5,000 jobs from the Information Systems Division; in August he announced that an additional 35,000 to 45,000 positions would be cut around the world. In Timmer's view, Philips had grown too large and bureaucratic, and its employees, convinced of the company's invincibility, had become insulated and lost their creativity. Timmer hoped to infuse the company with a new entrepreneurial spirit; in his words, Philips employees needed to realize that "the outside world is a damn tough one."

It soon became apparent that Timmer's efforts were paying off. According to calculations published by *Financial*

World magazine in its third annual survey of the world's top brands, the value of the Philips brand name more than doubled between 1993 and 1994, to nearly $1.4 billion. The figure reflected the company's lower costs and increased marketing effort, as well as brand strength considerations such as the ability to "travel well" across geographic and cultural borders. *Financial World* ranked Philips ahead of such well-known global brands as Apple, Pioneer, and IBM. (The Kodak brand ranked number one in the high-tech category.)

Despite this good publicity, by mid-1994 Philips was still looking for a hit consumer electronics product. It had invested $500 million in Compact Disc Interactive (CD-i), an easy-to-use multimedia product that was designed to be attached to a television set and used as an interactive teaching aid, game console, and video player. The unit could also play standard and interactive music CDs. Product development had begun in the 1980s; initially, Japanese consumer electronics powerhouses, Sony and Matsushita collaborated on the CD-i project. Various problems arose, however, such as the reluctance of Philips engineers to share technical specifications with the Japanese. In the end, Philips severed ties with its Japanese partners and moved ahead on CD-i independently.

CD-i was introduced with great fanfare in the fall of 1991 as "The Imagination Machine." Despite CD-i's versatility, acceptance was generally cool in the United States and Europe. In the United States, Philips failed to persuade Dow Stereo/Video, a small but highly regarded chain of upscale consumer-electronics stores in southern California, to carry CD-i. CD-i was available at stores in the Macy's chain, at Radio Shack, and at Service Merchandise, a catalog showroom retailer. CD-i's sophisticated features meant that clerks had to spend considerable time explaining the product to prospective buyers. Another sales barrier was the hefty price tag—$799 in the United States. At one German retailer, the 47-store Mediamarkt-Saturn Chain, only 95 players were sold during all of 1993. To bolster the United States marketing effort, Philips spent about $20 million to produce and broadcast a 30-minute infomercial titled "The Great Wall" during which CD-i's various features were demonstrated. Philips broke new ground by purchasing air time for the infomercial during prime time instead of late at night. Viewers were invited to call a toll-free number for the name of their nearest dealer.

By mid-1994, 80 movies and 150 interactive titles were available in the CD-i format. Interactive titles, which carried a $49.98 list price in the United States, included "NFL Football Trivia," fantasy games such as "Zelda: The Wand of Gamelon," and a "dating and dress-up game" called "Girl's Club." The promise of CD-i could be seen in a first-of-its-kind interactive music disc by rock artist Todd Rundgren titled "No World Order." Listeners could customize the tempo, mood, and style of the performance they were listening to. Still, complained a marketing executive at FNAC, a Paris-based chain of consumer electronics stores, "There's never enough software." However, retailers were still backing the product; as a spokesperson for the 850-store Dixons and Curry's consumer electronics chain noted, "We can't overlook a major new technology."

Unfortunately for Philips, CD-i had to vie with other new technologies in the marketplace. For example, the popularity of CD-ROM drives increased dramatically during 1993 and 1994. CD-ROM was used in conjunction with a PC rather than a television set, but the discs were similar in capablity to those used with CD-i. Also in 1993, another expensive TV-based multimedia product appeared. 3DO, also priced at $799 and sold by Japan's Matsushita Electric Company, appeared to be CD-i's most direct competitor.

Philips executives remained upbeat about CD-i's prospects. The company promised that 100 new software titles would appear by the end of 1994. Despite worldwide CD-i sales of only 300,000 units since the product's introduction, the president of Philips's interactive-media division predicted that 1 million households around the world would own players by the end of 1994. To spur U.S. sales, a new Magnavox unit was introduced and priced at $299, less than half the price of the first CD-i players. "We're almost giving away the machines because we want to sell software," said Philips executive John Hawkins. A $15 million advertising campaign featuring comedian Phil Hartman was also planned for the last quarter of the year. Vowed Mr. Hawkins: "You aren't going to be able to avoid seeing us."

DISCUSSION QUESTIONS

1. Why has Philips repeatedly failed to capitalize on its major innovations in electronics? What is the problem?
2. What were the biggest marketing challenges facing Philips during the launch of CD-i?
3. What changes would you recommend to Philips to ensure more success with global marketing?

Sources: Martin du Bois and Cacilie Rohwedder, "Early Casualty?" *The Wall Street Journal* (Mar. 21, 1994), p. R19.

Nikhil Hutheesing, "Betamax versus VHS All Over Again?" *Forbes* (Jan. 3, 1994), pp. 88–89.

Steven Greenhouse, "An Anxious Philips," *The New York Times* (June 4, 1989), Sec. 3, p. 1, 10.

Jonathan Kapstein, "Enough with the Theory—Where's the Thingamajig?" *Business Week* (Mar. 21, 1989), pp. 154, 156, 158.

Jonathan B. Levine, "What's Behind the Bombshell at Philips," *Business Week* (May 28, 1990), pp. 38–39.

D. Kuin, "Philips Is Zichzelf Tegengekomen," *Financieel Dagblad* (Oct. 10, 1990), p. 7.

W. Van Enk, "De Nieuwe terugspeelbal van Philips-president Timmer," *Financieel Dagblad* (Oct. 10, 1990), p. 5.

Klaas Steenhuis, "Timmer Had Voor Harde Aanpak Geen Alternatief," *Financieel Telegraaf* (Oct. 27, 1990), p. 19.

James Lardner, *Fast Forward: Hollywood, the Japanese, and the VCR Wars* (NAL Penguin: New York, 1987).

*I*n the early 1990s, Philips Electronics NV's Consumer Electronics Division put the world on notice that it was seizing the new-product initiative with renewed vigor. First, Philips launched a new multimedia product known as Compact Disc Interactive, or CD-i. The device was similar to a standard CD player with an additional feature: When hooked up to a TV set, it could play video games, movies, and educational and entertainment software in a new disc format. Philips was also anxious to reclaim a leading role in the home stereo market with a new product called Digital Compact Cassette, or DCC. Philips believed DCC represented a new era in audiocassette recording and playback. DCC would provide clearer and quieter performance than was offered by even the best conventional analog cassette equipment; owners could make copies of their favorite CDs that were virtually indistinguishable from the originals.

Early in the development of DCC, Philips created a team to assess what the product should do. The team members knew that annual worldwide sales of standard analog cassette machines—personal and car stereos as well as home decks—totaled 200 million units. Also, consumers bought hundreds of millions of prerecorded cassettes every year. Gerry Wirtz was named coordinator in charge of the team. Recalling the effort, he said:

> I asked myself what my neighbors might buy. They might have a CD player at home and a cassette player in the car. They would not be interested in a completely new recorder just because it was digital. But if I came to them with a digital machine that would play a new type of cassette and it also played their old one— now they might be interested.

Accordingly, while DCC was designed to provide the sonic advantages of digital recording and playback, the unit would also play back conventional tapes since many potential buyers already owned large tape libraries.

Besides the compatibility issue, there were several other requirements for market success. One was price. Philips knew that DCC had to be reasonably close in price to existing cassette machines. Another issue was copyright agreements with major music companies; DCC would not sell unless prerecorded tapes were available in the new format. Philips's 80 percent interest in PolyGram Records gave the company access to many artists.

Late in 1989, Philips demonstrated DCC for representatives of other consumer electronics manufacturers and major record labels. Matsushita, whose consumer electronics brands include National, Panasonic, and Technics, agreed to support the project, giving Philips a boost for selling DCC in Japan. Because Matsushita also owned two record labels—MCA Music and Geffen—its support boosted the number of popular prerecorded titles that would be available in the DCC format.

Philips displayed working prototypes of DCC at the Winter Consumer Electronics show in Las Vegas in January 1992. However, a worldwide launch party in Paris scheduled for April 1992 was postponed until fall. Philips had planned to introduce portable versions as well as full-sized DCC units for home use. However, software problems kept the portable models off the market for several months.

Even as the DCC launch date was pushed back, two new complications had appeared. First, Sony announced that it was also developing a new digital recorder/player, the MiniDisc. Sony's system used small optical discs rather than cassettes; Sony's acquisition of CBS Records a few years earlier guaranteed that recordings by Michael Jackson, Mariah Carey, and other popular artists would be released in the MiniDisc format. Sony had also licensed its technology to a number of other companies, so that Aiwa, RCA, Sanyo, and Sharp could market the MiniDisc under their own brand names.

The second complication was legislation in the United States that would require a small royalty on the sale of every piece of digital recording equipment and every blank digital tape sold in the United States. The legislation had been introduced by the music industry, which was afraid that the new generation of digital recording equipment would allow widespread pirating of copyrighted music performances. Passage of the legislation was considered a prerequisite to getting widespread support for DCC by the recorded music industry.

In November 1992, after Philips had spent about $100 million on product development and marketing, the first DCC machines went on sale in the United States. Priced between $700 and $1,000, the units appeared on retailers' shelves in time for the Christmas season. Sony's MiniDisc was launched one month later. By mid-1993, it appeared that MiniDisc was outselling DCC by about two to one. Publicly, Philips expressed satisfaction with the launch; privately, however, the company took steps to shake up the marketing team. In particular, DCC advertising needed an overhaul. The early TV ads didn't show the product and failed to communicate DCC's "backwards compatibility," that is, its ability to play any analog cassette tape. The ads left many viewers—and potential buyers—confused.

Piet Bogels, a veteran Philips executive, became the new project coordinator in charge of worldwide marketing of DCC. In his view, the biggest problem with DCC was the delayed launch of the portable versions. Finally, in June 1993, portable DCC units went on sale in Japan; portables went on sale in the United States and Europe in the fall. Late in 1993, the Philips effort got a boost from Matsushita's "Listen and Win" Sweepstakes. Matsushita used direct mail to target 1,000 known early adopters with a mailing that included a hit album by Meat Loaf in the DCC format and a chance to be an instant winner. Recipients in New York, Los Angeles, and a dozen other major U.S. markets were urged to take the cassette to a designated retailer to preview the album and qualify for a prize. Several grand prizes with a value of $2,500 were offered in each market; winners received a Technics home DCC unit, plus Panasonic portable and car versions.

DISCUSSION QUESTIONS
1. What factors and forces played a critical role in the months leading up to the launch of the DCC?
2. Evaluate the marketing effort behind the launch.
3. Would you buy a DCC unit? Why or why not?

Sources: Jacob Schlesinger, "Matsushita, Pitting Itself Against Sony, Agrees to Back Philips's Digital Cassettes," *The Wall Street Journal* (July 9, 1991), p. B3.
Barry Fox, "The Face of a New Technology," *New Scientist* (July 19, 1993), pp. 30–34.
Patrick M. Reilly, "Sony's Digital Audio Format Pulls Ahead of Philips's, but Both Still Have Far to Go," *The Wall Street Journal* (Aug. 6, 1993), p. B1.
Richard Hudson, "Philips Executive Says Launch of DCC Was Flawed, Vows Comeback," *The Wall Street Journal* (Aug. 19, 1993), p. A7.
Kevin Goldman, "Philips Infomercial Does Its Thing in Popular TV-Watching Hours," *The Wall Street Journal* (Sept. 22, 1993), p. B8.
Patrick M. Reilly, "Skeptics Question Development Progress of Two New Digital-Recording Systems," *The Wall Street Journal* (Jan. 8, 1992), p. B1.
Gerry Khermouch, "Matsushita Wants to Drive DCC Adopters," *Brandweek* (Dec. 13, 1993), p. 5.

Pricing Decisions

For many people, the phrase "black market" conjures up images of a shadowy, underground economy in which goods are bought and sold in back alleys without the knowledge of government authorities. For better or for worse, global marketing has a distinctive color on its palette: gray. "Gray marketing" is the distribution of trademarked products in a country by unauthorized persons. Sometimes, gray marketers bring a product produced in one country—French champagne, for example—into a second country market in competition with authorized importers. The gray marketers sell at prices that undercut those set by the legitimate importers. This practice, known as parallel importing, may flourish when a product is in short supply or when producers attempt to set high prices. This has happened with French champagne sold in the United States; it is also true of the European market for pharmaceuticals, where prices vary widely from country to country. In the United Kingdom and the Netherlands, for example, parallel imports account for as much as 10 percent of the sales of some pharmaceutical brands.

In any country, three basic factors determine the boundaries within which market prices should be set. The first is product cost, which establishes a *price floor*, or minimum price. While it is certainly possible to price a product below the cost boundary, few firms can afford to do this for extended periods of time. Second, competitive prices for comparable products create a *price ceiling*, or upper boundary. International competition almost always puts pressure on the prices of domestic companies. A widespread effect of international trade is to lower prices. Indeed, one of the major arguments favoring international business is the favorable impact of international competition upon national price levels and, in turn, upon a country's rate of inflation. Between the lower and upper boundaries for every product there is an *optimum price*, which is a function of the demand for the product as determined by the willingness and ability of customers to buy. As the gray marketing example illustrates, however, sometimes the optimum price can be affected by arbitragers who exploit price differences in different countries.

The interplay of these factors is reflected in the pricing policies adopted by many companies in the mid-1990s. With inflation in the United States in the low single digits and demand forcing factories to run at or near capacity, companies should be able to raise prices. However, the domestic economic situation is not the only consideration. Worldwide, a combination of idle manufacturing capacity and many jobless workers make it difficult for U.S. companies to increase prices. Notes John Ballard, CEO of a California-based engineering company, "We thought about price increases. But our research of competitors and what the market would bear told us it was not worth pursuing."[1]

BASIC PRICING CONCEPTS

As CEO Ballard's experience shows, the global manager must develop pricing systems and pricing policies that address price floors, price ceilings, and optimum prices in each of the national markets in which his or her company operates. The following is a list of eight basic pricing considerations for marketing outside the home country.[2]

1. Does the price reflect the product's quality?
2. Is the price competitive?
3. Should the firm pursue market penetration, market skimming, or some other pricing objective?
4. What type of discount (trade, cash, quantity) and allowance (advertising, trade-off) should the firm offer its international customers?
5. Should prices differ with market segment?
6. What pricing options are available if the firm's costs increase or decrease? Is demand in the international market elastic or inelastic?
7. Are the firm's prices likely to be viewed by the host-country government as reasonable or exploitative?
8. Do the foreign country's dumping laws pose a problem?

The task of determining prices in global marketing is complicated by fluctuating exchange rates which may bear only limited relationship to underlying costs. According to the concept of purchasing power parity (PPP) outlined in Chapter 6, changes in exchange rates should be directly linked to changes in domestic prices. Thus, in theory, fluctuating exchange rates should not present serious problems for the global marketer, because a rise or decline in the value of the home-country currency should be offset by an opposite rise or decline in domestic price levels. In the real world, however, exchange rates do not move in lock-step fashion with inflation. This means that global marketers are faced with difficult decisions about how to deal with windfalls resulting from favorable exchange rates, as well as losses due to unfavorable exchange rates.

A firm's pricing system and policies must also be consistent with other uniquely global constraints. Those responsible for global pricing decisions must take into account international transportation costs, middlemen in elongated international channels of distribution, and the demands of global accounts for equal price treatment regardless of location. In addition to the diversity of national markets in all three basic dimensions—cost, competition, and demand—the international executive is also confronted by conflicting governmental tax policies and claims as well as various types of price controls. These include dumping legislation, resale price maintenance legislation, price ceilings, and general reviews of price levels. For example, Procter & Gamble encountered strict price controls in Venezuela in the late 1980s. Despite increases in the cost of raw materials, P&G was only granted about 50 percent of the price increases it requested; even then, months passed be-

---

[1]Lucinda Harper and Fred R. Bleakley, "Like Old Times: An Era of Low Inflation Changes the Calculus for Buyers and Sellers," *The Wall Street Journal* (Jan. 14, 1994), p. A1.
[2]Adapted from "Price, Quotations, and Terms of Sale Are Key to Successful Exporting," *Business America* (Oct. 4, 1993), p. 12.

fore permission to raise prices was forthcoming. As a result, by 1988 detergent prices in Venezuela were less than they were in the United States.[3]

While the "textbook" approach outlined above is used in part or in whole by most experienced global firms, it must be noted that the inexperienced or part-time exporter does not usually go to all this effort to determine the "best" price for a product in international markets. Such a company will frequently use a much simpler approach to pricing such as the cost-plus method explained later in this chapter. As managers gain experience and become more sophisticated in their approach, however, they realize that the factors identified here should be considered when making pricing decisions.

There is another important internal organizational consideration besides cost. Within the typical corporation there are many interest groups and, frequently, conflicting price objectives. Divisional vice presidents, regional executives, and country managers are each concerned about profitability at their respective organizational levels. Similarly, the director of international marketing seeks competitive prices in world markets. The controller and financial vice president are concerned about profits. The manufacturing vice president seeks long runs for maximum manufacturing efficiency. The tax manager is concerned about compliance with government transfer pricing legislation. And company counsel is concerned about the antitrust implications of international pricing practices.

Compounding the problem is the rapidly changing global marketplace and the inaccurate and distorted nature of much of the available information regarding demand. In many parts of the world, external market information is distorted and inaccurate. It is often not possible to obtain the definitive and precise information that would be the basis of an "optimal" price. The same may be true about internal information. In Russia, for example, market research is a fairly new concept. Historically, detailed market information was not gathered or distributed. Also, managers at newly privatized factories are having difficulty setting prices because cost accounting data relating to manufacturing are frequently unavailable.

There are other problems. When attempting to estimate demand, for example, it is important to consider product appeal relative to competitive products. While it is possible to arrive at such estimates after conducting market research, the effort can be costly and time-consuming. Company managers and executives have to rely on intuition and experience. One way of improving estimates of potential demand is to use analogy. As described in Chapter 7, this approach basically means extrapolating potential demand for target markets from actual sales in markets judged to be similar.

GLOBAL PRICING OBJECTIVES AND STRATEGIES

A number of different pricing strategies are available to global marketers. An overall goal must be to contribute to company sales and profit objectives worldwide. Customer-oriented strategies such as marketing skimming, penetration, and market holding can be used when consumer perceptions, as determined by the value equation, are used as a guide. Global pricing can also can be based on other external criteria such as the escalation in costs when goods are shipped long distances across national boundaries. The issue of global pricing can also be fully integrated in the product design process, an approach widely used by Japanese companies. Prices in global markets are not carved in stone; they must be evaluated at regular intervals and adjusted if necessary. Similarly, pricing objectives may vary depending on a product's life cycle stage and the country-specific competitive situation.

Market Skimming

The market skimming pricing strategy is a deliberate attempt to reach a market segment that is willing to pay a premium price for a product. In such instances, the product must create high value for buyers. This pricing strategy is often used in the introductory

[3]Alecia Swasy, "Foreign Formula: Procter & Gamble Fixes Aim on Tough Market: The Latin Americans," *The Wall Street Journal* (June 15, 1990), p. A7.

phase of the product life cycle when both production capacity and competition are limited. By setting a deliberately high price, demand is limited to early adopters—those who are willing and able to pay the price. One goal of this pricing strategy is to maximize revenue on limited volume and to match demand to available supply. Another goal of market skimming pricing is to reinforce customers' perceptions of high product value. When this is done, the price is part of the total product positioning strategy.

When Sony first began selling Betamax VCRs in the United States in 1976, it used a skimming strategy. Harvey Schein, who was president of Sony of America at the time, recalled the response to the $1,295 price tag.

> It was fantastic, really. When you have a new product that is as jazzy as a videotape recorder, you really skim off the cream of the consuming public. The Betamax was selling for over a thousand dollars. . . . But there were so many wealthy people who wanted to be the first in the neighborhood that it just went whoof—like a vacuum. It flew off the shelf . . ."[4]

The initial success of the Betamax proved that consumers in the United States, Japan, and elsewhere were willing to pay a high price for a piece of consumer electronics equipment that would allow them to watch their favorite television shows at any time of the day or night.

Penetration Pricing

Penetration pricing uses price as a competitive weapon to gain market position. The majority of companies using this type of pricing in international marketing are located in the Pacific Rim. Scale-efficient plants and low-cost labor allow these companies to "blitz" the market.

It should be noted that a first-time exporter is unlikely to use penetration pricing. The reason is simple: Penetration pricing often means that the product may be sold at a loss for a certain length of time. Companies that are new to exporting cannot absorb such losses. Nor are they likely to have the marketing system in place (including transportation, distribution, and sales organizations) that allows global companies like Sony to make effective use of a penetration strategy. However, a company whose product is not patentable may wish to use penetration pricing to achieve market saturation before the product is copied by competitors.

Market Holding

The market holding strategy is frequently adopted by companies that want to maintain their share of the market. In single-country marketing, this strategy often involves reacting to price adjustments by competitors. For example, when one airline announces special bargain fares, most competing carriers must match the offer or risk losing passengers. In global marketing, currency fluctuations often trigger price adjustments. Many U.S. companies used this strategy in the early to mid-1980s when the dollar appreciated against most other currencies. If U.S.-based companies marketing internationally had maintained their price levels, currency translations tied to the strong dollar would have automatically increased the price of many products. As a result, companies would have priced themselves out of many international markets. To avoid this, companies set prices based not on the U.S. price translated at the current exchange rate but, rather, on the competitive situation in each market and the ability and willingness of customers to pay.

From the mid- to late 1980s, as the dollar weakened against world currencies, the situation was reversed. Companies based in Japan, Germany, France, and elsewhere attempted to hold the line on U.S. prices. Needless to say, adjusting prices to fit the competitive situation may mean lower profit margins. When Max Imgruth, head of Charles

---

[4]James Lardner, *Fast Forward: Hollywood, the Japanese, and the VCR Wars* (New York: New American Library, 1987), p. 91.

■ GRAY MARKETING

*A*nother type of gray marketing occurs when a company manufactures a product in multiple locations—in the home-country market as well as in foreign markets. In this case, products manufactured abroad by the company's foreign affiliate for sales abroad are sometimes sold by a foreign distributor to gray marketers. The latter then bring the products into the producing company's home-country market where they compete with domestically produced goods. Even though the gray market goods carry the same trademarks as the domestically produced ones, they often differ in quality, ingredients, or some other way. For example, in the mid-1980s, Caterpillar's U.S. dealers found themselves competing with gray market construction equipment manufactured in Europe. The strong dollar had provided gray marketers with an opportunity to bring Caterpillar equipment into the United States at lower prices than domestically produced equipment.

As these examples show, the marketing opportunity that presents itself depends on gray market goods being priced lower than goods sold by authorized distributors or domestically produced goods. Clearly, buyers gain from lower prices and increased choice. However, gray market goods—especially cameras and consumer electronics equipment—may not be covered by manufacterers' warranties.

In the United States, gray market goods are subject to a 60-year-old law, the Tariff Act of 1930. Section 526 of the act expressly forbids importation of goods of foreign manufacture without the permission of the trademark owner. There are, however, several exceptions spelled out in the act; this provides the U.S. Customs Service, which implements the regulations, and the court system considerable leeway in decisions regarding gray market goods. For example, in 1988 the U.S. Supreme Court ruled that trademarked goods of foreign manufacture such as champagne could legally be imported and sold by gray marketers. In many instances, however, the court's interpretation of the law differs from that of the Customs Service.

Because of problems associated with regulating gray markets, one legal expert has argued that, in the name of free markets and free trade, the U.S. Congress should repeal Section 526. In its place, a new law should require gray market goods to bear labels clearly explaining any differences between them and goods that come through authorized channels. Other experts believe that, instead of changing the laws, companies should develop proactive strategic responses to gray markets. One such strategy would be improved market segmentation and product differentiation to make gray market products less attractive; another would be to aggressively identify and terminate distributors that are involved in selling to gray marketers.

Sources: Per-Henrik Mansson, "Supreme Court Upholds Gray Market Champagne," *Wine Spectator* (July 15, 1988), p. 5.
James E. Inman, "Gray Marketing of Imported Trademarked Goods: Tariffs and Trademark Issues," *American Business Law Journal* (May 1993), pp. 59–116.
Paul Lansing and Joseph Gabriella, "Clarifying Gray Market Gray Areas," *American Business Law Journal* (September 1993), pp. 313–337.

Jourdan USA, vetoed double-digit price increases for the company's shoes in 1992, he noted, "The American consumer is not going to swallow those price increases." Speaking of his company, he lamented, "We're taking a tremendous hit. We're living on air and inspiration."[5]

By early 1993, as the yen approached parity with the dollar (¥100 = $1), Nikon, Sharp, and other Japanese companies had abandoned the market holding strategy and raised prices. A strong home currency may also force a company to consider offshore manufacturing or licensing agreements, rather than exporting, to maintain market share. Ikea, the Swedish home furnishings company, sourced 50 percent of its products in the United States in 1992, compared with only 10 percent in 1989.[6] Market holding means that a company must carefully examine all its cost accounting to determine whether it can afford to continue marketing in a country.

Setting Prices: The Japanese Approach

When Sony developed the portable CD player in the mid-1980s, the cost per unit at initial sales volumes was estimated to exceed $600. Since this was a "no-go" price in the United States and other target markets, Sony chairman Akio Morita instructed management to price the unit in the $300 range to achieve penetration. Because Sony was a global

---

[5]Joan E. Rigdon and Valerie Reitman, "Pricing Paradox: Consumers Still Find Imported Bargains Despite Weak Dollar," *The Wall Street Journal* (Oct. 7, 1992), p. A1. See also Valerie Reitman, "Currency Waves: Global Money Trends Rattle Shop Windows in Heartland America," *The Wall Street Journal* (Nov. 26, 1993), pp. A1, A8.
[6]Ibid., p. A6.

marketer, the sales volume it expected to achieve in these markets led to scale economies and lower costs.

The Sony example illustrates a fundamental difference in the approach to pricing issues adopted by Japanese companies. As shown in Figure 14–1, they begin with market research and product characteristics. Up to this point, the processes are parallel in the United States and Japan. At the next step, the processes diverge. In Japan, the planned selling price minus the desired profit is calculated, resulting in a target cost figure. It is only at this point that design, engineering, and supplier pricing issues are dealt with; extensive consultation between all value chain members is used to meet the target. Once the necessary negotiations and tradeoffs have been settled, manufacturing begins, followed by continuous cost reduction. In the U.S. process, cost is typically determined after design, engineering, and marketing decisions have been made in sequential fashion; if the cost is too high, the process cycles back to "square one"—the design stage.[7]

Cost-Plus/Price Escalation

Companies new to exporting frequently use a strategy known as cost-plus pricing to gain a toehold in the global marketplace. There are two cost-plus pricing methods: The older is the historical accounting cost method that defines cost as the sum of all direct and indirect manufacturing and overhead costs. An approach used in recent years is known as the *estimated future cost method*.

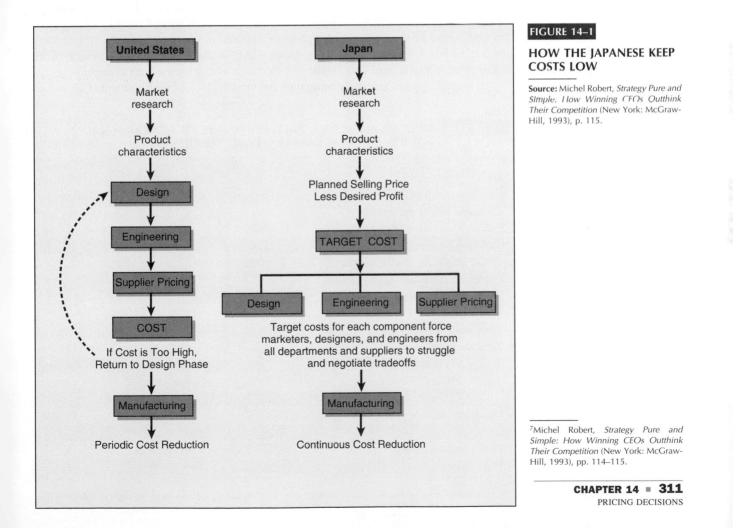

FIGURE 14–1

HOW THE JAPANESE KEEP COSTS LOW

Source: Michel Robert, *Strategy Pure and Simple. How Winning CEOs Outthink Their Competition* (New York: McGraw-Hill, 1993), p. 115.

[7]Michel Robert, *Strategy Pure and Simple: How Winning CEOs Outthink Their Competition* (New York: McGraw-Hill, 1993), pp. 114–115.

Cost-plus pricing requires adding up all the costs required to get the product to where it must go, plus shipping and ancillary charges and a profit percentage. The obvious advantage of using this method is its low threshold: It is relatively easy to arrive at a quote, assuming that accounting costs are readily available. The disadvantage of using historical accounting costs to arrive at a price is that this approach completely ignores demand and competitive conditions in target markets. Therefore, historical accounting cost-plus prices will frequently be either too high or too low in the light of market and competitive conditions. If historical accounting cost-plus prices are right, it is only by chance.

However, as noted in Chapter 9, novice exporters don't care—they are reactively responding to global market opportunities, not proactively seeking them. Experienced global marketers realize that nothing in the historical accounting cost-plus formula directly addresses the competitive and customer value issues that must be considered in a rational pricing strategy.

Price escalation is the increase in a product's price as transportation, duty, and distributor margins are added to the factory price. Table 14–1 is a typical example of the kind of price escalation that can occur when a product is destined for international markets. In this example, a distributor of agricultural equipment in Kansas City is shipping a container load of farm implements to Yokohama, Japan. A shipment of product that costs ex-works $30,000 in Kansas City ends up having a total retail price in excess of US $50,000 in Yokohama—almost double the ex-works Kansas City price. (*Ex-works* and other trade terms are explained in Appendix 14–A at the end of this chapter.)

Let us examine this shipment to see what happened. First, there is the total shipping charge of $5,453.07, which is 18 percent of the ex-works Kansas City price. The principal component of this shipping charge is a combination of land and ocean freight totaling $5,267.80. A currency adjustment factor (CAF) is charged due to the strength of the dollar relative to the yen. This figure will fluctuate as currency values change.

All import charges are assessed against the landed price of the shipment (CIF value).

TABLE 14–1 **PRICE ESCALATION: A 20-FT. CONTAINER OF AGRICULTURAL EQUIPMENT FROM KANSAS CITY TO YOKOHAMA***

Item			Percentage of FOB Price
Ex-works Kansas City		$30,000.00	100
Container freight charges from K.C. to Seattle	$1,475.00		
Terminal handling fee	350.00		
Ocean freight for 20-ft. container	2,280.00		
Currency adjustment factor (CAF) (51% of ocean freight)	1,162.80		
Insurance (covers 110% of CIF value)	35.27		
Forwarding fee	150.00		
Total shipping charges		5,453.07	18
Total CIF Yokohama value		$35,453.07	
V.A.T. (3% of CIF value)		1,063.69	3
		$36,516.76	
Distributor markup (10%)		3,651.67	12
		$40,168.43	
Dealer markup (25%)		10,042.10	33
Total retail price		$50,210.53	166

*This was loaded at the manufacturer's door, shipped by stack train to Seattle, and then via ocean freight to Yokohama. Total transit time from factory door to foreign port is about 28 days.

Note that there is no line item for duty in this example; no duties are charged on agricultural equipment sent to Japan.[8] Duties may be charged in other countries. A nominal distributor markup of 10 percent ($3,652) actually represents 12 percent of the CIF Yokohama price, because it is a markup not only on the ex-works price but on freight and VAT as well. (It is assumed here that the distributor's markup includes the cost of transportation from the port to Yokohama.) Finally, a dealer markup of 25 percent adds up to $10,042—33 percent—of the CIF Yokohama price. Like distributor markup, dealer markup is based on the total landed cost.

The net effect of this add-on accumulating process is a total retail price in Yokohama of $50,210, or 166 percent of the ex-works Kansas City price. This is price escalation. The example provided here is by no means an extreme case. Indeed, as discussed in Chapter 15, longer distribution channels, or channels that require a higher operating margin—as are typically found in export marketing—can contribute to price escalation. Because of the layered distribution system in Japan, the markups in Yokohama could easily result in a price that is 200 percent of the CIF value.

The example of cost-plus pricing presented above shows an approach that a beginning exporter might use to determine the CIF price. However, experienced global marketers view price as a major strategic variable that can help achieve marketing and business objectives.

Using Sourcing as a Strategic Pricing Tool

The global marketer has several options when addressing the problem of price escalation described in the previous section. The choices are dictated in part by product and market competition. Marketers of domestically manufactured finished products may be forced to switch to offshore sourcing of certain components to keep costs and prices competitive. In particular, the Far East and South America are emerging as attractive low-cost sources of production.

Another option is to source 100 percent of a finished product offshore near or in local markets. The manufacturer could enter into one of the arrangements discussed in Chapter 10 such as licensing or a joint venture. This allows the manufacturer to establish a presence in the market it is trying to penetrate while avoiding price escalation due to transportation charges or high home-country manufacturing costs.

The third option is a thorough audit of the distribution structure in the target markets. A rationalization of the distribution structure can substantially reduce the total markups required to achieve distribution in international markets. Rationalization may include selecting new intermediaries, assigning new responsibilities to old intermediaries, or establishing direct marketing operations. For example, Toys 'Я' Us successfully entered the Japanese toy market because it bypassed layers of distribution and adopted a warehouse style of selling similar to its U.S. approach. Toys 'Я' Us has been viewed as a test case of the ability of Western retailers—discounters in particular—to change the rules of distribution (for more on Toys 'Я' Us in Japan, see Case 15–1).

DUMPING

Dumping is an important global pricing strategy issue. GATT's 1979 Antidumping Code defined dumping as the sale of an imported product at a price lower than that normally charged in a domestic market or country of origin. In addition, many countries have their own policies and procedures for protecting national companies from dumping. The U.S. antidumping act of 1921, which is enforced by the U.S. Treasury, did not define dumping specifically but instead referred to unfair competition. However, Congress has

---

[8]Since the Uruguay Round of GATT negotiations, Japan will lower or eliminate duties on 6,000 categories of imports. Japan's average duty rate as of 1994 is 2.5%, one of the lowest in the world.

defined dumping as an unfair trade practice that results in "injury, destruction, or prevention of the establishment of American industry." Under this definition, dumping occurs when imports sold in the U.S. market are priced either at levels that represent less than the cost of production plus an 8 percent profit margin or at levels below those prevailing in the producing country.

Dumping was a major issue in the Uruguay Round of GATT negotiations. Many countries disapproved of the U.S. system of antidumping laws, in part because the Commerce Department historically almost always ruled in favor of a U.S. company filing a complaint. For example, in 1993 alone, more than 80 rulings were issued; in most instances, foreign firms were found guilty of dumping.[9] Another issue was the fact that U.S. exporters were often targeted in antidumping investigations in countries with few formal rules for due process. The U.S. negotiators hoped to improve the ability of U.S. companies to defend their interests and understand the bases for rulings.

The result of the GATT negotiations was an Agreement on Interpretation of Article VI. From the U.S. point of view, one of the most significant changes between the agreement and the 1979 code is the addition of a "standard of review" that will make it harder for GATT panels to dispute U.S. antidumping determinations. There are also a number of procedural and methodological changes. In some instances, these have the effect of bringing GATT regulations more in line with U.S. law. For example, in calculating "fair price" for a given product, any sales of the product at below-cost prices in the exporting country are not included in the calculations; inclusion of such sales would have the effect of exerting downward pressure on the "fair price." The agreement also brings GATT standards into line with U.S. standards by prohibiting governments from penalizing differences between home-market and export-market prices of less than 2 percent.

As the nature of these issues and regulations suggests, some countries use dumping legislation as a legitimate device to protect local enterprise from predatory pricing practices by foreign companies. In other nations, they represent protectionism, a device for limiting foreign competition in a market. The rationale for dumping legislation is that dumping is harmful to the orderly development of enterprise within an economy. Few economists would object to long-run or continuous dumping. If this were done, it would be an opportunity for a country to take advantage of a low-cost source of a particular good and to specialize in other areas. However, continuous dumping only rarely occurs; the sale of agricultural products at international prices with farmers receiving subsidized higher prices is an example of continuous dumping. The type of dumping practiced by most companies is sporadic and unpredictable, and does not provide a reliable basis for national economic planning. Instead it may injure a domestic enterprise.

The dumping issue has been dealt with in various ways in the United States. For example, when the Japanese share of the U.S. color TV market jumped from 11 percent to 29 percent in the first six months of 1976, U.S. manufacturers filed complaints with the International Trade Commission and brought suit against the Japanese companies for dumping and illegal price fixing. U.S. labor unions formed committees to petition the commission for tariffs and quotas on TVs.

In 1976, the U.S. Treasury Department also investigated foreign car pricing practices. It concluded that 23 out of 28 foreign automakers had been dumping cars in the United States and demanded an increase in prices by 1977. Volkswagen, for example, was forced to raise its 1977 car prices an average of 2.5 percent. In a similar case that same year, the ITC ruled that Japanese steelmakers were engaged in unfair competition. It ordered them to stop "predatory" pricing of their estimated $20 million steel exports to the United States, and forced the steel companies to provide detailed production and pricing figures. Citing the 1974 Trade Act provision that calls for the establishment of reference prices below

[9]James Bovard, "Clinton's Dumping Could Sink GATT," *The Wall Street Journal* (Dec. 9, 1993), p. A20.

South Korea's Kia Motor Corporation is staking a claim to the low-priced car segment once dominated by Japan. (Goldberg Moser O'Neill. Awarded an EFFIE in 1995.)

which importers will be charged with dumping, the Treasury Department then set minimum steel import price levels.

As noted, the last few years have seen a great incidence of antidumping investigation and penalties, imposed primarily in the United States but also in the EU, Canada, and Australia. Although many of the dumping cases in the United States involved manufactured goods from the Far East, they are by no means limited to Asia. Since 1990, there have been dumping cases involving iron castings from India, salmon from Norway, neoprene from France, nylon belts from Germany, wool from Argentina, and textiles from Mexico. The list could go on and on. Most of the cases involved a single or very narrowly defined group of products and were initiated by U.S. companies that claimed to be materially damaged by the low-priced imports. In some cases, like tungsten from China and nitrocellulose from Yugoslavia, the U.S. company bringing action was the sole U.S. producer.

One U.S. company, Smith Corona Corporation of New Canaan, Connecticut, filed an antidumping complaint against Brother Industries of Japan in 1974 and has been involved in dumping-related litigation ever since. One of the lessons from this saga is that it can take years to get relief from the ITC. Smith Corona had to refile its original complaint; the ITC finally found in its favor in 1980, ordering a 48.7 percent duty on imports of portable typewriters. However, the duties only applied to typewriters; Brother responded by designing new products with chip-based memory functions. Because this new product was no longer classified as a typewriter—rather, it was a "word processor"—Brother effectively sidestepped the duties. Brother also began assembling typewriters and word processors from imported parts in a plant in Tennessee. This example shows to what lengths a company will go to get around dumping regulations; Brother used both product innovation and a new sourcing strategy. Finally, in an ironic twist, Brother turned the tables on Smith Corona by accusing the latter of dumping. The rationale: Many of Smith Corona's typewriters are imported from a plant in Singapore; Brother pointed to its own U.S. plant as evidence that it was the true U.S. producer![10]

For a positive proof of dumping occurring in the United States, both price discrimination and injury must be demonstrated. The existence of either one without the other is an insufficient condition to constitute dumping. Companies concerned with running afoul of antidumping legislation have developed a number of approaches for avoiding the dumping laws. One approach is to differentiate the product sold from that in the home market. An example of this is an auto accessory that one company packaged with a wrench and an instruction book, thereby changing the "accessory" to a "tool." The tariff rate in the export market happened to be lower on tools, and the company also acquired immunity from antidumping laws because the package was not comparable to competing goods in the target market. Another approach is to make nonprice competitive adjustments in arrangements with affiliates and distributors. For example, credit can be extended and essentially have the same effect as a price reduction.

ENVIRONMENTAL INFLUENCES ON PRICING DECISIONS

Global marketers must deal with a number of environmental considerations when making pricing decisions. Among these are currency fluctuations, inflation, government controls and subsidies, and competitive behavior. Some of these factors work in conjunction with others; for example, inflation may be accompanied by government controls. Each consideration is discussed in detail below.

Currency Fluctuations

As discussed in Chapter 6, price adjustments may be appropriate when currencies strengthen or weaken. In some instances, a slight strengthening of a country's currency has little effect upon export performance. Price increases are passed on to international customers without significant decreases in sales volume. In more competitive market situations, companies in the strong-currency country will often absorb the price increase by maintaining international market prices at pre-revaluation levels. In actual practice, a manufacturer and its distributor may work together to maintain market share in international markets. Either party, or both, may choose to take a lower profit percentage. The distrib-

[10]Eduardo Lachica, "Legal Swamp: Anti-Dumping Pleas Are Almost Useless, Smith Corona Finds," *The Wall Street Journal* (June 18, 1992), pp. A1, A8.

utor may also choose to purchase more product to achieve volume discounts; another alternative is to maintain leaner inventories if the manufacturer can provide just-in-time delivery. By using these approaches, it is possible to remain price competitive in markets where revaluation is a price consideration.

If a country's currency weakens relative to a trading partner's currency, a producer in a weak-currency country can cut export prices to increase market share or leave prices alone for healthier profit margins. For example, Italian automaker Alfa Romeo featured a "currency exchange adjustment" in its U.S. advertising during the dollar's heyday in 1984. The experience of Campbell Soup Company in Japan also illustrates price strategy options presented by currency devaluation. In 1985, when the dollar was strong and the exchange rate was ¥240/$1, a can of Campbell's soup sold in Japan for ¥220, which was the equivalent of $.91 (220/240 = .91). By 1987, the exchange rate was ¥142/$1, reflecting a weaker dollar (one that bought fewer yen) and a stronger yen (fewer yen could buy $1). If Campbell had not adjusted its prices in Japan, it would have enjoyed windfall revenues: The can of soup priced at ¥220 would translate into $1.69—an increase of 85 percent (220/142 = 1.69). Campbell adopted a proactive approach and *lowered* the yen price of a can of soup to ¥185; but even with the lower price, the stronger yen *still* translated that yen price into $1.30 per can (185/142 = 1.30), versus $.91 at the old exchange rate. Campbell opted to use price as a strategic variable to increase sales volume; the company also reinvested the extra profit by increasing its sales staff and offering deals to retailers in an effort to gain wider distribution.[11]

Inflationary Environments

Inflation, or a persistent upward change in price levels, is a worldwide phenomenon. Inflation requires periodic price adjustments. These adjustments are necessitated by rising costs that must be covered by increased selling prices. An essential requirement when pricing in an inflationary environment is the maintenance of operating profit margins. Regardless of cost accounting practices, if a company maintains its margins, it has effectively protected itself from the effects of inflation. To keep up with inflation in Peru, for example, Procter & Gamble has resorted to biweekly increases in detergent prices of 20 to 30 percent.[12]

Within the scope of this chapter it is only possible to touch on the many accounting issues and conventions relating to price adjustments in international markets. In particular, it is worth noting that the traditional FIFO (first-in, first-out) costing method is hardly appropriate for an inflationary situation. A more appropriate accounting practice under conditions of rising prices is the LIFO (last-in, first-out) method, which takes the most recent raw material acquisition price and uses it as the basis for costing the product sold. In highly inflationary environments, historical approaches are less appropriate costing methods than replacement cost. The latter amounts to a next-in, first-out approach. Although this method does not conform to generally accepted accounting principles, it can be used to estimate future prices that will be paid for raw and component materials. These replacement costs can then be used to set prices. While this approach is useful in managerial decision making, it cannot be used in financial statements. Regardless of the accounting methods used, an essential requirement under inflationary conditions of any costing system is that it maintain gross and operating profit margins. Managerial actions can maintain these margins subject to the following constraints.

Government Controls and Subsidies

If government action limits the freedom of management to adjust prices, the maintenance of margins is definitely compromised. Under certain conditions, government action is a real threat to the profitability of a subsidiary operation. In a country that is undergoing severe financial difficulties and is in the midst of a financial crisis (for example, a

[11]Damon Darlin, "Trade Strategies: Most U.S. Firms Seek Extra Profits in Japan, at the Expense of Sales," *The Wall Street Journal* (May 15, 1987), p. A1.
[12]Swasy 1990, p. A1.

■ THE CONTRARIAN VIEWS OF JAMES BOVARD

OPEN TO DISCUSSION

James Bovard might be considered the Ralph Nader of global marketing. He is a tireless advocate of unrestricted trade and a vocal critic of U.S. trade policy who campaigns to influence the views of policy makers and the general public. In his recent book *The Myth of Fair Trade* and numerous articles and essays, Bovard argues that U.S. trade laws are hypocritical because they reduce, rather than encourage, competition. The result, he asserts, is higher prices for U.S. consumers. His positions and opinions on two trade issues, dumping and Super 301, are summarized below, along with a sampling of responses.

Dumping. Bovard believes the U.S. antidumping laws should be repealed. Calling antidumping laws a relic of the fixed exchange rate era, he notes that the U.S. Commerce Department can convict a company of dumping on the basis of "dumping margins" (price differences) as small as one-half of one percent, even though the dollar can experience double-digit fluctuations relative to other world currencies. Moreover, a dumping conviction can restrict a company's market access for 15 years, long after an offense has occurred. Bovard cautions that other nations may copy U.S. antidumping regulations, to the ultimate detriment of U.S. companies.

While the Uruguay Round of GATT negotiations resulted in some changes addressing Bovard's specific concerns, the broader issue is still open. Should the U.S. antidumping laws be repealed? Not according to Don E. Newquist, former chairman of the U.S. International Trade Commission. He argues that antidumping laws help preserve the United States' manufacturing and technology base. He warns that without

the laws, foreign producers that are sheltered from import competition in their home markets—e.g., Japanese companies—can use excess profits from domestic sales to subsidize low-cost exports to the United States. This could lead to market share losses, cash flow reductions, and even plant closings in the United States.

Super 301 and Section 301. In March 1994, Bovard blasted the Clinton administration's decision to reinstate Super 301 to punish Japan for unfair trade practices. Super 301 was a 1988 trade provision that allowed the United States to single out individual nations as unfair traders and impose 100 percent tariffs on exports from those nations unless U.S. demands were granted. An earlier regulation, Section 301 of the Trade Act of 1974, allowed the U.S. government to investigate and retaliate against unfair trade barriers in other nations. Bovard's specific complaint about President Clinton's action was that both 301 provisions have been ineffective, and that threats of retaliation have brought results in only a handful of cases.

Bovard has also frequently argued that the United States is hypocritical when it comes to trade policy, citing numerous examples of U.S. trade practices over the past 20 years to support his claim. For example, in 1990, the United States initiated a case against Canada for limiting U.S. beer imports, even though the United States imposes its own complicated regulations on Canadian beer imports. In 1989, the United States threatened Japan with Section 301 on the grounds that Motorola had not been granted a large enough geographical selling area. Bovard ascribed Motorola's sales problems in Japan to a simple lack of product adaptation: The company initially exported cellular phones designed for U.S. frequencies; Japanese cellular phone exports to the United States are designed for U.S. frequencies.

Sources: James Bovard, "Trade Quotas Build New Chinese Wall," *The Wall Street Journal* (Jan. 10, 1994), p. A12. James Bovard, "A U.S. History of Trade Hypocrisy," *The Wall Street Journal* (Mar. 8, 1994), p. A1.

foreign exchange shortage caused in part by runaway inflation), government officials are under pressure to take some type of action. This has been true in Brazil for many years. In some cases, governments will take expedient steps rather than getting at the underlying causes of inflation and foreign exchange shortages. Such steps might include the use of broad or selective price controls. When selective controls are imposed, foreign companies are more vulnerable to control than local businesses, particularly if the outsiders lack the political influence over government decision making possessed by local managers.

Government control can also take the form of prior cash deposit requirements imposed on importers. As discussed in Chapter 9, this is a requirement that a company has to tie up funds in the form of a non–interest-bearing deposit for a specified period of time if it wishes to import products. Such requirements clearly create an incentive for a company to minimize the price of the imported product; lower prices mean smaller deposits. Other government requirements that affect the pricing decision are profit transfer rules that restrict the conditions under which profits can be transferred out of a country. Under such rules, a high transfer price paid for imported goods by an affiliated company can be interpreted as a device for transferring profits out of a country.

Government subsidies can also force a company to make strategic use of sourcing to be price competitive. In Europe, government subsidies to the agricultural sector make it difficult for U.S. distributors of processed food to compete on price when exporting to the EU. In the United States some, but not all, agricultural sectors are subsidized. For example, U.S. poultry producers and processors are not subsidized, a situation that makes their prices noncompetitive in world markets. One Midwestern chicken processor with European customers sourced its product in France for resale in the Netherlands. By doing so, the company took advantage of lower costs derived from subsidies and eliminated price escalation due to tariffs and duties.

Competitive Behavior

As noted at the beginning of this chapter, pricing decisions are bounded not only by cost and the nature of demand but also by competitive action. If competitors do not adjust their prices in response to rising costs, management—even if acutely aware of the effect of rising costs on operating margins—will be severely constrained in its ability to adjust prices accordingly. Conversely, if competitors are manufacturing or sourcing in a lower-cost country, it may be necessary to cut prices to stay competitive.

TRANSFER PRICING

Transfer pricing refers to the pricing of goods and services bought and sold by operating units or divisions of a single company. In other words, transfer pricing concerns intracorporate exchanges—transactions between buyers and sellers that have the same corporate parent. For example, Toyota subsidiaries sell to, and buy from, each other. The same is true of other companies operating globally. As companies expand and create decentralized operations, profit centers become an increasingly important component in the overall corporate financial picture. Appropriate intracorporate transfer pricing systems and policies are required to ensure profitability at each level. When a company extends its operations across national boundaries, transfer pricing takes on new dimensions and complications. In determining transfer prices to subsidiaries, global companies must address a number of issues, including taxes, duties and tariffs, country profit transfer rules, conflicting objectives of joint venture partners, and government regulations.

There arc three major alternative approaches to transfer pricing. The approach used will vary with the nature of the firm, products, markets, and the historical circumstances of each case. The approaches are: (1) cost-based transfer pricing, (2) market-based transfer pricing, and (3) negotiated transfer pricing.

Cost-based Transfer Price

Because companies define costs differently, some companies using the cost-based approach may arrive at transfer prices that reflect variable and fixed manufacturing costs only. Alternatively, transfer prices may be based on full costs, including overhead costs from marketing, R&D, and other functional areas. The way costs are defined may have an impact on tariffs and duties of sales to affiliates and subsidiaries by global companies.

Cost-plus pricing is a variation of the cost-based approach. Companies that follow the cost-plus pricing method are taking the position that profit must be shown for any product or service at every stage of movement through the corporate system. In such an instance, transfer prices may be set at a certain percentage of fixed costs, such as "110 percent of cost." While cost-plus pricing may result in a price that is completely unrelated to competitive or demand conditions in international markets, many exporters use this approach successfully.

Market-based Transfer Price

A market-based transfer price is derived from the price required to be competitive in the international market. The constraint on this price is cost. However, as noted above, there is a considerable degree of variation in how costs are defined. Since costs generally decline with volume, a decision must be made regarding whether to price on the basis of current or planned volume levels. To use market-based transfer prices to enter a new market that is too small to support local manufacturing, third-country sourcing may be required. This enables a company to establish its name or franchise in the market without committing to a major capital investment.

Negotiated Transfer Price

A third alternative is to allow the organization's affiliates to negotiate transfer prices among themselves. In some instances, the final transfer price may reflect costs and market prices, but this is not a requirement.[13]

Tax Regulations and Transfer Prices

Since the global corporation conducts business in a world characterized by different corporate tax rates, there is an incentive to maximize system income in countries with the lowest tax rates and to minimize income in high-tax countries. Governments, naturally, are well aware of this situation. In recent years, many governments have tried to maximize national tax revenues by examining company returns and mandating reallocation of income and expenses.

While a full treatment of tax issues is beyond the scope of this book, students should understand that a basic pricing question facing global marketers is, "What can a company do in the international pricing area in the light of current tax law?" It is important to note that U.S. Treasury regulations do not have the weight of law until they are upheld by the courts. Global marketers must examine the regulations carefully, not only because they are the tax law but because they guide the IRS when it reviews transactions between related business organizations. In the United States, Section 482 of the tax code and the accompanying regulations are devoted to transfer pricing. The complete text of Section 482 appears in Appendix 14–B.

Sales of Tangible and Intangible Property

Section 482 of the U.S. Treasury regulations deals with controlled intracompany transfers of raw materials and finished and intermediate goods, as well as intangibles such as charges for the use of manufacturing technology. The general rule that applies to sales of tangible property is known as the "arm's-length" formula, defined as the price that would have been charged in independent transactions between unrelated parties under similar circumstances. Three methods—listed below in order of priority—are spelled out in the regulations for establishing an arm's-length price. The regulations require that a company disprove the applicability of one method before utilizing a lower-priority one.

According to the *comparable uncontrolled price* method, uncontrolled sales (between unrelated seller and buyer) are considered comparable to controlled sales (sales between related parties) if the property and circumstances involved are identical or nearly identical to those in controlled sales. Frequently, no comparable uncontrolled sale is available to use as a reference. In such instances, it may be necessary to determine an *applicable resale price*—the price at which property purchased in a controlled sale is resold by the buyer in an uncontrolled sale. Using this approach, which is sometimes referred to as "retail price minus," an arm's-length price can be established by reducing the applicable re-

[13]Charles T. Horngren and George Foster, *Cost Accounting, A Managerial Approach* (Upper Saddle River, N.J.: Prentice Hall, 1991), p. 856.

sale price by an amount that reflects an appropriate markup. This is the "resale price method" of determining transfer prices. The third and lowest-priority method is the *cost-plus method*. When the quest for an arm's-length price brings a global company to cost-plus, it has come full circle to the basic transfer pricing methods described above.

Table 14–2 summarizes the results of recent studies comparing transfer pricing methods by country. As shown in the table, nearly half of U.S.-based companies doing business internationally use some form of cost-based transfer pricing

Competitive Pricing

Because Section 482 places so much emphasis on arm's-length price, a manager at a U.S. company who examines the regulations might wonder whether the spirit of these regulations permits pricing decisions to be made with regard to market and competitive factors. Clearly, if only the arm's-length standard is applied, a company may not be able to respond to competitive factors existing in every market, domestic and global. Fortunately, the regulations provide an opening for the company that seeks to be price competitive or to aggressively price U.S.-sourced products in its international operations. Many interpret the regulations to mean that it is proper for a company to reduce prices and increase marketing expenditures through a controlled affiliate to gain market share even when it would not do so in an arm's-length transaction with an independent distributor. This is because market position represents, in effect, an investment and an asset. A company would invest in such an asset only if it controlled the reseller—that is, if the reseller is a subsidiary. The regulations may also be interpreted as permitting a company to lower its transfer price for the purpose of entering a new market or meeting competition in an existing market either by instituting price reductions or by increased marketing efforts in the target markets. Companies must have and use this latitude in making price decisions if they are to achieve significant success in international markets with U.S.-sourced goods.

Importance of Section 482 Regulations

Whatever the pricing rationale, it is important that executives and managers involved in international pricing policy decisions familiarize themselves with the Section 482 regulations. The pricing rationale must conform with the intention of these regulations. In an effort to develop more workable transfer pricing rules, the IRS issued temporary regulations on January 13, 1993, calling for "contemporaneous documentation" that supports transfer price decisions. Such documentation will require participation of management and marketing personnel in transfer pricing decisions, as opposed to the tax department. Companies should be prepared to demonstrate that their pricing methods are the result of informed choice, not oversight.

It is true that Treasury regulations and IRS enforcement policy often seem perplexingly inscrutable. However, there is ample evidence that the government simply seeks to

TABLE 14–2 **TRANSFER PRICING METHODS USED IN SELECTED COUNTRIES (PERCENTAGE)**

Method	United States	Canada	Japan	United Kingdom
Cost-based	46	33	41	38
Market-price–based	35	37	37	31
Negotiated	14	26	22	20
Other	5	4	NA	11
	100	100	100	100

Source: Adapted from Charles T. Horngren and George Foster, *Cost Accounting, A Managerial Approach* (Upper Saddle River, N.J.: Prentice Hall, 1991), p. 866.

prevent tax avoidance and to ensure fair distribution of income from the operations of companies doing business internationally. Still, the government does not always succeed in its efforts to enforce Section 482 by reallocating income. In one recent court decision, Merck & Co. sued the U.S. government on the grounds that the IRS's allocation of 7 percent of the income from a wholly owned subsidiary to the parent company was "arbitrary, capricious, and unreasonable." The IRS had argued that Merck artificially shifted income to the subsidiary by sharing costs associated with R&D, marketing facilities, and management personnel. The court agreed with Merck and ordered the IRS to issue a tax refund.

As the Merck case demonstrates, even companies that make a conscientious effort to comply with the regulations and that document this effort may find themselves in tax court. Should a tax auditor raise questions, executives should be able to make a strong case for their decisions. Fortunately, consulting services are available to help managers deal with the arcane world of transfer pricing. It is not unusual for large global companies to invest hundred of thousands of dollars and hire Big Eight accounting firms for a review of transfer pricing policies. For companies with tighter budgets, Worldwide Transfer Pricing Institute in Schaumburg, Illinois, offers a package of software, documentation, and training.

Transfer pricing to minimize tax liabilities can lead to unexpected and undesired distortions. A classic example is a major U.S. company with a decentralized, profit-centered organization that promoted and gave frequent and substantial salary increases to its divisional manager in Switzerland. The reason for the manager's rapid rise was his outstanding profit record. His stellar numbers were picked up by the company's performance appraisal control system, which in turn triggered the salary and promotion actions. The problem in this company was that the financial control system had not been adjusted to recognize that a Swiss "tax haven" profit center had been created. The manager's sky-high "profits" were simply the result of artificially low transfer pricing into the tax haven operations and artificially high transfer pricing out of the Swiss tax haven to operating subsidiaries. It took a team of outside consultants to discover the situation. In this case the company's profit and loss records were a gross distortion of true operating results. The company had to adjust its control system and use different criteria to evaluate managerial performance in tax havens.

Duty and Tariff Constraints

Corporate costs and profits are also affected by import duties. The higher the duty rate, the more desirable a low transfer price. The high duty creates an incentive to reduce transfer prices to minimize the customs duty. As discussed in Chapter 9, duties in many industry sectors were substantially reduced or eliminated by the Uruguay Round of GATT negotiations. Many companies tend to downplay the influence of taxes when developing pricing policies. There are a number of reasons for this. First, some companies consider tax savings to be trivial in comparison with the earnings that can be obtained by concentrating on effective systems of motivation and corporate resource allocation. Second, management may consider any effort at systematic tax minimization to be unethical. Another argument is that a simple, consistent, and straightforward pricing policy minimizes the tax investigation problems that can develop if sharper pricing policies are pursued. According to this argument, the savings in executive time and the costs of outside counsel offset any additional taxes that might be paid using such an approach. Finally, after analyzing the worldwide trend toward harmonization of tax rates, many CFOs have concluded that any set of policies appropriate to a world characterized by wide differentials in tax rates will soon become obsolete. They have therefore concentrated on developing pricing policies that are appropriate for a world that is very rapidly evolving toward relatively similar tax rates.

Joint Ventures

Joint ventures present an incentive to set transfer prices at higher levels than would be used in sales to wholly owned affiliates because a company's share of the joint venture earnings is less than 100 percent. Any profits that occur in the joint venture must be shared. The increasing frequency of tax authority audits is an important reason for working out an agreement that will also be acceptable to the tax authorities. The tax authorities' criterion of "arm's-length" prices is probably most appropriate for the majority of joint ventures.

To avoid potential conflict, companies with joint ventures should work out pricing agreements in advance that are acceptable to both sides. The following are several considerations for joint venture transfer pricing (Doorley & Collins 1991, 212–213):

1. The way in which transfer prices will be adjusted in response to exchange rate changes.
2. Expected reductions in manufacturing costs arising from learning curve improvements and the way these will be reflected in transfer prices.
3. Shifts in the sourcing of products or components from parents to alternative sources.
4. The effects of competition on volume and overall margins.

GLOBAL PRICING: THREE POLICY ALTERNATIVES

What pricing policy should a global company pursue? Viewed broadly, there are three alternative positions a company can take on worldwide pricing.

Extension/Ethnocentric

The first can be called an *extension/ethnocentric* pricing policy. This policy requires that the price of an item be the same around the world and that the importer absorb freight and import duties. This approach has the advantage of extreme simplicity because no information on competitive or market conditions is required for implementation. The disadvantage of this approach is directly tied to its simplicity. Extension pricing does not respond to the competitive and market conditions of each national market and, therefore, does not maximize the company's profits in each national market or globally.

Adaptation/Polycentric

The second pricing policy can be termed *adaptation/polycentric*. This policy permits subsidiary or affiliate managers to establish whatever price they feel is most desirable in their circumstances. Under such an approach, there is no control or firm requirement that prices be coordinated from one country to the next. The only constraint on this approach is in setting transfer prices within the corporate system. Such an approach is sensitive to local conditions, but it does present problems of product arbitrage opportunities in cases where disparities in local market prices exceed the transportation and duty costs separating markets. When such a condition exists, there is an opportunity for the enterprising business manager to take advantage of these price disparities by buying in the lower-price market and selling in the more expensive market. There is also the problem that under such a policy, valuable knowledge and experience within the corporate system concerning effective pricing strategies are not applied to each local pricing decision. The strategies are not applied because the local managers are free to price in the way they feel is most desirable, and they may not be fully informed about company experience when they make their decision.

Invention/Geocentric

The third approach to international pricing can be termed *invention/geocentric*. Using this approach a company neither fixes a single price worldwide nor remains aloof from subsidiary pricing decisions, but instead strikes an intermediate position. A company pursuing this approach works on the assumption that there are unique local market factors that should be recognized in arriving at a pricing decision. These factors include local costs, income levels, competition, and the local marketing strategy. Local costs plus a return on invested capital and personnel fix the price floor for the long term. However, for the short term, a company might decide to pursue a market penetration objective and price at less than the cost-plus return figure using export sourcing to establish a market. Another short-term objective might be to estimate the size of a market at a price that would be profitable given local sourcing and a certain scale of output. Instead of building facilities, the target market might first be supplied from existing higher-cost external supply sources. If the price and product are accepted by the market, the company can then build a local manufacturing facility to further develop the identified market opportunity in a profitable way. If the market opportunity does not materialize, the company can experiment with the product at other prices because it is not committed to a fixed sales volume by existing local manufacturing facilities.

Selecting a price that recognizes local competition is essential. Many international market efforts have floundered on this point. A major U.S. appliance manufacturer introduced its line of household appliances in West Germany and, using U.S. sourcing, set price by simply marking up every item in its line by 28.5 percent. The result of this pricing method was a line that contained a mixture of underpriced and overpriced products. The overpriced products did not sell because better values were offered by local companies. The underpriced products sold very well, but they would have yielded greater profits at higher prices. What was needed was product line pricing, which took lower-than-normal margins in some products and higher margins in others to maximize the profitability of the full line.

For consumer products, local income levels are critical in the pricing decision. If the product is normally priced well above full manufacturing costs, the global marketer has the latitude to price below prevailing levels in low-income markets and, as a result, reduce the gross margin on the product. While no business manager enjoys reducing margins, margins should be regarded as a guide to the ultimate objective, which is profitability. In some markets, income conditions may dictate that the maximum profitability will be obtained by sacrificing "normal" margins. *The important point here is that in global marketing there is no such thing as a "normal" margin.*

The final factor bearing on the price decision is the local marketing strategy and mix. Price must fit the other elements of the marketing program. For example, when it is decided to pursue a "pull" strategy that uses mass-media advertising and intensive distribution, the price selected must be consistent not only with income levels and competition but also with the costs and extensive advertising programs.

In addition to these local factors, the geocentric approach recognizes that headquarters price coordination is necessary in dealing with international accounts and product arbitrage. Finally, the geocentric approach consciously and systematically seeks to ensure that accumulated national pricing experience is leveraged and applied wherever relevant.

Of the three methods, only the geocentric approach lends itself to global competitive strategy. A global competitor will take into account global markets and global competitors in establishing prices. Prices will support global strategy objectives rather than the objective of maximizing performance in a single country.

SUMMARY

Pricing decisions are a critical element of the marketing mix that must reflect costs and competitive factors. There is no absolute maximum price, but for any customer, price must correspond to the customer's perceived value of the product. The aim of most marketing strategies is to set a price that corresponds to customer's perception of value in the product and at the same time does not "leave money on the table." In other words, the objective is to charge what a product is worth to the customer and to cover all costs and provide a margin for profit in the process.

International pricing is complicated by the fact that businesses must conform to different rule-making bodies and to different competitive situations in each country. Both the countries and the competition are constraints on pricing decisions. Each company must examine the market, the competition, its own costs and objectives, and local and regional regulations and laws in setting prices that are consistent with the overall marketing strategy.

Dumping—selling products in international markets at prices below those in the home country or below the cost of production—and parallel importing are two particularly contentious pricing issues. Company managers must also set transfer prices that are appropriate to company profitability objectives that conform to tax regulations in individual country markets.

DISCUSSION QUESTIONS

1. What are the three basic factors affecting price in any market? What considerations enter into the pricing decision?

2. Define the various types of pricing strategies and objectives available to global marketers.

3. Identify some of the environmental constraints on global pricing decisions.

4. What is "dumping"? Why was dumping such an important issue during the Uruguay Round of GATT negotiations?

5. What is a transfer price? What is the difference, if any, between a transfer price and a "regular" price? What are three methods for determining transfer prices?

6. What are the three alternative approaches to global pricing? Which one would you recommend to a company that has global market aspirations?

7. If you were responsible for marketing CAT scanners worldwide (average price, $1,200,000) and the country of manufacture was experiencing a strong and appreciating currency against almost all other currencies, what options are available for adjusting prices to take into account the strong currency situation?

BIBLIOGRAPHY

Books

Abdallah, Wagdy M. *International Transfer Pricing Policies: Decision Making Guidelines for Multinational Companies.* New York: Quorum Books, 1989.

Doorley, Thomas L., III, and Timothy M. Collins. *Teaming Up for the '90s: A Guide to International Joint Ventures and Strategic Alliances.* Homewood, Ill.: Business One Irwin, 1991.

Nagle, Thomas T. *The Strategy and Tactics of Pricing: A Guide to Profitable Decision Making.* Upper Saddle River, N.J.: Prentice Hall, 1987.

Robert, Michel. *Strategy Pure and Simple: How Winning CEOs Outthink Their Competition.* New York: McGraw-Hill, 1993.

Seymour, Daniel T. *The Pricing Decision.* Chicago: Probus Publishing Co., 1989.

Articles

Cannon, Hugh M., and Fred W. Morgan. "A Strategic Pricing Framework." *Journal of Business and Industrial Marketing* 6, nos. 3, 4 (Summer–Fall 1991), pp. 59–70.

Cohen, Stephen S., and John Zysman. "Countertrade, Offsets, Barter and Buyouts." *California Management Review* 28, no. 2 (Winter 1986), pp. 41–55.

Glicklich, Peter A., and Seth B. Goldstein. "New Transfer Pricing Regulations Adhere More Closely to an Arm's-Length Standard." *Journal of Taxation* 78, no. 5 (May 1993), pp. 306–314.

Lancioni, Richard, and John Gattorna. "Strategic Value Pricing: Its Role in International Business." *International Journal of Physical Distribution and Logistics* 22, no. 6, 1992 pp. 24–27.

Marn, Michael V., and Robert L. Rosiello. "Managing Price, Gaining Profit." *Harvard Business Review* 70, no. 5 (September–October 1992), pp. 84–94.

Samli, A. Coskun, and Laurence Jacobs. "Pricing Practices of American Multinational Firms: Standardization vs. Localization Dichotomy." *Journal of Global Marketing* 8, no. 2 (1994), pp. 51–74.

Schuster, Falko. "Barter Arrangements with Money: The Modern Form of Compensation Trading." *Columbia Journal of World Business* 15, no. 3 (Fall 1980), pp. 61–66.

Seifert, Bruce, and John Ford. "Are Exporting Firms Modifying Their Product, Pricing and Promotion Policies?" *International Marketing Review* 6, no. 6, 1989, pp. 53–68.

Simon, Hermann. "Pricing Opportunities—and How to Exploit Them." *Sloan Management Review* 33, no. 2 (Winter 1992), pp. 55–65.

Simon, Hermann, and Eckhard Kucher. "The European Pricing Time Bomb: and How to Cope With It." *European Management Journal* 10, no. 2 (June 1992), pp. 136–145.

Sinclair, Stuart. "A Guide to Global Pricing." *Journal of Business Strategy* 14, no. 3 (May-June 1993), pp. 16–19.

Williams, Jeffrey R. "How Sustainable Is Your Competitive Advantage?" *California Management Review* 34, no. 3 (Spring 1992), pp. 29–51.

3DO is a classic Silicon Valley start-up story. Several years ago, William "Trip" Hawkins set out to develop the world's most technologically advanced home gaming system. The 3DO Interactive Multiplayer product packs twice the computing power—32 bits instead of 16—found in competing game systems from Sega and Nintendo. Also, 3DO software comes on CD-ROM instead of cartridges. Such features provide 3D realism and allow video games to incorporate video clips from movies and TV shows. Despite 3DO's sophistication, Hawkins hoped for broad market appeal. "This is not a product for the computer nerds. It's for the masses," he said.

When Hawkins first conceived of 3DO, he realized the "razors" wouldn't sell unless plenty of "blades" were available. In other words, Hawkins knew he would have to convince software developers to create popular games that would drive sales of 3DO machines. To do that, he took advantage of the developers' resentment at having to pay exorbitant fees—as much as $12 per cartridge—to Sega and Nintendo for every piece of software sold. Hawkins offered a licensing deal requiring fees of only $3 per game. Developers were also attracted by the fact that 3DO's disc format was cheaper to manufacture than game cartridges.

The first 3DO players went on sale in October 1993; manufactured in Japan by Matsushita and bearing the Panasonic brand, they carried a hefty price tag of $699. Despite Hawkins's success at lining up hundreds of software developers, only about 50 game titles were available during the first few months 3DO was on sale. None was an instant hit along the lines of Sonic the Hedgehog, a game character that helped propel sales of Sega's Genesis player. Despite the 3DO Multiplayer's impressive sound and graphics, the CD-ROM format precluded players from storing data on them (ROM stands for "read only memory"). Thus, some players preferred the Sega Genesis 16-bit version of games such as Madden Football because the cartridge format allowed players to compile statistics on players and teams throughout the football season. Then there was the issue of price: With 16-bit players from Sega and Nintendo selling for less than $100, even consumers who wanted to own 3DO players were hard-pressed to justify the price premium. About 300,000 3DO units were sold worldwide in the first year after the launch. Hawkins hoped that the November 1994 release of a new game, FIFA International Soccer, would boost yearend sales.

Limited consumer demand put a severe financial strain on Hawkins's company; 3DO posted a $51 million loss for the year ending March 31, 1994. The dismal performance prompted Bruce Ryon, an industry analyst with Dataquest, to declare, "I think 3DO is going to fail. It will be a footnote in the history of the business." By May 1994, the stock price of 3DO Co. had sunk to the mid-teens from its October 1993 high of $47. In mid-December 1994, the price had dipped below $11 per share. The picture was further clouded after Hawkins made several decisions that angered his suppliers. First, he launched an in-house software development program that put the company in direct competition with its outside developers. Even more damaging was his announcement that, in order to help cover manufacturing and advertising costs, the $3 per-unit software licensing fee would be doubled, to $6. After vendors expressed outrage, however, Hawkins was forced to scale back the increase to $1 instead of $3.

Some industry observers expected 3DO to make a solid showing during the 1994 holiday season. Korea's Goldstar began marketing a 3DO unit, and the players were available in about 6,000 stores—three times the number of outlets as in 1993. In addition, 100 game titles were available, including "Demolition Man," featuring actual footage from the Sylvester Stallone movie. An aggressive TV advertising campaign showed competing machines being dumped in a coffin as an announcer urged video game fans to "put away your toys." Perhaps most important, however, was the fact that the list price of 3DO machines had been cut about 40 percent, to $399.

Still, competitors had been developing their own new machines. Sony launched its own 32-bit CD-ROM machine in Japan during the 1994 Christmas season. When PlayStation went on sale in the U.S. in September 1995, it carried a list price of $299; an estimated 70,000 units were sold in the first month alone. The Sony player was selling much better than Sega's Saturn, which reached the U.S. market in May 1995. Perhaps the biggest industry surprise in 1995 was the strong market demand for new games designed specifically for the older 16-bit systems. About 40 million of the older Genesis and Super Nintendo players are still in use in the United States; several of Nintendo's new 16-bit games—including Donkey Kong Country and Killer Instinct—were runaway best-sellers. It appeared that 3DO might be caught in the middle between the older players and new 32-bit systems such as PlayStation. Meanwhile, anticipation was building for Nintendo's new system, the Ultra 64, that was scheduled to go on sale in the United States in September 1996 for $250. As industry consultant Paul Saffo summed up the situation, "Trip's cleared the runway. But he hasn't cleared the trees."

DISCUSSION QUESTIONS

1. What pricing strategy did Hawkins use when 3DO was first released?
2. What are some of 3DO's key product features?
3. Do you agree with Hawkins's decision to alter the fee arrangement with software suppliers?
4. Do you think 3DO will succeed during the next few years? Why or why not?

Sources: Jim Carlton, "Aging 16-Bit Players Manage to Hang On," *The Wall Street Journal* (Nov. 16, 1995), pp. B1, B10.
John Markoff, "For 3DO, a Make-or-Break Season," *The New York Times* (Dec. 11, 1994), Sec. 3, pp. 1, 6.
Ralph T. King, Jr., "3DO Faces Struggle to Keep Video-Game Player Alive," *The Wall Street Journal* (May 19, 1994), p. B4.
Jim Carlton, "3DO Faces Revolt by Game Developers over Fee to Cut Manufacturers' Losses," *The Wall Street Journal* (Oct. 24, 1994), p. B4.
Cleveland Horton and Ira Teinowitz, "Video Goes 3DO," *Advertising Age* (Jan. 11, 1993), pp. 1, 43.

TRADE TERMS

A number of terms covering the conditions of the delivery are commonly used in international trade. The internationally accepted terms of trade are known as Incoterms. Every commercial transaction is based upon a contract of sale, and the trade terms used in that contract have the important function of naming the exact point at which the ownership of merchandise is transferred from the seller to the buyer.

The simplest type of export sale is "ex-works" (manufacturer's location). Under this type of contract, the seller assists the buyer in obtaining an export license, but the buyer's responsibility ends there. At the other extreme, the easiest terms of sale for the buyer are "delivered duty paid" (named place of destination), including duty and local transportation to his or her warehouse. Under this contract, the buyer's only responsibility is to obtain an import license if one is needed and to pass the customs entry at the seller's expense. Between these two terms there are many expenses that accrue to the goods as they move from the place of manufacture to the buyer's warehouse. Following are some of the steps involved in moving goods from a factory to a buyer's warehouse:

1. Obtaining an export license if required (in the United States, nonstrategic goods are exported under a general license that requires no specific permit)
2. Obtaining a currency permit if required
3. Packing the goods for export
4. Transporting the goods to the place of departure (this would normally involve transport by truck or rail to a seaport or airport)
5. Preparing a land bill of lading
6. Completing necessary customs export papers
7. Preparing customs or consular invoices as required by the country of destination
8. Arranging for ocean freight and preparation
9. Obtaining marine insurance and certificate of the policy

Who carries out these steps? It depends on the terms of the sale. In the following paragraphs some of the major terms are defined. The following two terms are acceptable Incoterms for all modes of transportation:

Ex-works. In this contract, the seller places goods at the disposal of the buyer at the time specified in the contract. The buyer takes delivery at the premises of the seller and bears all risks and expenses from that point on.

Delivered duty paid. Under this contract, the seller undertakes to deliver the goods to the buyer at the place he or she names in the country of import with all costs, including duties, paid. The seller is responsible under this contract for getting the import license if one is required.

The following are acceptable Incoterms for sea and inland waterway transportation only:

FAS (free alongside ship) named port of shipment. Under this contract, the seller must place goods alongside, or available to, the vessel or other mode of transportation and pay all charges up to that point. The seller's legal responsibility ends once he or she has obtained a clean wharfage receipt.

FOB (free on board). In an FOB contract, the responsibility and liability of the seller does not end until the goods have actually been placed aboard a ship. Terms should preferably be "FOB ship (name port)." The term FOB is frequently misused in international sales. FOB means "goods must be loaded on board, *and* buyer pays freight." Since freight charges generally include loading the goods, in essence, a double payment is made; the buyer pays twice!

CIF (cost, insurance, freight) named port of importation. Under this contract, as in the FOB contract, the risk of loss or damage to goods is transferred to the buyer once the goods have passed the ship's rail. But the seller has to pay the expense of transportation for the goods up to the port of destination, including the expense of insurance.

CFR (cost and freight). The terminology is the same as CIF, except the seller is not responsible for risk of loss at any point outside the factory.

The following Incoterm is acceptable for air, rail, and multimodal shipments.

FCA (free carrier) named place. Seller fulfills obligations when he or she hands over goods cleared for exports to the carrier named by the buyer at the named place or point (e.g., airport, rail siding, or seller's factory).

SECTION 482 OF THE INTERNAL REVENUE CODE

In any case of two or more organizations, trades, or businesses (whether or not incorporated, whether or not organized in the United States, and whether or not affiliated) owned or controlled directly or indirectly by the same interests, the Secretary may distribute, apportion, or allocate gross income, deductions, credits, or allowances between or among such organizations, trades, or businesses, if he determines that such distribution, apportionment, or allocation is necessary in order to prevent evasion of taxes or clearly to reflect the income of any of such organizations, trades, or businesses. In the case of any transfer (or license) of intangible property (within the meaning of section 936(h)(3)(B)), the income with respect to such transfer or license shall be commensurate with the income attributable to the intangible.

Source: *Internal Revenue Code* (New York: The Research Institute of America, 1987), p. 695.

Global Marketing Channels and Physical Distribution

> *"Logistics is far more than trucks and checking stations. It's really a question of having the right inventory level to support customer demand and how to structure the supply chain—from where the supplier is based to how long it takes to get goods from the supplier to the store."*
>
> —Andrew Higginson,
> *global finance director,*
> *Laura Ashley Holdings*

Hypermarkets are giant stores as big as four or more football fields. Part supermarket, part department store, they feature a wide array of product categories—groceries, toys, furniture, fast food, and financial services— all under one roof. Hypermarkets have flourished in Europe for more than three decades. Carrefour SA, a French company, opened the first hypermarket in 1962; with help from the French government, zoning laws ensured that competing stores would be kept from the vicinity. By end of the 1990s, Carrefour and its chief rival, Euromarchè SA, together had about 150 of France's nearly 1,000 hypermarkets; the giant stores account for about 20 percent of all retail sales and nearly one-half of all grocery sales. Most of the European stores were established before competing outlets such as shopping malls and discount stores made the Atlantic crossing from America.

Hypermarkets are just one of the many elements the constitute distribution channels around the globe. The American Marketing Association defines *channel of distribution* as "an organized network of agencies and institutions which, in combination, perform all the activities required to link producers with users to accomplish the marketing task."[1] Distribution is the physical flow of goods through channels; as suggested by the definition, channels are comprised of a coordinated group of individuals or firms that perform functions adding utility to a product or service.

Distribution channels in markets around the world are among the most highly differentiated aspects of national marketing systems. On the opposite end of the spectrum from hypermarkets, for example, are small stores in Latin America called *pulperias*. The diversity of channels and the wide range of possible distribution strategies can present challenging problems to anyone designing a global marketing program. Smaller companies are often blocked by their inability to establish effective channel arrangements. In larger companies operating via country subsidiaries, channel strategy is the element of the marketing mix that headquarters understands the least. To a large extent, channels are an aspect of the marketing program that is locally led through the discretion of the in-country marketing management group. Nevertheless, it is important for managers responsible for world marketing programs to understand the nature of international distribution channels.

---

[1]Peter D. Bennett, *Dictionary of Marketing Terms* (Chicago: American Marketing Association, 1988), p. 29.

Channels and physical distribution are integral parts of the total marketing program and must be appropriate to the product design, price, and communications aspects of the total marketing program.

CHANNEL OBJECTIVES AND CONSTRAINTS

The general objective of marketing channels is to create utility for customers. The major categories of channel utility are *place* (the availability of a product or service in a location that is convenient to a potential customer); *time* (the availability of a product or service when desired by a customer); *form* (the availability of the product processed, prepared, ready to use, and in proper condition); and *information* (the availability of answers to questions and general communication about useful product features and benefits). Since these utilities can be a basic source of competitive advantage and product value, choosing a channel strategy is one of the key policy decisions marketing management must make.

Channel decisions are important because of the number and nature of relationships that must be managed. Channel decisions typically involve long-term legal commitments and obligations to other firms and individuals. Such commitments are often extremely expensive to terminate or change. Even in cases where there is no legal obligation, commitments may be backed by good faith and feelings of obligation, which are equally difficult to manage and painful to adjust. From the viewpoint of the marketer concerned with a single-country program, channel arrangements in different parts of the world are a valuable source of information and insight into possible new approaches for more effective channel strategies. (Of course, the same is true for the other elements of the marketing mix.) For example, self-service discount pricing in the United States was studied by retailers from Europe and Asia who then introduced the self-service concept in their own countries. Governments and business executives all over the world have examined Japanese trading companies with great interest to learn from their success.

The starting point in selecting the most effective channel arrangement is a clear focus of the company's marketing effort on a target market and a determination of its needs and preferences. Where are the potential customers located? What are their information requirements? What are their preferences for service? How sensitive are they to price? Customer preference must be carefully determined because there is as much danger to the success of a marketing program in creating too much utility as there is in creating too little. Moreover, each market must be analyzed to determine the cost of providing channel services. What is appropriate in one country may not be effective in another.

For example, an international manufacturer of construction products that emphasized the speedy service provided by a sales force in radio-equipped station wagons made the mistake of offering too much service in the United States. The company prided itself on the fact that a maximum of two hours elapsed between the receipt of a customer order from a construction site and the actual delivery by a salesperson. The cost of this service was included in the prices the company charged. While its service record was outstanding, the company discovered that in the United States its products were at a serious competitive price disadvantage. Customers gave the company high marks for its service, but in terms of actual buying behavior they preferred to buy from a competitor whose costs were much lower because of less speedy delivery service. The competitor passed these cost savings on to customers in the form of lower prices. In this particular example, price was more important than time utility to U.S. customers. This situation did not apply to European markets, where competition and customer preference made speedy delivery necessary.

Channel strategy in a global marketing program must fit the company's competitive position and overall marketing objectives in each national market. If a company wants to enter a competitive market, it has two basic choices:

1. Direct involvement (its own sales force, retail stores, etc.)
2. Indirect involvement (independent agents, distributors, wholesalers)

The first choice requires that the company must establish company-owned or franchised outlets. The second choice requires incentives to independent channel agents that will induce them to promote the company's product. The process of shaping international channels to fit overall company objectives is constrained by several factors: customers, products, middlemen, and the environment. Important characteristics of each of these factors are discussed briefly.

Customer Characteristics

The characteristics of customers are an important influence on channel design. Their number, geographical distribution, income, shopping habits, and reaction to different selling methods all vary from country to country and therefore require different channel approaches. Remember, channels create utility for customers.

In general, regardless of the stage of market development, the need for multiple channel intermediaries increases as the number of customers increases. The converse is also true: The need for channel intermediaries decreases as the number of customers decreases. For example, if there are only 10 customers for an industrial product in each national market, these 10 customers must be directly contacted by either the manufacturer or an agent. For mass-market products bought by millions of customers, retail distribution outlets or mail-order distribution is required. In a country with a large number of low-volume retailers, it is usually cheaper to reach them via wholesalers. Direct selling that bypasses wholesale intermediaries may be the most cost-effective means of serving large-volume retailers. While these generalizations apply to all countries, regardless of stage of development, individual country customs will vary. For example, Toys 'Я' Us faced considerable opposition from Japanese toy manufacturers who refused to engage in direct selling after the U.S. company built its first stores in Japan.

Product Characteristics

Certain product attributes such as degree of standardization, perishability, bulk, service requirements, and unit price have an important influence on channel design and strategy. Products with high unit price, for example, are often sold through a company sales force because the selling cost of this "expensive" distribution method is a small part of the total sale price. Moreover, the high cost of such products is usually associated with complexity or with product features that must be explained in some detail, and this can be done most effectively by a controlled sales force. For example, mainframe computers are expensive, complicated products that require both explanation and applications analysis focused on the customer's needs. A company-trained salesperson or "sales engineer" is well suited for the task of creating information utility for computer buyers.

Mainframe computers, photocopiers, and other industrial products may require margins to cover the costs of expensive sales engineering. Other products require margins to provide a large monetary incentive to a direct sales force. In many parts of the world, cosmetics are sold by door-to-door; company representatives call on potential customers. The reps must create customer awareness of the value of cosmetics and evoke a feeling of need for this value that leads to a sale. The sales activity must be paid for. Companies using direct distribution for consumer products rely upon wide gross selling margins to generate the revenue necessary to compensate sales people. Amway and Avon are two companies that have succeeded in extending their direct sales systems outside the United States.

Perishable products impose special form utility demands on channel members. Such products usually need relatively direct channels to ensure satisfactory condition at the time of customer purchase. In less-developed countries, producers of vegetables, bread, and other food products typically sell their goods in public marketplaces. In developed countries, perishable food products are distributed by controlled sales forces, and stock is checked by these sales distributor organizations to ensure that it is fresh and ready for purchase.

In 1991, Andersen Consulting assisted the Moscow Bread Company in improving its ability to distribute bread in the Russian capital. For Russians, bread is truly the "staff of life," with consumers queuing up daily to buy fresh loaves at numerous shops and kiosks. Unfortunately, distribution was often hampered by excessive paperwork that resulted in the delivery of stale bread; Andersen found that as much as one-third of the bread produced was wasted. The consulting team arrived at a simple solution: plastic bags to keep the bread fresh. The team found that, although 95 percent of food is packaged in developed countries, the figure was only 2 percent in the former Soviet Union, where open-air markets are the norm. Russian consumers responded favorably to the change; not only did the bags guarantee freshness and extend the shelf life of the bread by 600 percent, the bags themselves created utility. In a country where such extras are virtually unknown, the bags constituted a reusable "gift."[2]

Bulky products usually require channel arrangements that minimize the shipping distances and the number of times products change hands between channel intermediaries before they reach the ultimate customer. Soft drinks and beer are examples of bulky products whose widespread availability is an important aspect of an effective marketing strategy.

Middleman Characteristics

Channel strategy must recognize the characteristics of existing middlemen. Middlemen are in business to maximize their own profit and not that of the manufacturer. They are notorious for "cherry picking," that is, the practice of taking orders from manufacturers whose products and brands are in demand to avoid any real selling effort for a manufacturer's products that may require "push." This is a rational response by the middleman, but it can present a serious obstacle to the manufacturer attempting to break into a market with a new product. The "cherry picker" is not interested in building a market for a new product. This is a problem for the expanding international company. Frequently, a manufacturer with a new product or a product with a limited market share is forced to set up some arrangement for bypassing the "cherry picking" segment of the channel. In some cases, manufacturers will set up an expensive direct distribution organization to obtain a share of the market. When they finally obtain a share of the target market, they may abandon the direct distribution system for a more cost-effective intermediary system. The move does not mean that intermediaries are "better" than direct distribution. It is simply a response by a manufacturer to cost considerations and the newly acquired attractiveness of the company's product to independent distributors.

An alternative method of dealing with the "cherry picking" problem does not require setting up an expensive direct sales force. Rather, a company may decide to rely on a distributor's own sales force by subsidizing the cost of the sales representatives the distributor has assigned to the company's products. This approach has the advantage of holding down costs by tying missionary and support selling in with the distributor's existing sales management team and physical distribution system. With this approach it is possible to place managed direct selling support and distribution support behind a product at the expense of only one salesperson per selling area. The distributor's incentive for cooperat-

---

[2]"Case Study: Moscow Bread Company," Andersen Consulting (1993).

ing in this kind of arrangement is that he or she obtains a "free" sales representative for a new product with the potential to be a profitable addition to his or her line. This cooperative arrangement is ideally suited to getting a new export-sourced product into distribution in a market.

Environmental Characteristics

The general characteristics of the total environment are a major consideration in channel design. Because of the enormous variety of economic, social, and political environments internationally, there is a need to delegate a large degree of independence to local operating managements or agents. A comparison of food distribution in countries at different stages of development illustrates how channels reflect and respond to underlying market conditions in a country. In the United States, several factors combine to make the supermarket or the self-service one-stop food store the basic food retailing unit. These factors include high incomes, large-capacity refrigerator/freezer units, automobile ownership, acceptance of frozen and convenience foods, and attitudes toward food preparation. Many shoppers want to purchase a week's worth of groceries in one trip to the store. They have the money, ample storage space in the refrigerator, and the hauling capacity of the car to move this large quantity of food from the store to the home. The supermarket, because it is efficient, can fill the food shoppers' needs at lower prices than are found in butcher shops and other traditional full-service food stores. Additionally, supermarkets can offer more variety and a greater selection of merchandise than can smaller food stores, a fact that appeals to affluent consumers.

The 1970s saw a severe drop in grocery outlet density in nearly all countries. Six countries—Australia, the United States, South Africa, the Netherlands, Great Britain, and Sweden—now have one outlet or fewer per thousand population. Ireland, Belgium, Germany, and a number of other countries have experienced more than 50 percent reduction in outlet density.

The trend continues even in countries with a low density of stores already. For example, in the United States, thousands of stores have disappeared in the past several years. Industry observers expect this trend of fewer grocery stores to continue in the future at varying rates in different countries. Stabilization may come at above or below the U.S. level.

SELECTION AND CARE OF DISTRIBUTORS AND AGENTS

The selection of distributors and agents in a target market is a critically important task. A good commission agent or stocking distributor can make the difference between realizing zero performance and performance that exceeds 200 percent of what is expected. At any point in time, some of any company's agents and distributors will be excellent, others will be satisfactory, and still others will be unsatisfactory and in need of replacement.

To find a good distributor, a firm can begin with a list provided by the U.S. Department of Commerce or its equivalent in other countries. The local chamber of commerce in a country can also provide lists, as can local trade associations. It is a waste of time to try to screen the list by mail. Go to the country and talk to end users of the products you are selling and find out which distributors they prefer and why they prefer them. If the product is a consumer product, go to the retail outlets and find out where consumers are buying products similar to your own and why. Two or three names will keep coming up. Go to these two or three and see which of them would be available to sign. Before signing, make sure there is someone in the organization who will be the key person for your product. The "key person" is someone who will make it a personal objective to achieve success with your product.

This is the critical difference between the successful distributor and the worthless distributor. There must be a personal, individual commitment to the product. The second and related requirement for successful distributors or agents is that they must be successful with the product. Success means that they can sell the product and make money on it. In any case, the product must be designed and priced to be competitive in the target market. The distributor can assist in this process by providing information about customer wants and the competition and by promoting the product he or she represents.

The RF Division of Harris Corporation achieved great success in international markets with its short-wave radios. One of the reasons for its success was the quality of agents in key markets and their commitment to the Harris product. They were attracted to Harris because the company made a product that was as good as or better than any other product on the market. Also, Harris offered commissions of 33 percent on all sales—at least 15 percent higher than commissions offered by any other competitor. This was certainly one of the single most important factors in ensuring Harris's success. The generous commission motivated the agents to sell Harris products and provided the financial resources to support a strong marketing effort.

The only way to keep a good distributor is to work closely with him or her to ensure that he or she is making money on the product. Any distributor who does not make money on a line will drop it. It is really quite simple. In general, if a distributor is not working out, it is wise to terminate the agreement and find another one. Few companies are large enough to convert a mediocre distributor or agent into an effective business representative. Therefore, the two most important clauses in the distributor contract are the performance and cancellation clauses. Make sure they are written in a way that will make it easy to enforce or, if necessary, terminate the agreement. There is a myth that it is expensive or even impossible to terminate distributor and agent agreements. Some of the most successful global marketers have terminated hundreds of agreements and know success is based on their willingness to terminate if a distributor or agent does not perform. The key factor is performance: Distributors who do not perform must either shape up or be replaced.

DISTRIBUTION CHANNELS: TERMINOLOGY AND STRUCTURE

Distribution channels are systems that link manufacturers to customers. Although channels for consumer products and industrial products are similar, there are also some distinct differences, as discussed below. Consumer channels are designed to put products in the hands of people for their own use; industrial channels deliver products to manufacturers or organizations that use them in the production process or day-to-day operations.

Consumer Products

Figure 15–1 summarizes channel structure alternatives for consumer products. A consumer products manufacturer can sell to customers directly (using a door-to-door sales force), through mail-order selling (using a catalog or other printed materials), or through manufacturer-owned stores. Of the first three direct alternatives, the mail-order business is the most widely used. Some observers predict that the importance of direct mail distribution will grow considerably in the next few years because time, one of the most valuable resources, has become increasingly scarce. As consumers trade off the time cost of in-store shopping against the time demands of leisure activity, they are increasingly attracted to the time and place utility created by direct mail marketing.

Door-to-door selling is a relatively expensive form of distribution that, as noted above, requires high gross margins and can result in higher prices to the customer. In the United States, it is a form of selling that is mature. Certain items—household brushes, vacuum cleaners, and cosmetics—continue to be sold in this manner. Door-to-door selling is, how-

FIGURE 15–1

MARKETING CHANNEL
ALTERNATIVES:
CONSUMER PRODUCTS

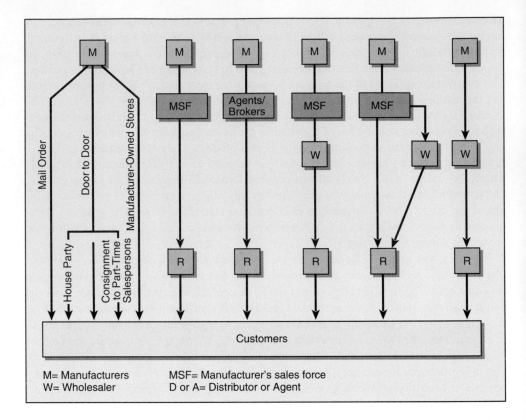

Figure 15–1 Marketing Channel Alternatives: Consumer Products

M= Manufacturers   MSF= Manufacturer's sales force
W= Wholesaler   D or A= Distributor or Agent

ever, growing in popularity outside the United States. For example, Avon has successfully used this approach in more than 50 countries identified by company executives as having weak retail infrastructures. Also, it recognized that low levels of discretionary income translate into low levels of expenditures on cosmetics and toiletries. Thus, the role of the sales force is to communicate the benefits of cosmetics and build demand. In such countries as China, Hungary, the Czech Republic, and Russia, home direct-selling is the perfect channel strategy. In fact, Avon became the first company permitted to sell door to door in China. Since 1990, Avon has operated a joint venture with Guangzhou Cosmetics Factory in the province of Old Canton.

U.S. automobile manufacturers attempting to penetrate the Japanese market aren't faced with high tariffs. Rather, they are confronted with the fact that half the nation's cars are sold door to door. Toyota and its eight Japanese competitors maintain showrooms, but they also employ more than 100,000 car salespeople. Unlike their American counterparts, many Japanese car buyers never visit dealerships. In fact, the close, long-term relationships between auto salespersons and the Japanese people can be thought of as a consumer version of the *keiretsu* system discussed in Chapter 11. Car buyers expect numerous face-to-face meetings with a sales representative, during which trust is established. The relationship continues after the deal is closed; sales reps send cards and continually seek to ensure the buyers' satisfaction. U.S. rivals such as Ford, meanwhile, try to generate showroom traffic. Nobumasa Ogura, who manages a Ford dealership in Tokyo, says, "We need to come up with some ideas to sell more cars without door-to-door sales, but the reality is that we haven't come up with any."[3]

A third direct selling alternative is the *manufacturer-owned store* or *independent franchise store*. For example, the Walt Disney company owns stores that sell apparel, videos,

[3]Valerie Reitman, "Toyota Calling: In Japan's Car Market, Big Three Face Rivals Who Go Door-to-Door," *The Wall Street Journal* (Sept. 28, 1994), pp. A1, A6.

toys, and other merchandise relating to the company's trademarked characters. As noted in Chapter 11, Japanese consumer electronics companies integrate stores into their distribution groups. Some companies such as Nike and Levi Strauss establish one or a few "flagship" retail outlets as a showcase or means of obtaining marketing intelligence rather than as a distribution strategy. If a manufacturer's product line is sufficiently broad to support a retail outlet, this form of distribution can be very attractive. The shoe store, for example, is a viable retail unit, and shoe manufacturers typically have established their own direct outlets as a major element in their distribution strategy, both at home and in important world markets. One of the first successful U.S.-based international companies, Singer, established a worldwide chain of company-owned and -operated outlets to sell and service sewing machines.

The other channel structure alternatives for consumer products are various combinations of a manufacturer's sales force and wholesalers calling upon retail outlets, which in turn sell to customers. In a given country at a particular point in time, various product classes will have characteristic distribution patterns associated with them. In Japan, for example, several layers of small wholesalers play an important role in the distribution of food. Attempts to bypass these apparently unnecessary units in the channel have failed because the cost to a manufacturer of providing their service (frequent small deliveries to small grocery outlets) is greater than the margin they require. Channel patterns that appear to be inefficient may reflect rational adjustment to costs and preferences in a market, or they may present an opportunity to the innovative global marketer to obtain competitive advantage by introducing more effective channel arrangements.

Global Retailing

Global retailing is any retailing activity that crosses national boundaries. Today there is a growing interest among successful retailers to expand globally, but this not a new phenomenon. For centuries, venturesome merchants have gone abroad both to obtain merchandise and ideas and to operate retail establishments. The development of trading company operations in Africa and Asia by British, French, Dutch, Belgian, and German retailing organizations progressed extensively during the 19th and early 20th centuries. International trading and retail store operation were two of the economic pillars of the colonial system of that era. The big change taking place in international retailing today involves the gradual dissolution of the colonial retailing structure and, in its place, the creation of international retailing organizations operating in the industrialized countries.

Retail stores can be divided into categories according to the amount of square feet of floor space, the level of service offered, and width and depth of product offerings. In practice, stores have many different names in different countries, and definitions based on selling area also vary. A variety of terms is used to refer to large stores, including hypermarkets, mass merchandisers, discounters, supermarkets, and superstores.

In general, countries where the proportion of store numbers is low relative to their share of turnover are those which joined the supermarket revolution many years after it began. France, Belgium, Spain, Brazil, and Colombia are some of the countries in which supermarket retailing sprang up as large, modern, highly efficient units were built. In Italy, where worker protective legislation limiting the opening of large supermarkets is a factor, large surface stores grew in popularity more gradually. They have more than half of the grocery market share today, up from only 25 percent several years ago. In other countries, supermarkets have existed for more than two decades. Some of the smaller units have been closed down and new, very large stores have appeared in their place.

The large number of unsuccessful international retailing ventures suggests that anyone contemplating a move into international retailing should do so with a great deal of caution. Speaking of global opportunities for U.S.-based retailers, one industry analyst noted, "It's awfully hard to operate across the water. It's one thing to open up in Mexico and

Dell rings up $5 billion in sales of made-to-order PC systems; business sales comprise 90 percent of the total. Michael Dell calls Asia "the center of the universe for the computer industry." He hopes to achieve success there using the same direct-sales approach that has been effective in more than 100 countries. (Goldberg Moser O'Neill. Awarded an EFFIE in 1995.)

Canada, but the distribution hassles are just too big when it comes to exporting an entire store concept overseas."[4] The critical question for the would-be international retailer is, "What advantages do we have relative to local competition?" The answer will often be "Nothing," when local laws governing retailing practice are taken into account. In such cases there is no reason to expect highly profitable operations to develop from a venture into international retailing.

On the other hand, the answer may indicate that potential advantages do exist. Basically, a retailer has two things to offer consumers. One is the selection of goods at a price, and the second is the overall manner in which the goods are offered in the store setting. This includes such things as the store site, parking facilities, in-store setting, and customer service. JC Penney is expanding retailing operations internationally for both reasons. After touring several countries, JC Penney executives realized that retailers outside the United States often lack marketing sophistication in terms of displaying products, locating aisles to optimize customer traffic, and grouping products. For example, in Istanbul, Turkey, a visiting team noted that one store featured lingerie next to plumbing equipment. According to William R. Howell, Penney chairman and CEO, Penney's advantage in such instances is its ability to "develop an environment that invites the customer to shop."[5]

1MB video RAM with 32-bit local bus means faster video performance.

Swappable hard drives make it easy to share a Latitude XP without having to share all your files.

DELL LATITUDE XP
INTEL DX4 75MHz SYSTEM

$3399

BUSINESS LEASE: $126/MO.
• 9.5" DUAL SCAN STN COLOR
• 8MB RAM
• 340MB HARD DRIVE
• 3 YEAR WARRANTY
• NEW LITHIUM ION BATTERY
ORDER CODE #600011

For programs requiring major RAM, we offer **RAM expansion up to 36MB** on Latitude XP!

CommWorks, RadioMail and America OnLine free and pre-installed so you never have to be out of touch.

DELL
To Order, Call
800-285-6840
In Canada? Call 800-668-3021
Mon-Fri 7am-9pm CT • Sat 10am-6pm CT • Sun 12pm-5pm CT
In Mexico City? Call 800-228-2441
Keycode #IBC13

Industrial Products

Figure 15–2 summarizes marketing channel alternatives for the industrial product company. Three basic elements are involved: the manufacturer's sales force, distributors or agents, and wholesalers. A manufacturer can reach customers with its own sales force, or a sales force that calls on wholesalers who sell to customers, or a combination of these two arrangements. A manufacturer can sell directly to wholesalers without using a sales force, and wholesalers in turn can supply customers. Finally, a distributor or agent can call on wholesalers or customers for the manufacturer.

Patterns vary from country to country. Before deciding which pattern to use and which wholesalers and agents to select, managers must study each country individually. In general, the larger the market, the more feasible it is for a manufacturer to use its own sales force. Kyocera Corp. of Kyoto, Japan, has successfully used its own sales force at home and in the United States to achieve leadership in the $1.2 billion global market for ceramic microchip covers. Company founder Kazuo Inamori goes to great lengths to make sure the spiritual drive of Kyocera's unique corporate culture extends to all parts of the company, including the sales force.

[4]Neil King, Jr., "Kmart's Czech Invasion Lurches Along," *The Wall Street Journal* (June 8, 1993), p. A11.
[5]Bob Ortega, "Foreign Forays: Penney Pushes Abroad in Unusually Big Way as It Pursues Growth," *The Wall Street Journal* (Feb. 1, 1994), pp. A1, A7.

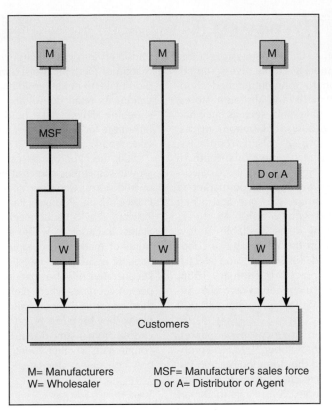

FIGURE 15–2

MARKETING CHANNEL
ALTERNATIVES:
INDUSTRIAL PRODUCTS

M= Manufacturers
W= Wholesaler

MSF= Manufacturer's sales force
D or A= Distributor or Agent

INTERNATIONAL CHANNEL INNOVATION

As noted at the beginning of this chapter, distribution channels around the world are highly differentiated. On the surface, it appears this differentiation can only be explained in terms of culture and the income level that exists in the market. However, the incidence and rate of innovation in retail channels can be explained in terms of the following four observations:

1. Innovation takes place only in the most highly developed systems. In general, channel agents in less-developed systems will adapt developments already tried and tested in more highly developed systems.
2. The ability of a system to successfully adapt innovations is directly related to its level of economic development. Certain minimum levels of economic development are necessary to support anything beyond the most simple retailing methods.
3. When the economic environment is favorable to change, the process of adaptation may be either hindered or helped by local demographic/geographic factors, social mores, government action, and competitive pressures.
4. The process of adaptation can be greatly accelerated by the actions of aggressive individual firms.

Self-service—the provision for customers to handle and select merchandise themselves in a store with minimal assistance from sales personnel—is a major 20th century channel innovation. It provides an excellent illustration of the postulates just outlined. Self-service was first introduced in the United States. The spread of self-service to other countries supports the hypothesis that the ability of a system to accept innovations is directly related to the level of economic development in the system. Self-service was first introduced internationally into the most highly developed systems. It has spread to the coun-

■ HYPERMARKETS

*I*n the United States, retailing channels are quite diverse. In addition to long-entrenched shopping malls and discount stores, wholesale clubs such as Pace and Sam's offer rock-bottom prices, and Toys 'Я' Us, Circuit City, and other "category killers" offer tremendous depth in particular product categories. Sensing a market opportunity, Euromarché opened its first U.S. hypermarket in October 1984. Bigg's, in Cincinnati, was one and a half times the size of a football field with 75 aisles, 40 checkout lanes, and 60,000 different items available at low prices. One shopper summed up the advantage of shopping at Bigg's: "I can buy bread, lunchmeat, and electrical equipment all at the same place." In February 1988, Carrefour ("Crossroads" in French) opened its own U.S. hypermarket, a gigantic store in Philadelpia with 330,000 square feet of floor space.

Carrefour soon built a second American hypermarket, but then shut down both stores in October 1993. The problem? Many shoppers simply found the stores too big and too overwhelming. Moreover, big scale changed the economics of profitable operation. For example, consultants for Kmart noted that its hypermarket near Atlanta could only succeed if it attracted four times as many shoppers as a regular discount department store and if the average transaction equaled $43—double the average for discount stores. Meanwhile, costs associated with running the huge stores translated into gross margins of around 8 percent—half the margin of the typical discount store. Finally, Americans just didn't take to mixing food and nonfood purchases in one location. As retail consultant Kurt Barnard noted, "One-stop shopping did not take hold easily. Working parents don't have time for their kids, let alone a shopping expedition that takes hours."

Still, the hypermarket concept is thriving overseas where growth sometimes comes at the expense of traditional family-owned stores. Carrefour operates a network of 240 stores in France, Spain, Portugal, Italy, Turkey, Brazil, Argentina, and Taiwan. Why is the concept so successful outside the United States? In countries where shoppers must visit many smaller stores or markets to complete the shopping, the mega-store concept is viewed as a welcome innovation. Also, hypermarket operators offer free parking in spacious lots, a lure to shoppers in countries where parking spaces are in short supply. A third reason is demographic: as more women enter the workplace, they have less time to shop. While U. S. shoppers can choose from many discount stores and supermarkets, their counterparts in other countries find that hypermarkets are the only convenient alternative to shopping store-to-store.

Sources: Laurie Underwood, "Consumers at a Crossroad," *Free China Review* (Feb. 2, 1995), pp. 66–67.

Steven Greenhouse, " 'Hypermarkets' Come to U.S.," *The New York Times*, (Feb. 7, 1985), p. 29

Laurie M. Grossman, "Hypermarkets: A Sure-Fire Hit Bombs," *The Wall Street Journal* (June 25, 1992), p. B1.

Anthony Ramirez, "Will American Shoppers Think Bigger Is Really Better?" *The New York Times* (Apr. 1, 1990), Sec. 3, p. 11.

---

tries at middle and lower stages of development but serves very small segments of the total market in these countries.

If a marketing system has reached a stage of development that will support a channel innovation, it is clear that the action of well-managed firms can contribute considerably to the diffusion of the channel innovation. The rapid growth of Benetton and McDonald's is a testament to the skill and competence of these firms as well as to the appeal of their product. In some instances, channel innovations are improved, refined, and expanded outside the home country. For example, 7-Eleven stores in Japan are half the size of U.S. stores, carry one-third the inventory, yet ring up twice as much in sales. They boast a fourth-generation point-of-sale (POS) information system that is more sophisticated than the system used in the United States. Another Japanese 7-Eleven innovation: an in-store catalog, Shop America, that allows Japanese shoppers to order imported luxury products from companies like Tiffany's and Cartier. The Japanese successes came even as Southland Corporation, the U.S.-based parent company, slipped into financial difficulty. Retailing analyst Takayuki Suzuki has been critical of Southland, noting, "Their merchandising has been really backwards, and the gap between us is rather large. The biggest reason is that they kept their old style and did not improve their methods and adapt to consumers' changing tastes. They became really rigid." Eventually 7-Eleven Japan acquired the U.S.-based parent company.[6]

[6]James Sterngold, "New Japanese Lesson: Running a 7-11," *The New York Times* (May 9, 1991), p. C7.

A MATTER OF CULTURE ▼

*O*ne of the conspicuous features of retail channels in less-developed countries is the remarkable number of people engaged in selling very small quantities of merchandise. In Ethiopia and other East African countries, for example, an open window in the side of a building is likely to be a *souk*, a small walk-up store whose proprietor sells everything from toilet paper and playing cards to rice and eggs. To maximize sales, *souks* are strategically interspersed throughout neighborhood areas. The proprietors know what customers want and need. For example, early in the day they may sell incense and a paper cone with enough coffee for the morning coffee ceremony. In the evening, cigarettes and gum may be in demand, especially if the *souk* is located near a neighborhood nightclub. If a *souk* is closed, it is often possible to rouse the proprietor by knocking on the window, since the store also serves as the proprietor's domicile. Some *souk* owners will even provide "curb service" and bring items to a customer waiting in a car.

By comparison, government department stores in East Africa are less likely to display such a service orientation. Government stores may be stocked with mass quantities of items that are slow to sell. For example, the shelves may hold row after row of tinned tomatoes, even though fresh tomatoes are readily available year around in the market. Customers must go through several steps before actually taking possession of their purchases: determining what goods are available, making a purchase decision, moving to another area to pay, and finally, actually taking possession of the goods. This usually involves a substantial number of papers, seals, and stamps, as well as interaction with two or three clerks. Clerk jobs are highly prized in countries where jobs are scarce; compared to the *souk* proprietor, who is willing to work from dawn to dusk, the government employee works from 9:00 A.M. to 5:00 P.M. with two hours off for lunch.

In Costa Rica, the privately owned *pulperia* is similar to the Western-style general store that was popular in the first part of the century. Customers enter the store, tell clerks what items are desired, and the clerks fetch the items—which may range from chicken feed to thumb tacks. A typical *pulperia* stocks staples such as sugar and flour in 50-kilo bags which the proprietor resells in smaller portions. Most *pulperias* have a refrigeration unit so they can sell ice cream novelties; in areas where there is no electricity, the *pulperia* owner will use a generator to provide power for the refrigerator. *Pulperias* are serviced by a fleet of private wholesalers; on any given day, the soft drink truck, the candy truck, or the staples truck may make deliveries. The *pulperia* serves as a central gathering place for the neighborhood, and generally has a public telephone from which patrons can make calls for a fee. This attracts many people to the store in communities where there are few, if any, private telephones.

Both the *souk* and the *pulperia* typically offer an informal system of credit. People who patronize these shops usually live in the neighborhood and are known to the proprietor. Often the proprietor will extend credit if he or she knows that a customer has suffered a setback such as loss of a job or a death in the family. Informally, the proprietors of private retail shops fulfill the role of a lender, especially for people who do not have access to credit through regular financial institutions.

Source: Private communication from Brian Larson of CARE Niger.

CHANNEL STRATEGY FOR NEW MARKET ENTRY

A global company expanding across national boundaries often finds itself in the position of entering a market for the first time. The company must use established channels, build its own channels, or abandon the market. Channel obstacles are often encountered when a company enters a competitive market where brands and supply relationships are already established. As noted above, there is little immediate incentive for an independent channel agent to take on a new product when established names are accepted in the market and are satisfying current demands. The global company seeking to enter such a market must either provide some incentive to channel agents or establish its own direct distribution system. Each of these alternatives has its disadvantages.

A company may decide to provide special incentives to independent channel agents; however, this approach can be extremely expensive. The company might offer outright payments—either direct cash bonuses or contest awards—tied to sales performance. In competitive markets with sufficiently high prices, incentives could take the form of gross margin guarantees. Both incentive payments and margin guarantees are expensive. The incentive payments are *directly* expensive; the margin guarantees can be *indirectly* expensive because they affect the price to the consumer and the price competitiveness of a manufacturer's product.

Establishing direct distribution in a new market can also be expensive. Sales representatives and sales management must be hired and trained. The sales organization will inevitably be a heavy loser in its early stage of operation in a new market because it will not have sufficient volume to cover its overhead costs. Therefore, any company contemplating establishing a direct sales force, even one assigned to distributors, should be prepared to underwrite losses for this sales force for a reasonable period of time.

The expense of a direct sales force acts as a deterrent to establishing direct distribution in a new market. Nevertheless, it is often the most effective method. Indeed, in many instances direct distribution is the only feasible way for a new company to establish itself in a market. By using a sales force, the manufacturer can ensure aggressive sales activity and attention to its products. Sufficient resource commitment to sales activity, backed up by appropriate communications programs (including advertising) may in time allow a manufacturer with competitive products and prices to obtain a reasonable share of market. When market share objectives have been reached, the manufacturer may consider shifting from the direct sales force to reliance on independent intermediaries. This shift becomes a possibility when market share and market recognition make the manufacturer's brand attractive to independent intermediaries.

Kyocera achieved great success in the U.S. market by custom-tailoring ceramic chip housings to each customer's needs. Kyocera also has become legendary for its service among California's Silicon Valley chipmakers. Instead of following the electronics industry norm of using distributors for its products, Kyocera relies on a salaried sales force. Kyocera backs up its $100-million-per-year R&D expenditures with sales forces in both the United States—50 direct salespersons at 12 direct sales offices—and Japan that place unwavering emphasis on quality and customer service. Early on, Kyocera earned a reputation for answering customer questions overnight, while U.S. suppliers often took weeks to respond. Employees would work around the clock to satisfy customer requests for samples. Another hallmark: No company is too small for Kyocera to serve. Jerry Crowley of Gazelle Microcircuits in Santa Clara reported, for example, that Kyocera salespeople began calling on him when he had only 11 employees. Gazelle has been buying custom chip packages from Kyocera ever since.

PHYSICAL DISTRIBUTION AND LOGISTICS

The value chain and value system are conceptual tools that provide a framework integrating various organizational activities, including distribution and physical transportation (see Table 15–1). Physical distribution issues include order processing, warehousing, inventory management, and transportation. Warehouses are used to store goods until they are sold; another type of facility, the distribution center, is designed to efficiently receive goods from suppliers and then fill orders for individual stores. A company may have its own warehouses and distribution centers, or pay a specialist to provide these facilities. Proper inventory management ensures that a company neither runs out of manufacturing components or finished goods nor incurs the expense and risk of carrying excessive stocks of these items. Finally, transportation decisions concern which of five methods a company should use to move its products: rail, truck, air, water, or pipeline.

When contemplating market expansion outside the home country, management's inclination may be to configure these aspects of the value chain exactly as they are at home. However, this may not be the most effective solution because the organization may lack the necessary skill and experience to conduct all value chain activities in target markets. A company with home market competitive advantages in both upstream activities and

TABLE 15-1	DISTRIBUTION FUNCTIONS IN THE VALUE CHAIN

Purchasing

In-bound Logistics

R&D

Assembly and Manufacturing

Out-bound Logistics

Marketing

   Information and Research

   Target Market Selection

   Product Policy and Strategy

   Pricing Policy and Strategy

   Distribution Policy and Strategy

   Communications Policy and Strategy

     Messages, Appeals

     Media Strategy and Plan

     Advertising Plan

     Promotion Plan

     Personal Selling

     Direct Marketing Plan

       Direct Mail

       Telemarketing

Installation and Testing Service

Margin

downstream activities—manufacturing and distribution, for example—may be forced to reconfigure distribution activities to successfully enter new global markets. For example, Wal-Mart's expansion into Mexico has been hampered by the fact that most Mexican suppliers ship directly to stores rather than to retailer warehouses and distribution centers. Thus Wal-Mart lacks the control that is the key to its low prices in the United States. Notes Sam Dunn, director of administration for Wal-Mart de Mexico, "The key to this market is distribution. The retailer who solves that will dominate."[7]

Among U.S. companies, 3M does an excellent job of managing the physical distribution aspects of the value chain to support global market exports. Outbound logistics, for example, represent just one aspect of the company's overall global strategic plan to support burgeoning exports to Europe. In St. Paul, 3M's international distribution center receives more than 5,000 orders per week. In 1985, export orders took 11 days to get through the center. By 1990, only 5.5 days were required; shipping mistakes were cut 71 percent, despite the fact that volume was up 89 percent. In Europe, meanwhile, 3M set up a distribution center in Breda, Netherlands, to receive containers from Norfolk, Virginia, and other ports. Logistics managers convinced 3M to spend as much as $1 million per year for additional trucks to provide daily delivery service to each of 3M's 19 European subsidiaries. The outlay was approved after the managers demonstrated that savings could be achieved—due to lower inventories and faster deliveries—even if trucks were not filled to capacity.[8]

Laura Ashley, the global retailer of traditional English-style clothing for women, re-

[7]Bob Ortega, "Tough Sale: Wal-Mart Is Slowed by Problems of Price and Culture in Mexico," *The Wall Street Journal* (July 28, 1994), pp. A1, A5.
[8]Robert L. Rose, "Success Abroad: 3M, by Tiptoeing into Foreign Markets, Became a Big Exporter," *The Wall Street Journal* (Mar. 29, 1991), p. A10.

BEHIND THE SCENES

■ A CASE OF WINE: ADDING UTILITY THROUGH DISTRIBUTION CHANNELS

*E*ach year, wine and spirits worth more than $1 billion are exported from France, Germany, Italy, and other European countries to all parts of the world. Have you ever wondered how a case of wine finds its way from, say, France to your local liquor store? In fact, after leaving the winery, the wine may pass through many hands before it finishes its journey at your local retailer.

In France, the structure of the wine industry is quite complex. An intermediary called a ***négociant*** plays an important role that varies according to region. *Négociants* sometimes act as brokers and have standing contracts to buy specified quantities of finished wine on behalf of various United States **importers**. The *négociant* also functions somewhat like a banker, paying the producer as much as 25 percent in advance of delivery. *Négociants* may also buy grapes from growers to make their own wines, blending and bottling them under their own labels. Wine may be bottled and packed in cases by the producer or by the *négociant*.

Wine destined for France or other European markets travels by truck. If the wine is to be exported to the United States or Japan, a **freight forwarder** or **shipping agent** sends a truck to the winery to pick up the wine. For the largest producers, a truck carrying a 20- or 40-foot shipping container is backed up to the door of the winery and loaded there for the ocean voyage. For smaller producers, the wines are picked up and then delivered to a warehouse. There, the shipping agent consolidates various deliveries before filling a container for the shipping line of the importer's choosing.

Shipping dates and rates will vary depending on the availability of containers. In general, a 20-foot container can hold 800 cases of wine; a single 40-foot container can take up to 1,300 cases. The weight of the wine is a consideration when determining how many cases to ship in a given container. Not only do wine bottles vary in size (750 ml bottles are the most common, with 12 bottles in a case), but there is likely to be a difference in weight between two cases of different types of wine. For example, heavier bottles are required for champagne and other sparkling wines since the contents are under pressure; bottles of fine Bordeaux are packaged in wooden crates that weigh more than ordinary cardboard cartons.

Shipping wine is a challenging venture because of the volatile and perishable nature of the product. Proper storage and transportation are vital; light, heat, and temperature fluctuations are wine's worst enemy. Ideally, wine should be kept at a constant temperature near 55 degrees. To prevent improper shipping from ruining a shipment, temperature-controlled containers (known as "reefers") are often used, even though they add about $3 per case to the cost of the shipment. To further protect the wine, some importers avoid shipping during the hot summer months. Because ownership of the wine is transferred to the importer at the moment the wine leaves the French storage warehouse, it is important to insure the shipment. Wine shipments can even be insured against possible losses due to war and terrorism. The best importers arrange for proper warehouse storage even before taking title to the wines.

The trans-Atlantic trip for U.S.-bound wine takes a week or more. The port of entry depends on the location of the importer or **wholesaler/distributor**. The Port of New York is used when wines are destined for the East Coast. Wine bound for the nation's midsection often enters through Baltimore or Norfolk, Virginia. Ships going to a western destination may chart a course through the Gulf of Mexico on their way to Houston; wines bound for the Port of San Francisco pass through the Panama Canal. Once the wine enters the United States, it must clear U.S. customs. Customs agents and the importer or wholesaler make sure the shipment meets all government regulations and that paperwork is properly prepared.

After it has cleared customs, the wine is then shipped to the wholesaler's warehouse. If the wholesaler is too busy to pick the container up immediately, it may sit on the dock for a week or more in warm weather; without refrigeration, the wine—and the importer's investment—might be lost. If the distributor is located in Chicago, the wine often enters the country in Baltimore and completes the next leg of the trip via rail. Sometimes, trucks will bring a shipment of wine to the Midwest from the East Coast and return full of meat in order to make the trip cost effective. After the wine has been unloaded at the warehouse, the distributor's sales staff arranges for the cases of wine to be delivered by truck or van to individual **retailers**.

There is as much variety among retail channels for wine as there is among wine producers. Outlets vary from "mom and pop" grocery stores, to wine sections in large supermarkets, to huge wine and liquor discounters, with considerable variety in between. In some stores, wine is stored and displayed haphazardly, often in sunny windows or near heating vents. One large retailer, Big Y in Northampton, Massachusetts, even goes so far as to keep the entire store at 55 degrees year around.

There are still other factors that have a major influence on sales. One is the marketing and merchandising skill of the retailer: Point-of-sale help from an informed retailer is important in selling fine wines. Also, the industry press can have a huge impact on sales. A good rating in publications such as *Wine Spectator* or *The Wine Advocate* can make the difference between obscurity and a sellout in a particular wine. Often, savvy wine retailers will display a press clipping with a positive rating right on the bin of a certain wine so customers can educate themselves as they shop.

cently reconfigured its supply chain. The company has more than 500 company-owned retail stores around the world, supplying them with goods manufactured in 15 different countries. In the past, Laura Ashley's suppliers all sent goods to the company's distribution center in Wales. This meant that blouses manufactured in Hong Kong were first sent to Wales; blouses bound for the company's Tokyo store then had to be sent back to the Far East. Not surprisingly, this was not an effective arrangement; Laura Ashley stores were typically sold out of 20 percent of goods even though the company's warehouses were full. To cut costs and improve its inventory management, Laura Ashley has subcontracted physical distribution to Federal Express's Business Logistics Service. FedEx's information system is tied in with the retail stores; when a Laura Ashley buyer orders blouses from Hong Kong, FedEx arranges shipment from the manufacturer directly to the stores.[9]

CASE EXAMPLE: JAPAN

Japan has presented an especially difficult distribution challenge to foreign companies. Japanese distribution is a highly developed system that has evolved to satisfy the needs of the Japanese consumer. The total number of retail outlets in Japan—1.6 million stores—represents about 5 percent more stores than in the United States for a population that is half the size. Japan has 132 retail stores per 10,000 people, compared to 65 stores per 10,000 people in the United States. A correspondingly high number of intermediaries, including more than 400,000 wholesalers, is needed in Japan to service this fragmented system of outlets (Kaikati 1993).

The categories of wholesalers and retailers in Japan are very finely divided. For example, meat stores in Japan do about 80 percent of their business in meat items. Similar specialization exists in other specialty stores as well. This kind of concentration is also true at the wholesale level. This very high degree of specialization in Japan is made possible by the clustering of various types of stores at major street intersections or stops along commuter rail lines.

There are, of course, many instances in which overseas firms have entered the Japanese market and have been able to overcome difficulties presented by the distribution system. Unfortunately, problems in coping with and adapting to Japanese distribution have also prevented a number of firms from achieving the success they might have had. Historically, foreign marketers in Japan make two basic mistakes. The first is their assumption that distribution problems can be solved the same way they would be in the West, that is, by going as directly as possible to the customer and thus cutting out the middleman. In Japan, because of the very fragmented nature of retailing, it is simply not cost effective to go direct.

The second mistake often made is in treating the Japanese market at arm's length by selling to a trading company. The trading company may sell in low volumes to a very limited segment of the market, such as the luxury segment, with the result that there is usually limited interest on the part of the trading company. The experience is likely to be disappointing to all parties involved.

Successful distribution in Japan (or any other market) requires adaptation to the realities of the marketplace. In Japan, this means first and foremost adaptation to the reality of fragmented distribution. Second, it requires research into the market itself including customer needs and competitive products. Then a company must develop an overall marketing strategy that (1) positions the product vis-à-vis market segment identified according to need, price, and other issues; (2) positions the product against competitors; and (3) lays out a marketing plan—including a distribution plan—for achieving volume and share-of-market objectives.

[9]Stephanie Strom, "Logistics Steps onto Retail Battlefield," *The New York Times* (Nov. 3, 1993), pp. D1, D2.

Devising a Japanese Distribution Strategy

In the 1970s, Shimaguchi and Rosenberg identified several considerations for any company formulating and implementing a Japanese distribution strategy. The first called for finding a Japanese partner such as an import agent to help navigate the unfamiliar waters. Import agents range in size from small local distributors to the giant *sogo-sosha* (general trading companies). The authors also advised companies to pursue a strategy of offering better quality, lower price, or a distinctive positioning as a foreign product. Foreigners are advised to prepare for a long-term effort and modest returns; nothing happens quickly in Japanese distribution, and patience is required. Finally, the authors advised cultivating personal relationships in distribution. Loyalty and trust are important.[10]

While these consideration are still relevant today, some recent studies have described ways to bypass the Japanese distribution quagmire by pursuing alternative distribution channels. For example, foreign companies may wish to follow the example of Toys 'Я' Us and establish their own retail stores in Japan. Toys 'Я' Us attempted to circumvent the multilayer wholesale system by buying direct from manufacturers (see Case 15–1). A second approach is to use direct marketing techniques. While telemarketing is relatively new and has proven more successful with business-to-business rather than consumer marketing, mail order in Japan has been experiencing 17 percent annual growth. L.L. Bean sells a substantial amount of merchandise in Japan despite the fact that it has never published a Japanese catalog. Door-to-door selling is a third alternative channel strategy in Japan that has been successfully pursued by Amway. Amway has established its own system of independent distributors; most of the 150-plus products sold are imported from the United States. Finally, a company may wish to explore creative ways of piggybacking with other successful companies. For example, Shop America successful launched a specialty catalog business by piggybacking with Japan's 7-Eleven convenience stores (Kaikati 1993).

[10]Mitsuaki Shimaguchi and Larry R. Rosenberg, "Demystifying Japanese Distribution," *Columbia Journal of World Business* (Spring 1979), pp. 38–41.

SUMMARY

Channel decisions are difficult to manage globally because of the variation in channel structures from country to country. Nevertheless, certain patterns of change associated with market development offer the astute global marketer the opportunity to create channel innovations and gain competitive advantage. The characteristics of customers, products, middlemen, and environment all impact channel design and strategy. Consumer channels may be relatively direct, utilizing direct mail or door-to-door selling as well as manufacturer-owned stores. A combination of manufacturer's sales force, agents/brokers, and wholesalers may also be used. Channels for industrial products are less varied, with manufacturer's sales force, wholesalers, and dealers or agents being utilized.

In developed countries, retail channels are characterized by the substitution of capital for labor. This is evident in self-service stores, which offers a wide range of items at relatively low gross margins. The opposite is true in less-developed countries with abundant labor. Such countries disguise their unemployment in "inefficient" retail and wholesale channels suited to the needs of consumers; such channels may have gross margins that are 50 percent lower than those in self-service stores in developed countries. A global marketer must either tailor the marketing program to these different types of channels or introduce new retail concepts.

Transportation and physical distribution issues are critically important in global marketing because of the geographical distances involved in sourcing products and serving customers in different parts of the world. Today, many companies are reconfiguring their supply chains to cut costs and improve efficiency.

DISCUSSION QUESTIONS

1. In what ways can channel intermediaries create utility for buyers?
2. What factors influence the channel structures and strategies available to global marketers?
3. What is "cherry picking"? What approaches can be used to deal with this problem?
4. Compare and contrast the typical channel structures for consumer products and industrial products.
5. Briefly discuss the global issues associated with physical distribution and transportation logistics. Cite one example of a company that is making efficiency improvements in its channel or physical distribution arrangements.
6. What special distribution challenges exist in Japan? What is the best way for a non-Japanese company to deal with these challenges?

BIBLIOGRAPHY

Books

Bauer, P. T. *West African Trade*. Cambridge: Cambridge University Press, 1954.

Fields, George. *From Bonsai to Levi's: An Insider's Surprising Account of How the Japanese Live*. New York: Macmillan, 1983.

Harvey, Michael G., and Robert F. Lusch, eds. *Marketing Channels: Domestic and International Perspectives*. Norman, Okla.: Center for Economic & Management Research, 1982.

Stern, Louis W., and Adel L. El-Ansary. *Marketing Channels* (3d ed.). Upper Saddle River, N.J.: Prentice Hall, 1988.

Waldman, Charles. *Strategies for International Mass Retailers*. New York: Prager Publishers, 1978.

Articles

Allen, Randy L. "The Why and How of Global Retailing," *Business Quarterly* 57, no. 4 (Summer 1993), pp. 117–122.

Bello, Daniel C., David J. Urban, and Brohislaw J. Verhage. "Evaluating Export Middlemen in Alternative Channel Structures." *International Marketing Review* 8, no. 5 (1991), pp. 49–64.

Cavusgil, S. Tamer. "The Importance of Distributor Training at Caterpillar." *Industrial Marketing Management* 19, no. 1 (February 1990), pp. 1–9.

Fernie, John. "Distribution Strategies for European Retailers." *European Journal of Marketing* 26, nos. 8, 9, (1992), pp. 35–47.

Frazier, Gary L., James D. Gill, and Sudhir H. Kale. "Dealer Dependence Levels and Reciprocal Actions in a Channel of Distribution in a Developing Country." *Journal of Marketing* 53, no. 1 (January 1989), pp. 50–69.

Gentry, Julie R., Janjaap Semeijn, and David B. Vellenga. "The Future of Road Haulage in the New European Union—1995 and Beyond." *The Logistics and Transportation Review* 31, no. 2 (1995), pp. 145–160.

Hill, John S., Richard R. Still, and Unal O. Boya. "Managing the Multinational Sales Force." *International Marketing Review* 8, no. 1 (1991), pp. 19–31.

Kaikati, Jack G. "Don't Crack the Japanese Distribution System—Just Circumvent It." *Columbia Journal of World Business* 28, no. 2 (Summer 1993), pp. 34–45.

Kale, Sudhir, and Roger P. McIntyre. "Distribution Channel Relationships in Diverse Cultures." *International Marketing Review* 8, no. 3 (1991), pp. 311–45.

Klein, Saul. "Selection of International Marketing Channels." *Journal of Global Marketing* 4, no. 4 (1991), pp. 21–37.

Klein, Saul, and Victor Roth. "Satisfaction with International Marketing Channels." *Journal of the Academy of Marketing Science* 21, no. 1 (Winter 1993), pp. 39–44.

Murphy, Paul R., James M. Daley, and Douglas R. Dalenberg. "Doing Business in Global Markets: Perspectives of International Freight Forwarders." *Journal of Global Marketing* 6, no. 4 (1993), pp. 53–68.

Novich, Neil S. "Leading-Edge Distribution Strategies." *Journal of Business Strategy* 11, no. 6 (November–December 1990), pp. 48–53.

Olsen, Janeen E., and Kent L. Granzin. "Economic Development and Channel Structure: A Multinational Study." *Journal of Macromarketing* 10, no. 2 (Fall 1990), pp. 61–77.

Raguraman K., and Claire Chan. "The Development of Sea-Air Intermodal Transportation: An Assessment of Global Trends." *The Logistics and Transportation Review* 30, no. 4 (December 1994), pp. 379–396.

Rosenbloom, Bert. "Motivating Your International Channel Partners." *Business Horizons* 33, no. 2 (March–April 1990), pp. 53–.

Sachdev, Harash J., Daniel C. Bello, and Bruce K. Pilling. "Control Mechanisms within Export Channels of Distribution." *Journal of Global Marketing* 8, no. 2 (1994), pp. 31–50.

Samiee, Saeed. "Retailing and Channel Considerations in Developing Countries: A Review and Research Propositions." *Journal of Business Research* 27, no. 2 (June 1993), pp. 103–129.

Sherwood, Charles, and Robert Bruns. "Solving International Transportation Problems." *Review of Business* 14, no. 1 (Summer/Fall 1992), pp. 25–30.

Weigand, Robert E. "Parallel Import Channels—Options for Preserving Territorial Integrity." *Columbia Journal of World Business* 26, no. 1 (Spring 1991), pp. 53–60.

In fall 1989, Toys 'Я' Us executives announced plans to form a joint venture with McDonald's Japanese subsidiary and open a store in Japan. Company officials were attracted by the prospect of having stores in the world's second-largest toy market, where annual sales amounted to $6 billion. Starting with the first store in Niigata, they hoped to add 10 new stores each year through the end of the decade. The announcement marked the first such move by a major U.S. retailer, and it was widely regarded on both sides of the Pacific as a test case of whether Japan's notoriously closed wholesaling and retailing system could be penetrated by an outsider.

Toys 'Я' Us Chairman Charles Lazarus had revolutionized the way children's toys were sold in the United States. The company bypassed distributors and dealt directly with manufacturers. The stores themselves were often located in suburban areas with plenty of parking. This unique approach resulted in economies that allowed Toys 'Я' Us to discount prices by as much as 30 percent. Toys 'Я' Us opened its first store outside the United States in 1984; it quickly expanded operations to Europe, Hong Kong, and Singapore. At the time of the announcement, Toys 'Я' Us had nearly 500 stores around the world. Many observers wondered whether the system could be successfully replicated in Japan.

Toys 'Я' Us executives knew that "location, location, location" is key in their business; accordingly, they set out to find a Japanese partner who was savvy to local real estate. That partner turned out to be Den Fujita, the bilingual, bicultural president of McDonald's Japanese operation. Mr. Fujita had built a $1.3 billion fast food empire in Japan in a little more than two decades. His importance as a partner was reflected in the remarks of an industry observer, who noted, "This is really a real estate deal, not a retailing deal." Mr. Fujita recognized the similarity between the target markets for McDonald's and Toys 'Я' Us, and hoped to "piggyback" by putting his restaurants near the toy stores. The typical "mom and pop" Japanese store covered about 3,200 square feet of floor space and stocked 1,000 to 2,000 different items. Toys 'Я' Us intended build a 54,000-square-foot superstore, with about 8,000 different toys.

Before breaking ground, however, the company had to contend with Japan's Large-scale Retail Law, which required builders—even Japanese—to obtain approval from other retailers before building a large store in a particular neighborhood. Delays in obtaining approval had been known to drag on for as long a decade. The law was on the books because, traditionally, small shopkeepers were strong supporters of the Liberal Democratic Party; the law was a form of quid pro quo. After Toys 'Я' Us formally applied for permission to build the first store in Niigata, local merchants did more than invoke the law. They also formed a lobbying group, the Japan Association of Specialty Toy Shops, in an effort to block the newcomer. One local merchant expressed a commonly held fear in saying, "If Toys 'Я' Us comes in, Japanese toy shops will be wiped out."

This situation prompted company officials to seek the support of Carla Hills, the United States Trade Representative; the resulting political pressure (under the aegis of the Structural Impediments Initiative) led to considerable publicity that painted the Japanese as protectionist and unfair traders. This action, too, met with disapproval by local merchants. "Toys 'Я' Us is trying to make this a political problem," complained one retailer. "They are calling on Carla Hills, trying to mix business and politics. But toys are more than that. Toys are culture." Despite such reactions, in spring 1990 the Ministry of International Trade and Industry (MITI) changed the law so that the longest a proposed store opening could be delayed was 18 months.

Having overcome this barrier, Toys 'Я' Us officials still met with opposition. Talks had to be conducted with the local chamber of commerce at each site. In Kanagawa Prefecture, Sagamihara City, for example, talks began in May 1990. In August, Toys 'Я' Us representatives had to answer questions at a public meeting. Then they made presentations at four different meetings of the commercial activities council. In June, the company finally was granted permission to open a store after December 1.

While these negotiations continued, Toys 'Я' Us was struggling to convince Japanese toy manufacturers to sell direct and bypass the multilayered distribution system for which Japan is famous. Once again, opposition was strong; Bandai, the number one toy maker, joined with other manufacturers in refusing to sell directly to Toys 'Я' Us. Finally, Nintendo broke with the group and became the first manufacturer to sign on—in large part because Toys 'Я' Us was a major retail account in the United States. However, Nintendo's direct-sale prices are not discounted enough to "rock the boat" in Japan.

Toys 'Я' Us finally opened its first Japanese store on December 20, 1991. The location was not Niigata, however, where local opposition had pushed the opening into 1993. Instead, the first Toys 'Я' Us was opened in the city of Ami, Ibaraki Prefecture, 40 miles north of Tokyo (a second store opened on January 4, 1992). Besides a parking lot large enough to hold nearly 1,000 cars, the familiar English-language Toys 'Я' Us sign was prominently displayed. More than one thousand shoppers were waiting at the doors on opening day. Shoppers found lower prices than at the smaller retailers, but only 10 to 20 percent lower. Two-thirds of the product assortment consisted of Japanese toys; the rest—Barbie dolls and Huffy bikes, for example—were imports. Once the "unthinkable" had come to pass, local opposition seemed to cool. A Japanese toystore owner near the Ami store said, "An integrated store for children is a good thing. My wife can't wait to go shopping there for our kids."

Still, it remains to be seen whether Toys 'Я' Us can offer the level of service Japanese consumers have come to expect from the mom-and-pop stores. The latter have been known to replace defective or broken-down goods even after warranties have expired. Repair services are also performed at no cost. Above all, however, Japanese consumers are among the most discriminating. A package that is scratched or marred reflects poorly on the manufacturer. Clearly, Toys 'Я' Us has won an important victory by setting up shop in Japan. Now, the marketplace will determine the ultimate success or failure of the venture.

DISCUSSION QUESTIONS

1. Summarize the steps Toys 'Я' Us has taken to develop its retailing system in Japan.
2. What is your reaction to the complaint of the Japanese shopkeeper that Toys 'Я' Us was "trying to make this a political problem"?
3. Now that Toys 'Я' Us has "broken the ice," do you think other major U.S. retailers will attempt to enter the market? Why or why not?
4. What advice would you offer a Japanese retailer for competing with Toys 'Я' Us?

Sources: Kathryn Graven, "For Toys 'Я' Us, Japan Isn't Child's Play," *The Wall Street Journal* (Feb. 7, 1990), p. B1.
Robert Neff, "Guess Who's Selling Barbies in Japan Now?" *Business Week* (Dec. 9, 1991), pp. 72+.
Edmund W. Schuster, "You Can't Remove Cultural Barriers," *Transportation and Distribution* (June 1991), pp. 43–45.
Mark Mason, "United States Direct Investment in Japan: Trends and Prospects," *California Management Review* (Fall 1992), pp. 98–115.
"Retailing in Japan: Toy Joy," *The Economist* (Jan. 4, 1992), p. 62.
James Sterngold, "Den Fujita, Japan's Mr. Joint Venture," *The New York Times* (Mar. 22, 1992), Sec. 3, pp. 1, 6.

CHAPTER 18

Global Marketing Communications Decisions: Advertising, Public Relations, Sales Promotion, and Personal Selling

"Eighteen-year-olds in Paris have more in common with 18-year-olds in New York than with their own parents. They buy the same products, go to the same movies, listen to the same music, sip the same colas. Global advertising merely works on that premise."[1]

—*William Roedy, Director, MTV Europe*

In February 1993, a group of investors headed by Robert Louis-Dreyfus, former CEO of Saatchi & Saatchi Advertising, bought a controlling interest in Adidas AG. Adidas markets sports shoes, athletic clothing, and equipment in 160 countries. The German company has an illustrious history dating back many decades; in fact, Jesse Owens was wearing Adidas track shoes when he won four gold medals at the 1936 Olympic games. Such public triumphs helped make Adidas the world leader in the sports shoe market; today, the company commands a 26 percent share of the global market. In Europe alone, about half of Adidas's $2.13 billion in 1994 revenues came from footwear sales.

Although impressive, these numbers might be even higher but for years of financial controversy and changing ownership that diverted management's attention from the market and gradually eroded the company's fortunes. In Germany, Adidas's share of the sports shoe sales declined from 60 percent to 40 percent over the past decade, including a 10-point slide in a two-year period. In Europe, where sneaker sales have doubled since 1985, Nike and Reebok today command 50 percent of the market, compared with only 5 percent a decade ago—despite very high import duties. The Americans' success is due in part to big spending on advertising. Nike and Reebok each spend nearly $100 million annually to promote their shoes in Europe; Adidas's ad spending in Europe totals about $60 million. The popularity of American sneakers got an extra boost thanks to the high visibility of the American Dream Team at the 1992 Olympics; NBA stars endorse both Reebok and Nike.

Clearly, advertising, publicity, and other forms of communication are critical tools in the global sneaker wars. Marketing communications—the promotion "P" of the marketing mix—refers to all forms of communication used by organizations to inform, remind, explain, persuade, and influence the attitudes and buying behavior of customers and other persons. The primary purpose of marketing communications is to tell customers about the benefits and values that a product or service offers. The elements of the promotion mix are advertising, public relations, personal selling, and sales promotion. All of these elements can be utilized in global marketing, either

[1]Ken Wells, "Selling to the World: Global Ad Campaigns, After Many Missteps, Finally Pay Dividends," *The Wall Street Journal* (Aug. 27, 1992), p. A1.

alone or in varying combinations. The environment in which marketing communications programs and strategies are implemented also varies from country to country. The challenge of effectively communicating across borders is one reason Nike, Nestlè, Microsoft, and other companies are embracing a concept known as *integrated marketing communications* (IMC). Adherents of an IMC approach explicitly recognize that the various elements of a company's communication strategy must be carefully coordinated (Duncan & Everett 1993). In this chapter, we will examine the promotion mix elements from the perspective of the global marketer.

GLOBAL ADVERTISING AND BRANDING

Advertising may be defined as any sponsored, paid message placed in a mass medium. **Global advertising** is the use of the same advertising appeals, messages, art, copy, photographs, stories, and video segments in multiple country markets. A global company that has the ability to successfully transform a domestic campaign into a worldwide one, or to create a new global campaign from the ground up, has a critical advantage. There are powerful reasons to try to create an effective global campaign. The creative process will force a company to determine whether there is a global market for its product. The first company to find a global market for any product is always at an advantage over competitors making the same discovery later. *The search for a global advertising campaign can be the cornerstone of the search for a coherent global strategy.* Such a search should bring together everyone involved with the product to share information and leverage their experiences.

Because advertising is often designed to add psychological value to a product or brand, it plays a more important communications role in marketing consumer products than in marketing industrial products. Frequently purchased, low-cost products generally require heavy advertising support to remind consumers about the product. Not surprisingly, consumer products companies top the list of big global advertising spenders. Procter & Gamble, Philip Morris, and Unilever are just a few of the companies with significant advertising expenditures outside the home-country markets.

There are several reasons for global advertising's growing popularity. Global campaigns attest to management's conviction that unified themes not only spur short-term sales but also help build long-term product identities and offer significant savings in production costs.[2] Regional trading centers such as Europe are experiencing an influx of internationalized brands as companies align themselves, buy up other companies, and get their pricing policies and production plans organized for a united region. From a marketing point of view, there is a great deal of activity going on that will make brands truly pan-European in a very short period of time. This phenomenon is accelerating the growth of global advertising.[3]

The potential for effective global advertising also increases as companies recognize and embrace new concepts such as "product cultures." Companies realize that some market segments can be defined on the basis of global demography—youth culture, for example—rather than ethnic or national culture. Athletic shoes and other clothing products, for example, can be targeted to a worldwide segment of 18- to 25-year-old males. As noted in the quote at the beginning of this chapter, William Roedy, director of MTV Europe, sees clear implications of such "product cultures" for advertising. MTV is just one of the media vehicles that enable people virtually anywhere to see

[2]Ibid., A8.
[3]Ann Cooper, "As the World Turns," *Advertising Age* (Apr. 2, 1990), pp. SS16–SS19, SS22–SS23, SS35.

CHAPTER 16 ■ **349**
GLOBAL MARKETING
COMMUNICATIONS DECISIONS:
ADVERTISING, PUBLIC
RELATIONS, SALES PROMOTION,
AND PERSONAL SELLING

■ ADIDAS

*T*he American athletic shoe companies are skilled global marketers. Reebok is the market leader in France, Spain, and England, but Nike is number one in many other European countries. Industry observers believe that, despite the recent recession, the two companies will reach $3 billion in worldwide sales by 1996. Although advertising tag lines such as "Just Do It" and "Planet Reebok" are presented in English, other parts of the message are adapted to reflect cultural differences. In France, for example, violence in ads is unacceptable, so Reebok replaced boxing scenes with images of women running on a beach. Also, European participation in sports is lower than in America; accordingly, Europeans are less likely to visit sporting goods stores. In France, Reebok shoes are now sold in nearly 1,000 traditional shoe stores.

Even in the face of such tough and growing competition, Adidas still enjoys high brand loyalty among older Europeans. The company recruits young people and pays them to wear Adidas shoes in public; they are also paid to work at sporting goods stores and promote Adidas products in other ways. Adidas also updated its image among younger European consumers by creating a new sport called Streetball. Ads airing on MTV Europe feature players outfitted in the company's new Streetball apparel line. Unlike its American rivals, Adidas does not utilize a global ad campaign. For example, a 1995 campaign that ran outside the United States featured Emil Zatopke, a Czechoslovakian Olympic runner.

The company does, however, maintain a single advertising agency—London-based Leagas Delany—for all its global markets. Bruce Haines, the agency's chief executive, notes, "Adidas is structured by geographic territories and sports-based business units. We're anxious to make sure there's one hand writing one signature whatever the work, whatever the sport." In a move that indicated optimism about Adidas's future, in 1995 Dreyfus's group raised its stake to full ownership. Meanwhile, Adidas was hard at work on a new "barefoot wear" product. As Dreyfus said in an interview on CNN, "The idea is there is nothing better than the foot as an instrument for running. The only problem is abrasion. So they are very revolutionary shoes and it will have a huge campaign behind it after June [1996]."

Sources: Dagmar Mussey, "Adidas Strides on its Own Path," *Advertising Age* (Feb. 13, 1995), p. 6.
Kevin Goldman, "Adidas Tries To Fill its Rivals' Big Shoes," *The Wall Street Journal* (Mar. 17, 1994), p. B5.
Joseph Pereira, "Off and Running: Pushing U.S. Style, Nike and Reebok Sell Sneakers to Europe," *The Wall Street Journal* (July 22, 1993), pp. A1, A8.
Stephen Barr, "Adidas on the Rebound," *CFO* (September 1991), pp. 48–56.
Igor Reichlin, "Where Nike and Reebok Have Plenty of Running Room," *Business Week* (Mar. 11, 1991), pp. 56–60.

how the rest of the world lives and to learn about products popular in other cultures. Many human wants and desires are very similar if presented within recognizable experience situations. People everywhere want value, quality, and the latest technology made available and affordable; everyone everywhere wants to be loved and respected, gets hungry, and so on.[4]

Global advertising also offers companies economies of scale in advertising as well as improved access to distribution channels. In cases where shelf space is at a premium, as with food products, a company has to convince retailers to carry its products rather than those of competitors. A global brand supported by global advertising may be very attractive since, from the retailer's standpoint, a global brand is less likely to languish on the shelves. Landor Associates, a company specializing in brand identity and design, recently determined that Coke has the number one brand awareness and esteem position in the United States, number two in Japan, and number six in Europe. However, standardization is not always required or even advised. Nestlè's Nescafé is marketed as a global brand even though advertising messages and product formulation vary to suit cultural differences.

Global Advertising Content: The "Extension" versus "Adaptation" Debate

Communication experts generally agree that the overall requirements of effective communication and persuasion are fixed and do not vary from country to country. The same thing is true of the components of the communication process: The marketer's/sender's message must be encoded, conveyed via the appropriate channel(s), and decoded by the customer/receiver. Communication takes place only when meaning is transferred. Four

GLOBAL MARKETING
COMMUNICATIONS DECISIONS:
ADVERTISING, PUBLIC
RELATIONS, SALES PROMOTION,
AND PERSONAL SELLING

---

[4]Dean M. Peebles, "Executive Insights: Don't Write Off Global Advertising," *International Marketing Review* 6, no. 1 (1989), pp. 73–78.

major difficulties can compromise an organization's attempt to communicate with customers in any location:

1. The message may not get through to the intended recipient. This problem may be the result of an advertiser's lack of knowledge about appropriate media for reaching certain types of audiences. For example, the effectiveness of television as a medium for reaching mass audiences will vary proportionately with the extent to which television viewing occurs within a country.

2. The message may reach the target audience but may not be understood or may even be misunderstood. This can be the result of an inadequate understanding of the target audience's level of sophistication or improper encoding.

3. The message may reach the target audience and may be understood but still may not induce the recipient to take the action desired by the sender. This could result from a lack of cultural knowledge about a target audience.

4. The effectiveness of the message can be impaired by *noise*. Noise in this case is an external influence such as competitive advertising, other sales personnel, and confusion at the receiving end which can detract from the ultimate effectiveness of the communication.

The key question for global marketers is whether the *specific* advertising message and media strategy must be changed from region to region or country to country because of environmental requirements. Proponents of global advertising believe that the era of the global village is fast approaching, and that tastes and preferences are converging. According to the standardization argument, since people everywhere want the same products for the same reasons, companies can achieve great economies of scale by unifying advertising around the globe. Advertisers who follow the localized approach are skeptical of the "global village" argument. Rather, they assert that consumers still differ from country to country and must be reached by advertising tailored to their respective countries. Proponents of localization point out that most blunders occur because advertisers have failed to understand—and adapt to—foreign cultures.

During the 1950s, the widespread opinion of advertising professionals was that effective international advertising required assigning responsibility for campaign preparation to a local agency. In the early 1960s, this idea of local delegation was repeatedly challenged. For example, Eric Elinder, head of a Swedish advertising agency, wrote: "Why should three artists in three different countries sit drawing the same electric iron and three copywriters write about what after all is largely the same copy for the same iron?"[5] Elinder argued that consumer differences between countries were diminishing and that he would more effectively serve a client's interest by putting top specialists to work devising a strong international campaign. The campaign would then be presented with insignificant modifications that mainly entailed translating the copy into language well suited for a particular country.

As the decade of the 1980s began, Pierre Liotard-Vogt, former CEO of Nestlè, expressed similar views in an interview with *Advertising Age*.

Advertising Age: Are food tastes and preferences different in each of the countries in which you do business?

Liotard-Vogt: The two countries where we are selling perhaps the most instant coffee are England and Japan. Before the war they didn't drink coffee in those countries, and I heard people say that it wasn't any use to try to sell instant coffee to the English because they drink only tea and still less to the Japanese because they drink green tea and they're not interested in anything else.

When I was very young, I lived in England and at that time, if you spoke to an

[5]Eric Elinder, "International Advertisers Must Devise Universal Ads, Dump Separate National Ones, Swedish Ad Man Avers," *Advertising Age* (Nov. 27, 1961), p. 91.

CHAPTER 16 ■ 351
GLOBAL MARKETING
COMMUNICATIONS DECISIONS:
ADVERTISING, PUBLIC
RELATIONS, SALES PROMOTION,
AND PERSONAL SELLING

Englishman about eating spaghetti or pizza or anything like that, he would just look at you and think that the stuff was perhaps food for Italians. Now on the corner of every road in London you find pizzerias and spaghetti houses.

So I do not believe [preconceptions] about "national tastes." They are "habits," and they're not the same. If you bring the public a different food, even if it is unknown initially, when they get used to it, they will enjoy it too.

To a certain extent we know that in the north they like a coffee milder and a bit acid and less roasted; in the south, they like it very dark. So I can't say that taste differences don't exist. But to believe that those tastes are set and can't be changed is a mistake.[6]

The "standardized versus localized" debate picked up tremendous momentum after the publication in 1983, noted in earlier chapters, of Professor Ted Levitt's *Harvard Business Review* article titled "The Globalization of Markets." In contrast to the view expounded by Levitt and Liotard-Vogt, some recent scholarly research suggests that the trend is toward the increased use of *localized* international advertising. Ali Kanso reached that conclusion in a study surveying two different groups of advertising managers—those taking localized approaches to overseas advertising and those taking standardized approaches.[7] Another finding was that managers who are attuned to cultural issues tended to prefer the localized approach, while managers less sensitive to cultural issues preferred a standardized approach. Bruce Steinberg, ad sales director for MTV Europe, has discovered that the people responsible for executing global campaigns locally can exhibit strong resistance to a global campaign. Steinberg sometimes has to visit as many as 20 marketing directors from the same company to get approval for a pan-European MTV ad.[8]

As Kanso correctly notes, the controversy over advertising approaches will probably continue for years to come. Localized and standardized advertising both have their place and both will continue to be used. Kanso's conclusion: What is needed for successful international advertising is a global commitment to local vision. In the final analysis, the decision of whether to use a global or localized campaign depends on recognition by managers of the trade-offs involved. On the one hand, a global campaign will result in the substantial benefits of cost savings, increased control, and the potential creative leverage of a global appeal. On the other hand, localized campaigns have the advantages of appeals that focus on the most important attributes of a product in each nation or culture. The question of *when* to use each approach depends on the product involved, an issue that is discussed later in the chapter.

Selecting an Advertising Agency

Another global advertising issue companies face is whether to invite advertising agencies to serve product accounts on a multicountry or even global basis. It is possible to select a local agency in each national market or an agency with both domestic and overseas offices. When Coca-Cola Company crossed the oceans, McCann-Erickson Worldwide followed. When Ford Motor Co. entered overseas markets, J. Walter Thompson Co. was close behind. Today, there is a growing tendency for clients to designate global agencies for product accounts in order to support the integration of the marketing and advertising functions. For example, in 1995, Colgate-Palmolive consolidated its $500 million in global billings with Young & Rubicam. Similarly, Bayer AG consolidated most of its $300 million consumer products advertising with BBDO Worldwide; Bayer had previously relied on 50 agencies around the globe. Agencies are aware of this trend and are themselves pursuing international acquisitions and joint ventures to extend their geographic reach and

GLOBAL MARKETING
COMMUNICATIONS DECISIONS:
ADVERTISING, PUBLIC
RELATIONS, SALES PROMOTION,
AND PERSONAL SELLING

[6]"A Conversation with Nestlé's Pierre Liotard-Vogt," *Advertising Age* (June 30, 1980), p. 31.
[7]Ali Kanso, "International Advertising Strategies: Global Commitment to Local Vision," *Journal of Advertising Research* (January–February 1992), pp. 10–14.
[8]Wells 1992.

their ability to serve clients on a global account basis. The 20 largest global advertising organizations ranked by 1994 gross income are shown in Table 16–1.

The organizations identified in Table 16–1 may include one or more "core" advertising agencies as well as units specializing in direct marketing, public relations, or research. The "family tree" of Adidas AG's advertising agency reflects the structure that is typical of agency ownership today: Leagas is owned by Abbott Mead Vickers/BBDO, which in turn is a unit of BBDO Worldwide, whose parent is the Omnicom Group. Individual agencies (agency "brands") are ranked in Table 16–2 by 1994 worldwide income.

In selecting an advertising agency, the following issues should be considered:

Company organization. Companies that are decentralized may want to leave the choice to the local subsidiary.

National responsiveness. Is the global agency familiar with local culture and buying habits in a particular country, or should a local selection be made?

Area coverage. Does the candidate agency cover all relevant markets?

Buyer perception. What kind of brand awareness does the company want to project? If the product needs a strong local identification, it would be best to select a national agency.

Despite an unmistakable trend toward using global agencies to support global marketing efforts, companies with geocentric orientations will adapt to the global market requirements and select the best agency or agencies accordingly. For example, Colgate recently acquired the Kolynos line of oral-care products in Latin America; McCann-Erickson Worldwide will be responsible for that account even though Young & Rubicam has the bulk of Colgate's business elsewhere.[9] Western agencies still find markets such as South Korea and Japan very complex; similarly, Japanese and Korean agencies find it just as difficult to establish local agency presence in Western markets. Not surprisingly,

TABLE 16–1 TOP 20 GLOBAL ADVERTISING ORGANIZATIONS (US$ MILLIONS)	
Organization and Headquarters Location	**Gross Income**
1. WPP Group (London)	$2,768.2
2. Interpublic Group of Cos. (New York)	2,211.0
3. Omnicom Group (New York)	2,052.6
4. Dentsu Inc. (Tokyo)	1,641.7
5. Cordiant (London)	1,431.5
6. Young & Rubicam (New York)	1,059.7
7. Euro RSCG (Levallois-Perret)	813.3
8. Grey Advertising (New York)	808.7
9. Hakuhodo (Tokyo)	774.2
10. Leo Burnett (Chicago)	677.5
11. True North Communications (Chicago)	619.0
12. D'Arcy Masius Benton & Bowles (New York)	608.4
13. Publicis Communication (Paris)	529.3
14. Bozell, Jacobs, Kenyon & Eckhardt (New York)	329.6
15. BDDP Group (Paris)	243.8
16. Tokyu Agency (Tokyo)	212.1
17. Assatsu Inc. (Tokyo)	191.0
18. Daiko Advertising (Tokyo/Osaka)	182.6
19. Dentsu, Young & Rubicam Partnerships (Tokyo/Singapore)	146.0
20. Dai-Ichi Kikaku (Tokyo)	139.3

Source: "World's Top 50 Advertising Organizations," *Advertising Age* (Apr. 10, 1995), p. S18.

[9]Sally Goll Beatty, "Young & Rubicam Is Only One for Colgate," *The Wall Street Journal* (Dec. 1, 1995), p. B6.

TABLE 16–2	TOP 25 GLOBAL ADVERTISING AGENCY BRANDS (US$ MILLIONS)
Agency	**Gross Income**
1. Dentsu Inc.	$1,568.7
2. McCann-Erickson Worldwide	1,063.4
3. J. Walter Thompson Co.	881.4
4. Hakuhodo	774.2
5. BBDO Worldwide	736.5
6. Grey Advertising	700.7
7. Leo Burnett Co.	677.5
8. Lintas Worldwide	665.5
9. Euro RSCG	639.6
10. DDB Needham Worldwide	629.1
11. Ogilvy & Mather Worldwide	611.1
12. Saatchi & Saatchi Advertising	602.4
13. True North Communications	549.1
14. Publicis Communication	529.3
15. Young & Rubicam	506.6
16. D'Arcy Masius Benton & Bowles	500.2
17. Bates Worldwide	494.1
18. Lowe Group	300.3
19. Bozell Worldwide	229.7
20. Tokyu Agency	212.1
21. Asatsu Inc.	191.0
22. Daiko Advertising	182.6
23. TBWA Advertising	182.5
24. BDDP Advertising	171.6
25. Wunderman Cato Johnson Worldwide	167.5

Source: "World's Top 25 Agency Brands," *Advertising Age* (Apr. 10, 1995), p. S20.

as the Saturn unit of General Motors prepared for its 1997 entry into the Japanese market, it hired the Tokyo-based Dai-Ichi Kikaku as its agency.

Advertising Appeals and Product Characteristics

Advertising must communicate appeals that are relevant and effective in the target market environment. Because products are frequently at different stages in their life cycle in various national markets, and because of the basic cultural, social, and economic differences that exist in markets, the most effective appeal for a product may vary from market to market. Yet, global marketers should attempt to identify situations where (1) potential cost reductions exist because of the presence of economies of scale, (2) barriers to standardization such as cultural differences are not significant, and (3) products satisfy similar functional and emotional needs across different cultures. Green, Cunningham, and Cunningham conducted a cross-cultural study to determine the extent to which consumers of different nationalities use the same criteria to evaluate two common consumer products, soft drinks and toothpaste. Their subjects were college students from the United States, France, India, and Brazil. Compared to France and India, the U.S. sample placed more emphasis on the subjective and less on functional product attributes, and the Brazilian sample appeared even more concerned with the subjective attributes than did the U.S. sample. The authors concluded that advertising messages should not use the same appeal for these countries if the advertiser is concerned with communicating the most important attributes of its product in each market.[10]

Effective advertising may also require developing different creative executions or presentations using a product's basic appeal or selling proposition as a point of departure. In other words, there can be differences between *what* one says and *how* one says it. If the creative execution in one key market is closely tied to a particular cultural attribute, the execution may have to be adapted to other markets. For example, the selling proposition for many products and services is fun or pleasure, and the creative presentation should show people having fun as appropriate for a country or culture. Club Med attempted to use a unified global advertising campaign featuring beautiful photos of vacationers in revealing swimming suits. Many Americans—for whom modesty in public is important— saw the ads as risqué and titillating, with appeal only to "swinging singles." Europeans are accustomed to partial nudity on public beaches and did not consider the ads to be improper. Although Club Med keyed its basic selling proposition to the theme "The antidote to civilization," the creative execution had to be brought in line with the tastes, perceptions, and experiences of the American market.

According to one recent survey, experienced advertising executives indicated that strong selling propositions can be transferred more than 50 percent of the time. An example of a selling proposal that transfers well is "top quality." The promise of low price or of value-for-money regularly surmounts national barriers. In the same survey, most executives indicated that they did not believe that creative presentations traveled well. The obstacles are cultural barriers, communications barriers, legislative problems (for example, children cannot be used in France to merchandise products), competitive positions (the advertising strategy for a leading brand or product is normally quite different from that for a minor brand), and execution problems.

Food is the product category most likely to exhibit cultural sensitivity. Thus, marketers

[10]Robert T. Green, William H. Cunningham, and Isabella C. M. Cunningham, "The Effectiveness of Standardized Global Advertising," *Journal of Advertising* (Summer 1975), pp. 25–30.

■ GLOBAL CAMPAIGNS FOR GLOBAL PRODUCTS

GLOBAL MARKETING IN ACTION

Certain consumer products lend themselves to advertising extension. If a product appeals to the same need around the world, there is a possibility of extending the appeal to that need. The list of products "going global," once confined to a score of consumer and luxury goods, is growing. Global advertising is partly responsible for increased worldwide sales of disposable diapers, diamond watches, shampoos, and athletic shoes. Some longtime global advertisers are benefiting from fresh campaigns. Jeans marketer Levi Strauss & Co. racked up record sales in Europe in 1991 on the strength of a campaign extended unchanged to Europeans, Latin Americans, and Australians. The basic issue is whether there is in fact a global market for the product. If the market is global, appeals can be standardized and extended. Soft drinks, Scotch whisky, Swiss watches, and designer clothing are examples of product categories whose markets are truly global. For example, Seagrams recently ran a global campaign keyed to the theme line, "There will always be a Chivas Regal." The campaign ran in 34 countries and was translated into 15 languages. In 1991, Seagrams launched a global billboard campaign to enhance the universal appeal for Chivas. The theory: The rich all over will sip the brand, no matter where they made their fortune.

Gillette Co. took a standardized "one product/one brand name/one strategy" global approach when it introduced the Sensor razor in 1990. The campaign slogan was "Gillette. The Best a Man Can Get," an appeal that was expected to cross boundaries with ease. Peter Hoffman, marketing vice president of the North Atlantic Shaving Group, noted in a press release: "We are blessed with a product category where we're able to market shaving systems across multinational boundaries as if they were one country. Gillette Sensor is the trigger for a total Gillette megabrand strategy which will revolutionize the entire shaving market." In the Japanese market, Gillette's standardized advertising campaign differs strikingly from that of arch-rival Schick. Prior to the Sensor launch, Gillette custom-made advertising for the Japanese market; now, except that the phrase, "The best a man can get," is translated into Japanese, the ads shown in Japan are the same as those shown in the United States and the rest of the world. Schick, meanwhile, uses Japanese actors in its ads.

of food and food products must be alert to the need to localize their advertising. A good example of this is the recent effort by H.J. Heinz Co. to develop the overseas market for ketchup. Heinz's strategy called for adapting both the product and advertising to target country tastes.[11] In Greece, for example, ads show ketchup pouring over pasta, eggs, and cuts of meat. In Japan, they instruct Japanese homemakers in using ketchup as an ingredient in Western-style food such as omelets, sausages, and pasta. Barry Tilley, London-based general manager of Heinz's Western Hemisphere trading division, says Heinz uses focus groups to determine what foreign consumers want in the way of taste and image. Americans like a relatively sweet ketchup, but Europeans prefer a spicier, more piquant variety. Significantly, Heinz's foreign marketing efforts are most successful when the company quickly adapts to local cultural preferences. In Sweden, the made-in-America theme is so muted in Heinz's ads that "Swedes don't realize Heinz is American. They think it is German because of the name," says Mr. Tilley. In contrast to this, American themes still work well in Germany. Kraft and Heinz are trying to outdo each other with ads featuring strong American images. In Heinz's latest TV ad, American football players in a restaurant become very angry when the twelve steaks they ordered arrive without ketchup. The ad ends happily, of course, with plenty of Heinz ketchup to go around.[12]

In general, the fewer the number of purchasers of a product, the less important advertising is as an element of the promotion mix. For example, successful marketing of expensive and technically complex industrial products generally requires a highly trained direct sales force. The more sophisticated and technically complicated an industrial product is, the more necessary this becomes. For such products, there is no point in letting national agencies duplicate each other's efforts. Advertising of industrial products—computers and telecommunications equipment, for example—does play an important role in setting the stage for the work of the sales force. A good advertising campaign can make it significantly easier for a salesperson to get in the door and, once inside, make the sale.

Creating Advertising

ART DIRECTION • Art direction is concerned with visual presentation—the "body language" of print and broadcast advertising. Some forms of visual presentation are universally understood. Revlon, for example, has used a French producer to develop television commercials in English and Spanish for use in international markets. These commercials, which are filmed in Parisian settings, communicate the universal appeal and specific advantages of Revlon products. By producing its ads in France, Revlon obtains effective television commercials at a much lower price than it would have to pay for similar-length commercials produced in the United States. PepsiCo has used four basic commercials to communicate its advertising themes. The basic setting of young people having fun at a party or on a beach has been adapted to reflect the general physical environment and racial characteristics of North America, South America, Europe, Africa, and Asia. The music in these commercials has also been adapted to suit regional tastes, ranging from rock 'n' roll in North America to bossa nova in Latin America to high life in Africa.

The international advertiser must make sure that visual executions are not inappropriately extended into markets. Benetton recently encountered a problem with its "United Colors of Benetton" campaign. The campaign appeared in 77 countries, primarily in print and on billboards. The art direction focused on striking, provocative interracial juxtapositions—a white hand and a black hand handcuffed together, for example. Another version of the campaign, depicting a black woman nursing a white baby, won advertising awards in France and Italy. However, because the image evoked the history of slavery in America, that particular creative execution was not used in the U.S. market (for more on the Benetton story, see Case 16–1 on page 370).

356 ▪ **CHAPTER 16**
GLOBAL MARKETING
COMMUNICATIONS DECISIONS:
ADVERTISING, PUBLIC
RELATIONS, SALES PROMOTION,
AND PERSONAL SELLING

[11]Gary Levin, "Ads Going Global," *Advertising Age* (July 22, 1991), pp. 4, 42.
[12]Gabriella Stern, "Heinz Aims to Export Taste for Ketchup," *The Wall Street Journal* (Nov. 20, 1992), p. B1.

■ REGULATION OF TOBACCO ADVERTISING

OPEN TO DISCUSSION

China. Effective October 31, 1994, the Chinese government banned all types of tobacco advertising. With a population of 1.2 billion people and having one out of every three smokers in the world, China is considered to be a massive potential market for cigarette manufacturers at a time when Western markets are shrinking. The ban—which prohibits advertising in the media and public places such as theatres and sporting events—was part of China's first Law of Advertisements. The law means that the green neon sign for RJR's Salem brand will be removed from the Shanghai airport, where freelance anti-smoking police are employed to collect fines from violators of the smoking ban.

Central and Eastern Europe. The recent flood of Western goods, from Mars candy bars and Winston cigarettes to Mercedes cars, has begun to cause some hard feelings in Russia. As one observer noted, hostility to Western advertising and sales goes back to the communist era, when the Soviets were afraid of being cheated in arms talks or trade agreements. Now that the Cold War is over, the animosity is manifesting itself at the consumer level. Advertising opponents are receiving help from the West: Late in 1993, TV spots advocating a ban on all types of cigarette advertising began appearing on most Russian channels. The ads were financed by Andrew Tobias, a *Time* columnist and financial guru, and Smokefree Educational Services, a U.S. anti-smoking group.

A spokeswoman for RJR in Winston-Salem, North Carolina, said the company is simply fulfilling a need that was already there. The company was asked by the Russian government to help fill a demand after riots over a cigarette shortage several years ago. Still, many Russians believe Western tobacco companies spend heavily on ads in their country because they know there are enormous profits to be made from Russian smokers. As one Russian noted, "In most countries, tobacco advertising is banned. Is our health worth less than theirs? Please, President Yeltsin, put a stop to cigarette advertising."

There have been efforts in other countries such as Hungary and Romania to crack down on tobacco advertising with bans or partial bans, but the new laws tend to be so confusing and poorly enforced that marketers frequently ignore them. Nonetheless, some tobacco marketers have already prepared for growing restrictions on tobacco advertising by eliminating all mention of cigarettes and even the pack itself from their ads. As one example, Philip Morris's Marlboro ads are widely recognizable from just their red and white logo.

Australia. In June 1994, the Philip Morris Company began legal action to overturn the Australian government's ban on cigarette advertising, contending that it infringes on the company's freedom of speech. Under legislation passed in 1992, tobacco advertising and sponsorship in Australia are being phased out and will be banned entirely by 1996, except for international events such as Formula One racing. Philip Morris is trying to have the Commonwealth Tobacco Advertising Prohibition Act declared invalid. Vice president David Davies believes the act goes beyond preventing cigarette advertising and imposes a wide array of restrictions that infringe on basic rights. According to Davies, "The Philip Morris Australian subsidiary says the anti-tobacco laws breach the Australian Constitution's implied guarantee of freedom of communication, breaches the states and is beyond the powers of the federal Government."

European Union. A tobacco ad ban proposal was introduced in mid-1991 with the aim of fulfilling single-market rules of the Maastricht Treaty on European Union. Not surprisingly, the ban has been opposed by international tobacco and advertising associations. The Commission justified the ban, noting that various countries had or were considering restrictions on tobacco advertising and that there was a need for common rules on cross-border trade.

The hotly debated directive to ban tobacco advertising across the EU is losing steam and was sent back to the negotiating table. Greece, a country that has opposed the ban, officially took over the EU presidency in January 1994 and set the agenda for the EU negotiations. A big campaign to save the tobacco directive is highly unlikely. EU members are coming to the conclusion that each country should individually handle the ban rather than blindly following the EU directive. For example, in January 1994, the Dutch prime minister pressed leaders at the Brussels European Council to withdraw the tobacco directive and allow countries to decide their own fates.

For RJ Reynolds International, Philip Morris International, B.A.T, and other tobacco marketers, the receding threat of a pan-European ban on tobacco ads is welcome news. The industry spends between $600 million and $1 billion on advertising in the EU annually. An EU ban would have hurt them most in the countries where they compete with entrenched state tobacco monopolies, namely France, Italy, and Spain.

Sources: "Australia's Ad Ban Is Fought," *The New York Times* (June 7, 1994), p. 19. Marcus Brauchli, "China Passes Law in Move to Prohibit Ads for Tobacco," *The Wall Street Journal* (Oct. 31, 1994), p. B10.
Lili Cui, "Mass Media Boycott Tobacco Ads," *Beijing Review* (June 6, 1994), p. 8.
Amy Haight, "EC Ad Ban May Go Up In Smoke," *Advertising Age* (Jan. 17, 1994), p. 18.
Steven Gutterman, "After the Russian Thaw, a New Big Chill to the West." *Advertising Age* (Jan. 24, 1994), pp. 3, 44.
"Tobacco Adverts: Fuming," *The Economist* (Feb. 5, 1994), pp. 60–61.

COPY • Translating copy, or the written text of an advertisement, has been the subject of great debate in advertising circles. Copy should be relatively short and avoid slang or idioms. This is because other languages invariably take more space to convey the same message; thus the increased use of pictures and illustrations. More and more European and Japanese advertisements are purely visual, conveying a specific message and invoking the company name.[13] Low literacy rates in many countries seriously compromise the use of print as a communication device and require greater creativity in the use of audio-oriented media.

It is important to recognize overlap in the use of languages in many areas of the world (e.g., the EU, Latin America, and North America). Capitalizing on this, global advertisers can realize economies of scale in producing advertising copy with the same language and message for these markets. Of course, the success of this approach will depend in part on avoiding unintended ambiguity in the ad copy. On the other hand, in some situations ad copy must be translated into the local language. Advertising slogans often present the most difficult translation problems. The challenge of encoding and decoding slogans and tag lines in different national and cultural contexts can lead to hilarious errors. For example, Kentucky Fried Chicken's "Finger-lickin' good" came out in Chinese as "Eat your fingers off"; the Asian version of Pepsi's "Come Alive" copy line was rendered as a call to bring ancestors back from the grave.[14]

Before deciding whether to prepare new copy for a foreign market or simply to translate the English copy, an advertiser must consider whether the message as translated can be received and comprehended by the intended foreign audience. Anyone with a knowledge of foreign languages realizes that the ability to think in that language facilitates accurate communication. One must understand the connotations of words, phrases, and sentence structures, as well as their translated meaning, in order to be confident that a message will be understood correctly after it is received. The same principle applies to advertising—perhaps to an even greater degree. A copywriter who can think in the target language and understands the consumers in the target country will be able to create the most effective appeals, organize the ideas, and craft the specific language, especially if colloquialisms, idioms, or humor are involved. For example, in southern China, McDonald's is careful not to advertise prices with multiple occurrences of the number four. The reason is simple: In Cantonese, the pronunciation of the word "four" is similar to that of the word "death."[15]

When formulating television and print advertising for use in industrialized countries such as the United States and Japan, the advertiser must recognize major style and content differences. American ads make more frequent use of spokespersons and direct product comparisons, and use logical arguments to try to appeal to the reason of audiences. Japanese advertising is more image-oriented and appeals to the sentiment of the audience. Ads that look irritating to the Japanese viewer may not necessarily be perceived that way by an American, and vice versa. What is most important frequently is not what is stated explicitly but, rather, what is implied.

CULTURAL CONSIDERATIONS • Knowledge of cultural diversity, especially the symbolism associated with cultural traits, is essential when creating advertising. Local country managers will be able to share important information, such as when to use caution in advertising creativity. Use of colors and man/woman relationships can often be stumbling blocks. For example, white in Asia is associated with death. In Japan intimate scenes between men and women are considered to be in bad taste; they are outlawed in Saudi Arabia. Veteran adman John O'Toole offers the following insights to global advertisers:

> Transplanted American creative people always want to photograph European men kissing women's hands. But they seldom know that the nose must never touch the hand or that this rite is reserved solely for married women. And how do you know that the

[13]Vern Terpstra and Ravi Sarathy, *International Marketing* (Orlando, Fla.: The Dryden Press, 1991), p. 465.
[14]Richard N. Weitz, "How Do You Say 'Oops!' " *Business Marketing* (October 1990), pp. 52–53.
[15]Jeanne Whalen, "McDonald's Cooks Worldwide Growth," *Advertising Age International* (July–August 1995), p. 14.

GLOBAL MARKETING
COMMUNICATIONS DECISIONS:
ADVERTISING, PUBLIC
RELATIONS, SALES PROMOTION,
AND PERSONAL SELLING

woman in the photograph is married? By the ring on her left hand, of course. Well, in Spain, Denmark, Holland, and Germany, Catholic women wear the wedding ring on the right hand.

When photographing a couple entering a restaurant or theater, you show the woman preceding the man, correct? No. Not in Germany and France. And this would be laughable in Japan. Having someone in a commercial hold up his hand with the back of it to you, the viewer, and the fingers moving toward him should communicate "come here." In Italy it means "good-bye."[16]

Tamotsu Kishii identified seven characteristics that distinguish Japanese from American creative strategy.[17]

1. Indirect rather than direct forms of expression are preferred in the messages. This avoidance of directness in expression is pervasive in all types of communication among the Japanese, including their advertising. Many television ads do not mention what is desirable about the brand in use and let the audience judge for themselves.

2. There is often little relationship between ad content and the advertised product.

3. Only brief dialogue or narration is used in television commercials, with minimal explanatory content. In the Japanese culture, the more one talks, the less others will perceive him or her as trustworthy or self-confident. A 30-second advertisement for young men's wear shows five models in varying and seasonal attire, ending with a brief statement from the narrator: "Our life is a fashion show!"

4. Humor is used to create a bond of mutual feelings. Rather than slapstick, humorous dramatizations involve family members, neighbors, and office colleagues.

5. Famous celebrities appear as close acquaintances or everyday people.

6. Priority is placed on company trust rather than product quality. The Japanese tend to believe that if the firm is large and has a good image, the quality of its products should also be outstanding.

7. The product name is impressed on the viewer with short, 15-second commercials.

Global Media Considerations

MEDIA VEHICLES AND EXPENDITURES • Appendix 16–A gives statistics on world advertising expenditures in 1990. The total for the 53 countries reported exceeded $265 billion. The United States, with expenditures of more than $128 billion, spent as much on advertising as the next 19 countries combined (see Table 1 in Appendix 16–A). As might be expected, the largest per capita advertising expenditures occurred mostly in the highly developed countries of the world. The lowest per capita expenditures were in the less-developed countries.

Per capita advertising expenditures in 1990 (see Table 2 in Appendix 16–A) averaged $110 for the 53 countries covered, and a total of 19 countries each spent more than $100 per capita on media advertising. Thirteen of these spent more than $200 per capita. Switzerland tops the list with more than $600 in per capita advertising expenditures. Spain and the United States spent more than 2 percent of their GNP on advertising in 1990; 21 other countries reported percentages in excess of 1 percent (see Table 3 of Appendix 16–A).

---

[16]John O'Toole, *The Trouble with Advertising* (New York: Chelsea House, 1981), pp. 209–210.
[17]C. Anthony di Benedetto, Mariko Tamate, and Rajan Chandran, "Developing Creative Advertising Strategy for the Japanese Marketplace," *Journal of Advertising Research* (January–February 1992), pp. 39–48. A number of recent studies have been devoted to comparing ad content in different parts of the world, including Mary C. Gilly, "Sex Roles in Advertising: A Comparison of Television Advertisements in Australia, Mexico, and the United States," *Journal of Marketing* (April 1988), pp. 75–85; and Marc G. Weinberger and Harlan E. Spotts, "A Situation View of Information Content in TV Advertising in the U.S. and U.K.," *Journal of Advertising* 53 (January 1989), pp. 89–94.

CHAPTER 16 ■ 359
GLOBAL MARKETING
COMMUNICATIONS DECISIONS:
ADVERTISING, PUBLIC
RELATIONS, SALES PROMOTION,
AND PERSONAL SELLING

A key issue in advertising is that of which of the measured media—print, broadcast, transit, etc.—to utilize. Print advertising (see Table 4 in Appendix 16–A) continues to be the number one advertising vehicle in most countries. However, spending on print media in the United States dropped from more than $50 billion in 1989 to $42 billion in 1990. Thirteen other nations surpassed the $1 billion spending mark for print media. Per capita print expenditures (see Table 5 in Appendix 16–A) were highest in Switzerland, Finland, and Sweden.

The use of newspapers for print advertising is so varied around the world as to almost defy description. In Mexico, an advertiser that can pay for a full-page ad may get the front page, while in India, paper shortages may require booking an ad six months in advance.

In some countries, especially those where the electronic media are government-owned, television and radio stations can broadcast only a restricted number of advertising messages. In Saudi Arabia, no commercial television advertising was allowed prior to May 1986; currently, ad content and visual presentation are restricted. In such countries, the proportion of advertising funds allocated to print is extremely high. In April 1995, Russia's national Channel 1 banned all commercial advertising; the ban was subsequently lifted.

The United States and Japan continued to be the two leaders in television advertising during 1990. Their combined expenditure was more than $39 billion and accounted for most of the world's expenditures in this medium (see Table 7 in Appendix 16–A). On a per capita basis, advertisers in the United States were the foremost users of television, with per capita expenditures exceeding $113. It is interesting to note that in Japan, per capita spending on television advertising between 1984 and 1990 more than doubled, from $37.4 to $90.4 (see Table 8 in Appendix 16–A).

Television is also important in the Latin American market (see Table 9 in Appendix 16–A). Of the 10 countries that allocated more than 50 percent of their measured media expenditures to television, the top 9 were located in Central/South America or the Caribbean. As ownership of television sets increases in other areas of the world such as Southeast Asia, television advertising will become more important as a communication vehicle.

Worldwide, radio continues to be a less important advertising medium than print and television. As a proportion of total measured media advertising expenditures, radio trailed considerably behind both print, television, and direct advertising. However, in countries where advertising budgets are limited, radio's enormous reach can provide a cost-effective means of communicating with a large consumer market. Also, radio can be effective in countries where literacy rates are low. Radio accounted for more than 20 percent of the total measured media in only two countries, both less-developed countries (see Table 12 in Appendix 16–A).

As countries add mass transportation systems and build and improve their highway infrastructures, advertisers are utilizing more indoor and outdoor posters and billboards to reach the buying public. Spending on outdoor and transit advertising in Japan is much higher than in other countries (see Table 13 in Appendix 16–A). Compared with the United States, spending on transit ads is four times higher in Japan ($4.3 billion vs. $1.1 billion); spending on billboards is more than double ($2.6 billion vs. $1.1 billion). Transit advertising was recently introduced in Russia, where drab streetcars and buses have been emblazoned with the bright colors of Western brands.

MEDIA DECISIONS • While markets are becoming increasingly similar in industrial countries, media situations still vary to a great extent. The availability of television, newspapers, and other forms of electronic and print media varies around the world. This can have an impact on media decisions. For example, the circulation figures of newspapers on a per capita basis cover a wide range. In Japan, where readership is high, there is one newspaper in circulation for every two people. There are approximately 65 million newspapers in daily circulation in the United States, a per capita ratio of approximately one to

GLOBAL MARKETING
COMMUNICATIONS DECISIONS:
ADVERTISING, PUBLIC
RELATIONS, SALES PROMOTION,
AND PERSONAL SELLING

four. The ratio is one paper to 10 to 20 people in Latin America and one to 200 people in Nigeria and Sweden.

Even when media availability is high, its use as an advertising vehicle may be limited. For example, in Europe, television advertising either does not exist or is very limited in Denmark, Sweden, and Norway. The time allowed for advertising each day varies from 12 minutes in Finland to 80 in Italy, with 12 minutes per hour per channel allowed in France and 20 in Switzerland, Germany, and Austria. Regulations concerning content of commercials vary, and there are waiting periods of up to two years in several countries before an advertiser can obtain broadcast time. In Germany, advertising time slots are reserved and paid for one year in advance.

In Saudi Arabia, where all advertising is subject to censorship, regulations prohibit a long list of subject matter which includes the following:

Advertisements of horoscope or fortune-telling books, publications, or magazines are prohibited.

Advertisements that frighten or disturb children are to be avoided.

Use of preludes to advertisements that appear to indicate a news item or official statement are to be avoided.

Use of comparative advertising claims is prohibited.

Noncensored films cannot be advertised.

Women may only appear in those commercials that relate to family affairs, and their appearance must be in a decent manner that ensures their feminine dignity.

Female children under six years of age may appear in commercials provided that their roles are limited to a childhood-like activity.

Women should wear a long suitable dress, which fully covers her body except face and palms. Sweat suits or similar garments are not allowed.[18]

PUBLIC RELATIONS AND PUBLICITY

A company's public relations effort should make use of publicity and other nonpaid forms of communication to foster goodwill and understanding among constituents both inside and outside the company. Any company that is increasing its activities outside the home country can utilize PR personnel as boundary spanners between the company and employees, unions, stockholders, customers, the media, financial analysts, governments, and suppliers. The basic tools of public relations include news releases, newsletters, tours of plants and other company facilities, articles in trade or professional journals, company publications and brochures, TV and radio talk show appearances by company personnel, and special events.

Many companies have their own in-house PR staff. Companies may choose to engage the services of an outside PR firm. Some PR firms are associated with advertising organizations; for example, Burston-Marsteller is a PR unit of Young & Rubicam, while Fleishman-Hillard is affiliated with D'Arcy Masius Benton & Bowles. Other PR firms, including the London-based Shandwick PLC and Edelman Public Relations Worldwide and Canada's Hill & Knowlton, are independent. Several independent PR firms in the United Kingdom, Germany, Italy, Spain, Austria, and the Netherlands have joined together in a network known as Globalink. The purpose of the network is to provide members with various forms of assistance such as press contacts, event planning, literature design, and suggestions for tailoring global compaigns to local needs in a particular country or region.[19]

---

[18]National Trade Data Bank: The Export Connection, USDOC, *International Trade Administration*, Market Research Reports (Oct. 2, 1992). See also Mushtag Luqmani, Ugur Yavas, and Zahir Quraeshi, "Advertising in Saudi Arabia: Content and Regulation," *International Marketing Review* 6, no. 1 (1989), pp. 59–72.
[19]Joe Mullich, "European Firms Seek Alliances for Global PR," *Business Marketing* 79 (August 1994), pp. 4, 31.

CHAPTER 16 ■ 361
GLOBAL MARKETING
COMMUNICATIONS DECISIONS:
ADVERTISING, PUBLIC
RELATIONS, SALES PROMOTION,
AND PERSONAL SELLING

Panasonic paid $40 million to be an official worldwide sponsor of the 1996 Olympics. A $10 million TV advertising campaign featured athletes and national anthems from around the world. The 60-second ad cost $1 million to produce and featured a customized ending for individual countries. (Courtesy of Matsushita Electric Corporation of America.)

362 ■ **CHAPTER 16**
GLOBAL MARKETING
COMMUNICATIONS DECISIONS:
ADVERTISING, PUBLIC
RELATIONS, SALES PROMOTION,
AND PERSONAL SELLING

The Growing Role of Public Relations in Global Marketing Communications

Public relations professionals with international responsibility must go beyond media relations and serve as more than a company mouthpiece; they are called upon to simultaneously build consensus and understanding, create trust and harmony, articulate and influence public opinion, anticipate conflicts, and resolve disputes (Nessman 1995, 154). As companies become more involved in global marketing and the globalization of industries continues, it is important that company management recognize the value of international public relations. One recent study found that, internationally, PR expenditures are growing an average of 20 percent annually. Fueled by soaring foreign investment, industry privatization, and a boom in initial public offerings (IPOs), PR expenditures in India are reported to be growing by 200 percent annually.

The number of international PR associations is growing as well. The new Austrian Public Relations Association is a case in point; many European PR trade associations are part of the Confédération Européenne des Relations Publiques and the International Public Relations Association. Another factor fueling the growth of international PR is increased governmental relations among countries. Governments, organizations, and societies are dealing with broad-based issues of mutual concern such as the environment and world peace. Finally, the technology-driven communication revolution that has ushered in the information age makes public relations a profession with truly global reach. Faxes, satellites, high speed modems, and the Internet allow PR professionals to be in contact with media virtually anywhere in the world.

In spite of these technological advances, PR professionals must still build good personal working relationships with journalists and other media representatives as well as leaders of other primary constituencies. Therefore, strong interpersonal skills are needed. One of the most basic concepts of the practice of public relations is to "know the audience." For the global PR practitioner, this means knowing the audiences in both the home country and the host country or countries. Specific skills needed include the ability to communicate in the language of the host country and familiarity with local customs. Obviously, a PR professional who is unable to speak the language of the host country will be unable to communicate directly with a huge portion of an essential audience. Likewise, the PR professional working outside the home country must be sensitive to nonverbal communication issues in order to maintain good working relationships with host-country nationals. Commenting on the complexity of the international PR professional's job, one expert notes that, in general, audiences are "increasingly more unfamiliar and more hostile, as well more organized and powerful . . . more demanding, more skeptical and more diverse." In other words, international PR practitioners must be "bridges over the shrinking chasm of the global village" (Grunig 1992, 130).

How Public Relations Practices Differ Around the World

Public relations practices in specific countries can be affected by cultural traditions, social and political contexts, and economic environments. As noted earlier in the chapter, the mass media and the written word are important vehicles for information dissemination in many industrialized countries. In developing countries, however, the best way to communicate might be through the gongman, the town crier, the market square, or the chief's courts. In Ghana, dance, songs, and storytelling are important communication channels. In India, where half of the population cannot read, press releases will not be the most effective way to communicate (Botan 1992, 150–151). In Turkey, the practice of PR is thriving in spite of that country's reputation for harsh treatment of political prisoners. Although the Turkish government still asserts absolute control as it has for generations, corporate PR and journalism are allowed to flourish so that Turkish organizations can compete globally.

Even in industrialized countries, there are some important differences between PR practices. In the United States, much of the news in a small, local newspaper is placed by means of the hometown news release. In Canada, on the other hand, large metropolitan population centers have combined with Canadian economic and climatic conditions to thwart the emergence of a local press. The dearth of small newspapers means that the practice of sending out hometown news releases is almost nonexistent (Sharpe 1992, 104–105). In the United States, PR is increasingly viewed as a separate management function. In Europe, that perspective has not been widely accepted; PR professionals are viewed as part of the marketing function rather than distinct and separate specialists in a company. In Europe, fewer colleges and universities offer courses and degree programs in public relations than in the United States. Also, European coursework in PR is more theoretical; in the United States, PR programs are often part of mass communication or journalism schools and there is more emphasis on practical job skills.

A company that is ethnocentric in its approach to PR will extend home-country PR activities into host countries. The rationale behind this approach is that people everywhere are motivated and persuaded in much the same manner. Obviously, this approach does not take cultural considerations into account. A company adopting a polycentric approach to PR gives the host-country practitioner more leeway to incorporate local customs and practices into the PR effort. Although such an approach has the advantage of local responsiveness, the lack of global communication and coordination can lead to a PR disaster (Botan 1992, 155).

The ultimate test of a company's understanding of the power and importance of public relations occurs during a time of environmental turbulence, especially a potential or actual crisis. When disaster strikes, a company or industry often finds itself thrust into the

CHAPTER 16 ▪ **363**
GLOBAL MARKETING
COMMUNICATIONS DECISIONS:
ADVERTISING, PUBLIC
RELATIONS, SALES PROMOTION,
AND PERSONAL SELLING

spotlight. A company's handling of communications during such times can have significant implications. The best response is to be forthright and direct, reassuring the public and providing the media with accurate information.

In the fall of 1994, computer chip maker Intel showed a poor understanding of public relations basics after a college professor discovered a technical defect in the company's flagship Pentium chip. The professor, Thomas Nicely, contacted Intel and asked for a replacement chip, but his request was refused. Intel acknowledged that Pentium had a flaw but insisted it would cause a computing error only once in 27,000 years. Having received no satisfaction from the semiconductor giant—Intel commands an 80 percent share of the global semiconductor market—Nicely posted his complaint on the Internet. Word about the Pentium flaw and Intel's response spread quickly. Intel CEO Andrew Grove added fuel to the fire when he issued an apology via the Internet. Grove said, "No chip is ever perfect," and offered to replace defective chips if customers could prove they used computers to perform complicated mathematical calculations. Grove's lack of humility, coupled with revelations that the chipmaker itself had been aware of the Pentium flaw for months, only worsened the public's perception of the company. After weeks of negative publicity around the world, Intel finally announced that new Pentium chips would be available to anyone who requested them.

Although the furor died down without permanent damage to Intel's reputation, a similar poor handling of a PR crisis ultimately cost France's Perrier Group its independence. In 1990, Perrier was forced to recall all U.S. shipments of its sparkling water after traces of benzene contamination were found. Eventually, the recall spread to the rest of the world, and a total of 160 million bottles were recalled. Perrier botched its communication effort in the early days of the crisis; management claimed that a technician had contaminated a tank during routine cleaning. Ultimately, company executives acknowledged that the company's water contains benzene when it comes out of the ground; the chemical has to be removed by filtration. Needless to say, competitors such as Evian capitalized on Perrier's woes, and Nestlè acquired Perrier in 1992. While overall U.S. bottled water sales increased 13.8 percent in 1993, Perrier was the only brand in the top 10 to experience a sales decline.[20]

In 1995, Japanese car marketers hired Hill & Knowlton to create a PR campaign designed to convince President Clinton that his plan to impose 100 percent tariffs on 13 luxury cars was ill-advised and could even cost him California's 54 electoral votes in the 1996 election. Nissan and other companies also sent position papers and information pack-

Photo for *AIADA*. Reprinted by permission of *AIADA*.

Meet the first casualties of U.S. trade sanctions on Japan.

They're just a few of the thousands of hard-working Americans who service and sell cars made by Acura, Infiniti, Lexus, Mazda and Mitsubishi. If the Clinton Administration has its way on auto trade sanctions, chances are many people just like them will be out of a job.

The Administration plans to levy a punitive 100 percent tariff on Japanese luxury cars—effectively doubling their price—in an attempt to open Japanese markets. The goal is simple: make these cars so expensive no one will buy them.

But in aiming at Japan, the Clinton Administration is hitting American small businesspeople and their employees. Because while Japan can weather these sanctions, many American car dealers can't. If nobody can afford their cars, they go out of business—and their employees are out of a job.

There is a better way. Last year, President Clinton fought long and hard for the creation of the World Trade Organization (WTO) to mediate disputes just like this one. Why impose sanctions that only hurt American small businesses and jobs when a reasonable alternative exists? Why not let the WTO decide who's right?

U.S. Trade Sanctions on Japan: There's a Better Solution

AMERICAN INTERNATIONAL AUTOMOBILE DEALERS ASSOCIATION

364 ■ CHAPTER 16
GLOBAL MARKETING
COMMUNICATIONS DECISIONS:
ADVERTISING, PUBLIC
RELATIONS, SALES PROMOTION,
AND PERSONAL SELLING

---

[20]Marcy Magiera, "Water Everywhere," *Advertising Age* (Feb. 7, 1994), p. S-6.

ets to dealers and the media. Interviews with representatives from auto dealers were carried by both print and electronic media.

SALES PROMOTION

Sales promotion refers to any consumer or trade program of limited duration that adds tangible value to a product or brand. The tangible value created by the promotion may come in various forms, such as a price reduction or a "Buy one, get one free" offer. Mail-in refunds, samples, and coupons are also commonly used in the United States. The purpose of a sales promotion may be to stimulate nonusers to sample a product or to increase overall consumer demand. Trade promotions are designed to increase product availability in distribution channels.

The increasing popularity of sales promotion as a marketing communication tool outside the United States can be explained in terms of several strengths and advantages. Besides providing a tangible incentive to buyers, sales promotion also reduces the perceived risk buyers may associate with purchasing the product. From the point of view of the company, sales promotion provides accountability; the manager in charge of the promotion can immediately track the results of the promotion. Moreover, some consumer sales promotions, including sweepstakes and rebates, require buyers to fill out a form and mail it to the company. This allows a company to build up information in its database which it can use when communicating with customers in the future.

Companies must take extreme care when designing sales promotions. A 1992 promotion sponsored by Maytag Corporation's Hoover European Appliance Group was a smashing success that turned into a financial and public relations fiasco. Over a period of several months, Hoover offered free round-trip airline tickets to the United States and Europe to purchasers of vacuum cleaners or other Hoover appliances. The promotion was designed to take advantage of low-cost, "space available" tickets; executives hoped that the cost of the tickets would be offset by commissions paid to Hoover when customers rented cars or booked hotel rooms. Finally, it was expected that a percentage of customers who bought appliances would fail to meet certain eligibility requirements and thus be denied free tickets.

In the United Kingdom, the word "Hoover" is both a brand name and a verb (as in, "Hoover the carpet"). The number of people who actually qualified for the free tickets—more than 200,000 in all—exceeded company forecasts, while the number of car rentals and hotel bookings was lower than expected. Hoover was swamped by the volume of inquiries; many customers were angered by long delays in responses to their requests for the tickets. The bottom line was that Hoover had failed to budget enough for the promotion, forcing Maytag CEO Leonard Hadley to take pretax charges of $72.6 million. In an effort to honor its commitment to Hoover customers, Maytag bought several thousand seats on various airlines. "The Hoover name in the United Kingdom is valuable, and this investment in our customer base there is essential to our future," Hadley said.

Hadley fired the president and director of marketing services at Hoover Europe and the vice president of marketing at Hoover UK. Fallout from the promotion became an ongoing PR nightmare, as headlines in the London Daily Mail trumpeted "Hoover fiasco: Bosses sacked" and "How dumb can you get?" Meanwhile, complaints from angry Europeans poured into Maytag's Newton, Iowa, headquarters. A Hoover Holiday Pressure Group was rumored to have thousands of members; three people even traveled to Newton in an unsuccessful attempt to meet with CEO Hadley. By May 1995, Hadley was ready to throw in the towel: He decided to sell Hoover Europe to Italy's Candy SpA for $170 million. Hadley intends to refocus Maytag on the North American market.[21]

---

[21]Rick Jost, "Maytag Wrings Out after Flopped Hoover Promotion," *The Des Moines Register* (Apr. 5, 1993), p. 3B. Rick Jost, "Mail Flying In from Britons Upset by Maytag Promotion," *The Des Moines Register* (July 11, 1994), p. B3.

CHAPTER 16 ■ 365
GLOBAL MARKETING
COMMUNICATIONS DECISIONS:
ADVERTISING, PUBLIC
RELATIONS, SALES PROMOTION,
AND PERSONAL SELLING

Many international managers have learned about American-style promotion strategies and tactics by attending seminars such as those offered by the Promotional Marketing Association of America (PMAA). Sometimes adaptation to country-specific conditions is required; for example, TV ads in France cannot have movie tie-ins. Ads must be designed to focus on the promotion rather than the movie. According to Joseph Potacki, who teaches a "Basics of Promotion" seminar for the PMAA, the biggest difference between promotion in the United States and in other countries pertains to couponing. In the United States, couponing accounts for 70 percent of consumer promotion spending. That percentage is much lower outside the United States. According to Potacki, "It is far less—or nonexistent—in most other countries simply because the cultures don't accept couponing." Potacki notes that couponing is gaining importance in countries such as the United Kingdom as retailers learn more about couponing.[22]

Sales promotion in Europe is highly regulated, as shown in Table 16–3. Sales promotions are popular in Scandinavia because broadcast advertising is highly regulated. On the other hand, promotions in the Nordic countries are themselves subject to regulations. If such regulations are relaxed as the single market develops in Europe and regulations are harmonized, companies may be able to roll out pan-European promotions.

PERSONAL SELLING

Personal selling is person-to-person communication between a company representative and a prospective buyer. The seller's communication effort is focused on informing and persuading the prospect with the goal of making a sale. The salesperson's job is to correctly understand the buyer's needs, match those needs to the company's product(s), and then persuade the customer to buy. Because selling provides a two-way communication channel, it is especially important in marketing industrial products which may be expensive and technologically complex. Personal selling is also a popular marketing communication tool in countries with restrictions on advertising and in countries where low wage rates allow large local sales forces to be hired.[23]

Sales personnel can also convey information from the market back to the company. Effective personal selling in a salesperson's home country requires building a relationship with the customer; global marketing presents additional challenges because the buyer and seller may come from different national or cultural backgrounds. It is difficult to overstate the importance of a face-to-face, personal selling effort for industrial products in global markets. In 1993, a Malaysian developer, YTL Corp., sought bids on a $700 million contract for power-generation turbines. Siemens AG of Germany and General Electric were among the bidders. Datuk Francis Yeoh, managing director of YTL, requested meetings with top executives from both companies. "I wanted to look them in the eye to see if we can do business," Yeoh said. Siemens complied with the request. GE did not send an executive, and Siemens was awarded the contract.[24]

The personal selling process is typically divided into several stages: prospecting, preapproach, problem solving, approaching, presenting, handling objections, closing the sale, and following up. The relative importance of each stage can vary by country or region. Experienced American sales reps know that persistence is one tactic often required to win an order in the United States; however, persistence in the United States often means "tenacity," as in, "Don't take 'no' for an answer." Persistence is also required if a global industrial marketing effort is to succeed; in some countries, however, persistence often means

[22]Leslie Ryan, "Sales Promotion: Made in America," *Brandweek* (July 31, 1995), p. 28.

[23]John J. Burnett, *Promotion Management* (Houghton Mifflin: Boston, 1993), p. 710.

[24]Marcus W. Brauchli, "Looking East: Asia, on the Ascent, Is Learning to Say No to 'Arrogant' West," *The Wall Street Journal* (Apr. 13, 1994), pp. A1, A8.

	U.K.	Ireland	Spain	Portugal	Greece	France	Italy	Nether-lands	Denmark	Belgium	West Germany	Luxem-bourg
In-pack premiums	P	P	P	P	P	M	P	M	M	M	M	N
Multiple-purchase offers	P	P	P	P	P	P	P	P	M	M	M	N
Extra product	P	P	P	P	P	P	P	M	P	M	M	P
Free product	P	P	P	P	P	P	P	P	P	M	P	P
Free mail-ins	P	P	P	P	P	P	P	P	M	M	N	M
With-purchase premiums	P	P	P	P	P	P	P	M	M	M	M	N
Cross-product offers	P	P	P	P	P	P	P	M	M	N	N	N
Collector devices	P	P	P	P	P	M	P	M	M	M	N	N
Competitions	P	P	P	P	P	M	P	M	M	P	M	M
Free drawings	P	P	P	P	P	P	P	N	N	N	N	N
Share-outs	P	P	P	P	P	M	M	N	N	N	N	N
Sweepstakes/ lottery	M	M	M	M	M	M	M	M	N	M	M	N
Money-off vouchers	P	P	P	P	P	P	M	P	M	P	N	M
Money-off next purchases	P	P	P	P	P	P	M	P	N	P	N	N
Cash backs	P	P	P	P	P	P	N	P	P	P	M	N

P Permitted
M May be permitted
N Not permitted

Source: "Europe's Promotion Maze," *Advertising Age* (Apr. 30, 1990), p. S-11.

"endurance," a willingness to patiently invest months or years before the effort results in an actual sale. For example, a company wishing to enter the Japanese market must be prepared for negotiations to take from three to ten years.

Prospecting is the process of identifying leads—customers or others who might be interested in the product. Problem solving involves understanding the match between the customers' needs and the company's products and developing a sales presentation. The next two steps, the approach and the presentation, involve one or more meetings between seller and buyer. In global selling, it is absolutely essential for the salesperson to understand cultural norms and proper protocol. In some countries, the approach is drawn out as the buyer gets to know or "takes the measure" of the salesperson on a personal level with no mention of the pending deal. In such instances, the presentation comes only after rapport has been firmly established.

During the presentation, the salesperson must deal with objections. Objections may be business-related or of personal nature. A common theme in sales training is the notion of active listening; naturally, in global sales, verbal and nonverbal communication barriers of the type discussed in Chapter 4 present special challenges for the salesperson. When

CHAPTER 16 ■ 367
GLOBAL MARKETING
COMMUNICATIONS DECISIONS:
ADVERTISING, PUBLIC
RELATIONS, SALES PROMOTION,
AND PERSONAL SELLING

objections are successfully overcome, the salesperson moves on to the close and asks for the order. A successful sale does not end there, however; the final step of the selling process involves following up with the customer to ensure his or her ongoing satisfaction with the purchase.

SUMMARY

Marketing communications—the promotion "P" of the marketing mix—includes advertising, public relations, sales promotion, and personal selling. While marketers may identify opportunities for global advertising campaigns, local adaptation or distinct local campaigns may also be required. A powerful reason to try to create a global campaign is that the process forces a company to attempt to identify a global market for its product. In addition, the identification of global appeals and benefits forces a company to probe deeply to identify basic needs and buying motives. When creating advertising, care must be taken to ensure that the art direction and copy are appropriate for the intended audiences in target countries. Advertisers may place a single global agency in charge of worldwide advertising; it is also possible to use one or more agencies on a regional or local basis. Advertising intensity varies from country to country. The United States, for example, accounts for less than 25 percent of gross world product but almost 50 percent of world advertising expenditures. Media availability varies considerably from country to country. Television is the leading medium in many markets, but its availability for advertising is severely restricted or nonexistent in others.

Public relations, sales promotion, and personal selling are also important tools in global marketing. Corporate communications must be designed to foster goodwill and provide accurate, timely information, especially in the event of a crisis. Sales promotions must conform with regulations in each country market. An ill-designed promotion can result in unwanted publicity. Finally, personal selling, or one-on-one communication, requires company representatives to be well versed in the culture of countries in which they do business. Behavior in each stage of the selling process may have to be appropriately tailored to individual country requirements.

DISCUSSION QUESTIONS

1. In what ways can global brands and global advertising campaigns benefit a company?
2. How does the "standardized versus localized" debate apply to advertising?
3. When creating advertising for world markets, what issues must art directors and copywriters take into account?
4. How do the media options available to advertisers vary in different parts of the world? What can advertisers do to cope with media limitations in certain countries?
5. What are some of the ways public relations practices vary in different parts of the world?
6. What roles can sales promotion and personal selling play in the global marketing mix?

BIBLIOGRAPHY

Books

Mooij, Marieke K. de. *Advertising Worldwide: Concepts, Theories, and Practice of International, Multinational and Global Advertising*, 2d ed. Upper Saddle River, NJ: Prentice Hall, N.J.: 1994.

Mueller, Barbara. *International Advertising: Communicating across Cultures*. Belmont, Calif.: Wadsworth Publishing Company, 1995.

Articles

Alden, Dana L., Wayne D. Hoyer, and Chol Lee. "Identifying Global and Culture-Specific Dimensions of Humor in Advertising: A Multinational Analysis." *Journal of Marketing* 57, no. 2 (April 1993), pp. 64–75.

Andrews, J. Craig, Srinivas Durvasula, and Richard G. Netemeyer. "Testing the Cross-National Applicability of U.S. and Russian Advertising." *Journal of Advertising* 23, no. 1 (March 1994), pp. 71–82.

Banerjee, Anish. "Transnational Advertising Development and Management: An Account Planning Approach and Process Framework." *International Journal of Advertising* 13, no. 2 (1994), pp. 95–124.

Botan, Carl. "International Public Relations: Critique and Reformulation." *Public Relations Review* 18, no. 2 (Summer 1992), pp. 149–159.

Bovet, Susan Fry. "Building an International Team." *Public Relations Journal* (August–September 1994), pp. 26+.

Duncan, Thomas R., and Stephen E. Everett. "Client Perception of Integrated Marketing Communications." *Journal of Advertising Research* (May–June 1993), pp. 119–122.

Epley, Joe S. "Public Relations in the Global Village: An American Perspective." *Public Relations Review* 18, no. 2 (Summer 1992), pp. 109–116.

Grunig, Larissa A. "Strategic Public Relations Constituencies on a Global Scale." *Public Relations Review* 18, no. 2 (Summer 1992), pp. 127–136.

Hiebert, Ray E. "Advertising and Public Relations in Transition from Communism: The Case of Hungary, 1989–1994." *Public Relations Review* 20, no. 4 (Winter 1994), pp. 357–372.

Hill, John S., and Alan T. Shao. "Agency Participants in Multicountry Advertising: A Preliminary Examination of Affiliate Characteristics and Environments." *Journal of International Marketing* 2, no. 2 (1994), pp. 29–48.

Huneycutt, Earl D., Jr., and John B. Ford. "Guidelines for Managing an International Sales Force. *Industrial Marketing Management* 24 (March 1995), pp. 135–144.

Johansson, Johny K. "The Sense of 'Nonsense': Japanese TV Advertising." *Journal of Advertising* 23, no. 1 (March 1994), pp. 17–26.

Josephs, Ray, and Juanita W. Josephs. "Public Relations, the U.K. Way." *Public Relations Journal* (April 1994), pp. 14–18.

Kashani, Kamran, and John A. Quelch. "Can Sales Promotion Go Global?" *Business Horizons* (May–June 1990), pp. 37–43.

Lohtia, Ritu, Wesley J. Johnston, and Linda Aab. "Creating an Effective Print Advertisement for the China Market: Analysis and Advice." *Journal of Global Marketing* 8, no. 2, (1994), pp. 7–30.

Luqmani, Mushtag, Ugur Yavas, and Zahir Quraeshi. "Advertising in Saudi Arabia: Content and Regulation." *International Marketing Review* 6, no. 1 (1989), pp. 59–72.

McGuinness, Dalton, Mike Brennan, and Philip Gendall. "The Effect of Product Sampling and Couponing on Purchase Behavior: Some Empirical

Evidence." *International Journal of Advertising* 14, no. 3 (1995), pp. 219–230.

Nessmann, Karl. "Public Relations in Europe: A Comparison with the United States." *Public Relations Review* 21, no. 2 (Summer 1995), pp. 151–160.

Newsom, Doug, and Bob Carrell. "Professional Public Relations in India: Need Outstrips Supply." *Public Relations Review* 20, no. 2 (Summer 1994), pp. 183–188.

Parameswaran, Ravi, and R. Mohan Pisharodi. "Facets of Country of Origin Image: An Empirical Assessment," *Journal of Advertising* 23, no. 1 (March 1994), pp. 43–56.

Samli, A. Coskun, Gregory P. Wirth, and James R. Wills, Jr. "High-Tech Firms Must Get More Out of Their International Sales Efforts." *Industrial Marketing Management* 23 (October 1994), pp. 333–342.

Sharpe, Melvin L. "The Impact of Social and Cultural Conditioning on Global Public Relations." *Public Relations Review* 18, no. 2 (Summer 1992), pp. 103–107.

Tansey, Richard, and Michael R. Hyman. "Dependency Theory and the Effects of Advertising by Foreign-based Multinational Corporations in Latin America." *Journal of Advertising* 23, no. 1 (March 1994), pp. 27–42.

Wells, Ludmilla Gricenko. "Western Concepts, Russian Perspectives: Meanings of Advertising in the Former Soviet Union." *Journal of Advertising* 23, no. 1 (March 1994), pp. 83–95.

Zandpour, Fred. "Global Reach and Local Touch: Achieving Cultural Fitness in TV Advertising." *Journal of Advertising Research* 34, no. 5 (September–October 1994), pp. 35–63.

Zavrl, Frani, and Dejan Vercic. "Performing Public Relations in Central and Eastern Europe." *International Public Relations Journal* 18, no. 2 (1995), pp. 21–23.

*B*enetton Group SpA, the Italy-based global clothing retailer, seems to have fallen on hard times. Until recently, financial results were excellent: Worldwide sales of Benetton's brightly-colored knitware and contemporary clothing doubled between 1988 and 1993 to 2.75 trillion lire ($1.63 billion). In 1993 alone, sales were up about 10 percent, and net income increased by 13 percent. The strong showing in 1993 was due in part to the devaluation of the Italian lira, which enabled Benetton to cut prices for its clothing around the world.

By contrast, 1994 results were discouraging. Sales were flat at $1.69 billion, operating profits fell 5 percent, to $245 million, and margins narrowed to 13.9 percent down from 14.7 percent during the three-year period 1991–1993. The sales slump was surprising in view of the fact that Benetton had opened stores in China, Eastern Europe, and India, and extended the brand into new categories such as footwear and cosmetics. Some industry observers believed that Benetton's wounds were self-inflicted. According to this view, 1994's results represented the backlash from Benetton's highly controversial global advertising campaigns, now several years old, keyed to the theme "The United Colors of Benetton."

Various executions of the ads, in magazines and on posters and billboards, featured provocative, even shocking photos designed to focus public attention on social and political issues such as the environment, terrorism, racial issues, and sexually transmitted diseases. The creative concept of the ads reflected the views of Oliviero Toscani, creative director and chief photographer for Benetton. "I have found out that advertising is the richest and most powerful medium existing today. Therefore, I feel responsible to do more than say, 'Our sweater is pretty,'" he told *The New York Times*. Noted Vittorio Rava, worldwide advertising manager, "We believe our advertising needs to shock, otherwise people will not remember it."

One of the first ads to stir controversy depicted a white hand and a black hand joined by handcuffs; another showed an angelic white child embracing a black child whose hair was unmistakably styled to resemble the horns of a devil. An ad with a picture of a black woman nursing a white baby appeared in 77 countries; while not used in the United States and the United Kingdom, the ad won awards in France and Italy. In fall 1991, several U.S. magazine publishers refused to carry some of the ads; one depicted a nun kissing a priest. A picture of a newborn baby covered with bloody placenta was also rejected. According to Benetton's Ravo, "We didn't envision a political idea when we started this 'Colors' strategy five years ago, but now, with racist problems becoming more important in every country it has become political on its own."

With its next series of ads, Benetton began using images associated with sexuality. As Peter Fressola, director of communications, explained the message strategy, "We're saying there are two important issues to be addressed, and they are overpopulation and sexually transmitted diseases such as AIDS. I think it is time to take the gloves off and put on the rubbers and address these issues." In an interview with *Advertising Age*, Mr. Toscani explained, "Everybody uses emotion to sell a product. The difference here is we are not selling a product. We want to show, in this case, human realities that we are aware of." The ads broke new ground for the images they presented: A man dying of AIDS surrounded by his family; a montage of multicolored condoms; a group of people with the initials "HIV" stamped on their arms; test tubes filled with blood labeled with the names of world leaders.

In France, the HIV ad caused a great deal of controversy. One man who was dying of AIDS ran an ad with a picture of his own face above a tagline that read "during the agony, the sales continue." In the United States, where the number of Benetton stores had been slowly dwindling, the ads were

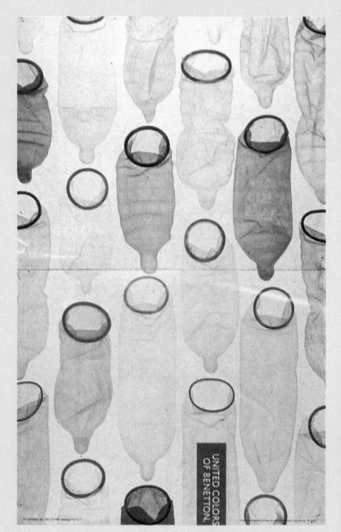

United Colors of Benetton. Concept: O. Toscani. Spring 1991. Photo: Theresa Frare. Reprinted by permission.

United Colors of Benetton. Spring 1994. Photo: O. Toscani. Reprinted by permission.

poorly received by many customers and Benetton retailers. The manager of a Benetton store in Biloxi, Mississippi, received telephone calls from people who said they refused to shop at stores selling products from a "sick" company. In Florida, one franchisee closed a dozen Benetton locations, noting, "It is not our function as retailers to raise the consciousness of people. I've had long, hard fights with Italy over the advertising." In an effort to help mollify its American licensees, Benetton began providing them with local ads featuring clothing instead of social issues. At the national level, however, Benetton continued the controversial ads. When asked about the possible negative impact of customer boycotts, Luciano Benetton, president of the company's U.S. division, said, "It's silly to change direction because someone in the market thinks it's not right. We are sincere, and we are consistent in pursuing it this way."

In the spring of 1994, it appeared that Benetton had finally gone too far. A new $15 million ad campaign that ran in 25 countries featured a picture of the bloody uniform of a Croatian soldier who had died in the Bosnian civil war. While Benetton executives had come to expect criticism, they were unprepared for the latest reaction. The company was accused of exploiting the war for the sake of profit. In France, many of the offending posters were pulled down or covered with grafitti reading "Boycott Benetton" and "This is blood for money." The French minister for humanitarian affairs even made a public announcement discouraging people from buying Benetton sweaters; he called for his fellow citizens to "pull [the sweaters] off people who are going to wear them." In some parts of Germany and Switzerland, the company's products were banned. Some media reports in Europe questioned the authenticity of the uniform, alleging it did not belong to the fallen soldier named in the ad. The Vatican newspaper charged Benetton with "advertising terrorism."

Mr. Benetton acknowledged that "this is not what a corporate communications campaign should do. It should create interest." Still, he vowed the company would continue "to search for new facts and new emotions" to include in its ads. Indeed, when the Sarajevo daily newspaper *Oslo bodhenie* ("Liberation") requested posters of the ad to put up around the city, Benetton supplied 10,000 copies. In France, however, a court ordered the company to pay $32,000 to French HIV victims; a German court banned several of the most controversial ads.

DISCUSSION QUESTIONS

1. What is your personal reaction to the controversial Benetton ads?
2. Do you believe Benetton is "sincere" in its campaign, or is the company just exploiting human misery?
3. There is a saying in the marketing world that "there is no such thing as bad publicity." Does that apply in the Benetton case?
4. From a marketing (as opposed to personal) point of view, advise Benetton on its campaign. Should the company continue, expand, change, or terminate the campaign?

Sources: John Rossant, "The Faded Colors of Benetton," *Business Week* (Apr. 10, 1995), pp. 87, 90.

Peter Gumbel, "Benetton Is Stung by Backlash over Ad," *The Wall Street Journal* (Mar. 4, 1994), p. A8.

Gary Levin, "Benetton Ad Lays Bare the Bloody Toll of War," *Advertising Age* (Feb. 21, 1994).

Judith Graham, "Benetton 'Colors' the Race Issue," *Advertising Age* (Sept. 11, 1989), p. 3.

Kim Foltz, "Campaign on Harmony Backfires for Benetton," *The New York Times* (Nov. 20, 1989), p. 32.

Dennis Rodkin, "How Colorful Can Ads Get?" *Mother Jones* (January 1990), p. 52.

Stuart Elliott, "Benetton Stirs More Controversy," *The New York Times* (July 23, 1991), p. 19.

Gary Levin, "Benetton Brouhaha," *Advertising Age* (Feb. 17, 1992), p. 62.

Teri Agins, "Shrinkage of Stores and Customers in U.S., Causes Italy's Benetton to Alter Its Tactics," *The Wall Street Journal* (June 24, 1992), pp. B1, B10.

WORLD ADVERTISING EXPENDITURES[25]

Table 1 shows, by rank, the 27 top-spending countries in advertising in 1990, including all print, television, radio, cinema, outdoor/transit, direct advertising, and miscellaneous expenditures reported. Advertising expenditures in each of these countries exceeded $500 million.

PER CAPITA ADVERTISING EXPENDITURES

Details on per capita expenditures selected countries are shown in Table 2.

---

[25] This information is excerpted from *World Advertising Expenditures*, 1990 edition, sponsored by Starch *INRA* Hooper Inc., in cooperation with the International Advertising Association. Copyright © 1990, by Starch INRA Hooper, used with permission.

TABLE 1 — TOTAL ADVERTISING EXPENDITURES

Country	US$ Millions
United States	$128,640.0
Japan	38,433.6
United Kingdom	15,816.0
West Germany	13,944.4
France	12,891.9
Spain	10,350.2
Italy	5,709.7
Netherlands	4,334.7
Switzerland	4,098.0
Australia	3,847.9
Brazil	3,186.5
South Korea	2,826.1
Sweden	2,719.3
Mexico	2,199.3
Finland	1,800.2
Taiwan	1,569.3
Denmark	1,377.2
Belgium	1,283.2
Norway	1,233.2
Austria	1,012.0
India	895.8
Hong Kong	861.4
Argentina	829.7
New Zealand	624.5
Israel	587.9
Greece	526.1
China	523.0

Per Capita Advertising Expenditures

TABLE 2 — PER CAPITA ADVERTISING EXPENDITURES, 1990

Country	US$
Switzerland	$613
United States	513
Finland	362
Sweden	319
Japan	311
Norway	291
Netherlands	290
United Kingdom	275
Denmark	268
Spain	263
France	228
Australia	226
West Germany	225
New Zealand	183
Hong Kong	149
Austria	132
Belgium	128
Israel	127
Singapore	116

TABLE 3 — ADVERTISING EXPENDITURES AS A PERCENTAGE OF GNP, 1990

Country	Percent of GNP
Spain	2.4
United States	2.4
Switzerland	1.9
United Kingdom	1.7
Netherlands	1.7
New Zealand	1.4
Bolivia	1.4
Finland	1.4
Sweden	1.3
Australia	1.3
Hong Kong	1.3
Costa Rica	1.3
Norway	1.3
Japan	1.2
South Korea	1.2
Panama	1.2
Denmark	1.2
France	1.2
Colombia	1.2
Israel	1.2
Argentina	1.1
Mexico	1.0
Dominican Republic	1.0

TABLE 4 — ADVERTISING EXPENDITURES IN PRINT MEDIA, 1990

Country	US$ Millions
United States	$42,174.0
Japan	11,971.1
United Kingdom	9,055.6
West Germany	8,429.8
Spain	4,051.8
France	3,627.0
Italy	2,466.9
Netherlands	2,232.4
Switzerland	1,895.3
Australia	1,869.7
Sweden	1,706.8
South Korea	1,370.0
Finland	1,167.3
Brazil	1,121.8

TABLE 5 — PER CAPITA PRINT ADVERTISING EXPENDITURES, 1990

Country	US$
Switzerland	$283.3
Finland	234.4
Sweden	199.6
Denmark	174.6
Norway	172.3
United States	168.1
United Kingdom	157.5
Netherlands	149.5
West Germany	136.0
Australia	109.9
Spain	103.0

TABLE 6 — PERCENT OF MEASURED MEDIA ADVERTISING EXPENDITURES ALLOCATED TO PRINT MEDIA, 1990

Country	Percent
Norway	93.0
Sweden	92.9
Denmark	83.0
Zambia	82.5
Netherlands	82.3
Israel	81.1

ADVERTISING EXPENDITURES AS A PERCENT OF GNP

The countries in which the proportion of GNP allocated to advertising was the lowest were the less-developed countries of Africa and Asia and some of the oil-rich countries of the Middle East. Table 3 shows, in rank order, those countries with advertising expenditures exceeding 1 percent of GNP.

Some dramatic changes in ranking have taken place over the years. In the mid-1980s, for example, Finland ranked second behind the United States with expenditures slightly exceeding 2 percent of GNP; in 1990 Finland ranked eighth with 1.4 percent.

PRINT ADVERTISING

Table 4 shows the 14 countries that spent more than $1 billion on advertising with print media in 1990, and Table 5 shows the countries where such expenditures were over $100 per capita.

The countries in Table 6 each expended over 80 percent of their 1990 measured media advertising expenditures in print.

TELEVISION ADVERTISING

As noted in Chapter 16, the United States and Japan lead the world in television advertising expenditures.

TABLE 7 ADVERTISING EXPENDITURES IN TELEVISION MEDIA, 1990

Country	US$ Millions
United States	$28,405.0
Japan	11,164.4
United Kingdom	4,149.4
Italy	2,908.1
France	2,523.3
Spain	2,393.8
Brazil	1,825.9
West Germany	1,798.2
Mexico	1,649.1
Australia	1,357.9

TABLE 8 PER CAPITA TELEVISION ADVERTISING EXPENDITURES, 1990

Country	US$
United States	$113.2
Japan	90.4
Australia	79.9
Hong Kong	73.0
United Kingdom	72.2
New Zealand	61.7
Spain	60.9
Italy	50.5
France	44.7
Finland	42.2
Singapore	35.0
Austria	34.6
Belgium	32.1

TABLE 9 PERCENT OF MEASURED MEDIA ADVERTISING EXPENDITURES ALLOCATED TO TELEVISION MEDIA, 1990

Country	Percent
Mexico	75.0
Bolivia	72.3
Ecuador	66.2
Venezuela	65.0
Dominican Republic	64.4
Guatemala	64.0
Colombia	59.5
Panama	59.3
Brazil	57.7
Italy	50.9

RADIO ADVERTISING

As shown in Table 10, eight countries reported radio advertising expenditures of more than $200 million in 1990, and only three others reported a radio budget of over $100 million.

Per capita radio expenditures in 1990 were $10 or more in nine countries and $5 or more in six others (see Table 11).

TABLE 10 ADVERTISING EXPENDITURES IN RADIO MEDIA, 1990

Country	US$ Millions
United States	$8,726.0
Japan	1,612.7
Spain	784.7
France	619.8
West Germany	550.8
Australia	335.2
United Kingdom	290.2
Mexico	235.8
Brazil	153.0
South Korea	134.7
Austria	119.3

TABLE 11 PER CAPITA RADIO ADVERTISING EXPENDITURES, 1990

Country	US$
United States	$34.8
New Zealand	24.6
Spain	20.0
Australia	19.7
Austria	15.6
Japan	13.1
Finland	12.6
France	11.0
Ireland	10.0
West Germany	8.9
Hong Kong	6.6
Israel	6.5
Switzerland	6.1
Taiwan	5.3
United Kingdom	5.1

TABLE 12 PERCENT OF MEASURED MEDIA ADVERTISING EXPENDITURES ALLOCATED TO RADIO MEDIA, 1990

Country	Percent
Trinidad and Tobago	22.6
Kenya	21.7

OUTDOOR AND TRANSIT ADVERTISING

Table 13 gives the top 10 countries spending more than $100 million for posters and billboards and transit advertising.

TABLE 13	1990 OUTDOOR EXPENDITURES IN OUTDOOR AND TRANSIT MEDIA (US$ MILLIONS)		
Country	Transit	Billboards	Transportation
Japan	$4,347.7	$2,634.8	$1,712.8
France	1,138.6	N/A	N/A
United States	1,084.0	1,084.0	N/A
United Kingdom	503.3	330.2	173.1
South Korea	476.3	N/A	476.3
West Germany	420.9	N/A	N/A
Spain	363.0	229.0	134.0
Switzerland	299.5	N/A	N/A
Australia	221.9	N/A	N/A
Italy	243.0	N/A	N/A

CHAPTER 17

Leading, Organizing, and Controlling the Global Marketing Effort

> *"Rupert Murdoch has established the norm for the worldwide, vertically-integrated strategy."[1]*
>
> —John Malone, CEO, TeleCommunications Inc.

Rupert Murdoch has been described as a media visionary. Murdoch is chairman and CEO of the News Corporation Ltd., a global powerhouse that produces and distributes news and entertainment around the world. Murdoch's empire includes important print media companies such as HarperCollins Publishers and London's *Herald & Weekly Times*. The Fox Film Entertainment Group produces movies, TV shows, and animated features that can be shown on the Fox TV network. Murdoch purchased 12 TV stations in the United States that now serve as network affiliates and carry Fox-produced programming; in 1994, he startled the broadcast world by bidding $1.6 billion for the rights to NFL broadcasts that had previously belonged to CBS. Outside the United States, Murdoch's company has stakes in several satellite systems, including British Sky Broadcasting in the United Kingdom and the Hong Kong–based Star TV that services Asia and India. Murdoch's biographer describes him as "an extraordinarily energetic person." Jessica Reif, a media analyst with Merrill Lynch, says of Murdoch, "He has an uncanny ability to see the world in different ways."

This chapter focuses on the integration of each element of the marketing mix into a total plan that addresses opportunities and threats in the global marketing environment. Rupert Murdoch illustrates the critical role of leadership in a global firm. Leaders must be capable of articulating a coherent global vision and strategy that integrate local responsiveness, global efficiency, and leverage. The leader is also the architect of an organization design that is appropriate for the company's strategy. The leader must also ensure that appropriate control mechanisms are in place so that, in a world in which industries and markets are rapidly globalizing, organizational goals can be achieved.

---

[1]Kevin Maney, "Media Firms Shift to Gain Product Control," *USA Today* (Sept. 14, 1995), p. 2B.

LEADERSHIP

Global marketing demands exceptional leadership. As we have said throughout this book, the hallmark of a global company is the capacity to formulate and implement global strategies that leverage worldwide learning, respond fully to local needs and wants, and draw on the talent and energy of every member of the organization. This is a heroic task requiring global vision and a sensitivity to local needs. Overall, the leader's challenge is to direct the efforts and creativity of everyone in the company toward a global effort that best utilizes organizational resources to exploit global opportunities. Beliefs, values, and the intended geographic scope of activities should be clearly articulated in a company's mission statement. Using the mission statement or similar document as a reference and guide, members of each operating unit must address their immediate responsibilities and at the same time cooperate with functional, product, and country experts in different locations.

At Levi Strauss & Co. an Aspirations Statement that reflects the vision of chairman and CEO Robert Haas is clearly posted in every company facility. The statement spells out Levi's values-based formula for achieving profit and making the world a better place; it addresses issues ranging from workforce diversity and employee empowerment to honest communication and ethical management practices. Levi recently announced that it would cancel operations in China due to the Chinese government's record of human rights violations. According to David Schmidt, Levi's vice president for corporate marketing, "There are wonderful commercial opportunities in China. But when ethical issues collide with commercial appeal, we try to ensure ethics as the trump card. For us, ethical issues precede all others."[2] Levi's stance is particularly striking in view of the fact that, in 1994, the U.S. government granted China most-favored-nation trading status despite its human rights record. Levi is also applying its ethics code in other parts of the world. About half of the apparel sold by the company is manufactured in plants located in low-wage countries such as Bangladesh, Indonesia, and Malaysia. Levi is strict about enforcing International Labor Organization standards that prohibit hiring children below the age of 14. However, company personnel are also sensitive to the economic issues that lead to ILO violations. In one instance, Levi executives learned that some underage factory employees in Bangladesh were the sole breadwinners in small families. Instead of firing the children, Levi arranged to pay their wages while they returned to school. Levi's intent was to hire the youths back after they turn 14.

Top Management Nationality

Many globally minded companies realize that the best person for a top management job is not necessarily someone born in the home country. Speaking of U.S. companies, Christopher Bartlett of the Harvard Business School notes, "Companies are realizing that they have a portfolio of human resources worldwide, that their brightest technical person might come from Germany, or their best financial manager from England. They are starting to tap their worldwide human resources. And as they do, it will not be surprising to see non-Americans rise to the top" (Peckter 1993, 56). The ability to speak foreign languages is one difference between managers born and raised in the United States and those born and raised elsewhere. For example, according to one recent report, 20,000 Japanese businesspersons who are fluent in English are working in the United States, while only 200 American businesspersons doing business in Japan can speak Japanese.[3] Roberto Goizeta, the Cuban-born CEO of Coca-Cola, speaks English, Spanish, and Portuguese;

---

[2]Michale Janofsky, "Levi Strauss: American Symbol with a Cause," *The New York Times* (Jan. 3, 1994), p. C4. See also Russell Mitchell, "Managing by Values: Is Levi Strauss' Approach Visionary—or Flaky?" *Business Week* (Aug. 1, 1994), pp. 46–52; William Beaver, "Levi's Is Leaving China," *Business Horizons 38*, no. 2 (March–April 1995), pp. 35–40.
[3]Charlene Marmer Solomon, "Success Abroad Depends on More than Job Skills," *Personnel Journal* (April 1994), p. 52.

Ford's chief executive, Alexander Trotman, was born in England and speaks English, French, and German.

Sigismundus W.W. Lubensen, the Dutch-born president and CEO of Quaker Chemical Corporation, is a good example of today's cosmopolitan executive. Educated in Rotterdam as well as New York, Lubensen, who speaks Dutch, English, French, and German, says, "I was lucky to be born in a place where if you drove for an hour in any direction, you were in a different country, speaking a different language. It made me very comfortable traveling in different cultures." It is perhaps not surprising that Lubensen favors a global approach to organizational design over a domestic/international approach. He advised Peter A. Benoliel, his predecessor CEO, to have units in the Netherlands, France, Italy, Spain, and England report to a regional vice president in Europe. "I saw that it would not be a big deal to put all of the European units under one common denominator," Lubensen recalls (Peckter 1993, 58).

Leadership and Core Competence

Core competence, a concept developed by global strategy experts C. K. Prahalad and Gary Hamel, was introduced in Chapter 11. In the 1980s, many business executives were assessed on their ability to reorganize their corporations. In the 1990s, Prahalad and Hamel believe executives are judged on their ability to identify, nurture, and exploit the core competencies that make growth possible. Core competence must provide potential access to a wide variety of markets, make a significant contribution to the perceived customer benefits of the end product, and be difficult for competitors to imitate. Few companies are likely to build world leadership in more than five or six fundamental competencies. In the long run, an organization will derive its global competitiveness from its ability to bring high-quality, low-cost products to market faster than its competitors. In order to do this, an organization must be viewed as a portfolio of competencies rather than a portfolio of businesses. Many companies have the technical resources to build competencies but key executives lack the vision to do so. The concept of distinctive competencies challenges executives to rethink the concept of the corporation itself. It also requires redefining the task of management as building both competencies and the administrative means for assembling resources spread across multiple businesses (Prahalad & Hamel 1990, 79–86).

ORGANIZATION

The goal in organizing for global marketing is to find a structure that enables the company to respond to relevant market environment differences while ensuring the diffusion of corporate knowledge and experience from national markets throughout the entire corporate system. The pull between the value of centralized knowledge and coordination and the need for individualized response to the local situation creates a constant tension in the global marketing organization. A key issue in global organization is how to achieve balance between autonomy and integration. Subsidiaries need autonomy in order to adapt to their local environment. But the business as a whole needs integration to implement global strategy (Yip 1992, 179).

When management at a domestic company decides to pursue international expansion, the issue of how to organize arises immediately. Who should be responsible for this expansion? Should product divisions operate directly or should an international division be established? Should individual country subsidiaries report directly to the company president or should a special corporate officer be appointed to take full-time responsibility for international activities? After the decision of how to organize initial international operations has been reached, a growing company is faced with a number of reappraisal points during the development of its international business activities. Should a company abandon its international division, and if so, what alternative structure should be adopted?

LEADING, ORGANIZING, AND
CONTROLLING THE GLOBAL
MARKETING EFFORT

Should an area or regional headquarters be formed? What should be the relationship of staff executives at corporate, regional, and subsidiary offices? Specifically, how should the marketing function be organized? To what extent should regional and corporate marketing executives become involved in subsidiary marketing management?

It is important to recognize that there is no single correct organizational structure for global marketing. Even within an industry, worldwide companies have developed very different strategic and organizational responses to changes in their environments (Bartlett & Ghoshal 1989, 3). Still, it is possible to make some generalizations. Leading-edge global competitors share one key organizational design characteristic: Their corporate structure is flat and simple, rather than tall and complex. The message is clear: The world is complicated enough, so there is no need to add to the confusion with a complex internal structuring. Simple structures increase the speed and clarity of communication and allow the concentration of organizational energy and valuable resources on learning, rather than on controlling, monitoring, and reporting.[4] According to David Whitwam, CEO of Whirlpool, "You must create an organization whose people are adept at exchanging ideas, processes, and systems across borders, people who are absolutely free of the 'not-invented-here' syndrome, people who are constantly working together to identify the best global opportunities and the biggest global problems facing the organization" (Maruca 1994, 136–137).

A geographically dispersed company cannot limit its knowledge to product, function, and the home territory. Company personnel must acquire knowledge of the complex set of social, political, economic, and institutional arrangements that exist within each international market. Most companies, after initial ad hoc arrangements—for example, all foreign subsidiaries reporting to a designated vice president or to the president—establish an international division to manage their geographically dispersed new business. It is clear, however, that the international division in the multiproduct company is an unstable organizational arrangement. As a company grows, this initial organizational structure frequently gives way to various alternative structures (Stopford & Wells 1972).

In today's fast-changing competitive global environment, corporations are having to find new and more creative ways to organize. New forms of flexibility, efficiency, and responsiveness are required to meet the market demands. The need to be cost effective, to be customer-driven, to deliver the best quality, and to deliver that quality quickly are some of today's global realities. Recently, several authors have described new organizational designs that represent responses to the competitive environment of the late 20th century. These designs acknowledge the need to find more responsive and flexible structures, to flatten the organization, and to employ teams. There is the recognition of the need to develop networks, to develop stronger relationships among participants, and to exploit technology. These designs also reflect an evolution in approaches to organizational effectiveness. At the turn of the century, Fredrick Taylor claimed that all managers had to see the world the same way. Then came the contingency theorists who said that effective organizations design themselves to match their conditions. These two basic theories are reflected in today's popular management writings. As Henry Mintzberg has observed, "To Michael Porter, effectiveness resides in strategy, while to Tom Peters it is the operations that count—executing any strategy with excellence" (Mintzberg 1991, 54–55). We believe that successful companies, the real global winners, must have both: good strategies and good execution.

Patterns of International Organizational Development

Organizations vary in terms of the size and potential of targeted global markets and local management competence in different country markets. Conflicting pressures may arise from the need for product and technical knowledge, functional expertise in market-

---

[4]Vladimir Pucik, "Globalization and Human Resource Management," in V. Pucik, N. Tichy, and C. Barnett, *Globalizing Management: Creating and Leading the Competitive Organization* (New York: J. Wiley & Sons, 1992), p. 70.

*I*t takes more than one person to run News Corporation's far-flung empire. Murdoch exerts control by keeping things simple and delegating authority to a small inner circle of close associates who are known inside the company as "clones." "You can't build a strong corporation with a lot of committees and a board that has to be consulted at every turn. You have to make your own decisions," he says. He expects newcomers to hit the ground running. "He gives you great freedom, but he lets you know from the beginning that you have no safety net under you," says one manager. Executives at News Corporation's various units know that, at any moment, they are likely to receive a telephone call that begins, "Murdoch here. How're things at your shop?" A former Fox TV executive recalls, 'The atmosphere is sort of like a monarchy. Everybody works for the king, and nothing else matters."

The Wall Street Journal has called Murdoch's approach "micromanagement on a global scale." Murdoch is viewed as an autocratic leader who often relies on his own intuition when making major decisions. He tends to focus on the News Corporation's various businesses one at a time, immersing himself in the most minute details. "If you're going to get into a business, you should get as close to it as possible, even run it yourself for a period," Murdoch says. Murdoch also has a propensity for making quick decisions. "I like to be able to move fast," he explains. "Sometimes it leads to making mistakes, but other times it leads to getting an opportunity before other people see it." Frank Barlow, a director at competitor Pearson PLC, says, "Most corporations are much more analytical about making acquisitions, while Rupert is instinctive."

Not surprisingly, Murdoch's style of leadership has invited criticism. He has been known to use his newspapers as public outlets for his own views and opinions. Sometimes he rushes into deals that don't work out; in other instances, industry observers say, he pays too much for his acquisitions. In 1995, he shocked the broadcast industry by paying $565 million for the rights to broadcast major league baseball through 1999 (meanwhile, News Corporation took a $350 million writeoff in 1995 for losses on its NFL broadcasts). The move reflects Murdoch's goal of transforming News Corporation into a global sports programming leader; other sports investments include $375 million to start a rugby team in Australia and $400 million for broadcast rights to professional soccer games in Great Britain. Murdoch's plans for the near future include launching a 24-hour news channel to compete head-to-head with CNN and starting up a direct-broadcast satellite television service in the United States.

Sources: Meg Cox, "One-Man Show: How Do You Tame a Global Company? Murdoch Does It Alone," *The Wall Street Journal* (Feb. 14, 1994), pp. A1, A6.
Richard W. Stevenson, "Networking, Globally and Relentlessly," *The New York Times* (May 29, 1994), Sec. 3, pp. 1, 3.
Albert Scardino, "How Murdoch Makes It Work," *The New York Times* (Aug. 14, 1988), Sec. 3, pp. 1, 5.

ing, finance, and operations, and area and country knowledge. Because the constellation of pressures that shape organizations is never exactly the same, no two organizations pass through organizational stages in exactly the same way, nor do they arrive at precisely the same organizational pattern. Nevertheless, some general patterns have developed.

A company engaging in limited export activities will often have a small in-house export department as a separate functional area. Most domestically oriented companies undertake initial foreign expansion by means of foreign sales offices or subsidiaries that report directly to the company president or other designated company officer. This person carries out his or her responsibilities without assistance from a headquarters staff group. This is a typical initial arrangement for companies getting started in international marketing operations.

INTERNATIONAL DIVISION STRUCTURE • As a company's international business grows, the complexity of coordinating and directing this activity extends beyond the scope of a single person. Pressure is created to assemble a staff group that will take responsibility for coordination and direction of the growing international activities of the organization. Eventually, this pressure leads to the creation of the international division, as illustrated in Figure 17–1. As shown in the figure, the executive in charge of the international division typically has a direct reporting relationship to corporate staff and thus ranks at the same level as the executives in charge of finance, marketing, operations, and other functional areas. Levi Strauss & Co. has an international division structure similar to the one shown here.

Four factors contribute to the establishment of an international division. First, top management's commitment to global operations has increased enough to justify an organizational unit headed by a senior manager. Second, the complexity of international operations

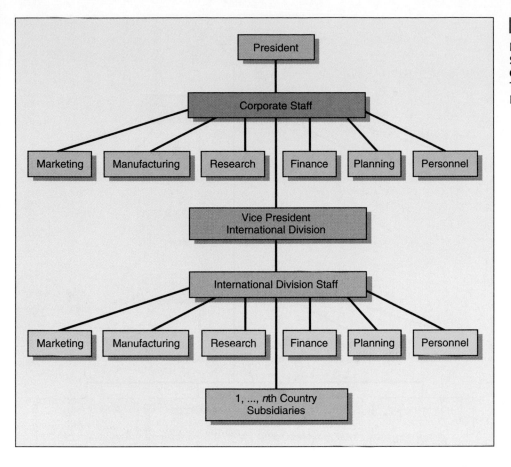

requires a single organizational unit whose management has sufficient authority to make its own determination on important issues such as which market entry strategy to employ. Third, an international division is frequently formed when the firm has recognized the need for internal specialists to deal with the special demands of global operations. A fourth contributing factor arises when management exhibits the desire to develop the ability to scan the global horizon for opportunities and competitive threats rather than simply respond to situations that are presented to the company.

REGIONAL MANAGEMENT CENTERS • When business is conducted in a single region that is characterized by similarities in economic, social, geographical, and political conditions, there is both justification and need for a management center. Thus, another stage of organizational evolution is the emergence of an area or regional headquarters as a management layer between the country organization and the international division headquarters. The increasing importance of the European Union as a regional market has prompted a number of companies to change their organizational structures by setting up regional headquarters there. Quaker Oats recently established its European headquarters in Brussels; Electrolux, the Swedish home appliance company, has also regionalized its European operations.[5] A regional center typically coordinates decisions on pricing, sourcing, and other matters. Executives at the regional center also participate in the planning and control of each country's operations with an eye toward applying company knowledge on a regional basis and optimal utilization of corporate resources on a regional basis. This organizational design is illustrated in Figure 17–2.

---

[5]". . . And Other Ways to Peel the Onion," *The Economist* (Jan. 7, 1995), pp. 52–53.

FIGURE 17–2

FUNCTIONAL CORPORATE
STRUCTURE, DOMESTIC
CORPORATE STAFF ORIEN-
TATION, INTERNATIONAL
DIVISION, AREA
DIVISIONS

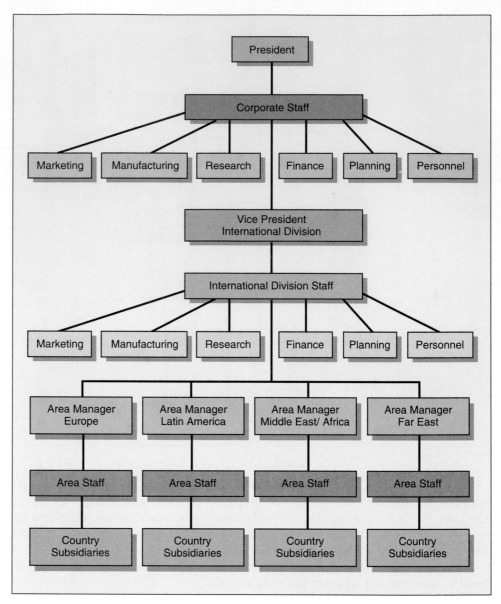

Regional management can offer a company several advantages. First, many regional managers agree that an on-the-scene regional management unit makes sense where there is a real need for coordinated, pan-regional decision making. Coordinated regional planning and control is becoming necessary as the national subsidiary continues to lose its relevance as an independent operating unit. Regional management can probably achieve the best balance of geographical, product, and functional considerations required to implement corporate objectives effectively. By shifting operations and decision making to the region, the company is better able to maintain an insider advantage (see Morrison, Ricks, & Roth 1991, 17–29).

A major disadvantage of a regional center is its cost. The cost of a two-person office could exceed $600,000 per year. The scale of regional management must be in line with the scale of operations in a region. A regional headquarters is inappropriate if the size of the operations it manages is inadequate to cover the costs of the additional layer of management. The basic issue with regard to the regional headquarters is, "Does it contribute enough to organizational effectiveness to justify its cost and the complexity of another layer of management?"

GEOGRAPHICAL STRUCTURE • The geographical structure involves the assignment of operational responsibility for geographic areas of the world to line managers. The corporate headquarters retains responsibility for worldwide planning and control, and each area of the world—including the "home" or base market—is organizationally equal. For the company with French origins, France is simply another geographic market under this organizational arrangement. The most common appearance of this structure is in companies with closely related product lines that are sold in similar end-use markets around the world. For example, the major international oil companies utilize the geographical structure, which is illustrated in Figure 17–3.

WORLDWIDE PRODUCT DIVISION STRUCTURE • When an organization assigns worldwide product responsibility to its product divisions, the product divisions must decide upon one of two possible designs. The first is to rely upon an international division, thereby dividing the world into domestic and foreign; the second is to rely upon an area structure with each region of the world organizationally treated on an equal basis. In most cases, when a divisional company shifts from a corporate international division to worldwide product divisions, there are two stages in the internationalization of the product divisions. The first stage occurs when international responsibility is shifted from a corporate international division to the product division international departments. The second occurs when the product divisions themselves shift international responsibility from international departments within the divisions to the total divisional organization. In effect, this shift is the utilization of a geographical structure within each product division. The

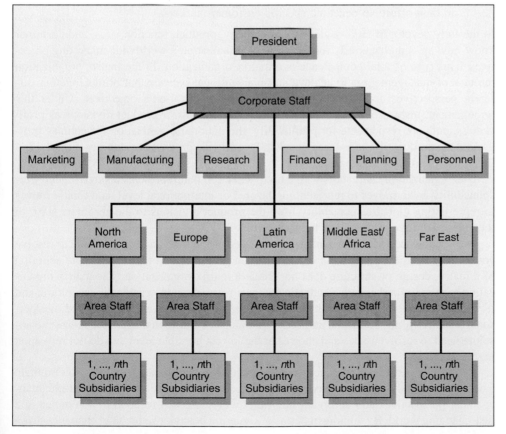

FIGURE 17–3

GEOGRAPHIC CORPO-RATE STRUCTURE, WORLD CORPORATE STAFF ORIEN-TATION, AREA DIVISIONS WORLDWIDE

product structure works best when a company's product line is widely diversified, when products go into a variety of end-use markets, and when a relatively high technological capability is required.

THE MATRIX DESIGN • The matrix form of organization can be well suited to global companies because it can be used to establish a multiple-command structure that gives equal emphasis to functional and geographical departments. The most sophisticated form of matrix integrates four basic competencies on a worldwide basis:

1. *Geographic knowledge.* An understanding of the basic economic, social, cultural, political, and governmental market and competitive dimensions of a country is essential. The country subsidiary is the major structural device employed today to enable the corporation to acquire geographic knowledge.
2. *Product knowledge and know-how.* Product managers with a worldwide responsibility can achieve this level of competence on a global basis. Another way of achieving global product competence is simply to duplicate product management organizations in domestic and international divisions, achieving high competence in both organizational units.
3. *Functional competence in such fields as finance, production, and, especially, marketing.* Corporate functional staff with worldwide responsibility contributes toward the development of functional competence on a global basis. In a handful of companies, the appointment of country subsidiary functional managers is reviewed by the corporate functional manager who is responsible for the development of his or her functional activity in the organization on a global basis.
4. *A knowledge of the customer or industry and its needs.* In certain large and very sophisticated global companies, staff with a responsibility for serving industries on a global basis exists to assist the line managers in the country organizations in their efforts to penetrate specific customer markets.

In the fully developed large-scale global company, product, function, area, and customer know-how are simultaneously focused on the organization's worldwide marketing objectives. This type of total competence is a matrix organization. In the matrix organization the task of management is to achieve an organizational balance that brings together different perspectives and skills to accomplish the organization's objectives. Under this arrangement, instead of designating national organizations or product divisions as profit centers, both are responsible for profitability: the national organization for country profits, and the product divisions for national and worldwide product profitability. Figure 17–4 illustrates the matrix organization.

This organization chart starts with a bottom section that represents a single-country responsibility level, moves to representing the area or international level, and finally moves to representing global responsibility from the product divisions to the corporate staff, to the chief executive at the top of the structure.

The key to successful matrix management is ensuring that managers are able to resolve conflicts and achieve integration of organization programs and plans. The mere adoption of a matrix design or structure does not create a matrix organization. The matrix organization requires a fundamental change in management behavior, organizational culture, and technical systems. In a matrix, influence is based on technical competence and interpersonal sensitivity, not on formal authority. In a matrix culture, managers recognize the absolute need to resolve issues and choices at the lowest possible level and do not rely upon higher authority.

As the 21st century approaches, an important task of top management is to eliminate a one-dimensional approach to decisions and encourage the development of multiple management perspectives and an organization that will sense and respond to a complex and fast-changing world. By thinking in terms of changing behavior rather than changing struc-

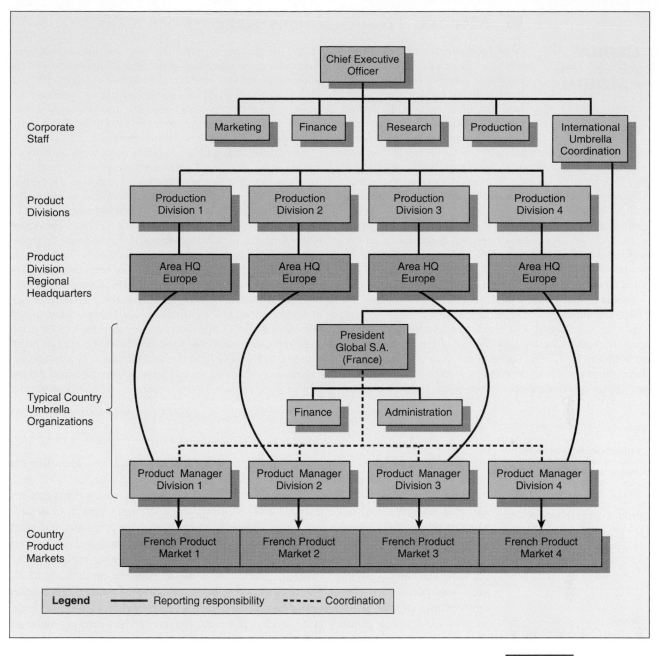

Corporate Staff

Chief Executive Officer

Marketing | Finance | Research | Production | International Umbrella Coordination

Product Divisions

Production Division 1 | Production Division 2 | Production Division 3 | Production Division 4

Product Division Regional Headquarters

Area HQ Europe | Area HQ Europe | Area HQ Europe | Area HQ Europe

Typical Country Umbrella Organizations

President Global S.A. (France)

Finance | Administration

Product Manager Division 1 | Product Manager Division 2 | Product Manager Division 3 | Product Manager Division 4

Country Product Markets

French Product Market 1 | French Product Market 2 | French Product Market 3 | French Product Market 4

Legend —— Reporting responsibility ----- Coordination

FIGURE 17–4

THE MATRIX STRUCTURE

tural design, company management can free itself from the limitations of the structural chart and focus instead on achieving the best possible results with available resources.

GLOBAL MARKETING MANAGEMENT CONTROL

Global marketing presents formidable problems to managers responsible for marketing control. Each national market is different from every other market. Distance and differences in language, custom, and practices create communication problems. As noted earlier in the chapter, in larger companies, the size of operations and number of country subsidiaries often result in the creation of an intermediate headquarters. This adds an organizational level to the control system. This section reviews global marketing control

*T*he increasing need for responsiveness to local markets has prompted many companies to transfer global headquarters of key business units outside the home country. Hyundai Electronics has transferred its personal computer headquarters from South Korea to California, while Hewlett-Packard moved its desktop PC headquarters from the United States to France. Germany's Siemens has moved its nuclear medicine products division to the United States. Du Pont has also transfered several units out of the United States; headquarters for the company's electronics unit is now in Japan and its Lycra and agricultural products businesses are now based in Switzerland. In 1995, RJR Nabisco consolidated its international tobacco business by merging two regional offices in Geneva, Switzerland, and eliminating duplicate jobs in Winston-Salem, North Carolina.

Such organizational changes can result in cost savings by eliminating duplication and also bring managers closer to important markets. Notes Jack Malloy, a senior vice president with Du Pont, "The name of the game is to get close to the customer and to understand the customer." At the same time, employees have the opportunity to gain a much-needed global perspective on their industry and line of business. Electronic communications technology helps executives cut down on travel and maintain control. For example, Philip J. Chauveau heads up AT&T's corded telephone business from an office near the French Riviera. He makes a weekly conference call to France, Thailand, and the United States to review sales figures with senior managers.

Sometimes headquarters transfers don't work as planned and must be reversed. Cadbury Schweppes PLC moved its beverage business headquarters from London to the United States in 1987, but moved it back to London in 1991. The original shift reflected the axiom "structure follows strategy." John Carson, the current president of Cadbury Beverages North America, recalled that the goal was to create "a strategic, coherent approach to the business and be in the backyard of where the big guys are." Cadbury had acquired stakes in Canada Dry and Dr Pepper/Seven-Up, aiming to become the world's leading non-cola producer with a strong presence in the $47 billion U.S. soft-drink market. However, the growth objectives of James P. Schadt, president of the U.S. division at the time, may have conflicted with those of corporate headquarters. A Cadbury official noted that the return to London "allows our chief executive to have his top managers around him" and cuts down on the amount of international travel.

Sources: "... And Other Ways to Peel the Onion," *The Economist* (Jan. 7, 1995), pp. 52–53.
"RJR Moving International Tobacco Unit to Europe," *The New York Times* (Oct. 14, 1995), p. A35.
Joann S. Lublin, "Firms Ship Unit Headquarters Abroad," *The Wall Street Journal* (Dec. 9, 1992), pp. B1, B8.
Judith Valente, "Cadbury Hopes Dr Pepper Will Satisfy Its Sweet Tooth," *The Wall Street Journal* (Nov. 26, 1993), p. B3.

practices, compares these practices with domestic marketing control, and identifies the major factors that influence the design of a global control system.

In the managerial literature, **control** is defined as the process by which managers ensure that resources are used effectively and efficiently in the accomplishment of organizational objectives. Control activities are directed toward marketing programs and other programs and projects initiated by the planning process. Data measures and evaluations generated by the control process are also a major input to the planning process. Thus, planning and control are intertwined and interdependent. The planning process can be divided into two related phases. *Strategic* planning is the selection of product and market opportunities and the commitment of human and financial resources to achieve these objectives. *Operational* planning is the process in which strategic product/market objectives and resource commitments to these objectives are translated into specific projects and programs. The relationship among strategic planning, operational planning, and control is illustrated in Figure 17–5.

For companies with global operations, marketing control presents additional challenges. The rate of environmental change in a global company is a dimension of each of the national markets in which it operates. In Chapters 2 through 6 of this book, we examined these environments; each is changing at a different rate and each exhibits unique characteristics. The multiplicity of national environments challenges the global marketing control system with much greater environmental diversity and, therefore, greater complexity in its control. Finally, global marketing can create special communications problems associated with the great distance between markets and headquarters and differences among managers in languages, customs, and practices.

When company management decides that it wants to develop a global strategy, it is essential that control of subsidiary operations be shifted from the subsidiary to the headquarters. The subsidiary will continue to make vital inputs into the strategic planning process; even so, such a shift in the organization's balance of power may result in strong resistance to change. In many companies, a tradition of subsidiary autonomy and self-sufficiency limits the influence of headquarters. To overcome such limits, headquarters must facilitate the shift in the perception of self-interest from subsidiary autonomy to global business performance. The conflicts that inevitably arise should be anticipated to the extent possible and the appropriate interventions made. In addition, headquarters can use both formal and informal approaches to maintain control.

FIGURE 17–5

RELATIONSHIPS OF STRATEGIC CONTROL AND PLANNING

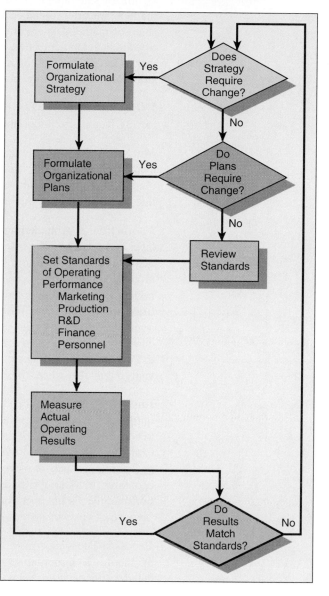

Formal Control Methods

Planning and budgeting are two basic tools of formal marketing control. Planning involves expressing desired sales and profit objectives and projected marketing program expenditures in unit and money terms. The formal document in which these objectives and expenditures are expressed is a budget. How is the budget established? In practice, many companies place heavy reliance upon two standards: last year's actual performance and some kind of industry average or historical norm. For global companies, a better approach is for headquarters to develop an estimate of the kind of growth that would be desirable and attainable in each national market. This estimate can be based upon company studies of national and industry growth patterns.

Control consists of measuring actual sales and expenditures. In the case of no variance (or if there is a favorable variance) between actual and budget, no action is usually taken. An unfavorable variance—lower unit sales than planned, for example—acts as a red flag that attracts the attention of line and staff executives at regional and international headquarters. They will investigate and attempt to determine the cause of the unfavorable variance and what might be done to improve performance.

Larger companies may have sufficient business volume to justify staff product specialists at corporate headquarters who follow the performance of products worldwide. Global marketing product managers have staff responsibility for their product(s) from introduction to termination. Because markets are at different stages of development, a company's products may be at different stages of the product life cycle in different geographic areas. A major responsibility of staff specialists is to ensure that lessons learned in world markets are applied to the management of products worldwide. The task of the global marketing product manager is to try to avoid making the same mistake twice and to capitalize on what the company has learned in world markets—in short, to ensure that all learning is applied wherever relevant. This includes transfers from markets that are at similar stages of development as well as transfers across stages of development.

Smaller companies focus on key products in key markets. Key products are those that are important to the company's sales, profit objectives, and competitive position. They are frequently new products that require close attention in their introductory stage in a market. If any budget variances develop with a key product, headquarters intervenes directly to learn about the nature of the problem and to assist local management in dealing with the problem.

Another principal measure of marketing performance is share of market. This is a valuable measure because it provides a comparison of company performance with that of other competitors in the market. Companies that do not obtain this measure, even if it is an estimate, are flying blind. In larger markets, data are reported for subsidiaries and, where significant sales are involved, on a product-by-product basis. Share-of-market data in larger markets are often obtained from independent market audit groups. In smaller markets, share-of-market data are often not available because the market is not large enough to justify the development of an independent commercial marketing audit service. In smaller markets, it is possible for a country manager or agent to hide a deteriorating market position or share of market behind absolute gains in sales and earnings.

INFLUENCES ON MARKETING BUDGETS • In preparing a budget or plan, the following factors are important:

Market Potential • How large is the potential market for the product being planned? In every domestic market, management must address this question in formulating a product plan. A company that introduces a product in more than one national market must answer this question for each market.

Competition • A marketing plan or budget must be prepared in light of the competitive level in the market. The more entrenched the competition, the more difficult it is to achieve market share and the more likely that a competitive reaction will occur to any move that promises significant success in the target market. Competitive moves are particularly important as a variable in international market planning because many companies are moving from strong competitive positions in their base markets to foreign markets where they have a minor position and must compete against entrenched companies. Domestic market standards and expectations of marketing performance are based on experience in markets where the company has a major position. These standards and expectations are simply not relevant to a market where the company is in a minor position trying to break into the market.

Impact of Substitute Products • One of the sources of competition for a product in a market is the frequent existence of substitute products. As a product is moved into markets at different stages of development, improbable substitute products often emerge. For example, in Colombia a major source of competition for manufactured boxes and other packaging products is woven bags and wood boxes made in the handicraft sector of the economy. Marketing officials of multinational companies in the packaging industry report that the garage operator producing a handmade product is very difficult competition because of costs of materials and labor in Colombia.

Process • The manner in which performance targets are communicated to subsidiary management is as important as the way in which they are derived. One of the most sophisticated methods used today is the so-called *indicative planning method*. Headquarters estimates of regional potential are disaggregated and communicated to subsidiary management as *guidance*. The subsidiaries are in no way bound by guidance. They are expected to produce their own plan, taking into account the headquarters guidance that is based on global data and their own data from the market, including a detailed review of customers, competitors, and other relevant market developments. This method produces excellent results because it combines a global perspective and estimate with specific country marketing plans that are developed from the objective to the program by the country management teams themselves.

Headquarters, in providing guidance, does not need to understand a market in depth. For example, it is not necessary that the headquarters of a manufacturer of electrical products know how to sell electric motors to a French consumer. What headquarters can do is gather data on the expected expansion in generating capacity in France and use experience tables drawn from world studies that indicate what each megawatt of additional generating capacity will mean in terms of the growth in demand in France for electric motors. The estimate of total market potential together with information on the competitiveness of the French subsidiary can be the basis for guidance in terms of expected sales and earnings in France. The guidance may not be accepted by the French subsidiary. If the indicative planning method is used properly, the subsidiary educates headquarters if its guidance is unrealistic. If headquarters does its job well, it will select an attainable but ambitious target. If subsidiary personnel doubt they can achieve the headquarters goal, discussion and headquarters involvement in the planning process will either lead to a plan that will achieve the guidance objective or a revision of the guidance by headquarters.

Informal Control Methods

In addition to budgeting, informal control methods play an important role. The main informal control method is the transfer of people from one market to another. When people are transferred, they take with them their experience in previous markets, which will normally include some standards for marketing performance. When investigating a new market that has lower standards than a previous market, the investigation will lead to revised standards or to discovery of why there is a difference. Another valuable informal control device is face-to-face contact between subsidiary staff and headquarters staff as well as contact among subsidiary staff. These contacts provide an opportunity for an exchange of information and judgments that can be a valuable input to the planning and control process. Annual meetings that bring together staff from a region of the world often result in informal inputs to the process of setting standards.

THE GLOBAL MARKETING AUDIT

A **global marketing audit** can be defined as a comprehensive, systematic examination of the marketing environment and company objectives, strategies, programs, policies, and activities. The audit can be company-wide in scope, or it can encompass a particular line of business or organizational subunit. The objective of periodic audits is to identify existing and potential problems and opportunities in a company's marketing performance and to recommend a plan of action for improving that performance. In other words, the global marketing audit is a tool for evaluating and improving a company's (or business unit's) global marketing operations.

A full marketing audit has two basic characteristics. First, it is formal and systematic. Asking questions at random as they occur to the questioner may result in useful insights, but this is not a marketing audit. The effectiveness of an audit normally increases to the extent that it involves a sequence of orderly diagnostic steps. Second, a marketing audit should be conducted periodically. Most companies in trouble are well on their way to disaster before the trouble is fully apparent. An audit can reveal such troubles while there is still time to deal with them. The audit may be broad, or it may be a narrowly focused assessment. A full marketing audit is comprehensive. It reviews the company's marketing environment, competition, objectives, strategies, organization, systems, procedures, and practices in every area of the marketing mix including product, pricing, distribution, communications, customer service, and research strategy and policy.

There are two types of audit: independent and internal. An independent marketing audit is conducted by someone who is free from influence of the organization being audited. The independent audit may or may not be objective: It is quite possible for company management to influence the consultant or professional firm that has been engaged. The company that wants a truly independent audit should understand the importance of objectivity.

A potential limitation of an independent marketing audit is the lack of understanding of the industry by the auditor. In many industries, there is no substitute for experience: An industry outsider may simply not see the subtle clues that an industry veteran would easily recognize. On the other hand, the independent auditor may see obvious indicators that the veteran may be unable to see.

An internal or self-audit may be quite valuable because it is conducted by marketers who understand the industry. On the other hand, it may lack the objectivity of an independent audit. Because the two types of audits have complementary strengths and limitations, both should be conducted periodically for the same scope and time period so that the results may be compared. The comparison may lead to insights on how to strengthen the performance of the marketing team.

Setting Objectives and Scope of the Audit

The first step of an audit is a meeting between company executives and the auditor to agree on objectives, coverage, depth, data sources, report format, and time period for the audit.

GATHERING DATA • One of the major tasks in conducting an audit is data collection. A detailed plan of interviews, secondary research, review of internal documents, and so forth is required. This effort usually involves an auditing team. A basic rule in data collection is not to rely solely on the opinion of people being audited for data. In auditing a sales organization, it is absolutely essential to talk to field sales personnel as well as sales management, and of course, no audit is complete without direct contact with customers and suppliers.

Creative auditing techniques should be encouraged and explored by the auditing team. For example, if an auditor wants to determine whether top executives are really in touch with the organization and all of its activities, the audior should speak with the mailroom personnel and find out if chief executives have ever visited the facility. If they have never been there, it speaks volumes about the management style and the degree of hands-on management in the organization. Similarly, if an organization has developed an elaborate marketing incentive program that is purported to generate results with customers, an audit should involve customer contact to find out if indeed the program is having any impact.

PREPARING AND PRESENTING THE REPORT • The next step after data collection and analysis is the preparation and presentation of the audit report. This presentation should restate the objectives and scope of the audit, present the main findings, and present major recommendations and conclusions as well as major headings for further study and investigation.

COMPONENTS OF THE MARKETING AUDIT • There are six major components of a full global marketing audit. They are:

1. The Marketing Environment Audit
2. The Marketing Strategy Audit
3. The Marketing Organization Audit
4. The Marketing Systems Audit
5. The Marketing Productivity Audit
6. The Marketing Function Audit

PROBLEMS, PITFALLS, AND POTENTIAL OF THE GLOBAL MARKETING AUDIT • The marketing audit presents a number of problems and pitfalls. Setting objectives can be a pitfall, if indeed the objectives are blind to a major problem. It is important for the auditor to be open to expand or shift objectives and priorities while in the conduct of the audit itself. Similarly, new data sources may appear during the course of an audit, and the auditor should be open to such sources. The approach of the auditor should be simultaneously systematic, following a predetermined outline, and perceptive and open to new directions and sources that appear in the course of the audit investigation.

REPORT PRESENTATION • One of the biggest problems in marketing auditing is that the executive who commissions the audit may have unrealistically high expectations about what the audit will do for the company. An audit is valuable even if it does not identify major new directions or offer cure-alls. It is important for all concerned to recognize that improvements at the margin are what truly make a difference between success and mediocrity. Experienced marketers don't look for dramatic revolutionary findings or cure-alls; rather, they recognize and accept that incremental improvement can lead to success in global marketing. Global marketers, even more than their domestic counterparts, need marketing audits to assess far-flung efforts in highly diverse environments. The global marketing audit should be at the top of the list of programs for strategic excellence and implementation excellence for the winning global company.

SUMMARY

To respond to the opportunities and threats in the global marketing environment a firm must have a global vision and strategy. By providing leadership, organizing a global effort, and establishing control procedures, a firm can exploit global opportunities. Leaders must have the vision in addition to the technical resources to build global competencies. In organizing the global marketing effort, a structure that enables the company to respond to relevant differences in international market environments and enables the company to extend valuable corporate knowledge is the goal. A balance between autonomy and integration must be established. Within this organization firms must establish core competencies to be competitive. The differences between global marketing control practices and purely domestic control must be recognized to be effective. Appropriate adjustments should be made to the way in which global planning and control practices are formulated and implemented. The global marketing audit can be an effective tool for improving global marketing performance.

DISCUSSION QUESTIONS

1. Are top executives of global companies likely to be home-country nationals?
2. In a company involved in global marketing, which activities should be centralized at headquarters and which should be delegated to national or regional subsidiaries?
3. Identify some of the factors that lead to the establishment of an international division as an organization increases its global business activities.
4. "A matrix structure integrates four competencies on a worldwide scale." Explain.
5. In preparing a marketing budget or plan, what are some factors managers should take into account?

BIBLIOGRAPHY

Books

Abrahams, Jeffrey. *The Mission Statement Book*. Berkeley, Calif.: Ten Speed Press, 1995.

Bartlett, Christopher A., and Sumantra Ghoshal. *Managing across Borders: The Transnational Solution*. Boston: Harvard Business School Press, 1989.

Davidow, William H., and Michael S. Malone. *The Virtual Corporation*. New York: Harper Business, 1993.

Gerlach, Michael L. *Alliance Capitalism: The Social Organization of Japanese Business*. Berkeley and Los Angeles: University of California Press, 1992.

Going Global: Succeeding in World Markets. Boston: Harvard Business School Press, 1991.

Hammer, Michael, and James Champy. *Reengineering the Corporation*. New York: HarperCollins Publishers, 1993.

Katzenbach, Jon R., and Douglas K. Smith. *The Wisdom of Teams: Creating the High Performance Organization*. Boston: Harvard Business School Press, 1993.

Nakatani, Iwao. *The Japanese Firm in Transition*. Tokyo: Asian Productivity Organization, 1988.

Robock, Stefan H., and Kenneth Simmonds. *International Business and Multinational Enterprises*. Homewood, Ill.: Irwin, 1989.

Snyder, Neil. *Vision, Values, and Courage*. New York: Free Press, 1995.

Stopford, John M., and Louis T. Wells. *Managing the Multinational Enterprise*. New York: Basic Books, 1972.

Tuller, Lawrence W. *Going Global: New Opportunities for Growing Companies to Compete in World Markets*. Homewood, Ill.: Business One Irwin, 1991.

Yip, George S. *Total Global Strategy*. Upper Saddle River, N.J.: Prentice Hall, 1992.

Articles

Beaver, William. "Levi's Is Leaving China." *Business Horizons 38*, no. 2 (March–April 1995), pp. 35–40.

Birkinshaw, Julian. "Encouraging Entrepreneurial Activity in Multinational Corporations." *Business Horizons 38*, no. 3 (May–June 1995), pp. 32–38.

Byrne, John A. "The Horizontal Corporation." *Business Week* (Dec. 20, 1993).

———. "The Virtual Corporation." *Business Week* (Feb. 8, 1993).

Cohen, Susan G. "Designing Effective Self-Managing Work Teams." *CEO Publication—University of Southern California*, pp. G93–99.

Florida, Richard. "The New Industrial Revolution." *Futures* (July–August 1991).

Halal, William E. "Global Strategic Management in a New World Order." *Business Horizons* 36, no. 6 (November–December 1993).

Hax, Arnoldo C. "Building the Firm of the Future." *Sloan Management Review* 30, no. 3 (Spring 1989), pp. 75–82.

Kashani, Kamran. "Beware the Pitfalls of Global Marketing." *Harvard Business Review* 67, no. 5 (September–October 1989), pp. 91–98.

Katzenbach, Jon R., and Douglas K. Smith. "The Discipline of Teams." *Harvard Business Review* 71, no. 2 (March–April 1993).

Krugman, Paul. "Competitiveness: A Dangerous Obsession." *Foreign Affairs* 73, no. 2 (March–April 1994), pp. 28–44.

Kuniyasu, Sakai. "The Feudal World of Japanese Manufacturing." *Harvard Business Review* 60, no. 6 (November–December 1990), pp. 38–49.

Maruca, Regina Fazio. "The Right Way to Go Global: An Interview with Whirlpool CEO David Whitwam." *Harvard Business Review* 72, no. 2 (March–April 1994), pp. 134–145.

Mintzberg, Henry. "The Effective Organization: Forces and Forms." *Sloan Management Review* (Winter 1991).

Morrison, Allen J., David A. Ricks, and Kendall Roth. "Globalization Versus Regionalization: Which Way for the Multinational?" *Organizational Dynamics* (Winter 1991), pp. 17–29.

O'Reilly, Anthony J. F. "Leading a Global Strategic Charge." *Journal of Business Strategy 12*, no. 4 (July–August 1991), pp. 10–13.

Peckter, Kerry. "The Foreigners Are Coming." *International Business* (September 1993), pp. 55–60.

Peters, Tom. "Time Obsessed Competition." *Management Review* (September 1990).

Prahalad, C. K., and Gary Hamel. "The Core Competence of the Corporation." *Harvard Business Review 68*, no. 3 (May–June 1990), pp. 79–93.

Quigley, Philip J. "The Coming of the Rabbiphant toward Decentralized Corporations." *Vital Speeches* (June 15, 1990).

Schill, Ronald L., and David N. McArthur. "Redefining the Strategic Competitive Unit: Towards a New Global Marketing Paradigm?" *International Marketing Review 9*, no. 3, pp. 5–24.

Thurow, Lester. "Who Owns the Twenty-First Century?" *Sloan Management Review 33*, no. 3 (Spring 1992), pp. 5–17.

Webster, Frederick E., Jr. "The Changing Role of Marketing in the Corporation." *Journal of Marketing* 56, no. 4, pp. 1–17.

VOLKSWAGEN AG: ROUGH ROAD FOR A WOULD-BE GLOBAL AUTOMAKER

Volkswagen AG enjoys the distinction of being the number one carmaker in Europe and the fourth largest in the world. The compact Golf is the best-selling car in Europe, where VW commands a 17 percent market share. Initial European demand for a new midsized model, the Passat, was so strong that there was an eight-month waiting list. The company can boast that its giant Wolfsburg plant is home to the most automated production line in the world, capable of completing 80 percent of a car's assembly by machine. VW ranks as the second-largest company in the new Germany; only Daimler-Benz is bigger. Outside Europe, Volkswagen has also achieved considerable success. In Mexico, for example, the company's share of the passenger car market is 40 percent. Volkswagen is also the number one Western auto manufacturer in China, where it commands 55 percent of the market.

Despite its stature in the global auto industry, VW's financial performance has been erratic in recent years. In 1992, vehicle sales reached an all-time high of 3.5 million units. In 1993, VW was in the red due to a 1.84 billion deutsche mark loss at its Sociedad Española de Automoviles de Turisme (SEAT) unit in Spain. In 1994, net income rebounded to 150 million marks on sales of 80 billion marks. As these results suggest, VW faces enormous challenges in the 1990s. The company has been forced to confront the fact that its costs are out of control. Much of the huge Wolfsburg assembly plant, parts of which date to 1938, is woefully inefficient in comparison to lean-production facilities operated by competitors like Toyota and Nissan. VW's German plants must run at 90 percent of production capacity for the company to break even; European rivals can break even at production levels of 70 percent. Meanwhile, Japanese production capacity in Europe is approaching 1 million vehicles. The advent of the Single Market brought an end to trade barriers and quotas; as a result, competition in Europe is heating up.

VW has also been plagued by headaches as plans to source cars in lower-wage countries such as Portugal and Mexico have gone awry. Despite efforts to train Mexican workers to be quality conscious, manufacturing problems with new Jetta and Golf models made in Puebla, Mexico, caused a severe shortage of vehicles in North America during the 1993 model year. The situation only worsened Volkswagen's fortunes in the United States, where the company was clinging to a market share of barely 1 percent.

These and other problems can be traced in part to former chairman Carl Hahn's attempts to implement his vision of VW as Europe's first global automaker. As described in an interview with *Harvard Business Review*, Hahn's strategic plan called for a decentralized structure composed of four autonomous divisions. In pursuit of this vision, Hahn invested tens of billions of dollars in Czechoslovakia's Skoda au-

toworks and SEAT in Spain. The Volkswagen, Audi, Skoda, and SEAT units each would have its own chief executive. As a whole, the company would be capable of turning out more than four million cars annually in low-cost plants located close to buyers. The company's R&D center, however, would continue to be in Germany. Highly automated plants in Germany would provide components such as transmissions, engines, and axles to assembly operations in other parts of the world.

In Spain, VW hoped to take advantage of labor rates 50 percent lower than in then West Germany and roughly on a par with those paid by Japanese companies with factories in Britain. Because labor makes up a larger share of production costs for subcompacts than for larger models, and because annual demand in Spain amounts to 500,000 cars, Spain was an attractive location for small-car production. Besides serving the domestic market, VW hoped to use Spain as a production source that would allow it to cut prices and boost margins on the Continent. Between 1986 and 1990, VW paid the Spanish government a total of $600 million in exchange for 100 percent ownership of SEAT. The company increased Spanish production from 350,000 to 500,000 vehicles; the popular Golf model represents about one-quarter of the output. VW invested $1.9 billion in a new plant in Martorell capable of producing 300,000 cars each year.

Hahn also earmarked $3 billion for a project in which he took a keen personal interest: investment in the former East Germany, where he was born. On October 3, 1990, German reunification added 16 million people to Volkswagen's home-country market virtually overnight. Under communism, the citizens of East Germany had a choice of basically one car: the notoriously low-quality Trabant. Hahn's strategy for a reunited Germany included building a new $1.9 billion factory that would employ 6,500 workers and produce a quarter of a million Golf and Polo models each year. The investment was justified in part by forecasts that East Germans would buy 750,000 cars each year; VW aimed to capture a third of the market, equal to its share in West Germany.

Unfortunately, Hahn's vision did not anticipate a global recession. First quarter 1993 sales in Germany were off by 25 percent; across Europe, sales declined by 17 percent. Needless to say, Hahn's multibillion-dollar investments weren't paying off. In January 1993, Hahn was succeeded as chairman by Ferdinand Piech, head of VW's Audi AG subsidiary and grandson of Ferdinand Porsche, designer of both the legendary cars that bear his name as well as the Volkswagen Beetle. Piech, who has been described as "steely eyed and intense," immediately declared a state of crisis in the company and began taking drastic actions; cost cutting topped the list. Piech planned to trim VW's worldwide employment of about 274,000, starting with 20,000 jobs in

1993. Despite sales increases in the Spanish market, SEAT was such a money loser that VW was forced to lay off several thousand workers. Unfortunately, Spain's rigid labor laws make layoffs so costly that Piech was forced to ask the Spanish government for a subsidy of more than 30 billion pesetas ($230 million) to pay for the restructuring.

Meanwhile, the new chairman was facing a different kind of challenge. With great fanfare, VW announced in March 1993 that it had succeeded in luring a new production chief away from General Motors. José Ignacio López de Arriortúa was expected to play a major role in cost cutting at VW, but he arrived amid accusations of industrial espionage. Specifically, GM alleged that López and several colleagues had left with secret information on product development and and other sensitive issues. The controversy did not stop López from doing what he had been hired to do. He broke long-term contracts with many of VW's suppliers and put new contracts up for bid; as a result, a higher percentage of components are now sourced outside of Germany. At VW's new General Pachecho plant in Buenos Aires, López has subcontracted various aspects of production to a dozen outside companies. VW workers will build a few crucial parts such as the chassis and powertrain; suppliers will be responsible for various other tasks such as assembling instrument panels. López anticipates a 50 percent reduction in costs.

Maryann Kellar, author of a book about VW, calls the Argentina experiment "something that has been talked about for years as the next great productivity and cost enhancement move by the industry." The strong leadership effort by VW's top executives is one reason why many observers remain bullish on the company, despite overall slow growth in the European auto market. Piech has pledged to slash the number of auto platforms VW offers in its various nameplates from 16 to 4 by 1998. Mexican production of a new version of the legendary Beetle is scheduled to begin in 1997. Piech also won concessions from IG Metall, the German autoworkers union. The union agreed to 2.5 percent annual pay raises and a pledge of job security through the end of 1997. In addition, the work shift for many assembly line workers has been reduced to five hours and 46 minutes—in essence, a four-day week. The union also agreed that paid hourly breaks would be cut to 2.5 minutes from 5 minutes. CFO Bruno Adelt estimated that all the agreed-upon changes would boost productivity 4 to 5 percent.

DISCUSSION QUESTIONS

1. Evaluate Volkswagen's goal of becoming Europe's first global automaker. What was the rationale behind the strategy?
2. What is the biggest challenge currently facing Volkswagen management?
3. VW's new version of the Beetle is expected to sell for $12,000. Evaluate its chances for market success.

Sources: David Woodruff, "VW Is Back—But for How Long?" *Business Week* (Mar. 4, 1996), pp. 66–67.
Jonathan Friedland, "VW Puts Suppliers on Production Line," *The Wall Street Journal* (Feb. 15, 1996), p. A11.
James Bennet, "Eurocars: On the Road Again," *The New York Times* (Aug. 20, 1995), Sec. 3, p. 1.
Steven Greenhouse, "Carl Hahn's East European Homecoming," *The New York Times* (Sept. 23, 1990), Sec. 3, pp. 1, 6.
Bernard Avishai, "A European Platform for Global Competition: An Interview with VW's Carl Hahn," *Harvard Business Review* (July–August 1991), pp. 103–113.
Ferdinand Protzman, "New Leadership for Volkswagen," *The New York Times* (Mar. 30, 1992), pp. C1, C2.
Timothy Aeppel, "VW Chief Declares a Crisis and Prescribes Bold Action," *The Wall Street Journal* (Apr. 1, 1993), p. B3.

KAZUO INAMORI: SPIRITUAL LEADERSHIP AT KYOCERA CORP.

With headquarters in Kyoto, Japan, Kyocera Corp. is a $3.2 billion company that develops and manufactures products and product components containing high-tech synthetic ceramics. Although Kyocera (the name is short for Kyoto Ceramics) is unknown to most people, it is *the* world leader in the production and sales of ceramic housings for computer microchips—with a 65 percent share of a $1.5 billion global market. The housings serve as a ceramic "cocoon" to protect the fragile chips during transit. Thirty percent of the firm's sales are in America, where its biggest customers are Intel and Advanced Micro Devices.

Like many other Japanese companies, Kyocera's competitive advantage stems from its ability to make high-quality products faster and cheaper than competitors. In other ways, however, Kyocera "breaks the mold" usually associated with "Japan Inc." The company is one of only a handful of companies in Japan with foreign directors on its board. Its San Diego–based subsidiary is mostly run by Americans. Rather than recruit graduates of prestigious schools, Kyocera prefers to hire its employees from second-tier technical schools. Company founder Kazuo Inamori believes his employees work harder because they are grateful to be given a chance to work for a top company. And while most Japanese companies strive for consensus and adherence to company norms, Inamori encourages creativity and independence within Kyocera.

In Kyocera's early days, Inamori often spent a great deal of time on the plant floor, personally overseeing the kilns and the mixing of raw materials. It was precisely this approach that helped it win its first crucial contract, with Texas Instruments. Making chip packages is both an art and a science; they must be baked for 18 hours at temperatures as high as 1,600 degrees Celsius. Recalls Mr. Inamori, "We got the contract because we were so good at mixing and baking, because the top people in the company were in front of the kilns all the time, and they could control the variances and keep the quality consistent, which is very hard in ceramics." Inamori earned the nickname "Mr. A.M." because he stayed at work until 3 or 4 in the morning.

Despite this close attention to production details, as Inamori explains in his recently published autobiography, the secret to Kyocera's growth is not its grasp of technology. Rather, it is the "spiritual energy of the workers." In an interview with *Business Japan*, Inamori said, "I feel that the strength of an enterprise is determined by the number of workers who really understand the spiritual qualities which enable a business to succeed. That is why I always endeavor to get my thoughts across to them. My time is often taken up in that connection rather than in dealing with technological problems concerning ceramic manufacture."

Inamori exhorts his employees to ever-higher levels of performance with "Inamorisms," which include such statements as "When a company is no longer on the offensive,

that company is already beginning to go downhill." Part of Inamori's directness and driven nature may be explained by the fact that, as a young man, his goal was to become a kamikazee pilot (the term used to describe Japanese volunteers who flew suicide attacks) pilot during World War II. However, because the war ended before he could fulfill his dream, he dedicated his life to staging offensive maneuvers in the marketing, rather than military, arena. Inamori believes that when a company is first founded, the employees have a burning drive for work and military-style discipline. When such organizations grow in size, however, top management's attention shifts away from the maintenance of worker energy. According to Inamori, the spiritual drive that was present when Kyocera was founded has not waned. This fact distinguishes Kyocera from most other organizations—Japanese, American, or otherwise.

Inamori implements that spiritual drive by striving for efficiency. He insists that all employees work at holding down costs and engage in high-quality work. For example, instead of following the electronics industry norm of using distributors for its products, Kyocera relies on a salaried sales force. The result: Kyocera spends 12 to 13 percent of revenues on general, administrative, and sales expenses compared to the 20 percent that is normal for other companies. There has never been a layoff at Kyocera's U.S. plant in San Diego; in return, the company enjoys high employee loyalty. These are just a few of the reasons why Kyocera is such a tough competitor.

Kyocera's early opportunities were tied to the fledgling semiconductor industry in the United States; ceramic components play a significant role in high-technology products because they are heat-resistant and do not conduct electricity. The road to Kyocera's domination of the chip package market began in the mid-1960s, when it bid successfully against a West German firm for a Texas Instruments contract to build ceramic insulating rods for silicon transistors. Soon thereafter, Fairchild Semiconductor (the forerunner to Intel) drafted technically demanding designs for housings to protect the chips it manufactured. However, Fairchild was unable to find any U.S. company willing to build the housings for a reasonable price, even though Coors Electronic Packaging was the world leader in ceramic semiconductor package manufacturing at the time. Fairchild turned to Kyocera, which was anxious to expand into electronic applications for its ceramic business. Asa Jonishi, Kyocera's first U.S. salesman, worked hard for the account; not only was Kyocera willing to take on the Fairchild project for a low price, it delivered its first order against a seemingly impossible deadline of three months.

Kyocera's success in the U.S. market can also be attributed to its willingness to custom tailor chip housings to each customer's needs. Among California's Silicon Valley chipmakers, Kyocera has become legendary for its service.

Kyocera backs up its $100 million-per-year R&D expenditures with sales forces in both the United States—50 direct salespersons at 12 direct sales offices—and Japan that pay heed to Inamori's unwavering emphasis on quality and customer service. Early on, Kyocera earned a reputation for answering customer questions overnight, while U.S. suppliers often took weeks to respond. Employees would work around the clock to satisfy customer requests for samples.

Today, Kyocera is targeting new applications for ceramics, including replacements for human body parts, automobile engines, and knives. Despite its past successes, Kyocera faces new challenges in the future. New Japanese competitors are starting to nibble at its market share. Plastic packaging has replaced ceramics for some types of integrated circuits. Kyocera's tight-fisted financial management system has faced the challenge of a strong yen. Although profits and sales dropped in 1993, Kyocera's numbers were stronger than those of other Japanese companies in the electronics industry. The company has diversified, both internally and externally. It has manufactured laptop computers for Radio Shack and VCRs for Hitachi. The company has made several acquisitions, including Elco Corp., a U.S. manufacturer of electrical connectors, and Yashica Corp., a Japanese camera company. Although most of its acquisitions are profitable, some industry observers believe the diversification effort has lacked focus.

DISCUSSION QUESTIONS

1. What factors have helped Kyocera achieve success at serving organizational markets?
2. How is Kyocera different from the "typical" Japanese company?
3. How important is Inamori's "spiritual drive" to Kyocera's success? What will happen to the company's culture after Inamori retires?

Sources: Kazuo Inamori, *A Passion for Success: Practical, Inspiration, and Spiritual Insight from Japan's Leading Entrepreneur* (New York: McGraw-Hill, 1995).
George Taninecz, "Kazuo Inamori: 'Respect the Divine and Love People,' " *Industry Week* (June 5, 1995), pp. 47–51.
"Kyocera's Secrets: Flexibility, Spirituality and Teamwork," *Business Japan* (January 1987), pp. 31–32.
Gene Bylinsky, "The Hottest High-Tech Company in Japan," *Fortune* (Jan. 1, 1990), pp. 83+.
"Cult of Personality," *Business Month* (August 1990), pp. 42–44.
David Halberstam, "Coming In from the Cold War," *The Washington Monthly* (January–February 1991), pp. 32–34.
Jacob M. Schlesinger, "Kyocera Plays an Ambivalent Role in U.S. Weaponry," *The Wall Street Journal* (Feb. 5, 1991), p. A15.
Jonathan Friedland, "Samurai Sorcerer," *Far Eastern Economic Review* (June 3, 1993), pp. 60–65.

The Future of Global Marketing

The world economy has undergone revolutionary changes during the past 50 years. Perhaps the greatest and most profound change is the emergence of global markets and global competitors that have steadily displaced local ones. The changes continue. Within the past decade, there have been four major changes:

- The poor countries of the world, which have always been poor, are getting rich.
- The world economy is the dominant economic unit. The macroeconomics of the nation-state no longer control economic outcomes in countries, and even the large superpower countries like the United States can no longer dictate to poorer countries how they should behave.
- The old trade-cycle model, which said that as a product matures, the location of production must shift to low-wage countries, has been repealed.
- The 75-year "contest" between capitalism and socialism is over. The clear success of the capitalist system over the communist centrally controlled model has led to the collapse of communism as a model for the organization of economic activity and as an ideology.

The first change is that poor countries are getting rich! The emergence of the newly rich countries from among the ranks of the former less-developed group breaks the long monopoly of Western Europe, the United States and Canada, and Japan on the "rich nation" status. These countries are proving that it is not necessary to be European or Japanese to be rich. Countries like Singapore and Hong Kong are already high-income countries; East Asia in particular is home to many countries that are growing at annual rates of 7 percent or higher. A 7 percent real growth rate will double real income in a decade. The emerging rich countries include smaller countries like South Korea as well as the largest countries in the world, China and India. For the first time in the history of the world, there is the very real likelihood of a much broader *global* prosperity.

The second major change is the emergence of the world economy as the dominant economic unit. Companies and countries that recognize this fact have the greatest chance of success. The United States is still a superpower, but it is no longer in a position to tell other successful nations how to behave in matters of internal affairs. As the poor countries grow richer, they assume that their values are responsible for their success, and they do not listen to lectures from their less-successful former world leaders. Wealth creates the foundation for political and military power and the basis for an assumption of moral superiority. The attitude of politicans and businesspeople from rich countries and from countries that are successfully developing is, "if we are rich or fast growing we must be doing something right."

Changes in global competition are bringing countries into more direct confrontation with their main economic rivals than was the case in the past. Yesterday's global forces were founded on exports of products and services not available to competing nations. In the past, countries would export agricultural products others could not grow, raw materials others didn't have, and high-tech products others could not build. Today, companies in the same industries in different countries and regions compete ferociously with each other in manufactured goods, agricultural products, natural resources, and services.

There are the new economic realities. The rich are getting richer, and the poor are getting richer, and the world is becoming more and more integrated. This means new opportunities and new challenges for companies and countries.

CAREERS IN GLOBAL MARKETING

There has never been a better time to prepare for a career in global marketing. Now that you are completing this book, the authors want to offer a few suggestions on how to jump-start your global marketing career.

First, remember that times have changed. Until very recently, one sure way to put your career at risk in many companies (especially U.S. companies) was to go overseas. There was nothing wrong with being overseas per se, but the problem for careers in U.S. companies was that management did not recognize the value of global experience and turned to executives who were close at hand when making promotions. "Out of sight, out of mind" seemed to be the operative phrase.

Today this has changed. Global experience counts. Only the truly lost do not recognize that we are in a global market with global competition, and those with global experience have a definite advantage. Top U.S. executives with international experience include Samir F. Gibara, president and CEO of Goodyear Tire & Rubber; Michael Hawley, president and COO of Gillette; Harry Bowman, chairman, president, and CEO of Outboard Marine; Lucio A. Noto, chairman and CEO of Mobil; and Raymond G. Viault, vice chairman of General Mills.[1]

Ray Viault was a vice president of General Foods in charge of the Maxwell House Coffee Division. When Philip Morris acquired General Foods, it kept Viault on as president of the Maxwell House division. Later, when Philip Morris acquired Jacob Suchard, the Zurich-based chocolate and coffee company, it chose Viault as the new CEO of the acquired company. Viault was able to take his grounding in the U.S. coffee market to Europe and did an outstanding job of leading the global marketing effort of Jacob Suchard.

How do you establish a career in global marketing? There are two broad paths:

1. Get directly into a job outside your home country or into a multicountry headquarters job in a global company.

[1]Joann S. Lublin, "An Overseas Stint Can Be a Ticket to the Top," *The Wall Street Journal* (Jan. 29, 1996), p. B1.

■ Is Competitiveness a Dangerous Obsession?

OPEN TO DISCUSSION

*S*tanford University economist Paul Krugman wants every student of international trade to reflect carefully on the following proposition:

Today, America is part of a truly global economy. To maintain our standard of living, America must learn to compete in an ever tougher world marketplace. That's why high productivity and product quality have become essential. We can only be competitive in the new global economy if we forge a new partnership between government and business.

To many, this proposition will sound reasonable. In style and substance, it echoes assertions being made in the 1990s by such well-known figures as economist Lester Thurow, presidential advisor Ira Magaziner, and U.S. Secretary of Labor Robert Reich. Krugman, however, says that the proposition is "baloney." In his words, it represents "the rhetoric of competitiveness," in which the United States is likened to a large corporation like GM. According to the rhetoric of competitiveness, America—like GM—is suffering because of global competition, and the nation's standard of living has stagnated as a result.

In numerous articles and a recent book, Krugman offers a painstaking analysis of what he believes to be a mistakenly held proposition. In sorting out the salient issues, Krugman's reasoning flies in the face of positions held by Thurow, Magaziner, Reich, and others; Krugman calls these individuals "strategic traders" and "policy entrepreneurs." Surprisingly, Krugman's critiques are not based on partisan politics; he himself is a liberal. His complaint is that fundamental economic concepts—especially comparative advantage—are being misinterpreted, misapplied, or ignored altogether in the name of public policy.

First, Krugman disputes the assertion that America is "part of a truly global economy." The reason: Approximately 90 percent of the goods and services produced in the United States are for domestic consumption; only 10 percent are destined for world markets. Indeed, 70 percent of the U.S. economy is based on services, and services are less likely than manufactured products to be marketed abroad. Thus, despite all the talk about "global integration," the "global economy" is not as interconnected as people might think.

Next, Krugman attacks the notion that America itself "competes in the global marketplace." Krugman argues that Japan, the United States, and other nations of the world are not in competition with each other in the sense that, say, Coca-Cola and PepsiCo or Reebok and Nike are. Few Coca-Cola employees buy Pepsi products, and vice versa. Thus a company is not like a nation: No company sells 90 percent of its output to its own employees. In the "cola wars," PepsiCo can only win by taking customers away from Coca-Cola. The same cannot be said of nations, Krugman asserts. The world's major industrial nations can be successful without causing harm to each other because they are not just competitors; trading partners also represent export markets and sources of imports. In other words, every potential problem also presents opportunities, and those opportunities may outweigh the problems.

Third, Krugman objects to linking the issue of higher U.S. productivity with international trade. Contrary to the message coming out of Washington, the fact that productivity improvement rates in other nations exceed those in the United States does not make the United States less competitive or lessen Americans' standard of living. Krugman asserts quite simply that America needs to be productive to produce more. That may sound tautologous, but it is a plain and simple economic truth that would be valid even if the United States did not engage in international trade. In his writings, Krugman reviews the basics of comparative advantage to demonstrate that, in fact, no special problems are created for a country that is less productive than its trading partners.

Finally, Krugman argues that the issues relating to the "rhetoric of competitiveness" are not simply academic ones. If the strategic traders' "rhetoric of competitiveness" message is heeded, the results could have far-reaching, undesirable consequences. First, it could lead to wasteful government spending in a misguided effort to enhance competitiveness. In the interest of competitiveness, government support might be directed at manufacturing. Yet it is the service sector, which is not a major part of international trade, where productivity is lagging. Second, it could lead to protectionism and trade wars. Finally, it could lead to poor public policy decisions in a variety of areas—health care, for example—that are unrelated to trade.

Sources: Paul Krugman, "A Country Is Not a Company," *Harvard Business Review 74*, no. 1 (January–February 1996), pp. 40+.

Paul Krugman, "Competitiveness: A Dangerous Obsession," *Foreign Affairs* (March–April 1994), pp. 28–44.

Paul Krugman, "Competitiveness: Does It Matter?" *Fortune* (Mar. 7, 1994), pp. 109+.

Paul Krugman, *Peddling Prosperity: Economic Sense and Nonsense in the Age of Diminished Expectations* (New York: W.W. Norton & Co., 1994).

2. Get experience in a company in an industry which prepares you for promotion to a job with multicountry responsibility or to an assignment outside your home country.

For many, the second choice is better than the first. There is no substitute for solid experience in a company in an industry. Your best opportunity to get solid experience may be in your home country. You speak the language, understand the culture, and are trained in business and marketing. You are ready to learn.

An option is to get this basic experience in another country. The advantage of this move is that you will learn a new culture and language and broaden your international experience while you learn about a company and an industry.

APPENDIX I

JAPANESE "LEAN" AUTO PRODUCTION[2]

In the automobile industry, the differences between the old "craft" production processes and those of mass production provide a good case study in the use of the value chain and the value system to obtain competitive advantage. Figure 1 provides dramatic evidence of the productivity differences between the two systems. The mass producers gained their substantial advantage by changing their value chain in such a way that each worker was able to do far more work each day than the craft producers. They did this, for the most part, by installing the moving assembly line. Simple as this change might appear, it did require the originators to conceive of the production process in a totally different way than it had been up to that time, and to rearrange the organization of people, equipment, and supplies to accommodate the new concept.

By rearranging their value chain activities, the mass producers were able to achieve reductions in effort ranging from 62 percent to 88 percent over the craft producers. These productivity improvements provided an obvious competitive advantage.

LEAN PRODUCTION

The advantage of the mass producers lasted until the Japanese auto companies further revised the value chain and created "lean production," thereby gaining for themselves the kinds of dramatic competitive advantages that mass producers gained over craft producers. Figure 2 displays the productivity differences between a mass production operation (GM Framingham) and a lean production operation (Toyota Takaoka). In terms of order of magnitude, the differences are similar to those that characterized the advantages of mass production over craft production.

From Figure 2 we see that the lean producer, Toyota, is using about 50 percent of the effort of the mass producer, GM, to assemble a car, and that even with the reduced assembly time, the lean producer's car has two-thirds less defects than that of the mass producer. The lean producer is also using about 40 percent less factory space and maintaining only a fraction of the inventory stored by the mass producer. Again the competitive advantages are obvious. Whether the strategy is focused on differentiation or low cost, the lean producer has the advantage.

In order to achieve these gains, the lean producer made changes to operations within the auto companies themselves, to operations within supplier firms and the interfaces between assemblers and suppliers, and to the interfaces with distributors and dealers. Individual firm value chains were modified and interfaces between firms were optimized to create an extremely effective and efficient value system.

FIGURE 1 · CRAFT VS. MASS PRODUCTION, 1913 VS. 1914

Minutes of Effort to Assemble	Late Craft Production, Fall 1913	Mass Production, Spring 1914	Percent Reduction in Effort
Engine	594	226	62
Magneto	20	5	75
Axle	150	26.5	83
Major components into a complete vehicle	750	93	88

Source: James P. Womack, Daniel T. Jones, and Daniel Roos, *The Machine that Changed the World: The Story of Lean Production* (New York: Harper Collins, 1990), p. 29.

[2]This appendix is adapted from the following sources: James P. Womack, Daniel T. Jones, and Daniel Roos, *The Machine That Changed the World: The Story of Lean Production* (New York: HarperCollins, 1990); Ranganath Nayak and John M. Ketteringham, *Breakthroughs!* (San Diego, Calif.: Pfeiffer & Company), 1994, Chapter 9; Michael Williams, "Back to the Past: Some Planets Tear Out Long Assembly Lines Switch to Craft Work," *The Wall Street Journal* (Oct. 24, 1994), pp. A1, A4.

FIGURE 2 **GM FRAMINGHAM ASSEMBLY PLANT VS. TOYOTA TAKAOKA ASSEMBLY PLANT, 1986**

	GM Framingham	Toyota Takaoka
Gross assembly hours per car	40.7	18.0
Adjusted assembly hours per car	31	16
Assembly defects per 100 cars	130	45
Assembly space per car (sq. ft.)	8.1	4.8
Average inventories of parts	2 weeks	2 hours

Source: James P. Womack, Daniel T. Jones, and Daniel Roos, *The Machine that Changed the World: The Story of Lean Production* (New York: Harper Collins, 1990), p. 81.

ASSEMBLER VALUE CHAINS

Within the lean production firms, mechanization, and particularly flexible mechanization, is increased. Workers receive considerable training to enable them to perform any job in their section of the assembly line, or area of the plant, and they are assigned to teams in which all members must be able to perform the functions of all other team members. Workers are also empowered to make suggestions and to take actions aimed at improving quality and productivity. In terms of quality control, every flaw is isolated and examined in detail to determine the "ultimate cause," and then corrected forever.

In contrast to the lean producers, the U.S. mass producers maintained operations that had greater direct labor content, less mechanization, and much less flexible mechanization. They also divided their employees into a large number of discrete specialties with no overlap. Employee initiative and teamwork was not encouraged. Quality control was expressed as an acceptable number of defects per vehicle. The advantages enjoyed by the lean producers can be seen in Figure 3.

Even when the comparisons are based on industry averages, the Japanese lean producers continue to enjoy substantial productivity and quality advantages. Again, these advantages put the lean producers in better position to exploit low cost or differentiation strategies. They are getting better productivity out of their workers and machines, and they are making better use of their factory floor space. (It should be noted that the large space per vehicle usage by the Japanese in North America is largely a function of the fact that they are using a number of old, inefficient, American plants for their operations, rather than building new

ones.) The relatively small size of the repair area reflects the higher quality of their products. Remember that repair area is used solely to repair defects that were created on the assembly line.

The "Suggestions Per Employee" section of Figure 3 provides some insight into why lean producers outperform mass producers. They invest a great deal more in the training of their workers. They rotate all workers through all jobs for which their teams are responsible. They encourage all workers to make suggestions, and they act on those suggestions. These changes to the value chain create major improvements in the value of their products.

DOWNSTREAM VALUE CHAINS

The differences between lean producers and U.S. mass producers in the way they deal with their respective dealers, distributors, and customers is as dramatic as those in the way they deal with their suppliers. U.S. mass producers follow the basic industry model and maintain an "arm's-length" relationship with dealers that is often characterized by a lack of cooperation and even open hostility. There is often no sharing of information because there is no incentive to do so. The manufacturer is often trying to force on the dealer models the dealer knows will not sell. The dealer, in turn, is often trying to pressure the customer into buying models the customer does not want. All parties are trying to keep information about what they really want from the others. This does nothing to ensure that the industry is responsive to market needs.

The problem starts with the market research, which is often

FIGURE 3 **SELECTED ASSEMBLY PLANT CHARACTERISTICS, VOLUME PRODUCERS**

	Japanese Firms in Japan	Japanese Firms in North America	U.S. Firms in North America	All Europe
Productivity (hours/vehicle)	16.8	21.2	25.1	36.2
Defects/100 vehicles	60.0	65.0	82.3	97.0
Suggestions/employee	61.1	1.4	.4	.4
Painting automation (% of direct steps)	54.6	40.7	33.6	38.2

Source: Adapted from James P. Womack, Daniel T. Jones, and Daniel Roos, *The Machine that Changed the World: The Story of Lean Production* (New York: HarperCollins, 1990), p. 92.

in error. It is compounded by the fact that the marketing divisions have little feedback from dealers regarding real customer desires. It continues to worsen when the product planning divisions make changes to the models without consulting the marketing divisions or the dealers. This process invariably results in the production of models that are very unpopular and almost impossible to sell. The manufacturer uses various schemes to force the dealers to accept the unpopular models, like making the dealers accept one unpopular model for every five popular models it orders. The dealer then has the problem of convincing customers that they want the unpopular models.

Within the mass assembler's value chain, the linkage between the marketing elements and the product planners is broken. The external linkage between the sales divisions and the dealers is also broken. The production process portion of the value chain is also broken in that it relies on the production of thousands of unsold models which then sit on dealer lots, at enormous cost, while the dealer works to find customers.

Within the dealerships there are even more problems. The relationship between the salesperson and the customer is based on sparring and trying to outsmart each other on price. It is very much like the relationship between the dealer and the manufacturer. Each is withholding information from the other in the hope of outsmarting the other. Salespeople are not real professionals. Most do not look at their positions as careers, but rather, they view their jobs as short-term, make-as-much-as-you-can-quickly jobs. They frequently know very little about the products they are selling. They do not investigate the customer's real needs and try to find the best product to satisfy those needs. Rather, they provide only as much information as is needed to close the deal. Once the deal is closed, the salesperson has virtually no further contact with the customer. There is no attempt to optimize the linkage between dealers and manufacturers or the linkage between dealers and customers.

The contrast with the lean producer is again striking. In Japan, the dealer's employees are true product specialists. They know their products and deal with all aspects of the product, including financing, service, maintenance, insurance, registration and inspection, and delivery. A customer deals with one person in the dealership and that person takes care of everything from the initial contact through eventual trade-in and replacement and all the problems in between. Dealer representatives are included on the manufacturer's product development teams and provide continuous input regarding customer desires. The linkages between dealers, marketing divisions, and product development teams are totally optimized.

The stress of large inventories of finished cars is also absent. A car is not built until there is a customer order for it. Each dealer has only a stock of models for the customer to look at. Once the customer has decided on the car he or she wants, the order is sent to the factory, and in a matter of a couple of weeks the car is delivered, by the salesperson, to the customer's house.

Once a Japanese dealer gets a customer, it is absolutely determined to hang on to that customer for life. It is also determined to acquire all of the customer's family members as customers. A joke among the Japanese says that the only way a person can escape from the salesperson who sold one a car is to leave the country. Japanese dealers maintain extensive databases on actual and potential customers. These databases deal with demographic data and preference data. Customers are encouraged to help keep the information in the database current, and they cooperate in this. This elaborate store of data becomes an integral part of the market research effort and helps ensure that products match customer desires.

The fact that there are no inventories of unpopular models and that every car is custom-ordered for each customer, and the fact that the dealer has elaborate data on the needs and desires of its customers change the whole nature of the interaction between the customer and the dealer. The customer literally builds the car he or she wants and can afford. There is no need to try to outsmart each other.

The differences between the U.S. mass producers and the Japanese lean producers reflect their fundamental differences in business objectives. The U.S. producers focus on short-term income and return on investment. Today's sale is a discrete event that is not connected to upstream activities in the value chain and has no value in tomorrow's activities. Efforts are made to reduce the cost of the sales activities. The Japanese see the process in terms of a long-term perspective. There are two major goals of the sales process. The first is to maximize the income stream from each customer over time. The second is to use the linkage with the production processes to reduce production and inventory costs and to maximize quality, and therefore differentiation.

Glossary

adopter categories. The categories of buyers in the adoption process developed by Everett Rogers at different stages of the "adoption" or product life cycle. The buyer or adoptor categories are: innovators, early adopters, early majority, late majority, and laggards. These buyer categories correspond to the introduction, growth, maturity, and decline stages of the product life cycle.

adoption process. A model developed by Everett Rogers which describes the "adoption" or purchase decision process. The stages consist of awareness, interest, evaluation, trial, and adoption.

analogy. A type of market analysis that involves stating a partial resemblance between two or more markets.

Andean Group. A five-country common market that includes Bolivia, Colombia, Ecuador, Peru, and Venezuela.

Association of Southeast Asian Nations (ASEAN). A cooperation group including Brunei, Indonesia, Malaysia, the Philippines, Singapore, Thailand, and Vietnam.

BSB's Global Scan. A market segmentation study of 18 Triad countries conducted by Backer Spielvogel & Bates Worldwide.

back translation. A technique used to improve the comprehension of a survey instrument that is translated into different languages.

balance of payments. The record of all economic transactions between the residents of a country and the rest of the world.

barriers to entry. Obstacles that hinder or prevent a company from entering an industry.

barter. The least complex and oldest form of bilateral, nonmonetized countertrade consisting of a direct exchange of goods or services between two parties.

basket case. A country with economic, social, and political problems that are so serious as to make the country unattractive for investment and operations.

call option. The right to buy a specified number of foreign currency units at a fixed price, up to the option's expiration date.

capital account. The part of the balance of payments that shows all long-term direct investment, portfolio investment, and other short- and long-term capital flows.

Caribbean Community and Common Market (CARICOM). A common market whose 13 members include Antigua and Barbuda, the Bahamas, Barbados, Belize, Dominica, Grenada, Guyana, Jamaica, Montserrat, St. Kitts and Nevis, St. Lucia, St. Vincent and the Grenadines, and Trinidad and Tobago.

Central American Common Market (CACM). A common market encompassing Costa Rica, El Salvador, Guatemala, Honduras, and Nicaragua.

Central European Free Trade Association (CEFTA). A cooperation agreement between Czechoslovakia, Hungary, and Poland.

civil-law country. A country in which the legal system is based on the codes that are considered to be the completely comprehensive, all-inclusive source of authority by reference to which disputes can be settled.

command allocation economic system. An economic system in which the state planners have broad powers to decide which products will be manufactured and how to make them.

common-law country. A country in which the legal system relies on past judicial decisions, or cases, to resolve disputes.

common market. A group of countries with economic cooperation that eliminates internal barriers to trade, establishes common external barriers, and allows free movement of factors of production.

comparative analysis. Comparisons of market potential and marketing performance in different country markets at the same point in time.

compensation trading (buyback). A countertrade deal typically involving sale of plant equipment or technology licensing in which the seller or licensor agrees to take payment in the form of the products produced using the equipment or technology for a specified number of years.

competitive advantage. The situation when there is a match between a firm's distinctive competencies and the factors critical for success within its industry.

concentrated global marketing. A strategy that calls for devising a marketing mix to reach a single segment of the global market.

counterpurchase. A monetized countertrade deal in which the seller agrees to purchase products of equivalent value which it must then sell in order to realize revenue from the original deal.

countertrade. An export transaction in which a sale results in product flowing in one direction to a buyer, and a separate stream of products and services, often flowing in the opposite direction.

current account. The part of the balance of payments that shows recurring trade in merchandise and service, private gifts, and public aid transactions between countries.

customs union. A group of countries with economic cooperation that eliminates internal barriers to trade and establishes common external tariffs (CET).

DMBB's Euroconsumer Study. A segmentation study of 15 European countries conducted by D'arcy Massius Benton & Bowles.

depreciation. The accounting term meaning the same thing as devaluation.

devaluation. The decline in value of a currency relative to other currencies.

differentiated global market. A strategy that calls for targeting two or more distinct market segments with multiple marketing mix offerings.

dumping. The sale of a product in an export market at a price lower than that normally charged in the domestic market or country of origin.

Economic Community of West African States (ECOWAS). A free trade area that includes Benin, Burkina Faso, Cape Verde, The Gambia, Ghana, Guinea, Guinea-Bissau, Ivory Coast, Liberia, Mali, Mauritania, Niger, Nigeria, Senegal, Sierra Leone, and Togo.

economic (operating) exposure. The degree to which exchange rates affect a company's market value as measured by its stock price.

economic union. A group of countries with economic cooperation that eliminates internal tariff barriers, establishes common external barriers, allows the free flow of factors of production, and coordinates and harmonizes economic and social policy within the union.

economies of scale. The decline in per-unit product costs as the absolute volume of production per period increases.

environmental sensitivity. The extent to which products must be adapted to the culture-specific needs of different national markets.

ethnocentric orientation. The view

that one's home country is superior to the rest of the world.

European Economic Area (EEA). A free trade area encompassing the EU nations and Iceland, Liechtenstein, and Norway.

European Union (EU). An 5-nation economic union consisting of Austria, Belgium, Denmark, Finland, France, Germany, Greece, Ireland, Italy, Luxembourg, Portugal, Spain, Sweden, and the United Kingdom.

existing market. A market in which customer needs are already being served.

export marketing. Exporting using the product offered in the home market as a starting point and modifying it as needed to meet the preferences of international target markets.

export selling. Exporting without tailoring the product, the price, or the promotional material to suit individual country requirements.

export subsidies. Direct or indirect financial contributions that benefit producers and allow them to compete more effectively in world markets.

Foreign Corrupt Practices Act (FCPA). A law that makes it illegal for U.S. corporations to bribe an official of a foreign government or political party to obtain or retain business.

forward market. A mechanism for buying and selling currencies at a preset price for future delivery.

free trade area. A group of countries with economic cooperation that abolishes all internal barriers to trade but allows member countries to maintain independent trade policies vis-à-vis other countries.

General Agreement on Tariffs and Trade (GATT). A treaty and an organization to promote international trade by lowering tariffs and removing other barriers. The GATT organization was replaced by the World Trade Organization (WTO) in 1995.

generic strategies. Michael Porter's model of four routes to competitive advantage, including cost leadership, product differentiation, cost focus, and focused differentiation.

geocentric orientation. The view that the entire world is a potential market; the company seeks to develop integrated world market strategies.

global advertising. Designing an ad for

multiple country markets using the same advertising appeals, messages, art, copy, photographs, stories, and video segments.

global marketing. The process of focusing an organization's resources on global market opportunities and threats.

gray marketing. The distribution of trademarked products in a country by unauthorized persons.

Gulf Cooperation Council (GCC). A six-nation organization whose members include Bahrain, Kuwait, Oman, Qatar, Saudi Arabia, and the United Arab Emirates.

hedging. The use of various techniques to reduce exchange rate exposure by ensuring that the loss of one currency position is offset by a corresponding gain in some other currency.

high-context culture. A culture in which messages and knowledge are more implicit and in which less information is contained in the verbal part of a message and more information resides in the context of communication.

high-income country. A country with GNP per capita above $14,000.

hypercompetition. A term used by Richard D'Aveni to describe a dynamic competitive world in which no action or advantage can be sustained for long.

incipient market. A market that will emerge if a particular economic, political, or socio-cultural trend continues.

investigation. A limited and informal type of search.

joint venture. A market entry strategy in which partners share ownership of a commercial entity.

latent market. An undiscovered market segment in which demand for a product would materialize if an appropriate product were offered.

letter of credit (L/C). A payment method in export/import in which a bank substitutes its creditworthiness for that of the buyer.

licensing. A contractual arrangement whereby one company (the licensor) makes an asset available to another company (the licensee) in exchange for royalties or some other form of compensation.

low-context culture. A culture in which messages and knowledge are more explicit and words carry most of the information in communication.

lower-middle-income country. A

country with GNP per capita of more than $500 and less than $2,500.

low-income country. a country with GNP per capita of less than $500.

market allocation economic system. An economic system in which free consumer choice determines how resources are allocated.

market-based transfer price. A transfer price derived from the price required to be competitive in the international market.

market holding. A pricing strategy adopted by companies that want to maintain their share of the market by adjusting prices as demanded by competitive or economic considerations.

market segmentation. The process of identifying and categorizing groups of customers and countries according to common characteristics.

market skimming. A pricing strategy by which a company attempts to reach a market segment willing to pay a premium price for a product.

marketing information system. A system (automated or otherwise) that provides a continuous flow of information about company activities.

Mercosur. A common market encompassing Argentina, Brazil, Paraguay, and Uruguay.

mixed allocation economic system. An economic system containing elements of both market and command allocation systems.

monitoring. The scanning mode whereby a particular story is tracked.

most-favored-nation status (MFN). A privileged trading status in which a GATT signatory nation agrees to apply its favorable tariff or lowest tariff rate to all nations that are also signatories to GATT.

nontariff trade barrier (NTB). A measure, other than a tariff or free competition from other independent firms, that is a deterrent or obstacle to the sale of products in a foreign market.

North American Free Trade Agreement (NAFTA). A free trade area encompassing Canada, Mexico, and the United States.

offset. A countertrade deal in which a government recoups hard-currency expenditures by requiring some form of cooperation by the seller, such as importing products or transferring technology.

ownership. A market entry strategy which may either be a "green field" start-up or build-from-scratch establishment of a business, or the acquisition of an existing business.

penetration pricing. The use of low price as a competitive weapon to gain market position.

piggyback marketing. An arrangement whereby one manufacturer obtains distribution of products through another's distribution channels.

polycentric orientation. The view that each country in which a company does business is unique.

price escalation. The increase in a product's price as transportation, duty, and distributor margins are added to the factory price.

primary data. Data gathered through original research pertaining to the particular problem, decision, or issue under study.

product differentiation. A product's perceived uniqueness.

product saturation level. The percentage of potential buyers or households who own a particular product.

psychographic segmentation. The process of grouping people in terms of their attitudes, values, and lifestyles.

purchasing power parity. A concept that permits adjustment of national income measurements in various countries to reflect what a unit of each country's currency can actually buy.

put option. The right to sell a specified number of foreign currency units at a fixed price, up to the option's expiration date.

regiocentric orientation. The view that each region in which a company does business is unique; the company seeks to develop an integrated regional strategy.

research. A formally organized effort to acquire specific information for a specific purpose.

search. The scanning mode characterized by formal information gathering activity.

secondary data. Existing data in personal files, libraries, and databases.

Section 482. The section of U.S. Treasury regulations that deals with intracompany transfers of raw materials and finished and intermediate goods and that attempts to prevent tax avoidance and to ensure fair distribution of income.

self-reference criterion. The unconscious reference to one's own cultural values.

South African Development Coordination Conference (SADCC). An economic cooperation arrangement between Angola, Botswana, Lesotho, Malawi, Mozambique, Namibia, Swaziland, Tanzania, Zambia, and Zimbabwe.

special drawing rights (SDRs). Reserve assets created by the International Monetary Fund.

standardized global marketing. A strategy that calls for creating the same marketing mix for a broad mass market of potential buyers around the world.

strategic intent. Hamel and Prahalad's model for achieving competitive advantage by means of ambition and obsession with winning.

Super 301. A trade provision that allows the United States to single out individual nations as unfair traders and impose 100 percent tariffs on exports from those nations unless they comply with U.S. demands.

surveillance. The scanning mode in which a marketer engages in informal information gathering.

switch trading. A transaction in which a professional switch trader, switch trading house, or bank steps into a simple barter arrangement or other countertrade arrangement where-in one of the parties is not willing to accept all the goods received in the transaction.

switching costs. A barrier to entry into an industry created by the need to change suppliers and products.

targeting. The process of evaluating market segments and focusing marketing efforts on a country, region, or group of people.

tax incentives. Preferential treatment earnings from export activities.

time-series displacement. An analogy technique based on the assumption of an analogy between markets at different time periods.

trade secrets. Confidential information or knowledge that has commercial value, is not in the public domain, and for which steps have been taken to keep it secret.

transaction exposure. The degree to which exchange rates affect a company's market value when company activities result in sales or purchases denominated in foreign currencies.

transfer pricing. The pricing of goods and services bought and sold by operating units or divisions of a single company.

translation exposure. The degree to which exchange rate fluctuations affect a company's book value when financial statements of global operations are consolidated and stated in the company's home currency.

upper-middle-income country. A country with GNP per capita of between $2,500 and $14,000.

usage rate. A behavior segmentation variable that categorizes consumers as heavy, medium, light, or non-users of a product.

user status. A behavior segmentation variable that categorizes consumers into categories such as potential users, non-users, ex-users, regular users, first-timer users, and users of competitors' products.

value chain. Organizational activities that create value, including product design, manufacture, marketing, and after-sales service.

value equation. $V = B/P$, where $V =$ Value, $B =$ Benefits, and $P =$ Price.

viewing. The scanning mode characterized by general exposure to information.

World Trade Organization (WTO). The successor to GATT

Y&R's 4Cs. A 20-country psychographic market segmentation study titled Cross Cultural Consumer Characterizations conducted by Young & Rubicam.

Author/Name Index

Subject/Company Index

THE WORLD IN 1997

180° 160°W 140°W 120°W 100°W 80°W 60°W 20°W

80°N

GREENLAND
(Den.)

Arctic Circ

ICELAND Inset: Be

ALASKA
(U.S.)

60°N

CANADA

MOROCCO

40°N

UNITED STATES

ATLANTIC

OCEAN

W. SAHARA
(Mor.)

A

Inset: Below, left

BAHAMAS

CAPE
VERDE MAURITANIA

Tropic of Cancer

20°N

CUBA

MEXICO

BELIZE

SENEGAL

HAWAII
(U.S.)

HONDURAS

GAMBIA BUR

GUINEA- BISSAU GUINEA

PACIFIC

GUATEMALA

EL SALVADOR

SIERRA LEONE CÔTE
D'IVOIR

OCEAN

NICARAGUA

COSTA RICA

VENEZUELA

GUYANA
SURINAME

LIBERIA

EQUATORIAL G

PANAMA

FR. GUIANA
(Fr.)

Equator

SAO
& PRI

COLOMBIA

GALAPAGOS IS.
(Ecuador)

ECUADOR

KIRIBATI

TOKELAU
(N.Z.)

WESTERN *AMERICAN*
SAMOA *SAMOA*
(U.S.)

COOK
ISLANDS
(N.Z.)

FRENCH
POLYNESIA
(Fr.)

PERU

BRAZIL

BOLIVIA

TONGA

PARAGUAY

20°S

Tropic of Capricorn

CHILE

NIUE
(N.Z.)

URUGUAY

ARGENTINA

40°S

FALKLAND IS.
(U.K.)

S. GEORGIA
(U.K.)

CARIBBEAN INSET

85°W U.S. 75°W 70°W 65°W

25°N

BAHAMAS *ATLANTIC*

OCEAN

Tropic of Cancer

CUBA

TURKS & CAICOS IS.
(U.K.)

20°N 20°N

CAYMAN IS.
(U.K.)

VIRGIN
IS. (U.K.) ANGUILLA (U.K.)

PUERTO
RICO
(U.S.)

ST. MARTIN/MAARTEN (Fr., Neth.)

ST. BARTHELEMY (Fr.)

HAITI DOMINICAN
REPUBLIC

ANTIGUA &
BARBUDA

JAMAICA

VIRGIN IS. (U.S.)

SABA (Neth.)

MONTSERRAT (U.K.)

ST. EUSTATIUS (Neth.)

GUADELOUPE (Fr.)

HONDURAS

ST. KITTS
& NEVIS DOMINICA

Caribbean Sea

15°N

MARTINIQUE (Fr.)

NICARAGUA

ST. LUCIA

0 150 300 Miles

ARUBA
(Neth.)

CURAÇAO
(Neth.)

ST. VINCENT &
THE GRENADINES BARBADOS

0 150 300 Kilometers

BONAIRE
(Neth.)

GRENADA

COSTA RICA

TRINIDAD &
TOBAGO

10°N

PANAMA COLOMBIA VENEZUELA